MOON

ATLANTIC CANADA

ANDREW HEMPSTEAD

Contents

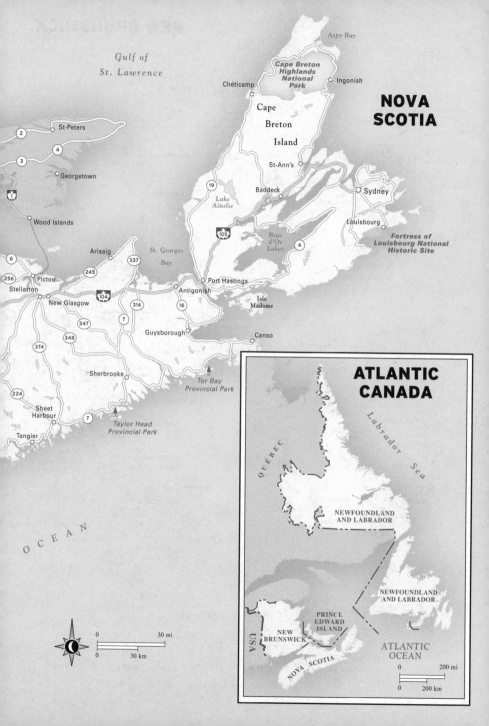

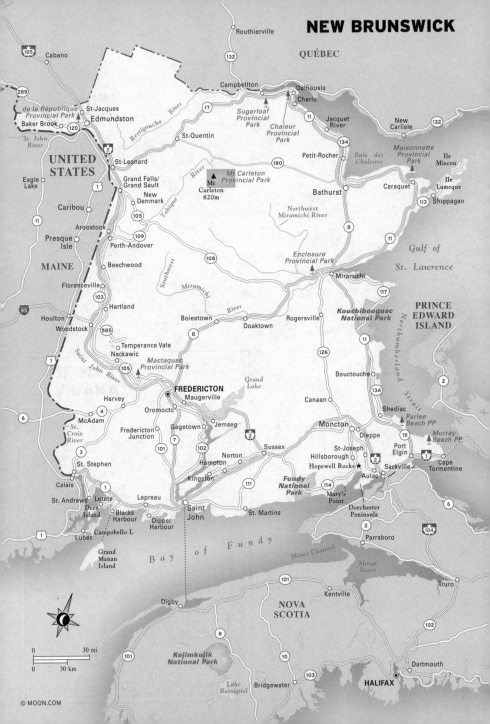

NEW BRUNSWICK

QUÉBEC

Routhierville

Cabano

de la République Provincial Park
Baker Brook
St-Jacques
Edmundston
St. John River

UNITED STATES

Eagle Lake

Caribou

Presque Isle

MAINE

Houlton

Campbellton
Dalhousie
Charlo

Sugarloaf Provincial Park
Chaleur Provincial Park

Jacquet River

New Carlisle

St-Quentin

St-Leonard

Grand Falls/ Grand Sault
New Denmark

Aroostook

Perth-Andover

Beechwood

Florenceville

Hartland

Mt Carleton Provincial Park
Mt Carleton 820m

Petit-Rocher

Baie des Chaleurs

Maisonnette Provincial Park

Ile Miscou

Ile Lamèque

Bathurst

Caraquet

Shippagan

Northwest Miramichi River

Gulf of St. Lawrence

PRINCE EDWARD ISLAND

Restigouche River

Tobique River

Saint John River

Southwest

Miramichi

River

Enclosure Provincial Park

Miramichi

Kouchibouguac National Park

Boiestown
Doaktown
Rogersville

Woodstock

Temperance Vale
Nackawic

Mactaquac Provincial Park

FREDERICTON
Maugerville

Harvey

McAdam

St. Croix River

Oromocto

Fredericton Junction

Gagetown

Jemseg

Grand Lake

Canaan

Bouctouche

Shediac
Parlee Beach PP

Moncton
Dieppe

Murray Beach PP

Northumberland Strait

Norton
Hampton

Sussex

St-Joseph
Hillsborough
Hopewell Rocks ★

Port Elgin

Cape Tormentine

St. Stephen

Calais

St. Andrews
Letete
Deer Island
Blacks Harbour
Campobello I.
Lubec

Grand Manan Island

Kingston

Lepreau

Dipper Harbour

Saint John

Fundy National Park

Mary's Point

Aulac

Dorchester Peninsula

Sackville

Parrsboro

St. Martins

B a y   o f   F u n d y

Minas Channel

Minas Basin

Truro

NOVA SCOTIA

Digby

Kentville

HALIFAX

Dartmouth

Kejimkujik National Park

Lake Rossignol

Bridgewater

© MOON.COM

0   30 mi
0   30 km

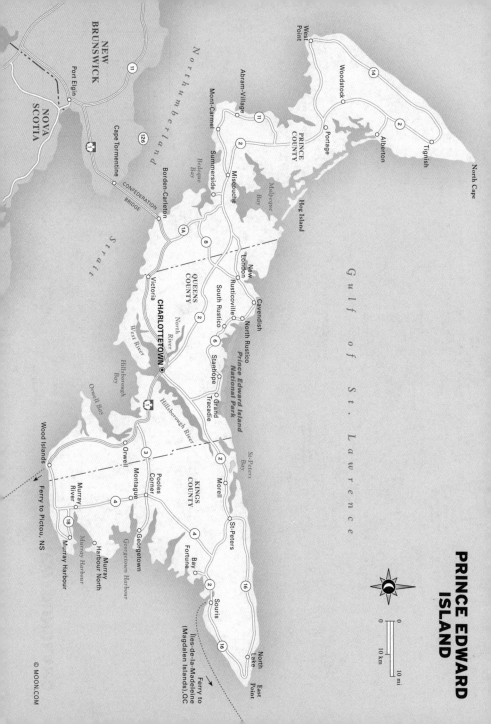

PRINCE EDWARD ISLAND

© MOON.COM

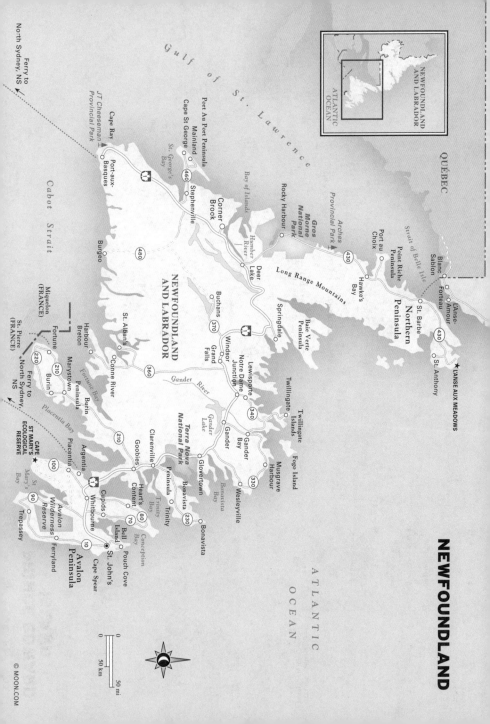

NEWFOUNDLAND

© MOON.COM

LABRADOR

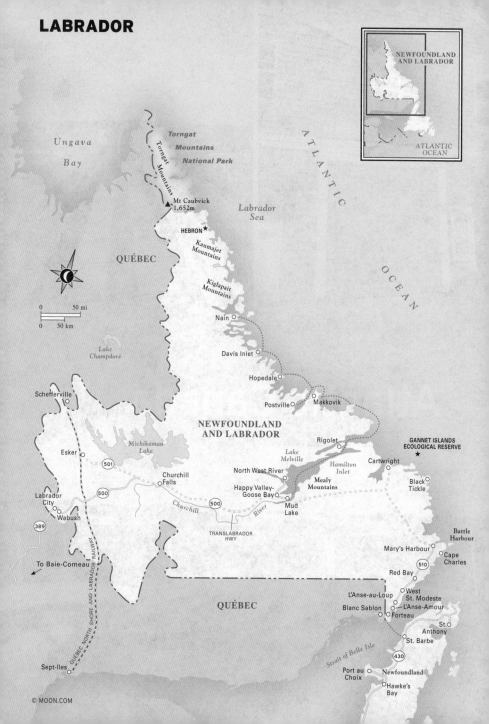

NEWFOUNDLAND
AND LABRADOR

ATLANTIC
OCEAN

*Ungava
Bay*

*Torngat
Mountains
National Park*

*Torngat
Mountains*

▲ Mt Caubvick
1,652m

*Labrador
Sea*

HEBRON ★

*Kaumajet
Mountains*

QUÉBEC

*Kiglapait
Mountains*

Nain ○

0   50 mi
0   50 km

*Lake
Champdoré*

Davis Inlet ○

Hopedale ○

Schefferville ○

Postville ○   ○ Makkovik

NEWFOUNDLAND
AND LABRADOR

Esker ○

*Michikamau
Lake*

Rigolet ○

*Lake
Melville*

GANNET ISLANDS
ECOLOGICAL RESERVE
★

○ 501

Churchill
Falls ○

North West River ○

*Hamilton
Inlet*

Cartwright ○

○ 500

Happy Valley-
Goose Bay ○

*Mealy
Mountains*

Black
Tickle ○

Labrador
City ○
○ Wabush

Churchill

500

Mud
Lake ○

River

○ 389

TRANSLABRADOR
HWY

Battle
Harbour ○

Mary's Harbour ○

510

Cape
Charles ○

To Baie-Comeau →

Red Bay ○

L'Anse-au-Loup ○   ○ West
St. Modeste

Blanc Sablon ○   ○ L'Anse-Amour
○ Forteau

St. ○
Anthony

St. Barbe ○

Strait of Belle Isle

430

Sept-Îles ○

QUÉBEC

Port au
Choix ○   ○ Newfoundland

○ Hawke's
Bay

QUÉBEC NORTH SHORE AND LABRADOR RAILWAY

© MOON.COM

ATLANTIC

OCEAN

DISCOVER

Atlantic Canada

Atlantic Canada, the sea-bound northeastern corner of North America, comprises four provinces—Nova Scotia, New Brunswick, Prince Edward Island, and Newfoundland and Labrador—that have their own personalities but are inextricably entwined in history, people, and place. Each province holds the promise of fabulous scenery and rich history.

The scene at Peggy's Cove on a foggy morning is alone worth the trip, and similarly memorable views of rugged coastline, forest-encircled lakes, and ancient landscapes present themselves at almost every turn. You can hike through flower-filled alpine meadows, stride the fairways of some of the world's best golf courses, and bike along red-clay lanes—or just take it easy, stepping back in time at historic attractions and soaking up culture in cosmopolitan cities.

The ocean is a defining feature of Atlantic Canada. It permeates all aspects of life on the edge of the continent, as it has done for centuries. Kayaking to an uninhabited island for a picnic lunch and searching out the world's rarest whales are just two possible watery adventures. Long stretches of sand are perfect for beach walking, and the warm waters of Northumberland Strait encourage

Clockwise from top left: whale-watching business; Summerville Beach Provincial Park; sign at Digby harbor; White Point Beach; downtown Lunenburg; kayaks on Prince Edward Island.

summer swimming. The surrounding waters also offer a veritable smorgasbord of seafood.

Some of your most treasured memories will be of the people. For centuries, the folk of Atlantic Canada have gone down to the sea to ply their trade on the great waters. The hard seafaring life has given them what so much of the modern world has thoughtlessly let slip through its fingers: nearness to nature's honest rhythms, replete with the old values of kindness, thrift, and rugged self-reliance. In a world crowded with too many people and too much development, Atlantic Canada remains a refuge of sorts, and its friendly people will make you feel welcome and comfortable.

Sure, you'll remember the sight and sound of bagpipers marching across Halifax's Citadel Hill, you'll snap the requisite photo of the lighthouse at Peggy's Cove, and you won't want to miss walking along the beaches of Prince Edward Island National Park. But there are many unexpected pleasures here as well: personal experiences that come about through intangible ingredients beyond the scope of any guidebook. In Atlantic Canada, you'll find adventures of your own making.

Clockwise from top left: Lunenburg Harbour; the Lobster Bar Restaurant in Pictou; Algonquin Golf Course in St. Andrews; Halifax Citadel National Historic Site.

10 TOP
EXPERIENCES

1 **Get close to icebergs at Twillingate:** This is one of the most accessible places in the world to see icebergs up close and personal—either from the shoreline or on a boat tour (page 392).

∨ ∨
∨ ∨

2 **Soak in the views at Peggy's Cove:** Hundreds of lighthouses line the rugged coastlines of Atlantic Canada, but there's something magical about the rocky setting of Peggy's Cove Lighthouse and the postcard-perfect village in its shadow (page 79).

3 **Cruise on the *Bluenose II*:** Set sail aboard a replica of Canada's most famous sailing ship and you are immersed in experiencing maritime history (page 90).

^ ^
^ ^ ^

4 **Drive the Cabot Trail:** The 311-kilometer (190-mile) Cabot Trail winds through Cape Breton Highlands National Park, a haven for outdoor enthusiasts and wildlife-loving visitors (page 180).

^
^
^

5 **Wander St. Andrews National Historic District:** The bright and cheery main street of St. Andrews is lined with historic wooden buildings filled with interesting boutiques and friendly cafés (page 211).

6 **Relax on the beaches of Prince Edward Island National Park:** The red-sand beaches and warm waters of the island's only national park make it a focal point for summer vacationers (page 296).

<<<

7 **Make a meal an adventure at the FireWorks Feast:** The FireWorks Feast at Inn at Bay Fortune takes you from a stroll through a farm, to an on-demand oyster bar, to a main meal cooked by one of Canada's best-known chefs (page 338).

8 **Get lost in time at the Colony of Avalon:** Journey back to the 17th century at this active archaeological dig (page 374).

9 **Dive deep at the Maritime Museum of the Atlantic:** This magnificent museum in Halifax tells the many stories of Atlantic Canada's links to the ocean, from the *Titanic* tragedy to fishing the Grand Banks (page 42).

10 **Follow in the footsteps of the Vikings at L'Anse aux Meadows:** A UNESCO World Heritage Site, the excavated remains of the Viking settlement signify the arrival of the first Europeans to step foot on North American soil over 1,000 years ago (page 415).

Planning Your Trip

Where to Go

Atlantic Canada is made up of four provinces, which makes dividing the region into manageable areas easy. But even among Canadians, there is sometimes confusion about the definition of "Atlantic Canada" versus "the Maritimes." The latter comprises New Brunswick, Nova Scotia, and Prince Edward Island, while Atlantic Canada comprises the Maritime provinces together with Newfoundland and Labrador.

coastline notched with innumerable coves and bays holding scores of picturesque fishing villages. It would be easy to spend an entire vacation exploring Nova Scotia, yet still leave feeling you hadn't seen everything. The cosmopolitan streets of **Halifax,** the colorful port of **Lunenburg,** the historical ambience of **Annapolis Royal,** and the wilds of **Cape Breton Island** are just a taste of what you can expect in this diverse province.

Nova Scotia

Nova Scotia typifies Atlantic Canada, with a dramatic, 7,459-kilometer-long (4,635-mile-long)

New Brunswick

New Brunswick is the largest of the Maritime provinces, but is the least known to outsiders.

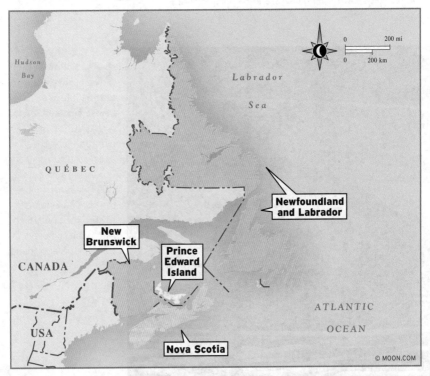

If You Have...

- **A WEEKEND:** Spend your time along the Halifax waterfront, Citadel Hill, and Point Pleasant Park.

- **ONE WEEK:** From Halifax, drive around the South Shore to the Fundy Coast.

- **TWO WEEKS:** Add Prince Edward Island—spend two days in Charlottetown and then enjoy some beach time in Cavendish.

- **THREE WEEKS:** Expand the two-week itinerary by catching a ferry to Newfoundland and traveling from St. John's to the tip of the Northern Peninsula.

Cavendish Beach

Although the province is mostly forested, it is its coastline and fertile **Saint John River valley** that attract the most attention. Here you'll find the elegant resort town of **St. Andrews,** the phenomenal **Fundy tides,** and **pristine beaches** such as **Parlee.** These attractions, along with the three main cities—**Fredericton, Saint John,** and **Moncton**—and a distinct Acadian flavor to the north coast, create a destination with something for everyone.

Prince Edward Island

Little PEI ranks as **Canada's smallest province,** as well as its most densely populated, most cultivated, most ribboned with roads, and most bereft of original wilderness. PEI also has the country's smallest provincial capital—**Charlottetown,** with a population of just 33,000. Tourism revolves around **Cavendish,** but the island's low-key charm is found elsewhere, along rural roads that end at the ocean and drift through neat villages that have changed little over the last century.

Newfoundland and Labrador

Three times the size of the Maritimes put together, this province redefines the region as Atlantic Canada. It comprises the island of Newfoundland as well as Labrador on the mainland. The Maritimes share a kindred climate, history, and lineage, but Newfoundland is different. About half of the island is **boreal forest,** while much of the rest is rocky, barren, or boggy. The people, many of whom live in the capital, **St. John's,** in some ways seem more akin to their Irish or English forebears than culturally blended or archetypically Canadian.

Know Before You Go

When to Go

Summer revolves around outdoor activities such as hiking, biking, swimming, canoeing, and fishing. **July** and **August** are especially busy. This is the time of year when school is out and the parks come alive with campers, the lakes and streams with anglers, the beaches with swimmers and sunbathers, the woods with wildlife, and the roadsides with stalls selling fresh produce.

Spring and **fall** are excellent times to visit Atlantic Canada. While **May-June** is considered a shoulder season, in many ways the province is at its blooming best in spring. After the first weekend in September, there is a noticeable decrease in travelers across the province. But **early fall** (Sept.-Oct.) provides pleasant daytime temperatures, reduced room rates, and uncrowded attractions. By late September, fall colors are at their peak, creating a mini-surge in visitors.

Officially, **winter** extends from late December into March, but in reality, most attractions and visitor information centers, as well as accommodations in resort towns, start closing in mid-October.

Passports and Visas

To enter Canada, a **passport** is required of citizens and permanent residents of the United States. For further information, see the website http://travel.state.gov. For current entry requirements to Canada, check the Citizenship and Immigration Canada website (www.cic.gc.ca).

All other foreign visitors must have a valid passport and may need a visa or visitors permit, depending on their country of residence and the vagaries of international politics. At present, visas are not required for citizens of the United States, the British Commonwealth, or Western Europe. The standard entry permit is for six months, and you may be asked to show onward tickets or proof of sufficient funds to last you through your intended stay.

Transportation

Visitors to Atlantic Canada have the option of arriving by road, rail, ferry, or air. The main gateway city for **flights** from North America and Europe is Halifax. **Ferries** cross to Yarmouth from Maine, while the **main rail line** enters the region from Québec and terminates at Halifax. **Driving,** whether in your own vehicle or a rental car, is by far the best way to get around Atlantic Canada, although some towns are served by bus.

ferry at Saint John Harbour

Mahone Bay

historic Digby

The Best of Atlantic Canada

Two weeks is an excellent length of time for visiting each of the four provinces and not feeling too rushed along the way. You could just spend the entire two weeks in the three Maritimes provinces, or only explore the far reaches of Newfoundland and Labrador, but this itinerary has it all.

Day 1

After arriving in **Halifax,** settle in at a historic downtown B&B such as The Halliburton. Spend the afternoon taking in sights such as **Halifax Citadel National Historic Site** and the **Maritime Museum of the Atlantic,** and make dinner reservations at a waterfront restaurant.

Day 2

Drive south through **Peggy's Cove** (take the obligatory lighthouse photo) and **Mahone Bay** (browse the arts and crafts shops, eat lunch at Rebecca's Restaurant) to **Lunenburg.** There's plenty to see en route, but arrive in time for an afternoon walk through the UNESCO-protected core of downtown, which is filled with colorful buildings. For the views alone, the Salt Shaker Deli & Inn is my favorite Lunenburg lodging.

Day 3

Drive across to **Annapolis Royal** to explore the historic town and visit **Fort Anne.** Stop in **Digby** for a meal of plump Digby scallops and board the afternoon ferry for New Brunswick and an overnight at one of the lodgings within walking distance of **Fundy National Park.**

Day 4

Mornings are a delight in Fundy National Park, so plan on a coastal hike and then drive through to **Fredericton.** Here, the **Historic Garrison District** packs in the past (and art lovers will want to schedule a stop at **Beaverbrook Art Gallery**), but the highlight of this day will be watching Loyalist history come to life at **Kings Landing Historical Settlement.** There's no advantage to staying right downtown, so reserve a room at On the Pond.

Day 5

Drive up the Saint John River, making a crossing at the **Hartland Covered Bridge,** then soaking up the wilderness of **Mount Carleton Provincial Park** en route to **Miramichi.** You'll learn about Acadians and their struggles at **Village Historique Acadien.**

Day 6

Drive to Prince Edward Island via the **Confederation Bridge.** Check in early to Charlottetown's Shipwright Inn and spend the afternoon on a rural jaunt through Cavendish, passing through **Prince Edward Island National Park** and stopping at **Green Gables Heritage Place.**

Day 7

Rise early to catch the ferry from Wood Islands to Caribou. Learn about the arrival of the early Scottish settlers at **Hector Heritage Quay** in Pictou, then drive through to **Baddeck,** on Cape Breton Island. Squeeze in a visit to **Alexander Graham Bell National Historic Site.** Most rooms at Baddeck's Water's Edge Inn have

balconies with views of the sun setting over the lake.

Day 8

Spend the day driving the famously scenic **Cabot Trail,** choosing between hiking coastal trails, relaxing on the beach, and a whale-watching trip. Catch the evening ferry to **Argentia** (reserve a cabin for extra comfort).

Day 9

You'll wake to your first views of Newfoundland as the ferry pulls into Argentia. There's plenty to see on the way to the capital, including the archaeological dig at the **Colony of Avalon.** Once in **St. John's,** head to **The Rooms** to learn about local history and **Signal Hill National Historic Site** for the views. Make reservations at **Mallard Cottage** for dinner. Still feeling energetic? The lively downtown bars of **George Street** come alive after dark.

Day 10

Head west, stopping at **Trinity,** a tiny fishing village where little has changed in over a century, en route to **Gros Morne National Park,** where during the long days of summer you have time for a walk through the **Tablelands** and can still be

Confederation Bridge

Fresh from the Sea

While the down-home cooking found across Atlantic Canada is irresistible, it is seafood that is the star. You'll find white-glove service at some seafood restaurants, but your most memorable meals will be less formal, including the following favorites.

NOVA SCOTIA

Almost completely surrounded by the sea, Nova Scotia offers up a wide variety of ocean delicacies.

- **Salty's:** Kick back on the Halifax harbor front with fish-and-chips at this casual restaurant.

- **Birch Street Seafoods:** This waterfront seafood market is the perfect place to try Digby's famous scallops.

NEW BRUNSWICK

Look for lobsters in the north and scallops along the Bay of Fundy.

- **Collins Lobster Shop:** In the village of Alma, try Collins Lobster Shop, where you can choose a lobster, wait until it's boiled to perfection, and then enjoy an outdoor feast overlooking the Bay of Fundy.

- **La Fine Grobe Sur-Mer:** Traditional French presentations of local seafood in a resort home overlooking the water create a memorable dining experience along the Acadian coast.

PRINCE EDWARD ISLAND

- **New Glasgow Lobster Suppers:** Lobster suppers are an island tradition. You'll see them advertised locally, or head to the popular New Glasgow Lobster Supper for a full lobster with all the trimmings.

- **Blue Mussel Café:** This rustic waterfront café overlooking North Rustico Harbour has tasty mussels steamed to order, as well as many other seafood delicacies.

- **Potato Country Kitchen:** Although this café is mostly about potatoes, save room for a slab of seaweed pie—but don't feel too guilty if you decide this island delicacy is not for you.

- **FireWorks Feast:** A truly unique dining experience, this dinner, hosted by the Inn at Bay Fortune, relies on farm-fresh produce and an abundance of local seafood.

NEWFOUNDLAND AND LABRADOR

Seal-flipper pie, moose burgers, and roasted wild game—partridge, rabbit, and caribou—are Newfoundland and Labrador highlights.

- **Lighthouse Picnics:** Head to the red-and-white lighthouse in Ferryland and order a picnic of crab cakes and other gourmet goodies.

- **Norseman Restaurant:** In L'Anse aux Meadows, this restaurant offers fresh, creative seafood dishes.

at Lobster Cove Head in time to watch the sunset. Gros Morne Cabins are a centrally located base in **Rocky Harbour.**

Day 11

Join a morning boat tour of **Western Brook Pond** and drive north along the Northern Peninsula. Make sure to stop at **Port au Choix National Historic Site** and the **thrombolites of Flowers Cove** en route to Southwest Pond Cabins in **L'Anse aux Meadows.** Dinner at the Norseman Restaurant is a must.

Day 12

Visit **L'Anse aux Meadows National Historic Site,** then drive to St. Barbe and put your feet up for a couple of hours on the ferry crossing to Labrador. Head north along the Labrador Straits to Mary's Harbour. Park your vehicle and pack an overnight bag for the short boat trip to **Battle Harbour,** an "outport" (remote fishing village) that was abandoned in the 1960s, but where

restoration efforts include a restaurant and an inn.

Day 13

Return to the mainland and spend the day exploring this remote stretch of coast. **Red Bay National Historic Site** should definitely be on your itinerary, as should the lighthouse at **L'Anse Amour.** Catch the ferry back to St. Barbe and continue south to Port-aux-Basques in time for the evening ferry back to Nova Scotia.

Day 14

Arriving in **North Sydney** around dawn, you have plenty of time to make an afternoon flight home from Halifax. If you're not flying out until the following morning, take Marine Drive along the Eastern Shore and spend the night along this remote stretch of coast, where **Sherbrooke Village** is a historical highlight and where the beaches of **Taylor Head Provincial Park** are perfect for a walk.

Green Gables Heritage Place

Maritime Museum of the Atlantic

While most visitors who choose Atlantic Canada for their vacations do so for the outdoors, there are a number of appealing cultural attractions to enjoy.

NOVA SCOTIA

- Take a tour of **Alexander Keith's Brewery,** Halifax.
- Explore the colorful architecture of **Lunenburg.**
- Wander along one of North America's best-preserved pre-1800s streets at **Annapolis Royal.**
- Soak up historic luxury at the **Keltic Lodge** on Cape Breton Island.

NEW BRUNSWICK

- Take in the sights and smells of **Kingsbrae Garden,** St. Andrews.
- Immerse yourself in Acadian culture at **Le Pays de la Sagouine.**

PRINCE EDWARD ISLAND

- Learn about the founding of Canada at **Province House,** Charlottetown.
- Step into the fictional shoes of Anne of Green Gables at **Cavendish.**

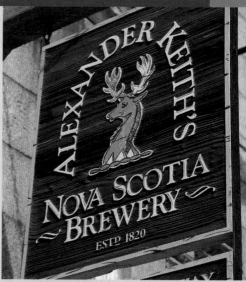
Alexander Keith's Brewery

NEWFOUNDLAND AND LABRADOR

- Dance the night away on bustling **George Street,** St. John's.
- Take an overnight excursion to the abandoned outport village of **Battle Harbour,** Labrador.

The Maritime Tour

It may be possible to touch down in all four provinces in one week, but such a rushed schedule is neither practical nor enjoyable. Therefore, in this itinerary, we'll stick to the three Maritime provinces (Nova Scotia, New Brunswick, and Prince Edward Island). This itinerary and those that follow assume you have your own vehicle or a rental.

the **Maritime Museum of the Atlantic** and a tour of **Alexander Keith's Brewery.** Enjoy your first evening in the city by tucking into seafood at an outdoor waterfront restaurant such as Salty's. For lodging, choose The Halliburton for historic charm or the Prince George Hotel for modern conveniences.

Day 1

Arrive in **Halifax** and spend the afternoon exploring the downtown precinct; include a visit to

Day 2

Rise early to beat the crowd to **Peggy's Cove,** then follow the scenic coastal route through

Chester to **Mahone Bay.** After lunch, spend time admiring the local arts and crafts scene and walk along the waterfront to view the trio of waterfront churches. At nearby **Lunenburg,** you'll find enough time for a sunset harbor cruise before turning in for the night at the Spinnaker Inn.

Day 3

Drive across southwestern Nova Scotia to **Annapolis Royal** and spend the afternoon exploring North America's oldest downtown street as well as attractions like **Port-Royal National Historic Site.** Guest rooms at the Garrison House reflect the town's gracious past.

Day 4

Catch the ferry from Digby to Saint John and drive down the coast to **St. Andrews,** where you can do what visitors have done for over a century—browse through the boutiques, enjoy **Kingsbrae Garden,** and dine on seafood. Have a room reserved at Seaside Beach Resort, unless it's a special occasion, in which case you'll want to spend the night at the Kingsbrae Arms.

Day 5

Drive along the Fundy Coast to **Fundy National Park.** Plan on at least one hike (Dickson Falls is an easy walk), and time your early afternoon departure for low tide at **Hopewell Rocks,** where you can "walk on the ocean floor." Continue north across the Confederation Bridge to the Shipwright Inn in **Charlottetown.**

Day 6

Spend some time in the island capital, where **Province House** is a highlight, but also head north to **Cavendish** to soak up the story of Anne of Green Gables at **Green Gables Heritage Place** and explore the beachfront national park. Splurge with an overnight stay at Inn at Bay Fortune and partake in its **FireWorks Feast.**

Day 7

Catch an early ferry back to the mainland and drive to Halifax. If time allows, fit in a few more city sights. The **Halifax Citadel National Historic Site** and the **Public Gardens** should be at the top of your list.

St. Andrews

A Family Affair

The most important thing to remember when traveling with children is not to try to fit too much in. Instead, sacrifice covering great distances for enjoying specific sights and towns for extended periods of time, and try to fit as many of these family-friendly attractions and activities into your itinerary as possible:

- **Harbour Hopper Tours,** Halifax, Nova Scotia

- **Museum of Natural History,** Halifax, Nova Scotia

- **Shubenacadie Wildlife Park,** near Truro, Nova Scotia

- **Hector Heritage Quay,** Pictou, Nova Scotia

- **Hopewell Rocks,** Fundy Coast, New Brunswick

- **Historic Garrison District,** Fredericton, New Brunswick

- **Magnetic Hill,** Moncton, New Brunswick

- **Parlee Beach,** Shediac, New Brunswick

- **Anne of Green Gables attractions,** Cavendish, Prince Edward Island

- **Prince Edward Island National Park,** Prince Edward Island

Hopewell Rocks

- **Attend a lobster supper,** Prince Edward Island

- **The Rooms,** St. John's, Newfoundland and Labrador

- **Norstead,** near St. Anthony's, Newfoundland and Labrador

Rugged Atlantic Canada

This 12-day itinerary is suited for outdoor enthusiasts with a love of nature. It is impossible to discuss adventures in the region without including Newfoundland, and so three days are spent on that island. If you have less time, plan on dedicating your next trip to Atlantic Canada to exploring the region's largest province. In keeping with the theme, I've added accommodations recommendations that keep you close to nature, but if cabins and cottages aren't your thing, you will find plenty of alternatives along the way.

Day 1

Pick up your rental car in **Halifax** and head for the **Eastern Shore.** Try surfing at **Lawrencetown Beach** or sea kayaking at **Tangier.** Enjoy a beachside picnic at **Taylor Head Provincial Park.** Stay at Paddler's Retreat

Bed and Breakfast and rent a kayak for an evening jaunt around the bay.

Day 2

Drive across **Cape Breton Island,** stopping for an outdoor lunch of steaming chowder at the Chowder House, and then spend the afternoon swimming and sunbathing at **Ingonish Beach.** Even if you don't pay for a room with water views at Glenghorm Beach Resort, the ocean is just a short walk from your front door.

Day 3

Day 3 is spent in **Cape Breton Highlands National Park.** In the process of reaching the best hikes, you'll drive the spectacular **Cabot Trail.** Leave the pavement behind on the **Skyline Loop Trail,** a moderate hike that leads to a stunning headland with sweeping water views. For a less energetic option, plan on walking to **Benjie's Lake** and spend the extra time exploring **Black Brook Cove.** Either way, allow three hours to reach North Sydney for the overnight ferry to **Port-aux-Basques.**

Day 4

The ferry arrives in **Newfoundland** as the sun rises, which makes the early morning drive north to **Gros Morne National Park** even more

enjoyable. In the afternoon, choose between exploring the **Tablelands** on foot and driving out to **Trout River** for rugged coastal scenery. Fresh seafood cooked on your barbecue at Mountain Range Cottages winds up this long day.

Day 5

The boat tour on **Western Brook Pond** is an absolute must, but allow time to reach the dock, which is only accessible on foot through a low-slung forest. Stop in at the **Discovery Centre** to learn about the park's geology and then hike to **Green Gardens.** Spend another night at Mountain Range Cottages.

Day 6

Even the adventurous need a day off, and this is it. Personally, I'd spend the time driving up the Northern Peninsula (**Port au Choix National Historic Site** makes a solid day trip while still allowing plenty of time for scenic stops), but you could also stay within the park and tackle the summit of **Gros Morne Mountain.** Drive back south to Port-aux-Basques and catch the evening ferry back to Nova Scotia.

Day 7

Hopefully you've not spent all night being entertained by the Celtic musicians in the onboard

Gros Morne National Park

lounge, because the ferry docks just before dawn and the morning is spent driving to Caribou, where you board the ferry to **Prince Edward Island.** The fossil cliffs of **Arisaig** make a worthwhile detour en route. Once on the island, stop at **Rossignol Estate Winery** for a bottle of wine and continue to Murray Harbour's Ocean Acres, where you can relax with a glass of chardonnay on your screened porch.

Day 8

Yes, you've seen the tourist brochures espousing the touristy wonders of Prince Edward Island, but on this visit you're chasing a more nature-oriented experience. In this regard, spend the morning on a **seal-watching** trip, stroll along the singing sands of the beach below **Basin Head,** and walk through the disappearing coastal forests of **Prince Edward Island National Park.** The Trailside Music Café and Inn, at Mount Stewart, is your overnight stop.

Day 9

Reserve an early tee time at the **Links at Crowbush Cove.** After lunch, strike out for the Confederation Bridge to New Brunswick and head to **Sackville Waterfowl Park** for its bird-watching opportunities. Walking through

the "flowerpots" at **Hopewell Rocks** is tide-dependent, but you can always kayak as a high-tide alternative. Spend the night in **Fundy National Park.**

Day 10

Continue down the coast to Saint John, where **Irving Nature Park** is a good example of what the entire coastline would have looked like before European settlement. You're staying in a city, so you may as well take advantage of the delightful harbor-front Hilton Saint John (which isn't as much of a splurge as you might imagine).

Day 11

Catch the ferry across the Bay of Fundy and drive out to **Brier Island,** taking the time to hike to **Balancing Rock** en route. An afternoon **whale-watching** trip can be combined with an evening of bird-watching. Stay at Brier Island Lodge, and dine in-house.

Day 12

The outdoor-oriented vacation is nearly over, but there's one more activity to try, and Atlantic Canada is the only place in the world you can do so—**riding the tidal bore** down the Shubenacadie River.

looking out over the Bay of Fundy

Best Scenic Drives

A great way to see Atlantic Canada is to hop in your car (or rental car) and explore. Scenic drives can be wonderful family vacation activities, too. See some of the beauty of Atlantic Canada while cruising along in these areas:

- **South Shore** (Nova Scotia, page 76). We devote an entire chapter to the South Shore of Nova Scotia, a scenic drive of epic proportions that extends between Halifax and Shelburne in 210 kilometers (130 miles) via Highway 103, but highlights such as Mahone Bay, Lunenburg, Crescent Beach, and numerous coastal provincial parks require detours—and at least two or three days.

- **Bras d'Or Lakes** (Nova Scotia, page 168). The two-hour drive from Canso Causeway to Sydney on Highway 105 gives travelers a taste of the Bras d'Or Lakes, but to fully appreciate the expansive water, plan on detouring to Iona and as far as Big Pond, adding an extra three hours driving time. Baddeck is a good base for exploring this area.

- **Cabot Trail** (Nova Scotia, page 180). For its stunning coastal scenery and abundant wildlife, the 311-kilometer (190-mile) Cabot Trail, which loops around the top end of Cape Breton Island, is generally regarded as one of the world's most scenic drives. You could make the loop in five or six hours, but two or three days are needed to fully appreciate the beauty of the region.

- **Saint John River Valley** (New Brunswick, page 240). The Trans-Canada Highway zooms up the Saint John River between Fredericton and Edmundston in 270 kilometers (165 miles), a three-hour drive, but travel upriver along the backroads and you'll pass through delightful villages such as Woodstock and Hartland.

- **Strait Coast** (New Brunswick, page 260). Named for Northumberland Strait, which separates Prince Edward Island from the mainland, the two-hour drive between Cape Tormentine and Miramichi is notable for warm swimming beaches, French-influenced attractions such as Le Pays de la Sagouine, and the barrier islands of Kouchibouguac National Park.

the Cabot Trail

- **North Cape** (Prince Edward Island, page 325). On the western portion of Prince Edward Island, all routes lead north to North Cape, but I suggest taking the coastal road (Highway 14) via West Point and Miminegash to the end of the road, where you enjoy sweeping ocean views, hiking trails, and even a restaurant. With scenic stops, allow a full day from Summerside for the 300-kilometer (185-mile) round-trip.

- **Irish Loop** (Newfoundland and Labrador, page 376). This 310-kilometer (190-mile) drive around the Avalon Peninsula starts and finishes in St. John's. It can be completed easily in a full day, but stopping to enjoy a boat tour of Witless Bay, the archaeological sites in Ferryland, and the wilderness of Mistaken Point would require an overnight stay en route.

- **Northern Peninsula** (Newfoundland and Labrador, page 410). For coastal scenery, charming seaside villages, and the splendor of Gros Morne National Park, the 420-kilometer (260-mile), five-hour trip between Deer Lake and St. Anthony in western Newfoundland is one of my favorite scenic drives in all of Canada. A lack of crowds and little-known attractions such as the thrombolites of Flowers Cove are a bonus.

Nova Scotia

Halifax

Halifax (pop. 425,000), the 250-year-old provin-

cial capital, presents Nova Scotia's strikingly modern face wrapped around a historic soul.

It's one of the most vibrant cities in Canada, with an exuberant cultural life and cosmopolitan population. The tourist's Halifax is tidily compact, concentrated on the manageable, boot-shaped peninsula the city inhabits. Its prettiest parts are clustered between the bustling waterfront and the short, steep hillside that the early British developed two centuries ago. In these areas you'll find handsomely historic old districts meshed with stylishly chic, new glass-sheathed buildings.

Halifax is more than a city, more than a seaport, and more than a provincial capital. Halifax is a harbor with a city attached, as the

Highlights

Look for ★ to find recommended sights, activities, dining, and lodging.

★ **Historic Properties:** The oldest waterfront warehouses in Canada have been brought to life with an impressive restoration project and are now filled with bustling boutiques, cafés, and a brewery (page 40).

★ **Maritime Museum of the Atlantic:** If you visit just one museum in Nova Scotia, make it this one, which tells the many stories of the region's links to the ocean, from the *Titanic* tragedy to fishing the Grand Banks (page 42).

★ **Alexander Keith's Brewery:** Tours of North America's oldest working brewery go beyond describing the beer-making process, delving deep into Halifax's history and its most colorful characters (page 44).

★ **Point Pleasant Park:** On the southern tip of the Halifax peninsula, this urban park is a favorite for walking and biking (page 45).

★ **Halifax Citadel National Historic Site:** Canada's most visited historic site lies atop downtown Halifax's highest point. It provides a glimpse into the city's past as well as sweeping harbor views (page 46).

★ **Public Gardens:** Strolling through these formal Victorian gardens is a morning rite for many locals (page 46).

★ **Fairview Cemetery:** Varying from three-digit numbers to moving family messages, the inscriptions on the headstones of more than 100

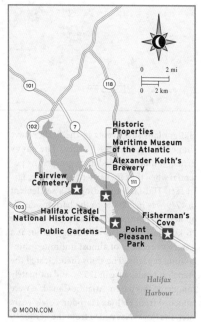

Titanic victims make this suburban cemetery a poignant place to visit (page 49).

★ **Fisherman's Cove:** If you're not planning to travel beyond Halifax, a visit to this historic fishing village will give you a taste of what you'll be missing farther afield (page 53).

Halifax

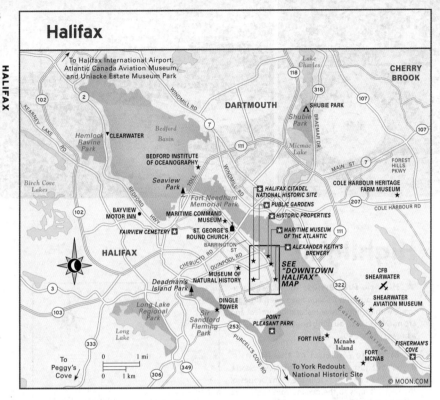

To Halifax International Airport,
Atlantic Canada Aviation Museum,
and Uniacke Estate Museum Park

CHERRY
BROOK

Lake
Charles

118

DARTMOUTH

SHUBIE PARK

107

Shubie
Park

107

102

2

7

318

Hemlock
Ravine
Park

CLEARWATER

Bedford
Basin

111

Micmac
Lake

MAIN ST

7

FOREST
HILLS
PKWY

Birch Cove
Lakes

BEDFORD INSTITUTE
OF OCEANOGRAPHY

Seaview
Park

Fort Needham
Memorial Park

COLE HARBOUR HERITAGE
FARM MUSEUM

HALIFAX CITADEL
NATIONAL HISTORIC SITE

207

COLE HARBOUR RD

102

BAYVIEW
MOTOR INN

MARITIME COMMAND
MUSEUM

PUBLIC GARDENS

HISTORIC PROPERTIES

FAIRVIEW CEMETERY

ST. GEORGE'S
ROUND CHURCH

MARITIME MUSEUM
OF THE ATLANTIC

111

HALIFAX

BARRINGTON ST

ALEXANDER KEITH'S
BREWERY

CFB
SHEARWATER

CHEBUCTO RD

QUINPOOL RD

SEE
"DOWNTOWN
HALIFAX"
MAP

322

3

MUSEUM OF
NATURAL HISTORY

SHEARWATER
AVIATION MUSEUM

Deadman's
Island Park

DINGLE
TOWER

Long Lake
Regional
Park

Sir
Sandford
Fleming
Park

253

POINT
PLEASANT PARK

Eastern Passage

FISHERMAN'S
COVE

103

Long
Lake

FORT IVES

Mcnabs
Island

FORT
MCNAB

333

To
Peggy's
Cove

0   1 mi

0   1 km

306

349

PURCELL'S COVE RD

To York Redoubt
National Historic Site

© MOON.COM

Haligonians say. Events in the harbor have shaped Nova Scotia's history. The savvy British military immediately grasped its potential when they first sailed in centuries ago. In fact, Halifax's founding as a settlement in 1749 was incidental to the harbor's development. From the first, the British used the 26-kilometer-long (16-mile-long) harbor as a watery warehouse of almost unlimited ship-holding capacity. The ships that defeated the French at Louisbourg in 1758—and ultimately conquered this part of Atlantic Canada—were launched from Halifax Harbour. A few years later, the Royal Navy sped from the harbor to harass the rebellious colonies on the Eastern Seaboard during the American Revolution. Ships from Halifax ran the blockades on the South's side during the American Civil War. And during World Wars I and II, the harbor bulged with troop convoys destined for Europe.

PLANNING YOUR TIME

Everyone has his or her own idea of how best to spend time in Halifax. History buffs will want to spend an entire week exploring the city's oldest corners, while outdoorsy types will want to hit the highlights before moving through to the rest of the province. Halifax has three attractions no one will want to miss, even if you have just one day. The first of these is the **Historic Properties,** a group of waterfront warehouses converted to restaurants and boutiques, while the nearby **Maritime**

Museum of the Atlantic is the place to learn about the city's seafaring traditions. The third is **Halifax Citadel National Historic Site.** These three attractions, along with time exploring the waterfront, could fill one day, but you'd be missing one of Halifax's best known attractions—its **pubs and breweries,** including **Alexander Keith's Brewery,** North America's oldest, which is open daily for tours.

Since it's both a gateway for air travelers and the hub of three highways, chances are you'll be passing through Halifax more than once on your travels through Nova Scotia. This allows you to break up your sightseeing and to plan your schedule around the weather. If, for example, the sun is shining when you first arrive, plan to visit **Point Pleasant Park,** the **Public Gardens,** and **Fairview Cemetery.** These spots and historic downtown attractions should fill two full days.

Across the harbor from downtown is the city of Dartmouth, where a seafood lunch at the fishing village of **Fisherman's Cove** makes a perfect getaway from the city.

HISTORY

The French learned about the area in the early 1700s, when local Mi'kmaq Indians escorted the French governor on a tour of what they called Chebuctook, the "Great Long Harbor," and adjacent waterways. But it was the British who saw the site's potential: In 1749, Colonel Edward Cornwallis arrived with about 2,500 settlers on 13 ships and founded Halifax along what is now Barrington Street. The settlement was named for Lord Halifax, then president of Britain's Board of Trade and Plantations. Early Halifax was a stockaded settlement backed by the Grand Parade, the town green where the militia drilled. More English settlers arrived in 1750, and by 1807 the city's population topped 60,000. A proper government setting—the sandstone Colonial Building (now Province House)—opened in 1819, followed by a number of noteworthy academic institutions. The harbor front acquired commercial legitimacy when native Haligonian Samuel Cunard, rich from lumbering, whaling, and

banking, turned his interests to shipping. By 1838 the Cunard Steamship Company handled the British and North American Royal Mail, and by 1840 Cunard's four ships provided the first regular transport between the two continents. The seaport's incorporation in 1841 ushered in a prosperous mercantile era. Granville Street, with its stylish shops, became, in its day, Atlantic Canada's Fifth Avenue. Less stylish brothels and taverns lined Brunswick, Market, and Barrack Streets, and the military police swept through the area often, breaking up drunken fistfights and reestablishing order.

By the 1960s, Halifax looked like a hoary victim of the centuries, somewhat the worse for wear. Massive federal, provincial, and private investment, however, restored the harbor to its early luster, with its warehouses groomed as the handsome Historic Properties. The city continued to polish its image, as sandblasting renewed the exterior of architectural treasures such as Province House. The Art Gallery of Nova Scotia moved from cramped quarters near the Public Archives and settled within the stunningly renovated former Dominion Building. Municipal guidelines sought to control the city's growth. The unobstructed view on George Street between the harbor and the Citadel was secured with a municipal mandate, and the height of the hillside's high-rise buildings was also restricted to preserve the cityscape. During this time, the waterfront evolved into a bustling tourist precinct, one that is also enjoyed by locals.

ORIENTATION

The layout of Halifax is easy to grasp. **Downtown** lines the western side of **Halifax Harbour.** Lower and Upper Water Streets and Barrington Street run through downtown parallel to the water. This is the core of the city, chock-full of historic attractions, the city's finest accommodations, and a wonderful choice of restaurants. The waterfront itself bustles day and night. From Historic Properties' wharves at the waterfront, sightseeing boats explore the harbor. The splendid

Maritime Museum and Art Gallery of Nova Scotia are close by.

A series of short streets rise like ramps from the waterfront, past the grassy Grand Parade and up **Citadel Hill.** Around the hill, a great swath of green space provides a welcome break from residential and commercial sprawl. Laid out by the city's original surveyor, **Central Common,** on the west side of the hill, marks a meeting of roads. Major thoroughfares merge here (Robie Street running north-south, Bell Road running southeast, and Cogswell Street running east-west). Locals refer to everything south of the commons as the South End, everything to the north the North End, and to the west the West End.

In the South End is the city's **academic area,** site of Dalhousie University, University of King's College, St. Mary's University, and the Atlantic School of Theology. At the southern tip of the downtown peninsula is **Point Pleasant Park,** an oasis of green surrounded by the grays of sprawling loading docks to the north and the surrounding sparkling blue waters of Halifax Harbour.

The **Northwest Arm** of Halifax Harbour nearly cuts the downtown area off from the rest of the city. At the head of this waterway is the **Armdale Rotary,** from where Herring Cove Road spurs south to **Purcells Cove Road,** which passes yacht-filled marinas, Sir Sandford Fleming Park, and York Redoubt National Historic Site.

Across Halifax Harbour from downtown is the city of **Dartmouth.** Linked to downtown by ferry and bridge, this commercial and residential area has a smattering of sights and is also worth visiting for the views back across to Halifax. Beyond the two bridges spanning Halifax Harbour is Bedford Basin, a large body of water surrounded by development. At the head of the basin is the residential area of Bedford and suburbs, including Lower Sackville and Waverly. Traveling down Highway 102 from Truro and **Halifax International Airport** (38 km/24 mi north of downtown), you'll pass exits for these and other towns.

Sights

Halifax is packed with attractions, all reasonably priced or absolutely free. The biggest concentration is within walking distance of the waterfront precinct and many accommodations. Beyond the downtown core are a number of interesting sights that are easy to miss but easy to reach by public transportation. Whatever your interests—searching out *Titanic*-related sights or exploring coastal parks—you will find plenty to do and see in the capital.

DOWNTOWN
The following sights are within walking distance of each other from the waterfront. You could easily spend a full day exploring this part of the city, taking time out to lunch at an outdoor harbor-front restaurant.

★ Historic Properties
Canada's oldest surviving group of waterfront warehouses is also one of the city's main tourist attractions, with excellent shopping and dining spread along a three-block expanse on Upper and Lower Water Streets. The wooden and stone warehouses, chandleries, and buildings once used by shipping interests and privateers have been restored to their early 1800s glory. They now house restaurants, shops, and other sites impressively styled with Victorian and Italianate facades. The history of the precinct is cataloged halfway along the Privateer Wharf building (on the inside) with interpretive panels.

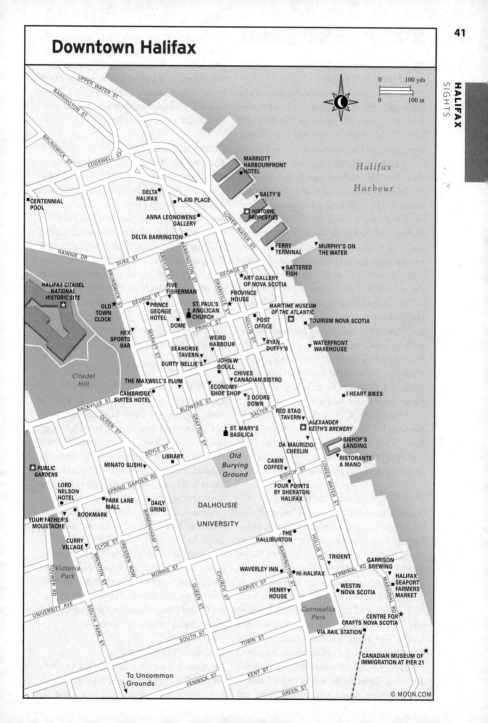

Downtown Halifax

Halifax Harbour

0   100 yds
0   100 m

UPPER WATER ST

BARRINGTON ST

BRUNSWICK ST

COGSWELL ST

MARRIOTT
HARBOURFRONT
HOTEL

■CENTENNIAL
POOL

DELTA
HALIFAX   PLAID PLACE

SALTY'S

ANNA LEONOWENS
GALLERY

HISTORIC
PROPERTIES

DELTA BARRINGTON

FERRY
TERMINAL

MURPHY'S ON
THE WATER

RAINNIE DR

DUKE ST

BATTERED
FISH

GEORGE ST

ART GALLERY
OF NOVA SCOTIA

HALIFAX CITADEL
NATIONAL
HISTORIC SITE

FIVE
FISHERMAN

PROVINCE
HOUSE

GRANVILLE ST

MARITIME MUSEUM
OF THE ATLANTIC

OLD
TOWN
CLOCK

PRINCE
GEORGE
HOTEL

ST. PAUL'S
ANGLICAN
CHURCH

TOURISM NOVA SCOTIA

POST
OFFICE

DOME

PRINCE ST

HFX
SPORTS
BAR

HOLLIS ST

WEIRD
HARBOUR

RYAN
DUFFY'S

WATERFRONT
WAREHOUSE

Citadel
Hill

SEAHORSE
TAVERN

JOHN W.
DOULL

DURTY NELLIE'S

MARKET ST

CHIVES
CANADIAN BISTRO

THE MAXWELL'S PLUM

ECONOMY
SHOE SHOP

I HEART BIKES

CAMBRIDGE
SUITES HOTEL

2 DOORS
DOWN

BLOWERS ST

SACKVILLE ST

SALTER ST

RED STAG
TAVERN

QUEEN ST

GRAFTON ST

ALEXANDER
KEITH'S BREWERY

ST. MARY'S
BASILICA

BISHOP'S
LANDING

DOYLE ST

LIBRARY

DA MAURIZIO/
CHEELIN

RISTORANTE
A MANO

PUBLIC
GARDENS

MINATO SUSHI

Old
Burying
Ground

CABIN
COFFEE

SPRING GARDEN RD

BISHOP ST

LORD
NELSON
HOTEL

PARK LANE
MALL

DAILY
GRIND

DALHOUSIE

FOUR POINTS
BY SHERATON
HALIFAX

BIRMINGHAM ST

BOOKMARK

UNIVERSITY

LOWER WATER ST

YOUR FATHER'S
MOUSTACHE

THE
HALLIBURTON

CURRY
VILLAGE

CLYDE ST

HOLLIS ST

TRIDENT

GARRISON
BREWING

Victoria
Park

BRENTON ST

DRESDEN ROW

MORRIS ST

WAVERLEY INN

HI-HALIFAX

TERMINAL RD

HALIFAX
SEAPORT
FARMERS'
MARKET

TOWER RD

BARRINGTON ST

HARVEY ST

HENRY
HOUSE

WESTIN
NOVA SCOTIA

MARGINAL RD

UNIVERSITY AVE

SOUTH PARK ST

QUEEN ST

CHURCH ST

Cornwallis
Park

CENTRE FOR
CRAFTS NOVA SCOTIA

VIA RAIL STATION

SOUTH ST

TOBIN ST

CANADIAN MUSEUM OF
IMMIGRATION AT PIER 21

To Uncommon
Grounds

FENWICK ST

KENT ST

GREEN ST

© MOON.COM

ARGYLE ST

BARRINGTON ST

GEORGE ST

★ Maritime Museum
 of the Atlantic

The seaport's store of nautical memorabilia lies within the sleek, burnished-red waterfront **Maritime Museum of the Atlantic** (1675 Lower Water St., 902/424-7490, http://maritimemuseum.novascotia.ca, summer daily 9:30am-5:30pm, the rest of the year Tues.-Sat. 9:30am-5pm, Sun. 1pm-5pm, adult $9.55, senior $8.50, child $5.15). The museum is one of the crowning achievements of the city's Waterfront Development Project. Most visitors find the *Titanic* display room most interesting. It contains the world's largest collection of artifacts from the floating palace deemed unsinkable by its owners; you will see the only deck chair recovered at the time of the sinking, a cribbage board, lounge paneling, and more. Also on display is a model of the *Titanic*, the wireless log taken as the vessel foundered, and a variety of information boards that tell the story of the ship's construction. *Titanic 3D*, a National Geographic documentary created from footage taken from the wreck, shows continuously.

Outside, the **CSS *Acadia*** is tied up at the wharf. This sturdy vessel spent its life as Canada's first hydrographic vessel, its crew surveying the east coast using sextants and graphing shoreline features.

Art Gallery of Nova Scotia

Atlantic Canada's largest and finest art collection is housed in two buildings separated by a cobbled courtyard just up from the harbor at the **Art Gallery of Nova Scotia** (1723 Hollis St., 902/424-5280, www.artgalleryofnovascotia.ca, summer daily 10am-5pm, fall-spring Tues.-Sat. 10am-5pm, Sun. noon-5pm, adult $12, senior $10, child $5). The main entrance is within Gallery South (also home to an excellent café). The vast majority of the collection is displayed in Gallery North, the sandstone Dominion Building. Some 2,000 works in oils, watercolors, stone, wood, and other media are

exhibited throughout its four floors of spacious galleries. The permanent collections give priority to current and former Nova Scotia residents and include works by Mary Pratt, Arthur Lismer, Carol Fraser, and Alex Colville. The mezzanine-level regional folk-art collection is a particular delight.

Province House

The seat of the provincial government, **Province House** (1726 Hollis St., 902/424-4661, July-Aug. Mon.-Fri. 9am-5pm, Sat.-Sun. 10am-4pm, the rest of the year Mon.-Fri. 9am-4pm, free) was completed in 1819. It's the smallest and oldest provincial legislature building in the country and features a fine Georgian exterior and splendid interior, resembling a rural English mansion more than an official residence. On his visit to modest but dignified Province House in 1842, author Charles Dickens remarked, "It was like looking at Westminster through the wrong end of a telescope . . . a gem of Georgian architecture."

St. Paul's Anglican Church

The stately white wooden **St. Paul's Anglican Church** (1749 Argyle St., 902/429-2240, www.stpaulshalifax.org, tours July-Aug. Mon.-Sat. 9am-4pm, free) was styled after the Palladian St. Peter's Church on Vere Street in London, England. Dating to 1749, it is the oldest surviving building in Halifax and was the first Anglican church in Canada. The interior is full of memorials to Halifax's early residents. Notice the bit of metal embedded above the door at the back of the north wall—it's a piece of shrapnel hurled from the *Mont Blanc*, 2 kilometers (1.2 miles) away, during the Halifax Explosion. The church is between Barrington and Argyle Streets at the edge of the Grand Parade; look for the square belfry topped by an octagonal cupola.

Old Burying Ground

Designated a national historic site in 1991, the **Old Burying Ground cemetery** (June-Sept. daily 9am-5pm, free) sits opposite

A Long Weekend in Halifax

Halifax is a major destination for conventioneers (modern facilities, well-priced accommodations, centrally located for delegates from both North America and Europe), and in this regard, you may find yourself wanting to hang around for a few days when the last meeting wraps up on Friday. Or, for leisure travelers, many flights to other parts of Atlantic Canada are routed through Halifax, so it will cost little or nothing to have a stopover before continuing to Newfoundland, Prince Edward Island, or elsewhere. This itinerary covers both scenarios, and you don't have to worry about driving.

DAY 1

You've been staying at an upscale downtown Halifax hotel such as Four Points by Sheraton Halifax, and suddenly it's not business anymore. No worries; rates drop dramatically come the weekend, so you won't break the bank by staying another two nights. Join the after-work crowd at the **Seahorse Tavern,** and then plan on dining next door at the **Economy Shoe Shop.**

DAY 2

Visit **Halifax Citadel National Historic Site** to get a feel for the city's colorful history, then walk over to the **Public Gardens.** After lunch, learn about the *Titanic* tragedy at the **Maritime Museum of the Atlantic** before visiting the graves of some of the victims at **Fairview Cemetery.** For a casual seafood dinner with a sublime view, walk along the waterfront to **Salty's.**

DAY 3

The local tour company Ambassatours operates an excellent full-day trip along the South Shore. It hits the highlights—scenic **Peggy's Cove** and the beautiful waterfront **churches of Mahone Bay**—while also allowing time to wander through the historic streets of downtown **Lunenburg,** where there's time for shopping and lunch. You'll be back in Halifax in time for dinner at **Chives Canadian Bistro,** which features lots of fresh seasonal produce.

DAY 4

Check the sailing schedule of the *Bluenose II* and make reservations for a morning cruise if this grand old lady is in port. Otherwise, you could start out with breakfast at the **Italian Market,** followed by shopping at downtown stores as varied as **NovaScotian Crystal** and **Rum Runners Rum Cake Factory.** Golfers may want to squeeze in a tee time at **Glen Arbour Golf Course,** which is on the way out to the airport.

Government House at Barrington Street and Spring Garden Road. Its history goes back to the city's founding. The first customer, so to speak, was interred just one day after the arrival of the original convoy of English settlers in 1749. Also among the thicket of age-darkened, hand-carved, old-fashioned headstones is the 1754 grave of John Connor, the settlement's first ferry captain. The most recent burial took place more than 160 years ago, in 1844.

St. Mary's Cathedral Basilica

Two popes and hundreds of thousands of parishioners have filed through the doors of the Gothic Revival **St. Mary's Cathedral Basilica** (1508 Barrington St., 902/429-9800, www.halifaxyarmouth.org/cathedral), whose spires cast an afternoon shadow over the Old Burying Ground. It was built in 1860; the title "Basilica" was bestowed during a visit by Pope Pius XII in 1950. The stained-glass windows, replaced after the originals were destroyed by the 1917 Halifax Explosion, are particularly impressive.

The *Titanic* Tragedy

"My God, the *Titanic* has struck a berg." With these fateful words, uttered on April 14, 1912, by wireless operator Jack Goodwin of Cape Race, Newfoundland, the outside world first heard about what would develop into the world's best-known maritime disaster—the sinking of the unsinkable ship on its maiden voyage between Southampton, England, and New York City. On board were 2,227 passengers and crew.

At the time of the wireless transmission, the vessel was 800 kilometers (495 miles) east of Halifax. Three Halifax ships were promptly chartered to search for the foundering vessel. By the time the first had arrived, the *Titanic* was lying on the bottom of the Atlantic Ocean. More than 1,500 passengers and crew perished while 702 lucky souls, mostly women and children, were rescued. Bodies were brought ashore at Karlsen's Wharf (2089 Upper Wharf St.) and Coaling Wharf No. 4 (north of the MacDonald Bridge), neither of which is open to the public. They were then transported in coffins to a variety of locations, including a curling rink (now an army

a headstone at Fairview Cemetery

surplus store, at 2660 Agricola St.) and Snow's Funeral Home (1750 Argyle St.), which is now a seafood restaurant. Some bodies were claimed by families, but most were buried in three local cemeteries. The largest concentration is in a plot donated by the White Star Line within Fairview Cemetery (corner of Connaught and Chisholm Aves.). Most of the black headstones simply note the date of the tragedy and a number that relates to the order in which bodies were pulled from the ocean. Others have moving tributes to the bravery of loved ones. John Clarke, a band member famous for continuing to play as the ship was sinking, is buried at Mount Olivet Cemetery (Mumford Rd., off Joseph Howe Dr.).

The *Titanic*'s owners, the White Star Line, maintained an office in Halifax at 1682 Hollis Street that still stands. It became a hive of activity when the bodies began arriving, as staff members were an important link between the victims and their families from around the world.

Funerals and services were held at a number of downtown churches, including St. George's Anglican Church (222 Brunswick St.), St. Paul's Anglican Church (1749 Argyle St.), and St. Mary's Cathedral Basilica (corner of Spring Garden Rd. and Barrington St.).

The best place to learn about the tragedy is the Maritime Museum of the Atlantic (1675 Lower Water St., 902/424-7490, http://maritimemuseum.novascotia.ca, May Mon.-Sat. 9:30am-5:30pm, June-Oct. daily 9:30am-5:30pm, Nov.-Apr. Tues.-Sat. 9:30am-5pm, Sun. 1pm-5pm, adult $9.55, senior $8.50, child $5.15), which has a dedicated display area with artifacts, such as the only deck chair recovered from the vessel. For archival records, including travel documents, photos, and correspondence related to *Titanic* passengers, visit the Nova Scotia Archives (6016 University Ave., 902/424-6060, Mon.-Fri. 8:30am-4:30pm, Sat. 9am-5pm, free).

★ Alexander Keith's Brewery

At the south end of downtown and one block back from the water, Alexander Keith's Brewery (1496 Lower Water St., 902/455-1474, www.alexanderkeithsbrewery.com, tours June-Oct. Mon.-Sat. noon-7:30pm, Sun. noon-5pm, Nov.-May Fri. 5pm-8pm, Sat. noon-8pm, Sun. noon-5pm, adult $25, senior $20, child $10) is North America's oldest operating brewery. Keith arrived in Halifax in 1795, bringing with him brewing techniques from his English homeland and finding a ready market among the soldiers and sailors living in the city. Although main brewing operations have been moved to the Oland Brewery, north of downtown, the original brewery, an impressive stone and granite edifice extending along an entire block, produces seasonal brews using traditional techniques. Tours are led by costumed guides, ending with a traditional toast to the "Father of Great Beer."

Canadian Museum of Immigration at Pier 21

As you continue south along Lower Water Street from the brewery (take the Harbourwalk for the full effect), beyond the statue of Samuel Cunard, the waterfront is dominated by Halifax's massive cruise-ship terminal. This 3,900-square-meter (41,979-square-foot) structure has a long and colorful history of welcoming foreigners in its original capacity as an "immigration shed," where more than a million immigrants, refugees, and war brides first set foot on Canadian soil between 1928 and 1971. It was also the main departure point for 500,000 Canadians who fought in World War II. Upstairs within the building is the **Canadian Museum of Immigration at Pier 21** (1055 Marginal Rd., 902/425-7770, www.pier21.ca, May-Nov. daily 9:30am-5:30pm, Dec.-Apr. Wed.-Sun. 10am-5pm, adult $13, senior $10, child $8). This vast immigration museum does a wonderful job of bringing to life the stories of those who traveled across the ocean to make a new home in Canada. The firsthand accounts begin with the decision to leave home, then go through voyage and arrival to describe onward journeys by rail across Canada. Allow time to view *Oceans of Hope*, a 30-minute film narrated by a fictional immigration officer.

Beside the street-level reception area is the **Research Centre,** which can be used by individuals whose families arrived in Canada through Pier 21. It contains a wide variety of documents, passenger logs, and historic images of passenger vessels.

Centre for Craft Nova Scotia

Beside the Canadian Museum of Immigration, provincial crafts development and innovation are nurtured at the **Centre for Craft Nova Scotia** (1061 Marginal Rd., 902/492-2522, www.craft-design.ns.ca, Tues.-Fri. 9am-5pm, Sat.-Sun. 11am-4pm, free), a workshop ensconced in the cruise-ship terminal geared to weaving, woodworking, metal, and multimedia production.

★ Point Pleasant Park

Before dawn on September 29, 2003, Hurricane Juan hit Halifax like no other storm in living memory. Seventy-five-hectare (185-acre) **Point Pleasant Park** (5718 Point Pleasant Dr., www.pointpleasantpark.ca, daily 6am-midnight), at the southern tip of the Halifax peninsula, took the full brunt of the storm. By daybreak the next morning, the full extent of the damage was first seen—more than 75,000 of the park's 100,000 trees had been destroyed, and the park's ecology had been changed forever. After the cleanup, a massive rejuvenation project that continues to this day began.

Although much of the forest may be gone, the park is still well worth visiting. To get to the main entrance, take South Park Street south from Sackville Street. South Park becomes Young Avenue, a tree-lined boulevard graced by magnificent mansions; turn left on Point Pleasant Drive. Marginal Road from downtown also terminates at the same waterside entrance. Views from the parking lot sweep across the harbor, with container terminals on one side and green space on the other. Forty kilometers (25 miles) of trails, many paved, allow for hiking, jogging, and cross-country skiing in winter. Bikes are allowed only Monday-Friday. Most of the main trails have reopened since the storm, allowing access to all corners of the spread, with terns, gulls, and ospreys winging overhead. A bit of real-estate trivia: The park is still rented from the British government, on a 999-year lease, for one shilling per year.

Point Pleasant's military significance is evidenced by the 1796 **Prince of Wales Martello Tower** (July-early Sept. daily

10am-6pm, free) and Fort Ogilvie, built in 1862, both part of Halifax's defensive system. The former, a thick-walled round tower based on those the British were building at the time to repel Napoleon's forces, was the first of its kind to be built in North America.

CITADEL HILL AND VICINITY

Walk up George Street from the harbor front to reach Citadel Hill. You'll know you're on the right street by the **Old Town Clock,** framed by the buildings of George Street at the base of Citadel Hill. Originally constructed as the official timekeeper for Halifax, the four-faced clock tower was completed in 1803 by order of the compulsively punctual Prince Edward. It is not open to the public but instead stands as a city landmark.

★ Halifax Citadel National Historic Site

Halifax's premier landmark, the **Citadel National Historic Site** (5425 Sackville St., 902/426-5080, www.pc.gc.ca, July-Aug. daily 9am-6pm, Sept.-June daily 9am-5pm, adult $12, senior $10.50, child $6, parking $3.15) is also the most visited national historic site in Canada. The Citadel crowns the hill at the top of George Street, commanding the strategic high ground above the city and harbor, with magnificent views of the entire area. This star-shaped, dressed-granite fortress, the fourth military works built on the site, was completed in 1856. In its heyday, the Citadel represented the pinnacle of defensive military technology, though its design was never tested by an attack.

In summer, students in period uniforms portray soldiers of the 78th Highlanders and the Royal Artillery, demonstrating military drills, powder magazine operation, changing of the sentries, and piping. At the stroke of noon each day, they load and fire a cannon with due military precision and ceremony, a shot heard round the city. Most of the fortress is open for exploration; exhibits include a museum, barrack rooms, a powder magazine, and

a 50-minute audiovisual presentation on the fort's history. Guided tours are included in the admission price, while within the grounds are a gift shop and café.

The grounds are open year-round, but no services are offered November-April.

Museum of Natural History

The rather plain exterior of the **Museum of Natural History** (1747 Summer St., 902/424-7353, http://naturalhistory.novascotia.ca, Tues.-Sun. 9am-5pm, adult $6.50, senior $5.70, child $4.05) belies a treasure trove of exhibits that bring the province's natural world to life. Opposite the ticket desk is a kid-friendly nature center with small critters in enclosures and tanks, and staff on hand to answer any questions. Beyond this point are exhibits that tell the story of Nova Scotia's first human inhabitants, Paleo Indians, who moved into the region 11,000 years ago. The dinosaur displays are a major draw for young and old. You'll also learn about modern-day creatures in a room full of stuffed animals and a large hall dominated by a pilot whale skeleton. Other highlights include a gem and mineral display and artifacts from Acadian culture. The museum is a five-minute walk from Citadel Hill, but it also has plenty of its own parking.

★ Public Gardens

South across Sackville Street from the Citadel grounds, the **Public Gardens** (www.halifaxpublicgardens.ca, May-mid-Oct. daily 8am-dusk, free) are an irresistibly attractive oasis spread over 7 hectares (17 acres) in the heart of the city. Bordered by Spring Garden Road, South Park Street, Summer Street, and Sackville Street, what started in 1753 as a private garden is reminiscent of the handsome parks of Europe and now considered one of the loveliest formal gardens in North America.

Inside the wrought-iron fence (main

1: Halifax Citadel National Historic Site; 2: Public Gardens

Halifax Harbour

From a maritime standpoint, Halifax Harbour is a jewel, the world's second-largest natural harbor (after Sydney Harbour in Australia). High rocky bluffs notched with coves rim the wide entrance where the harbor meets the frothy Atlantic. **McNabs Island** is spread across the harbor's mouth and is so large that it almost clogs the entrance. Many an unwary ship has foundered on the island's shallow, treacherous Eastern Passage coastline.

On the western side of McNabs Island, the harbor is split in two by Halifax's peninsula. The Northwest Arm, a fjord-like sliver of sea, cuts off to one side and wraps around the city's back side. Along its banks are the long lawns of parks, estates, yacht clubs, and several university campuses. The main channel continues inland, shouldered by uptown Halifax on one side and its sister city of Dartmouth on the other.

THE TOURIST'S HARBOUR

The harbor puts on its best show directly in front of downtown. White-hulled cruise ships nose into port and dock alongside Halifax's **Point Pleasant Park** at the peninsula's southern tip. Freighters, tugs, tour boats, and sailboats skim the choppy waters, and ferries cut through the sea traffic, scurrying back and forth between the two cities with their loads of commuters and sightseers.

The scene has a transfixing quality about it. Tourist season unofficially starts and ends when the harbor-front Halifax Sheraton hotel sets tables and chairs for alfresco dining on the waterfront promenade. Stiff summer breezes usually accompany lunch, but the view is worth it. Less hardy diners jostle for tables with a harbor view at **Salty's,** the nearby restaurant with its enviable wide-windowed dining room overlooking the same scene.

Beyond the tourist's realm and the two cities' harbor fronts, the spacious harbor compresses itself into **the Narrows.** Two high-flung steel expressways—the **MacDonald** and **MacKay Bridges**—cross the Narrows at either end. The MacDonald Bridge permits pedestrians and provides an aerial view of the **Maritime Command** and **Her Majesty's Canadian Dockyard** along the Halifax side.

The slender Narrows then opens into 40-square-kilometer (15.4-square-mile) **Bedford Basin,** 16 kilometers (9.9 miles) long and as capacious as a small inland sea. Sailboats cruise its waters now, but the expanse has seen a parade of ships cross its waters through the years—from the white-sailed British warships of centuries ago to the steel-hulled vessels of the Allies during both world wars.

HALIFAX HARBOUR FROM VARIED ANGLES

Halifax Harbour reveals itself in different views. Its pulse can be probed from one of the ferries or from the harbor front in either city. The approach from the Atlantic can be seen best from the historic fort at **York Redoubt** on Purcells Cove Road. You'll get a good view of the Northwest Arm's ritzy estate and university scene from Fleming Park's **Memorial Tower** on the same road. **Africville Park** beneath the MacKay Bridge overlooks the Narrows where that slender strait meets Bedford Basin.

entrance at the corner of South Park Street and Spring Garden Road), the setting revels in tulips that flower late May–early June, followed by rhododendrons, roses, and perennials through summer. Other highlights are the exotic and native trees, fountains, and lily ponds where ducks and geese make their homes. The ornate bandstand dates from Queen Victoria's Golden Jubilee and is the site of free Sunday afternoon concerts in July and August. Also during the summer, vendors of arts and crafts hawk their wares outside the gardens along Spring Garden Road.

NORTH OF DOWNTOWN

The following sights are north of Cogswell Street. It's a 2-kilometer (1.2-mile) walk from downtown to Fort Needham Memorial Park. Fairview Cemetery is not within walking distance.

St. George's Round Church

Architect William Hughes designed the unusual and charming timber-frame **St. George's Round Church** (Cornwallis and Brunswick Sts., www.roundchurch.ca, tours July-Aug. Mon.-Fri. 11am-4pm, free), which at once accommodated the overflow of parishioners from the nearby Dutch Church on Brunswick Street and satisfied Prince Edward's penchant for round buildings. The cornerstone was laid in 1800, and the chancel and front porch were added later. A fire in 1994 destroyed the dome, but it has since been replaced. St. George's is a few blocks north of downtown.

Maritime Command Museum

On the grounds of Canadian Forces Base Halifax, the **Maritime Command Museum** (Gottingen St. between North St. and Russell St., 902/721-8250, Mon.-Fri. 10am-3:30pm, free) is ensconced in the 30-room Admiralty House, built in the 1840s as a residence for the base's admiral. Exhibits include presentation swords, memorabilia from the World War II Battle of the Atlantic, a military gun collection, uniforms, ship models, and other artifacts relating to the history of the Canadian Maritime Military Forces.

Fort Needham Memorial Park

Continue north along Gottingen Street from the Maritime Command Museum and veer right onto Dartmouth Street to reach the **Fort Needham Memorial Park,** a high point of land with views across the head of Halifax Harbour. The park's most distinctive feature is a 14-bell carillon, a monument to the Halifax Explosion of 1917, at the time the largest human-created explosion the world had ever known. Stand in the break between the memorial's two halves to get views through a clearing to the harbor and the actual site of the explosion.

Africville Park

Halifax's peninsula is bookended by a pair of expansive green spaces. **Africville Park** is at the north end, overlooking Bedford Basin from the foot of the A. Murray MacKay Bridge. This was once the site of Africville, a community of Black Haligonians established in the 1840s but since demolished. The importance of the settlement is reflected in its designation as a national historic site. The only physical remainder of its history is a replica of the African United Church. As you head north from downtown along Barrington Street, access is along Service Road. A boat launch provides the only water access.

★ Fairview Cemetery

Take Windsor Street north from Quinpool Road to reach **Fairview Cemetery** (daily dawn-dusk), the final resting place of 121 *Titanic* victims. When the bodies were pulled from the Atlantic Ocean, they were given a number. These numbers, along with the date of the disaster, April 15, 1912 (it is assumed no one could have survived any longer than a day in the frigid ocean), adorn a majority of the simple black headstones paid for by the White Star Line, owners of the *Titanic*. Where identification was possible, a name accompanies the number (such as victim 227, J. Dawson, inspiration for the character Jack Dawson, played by Leonardo DiCaprio, in the movie *Titanic*). Some headstones are engraved with moving tributes, such as that to Everett Edward Elliott, aged 24, which reads, "Each man stood at his port while all the weaker ones went by, and showed once more to all the world how Englishmen should die."

The turn into the cemetery is easy to miss; get in the left lane by Connaught Avenue and turn against oncoming traffic to reach the cemetery's main entrance. The other option is to take Connaught Avenue off Windsor Street and park at the end of Chisholm Avenue. Once

Halifax Explosion

On the morning of Thursday, December 6, 1917, Halifax experienced a catastrophic explosion—at the time the largest human-created explosion in history, unrivaled until the detonation of the first atomic bomb. On that fateful morning, Halifax Harbour was busy with warships transporting troops, munitions, and other supplies bound for the war in Europe. A French ship, the *Mont Blanc*, filled to the gunwales with explosives—including 400,000 pounds of TNT—was heading through the Narrows toward the harbor mouth when it was struck by a larger vessel, the *Imo*, which was steaming in the opposite direction, and caught fire. The terrified crew of the *Mont Blanc* took immediately to the lifeboats as the burning ship drifted close to the Halifax shore.

A short time later, at 9:05am, the *Mont Blanc* cargo blew up, instantly killing an estimated 2,000 people, wounding another 10,000, and obliterating about 130 hectares (321 acres) of the North End of downtown Halifax. So colossal was the explosion that windows were shattered 80 kilometers (50 miles) away, and the shock wave rocked Sydney on Cape Breton, 430 kilometers (265 miles) northeast. The barrel of one of the *Mont Blanc*'s cannons was hurled 5.5 kilometers (3.4 miles), while its half-ton anchor shank landed more than 3 kilometers (1.9 miles) away in the opposite direction.

Serving as a memorial to the tragedy is **Fort Needham Memorial Park,** along Gottingen Street north from downtown. Here, a 14-bell carillon is on a high point of land from which the site of the original explosion can be seen. While the harbor-front **Maritime Museum of the Atlantic** has an exhibit dedicated to the explosion, one of the most interesting reminders is up the hill at **St. Paul's Anglican Church** (1749 Argyle St.), where a chunk of metal from the doomed *Mont Blanc* is embedded in the north-facing wall.

---

you're at the cemetery, the plot is well signposted, with an interpretive board describing the events leading up to identifying victims, even long after they were buried.

Hemlock Ravine Park

The rugged tract of forest known as **Hemlock Ravine Park** lies beside the western side of Bedford Basin between the busy Bedford and Bicentennial highways—but you'd never know urban civilization is so close as you walk along the five interconnecting walking trails. The park's namesake ravine, with its towering hemlocks, takes about 20 minutes to reach from the main parking lot, at the end of Kent Avenue, which branches off the Bedford Highway (Highway 2) 1 kilometer (0.6 mile) north of the Kearney Lake Road intersection. Beside the parking lot is a heart-shaped pond designed by Prince Edward, who spent his summers here with his companion Julie St. Laurent.

Uniacke Estate Museum Park

The splendid 930-hectare (2,298-acre)

Uniacke Estate Museum Park (758 Main Rd., Mount Uniacke, 902/866-0032, http://uniacke.novascotia.ca, June-early Oct. Tues.-Sat. 10am-5pm, Sun. 11:30am-5pm, adult $4, senior and child $3) is along Highway 1 beyond the city limits, 20 kilometers (12.4 miles) northwest from the intersection of Highway 102. The easiest way to get there is to take Exit 3 from Highway 101. The home's interior features original furnishings, including four-poster beds and family portraits. The grounds offer seven hiking trails.

Atlantic Canada Aviation Museum

Across the highway from the airport (take Exit 6 from Hwy. 102), the **Atlantic Canada Aviation Museum** (20 Sky Blvd., 902/873-3773, www.atlanticcanadaaviationmuseum.com, May-Sept. daily 9am-5pm, adult $5) is a good place to visit on the way north to Truro or before your flight home. On display are about 30 aircraft—everything from fighter planes to a homemade helicopter—and a couple of simulators.

WEST SIDE OF NORTHWEST ARM

Carefully make your way onto the Armdale Rotary at the west end of Quinpool Road and take the Herring Cove Road exit. A short distance south along this road, Purcells Cove Road veers off to the left. This winding road hugs the Northwest Arm for 9 kilometers (5.6 miles) to the fishing village of Herring Cove. Along the way are two yacht clubs filled with glistening white sailboats.

Sir Sandford Fleming Park

A 38-hectare (94-acre) grassy spread, the delightful **Sir Sandford Fleming Park** (daily 8am-dusk) is mostly forested, sloping to a seawall promenade fringing a quiet waterway. The land was donated by the Scottish-born Fleming, best known for establishing time zones. It is said a missed train led the enterprising Fleming to begin formulating a plan that would see the entire world operate on a 24-hour clock with time zones that related to longitude. Fleming, who also designed Canada's first postage stamp, lived in Halifax from the 1880s until his death in 1915.

On a slight rise above the bay is the 10-story **Dingle Tower** (June-Aug. daily 9am-5pm, free). A stairway winds up the interior of this stone edifice, presenting great views from the top.

The main entrance is off Purcells Cove Road; Dingle Road leads down through the wooded park to the waterfront.

York Redoubt National Historic Site

Set on a bluff high above the harbor entrance, **York Redoubt National Historic Site** (Purcells Cove Rd., 902/426-5080, www.pc.gc.ca, grounds mid-May-Oct. daily 9am-6pm, buildings mid-June-Aug. daily 10am-6pm, free) is 6 kilometers (3.7 miles) south of downtown. The setting draws visitors with walking paths that lead down the steep incline to picnic tables and protected coves. Up top are strategic fortifications dating to 1793, when Britain went to war with the French. Most of the fort is from later times, including massive muzzle-loading guns that were designed to fire nine-inch shells capable of piercing armored vessels.

MCNABS ISLAND

Whatever your interests, the 5-kilometer-long (3.1-mile-long) **McNabs Island,** at the entrance to Halifax Harbour, is a wonderful place to spend a day. The island is mostly

Atlantic Canada Aviation Museum

wooded, its forests filled with birdlife and its shoreline dotted with beaches and tidal pools. Archaeological evidence points to habitation by the Mi'kmaq at least 1,600 years ago, but the most obvious signs of human development are more recent, including two forts and the remains of a number of residences (including the summer home of Frederick Perrin, of Lea & Perrins Worcestershire sauce fame). Although many of the early residences have disappeared, signs of their formal gardens remain; look for ash, oak, and apple trees.

Recreation

Most visitors come to the island to go hiking. Ferries land at Garrison Pier, from which trails radiate in all directions. The top of Jenkin's Hill, easily reached in 10 minutes, is a good place to get oriented while also enjoying sweeping harbor views. At the 1864 **Fort Ives,** an easy 30-minute walk from the pier, cannons are still in place. **Fort McNab,** a similar distance south of the pier, was built in 1889 and is protected as a national historic site. Sandy **Mauger's Beach,** just south of Garrison Pier, is the best and most accessible of many island beaches.

Getting There

Year-round access to the island is provided by **McNabs Island Ferry** (902/465-4563, www. mcnabsisland.com, adult round-trip $20, senior and child round-trip $15), which departs on demand from Fisherman's Cove on the Dartmouth side of the harbor. The crossing takes less than 10 minutes. No services are available on the island, so bring your own food and drink and be prepared for changeable weather by bringing a rain jacket.

DARTMOUTH

Dartmouth is a large residential, commercial, and industrial area across the harbor from Halifax. The two cities are joined by a bridge and Metro Transit's Halifax-Dartmouth ferry from the foot of downtown's George Street to the Alderney Gate complex in Dartmouth. Ferries operate year-round Monday-Saturday 6:30am-midnight, and daily in summer. The fare is adult $2.50, senior and child $1.75 each way. The ferry arrives within walking distance of Dartmouth Heritage Museum properties and various shops and restaurants.

Dartmouth Heritage Museum

The **Dartmouth Heritage Museum** (www. dartmouthheritagemuseum.ns.ca) comprises two historic homes within walking distance of Alderney Gate. The 1867 **Evergreen House** (26 Newcastle St., 902/464-2300, summer Tues.-Sun. 10am-5pm, the rest of the year Tues.-Fri. 10am-5pm, adult $5), filled with period antiques, is the grander of the two. Built by a cooper (barrel maker) in 1785, **Quaker House** (57 Ochterloney St., 902/464-5823, summer Tues.-Sun. 10am-1pm and 2pm-5pm, adult $5) is one of Dartmouth's oldest residences. In addition to period furnishings, exhibits tell the story of the Quakers, who were drawn to Nova Scotia for its abundance of whales.

Bedford Institute of Oceanography

The government-run **Bedford Institute of Oceanography** (Baffin Blvd., 902/426-4306, www.bio.gc.ca, guided tours by appointment only May-Aug. Mon.-Fri. 9am-4pm, free) has a mandate that includes everything from helping maintain Canada's sovereignty to federal fisheries, but it is best known for its work on the sunken *Titanic*. On the guided tour, you'll get to learn about all this work, as well as step aboard a simulated ship's bridge and get up close and personal at the Touch Tank. To get there from downtown Halifax, cross the Narrows and take the Shannon Park exit from the MacKay Bridge (immediately after the toll gates); turn right and then left onto Baffin Boulevard, which crosses under the bridge to the institute. The easiest way to book a tour is through their website.

Shubie Park

In 1858, construction began on an ambitious canal system that linked Halifax Harbour with the Bay of Fundy via a string of lakes and the Shubenacadie River. The canal was abandoned just 12 years later. The canal between Lake Micmac and Lake Charles has been restored, complete with one of nine original locks. **Shubie Park** is laced with hiking and biking trails, but many visitors take to the water in canoes, kayaks, and paddleboards, paddling from the main day-use area to Lake Charles. Access is signposted from Braemar Drive, which branches north from Exit 6 of Highway 111.

Cole Harbour Heritage Farm Museum

Surrounded by a residential subdivision, the outdoor **Cole Harbour Heritage Farm Museum** (471 Poplar Dr., 902/434-0222, http://coleharbourfarmmuseum.ca, mid-May-mid-Oct. Mon.-Sat. 10am-4pm, Sun. noon-4pm, donation) is a great place for children. Buildings include a 200-year-old farmhouse, a blacksmith shop, various barns, and a tearoom, while garden plots represent early crops, with the produce used in the tearoom. Livestock is fenced, but rabbits, geese, and ducks roam free.

EASTERN PASSAGE

The Eastern Passage is a narrow waterway running between the Dartmouth side of Halifax Harbour and McNabs Island. From downtown Dartmouth, take Pleasant Street south to Highway 322. This route passes oil refineries and Canadian Forces Base Shearwater

before reaching the delightful Fisherman's Cove. Beyond this point, Highway 322 continues through an oceanfront residential area to Southeast Passage Provincial Park.

Shearwater Aviation Museum

At the entrance to Canadian Forces Base Shearwater, the **Shearwater Aviation Museum** (12 Wing Gate, Pleasant St., 902/720-1083, www.shearwateraviationmuseum.ns.ca, June-Aug. Mon.-Fri. 10am-5pm, Sat.-Sun. noon-4pm, Apr.-May and Sept.-Nov. Tues.-Fri. 10am-5pm, Sat. noon-4pm, donation) is home to 10 restored aircraft and an impressive collection of air force memorabilia. The museum is off Pleasant Street (Highway 322); turn left at the first set of lights beyond the Imperial oil refinery.

★ Fisherman's Cove

Fisherman's Cove is no different from the hundreds of picturesque fishing villages that dot the Nova Scotia coastline, with one exception—it's within the city limits of the capital. Lying along the Eastern Passage, 2 kilometers (1.2 miles) southeast of Dartmouth along Highway 322, the cove mixes the needs of working fishing vessels with a constant flow of curious visitors. You can drive along Government Wharf Road, which spurs right at the traffic lights in Eastern Passage, onto the main dock area, but it's much more enjoyable to explore the area on foot from the parking lot just beyond the cove's main entrance.

Recreation

WALKING AND HIKING

Even if you're not feeling overly energetic, plan to take a stroll along the downtown waterfront. A **seawall promenade** winds past docks filled with all manner of boats (tall ships, tugboats, and visiting yachts), harborfront restaurants, the Maritime Museum of the Atlantic, Historic Properties, and south to Pier 21. While it's possible to do all your downtown sightseeing on foot, an easier option is to catch a cab to Citadel Hill, from which it's downhill all the way back to the harbor. At Citadel Hill, take the time not only to visit the fort but also to walk around the perimeter, and then cross Sackville Street to the **Public Gardens,** a delightful place for a flower-filled stroll.

McNabs Island is a popular destination for day-tripping hikers.

Point Pleasant Park, 2.5 kilometers (1.6 miles) south of downtown, off Young Avenue, is laced with hiking and biking trails. The obvious choice is to stick to the water, along a 2-kilometer (1.2-mile) (one-way) trail that hugs the shoreline, passing Point Pleasant itself before winding around to the Northwest Arm. Other trails lead inland to historic fortifications and through the remains of forests devastated by Hurricane Juan in 2003.

Across the Northwest Arm from downtown, **Sir Sandford Fleming Park** flanks the water in an upscale neighborhood. Again, it's the seawall walk that is most popular, but another pleasant trail leads up through the forest to Frog Lake.

Take the Bedford Highway north from downtown and then 1 kilometer (0.6 mile) north of the Kearney Lake Road junction and watch for Kent Avenue (to the left), which leads into a dense old-growth forest protected as **Hemlock Ravine Park.** From the pond and picnic area, a world away from surrounding development, five trails branch off into the forest. Some are short and perfect for younger and older walkers, while others, including the trail to the hemlock-filled ravine, are steeper and can be slippery after rain.

BICYCLING

The local municipality, with its many lakes and harbor-side coves, has put considerable effort into making the city as bike-friendly as possible. The Halifax Regional Municipality website (www.halifax.ca) has a PDF bike map, or pick one up at the information center. A centrally located source for rentals and advice is **I Heart Bikes** (1507 Lower Water St., 902/406-7774, summer daily 10am-5pm). Standard bikes cost from $20 for two hours to $35 for a full day. Electric bikes are only slightly more expensive.

Freewheeling Adventures (902/857-3600 or 800/672-0775, www.freewheeling.ca, from $2,400 per person) is a local tour company that runs recommended guided bike trips along the South Shore, starting from Hubbards, just south of the city. Guests ride for up to six hours per day, stay in cottages or B&Bs, and have all meals included.

WATER SPORTS
Swimming and Sunbathing

In addition to indoor pools at most major downtown hotels, municipal swimming pools include the centrally located, 50-meter-long **Centennial Pool** (1970 Gottingen St., 902/490-7219, daily 7:45am-8:30pm), which has lots of times set aside for public swims, and **Needham Pool** (3372 Devonshire Ave., 902/490-4633, Mon.-Fri. 8:30am-6pm, Sun. 1:30pm-6:30pm).

Crystal Crescent Beach Provincial Park lies a half hour south of Halifax, off Highway 349, and is the locals' favorite Atlantic beach. Its sand is fine, and the sea is usually cold, but summer crowds heat up the action. Nature lovers will enjoy the 10-kilometer (6.2-mile) trail to remote Pennant Point, while naturists will want to gravitate to the farthest of the park's three beaches—one of Canada's few official nude beaches.

If you're visiting Fisherman's Cove, head east for 8 kilometers (5 miles) along Cow Bay Road to reach **Rainbow Haven Provincial Park.** The park protects wetlands at the mouth of Cole Harbour and an ocean-facing beach. The beach is often windy (it's not uncommon to see people sunbathing back in the dunes), but on calm days it's a delightful place to soak up some rays and maybe, if you're brave, take a dip in the water. At the end of the park access road are changing rooms and a concession selling beachy food (ice cream and hot dogs).

Canoeing and Kayaking
Based on the Northwest Arm, **St. Mary's Boat Club** (1641 Fairfield Rd., 902/490-4688, June-Sept. Sat.-Sun. 11am-7pm) rents canoes at no cost on a limited basis through summer. If you're interested in kayaking, call ahead for a schedule of evening events, which often include tours on Northwest Arm for $15 per person.

GOLFING
Halifax and the surrounding area are home to more than a dozen courses, varying from 9-hole public courses to exclusive 18-holers. The **Nova Scotia Golf Association** website (www.nsga.ns.ca) has links to all provincial courses.

The Courses
Glen Arbour Golf Course (Glen Arbour Way, off Hammonds Plains Rd., 1 km/0.6 mi west of Bedford, 902/835-4653) is one of Canada's finest links. Choose from five sets of tees, to a maximum of 6,800 yards. The course has abundant water hazards, 90 bunkers, and fairways lined by hardwood forests. Greens fees top out at $115 in midsummer, dropping as low as $60 for twilight golf in October.

Lost Creek Golf Club (310 Kinsac Rd., 902/865-4653) enjoys the same forested environment as Glen Arbour, but without the valet parking and high greens fees (golfing is just $52). To get there, take Exit 2 from Highway 101 and follow Beaverbank Road north for 10 kilometers (6.2 miles); turn right on Kinsac Road and then left on William Nelson Drive.

One of the region's most enjoyable layouts is **Granite Springs** (25 km/15.5 mi west of downtown, off Hwy. 333 at 4441 Prospect Rd., Bayside, 902/852-4653). This challenging course winds through 120 hectares (297 acres) of mature forest, with distant ocean views. Greens fees are $65 ($40 twilight).

WINTER SPORTS
In winter, walking paths become **cross-country ski trails** at Point Pleasant Park, Sir Sandford Fleming Park, and Hemlock Ravine Park. Dartmouth maintains groomed surfaces at Lake Charles, and several lakes in Halifax are great for skating.

Skiing and Snowboarding
The closest downhill skiing and boarding is at **Ski Martock** (902/798-9501, www.martock. com, Dec.-Mar. daily 9am-9pm, day passes adult $40, child $30), an hour's drive northwest of Halifax off Highway 101 (signposted from Exit 5). It's a popular family hill, with mostly beginner runs accessible by two lifts rising 180 vertical meters. Snowmaking covers the entire resort, while lights keep runs open nightly until 9pm.

Hockey
Through the long winter, when outside activities are curtailed by the weather, there is much interest in ice hockey (known in Canada simply as "hockey"). When they're not watching the National Hockey League on television (the closest teams are in Boston, Montréal, and Toronto), local fans flock to the Halifax Metro Centre to cheer on their own **Halifax Mooseheads** (5284 Duke St., 902/429-3267, www.halifaxmooseheads.ca, tickets from adult $20, senior $17, child $10), who play mid-September-mid-March in the Québec Major Junior Hockey League.

HARBOR CRUISES AND LAND TOURS

If you don't have a lot of time to explore Halifax or just want an introduction to the city, consider one of the many tours available—they'll maximize your time and get you to the highlights with minimum stress.

Bluenose II

The harbor front's premier attraction, the magnificent schooner *Bluenose II* (http://bluenose.novascotia.ca) divides her summer between Halifax, her home port of Lunenburg, and goodwill tours to other Canadian ports. The vessel is an exact replica of the famous *Bluenose*. The schooner is operated by the Lunenburg Marine Museum Society on behalf of the Province of Nova Scotia. When in Halifax, two-hour **harbor tours** (902/634-4794 or 800/763-1963, daily 9:30am and 1pm, adult $64, child $36) are available from the Maritime Museum of the Atlantic's wharf. Each sailing has 65 spots—which can be reserved online. Without a reservation, expect to line up for a spot.

Harbor Cruises

Harbour Hopper Tours (902/423-6242 or 800/565-9662, www.ambassatours.com, adult $37, senior $33, child $21) picks up passengers from the north side of the maritime museum for a quick trip around the historic streets of Halifax. Then the fun really starts, as the company's distinctive green and yellow amphibious vehicles plunge into the water for a cruise around the harbor. The trip lasts around one hour, with up to 20 departures daily May-October (9am-9:30pm). The ticket kiosk is on the waterfront just north of the maritime museum.

Many other sightseeing craft also offer harbor tours. **Ambassatours** (902/423-6242 or 800/565-9662, www.ambassatours.com) represents several vessels through a sailing season that runs mid-May-late October. The 23-meter (75-foot) wooden sailing ketch *Mar* departs up to six times daily (adult $37, senior $33, child $21). The *Harbour Queen I* is a 200-passenger paddle wheeler offering a narrated harbor cruise (adult $37, senior $33, child $21) and a variety of lunch and dinner cruises ($72 for dinner).

Bus Tours

Ambassatours (902/423-6242 or 800/565-9662, www.ambassatours.com) offers a downtown loop tour aboard an old British double-decker bus (mid-June-mid-Oct., adult $62, senior $57, child $32). You can get on and off as you please at any of the 17 stops on two loops, and tickets are valid for two days (a good plan is to ride the entire loop once, and then plan your stops for the second go-round). This same company also has a three-hour trip to Peggy's Cove (departs June-mid-Oct. Tues., Thurs., and Sun. 1pm, adult $52, senior $47, child $34) and a full-day trip that combines a stop in Mahone Bay with time in Lunenburg (departs June-Oct. Mon., Wed., Fri., and Sat. 9am, adult $90, senior $80, child $64).

Entertainment and Events

Halifax has a reputation as a party town, partly because of its large population of students. The city has dozens of pubs, many with local brews on tap and Celtic-inspired bands performing to small but raucous crowds. Most pubs close around midnight. The city also has a notable performing arts community. Although most seasons run through the cooler months, many companies put on events especially for summer crowds.

For complete listings of all that's happening around Halifax, pick up the free *Coast* (www.thecoast.ca). Friday and weekend editions of the *Chronicle Herald* (http://thechronicleherald.ca) also offer comprehensive entertainment listings.

Booths and Burgers

Beyond the white linens and perfectly presented seafood of Halifax's finer restaurants are a smattering of old-style diners. The following are my favorites—one downtown, another overlooking the city's most notorious intersection, and another handy for those traveling into downtown from the north.

In the heart of the central business district, the venerable **Bluenose II** (1824 Hollis St., 902/425-5092, Mon.-Fri. 7:30am-8:30pm, Sat. 8am-9pm, Sun. 8am-8pm, $9-16) is named for the famous schooner that calls Halifax home on a part-time basis. The booths fill with an eclectic crowd of locals for breakfast, but the space is bright and welcoming, and many regulars are families. Eggs Benedict is $8, steak and eggs $9.50, while the rest-of-the-day choices vary from a lobster sandwich ($12) to Greek specialties ($9-16).

Overlooking the confusing-even-for-the-locals Armdale Rotary is **Armview Restaurant** (7156 Chebucto Rd., 902/455-4395, Mon.-Wed. 11am-midnight, Thurs.-Sun. 8:30am-midnight, $8-21), which has been in business since the 1960s, which makes it one of Halifax's oldest restaurants. Although it's undergone renovations and the menu has been expanded to include options like mango halibut salad, you can still order no-frills breakfasts and burgers for around $10.

On Monday, Tuesday, and Wednesday, coupon-clipping retirees fill **Esquire Restaurant** (772 Bedford Hwy., 902/835-9033, daily 7:30am-8pm, $9-16) for specials such as home-style pork dinners for $10. The restaurant is across from the Bedford Basin, and there's plenty of parking, or, if you're staying across the road at the Esquire Motel, you need only to negotiate traffic zooming along the busy Bedford Highway.

PUBS AND BREWERIES

Halifax is renowned for its pubs and its great selection of locally brewed beers. Pubs range from historic homes to waterfront decks, but all are friendly and most also offer a good selection of food.

If you're going to have just one beer in Halifax, quaff it at the **Red Stag Tavern** (1496 Lower Water St., 902/422-0275, Sun.-Thurs. 11:30am-11pm, Fri.-Sat. 11:30am-10:30pm), part of the Keith's Brewery complex. Best known as North America's oldest working brewery, Keith's still uses traditional British brewing techniques. Its famous India Pale Ale is widely available on draught and in bottles across the country, but it's best enjoyed in the Red Stag, surrounded by a convivial atmosphere and with traditional maritime music in the background.

Henry House (1222 Barrington St., 902/423-5660, daily 11:30am-12:45am) is ensconced in a historic 1834 stone building a couple of blocks back from Alexander Keith's Brewery. The pub attracts a slightly older crowd of well-dressed locals and has a wide-ranging menu of food and beer, including gluten-free options.

In the harbor-front Historic Properties complex, **Gahan House** (1869 Upper Water St., 902/407-4278, daily 11am-midnight) is a big, bright room, with lots of outside waterfront seating. It has its own small brewery and offers a range of other local brews. The food here is also notable, ranging from traditional (lobster rolls) to modern (maple curry penne). Adjacent to Gahan House, live music at the **Lower Deck** (1887 Upper Water St., 902/425-1501, daily 11:30am-12:30am) keeps the crowds humming nightly at this waterfront pub within the historic Privateers Warehouse.

The Maxwell's Plum (1600 Grafton St., 902/423-5090, Sun.-Fri. 11am-2am, Sat. 10am-2am) has an excellent selection of imported draft beers (notably Beamish Irish Stout, John Courage, and Newcastle Brown Ale) and single-malt scotches. That alone may be reason enough to visit, but it's also a good venue for straight-ahead jazz, including Sunday afternoon jam sessions.

Best known for its rooftop patio, **Your Father's Moustache** (5686 Spring Garden

Rd., 902/423-6766, Mon.-Fri. 10:30am-midnight, Sat.-Sun. 10am-midnight) puts on excellent live, usually local, music most evenings. On Saturday afternoon, it hosts the popular Blues Matinee.

Aside from sidling up to the bar at the above pubs, beer connoisseurs visiting Halifax can buy directly from a number of small breweries scattered around the city. Generally, you can buy regular bottles, "growlers" (one- or two-liter jugs), or kegs up to 50 liters. **Garrison Brewing** (1149 Marginal Rd., 902/453-5343, Sun.-Fri. 10am-8pm, Sat. 8am-9pm) is in a touristy location south of downtown near Pier 21, but that doesn't stop the brewmaster from producing a wonderful range of ales. Garrison also has a large shop and tasting area.

Northwest of downtown, the **Granite Brewery** (6054 Stairs St., 902/422-4954, Mon.-Thurs. 10am-7pm, Fri.-Sat. 10am-8pm, Sun. noon-6pm) is tucked away between Robie and Kempt Streets, but it's well worth searching out for its excellent English-style ales that are sold to go.

NIGHTLIFE
Bars

In the basement of the Marquee Ballroom north of downtown is the **Seahorse Tavern** (2037 Gottingen St., 902/423-7200, Thurs.-Fri. 9pm-2am, Sat. 6pm-2am), which has been around since 1948 (although it has moved from its original location). Horsepower Beer, produced by the local Propeller Brewery, is available on tap only at the Seahorse, but most patrons are here for the music, with live performances Thursday-Saturday. Part of the same complex is the **Economy Shoe Shop** (1663 Argyle St., 902/423-8845, daily 11am-2am), a drinking and dining venue incorporating three restaurants and the Belgian Bar, with a gaudy but appealing tropical vibe.

HFX Sports Bar (1721 Brunswick St., 902/404-1404, Sun.-Fri. 4pm-2am, Sat. 11am-2am) is a cavernous sports bar anchored by a two-story wall of TV screens. It's arguably the best place in the city to go for U.S. sports,

but you can also watch British-oriented sports such as cricket and rugby. Food is typical pub fare, but is well priced.

Stayner's Wharf Pub & Grill (5075 George St., 902/492-1800, Sun.-Thurs. 11am-11pm, Fri.-Sat. 11am-1am) is in the heart of the tourist district, but since it's a smaller place, the casual visitor often misses this bar, which remains quiet until local jazz and blues bands hit the stage Wednesday-Sunday.

Nightclubs

Around midnight, when the pubs start closing their doors, the crowds move on to nightclubs spread through downtown.

The **Dome** (1726 Argyle St., 902/422-6907, Thurs.-Sat. 11pm-3:30am) is a mass of young heaving bodies who dance the night away in sync to one of Canada's most dynamic sound and light systems. It's also a bit of a pickup place. Under the same roof is **Cheers** (902/421-1655, daily 10pm-3:30am), which attracts an older crowd. Another multi-venue nightclub is **Pacifico** (corner of Barrington and Salter Sts., 902/422-3633, Thurs.-Sat. 9pm-2am), where **CraveBar** attracts serious dancers and the **Capitol** hosts a martini bar.

Starting out as a gay bar, **Reflections Cabaret** (5187 Salter St., 902/422-2957, Thurs.-Sun. 10pm-4am) now attracts an eclectic mix of locals of all persuasions. The biggest crowds are on weekends, when the resident DJ spins tunes until 4am.

Jazz and Blues

The **Seahorse Tavern** (2037 Gottingen St., 902/423-7200, Thurs.-Fri. 9pm-2am, Sat. 6pm-2am) hosts a blues jam every Thursday night. The Belgian Bar, within the **Economy Shoe Shop** (1663 Argyle St., 902/423-8845, daily 11am-2am) features no-charge Monday evening jazz.

The best blues bar in town is **Bearly's House of Blues and Ribs** (1269 Barrington St., 902/423-2526, Mon.-Sat. 11am-midnight,

---

1: Henry House; 2: Economy Shoe Shop; 3: the Granite Brewery; 4: Spring Garden Road

Sun. noon-midnight). As the name suggests, ribs ($16 for a half rack) are the dining specialty, but it is the music that draws an enthusiastic crowd. Weekends feature local talent, while weekdays except Monday and Wednesday the stage is turned over to traveling talent. On Saturday afternoons through winter, bluegrass musicians strum their stuff.

PERFORMING ARTS

Haligonians have a sweet and sometimes bittersweet Canadian sense of humor (somewhat like the British), and local theater revels in their brand of fun. A $52 admission will get you into dinner-theater musical productions at **Grafton Street Dinner Theatre** (1741 Grafton St., 902/425-1961), which operates daily except Monday in summer and Friday and Saturday only through the rest of the year.

The **Neptune Theatre** (1593 Argyle St., 902/429-7070) underwent a huge renovation in the 1990s, during which time the original 1915 auditorium was saved and renovated, while the surrounding structure was rebuilt. Today the theater hosts musicals, comedies, and Canadian premieres.

FESTIVALS AND EVENTS

Halifax hosts a number of well-known events that visitors plan their trips around, as well as many you probably haven't heard of but that are well worth attending if the dates correspond with your own travels. The most popular festivals are held outdoors and in summer, but the cooler months are the season for performing arts. For exact dates of festivals, check the event's website or **Tourism Nova Scotia** (www.novascotia.com).

Spring

The **Scotia Festival of Music** centers on the **Music Room** (6181 Lady Hammond Rd., 902/429-9467, www.scotiafestival.ns.ca) for two weeks from the last weekend in May. Chamber musicians present piano, cello, and violin recitals in a dignified yet casual atmosphere.

Summer

Nothing reflects Halifax's long military heritage better than the **Royal Nova Scotia International Tattoo** (902/420-1114, www.nstattoo.ca), held annually for 10 days at the beginning of July at the Scotiabank Centre (5284 Duke St.). A "tattoo" is an outdoor military exercise presented as entertainment. Here it involves competitions, military bands, dancers, gymnasts, and choirs. The event has grown to be regarded as one of the world's greatest indoor events, bringing together thousands of performers from around the world. You can buy tickets (around $35-60) through the **Scotiabank Centre Box Office** (902/451-1221, www.scotiabank-centre.com).

In mid-July, jazz fans descend on Halifax for the **Halifax Jazz Festival** (902/492-2225, www.halifaxjazzfestival.ca), the largest music festival east of Montréal. In addition to performing in a large tent set up on the waterfront along Lower Water Street at Salter Street, more than 400 musicians from around the world gather at venues as unique as a tugboat and as character-filled as local churches to perform traditional and contemporary jazz.

Halifax and Dartmouth come together to celebrate their birthdays with a civic holiday known as **Natal Day** (www.natalday.org), on the first Monday of every August. Events take place through the entire weekend, including a Saturday parade, talent shows, sporting events, and a grand finale fireworks presentation on the harbor Monday night.

Street performers fill five stages spread along the downtown waterfront for 11 days in early August during the **Halifax Busker Festival** (www.buskers.ca).

Summer finishes with the **Atlantic Fringe Festival** (902/423-4653, www.atlanticfringe.ca), featuring over 55 performers at various downtown venues through the first week of September.

Fall

The mid-September **Atlantic International Film Festival** (902/422-3456, www.atlanticfilm.com) has been wowing moviegoers for more than 35 years. It features the very best films from around the world, but the emphasis is on local and Canadian productions. Venues are mostly downtown theaters.

Celebrate **Alexander Keith's birthday** (902/455-1474, www.keiths.ca) on October 5 with hundreds of enthusiastic locals. Or pull up a barstool at any local pub and raise a toast of India Pale Ale to "The Great Man of Beer," who began brewing beer in Halifax in 1820. The brewery (check the website for locations) is the epicenter of celebrations, with plenty of foot-stomping, beer-drinking east coast music.

Winter

The middle weekend of November, the **Christmas Craft Village** (www. christmascraftvillage.com) fills Exhibition Park with hundreds of crafty booths selling everything from homemade preserves to self-published books to coastal antiques.

Shopping

Shopping in Halifax—the type visitors to the city will enjoy—centers on the **downtown waterfront,** with the exception being the boutiques and quirky shops along **Spring Garden Road.** Expect to find everything from lighthouse Christmas decorations made in China to original oil paintings, and everything in between.

Most shops and all major department stores are generally open Monday-Saturday 9:30am-5:30pm. Stores along the touristy harbor front usually have longer hours and are also open Sunday.

Arts and Crafts

The city's art galleries are superb, and most are located downtown. The newest fine arts trends are on exhibit at NSCAD University's **Anna Leonowens Gallery** (1891 Granville St., 902/494-8223, Mon.-Fri. 11am-5pm, Sat. noon-4pm). The gallery displays and sells the work of NSCAD University students. This downtown university, one of North America's oldest cultural institutions, was founded by the gallery's namesake, Anna Leonowens, in 1887. Leonowens, a one-time English teacher who was governess to the King of Siam in the 1860s, spent 20 years in Halifax, during which time she established NSCAD.

The city's definitive crafts source is **Jennifer's of Nova Scotia** (5635 Spring Garden Rd., 902/425-3119, Wed.-Fri. 9am-9pm, Sat. and Mon.-Tues. 9am-5:30pm, Sun. 11am-5pm), an outlet for over 100 provincial producers of handicrafts such as patchwork quilts, pottery, and soaps.

The **Gallery Shop** at street level of the **Art Gallery of Nova Scotia** (1723 Hollis St., 902/424-7542, Mon.-Sat. 10am-5pm, Sun. noon-5pm) is an inspiring room filled with the cream of provincial arts and crafts, as well as prints by folk artist Maude Lewis, books, cards, and other assorted arty gifts. Walking west down Hollis Street from the gallery is **Studio 21 Fine Art** (1273 Hollis St., 902/420-1852, Tues.-Fri. 11am-6pm, Sat. 10am-5pm), a good source of contemporary paintings by local artists.

For a unique combination of hand-built furniture and oddities such as porcelain dog dishes, head to **Bellissimo** (2743 Agricola St., 902/423-6014, Tues.-Sat. 10am-5pm).

Crystal

Canada's only traditional glassworks is **NovaScotian Crystal** (5080 George St., 902/492-0416, Mon.-Fri. 9am-8pm, Sat.-Sun. 10am-5pm), which is ensconced in a waterfront building that contains a showroom and workshop. You can watch master craftspeople at work every day, but Tuesday, Thursday, and Saturday are the days you won't want to miss—this is when the actual glassblowing takes place. Rather than taking a tour, interested folks crowd around open factory doors to watch the goings-on inside. The shop sells pieces such as Christmas ornaments, stemware, toasting flutes, candleholders, and bowls, many with Nova Scotian-inspired designs.

Clothing

Hundreds of clan fabrics and tartans in kilts, skirts, vests, ties, and other apparel are stocked at **Plaid Place** (1903 Barrington St., 902/429-6872, Mon.-Fri. 9:30am-5:30pm, Sat. 10am-5pm). For something a little less traditional, stop by the **Marine Heritage Store** (1675 Lower Water St., 902/423-9787, summer daily 9:30am-5:30pm, the rest of the year Tues.-Sat. 9:30am-5pm, Sun. 1pm-5pm), where you'll find casual clothing in a bright, subtly nautical-themed setting. Starting out by selling shirts from a log church, this local company has grown into a 30-store chain with outlets across Atlantic Canada. The downtown Halifax store is in the Maritime Museum of the Atlantic; another is at Halifax International Airport.

Markets

Halifax Seaport Farmers' Market (Pier 20, 1209 Marginal Rd., 902/492-4043, Mon.-Fri. 10am-5pm, Sat. 7am-3pm, Sun. 9am-3pm), North America's oldest such market (although the location is not the original), fills a massive waterfront building with local produce and handmade arts and crafts that make the perfect memento of your time in Nova Scotia.

Also at the Halifax Seaport, **Pavilion 22** (1031 Marginal Rd., 902/426-8222, May-Oct. when cruise ships have docked, see www.cruisehalifax.ca for a schedule) is designed as a market-style shopping experience for cruise-ship visitors, but is also worth stopping by if you are at this end of town.

Local Delicacies

You'll no doubt eat a lot of seafood while in Nova Scotia, but it can also make a great souvenir to take home for friends and family. Or plan a get-together upon your return and impress everyone with a Nova Scotian feast.

Clearwater (757 Bedford Hwy., 902/443-0333, daily 9am-7pm) is a high-profile supplier with a huge shopfront along the Bedford Highway waterfront. The outlet is anchored by a massive lobster tank divided into sections that make choosing the right-size lobster easy (from $10 per pound). You can also pick up cooked crab legs to go, attend cooking demonstrations, and buy all manner of seafood cookbooks. Better still for those departing Halifax International Airport, Clearwater has an airport location (902/873-4509, daily 5am-8pm) with a lobster tank. For an additional fee, live lobsters can be packaged for air travel. Clearwater also sells crabs, scallops, clams, and shrimp.

The days of Prohibition, when smuggling rum into the United States was a way to make a living for seafaring Nova Scotians, may be a distant memory, but at the **Rum Runners Rum Cake Factory** (Bishop's Landing, 1479 Lower Water St., 902/421-6079, mid-Apr.-late Dec. daily 10am-6pm), you can buy rum cakes from a rum-running family's recipe. The cakes are deliciously rich and sweet, and they travel well.

Outdoor and Camping Gear

Halifax's largest outdoor equipment store is **Mountain Equipment Co-op** (1550 Granville St., 902/421-2667, Mon.-Fri. 9:30am-9pm, Sat. 9am-6pm, Sun. 11am-5pm). This is a cooperative owned by its members; to make a purchase, you must be a member (a one-time $5 charge). The store holds a massive selection of clothing, climbing and mountaineering equipment, tents, backpacks, sleeping bags, books, and other accessories. To obtain a copy of the mail-order catalog, call 800/663-2667 or go online to www.mec.ca.

The Trail Shop (6112 Quinpool Rd., 902/423-8736, Mon.-Sat. 9am-6pm, Sun noon-4pm) has been a Halifax staple in the outfitting business since 1967. The selection of camping equipment, footwear, and field guides is particularly strong.

Food

Halifax may not have a reputation as a gastronomical wonderland, but the dining scene has improved greatly during the last decade. Not only is the standard of food high in many of the better restaurants, but prices are generally reasonable, with mains in even the very best restaurants rarely more than $40.

Naturally, seafood dominates many menus—especially lobster, crab, mussels, scallops, shrimp, halibut, and salmon, all of which are harvested in Nova Scotia. Some of the best seafood is found in the touristy waterfront precinct. You can also buy it fresh from trawlers at Fisherman's Cove and even pick up live lobsters packed for flying out at the airport.

DOWNTOWN
A Halifax Original
The stretch of Argyle Street between Sackville and Blowers Streets has emerged as a dining hot spot, with the utterly original ★ **Economy Shoe Shop** (1663 Argyle St., 902/423-8845, daily 11:30am-2am, $11-25) anchoring the strip. The unusual name originated when one of the owners was starting out in the restaurant business; with little cash to spare, he found an old neon sign bearing the name and hung it out front. The original space has grown to encompass three very different restaurants and a bar—one a bohemian-themed space, another a glass-roofed room enclosing a rainforest that adds a tropical vibe even in the dead of winter. On offer is everything from run-of-the-mill hamburgers to baked halibut and scallops Mornay. Throw entertaining servers into the mix and you get a unique dining experience without spending a fortune.

Seafood Along the Waterfront
In the Historic Properties, **Salty's** (1869 Lower Water St., 902/423-6818, daily 11:30am-10pm, $17-29) mixes seafood with succulent meat dishes in a sublime setting. Kick back with a margarita and watch the boats in the harbor. Sit indoors or out to enjoy some of the city's best food in a casual atmosphere, and don't miss the scrumptious desserts. The upstairs dining room is slightly more formal, with a menu and prices to match. Here, mains such as scallops roasted in red Thai curry and butter-poached halibut are in the $26-38 range.

Diners at **Murphy's on the Water** (1751 Lower Water St., 902/420-1015, daily 9am-10pm, $16-29) also enjoy panoramic harbor views, although it is slightly more touristy than Salty's. This restaurant fills a converted warehouse, with outside tables at the end of the pier. The emphasis is on seafood, such as lobster dip and fish cakes as starters and a unique lobster burger (a meat pattie topped with lobster meat).

Waterfront Warehouse (1549 Lower Water St., 902/425-7610, May-Oct. daily 11:30am-10pm, $17-44) is exactly that—a converted waterfront warehouse where tugboats were once repaired. The setting is casual yet refined, with white linens, nautical-themed furnishings, and an oversized fireplace. The seafood chowder is a hearty starter, while seafood-oriented mains include grilled salmon, seafood crepes, and the Seafood Tower to share.

Other Seafood Restaurants
★ **Five Fishermen** (1740 Argyle St., 902/422-4421, daily 5pm-10pm, $24-40) occupies one of Halifax's oldest buildings—it was built in 1816 and once used by famed governess Anna Leonowens (of *Anna and the King* fame) for her Victorian School of Art and Design. The restaurant is popular with seafood-loving Haligonians for its large-dish menu, which includes shellfish tagliatelle, pan-seared halibut, PEI oysters, and lobster-stuffed Digby scallops, as well as Alberta beef.

Contemporary

Chives Canadian Bistro (1537 Barrington St., 902/420-9626, daily 5pm-9:30pm, $20-29) is well worth searching out, and even though it's away from the touristy waterfront, you'll need a reservation. The menu revolves around seasonal ingredients and produce sourced from throughout Nova Scotia. Add immaculate presentation to fresh and healthy cooking styles, and you have a meal to remember. Mains such as cauliflower curry are all delicious and well presented. Save room for the lemon tart.

The unusual name, **2 Doors Down** (1533 Barrington St., 902/422-4224, Mon.-Fri. 11:30am-10pm, Sat.-Sun. 4:30pm-10pm, $15-26), comes from its location relative to the aforementioned Chives, which is part of the same ownership group. The 2 Doors Down space is unpretentious and simply decorated, leaving diners to focus on dishes that, like Chives, use local and seasonal ingredients, all sourced personally by the chef. Dishes such as arctic char smothered in corn sauce and the butter chicken burger are simple yet tasty. Rounding out an excellent choice for a well-priced dinner is a wine list that includes many Nova Scotian bottles.

Pub Dining

Durty Nelly's (1660 Argyle St., 902/406-7640, Mon.-Fri. 11:30am-2am, Sat.-Sun. 10:30am-2am, $12-19) is Irish in more than name. All furnishings in the traditionally stylish room were actually built in Ireland and transported across the Atlantic. The menu includes traditional treats such as lamb shank braised in Guinness, cottage pie, and bangers and mash, as well as local seafood.

It's a little away from the tourist precinct, but ★ **Henry House** (1222 Barrington St., 902/423-5660, daily 11:30am-12:30am, $17-29) offers excellent food in an intimate pub setting. Melt-in-your-mouth baby back ribs are a house specialty, or choose healthy options such as salmon baked in crushed cashews.

Steakhouses

For carnivorous cravings, prepare to splurge at **Ryan Duffy's** (1650 Bedford Row, 902/421-1116, daily 11:30am-2pm and 5pm-10pm, $20-55). Some cuts, such as the signature strip loin, are wheeled to your table by a waitperson, who asks how much of the loin you'd like before carving the cut and telling you the price. Back in the kitchen, it is cooked exactly the way you ordered it over charcoal coals. You'll be charged extra for accompanying vegetables.

Asian

Throughout downtown you'll find a smattering of good Asian restaurants. One of the best is **Cheelin** (1496 Lower Water St., 902/422-2252, Wed.-Mon. 11am-9pm, $11-24), within the Alexander Keith's Brewery complex. The atmosphere is informal, with chefs in an open kitchen churning out flavorful Chinese favorites. The steamed salmon with black bean sauce is a unique treat.

Hamachi Steakhouse (Bishop's Landing, 1477 Lower Water St., 902/422-1600, Mon.-Sat. 11am-10pm, Sun. noon-10pm, $23-45) is a contemporary Japanese restaurant specializing in *teppan* cooking. In the center of communal tables are grills; chefs slice, dice, and then grill your choice of a beef, chicken, or seafood main as you sample starters such as *niku balu* (tenderloin meatballs with pineapple-chili dipping sauce). For dessert, the Mount Fuji (a combination of brownie, ice cream, cream, and chocolate sauce) is an easy choice.

Italian

A traditional Italian restaurant in downtown Halifax is ★ **Ristorante a Mano** (Bishop's Landing, 1477 Lower Water St., 902/423-6266, www.ristorantemano.ca, Mon.-Sat. 11:30am-10pm, $17-30), a bustling space with typical Italian trattoria food at very reasonable prices. The menu changes regularly, but one staple is pasta and pizza handmade daily. On warm summer evenings, the outdoor tables are in high demand.

In the vicinity of Ristorante a Mano but more upscale, **Da Maurizio Dining Room** (1496 Lower Water St., 902/423-0859, Mon.-Sat. 5pm-10pm, $25-39) is a character-filled room within the historic Keith's Brewery building. Decorated in mellow hues, its walls are lined with Italian art, the wine rack filled with thoughtfully selected bottles from around the world, and the linen-draped tables highlighted by vases of fresh flowers. The menu represents the best of northern Italian cooking, with mains such as veal delicately sautéed with lobster in a brandy and cream sauce.

Cafés

You can get a caffeine hit at outlets of Second Cup and Tim Hortons spread throughout the city, but the absence of coffeehouse chains in downtown Halifax is refreshing.

A couple of blocks uphill from the harbor, **Weird Harbour** (1656 Barrington St., 902/555-5555, Mon.-Fri. 7am-6pm, Sat.-Sun. 8am-6pm) is a friendly little space with minimal furnishings but maximum quality when it comes to coffee.

The refined European vibe at **Pavia Espresso Bar & Cafe** (1273 Hollis St, 902/407-4008, Mon.-Fri. 8am-5pm, Sat.-Sun. 11am-4pm, lunches $7-10) is fitting for this café's location within the Art Gallery of Nova Scotia. The coffee is sourced by a well-known Italian roaster—and the baristas get their training in Florence—so you know this place is serious about pouring excellent coffee. The food is also notable, with choices such as an artichoke heart and pesto sourdough panini.

Step inside **Cabin Coffee** (1554 Hollis St., 902/422-8130, Mon.-Fri. 6:30am-6pm, Sat. 7:30am-5pm, Sun. 9am-5pm, lunches $6-10) and you'll be surprised by the relaxed and friendly ambience of this smaller café in the heart of downtown. In addition to top-notch coffee, the wraps, sandwiches, cinnamon buns, and muffins are all tasty and well priced.

Head down Bishop Street from Cabin Coffee to Bishop's Landing and you'll find ★ **Smiling Goat** (1475 Lower Water St., 902/446-3366, Mon.-Sat. 7am-8pm, Sun. 8am-8pm, lunches $6-9), a stylish espresso bar serving some of the very best coffee in Halifax. Either order it to go and enjoy along the adjacent waterfront or relax in the paved courtyard.

On the south side of downtown, **Trident** (1256 Hollis St., 902/423-7100, Mon.-Fri. 8am-5pm, Sat. 8:30am-5pm, Sun. 10am-3pm, lunches $6-10) is a secondhand bookstore on one side and an old-fashioned café with leather-backed chairs on the other—the perfect place to relax with a newly bought literary treasure, or to take advantage of the free wireless Internet.

SPRING GARDEN ROAD AND VICINITY

This restaurant-lined thoroughfare begins at Barrington Street and heads uphill past the main library and the Sexton Campus of Dalhousie University to the Public Gardens. Downstairs in **Spring Garden Place** is one of the city's better food courts.

Casual Dining

Your Father's Moustache (5686 Spring Garden Rd., 902/423-6766, Mon.-Fri. 10:30am-midnight, Sat.-Sun. 10am-midnight, $15-24) is a casual favorite with a reasonably priced menu of seafood, steaks, and pasta, and a popular brunch is served Sunday 11am-3pm. The beer-battered fish is also excellent. A huge patio and inexpensive kids' menu (everything $8) are also notable.

Asian

My favorite Indian restaurant in Halifax is **Curry Village** (1569 Dresden Row, 902/429-5010, Mon.-Sat. 11:30am-10pm, Sun. 4pm-9pm, $15-22), on the north side of Spring Garden Road, toward the Citadel. This place prepares chicken tandoori, *biryanis*, lamb *vindaloo*, and other Indian dishes to order.

For no-frills Japanese and Korean cooking at reasonable prices, consider a meal at **Minato Sushi** (1520 Queen St., 902/420-0331, Mon.-Sat. 11:30am-9pm, Sun. 1pm-8pm, $13-22). Dishes such as sautéed scallops and mushrooms in butter sauce are mostly under $20, and *bulkokee* (sweet beef teriyaki), a Korean dish, is $18.

Cafés

Within Halifax Central Library, **Pavia Espresso Bar & Cafe** (5440 Spring Garden Rd., 902/407-4008, Mon.-Thurs. 8am-9pm, Fri.-Sun. 9am-6pm, lunches $7-9) offers locally roasted, Italian-style coffee, along with delicious soups and salads, and grilled paninis on sourdough bread.

Just off the busy strip is **Daily Grind** (1479 Birmingham St., 902/429-6397, daily 9am-8pm, lunches $7-10), a longtime favorite with locals looking to avoid the chains. Cooked breakfasts are small, but the sandwiches, hot dishes such as quiche, and muffins are all delicious.

South of Spring Garden Road a few blocks, **Uncommon Grounds** (1030 South Park St., 902/404-3124, daily 7am-10pm, lunches $6-10) is a very popular spot—both for its excellent coffee and university district vibe.

NORTH OF DOWNTOWN
Delis

Well worth searching out, ★ **Italian Market** (6061 Young St., 902/455-6124, Mon.-Sat. 8am-7pm, Sun. 10am-6pm, lunches $7-13) is an absolute delight. Along one side is a deli counter with premade dishes, while another side is home to desserts and drinks. The shelves are lined with goodies imported from around the world. Choose from cabbage rolls, quiche, meatloaf, meatballs, sun-dried tomato-crusted chicken breasts, smoked salmon pâté, and more. Prices are reasonable, and there are a few tables at which to eat.

Cafés

A few blocks northwest of the Citadel, **Java Blend** (6027 North St., 902/423-6144, Mon.-Fri. 6:30am-6pm, Sat. 7:30am-5pm, Sun. 9am-4:30pm), in business as a coffee roaster since 1938, is well worth searching out if you appreciate coffee and its origins. Today, they roast over 30 blends of coffee—and many locals will tell you it's the best in town.

Head to Uncommon Grounds for great coffee.

DARTMOUTH AND VICINITY

Ask a local where to go for the best fish-and-chips, and many will direct you to **John's Lunch** (352 Pleasant St., 902/469-3074, Sun.-Wed. 10am-8pm, Thurs.-Sat. 10am-9pm, $7.50-18), a simple diner within walking distance of the ferry terminal that has been dishing up popular seafood dishes since 1969. Not much has changed since—seating choices include stools at the counter, vinyl booths, or picnic tables out front. Haddock is the fish of choice and is sourced daily at the market, but the deep-fried clams are also tasty. It's also remarkably inexpensive—fish (one piece)-and-chips is just $7.50, and a cup of coffee is $1.

From **Wooden Monkey** (88 Alderney Dr., 902/466-3100, Sun.-Thurs. 11:30am-9pm, Fri.-Sat. 11:30am-10pm, $22-30), views extend back across Halifax Harbour to downtown, a real treat when the nighttime lights of downtown are sparkling across the water. The menu is dominated by simple yet stylish dishes that will please all tastes, including vegetarians and vegans, all reasonably priced and well presented. The bacon-wrapped scallops are a good starter to share, while seafood chowder is a tasty yet inexpensive main. Wooden Monkey is on the upper floor of the Alderney Landing complex, where ferries from Halifax terminate. With ferries running until midnight, there's plenty of time to enjoy a meal before returning to your downtown accommodation.

Fisherman's Cove

At this historic fishing village, 2 kilometers (1.2 miles) southeast of Dartmouth alongside the Eastern Passage, it's no surprise that seafood dominates local menus. The most obvious place to eat is **Boondocks** (200 Government Wharf Rd., 902/465-3474, daily 11am-9pm, $13-26), a big, red-roofed building with a pleasant oceanfront patio. The menu offers the usual collection of seafood, including an excellent seafood chowder filled with Digby scallops, haddock tacos, pan-seared halibut and chips, and a decadently rich lobster stew.

Accommodations and Camping

Accommodations in Halifax vary from a hostel and budget-priced roadside motels to luxurious B&Bs. Downtown is home to a number of full-service hotels catering to top-end travelers and business conventions. In general, these properties offer drastically reduced rates on weekends—Friday and Saturday nights might be half the regular room rate. No matter when you plan to visit, arriving in Halifax without a reservation is unwise, but it's especially so in the summer, when gaggles of tourists compete for a relative paucity of rooms.

All rates quoted are for a double room in summer.

DOWNTOWN
Under $50

Also known as the Halifax Heritage House Hostel, **HI-Halifax** (1253 Barrington St., 902/422-3863, www.hihostels.ca) has 75 beds two blocks from the harbor and a 15-minute walk to attractions such as the Maritime Museum of the Atlantic and Citadel Hill. Facilities include a communal kitchen, a laundry room, television in the common room, and a storeroom for bikes. Beds in four- to eight-bed dorms are $36 per night ($41 for nonmembers), while those in private rooms are $66-78 s or d ($72-88 for nonmembers).

$150-200

Oscar Wilde and P. T. Barnum both slept (not together) at the **Waverley Inn** (1266 Barrington St., 902/423-9346 or 800/565-9346, www.waverleyinn.com, $155-240 s or d), which, at its completion in 1866, was one of the city's grandest residences. Rates for the 34 rooms include a cooked breakfast and wireless Internet, and tea, coffee, and snacks are offered all day and evening in the hospitality suite. Rooms are furnished with Victorian-era antiques, and deluxe rooms contain whirlpool tubs and feather beds. The least expensive single rooms are very small, while the deluxe twins are spacious and extravagantly luxurious.

★ **Cambridge Suites Hotel** (1583 Brunswick St., 902/420-0555 or 800/565-1263, www.cambridgesuiteshalifax.com, $185-235 s or d) is a modern, centrally located, all-suite hotel with 200 rooms. A few units are studios, but most have one or two separate bedrooms, and continental breakfast is included in the rates. Rooms are packed with amenities, including wireless Internet, beautiful bathrooms, lounge and work areas, and basic cooking facilities. The rooftop patio and a fitness center are pluses. Ask about rates that include free parking, full breakfast, and extras for traveling families.

★ **The Halliburton** (5184 Morris St., 902/420-0658 or 888/512-3344, www. thehalliburton.com, from $195 s or d) is a beautiful heritage property transformed into a boutique hotel. The 29 rooms come with super-comfortable beds topped with goosedown duvets and luxurious en suite bathrooms. Rates include continental breakfast, and wireless Internet is available throughout the building. The intimate in-house dining room, Stories, is open nightly (except Mon.) for dinner.

Halifax is home to two Delta properties. **Delta Barrington** (1875 Barrington St., 902/429-7410 or 888/236-2427, www.marriott. com, from $195 s or d) shares space with Barrington Place Mall in the historic area and has 200 comfortable rooms. Amenities include a fitness room, an indoor pool, a business center, a street-side café (with a summer seafood menu), and a lounge bar. Rack rates are around $190 s or d midweek and $160 on weekends. Nearby, the **Delta Halifax** (1990 Barrington St., 902/425-6700 or 888/236-2427,

www.marriott.com, $195 s or d) was one of the city's first grande dame hotels, and the old girl's still a handsome dowager. A highlight is the lavish indoor pool complex, complete with whirlpools and a sauna as well as an adjacent fitness room.

$200-250

In any other Canadian capital, you'd pay a lot more for a room of similar standard as those at the full-service **Prince George Hotel** (1725 Market St., 902/425-1986 or 800/565-1567, www.princegeorgehotel.com, from $235 s or d), one block below the Halifax Citadel and seven blocks uphill from the harbor. The rooms feature contemporary furnishings, and amenities include a midsize indoor pool, a business center with Internet access, a restaurant, a lounge, and quiet public areas off the main lobby. Although rack rates start at over $200, check the website for weekend specials, or upgrade to the Crown Service rooms for an extra $40.

Part of the Casino Nova Scotia complex, **Marriott Harbourfront Hotel** (1919 Upper Water St., 902/421-1700 or 800/943-6760, www.marriott.com, $245 s or d) is a modern edifice designed to resemble the garrison that once occupied the waterfront. Although many guests are from Atlantic Canada and are staying especially to play the tables, the hotel is also a convenient choice for leisure travelers. In addition to the casino, there is an upscale restaurant with harbor views, a stylish English pub, and live entertainment. Almost no one pays rack rates; check the website for a world of options starting at $149 s or d.

Over $250

If you're after modern accommodations, consider **Four Points by Sheraton Halifax** (1496 Hollis St., 902/423-4444, www.marriott. com, from $260 s or d), one block back from the harbor. The 177 guest rooms are filled with modern conveniences (free wireless

1: Waverley Inn; 2: Prince George Hotel's indoor pool

Internet, 27-inch TVs, multiple phones, and well-designed work areas), while other facilities include an indoor pool and fitness room. Disregard the rack rates and book online, and you'll pay as little as $175 s or d, even in midsummer.

Opened in 1930 to coincide with the arrival of the first passenger trains to Halifax, the station's adjacent **Westin Nova Scotian** (1181 Hollis St., 902/421-1000 or 888/627-8553, www.thewestinnovascotian.com, from $295 s or d) has been extensively renovated throughout. Linked to the railway station—many guests are still rail passengers—it oozes old-world charm throughout the public areas (poke your head into the Atlantic Ballroom) and the 300 guest rooms. Amenities include a fine-dining restaurant featuring contemporary cooking, a fitness room, an indoor pool, spa services, and a shuttle to the central business district (1 km/0.6 mi away).

CITADEL HILL AND VICINITY

The following accommodations are in the vicinity of Citadel Hill, from which it's downhill all the way to the harbor. Even the fittest visitors may not feel like tramping back up to the Citadel Hill area after a full day of sightseeing or a big meal at a downtown restaurant. No worries; a cab will cost around $7.

$50-100

A rambling old house directly opposite North Common has been renovated as **Fountain View Guest House** (2138 Robie St., between Williams St. and Compton Ave., 902/422-4169 or 800/565-4877, $40 s, $60 d), where the price is reflective of the rooms and services offered. The seven rooms share bathrooms, there is no kitchen or laundry, and parking is limited to what you can find on the street.

$100-150

Across North Common from Citadel Hill is the **Commons Inn** (5780 West St., 902/484-3466 or 877/797-7999, www.commonsinn.ca, $105-150 s or d), an older three-story building

with 40 basic guest rooms. The rooms are on the small side, but they are smartly outfitted with comfortable beds, en suite bathrooms, free local calls, cable TV, and wireless Internet. The spacious suite, complete with a separate sitting area and jetted tub, is an excellent value. Other pluses are free parking, two rooftop patios, and a continental breakfast buffet.

$200-250

The grandiose ★ **Lord Nelson Hotel** (1515 S. Park St., 902/423-5130 or 800/565-2020, www.lordnelsonhotel.ca, from $225 s or d) presides over a busy Spring Garden Road intersection and overlooks the famous Public Gardens. Originally opened in 1928, the Lord Nelson underwent a transformation in the late 1990s, reopening as one of the city's finest hotels. It is probably a little too far for some to walk to and from downtown, but location aside, it is one of Halifax's best and best-value accommodations. Beyond the extravagant marble-floored lobby are 260 elegantly furnished rooms, each with a large bathroom, wireless Internet access, a coffeemaker, and an iron. Other amenities include a fitness room, a restaurant and English-style pub, and room service. Parking is $18 per night. Check the website for specials under the "Our Packages" link.

NEAR THE AIRPORT

From the airport, it's only 40 minutes to downtown on the Airporter. Here are a few options just in case you must stay in the vicinity.

$100-150

Across the highway from the airport and linked by free shuttle is the **Quality Inn Halifax Airport Hotel** (60 Sky Blvd., 902/873-3000 or 800/667-3333, www.airporthotelhalifax.com, $145 s or d), which has regularly revamped rooms, indoor and outdoor pools, wireless Internet, a fitness room, and a restaurant where guests enjoy complimentary breakfast.

$150-200

★ **ALT Hotel** (40 Silver Dart Dr., 902/334-0136 or 855/258-5775, www.althotels.ca, $160 s or d) is a no-frills hotel located right at the airport. The rooms are simply decorated in a modern chic theme, while downstairs is a café filled with "grab and go" meals, and a smallish indoor pool. There's no room service or valet parking; in return there are no seasonal price adjustments.

Four kilometers (2.5 miles) south of the airport, **Hilton Garden Inn** (200 Pratt & Whitney Dr., Enfield, 902/873-1400, www.hilton.com, from $199 s or d) offers 24-hour shuttle service for guests. It's a newer property with a high standard of guest rooms, as well as a restaurant and a fitness room.

About halfway between the airport and downtown is **Inn on the Lake** (3009 Hwy. 2, Fall River, 902/861-3480 or 800/463-6465, www.innonthelake.com, from $189 s or d), which is a full-blown resort, complete with multiple dining rooms, recreational opportunities spread over 2 hectares (4.9 acres) of landscaped lakefront, and even a small sandy beach.

FISHERMAN'S COVE

If you don't need to be right downtown, consider the following oceanfront accommodation—it's both an excellent value and a world away from the bustle of the city.

$100-150

Overlooking the historic fishing village, the ★ **Inn at Fisherman's Cove** (1531 Shore Rd., Eastern Passage, 902/465-3455 or 866/725-3455, www.theinnatfishermanscove.com, $125-175 s or d) is a modern three-story building with its own private dock on the "crick" that has been chock-full of fishing boats for more than 200 years. Each room has an en suite bathroom and TV, while downstairs is a breakfast room that opens to the dock. Four of the eight guest rooms face the water and have private balconies. Rates include a light breakfast.

CAMPGROUNDS

A few commercial campgrounds lie within a 30-minute drive of downtown. Farther out are two provincial parks that offer camping without hookups.

Dartmouth

The closest camping to downtown is at ★ **Shubie Park Campground** (Jaybee Dr., Dartmouth, 902/435-8328, www.shubiecampground.com, mid-May-early Oct., tents $39, hookups $45-58). Facilities such as washrooms are clean and modern, while wireless Internet access and colorful landscaping add to the appeal. The adjacent beach on Lake Charles comes with supervised swimming, and the campground is linked to walking trails along the Shubenacadie Canal. On the downside, sites offer little privacy.

West

Woodhaven RV Park (1757 Hammonds Plains Rd., 902/835-2271, www.woodhavenrvpark.com, May-mid-Oct., $40-50) is 18 kilometers (11.2 miles) southwest from downtown and handy for an early morning start out to the South Shore. Facilities include 200 sites, coin-operated showers, two launderettes, a swimming pool, a playground, a games room, and wireless Internet access.

Halifax West KOA (3070 Hwy. 1, Upper Sackville, 902/865-4342, www.koa.com, mid-May-mid-Oct., campsites $36-58, cabins with shared bathrooms $68) is northwest of the city, farther out than Woodhaven and a 45-minute drive from downtown.

North

Laurie Provincial Park (coming from the north, take Exit 7 south to Hwy. 2, mid-June-early Sept., $27) lies on the southern shore of Grand Lake. Here, 71 sites are spread around a tree-lined loop. Each site has a picnic table and fire pit, while park amenities include toilets, a short walking trail, and a day-use area, but no showers or hookups.

Dollar Lake Provincial Park (mid-June-mid-Oct., $27) is farther from the city than

Laurie Provincial Park, but it has showers and a concession, as well as a nicer beach, with swimming, boating, walking trails, and a playground. Around 120 sites are spread around three loops, with Loop A closest to the water.

Information and Services

For information on Halifax, contact **Destination Halifax** (902/422-9334 or 877/422-9334, www.discoverhalifaxns.com). The **Halifax Regional Municipality** website (www.halifax.ca) has general information about the city, such as festivals and events, transportation, and park programs.

TOURIST INFORMATION
Downtown
Tourism Nova Scotia (1655 Lower Water St., 902/424-4248, daily 8:30am-6pm) operates an information center along the downtown waterfront at Sackville Landing. Its shelves are filled with province-wide information, so this is the place to get help planning your travels beyond the capital.

Airport
After retrieving your bags from the luggage carousels, you'll pass right by the **Airport Visitor Information Centre** (902/873-1223, daily 9am-9pm), which is a provincially operated facility. Most questions thrown its way relate to Halifax, but the center represents the entire province.

EMERGENCY SERVICES
The city's hospital services are coordinated under the auspices of the **Queen Elizabeth II Hospital** (1796 Summer St., 902/473-3383).

Municipal **police** are assigned to Halifax and Dartmouth; in emergencies, dial 911, and for nonemergency business, call 902/490-5026. The **Royal Canadian Mounted Police (RCMP)** can be reached by calling 911 or 902/426-1323.

ACCESS FOR TRAVELERS WITH DISABILITIES
The good news about Halifax is that its major attractions, as well as a small percentage of rooms in most major hotels, are wheelchair-accessible. Theaters and performing arts venues are also usually wheelchair-accessible. Halifax's public transit system, Metro Transit, has low-floor buses along all major routes as well as the **Access-A-Bus** program, providing wheelchair-accessible transportation on a door-to-door basis. Register at 902/490-6681.

BANKS
As Nova Scotia's capital, Halifax has banks by the dozens. **Scotiabank** (Mon.-Fri. 10am-5pm) has branches throughout the city and does not charge to convert foreign currency to Canadian dollars. The fee for cashing travelers checks is $2, so it pays to convert several checks at one time.

Hotel desks also exchange currency, but rates are more favorable at the banks.

Getting There

CAR

From Truro, it's 100 kilometers (63 miles) south to Halifax, a one-hour drive along wide, divided Highway 102. From Digby, the 230-kilometer (143-mile) drive takes under three hours along Highway 101, which enters Halifax from the northwest. If you are planning on catching the ferry from Maine to Yarmouth, it is 310 kilometers (190 miles) north along the South Shore (Highway 103) to Halifax (allow four hours). From Sydney, on Cape Breton Island, it's an easy five-hour drive to cover the 408 kilometers (255 miles) south to Halifax.

From other Canadian provinces, you will enter Nova Scotia along the Trans-Canada Highway east of Sackville. From Sackville, it's around 200 kilometers (124 miles) into downtown Halifax, a two-hour drive via Truro. From Charlottetown, on Prince Edward Island, allow four hours for the 330-kilometer (205-mile) drive to Halifax via the Confederation Bridge ($47 toll).

It's 260 kilometers (160 miles) to Halifax from Moncton, a three-hour drive along Highway 104 then 102. It's 410 kilometers (255 miles) from Saint John, 4.5 hours on Highway 1 then 104 and 102; the alternative to driving around the Bay of Fundy is to catch the Saint John-Digby ferry, although this takes longer and is more expensive. It's 430 kilometers (265 miles) from Fredericton, 4.5 hours on Highways 2, 104, and 102. It's 1,230 kilometers (760 miles) from Montréal, a 12-hour drive on the Trans-Canada Highway; and 1,800 kilometers (1,115 miles) from Toronto, 18 hours on the Trans-Canada Highway.

From the United States, you can either travel up I-95 through Bangor, Maine, to New Brunswick via Moncton (480 km/300 mi, 4.5 hours) or catch the ferry from Portland, Maine, to Yarmouth (11 hours sailing time, adult $139, vehicle $119, children free), from where it's 310 kilometers (190 miles) to Halifax along Highway 103 (allow four hours).

AIR

Halifax International Airport (YHZ, www. flyhalifax.com) is beside Highway 102, 38 kilometers (24 miles) north of Halifax. It is Atlantic Canada's busiest airport, handling more than 3.7 million passengers annually.

Beyond the baggage carousels are the car rental desks and an information counter specifically for helping out with airport transportation. The arrivals area is linked to the rest of the terminal by a short concourse. In between is the main concentration of food and retail shops, including a currency exchange (daily 7am-9pm); **Clearwater Seafood** (902/873-4509, daily 5am-8pm), which plucks live lobsters from a tank and packs them for air travel; a bookstore; and a variety of locally themed souvenir shops. There are also a play area and wireless Internet hotspots.

The airport's website has lots of information about the airport itself, as well as general travel-planning information and a nifty virtual flight map that tracks flights in real time as they arrive and depart from Halifax.

Airport Transportation

The **Halifax Airport Express** (902/429-2029, www.maritimebus.com/halifax-airport-shuttle) runs between the airport and major downtown hotels ($22 one-way, $40 round-trip) May-October at least once every hour between 5am and 1am. You need reservations only when returning to the airport from your hotel.

Taxi and limousine services are available curbside in the domestic arrivals area for all arriving flights. A one-way trip to Halifax city center is $60 by taxi or limousine.

Airport Car Rental

Once you've picked up your bags from

the baggage carousels, you'll find a row of check-in desks for major car rental companies immediately behind you. Airport phone numbers are **Avis** (902/429-0963), **Budget** (902/492-7553), **Enterprise** (902/873-4700), **Hertz** (902/873-2273), **National/Alamo** (902/873-3505), and **Thrifty** (902/873-3527).

Along the airport access road is a **Petro Canada** gas station, so you can avoid outrageous charges for not returning the vehicle with a full tank of gas.

Parking

Short-term covered airport parking within walking distance of the terminal costs $6 per hour, to a maximum of $21 per day and $105 per week. For long-term parking, nearby **Park'N Fly** (668 Barnes Dr., 902/873-4574, www.parknfly.ca) charges $15 per day and $75 per week, inclusive of a free ride to and from the airport. (Check the Park'N Fly website for a discount coupon.)

RAIL

Halifax is served by **VIA Rail** (416/366-8411 or 888/842-7245, www.viarail.ca) passenger trains from Montréal (22-24 hours, $175 pp). Trains run up to three times a week.

The **VIA Rail Station** is 1 kilometer (0.6 mile) south of downtown at the corner of Barrington and Cornwallis Streets. It's a classic old terminal with a colonnaded facade, high ceiling, and tiled floors, but it is only ever busy when a train rolls in. **Hertz** has a desk at the terminal, and a concourse links the terminal to the grand Westin hotel.

BUS

Long-distance bus services arrive and depart from the **VIA Rail Station** (corner of Barrington and Cornwallis Sts.), 1 kilometer (0.6 mile) south of downtown and within walking distance of HI-Halifax. The main carrier is **Maritime Bus** (902/429-2029, www.maritimebus.com), which has departures from Halifax to points throughout the province and beyond, including daily service to Wolfville (1.5 hours, $22), Moncton (4 hours, $54), and Sydney (7 hours, $78). Maritime runs as far as Québec, from where connections can be made to Greyhound buses.

Getting Around

PUBLIC TRANSPORTATION

Bus

Metro Transit (902/490-4000, www.halifax. ca) buses saturate city streets; charge adult $2.50, senior and child $1.75 (exact change only) with free transfers; and operate daily 6am-midnight. Main bus stops are on Water, Barrington, Cornwallis, Cogswell, and Duke Streets, Spring Garden Road, and Gottingen Street, with service to Quinpool Road and Bayers Street. If you're at a stop waiting for a bus, dial 465 followed by the four-digit route number (marked in red at every stop) for real-time information on when the next bus will be arriving.

Ferries

Metro Transit runs the **Halifax-Dartmouth ferry** from the foot of George Street (beside Historic Properties) to Alderney Drive in Dartmouth. It is the oldest saltwater passenger service in North America, having transported its first passengers by rowboat more than 200 years ago. Today, three modern vessels ply the route in just 12 minutes. The service runs year-round Monday-Saturday 6:30am-midnight, and June-September also on Sunday 6:30am-midnight. The one-way fare is the same as by bus—adult $2.50, senior and child $1.75.

Taxi

Cabs are easiest to flag outside major hotels or transportation hubs, such as the VIA Rail Station. All rides start at $3.50, with an additional $2.65 charged for each kilometer (0.6 mile) plus $0.60 for each additional person. Taxi fares within downtown usually run around $10, while the trip between the airport and downtown is $60. The two main companies are **Casino Taxi** (902/429-6666) and **Yellow Cab** (902/420-0000).

DRIVING

Getting into the city is made easy by a number of major arteries that spill right into downtown. Once in the commercial core, Haligonians are painstakingly careful and slow drivers—a wise way to go, as hillside streets are steep and many roads are posted for one-way traffic. Pedestrians have the right-of-way on crosswalks. Two **bridges** link Halifax and Dartmouth, the A. Murray MacKay and the Angus L. MacDonald; the toll is $1 one-way for vehicles, free for bicyclists and pedestrians.

Downtown Parking

Metered parking costs $1.50-2 per hour but is difficult to find during business hours. Most major hotels have underground public parking, and a few multistory parking lots are scattered throughout the city core. The most convenient parking lots are along Lower Water Street, at the foot of Prince and Salter Streets, but these are also the most costly ($5 per hour). If you're staying at a downtown hotel, expect to pay up to $24 per day for parking (ask about free parking for weekend reservations).

Car Rental

Each of the major car rental companies is represented at the airport and downtown. As always, book as far in advance as possible, and use the Internet to find the best deals. Vehicles rented from downtown are generally the same price as out at the airport, but the final bill comes with fewer taxes.

South Shore

Nova Scotians must have had this region in

mind when they coined the province's motto, "So Much to Sea."

The crashing Atlantic lays itself out in foaming breakers along the deeply scored Atlantic coastline that extends from Lunenburg to Yarmouth. It's a three-hour drive between these two towns, but you'll want at least two days and preferably more to explore the hidden corners of this quintessential corner of Nova Scotia. The seaports and towns follow one another, like a series of glossy, life-size picture postcards. There are those that outsiders will know by name—Peggy's Cove, Mahone Bay, and Lunenburg—but one of the joys of touring the South Shore is discovering your own Peggy's Cove.

The South Shore ends at Yarmouth, where the Atlantic meets the

Highlights

Look for ★ to find recommended sights, activities, dining, and lodging.

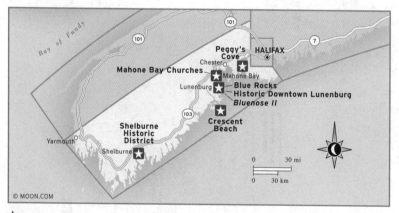

© MOON.COM

★ **Peggy's Cove:** Nova Scotia's most famous village is a photogenic gem you won't want to miss (page 79).

★ **Mahone Bay Churches:** Lining up along the waterfront, three historic churches reflect across the waters of charming Mahone Bay (page 83).

★ **Historic Downtown Lunenburg:** Designated a World Heritage Site by UNESCO, Lunenburg is as interesting as it is charming (page 89).

★ **Blue Rocks:** A world away from the crowds of Peggy's Cove, this picture-perfect fishing village clings to the shore of a rocky harbor (page 89).

★ *Bluenose II:* Lunenburg is a wooden-ships kind of town, and what better way to tour the harbor than aboard one (page 90)?

★ **Crescent Beach:** Just a short detour from the busy South Shore highway, this is my favorite beach among many choices south of Halifax (page 96).

★ **Shelburne Historic District:** A wonderful collection of 200-year-old wooden buildings brings the shipbuilding era to life (page 101).

South Shore

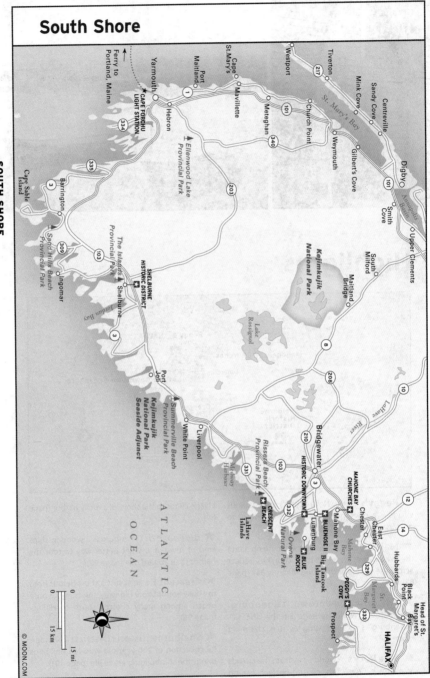

Ferry to
Portland, Maine

Yarmouth

★ CAPE FORCHU
LIGHT STATION

334

Hebron

335

Cape Sable
Island

3

Barrington

309

Ingomar

Sand Hills Beach
Provincial Park

103

The Islands
Provincial Park

SHELBURNE
HISTORIC DISTRICT

Shelburne

3

Jordan Bay

Port
Maitland

Cape
St. Mary's

1

Mavillette

Meteghan

101

Church Point

340

Westport

Tiverton

217

Mink Cove

Sandy Cove

Centreville

Weymouth

203

Ellenwood Lake
Provincial Park

Gilbert's Cove

Digby

101

Smith
Cove

Annapolis Basin

Upper Clements

South
Milford

Maitland
Bridge

Kejimkujik
National Park

Lake
Rossignol

8

LaHave River

10

208

Bridgewater

210

HISTORIC DOWNTOWN

103

332

MAHONE BAY
CHURCHES ✝

12

★ BUENOSE II

Mahone Bay

3

Lunenburg

BLUE
ROCKS

Big Tancook
Island

Chester

East
Chester

14

329

Hubbards

Black
Point

Head of St.
Margaret's
Bay

333

Peggy's Cove ✝

St.
Margaret's
Bay

Prospect

HALIFAX

Port
Joli

Kejimkujik
National Park
Seaside Adjunct

Summerville Beach
Provincial Park

White Point

Liverpool

Medway
Harbour

331

Risser's Beach
Provincial Park

LaHave
Islands

CRESCENT
BEACH ✝

Ovens
Natural Park

ATLANTIC

OCEAN

0
15 km

0
15 mi

© MOON.COM

Bay of Fundy. Locals say the Vikings came ashore a thousand years ago and inscribed the boulder that now sits at the Yarmouth County Museum's front door. Yarmouth's ragged coastline impressed early explorer Samuel de Champlain, who named the seaport's outermost peninsula Cap Forchu ("Forked Cape"). Like the Vikings, Champlain arrived and departed, as do thousands of visitors driving around the South Shore.

PLANNING YOUR TIME

It is possible to visit the best-known towns along this stretch of coast in a day and return to Halifax, but don't. More realistically, plan a day in each place that interests you. As elsewhere in Nova Scotia, dining at its best is superb, and the region's specialty is its abundance of top-notch country inns with public dining rooms. Many lodgings are in historic houses and mansions converted to country inns and in categories best described as better, best, and beautiful. But it is the towns themselves that are this region's highlight. Even with just one week to explore the entire province, plan to spend at least one night in **Mahone Bay** or **Lunenburg,** the former recognized for its three waterfront churches

and the latter a UNESCO World Heritage Site. While the detour to **Peggy's Cove** is almost de rigueur, you should work into your itinerary less publicized villages, such as **Blue Rocks,** near Lunenburg. Taking part in one of the highlights of the South Shore involves some planning—a sailing trip on the *Bluenose II* requires searching out the boat's schedule and making reservations well in advance.

Travelers on a tight schedule make Lunenburg a turnaround point, but the rest of the South Shore is well worth exploring and sets you up for exploring the Fundy Coast. This stretch of coast is dotted with coastal provincial parks and hideaways such as **Crescent Beach,** which is a long stretch of white sand. The major historic attraction between Lunenburg and Yarmouth is the **Shelburne Historic District.** If you are planning to circumnavigate southwestern Nova Scotia, Shelburne is an ideal location for an overnight stay. Couple that with a night in Lunenburg or Mahone Bay to give yourself three days for the South Shore—not enough time to see everything, but a chance to spend quality time visiting each of the highlights.

Halifax to Mahone Bay

From downtown Halifax, it's 105 kilometers (65 miles), a 1.5-hour drive along Highway 103 to Lunenburg, but for the most scenic views and interesting insights, forget the expressway and drive the secondary coastal routes. The best-known village in all of Nova Scotia is Peggy's Cove, a 40-minute drive southwest from downtown Halifax along Highway 333. Meanwhile, Highway 103 takes a direct route across to St. Margaret's Bay, from where secondary Highway 3 passes the charming towns set around Mahone Bay and its islands. One

of these, Oak Island, looms large in the world of treasure-hunting legends—pirates are believed to have buried incalculable booty on it in the 1500s.

★ PEGGY'S COVE

Atlantic Canada's most photographed site is a 40-minute drive southwest from Halifax, and the place is everything its fans say it is. With the houses of the tiny fishing village clinging

---

Previous: Peggy's Cove; Fisheries Museum of the Atlantic; Blue Rocks.

Halifax to Mahone Bay

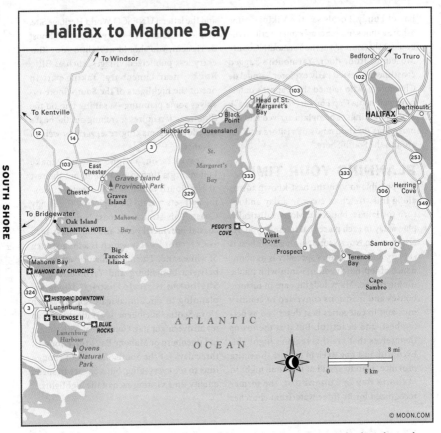

© MOON.COM

like mussels to weathered granite boulders at the edge of St. Margaret's Bay, the Atlantic lathering against the boulder-bound coast, the fishing boats moored in the small cove, and the white octagonal lighthouse overlooking it all, the scene is the quintessence of the Nova Scotia coast.

Sightseers clog the village during the daytime (to miss the worst of the crowds, get there before 9am or after 5pm), wandering along the wharves and around the weathered granite boulders surrounding the photogenic lighthouse. Peggy's Cove has a population of just 60 souls, so don't come expecting the services of a tourist town. The village has just one B&B, a restaurant, and the **deGarthe Gallery** (109 Peggy's Point Rd., 902/823-2256, May-Oct. daily 9am-4pm, free). The latter, along the

main road through town, displays the work of Finnish-born artist William deGarthe, whose stunning nautically themed oil paintings grace galleries the world over. Behind the gallery, deGarthe sculpted a 30-meter-long (98-foot-long) frieze on a granite outcropping. It depicts 32 of the seaside village's fishermen and families.

Peggy's Cove received worldwide attention in September 1998, when a Swissair MD-11 jetliner bound from New York City to Geneva crashed in shallow waters off the coast here, killing all 229 people aboard. A small memorial overlooks the ocean along Highway 333, 2 kilometers (1.2 miles) west of the village.

Food

The road through the village ends at the

Sou'Wester Restaurant (178 Peggy's Point Rd., 902/823-2561, June-Aug. daily 8am-9pm, Sept.-May daily 9am-8pm, $12-28), a cavernous room with a menu designed to appeal to the tourist crowd. And as the only place in town to eat, attract them it does—try to plan your meal before 10am or after 5pm. The menu does have a distinct maritime flavor, with dishes such as fish cakes, pickled beets, and eggs offered in the morning. The rest of the day, seafood continues to dominate, with haddock and chips for $16 and a full lobster supper for around $30.

Accommodations

The only accommodation has just five guest rooms, so book well ahead if you'd like to stay overnight in this delightful village. At the head of the actual cove, ★ Peggy's Cove Bed and Breakfast (17 Church Rd., 902/823-2265 or 877/725-8732, www.peggyscovebb.com, Apr.-mid-Nov., $160-175 s or d including breakfast) has well-furnished guest rooms with wireless Internet, a living area, a dining room, and a deck promising magnificent views across the cove.

Getting There

Peggy's Cove is about 45 kilometers (28 miles) southwest of Halifax on Highway 333. The drive takes about 40 minutes.

PEGGY'S COVE TO CHESTER

Highway 333 beyond Peggy's Cove winds north past a string of small fishing villages before reaching Highway 3 (Highway 103, the divided highway along the South Shore, takes an inland route, so turn at the older Highway 3). Rather than promising places at which you simply must stop, this route that lazily rounds St. Margaret's Bay is simply an enjoyable drive.

Continue west to Hubbards, where the ★ Trellis Café (22 Main St., 902/857-1188, daily 8am-9pm, $18-29) is a casual restaurant with colorful decor and occasional live entertainment on weekends. The namesake trellised deck is a good spot on warmer days. The morning starts out with great coffee and above-average breakfasts that include local specialties such as fish cakes. Lunch choices such as a lobster roll and a vegetarian coconut curry are all under $20. Dinner mains are generally less than $25, but you can spend less by ordering a combination of starters, such as seafood chowder and Caesar salad.

Beyond Hubbards, Queensland Beach is a popular stretch of sand with safe but chilly swimming and a freshwater lagoon that attracts lots of birdlife.

CHESTER AND VICINITY

The bayside town of Chester, first settled by New Englanders in 1759, lies at the northern head of Mahone Bay. Its first hotel was built in 1827, and the town, with its ideal sailing conditions and many vacation homes, has been a popular summer retreat ever since. Getting oriented beyond the downtown core can be confusing, so start your visit at the Tourist Information Centre (20 Smith Rd., 902/275-4616, May-early Oct. daily 10am-5pm), which is in a 1905 railway station on the Mahone Bay side of town (coming into town from Halifax, continue up the hill to the right of the downtown turnoff).

Recreation and Entertainment

Most visitors to Chester are content to browse through downtown shops and wander lazily along the Front Harbour waterfront.

An easy excursion is to Big Tancook Island (adult $6 round-trip, cash only) via ferries departing regularly from Front Harbour. Big Tancook is mostly residential, but it's a pleasant trip across, and walking paths lace the island.

Dating to 1914, Chester Golf Club (222 Golf Course Rd., Prescott Point, 902/275-4543) is an old-style golf course that opens up along the oceanfront to offer sweeping views on holes lapped by the water. Greens fees are a good value at $63.

Chester Playhouse (22 Pleasant St., 902/275-3933 or 800/363-7529, www.

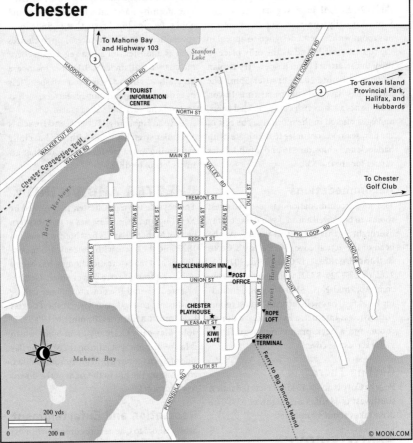

chesterplayhouse.ca) hosts some form of live entertainment weekly between March and December. Its Summer Theatre Festival draws professional talent in July and August. Past seasons have included musicals, Broadway-style revues, comedy improv, puppet shows, and children's programs.

Food

In downtown Chester, the **Kiwi Café** (19 Pleasant St., 902/275-1492, daily 8am-5pm, lunches $8-22) offers simple and healthy breakfasts and lunches along with a wide range of hot drinks, including chai tea and creamy hot chocolate; the lobster and haddock chowder is a lunchtime highlight. It's painted a cheery blue and kiwifruit green, with outside tables down one side.

The combination of excellent haddock chowder and stunning water views make **Rope Loft** (36 Water St., 902/275-3430, daily 11:30am-8pm, $14-30) the best choice in town for dinner. Housed in a 200-year-old waterfront building, the Rope Loft has a downstairs pub, but it is the upstairs restaurant with its wide deck that is the best place to dine. Beyond the chowder, expect the usual array of seafood and burger choices.

Accommodations and Camping

The most noteworthy of Chester's inns is ★ **Mecklenburgh Inn** (78 Queen St., 902/275-4638, www.mecklenburghinn.ca, May-Dec., $125-165 s, $135-165 d), a 120-year-old sea captain's home that has been given a bohemian-chic look. Guests tend to gather on the wide veranda to watch the world of Chester go by, and then, after dinner at a local restaurant, gravitate to the comfortable couches set around two fireplaces in the living room. Three of the four rooms have en suite bathrooms with claw-foot tubs, while the fourth has a private bathroom down the hall. A big breakfast of pancakes or smoked salmon eggs Benedict will set you up for a day of sightseeing.

Signposted from Highway 3, 3 kilometers (1.9 miles) northeast of Chester, **Graves Island Provincial Park** (mid-May-mid-Sept., $29) covers a small island connected to the mainland by a causeway. An open area at a high point of the island allows for pull-through RVs, while tent sites are scattered around the surrounding forest. If you're just visiting for the day, plan on a picnic at the waterfront day-use area just across the causeway.

Getting There

Chester is just off Highway 103 (take Exit 8), about 70 kilometers (43 miles) from Halifax, a 45-minute drive. It's around 70 kilometers (43 miles) from Peggy's Cove via Highway 333 and Highway 103.

Mahone Bay

The town of Mahone Bay (pop. 1,000), on the island-speckled bay of the same name, is one of the most charming in all of Nova Scotia. The town's prosperous past is mirrored in its architecture, with Gothic Revival, Classic Revival, and Italianate styles in evidence. Many of these buildings have been converted to restaurants specializing in seafood and shops selling the work of local artisans. The distinctive bayside trio of 19th-century churches reflected in the still water here has become one of the most photographed scenes in Nova Scotia.

SIGHTS AND EVENTS

Most visitors to Mahone Bay are quite happy to spend their time admiring the architecture, browsing through the shops, and enjoying lunch at one of the many cafés. If you are interested in the town's architectural highlights, ask for the three walking-tour brochures at the museum.

Mahone Bay Museum

Inside a 150-year-old wooden house, the **Mahone Bay Museum** (578 Main St., 902/624-6263, http://mahonebaymuseum.com, June-Sept. daily 10am-4pm, donation) describes the town's 250-year history. One room is dedicated to settlement of the area in the mid-1700s by German, French, and Swiss Protestants and the story of how they were enticed by the British government's offer of free land, farm equipment, and a year's "victuals." You'll also learn about the importance of shipbuilding to the area, which thrived in a dozen shipyards from the 1850s to the early part of the 20th century, and you can admire historic arts and crafts.

★ Mahone Bay Churches

From the flower-bedecked bandstand on Main Street, three churches can be seen shoulder to shoulder across the water. The oldest (and farthest from this viewpoint) is the **Trinity United Church** (Edgewater St., 902/624-9287), which dates to 1861 and was dragged by oxen to its current site in 1885. **St. John's Lutheran** (Edgewater St., 902/624-9660) is a symmetrical wooden structure

Mahone Bay

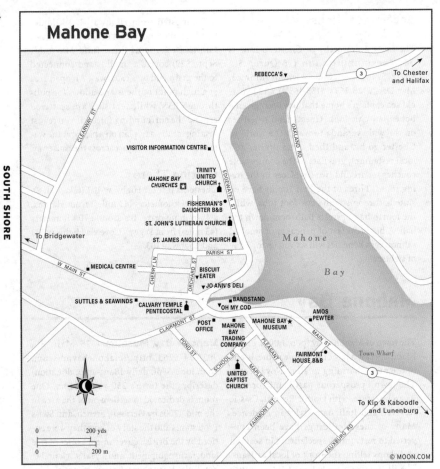

To Chester and Halifax

REBECCA'S ▾

VISITOR INFORMATION CENTRE ▪

MAHONE BAY CHURCHES ✠

TRINITY UNITED CHURCH ♦

FISHERMAN'S DAUGHTER B&B ▪

ST. JOHN'S LUTHERAN CHURCH ♦

ST. JAMES ANGLICAN CHURCH ♦

PARISH ST

Mahone

Bay

W. MAIN ST

To Bridgewater

MEDICAL CENTRE ▪

BISCUIT EATER ▾

JO-ANN'S DELI ▾

BANDSTAND ▪

OH MY COD ▾

SUTTLES & SEAWINDS ▪

CALVARY TEMPLE PENTECOSTAL ▪

AMOS PEWTER ▪

POST OFFICE ▪

MAHONE BAY TRADING COMPANY ▪

MAHONE BAY MUSEUM ★

FAIRMONT HOUSE B&B ▪

Town Wharf

UNITED BAPTIST CHURCH

To Kip & Kaboodle and Lunenburg

0   200 yds
0   200 m

© MOON.COM

standing in the middle of the three. Right on the corner is the Gothic Revival **St. James Anglican Church** (Edgewater St., 902/624-8614). This is the only one of the three open for tours (July-Aug. Thurs.-Sat. 11am-3pm, free).

Music at the Three Churches (www.threechurches.com, adult $25, child 12 and under free) is a series of classical music concerts hosted by the churches on select Friday and Sunday nights through summer. Visit the website or check with the visitor information center for a schedule and pay at the door.

If you walk along the waterfront beyond the information center, you'll see a different angle on the churches, as well as two others. Completed in 1875, the white spire you see rising above the trees is the **United Baptist Church** (56 Maple St., 902/624-9124), open for services Sunday at 11am. The **Calvary Temple Pentecostal** (at the traffic circle where Main and Edgewater Sts. meet, 902/624-8420) opens its doors Sunday at 7pm for hymn singing.

SHOPPING

Many artists are attracted to Mahone Bay for its scenic setting, and the main street has developed into a hub for shoppers. Most shops are open late spring-Christmas.

At **Amos Pewter** (589 Main St., 902/624-9547, summer Mon.-Sat. 9am-7pm, Sun. 10am-7pm, shorter hours and closed Sun. the rest of the year), you can watch artists at work as they cast, spin, and finish pewter pieces. Tea connoisseurs will be in their element at the **Tea Brewery** (525 Main St., 902/624-0566, Mon.-Sat. 11am-5:30 pm, Sun. 11am-5pm), while up the hill from the Tea Brewery, **Suttles and Seawinds** (466 Main St., 902/624-8375, Mon.-Sat. 10am-5pm, Sun. noon-5pm) sells stylish but colorful clothing.

FOOD

Mahone Bay's main street has a smattering of cafés, but most close in the late afternoon.

With a bag of carrots serving as a counterweight on the front door, ★ **Jo Ann's Deli** (9 Edgewater St., 902/624-6305, late May-late Oct. daily 9am-7pm) is a welcoming food shop filled with goodies. Locals come for organic produce, but everyone comes out with something—gourmet sandwiches, filled bagels, oatmeal cakes, brownies, homemade jams and preserves, ice cream, and more. If you're planning a picnic, this is the place to get everything together.

Away from the main street but worth the effort to find is the **Biscuit Eater** (16 Orchard St., 902/624-2665, Mon.-Sat. 9am-4pm, Sun. 10am-3pm, lunches $7-12), ensconced in a renovated 1775 residence (Mahone Bay's oldest building) and with a quiet patio surrounded by greenery. Lots of local ingredients and seasonal produce are used in a menu that ranges from a traditional ploughman's platter to creative sandwiches such as bacon, avocado, blue cheese, and fried egg on a ciabatta bun.

Oh My Cod (567 Main St., 902/531-2600, daily 11am-8pm, $14-20) is in the heart of the tourist precinct, and the food is surprisingly good at reasonable prices. The fish-and-chips comes with your choice of cod or haddock, while other options include a huge bowl of seafood chowder (that includes lobster), mussels by the pound, and scallop skewers. You can dine inside, but if the weather is nice, choose one of the two outside decks—one facing the street is good for people-watching, while the other overlooks the water.

A 10-minute waterfront walk from downtown, and with a classic view of all five Mahone Bay churches, ★ **Rebecca's Restaurant** (249 Edgewater St., 902/531-3313, Mon.-Sat. 11am-9pm, $19-33) sits at the head of the bay. The interior is beautifully decorated in a Rustic theme, but the most sought

Mahone Bay's photogenic churches

The Mystery of Oak Island

In 1795, on Oak Island, a small island in Mahone Bay, a young man came upon an area where the forest had been cut away. Besides the stumps, he found a large forked limb with an old tackle block and a "treenail," and the ground nearby was sunken in a pit. His first thought would have been buried treasure, as the bay was a known haunt for pirates such as "Captain" William Kidd, Sir Henry Morgan, and Edward "Blackbeard" Teach 100 years previously.

After hours of digging, Daniel McGinnis and two farmer friends reached a depth of 10 feet and hit wood. It turned out, however, not to be the rotted lid of a treasure chest but rather a platform of logs. So the men pressed on, convinced that the treasure lay just below. At a depth of 25 feet, digging became difficult, and they abandoned the effort.

The first organized dig occurred in 1804, when a boat loaded with equipment arrived. Another log platform was uncovered at the 30-foot level, and others 40 and then 50 feet from the surface. At 60 feet, the men uncovered a layer of coconut fiber, which hinted at cargo from warmer climes. At the 90-foot level, a large slab of granite (which was later verified as being from Europe) was uncovered. The next morning, the men returned to the pit to find it had filled with water. They had no success pumping the water out, so the search was halted until the following spring.

In 1805 a second shaft was dug, and at the 100-foot mark a horizontal tunnel was dug in the hope of reaching the treasure, but this search too was abandoned. It would be another 40 years

after tables on warm days are set out on a stone patio. The menu is wide ranging, with the emphasis on local game and produce, including one of the best seafood chowders I've tasted in Nova Scotia.

ACCOMMODATIONS

Through summer, especially on weekends, demand is high for a limited number of rooms, so plan accordingly and book as far in advance as possible.

$50-100

Mahone Bay is home to one of Nova Scotia's only privately operated backpacker lodges, ★ Kip and Kaboodle (9466 Hwy. 3, Mader's Cove, 902/531-5494 or 866/549-4522, www.kiwikaboodle.com, dorms $30, $65 s or d), which is 3 kilometers (1.9 miles) from the center of town toward Lunenburg. It's small, with facilities to match, but everything is well maintained, including a communal kitchen, living area, and outdoor pool. Other amenities include a barbecue and wireless Internet access. Rates include linens and a light breakfast.

$100-200

Opposite the town wharf, you can sit on the veranda of Fairmont House B&B (654 Main St., 902/624-8089, www.fairmonthouse. com, $125-185 s or d) and watch the world of Mahone Bay go by. A local shipbuilder built this Gothic Revival home in 1857, and it was converted to a B&B in 1991. In the ensuing years, its exterior has been given a coat of stately blue paint, and three guest rooms have been outfitted in stylish colored themes. All rooms have en suite bathrooms, air-conditioning, and niceties such as hair dryers and irons. Downstairs is a library with board games and a TV. Rates include a continental breakfast.

Nestled amid the famous three churches is ★ Fisherman's Daughter B&B (97 Edgewater St., 902/624-0660, www. fishermans-daughter.com, $140-150 s or d). Built in 1840 by a local shipbuilder, the home is understated but shows a restrained Gothic Revival style. A couple of the four guest rooms have funky layouts (such as beds nestled under the eaves), but this adds to the charm. A host of modern amenities and a full breakfast make this place an excellent choice.

A few kilometers north of Mahone Bay, back toward Chester, Oak Island Resort (off Hwy. 103 at 36 Treasure Dr., 902/627-2600 or

before the next serious attempt was made to retrieve whatever lay deep below Oak Island. While the secondary shafts filled with water only when linked to the original pit, it was noted that the level of water in all three shafts rose and fell with the tide. This deepened the mystery even further, but what the men found next amazed everyone present. Along the adjacent bay, just below the low-tide mark, were five drains that, it was later found, converged on a single tunnel. While it was understood that this simple man-made flooding system had been put in place after the treasure pit had been dug, this didn't help solve the mystery. Nor did it help the next round of investors, who spent the summer of 1863 in a futile attempt to reach below the 100-foot level, or the numerous other treasure seekers who attempted to get to the bottom of the pit during the next 140 years.

The saga has cost six lives, left many investors broke, and created numerous feuds between island property owners. Two treasure hunters, Dan Blankenship and Fred Nolan, spent a combined 100 years trying to outsmart those who designed the "Money Pit" many centuries ago. In 2005, Blankenship, who had sole road access to the island via a causeway, sold his share of the island to the government of Nova Scotia in the hopes that it would be opened to tourism. Incredibly, one of the world's great mysteries and longest treasure hunts continues to this day.

800/565-5075, www.oakislandresort.ca, $195-370 s or d) is one of Nova Scotia's only full-service resorts. Located right on the water and overlooking mystery-filled Oak Island, it offers indoor and outdoor pools, kayak rentals, boat tours, tennis courts, mini-golf, a children's program (summer only), and a restaurant with tables that spill out onto a huge ocean-facing deck. The main building holds standard guest rooms (some with balconies and ocean views), modern condos overlook the marina, and down a gravel road are two-bedroom cottages. The latter are right on the ocean, and each has a fire pit and picnic table out front.

INFORMATION AND SERVICES

The Visitor Information Centre (165 Edgewater St., 902/624-6151, summer Mon.-Sat. 9am-5pm, Sun. 11am-5pm) is in a small building just before you reach the first church.

GETTING THERE

Mahone Bay is about 30 kilometers (19 miles) from Chester. You can get there in 20 minutes via Highway 103 or Highway 3. From Halifax, follow Highway 103 to Exit 10. From there, Mahone Bay is a short drive south. Allow just over an hour for this 80-kilometer (50-mile) trip.

Lunenburg

Lunenburg (pop. 2,300) lies about equidistant between Halifax and Shelburne off Highway 103. Sited on a hilly peninsula between two harbors, this is one of the most attractive towns in Nova Scotia, with a wealth of beautiful homes painted in a crayon box of bold primary colors. In 1991, Lunenburg's Old Town was designated a national historic district, and in December 1995 the town received the ultimate honor when UNESCO designated it a World Heritage Site—one of only two cities in North America to enjoy that status (the other is Québec City). More recently, in 2005, the provincial government stepped in and bought a chunk of waterfront buildings and wharves, saving them from development that

Lunenburg

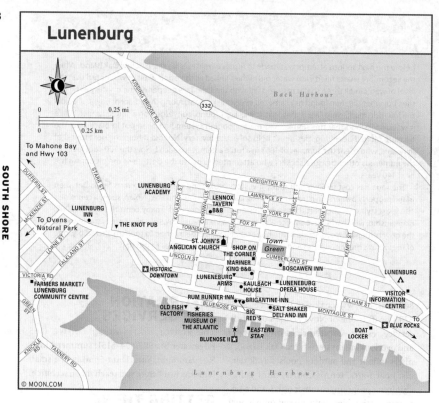

0.25 mi
0.25 km

To Mahone Bay and Hwy 103

Back Harbour

332

KISSING BRIDGE RD

DUFFERIN RD
STARR ST
MCKENZIE ST
LORNE ST
FALKLAND ST
VICTORIA RD
GREEN ST
KNICKLE RD
TANNERY RD

CREIGHTON ST

LUNENBURG ACADEMY ★

LENNOX TAVERN
■ B&B

LAWRENCE ST

KAULBACH ST
CORNWALLIS ST
DUKE ST
FOX ST
KING ST
YORK ST
PRINCE ST
HOPSON ST
KEMPT ST
PELHAM ST
MONTAGUE ST

LUNENBURG INN

▼ THE KNOT PUB

To Ovens Natural Park

TOWNSEND ST

ST. JOHN'S ⌂
ANGLICAN CHURCH

SHOP ON THE CORNER

Town Green

LINCOLN ST

MARINER KING B&B ●

★ HISTORIC DOWNTOWN

LUNENBURG ▼ ARMS

● BOSCAWEN INN

CUMBERLAND ST

■ FARMERS MARKET/ LUNENBURG COMMUNITY CENTRE

KAULBACH HOUSE ■
● LUNENBURG OPERA HOUSE

RUM RUNNER INN ●
● BRIGANTINE INN

BLUENOSE DR

OLD FISH ▼ FACTORY

FISHERIES MUSEUM OF THE ATLANTIC ★

BIG RED'S

● SALT SHAKER DELI AND INN

★ EASTERN STAR

BLUENOSE II ⌂

LUNENBURG ⌂

VISITOR INFORMATION CENTRE ■

To ↘ BLUE ROCKS ⌂

BOAT LOCKER ■

Lunenburg Harbour

© MOON.COM

would have taken away from the town's well-preserved history.

History

To understand what the fuss is all about, you have to go back in time a couple of centuries. Protestant German, Swiss, and French immigrants, recruited by the British to help stabilize their new dominion, settled the town in 1753; their influence is still apparent in the town's architectural details. With its excellent harbor—a protected inner arm of the Atlantic embraced by two long, curving peninsulas—Lunenburg became one of Nova Scotia's premier fishing ports and shipbuilding centers in the 19th century. In 1921, the famous schooner *Bluenose* was built here. The 49-meter (161-foot) fishing vessel won the International Fisherman's Trophy race that same year, and for the next 18 years it remained the undefeated champion of the Atlantic fleets. The ship has become the proud symbol of the province, and its image is embossed on the back of the Canadian dime.

Today, the fishing industry that fostered the town's growth and boatbuilding reputation is comatose, and the Atlantic fisheries are mere shadows of their former selves. But here in Lunenburg, the townspeople carry on the shipbuilding and shipfitting skills of their ancestors. The port is still known as a tall ship mecca, and big multimasted sailing ships, old and new alike from around the world, continue to put in here for repairs, shipfitting, or provisions—whatever excuse the owners can come up with. Underneath the tourist glitz, the community pride in this tradition runs strong and deep, and the town's international reputation among mariners remains formidable. Strike up a conversation with a local about sailing ships and see what happens.

★ HISTORIC DOWNTOWN

The port's oldest part is set on the hillside overlooking the harbor. The nine blocks of Old Town, designated a World Heritage Site by UNESCO, rise steeply from the water, and the village green spreads across the center. Bluenose Drive, the narrow lane along the harbor, and Montague Street, a block uphill, define the main sightseeing area. A mesh of one-way streets connects Old Town with the newer area built with shipbuilding profits. One of the pleasures of Lunenburg is strolling the residential and commercial streets, admiring the town's many meticulously preserved architectural gems. At the northern end of the harbor is the **Scotia Trawler Shipyard,** where the *Bluenose* was built. This shipyard, 16 other properties, and most of the wharves are off-limits, but the long-term plan is that the holdings will be opened to the public.

Fisheries Museum of the Atlantic

The spacious, bright red **Fisheries Museum of the Atlantic** (68 Bluenose Dr., 902/634-4794, mid-May-mid-Oct. daily 9:30am-5:30pm, adult $12, senior $9.50, child $3.50) boasts a trove of artifacts and exhibits on shipbuilding, seafaring, rum running, and marine biology. This thoroughly fascinating museum engages the visitor with demonstrations of fish filleting, lobster-trap construction, dory building, net mending, and other maritime arts. Inside are aquariums, tanks of touchable marine life, a gallery of ship models, full-size fishing vessels from around Atlantic Canada, a theater, a restaurant, and a gift shop. Tied up at the wharf outside are the fishing schooner *Theresa E. Connor*, built in Lunenburg in 1938; the steel-hulled trawler *Cape Sable*, an example of the sort of vessel that made the former obsolete; the *Royal Wave*, a Digby scallop dragger; and, when it's in its home port, the *Bluenose II*. All the vessels can be boarded and explored.

St. John's Anglican Church

St. John's Anglican Church (Cumberland and Cornwallis Sts., 902/634-4994, early June-Sept. daily 11am-7pm, free) stood for almost 250 years. In 2001, at the time the second-oldest church in Canada, it was destroyed by fire. It has been rebuilt and can be visited on volunteer-led tours.

Lunenburg Academy

High above the port and surrounded by parkland, the imposing **Lunenburg Academy** (97 Kaulbach St., no public access) is easily spotted from afar. Dating to 1885, this black-and-white wooden building, with its mansard roof and worn wooden stairways, was originally a prestigious high school. Today, it is the local elementary school, but it remains one of the oldest academies in Canada.

OTHER SIGHTS
★ Blue Rocks

Follow any of Lunenburg's downtown streets eastbound to link with a road that leads 8 kilometers (5 miles) to **Blue Rocks,** toward the end of the peninsula. This tiny fishing village is set along a jagged coastline wrapped with blue-gray slate and sandstone, and the combination of color and texture will inspire photographers. Blue Rocks has no official attractions or services. Instead, drive to the end of the road, from where you need to explore on foot to get the full effect of a part of Nova Scotia far removed from touristy Lunenburg and Peggy's Cove. The shoreline is littered with boats and fishing gear, such as nets and traps in various states of repair, while simple but colorful homes cling to the rocky foreshore.

Ovens Natural Park

A 15-minute drive south of Lunenburg on Highway 332, spectacular sea caves have been scooped out of the coastal cliffs. Early prospectors discovered veins of gold embedded in

The Famous *Bluenose*

Featured on Nova Scotian license plates and the back of the Canadian dime, the original *Bluenose* was launched from Lunenburg in 1921. Built as a fishing schooner, she was designed specifically for competing in the International Fisherman's Trophy, a racing series that pitted working ships from Canada and the United States against one another. Much to the joy of Canadians, the *Bluenose* won every racing competition she entered, while also serving as a working fishing boat. But by 1942, the era of the sail-powered fishing industry was giving way to that of modern steel-hulled trawlers, and the great *Bluenose* was sold to carry freight in the West Indies. Four years later, she foundered and was lost on a Haitian reef.

The ship herself was black. The name is thought to have originated from local fishermen, who, when conditions were cold and wet, would wipe their noses with their blue mittens, causing the dye to run.

In July 1963, the *Bluenose II* was re-created from the plans of the original and launched at Lunenburg. Some of the same craftspeople who had built the first *Bluenose* even participated in her construction.

the *Bluenose II*

the slate and white quartz cliffs, sparking a small gold rush in 1861. During the following several decades, the cliffs surrendered 15,500 grams of the precious metal, while the Cunard family, of shipping fame, had the beach sand transported to England to retrieve the gold. Today, **Ovens Natural Park** (902/766-4621, adult $10, senior and child $5) is privately owned, combining camping, cabins, hiking trails, and a restaurant on a 75-hectare (185-acre) site. Below the main parking lot, visitors can try their hand at panning for gold along Cunard's Beach. A trail leads along the sea cliffs and into one of the "ovens," and you can jump aboard an inflatable boat to get a sea-level view of the caves.

RECREATION

TOP EXPERIENCE

★ *Bluenose II*

To immerse yourself fully in the Lunenburg experience, set sail aboard the *Bluenose II*

(902/634-8483 or 877/441-0347, www.bluenose.novascotia.ca), an exact replica of the famous sailing ship. She underwent multiyear restorations from 2010 through 2014 to return to her former glory.

When not visiting other Canadian ports, the *Bluenose II* can be found here at her home berth, outside the Fisheries Museum of the Atlantic. Rather than separating you from the maritime experience with cushy reclining seats, acrylic windows, and a cocktail lounge, the *Bluenose II* takes you to sea as a sailor. Cruising out of the harbor under a fresh breeze—the sails snapping taut and the hull slicing through the chilly waters—you'll begin to understand and actually feel the history and lifeblood of Lunenburg.

When in Lunenburg, the *Bluenose II* departs twice daily (9:30am and 1:30pm, adult $64, child $36) for a two-hour harbor cruise. A total of 65 spots are offered on each sailing. Tickets are always in high demand, so making a reservation well in advance through the website or by phone is essential.

Other Boat Tours

The *Bluenose II* isn't always in port, and when she is, tickets sell fast. An excellent alternative is the *Eastern Star,* operated by **Star Charters** (waterfront, 902/634-3535, www.novascotiasailing.com, adult $40, child $20). The *Eastern Star* is a character-imbued 48-foot wooden ketch tended by an amiable and knowledgeable crew intent on perpetuating the seafaring tradition that put Lunenburg on the map. The *Eastern Star* makes four 90-minute cruises per day June-October, with a two-hour sunset cruise added in July and August.

Lunenburg Whale Watching Tours (902/527-7175, www.novascotiawhalewatching.com, adult $58, child $35) depart Government Wharf May-October four times daily. While whales are definitely the highlight, regular sightings are also made of sunfish, turtles, dolphins, seals, and puffins.

ENTERTAINMENT AND EVENTS

Nightlife

The seaport is usually quiet evenings and Sundays. Locals frequent **The Knot Pub** (4 Dufferin St., 902/634-3334, daily noon-11pm), a comfortable and lively place where you can get "knotwurst" and kraut with your draft beer. Up from the harbor, the **Lunenburg Arms** (94 Pelham St., 902/640-4040, daily 11am-close) has a lounge bar with tables that spill out onto a quiet patio.

Performing Arts

South Shore Players (www.southshoreplayers.ca), the local theater troupe, uses a variety of venues for its performances, including the Central United Church Hall on Lincoln Street. **Lunenburg Opera House** (290 Lincoln St., 902/640-6500, www.lunenburgoperahouse.com) hosts gigs by musicians from throughout Atlantic Canada. Cover charges range up to $20, and a schedule is posted on its website.

Lunenburg Folk Harbour Festival

For four days from the second Thursday in August, a roster of traditional, roots, and contemporary folk musicians come together for the **Lunenburg Folk Harbour Festival** (902/634-3180, www.folkharbour.com). They perform under a tent atop Blockhouse Hill, at the Lunenburg Opera House, in the downtown bandstand, and out on the wharf. Many performances are free, with big-name acts under the big tent costing $20.

SHOPPING

The **farmers market** at Lunenburg Community Centre (corner of Victoria Rd. and Green St., July-Oct. Thurs. 8am-noon) lures crowds for fresh produce, smoked meats, and crafts at the former railroad depot grounds; wares are high quality and priced accordingly.

Nautical gifts are available at the **Boat Locker** (280 Montague St., 902/640-3202, Mon.-Fri. 9am-5pm, Sat. 10am-4pm), which is also a full-service marine-supply center, and at the nonprofit ***Bluenose II* Company Store** (121 Bluenose Dr., 902/634-8483, mid-May-Oct. daily 9:30am-5pm), which sells all manner of *Bluenose* clothing, gifts, and art to support preservation of the vessel.

FOOD

Lunenburg has a great number of restaurants, nearly all serving seafood in a casual setting. Local specialties appearing on some menus include Solomon Gundy (pickled herring, usually served with sour cream), Lunenburg pudding (pork sausage), and fish cakes topped with rhubarb relish.

A couple of blocks uphill from the waterfront, **Shop on the Corner** (263 Lincoln St., 902/634-3434, Mon.-Fri. 8:30am-5pm, Sat. 9am-5pm, Sun. 10am-5pm, lunches $7-12) is an untouristy place that combines kitchen giftware with a small café offering a wide range of teas and the locally roasted, delightfully named Laughing Whale coffee.

Seafood

In the big red building down on the water, the **Old Fish Factory** (68 Bluenose Dr., 902/634-3333, mid-May-mid-Oct. daily 11am-9pm, $17-32) is a large restaurant in a converted fish storehouse. Specialties include creamy seafood chowder, beer-battered haddock, and fish baked on a cedar plank. After the Solomon Gundy, a sour-tasting local specialty, you'll be ready for Blueberry Grunt, sweet dumplings floating in a blueberry compote and topped with whipped cream. Non-seafood dishes with a Canadian twist are also offered, such as maple-glazed chicken. Lunch features similar offerings, but with lower prices.

One block back from the harbor, several restaurants line Montague Street. All have decks or floor-to-ceiling windows facing the water. **Big Red's** (80 Montague St., 902/634-3554, daily 10:30am-8pm, $14-28) is exactly that—a cavernous, family-friendly restaurant with a standard seafood menu and lots of pizza choices. Portions are generous and prices reasonable.

Grand Banker Bar & Grill (82 Montague St., 902/634-3300, daily 11am-midnight, $15-30) offers similarly great views from an enclosed dining room and serves a wide-ranging menu of seafood, salads, pastas, and sandwiches. The food is well prepared and the atmosphere pleasant and relaxed. Mains include crab cakes, Acadian seafood stew, and maple-pecan glazed salmon. A half dozen good beers and a couple of Nova Scotia wines are available. The Grand Banker puts on a fine brunch (Sat.-Sun. 11am-2pm, $10-20) that includes lobster eggs Benedict.

ACCOMMODATIONS AND CAMPING

Whatever Mahone Bay may lack in accommodations is more than made up for in Lunenburg, where more than 60 B&Bs—even more than Halifax, which has over 100 times the population—clog the historic streets. You should still try to make reservations ahead of time in summer, but be prepared for an answering machine in winter, when many lodgings are closed.

$50-100

Many of the B&Bs in the $100-150 range have rooms under $100 outside of summer, but in July and August, your choices are limited. Incorporating two (circa 1888 and 1905) buildings, the **Boscawen Inn** (150 Cumberland St., 902/634-3325 or 800/354-5009, www.boscawen.ca, $99-225 s or d) also has a couple of rooms under $100, but most are higher-priced. This European-style hotel occupies a scenic perch above the harbor and is surrounded by gardens. The five guest rooms in McLachlan House are less expensive than those across the road at what was originally known as the Boscawen Manor, but all guests enjoy a light breakfast included in the rates. Other amenities include a formal dining room and sun-soaked terrace, both open to the public for meals.

$100-150

Right downtown, above the Grand Banker restaurant, the tidy **Brigantine Inn and Suites** (82 Montague St., 902/634-3300 or 800/360-1181, www.brigantineinn.com, $110-200 s or d) provides excellent value. The inn offers seven nautically themed rooms, each with a private bathroom and named for a famous sailing ship. The smallest of the rooms is the brightly decorated Cutty Sark room, while the much larger Brigantine Romance room features a jetted tub on a glass-enclosed balcony overlooking the harbor. Part of the inn is a complex of seven suites one block from the main building. These have separate bedrooms, as well as sitting areas, coffeemakers, microwaves, and fridges.

One of the best in this price range is the ★ **Lennox Tavern B&B** (69 Fox St., 902/521-0214, www.lennoxtavernbb.ca, Apr.-Dec., $115-130 s or d), which dates to 1791, making it Canada's oldest inn. The owners breathed life into the building through a meticulous

1: the town of Lunenburg, protected as a UNESCO World Heritage Site; **2:** Blue Rocks

restoration using the original plans. Two guest rooms share a single bathroom, and the other two are en suite. Breakfast in what was originally the tavern is included in the rates.

With rooms and suites spread through three buildings on King Street, the ornately detailed **Mariner King B&B** (15 King St., 902/634-8509 or 800/565-8509, www. marinerking.com, $135-245 s or d) is right downtown. Its cheaper rooms are a little threadbare, but the character-filled Attic Suite is a gem. It even has its own rooftop patio.

Rum Runner Inn (66 Montague St., 902/634-9200 or 888/778-6786, www. rumrunnerinn.com, $139-199 s or d) is right along the busy restaurant strip opposite the waterfront. It's a historic building, but the 13 rooms are thoroughly modernized and look no different from a regular upscale motel. Each has a coffeemaker, a fridge, air-conditioning, and Internet connections. The most expensive rooms have a king bed and glassed-in veranda. A light breakfast is included.

If you're looking to stay in a historic building with a modern feel, consider the centrally situated ★ **Salt Shaker Deli and Inn** (126 Montague St., 902/634-8973, www.saltshakerdeli.com, $140-200 s or d). Overlooking the harbor, all four guest rooms have polished hardwood floors and antique-style beds. Two are split-level with jetted tubs in the en suite bathrooms and harbor views.

$150-200

The **Lunenburg Inn** (26 Dufferin St., 902/634-9419 or 800/565-3963, www. lunenburginn.com, Apr.-Oct., $159-199 s or d) is an elaborate Victorian home that has been taking in guests since 1924. It underwent serious renovations in the mid-1990s and now provides some of the nicest rooms in town, with rates including a full breakfast. If I had a choice, I'd stay in one of the two suites, which each have a sitting area with a TV, a jetted tub in the en suite bathroom, and a private entrance from the veranda. Guests enjoy a sitting room with a fireplace, a private bar, and wireless Internet.

Kaulbach House (75 Pelham St., 902/634-8818 or 800/568-8818, www.kaulbachhouse. com, $180-220 s or d) is one of Lunenburg's many historic treasures (circa 1880) converted to an inn, complete with the unique "Lunenburg bump," an enlarged dormer that extends past a building's eaves. Two blocks up from the harbor but with partial water views, the six antiques-filled rooms have en suite or private bathrooms, flat-screen TVs,

Lunenburg Inn

air-conditioning, and wireless Internet. A full breakfast is included in the rates.

Campgrounds

The **Lunenburg Campground** (Blockhouse Hill Rd., 902/634-8100, mid-May-early Oct., $32-48) sits on Blockhouse Hill, high above downtown and beside the information center. It's on the small side (55 sites), but the facilities are adequate (showers, views, Internet access).

A lot more than a campground, ★ **Ovens Natural Park** (off Hwy. 332, 902/766-4621, www.ovenspark.com, mid-May-mid-Oct.) has campsites (tents $35, hookups $50-75) and cabins varying from those with shared bathrooms (from $65 s or d) to self-contained two-bedroom chalets ($190). Amenities include lawn games, a playground, evening bonfires, a restaurant, and a gift shop. Stephen Chapin, younger brother of Harry Chapin (of "Cat's in the Cradle" fame) owns and operates the property with his family, making the evening sing-alongs a real treat. The middle weekend of August, the entire Chapin family comes together as a tribute to the singer, with everyone welcome to join in the fun.

INFORMATION AND SERVICES

Lunenburg Visitor Information Centre (Blockhouse Hill Rd., 902/634-8100, www. lunenburgns.com, late May-Sept. daily 9am-5pm) stocks locally written, informative literature about the port's historic architecture. Staff will help those without reservations find accommodations. The office can be a little hard to find. As you enter town, stay on Lincoln Street as it passes the signs for the waterfront, and you'll soon find yourself on Blockhouse Hill.

Fishermen's Memorial Hospital (14 High St., 902/634-8801) is between Dufferin and Green Streets. For the **RCMP,** call 902/634-8674.

GETTING THERE AND AROUND

Along divided Highway 103, it takes a little more than one hour to reach Lunenburg from Halifax (100 km/62 mi), taking Exit 10 via Mahone Bay for the final stretch.

If you're in Halifax without a vehicle, consider a six-hour tour with **Ambassatours** (902/423-6242 or 800/565-7173). These depart June-October Wednesday, Friday, and Saturday at 8:30am.

Lunenburg to Shelburne

Beyond Lunenburg, the divided highway continues south to Bridgewater, but the crowds thin out quickly. This is one of the best reasons to continue south—the rugged coastline is dotted with Peggy's Cove-like villages steeped in history but unaffected by tourism, and parks with designated hiking trails and sandy beaches beckon.

The 140-kilometer (87-mile) drive between Lunenburg and Shelburne takes less than two hours nonstop. As accommodations are limited along this stretch of coast, a sensible schedule is to plan to leave Lunenburg after breakfast, spend the day exploring the following parks and towns, and have a room booked in Shelburne for the night.

BRIDGEWATER

Situated on the LaHave River, west of Lunenburg, Bridgewater (pop. 8,200) is the main service town of the South Shore. Industry revolves around a Michelin tire plant, and if you're traveling south, this is the last place to fill up on fast food and do your mall shopping.

Sights

The 1860 **Wile Carding Mill** (242 Victoria

Rd., 902/543-8233, June-mid-Sept. Mon.-Sat. 9:30am-5:30pm, Sun. 1pm-5:30pm, adult $3.50, senior $2.25, child $2) was once a wool-processing mill. The wool was carded for spinning and weaving or made into batts for quilts. The original machinery is still in operation, powered by a waterwheel, and now demonstrates old carding methods. It's on the south side of the river (take Exit 13 from Highway 103).

Surrounded by parkland on the south side of downtown off King Street, **DesBrisay Museum** (130 Jubilee Rd., 902/543-4033, www.desbrisaymuseum.ca, June-Aug. Tues.-Sat. 9am-5pm, Sept.-May Wed.-Sun. 1pm-5pm, adult $3.50, senior $2.50, child $2) looks unappealing from the outside, but inside displays tell the story of Bridgewater's first European settlers and the importance of local industries. Highlights include Mi'kmaq quilting and a wooden plough dating to 1800.

Food and Accommodations

Waves Seafood & Grill (Eastside Plaza, 28 Davison Dr., 902/543-2020, Mon.-Fri. 11am-9pm, Sat.-Sun. 8am-9pm, $12-20) is open for the usual breakfast choices weekends only, but where this place really shines is with its inexpensive fish-and-chips, such as two pieces and chips for $15.

Bridgewater's premier bed and breakfast is **River Reflections** (225 King St., 902/527-2682 or 888/527-2682, www.riverreflectionsbandb.ca, $110-125 s or d), a gracious wooden building that dates to 1906. It has been beautifully restored, now with three simple guest rooms furnished with antiques. Rates include a full breakfast and the luxury of relaxing on a covered porch overlooking the LaHave River. To get there from Highway 103, take Exit 13 and follow Victoria Road to King Street in the heart of downtown.

About 6 kilometers (3.7 miles) east of town along Highway 331, on the south side of the LaHave River, the **Lighthouse Motel** (13 Conradin Dr., Conquerall Bank, 902/543-8151, www.lighthousemotel.ca, May-Oct., $95-120 s or d) combines standard motel rooms with suites and cottages. It occupies a prime riverside location, and guests have access to a private beach, a picnic area, and a playground.

Getting There

Bridgewater is about 20 kilometers (12.4 miles) west of Lunenburg via Highway 3. It's 110 kilometers (68 miles) southwest of Halifax, a 1.5-hour drive.

HIGHWAY 331 TO LIVERPOOL

Highway 331, which begins in downtown Bridgewater as King Street, follows the LaHave River to its mouth and then winds along the coast to Exit 17 of Highway 103. It adds just 30 minutes to the trip between Bridgewater and Liverpool, but you'll want to allow longer—it's a beautiful introduction to the untouristy South Shore beyond Lunenburg.

★ Crescent Beach

Around 20 minutes southeast of Bridgewater is **Crescent Beach,** a beautiful 2-kilometer (1.2-mile) stretch of finely ground quartz sand that links the mainland to the LaHave Islands. Like the rest of Nova Scotia, the water is cool, but on a hot summer's day, many people dive in for a swim. But it is the beach itself that is the draw, with sand dunes up to 2 meters (6.6 feet) high separating the beach from a shallow bay popular with kite surfers.

Crescent Beach is day-use only, but adjacent **Rissers Beach Provincial Park** boasts the same white sand and an area of pristine salt marsh laced with boardwalks. The park **campground** (902/688-2034, mid-May-mid-Oct., $29) fills every weekend through summer, but midweek even sites close to the sandy beach may remain empty. The park is just south of the turnoff to Crescent Beach.

1: Bridgewater and the LaHave River; **2:** Crescent Beach

GETTING THERE

Crescent Beach is about 30 kilometers (19 miles) southeast of Bridgewater, a 30-minute drive via Highway 331. It's 140 kilometers (87 miles) south of Halifax, just under two hours on Highways 103 and 331.

LaHave Islands

The causeway along Crescent Beach crosses to **Bush Island,** from where quirky old iron bridges provide access to **Bell Island** and **LaHave Island.** Just three of dozens of islands in the group, they are dotted with old fishing cottages inhabited by those who have escaped the rat race. On Bell Island, a museum filled with local history is in the church, while Bush Island Provincial Park is little more than a boat launch, but the rugged scenery and funky fishing cottages make the drive to the end of the road a delightful detour from the main South Shore tourist route.

LIVERPOOL

This historic town, at the mouth of the Mersey River, about 50 kilometers (31 miles) south of Bridgewater, doesn't get as much attention as it deserves. Throughout the compact downtown core are a number of interesting attractions, while Privateer Days (late June) provide a lively glimpse of the town's colorful past.

Sights and Events
THE PORT OF PRIVATEERS

Privateers were government-sanctioned pirates who had permission to capture enemy vessels. American privateers found their way to Nova Scotia during the American Revolution, but the British responded by attacking American boats. Privateers were required by law to take captured vessels to Halifax's Privateers Wharf, where the boats and cargo were auctioned off, a portion of which was handed back to the privateer and his crew. Liverpool local Simeon Perkins had a share in a privateering boat, along with dozens of others who used Liverpool as their home port. The most prolific of the privateer vessels was the *Liverpool Packet* captained by Joseph

Barss, which captured an estimated 200 vessels during its lifetime. With plundered goods from a single vessel selling for up to $1 million at auction, Liverpool became a wealthy town, and many of the grand homes still standing were financed by privateering.

OTHER SIGHTS

Well-known Canadian photographer Sherman Hines injected his own resources into developing the **Rossignol Cultural Centre** (205 Church St., 902/354-3067, July-Aug. Mon.-Sat. 10am-5:30pm, Sun. noon-5:30pm, adult $5, senior $4, child $3) in a school building once slated for demolition. One block south of Main Street along Old Bridge Street, it encompasses multiple small museums, including one devoted to outhouses (Hines is known for his outhouse photography) and others to folk art, the Mi'kmaq, and wildlife.

Built by infamous privateer Simeon Perkins, **Perkins House** (105 Main St.) is a classic example of a New England planter's adaptation to Nova Scotia. Built in 1766, it is furnished with antiques and displays that tell the story of Perkins's colorful life on the high seas. At the time of publication, the home was closed due to structural issues, but due to its age and interesting former owner, it is still worth viewing from the surrounding gardens.

Country music legend Hank Snow, who sold 70 million records, was born in nearby Brooklyn. Between Highway 103 and downtown, a railway station has been converted to the **Hank Snow Home Town Museum** (148 Bristol St., 902/354-4675, www.hanksnow.com, Mon.-Sat. 9am-5pm, Sun. 1pm-5pm, adult $5, senior $4, children free) in his memory. Displays catalog his life, from the earliest performances in Halifax through details of his seven number-one hits from 120 albums, to his Grand Ole Opry performances, his role in introducing Elvis Presley to the entertainment world, and, finally, the huge collection of awards accumulated through six decades of performing.

PRIVATEER DAYS

There's no better place to immerse yourself in the colorful history of Nova Scotia's privateers than **Privateer Days** (902/354-4500, www.privateerdays.ca), a Liverpool tradition held annually in late June. Walking tours led by locals in period dress and a re-creation of when two American privateer boats once invaded the town are highlights, but events go on all week, culminating with a bang during the final night's fireworks.

Food and Accommodations

Once home to a privateer, **Lane's Privateer Inn** (27 Bristol Ave., 902/354-3456 or 800/794-3332, www.lanesprivateerinn.com, mid-May-Oct., $120-175 s or d) has everything you need for an overnight stay under one roof. The 27 rooms all have en suite bathrooms and air-conditioning, while some have king beds and balconies overlooking the Mersey River. Downstairs is an excellent restaurant. Breakfast includes all the usual options, with Nova Scotian specialties such as smoked salmon sausage as a substitute for bacon. The lunch and dinner includes traditional Acadian *rappie* pie for $16, fish tacos for $17 and a lamb burger for $15, a lobster roll for $17, and lobster linguini for $24.

Getting There

Liverpool is about 50 kilometers (31 miles) south of Bridgewater via Highway 103. It's 160 kilometers (99 miles) south of Halifax, a two-hour drive, also via Highway 103.

LIVERPOOL TO PORT JOLI

If you've left Highway 103 to explore Liverpool, continue south through town along the older Highway 3 to reach White Point before rejoining the main route south at Summerville.

White Point

Activities at **White Point Beach Resort** (White Point Beach Resort Rd., 902/354-2711 or 800/565-5068, www.whitepoint.com) make this lodging a destination in itself. Stretching along a wide swath of white sand, it has indoor and outdoor pools, swimming in a freshwater lake, surfboard and kayak rentals, tennis courts, a nine-hole golf course, a games room, two restaurants, and nightly entertainment in the lounge. Most guests are families, many returning annually for summer vacation. Comfortable motel-like rooms are $175-210 s or d depending on the view, and cottages are $295-355.

Continuing along Highway 3 from White Point to Hunts Point, you'll come to **Hunts Point Beach Cottages** (Hwy. 3, 902/683-2077, www.huntspointbeach.com, mid-May-Sept., $145-180 s or d), a much quieter spot, where guests laze their time away on the grassy grounds, which extend to the beach. The newly renovated cottages have one or two bedrooms, kitchens, covered decks, and living rooms with TVs.

GETTING THERE

White Point is less than 10 kilometers (6.2 miles) south of Liverpool, a 10-minute drive via Highway 3. It's 170 kilometers (105 miles) south of Halifax, two hours via Highways 103 and 3.

Summerville Beach Provincial Park

Just before Highway 3 rejoins Highway 103, a short gravel road leads along the back of the small **Summerville Beach Provincial Park,** which protects a spit of sand jutting across Port Mouton. It's a day-use park with picnic tables and plenty of room to spread your towel on the beach.

Kejimkujik National Park Seaside Adjunct

About 25 kilometers (15.5 miles) southwest of Liverpool is one of the largest remaining undisturbed areas of Nova Scotian coastline. Affiliated with the inland Kejimkujik National Park (along Highway 8 between Liverpool and Annapolis Royal), the **Kejimkujik National Park Seaside Adjunct** encompasses unspoiled beaches and offshore isles. The park is accessible only on foot. The main access is along an easy 3-kilometer (1.9-mile) trail beginning at the parking lot on St. Catherine's Road (turn off in Port Joli) and ending at the southwest end of St. Catherine's River Beach. Some sections of this beach close late April-late July to protect piping plover nesting sites. The Seaside Adjunct has no visitor facilities, and camping is not permitted.

PORT JOLI

Port Joli is a picturesque coastal village with a seaside park that gets busy only on the hottest of summer weekends.

Thomas Raddall Provincial Park

This gem known as **Thomas Raddall Provincial Park** protects rock formations that suggest it was the point where the Gondwana and North American continents collided many millions of years ago. But for most, the beaches are the main draw. Left behind by the retreating ice cap at the end of the last ice age, banks of sand have washed ashore, forming beautiful stretches of beach now protected by the park.

The park has an 11-kilometer (6.8-mile) trail system, half of which is paved and set aside for both cyclists and walkers. The most popular destination is Sandy Bay, a short beach bookended by rocky headlands. If you can pull yourself away from the beach, follow the **Sandy Bay Trail** over the northern headland to the **Herring Rock Trail,** where the remains of a 1700s fishing station can be seen. Take both these trails and you'll be back on your beach towel within an hour. In the north of the park, beaches are lapped by the protected waters of Port Joli Harbour. Starting from the top end of the campground, the **Port Joli Trail** (1 km/0.6 mi each way) winds south past interpretive panels to Scotch Point Beach. To the north, a string of beaches spread out well beyond the park boundary.

The park **campground** (902/683-2664, mid-May-mid-Oct., $29) has 82 large sites, including a few designated for tents. Each site has a picnic table and fire pit, while other amenities include washrooms with showers, a playground, and firewood sales.

To get to the park, continue along Highway 103 south from Port Joli and turn south on East Port L'Herbert Road; it's 3 kilometers (1.9 miles) from the highway.

Getting There

Port Joli is 25 kilometers (15.5 miles) south of Liverpool, a 15-minute drive along Highway 103. It's 185 kilometers (115 miles) south of Halifax, two hours via Highway 103.

Shelburne and Vicinity

Like Lunenburg, 140 kilometers (87 miles) to the northeast, Shelburne (pop. 1,700) sits at the innermost end of a long harbor formed between two peninsulas. The seaport was established in 1783 when Loyalists fleeing the newly independent American colonies settled here by the thousands, establishing shipbuilding and fish processing businesses. But eventually the seaport began to show its age. Then Hollywood came to town. In 1992, the motley collection of historic buildings along the waterfront was used as a setting for Fairfield, Connecticut, circa 1780, in the American Revolution movie *Mary Silliman's War*. In 1995, Shelburne again hit the big screen as the setting for 1600s Boston in *The Scarlet Letter*, an adaptation of Nathaniel Hawthorne's novel. Demi Moore and Robert Duvall may be long gone, but the two movies created an impetus for preservation. While some "historic" buildings were added to the mix, many original buildings were spruced up, power lines were buried, and generally the town came together to promote its past.

Shelburne

★ SHELBURNE HISTORIC DISTRICT

Dock Street is dotted with some of Canada's oldest wooden buildings. The local historical society has done a wonderful job of breathing life into the **Shelburne Historic District,** while businesses such as a cooperage and boatbuilder help bring its history to life. In between are grassy areas, a waterfront pathway, and kayak rentals. Admission to each of the buildings is $4, or buy a ticket for $10 to visit all three.

Shelburne County Museum

The **Shelburne County Museum** (8 Maiden Ln., 902/875-3219, June-mid-Oct. daily 9:30am-5:30pm, mid-Oct.-May Tues.-Sat. 2pm-5pm) is the best place to make your first stop. It contains exhibits covering Shelburne's

Loyalist heritage and shipbuilding history. One highlight is the 250-year-old fire engine, believed to be the oldest in Canada.

Dory Shop Museum

First used in the mid-1800s, dories were small, skiff-like wooden boats that were essential to the success of fishing the Grand Banks. Rather than fishing from the mother vessel, a dozen or more dories would be transported to the fishing grounds, allowing hundreds of hooks to be laid out at once. Adding to their usability, they were inexpensive to make and stackable. On the waterfront across from the county museum, the **Dory Shop Museum** (11 Dock St., June-mid-Oct. daily 9:30am-5:30pm) is the last of seven once-thriving boat factories in town. The seven shops turned out thousands of handcrafted wooden fishing dories between 1880 and 1970. The shop now houses interpretive displays and gives demonstrations of the dying art.

Ross-Thomson House and Store Museum

The **Ross-Thomson House and Store Museum** (9 Charlotte Ln., 902/875-3141, June-mid-Oct. daily 9:30am-5:30pm) was built in 1785 as a Loyalist store. The last example of its kind today in Nova Scotia, it depicts the period setting with sample wares such as lumber and salted codfish, which were traded for tobacco, molasses, and dry goods. Upstairs is a military display, and outside, the garden has been planted as it would have been in the late 1700s.

Muir-Cox Shipyard

At the far south end of Dock Street, the small **Muir-Cox Shipyard** was closed at the time of publication. If it reopens in the near future, expect to see local men building traditional boats. It operated continuously between the 1820s and 1980s, launching square-rigged barques in its earliest days and wooden racing yachts in more modern times.

FOOD

If you're touring the historic waterfront precinct, you'll pass right by **Beandock** (32 Dock St., 902/875-1302, Mon.-Fri. 8:30am-4pm, Sat. 9am-4pm, Sun. 10am-4pm, lunches $7-10), in a rambling old wooden building with outdoor chairs that offer stunning water views. It's the best place in town for coffee, with food offerings including sandwiches, wraps, and desserts.

The bright and cheery ★ **Charlotte Lane Café** (13 Charlotte Ln., 902/875-3314, Tues.-Sat. 11:30am-2:30pm and 5pm-8pm, $19-33), between Water and Dock Streets, has an established reputation for fine dining. Its Swiss owner-chef, Roland Glauser, specializes in local seafood prepared with cooking techniques from around the world. The seafood chowder is one of the best I've tasted.

ACCOMMODATIONS AND CAMPING

Shelburne Harbourside Cottages (10 George St., 902/875-4555, www. shelburneharboursidecottages.com, $115 s or d) is an excellent lodging value. Each of its two modern cottages enjoys harbor views and has cooking facilities, a separate bedroom, a TV, and a deck. Extras include bike rentals and kayak rentals; the latter can be launched right from the cottages.

Cooper's Inn (36 Dock St., 902/875-4656 or 800/688-2011, www.thecoopersinn.com, Apr.-Oct., $140-220 s or d) is a two-story colonial beauty overlooking the harbor and next to the tourist bureau and museum. Built in 1784 by a merchant and restored and opened in 1988, the lodging has six rooms, all with private baths ($130-180), and a large top-floor suite with water views ($220). Rates include a full breakfast in the cheery dining room.

★ **Whispering Waves Cottages** (Black Point Rd., Ingomar, 902/637-3535 or 866/470-9283, www.novascotiacottages.info, $149-165 s or d) may be out of town, but an overnight stay at this welcoming waterfront property is as enjoyable as one could imagine. The modern cottages are stylishly furnished in wilderness, nautical, or romance themes, and each has a separate bedroom, kitchen, lounge room with a fireplace, and a deck with ocean views. A lobster dinner, delivered to your cottage door, is a delicious extra.

Campgrounds

Rustic and pretty, **The Islands Provincial Park** (off Hwy. 3, 5 km/3.1 mi west of Shelburne, 902/875-4304, mid-May-early

Shelburne Historic District

Sept., $29) faces the town across the upper harbor. It offers 64 unserviced sites with table shelters and grills, pit toilets, running water, and a spacious modern shower room.

GETTING THERE

Shelburne is 140 kilometers (87 miles) from Lunenburg along Highway 103. The drive takes less than two hours nonstop. It's 220 kilometers (136 miles) from Halifax, almost three hours via Highway 103.

SHELBURNE TO YARMOUTH

Barrington and Vicinity

Highway 103 takes a mainly inland route between Shelburne and Yarmouth. One place it does come in contact with the ocean is near Barrington, just off the main highway along Highway 3, where coastal views are exquisite. In Barrington itself, the **Old Meeting House Museum** (2408 Hwy. 3, 902/637-2185, June-Sept. Mon.-Sat. 9:30am-5:30pm, Sun. 1pm-5:30pm, donation) is a variation on planter life. Built by 50 Cape Cod families in 1765, the New England-style church is Canada's oldest nonconformist house of worship.

Beyond Barrington, at Villagedale, is **Sand Hills Beach Provincial Park,** so named for a complex dune system where wide tidal flats extend into the ocean. Time your arrival for high tide; the water is warm enough for swimming—in summer only, of course.

GETTING THERE

Barrington is about 35 kilometers (22 miles) southwest of Shelburne, a 25-minute drive on Highway 103. It's 255 kilometers (160 miles) from Halifax, three hours via Highway 103.

Cape Sable Island

At Barrington West, Cape Sable Island is well worth the detour, although there are limited services on the island, so plan on staying or dining in nearby Shelburne or Yarmouth. Connected to the mainland by a causeway, the island forms the southernmost point in Nova Scotia. Feared by early sailors because of its jagged shores, the island was settled by brick-making Acadians during the 17th century. The island also served as a summer base for fishermen from New England, and fishing prevails today as the community's main industry, with tourism a close second.

The island's four main beaches offer surfing, clam digging, swimming, fishing, and bird-watching. At **Hawk Beach,** on the eastern side (turn at Lower Clark's Harbour at Hawk Rd. and go left), you can see the **Cape Lighthouse** on a small nearby sandbar. The original tower, built in 1861, was Canada's first eight-sided structure; the present lighthouse, a protected heritage building, was constructed in 1923. At low tide on Hawk Beach, you can also see the remains of a 1,500-year-old forest.

Causeway Beach (turn right at the Corbett Heights subdivision) is a prime sunbathing and fishing (mackerel) spot. **Stoney Island Beach,** as the name implies, is not as popular with sunbathers as it is with seals, which like to sun themselves on the rocks. **South Side Beach** (turn on Daniel's Head Rd. in South Side) is also popular as a seal-watching and beachcombing locale.

GETTING THERE

Cape Sable Island is about 50 kilometers (31 miles) southwest of Shelburne along Highway 103, continuing on Highway 3 through Barrington. Allow 40 minutes. From Halifax, allow at least three hours for the 270-kilometer (165-mile) drive down Highway 103 and 3.

Yarmouth

Yarmouth (pop. 6,500) was the center of a shipbuilding empire during Canada's Great Age of Sail, when it ranked as the world's fourth-largest port of registry. Still the region's largest seaport, the town is a prosperous and orderly place supported by shipping—primarily lumber products, Irish moss, and Christmas trees—and fishing. Yarmouth's herring fleet is a major contributor to the local economy. The fleet sails at night and anchors with all its lights blazing farther up the Fundy Coast, creating a sight known as "herring city."

SIGHTS

If historic architecture interests you, take a leisurely walk along Main Street, where the commercial buildings demonstrate late 19th-century Classic Revival, Queen Anne Revival, Georgian, and Italianate styles. At the tourist information center on Forest Street, pick up the *Walking Tour of Yarmouth* brochure, which details about two dozen points of architectural and historical interest on a self-guided 4-kilometer (2.5-mile) walk.

Firefighters' Museum of Nova Scotia

The **Firefighters' Museum of Nova Scotia** (451 Main St., 902/742-5525, June and Sept. Mon.-Sat. 9am-5pm, July-Aug. Mon.-Sat. 9am-9pm, Sun. 10am-5pm, adult $5, senior $4, child $3) is a museum dedicated solely to firefighting equipment. Among the extensive vintage collection are an 1819 Hopwood and Tilley hand pump and other sparkling tools.

Yarmouth County Museum

An enjoyable walk from downtown through a tree-lined residential area east of Main Street leads to **Yarmouth County Museum** (22 Collins St., 902/742-5539, June-Sept. Mon.-Sat. 9am-5pm, Oct.-May Tues.-Sat. 2pm-5pm, adult $3, senior $2.50, child $1). It showcases

Canada's largest ship-portrait collection and exhibits a trove of seafaring lore, musical instruments, ship models, furniture, and more. The research library and archives store extensive records and genealogical materials.

Cape Forchu

The most scenic destination in the vicinity of Yarmouth is Cape Forchu, 10 kilometers (6.2 miles) south of town via Highway 304, where the red-and-white **Cape Forchu Light Station** guides ships into the harbor. Follow Main Street north and turn left at Vancouver Street. Just past the hospital complex, turn left on Grove Road. The Faith Memorial Baptist Church marks the site where the famous Yarmouth runic stone, believed to have been inscribed by Leif Eriksson's men, was found. Next you come to the lighthouse (July-Aug. daily 11:30am-7pm, free) perched on a stone promontory. The actual lighthouse is open to climb, and you get good views from the top. Below the lighthouse, a paved walking trail leads from the parking lot down to **Leif Ericson Picnic Park,** overlooking the rocky coast.

FOOD

Locals and visitors alike looking for quality tea and coffee in a refined setting gravitate to **Sip Cafe** (1 Collins St., 902/742-3579, Mon.-Fri. 7am-10pm, Sat.-Sun. 8am-10pm, lunches $6-9), which has indoor and outdoor seating, free Wi-Fi, and a range of sweet and savory pastries.

Rudder's (96 Water St., 902/742-7311, daily 11am-10:30pm, $16-30) is a large brew-pub set right on the water. It's a big room that manages to maintain a warm atmosphere, with even more tables spread across a veranda facing the harbor. The menu blends traditional pub food with Nova Scotian specialties—think maple-glazed salmon baked on a cedar plank, lobster and scallop crepes,

Yarmouth

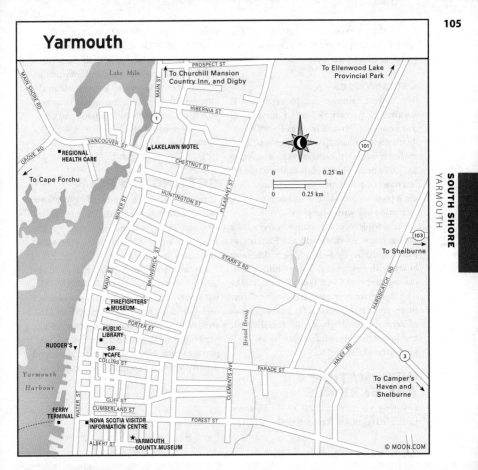

and steak and lobster. The lobster dinner is a major draw.

ACCOMMODATIONS AND CAMPING

North of downtown, where Vancouver Street crosses the head of Yarmouth Harbour, is the **Lakelawn Motel** (641 Main St., 902/742-3588 or 877/664-0664, www.lakelawnmotel.com, from $115-155 s or d). The centerpiece of this lodging is a grand 1864 mansion that holds a breakfast room and four upstairs B&B rooms. Spread around its perimeter is a U-shaped wing of 27 motel rooms that are a little worn but still a decent value.

Churchill Mansion Country Inn (44 Old Post Rd., Darlings Lake, 902/649-2818 or 888/453-5565, www.churchillmansion.com, May-mid-Nov., $179-249 s or d) was the hilltop summer home of Aaron Flint Churchill, who made his fortune in the shipping trade after establishing the Churchill Line out of Savannah, Georgia. Overlooking a lake and with distant ocean views, the house was converted to an inn in the 1980s. All the beautifully restored rooms are super spacious. The most expensive is Churchill's master bedroom, with a balcony overlooking the lake. A gourmet breakfast and evening snacks are included in the rates, while dinner is available for an extra charge in the restaurant. The town of Darlings Lake is 15 kilometers (9.3 miles) north of Yarmouth.

Campgrounds

The closest campground to Yarmouth is **Campers' Haven** (5 km/3.1 mi east of Yarmouth, off Hwy. 3 in Arcadia, 902/742-4848, www.campershavencampground.com, mid-May-mid-Oct., campsites $25-48, cottage $85-105 s or d). The lakeside campground offers more than 200 sites, as well as canoe rentals, a pool, a camp store, a launderette, and a recreation hall with a fireplace.

For a wilderness experience, travel a little farther out to **Ellenwood Lake Provincial Park** (mid-June-mid-Oct., $29), which has a beach with swimming, a short hiking trail through a mixed forest typical of the southwest region, showers, and a playground. To get there, drive 19 kilometers (11.8 miles) north of Yarmouth on Highway 101, take Exit 34, and follow the signs along Highway 340 for 7 kilometers (4.3 miles).

INFORMATION AND SERVICES

Greeting visitors as they arrive in town is the cavernous **Nova Scotia Visitor Information Centre** (228 Main St. at Forest St., 902/742-5033, May-June and Sept.-Oct. daily 8am-5pm, July-Aug. daily 8am-7pm), where you'll find literature and information on just about everything imaginable in the city and the province. In advance of your visit, visit www.yarmouthandacadianshores.com.

The **Regional Health Centre** (902/742-1540) is at 50 Vancouver Street. For the **RCMP,** call 902/742-8777.

GETTING THERE

Yarmouth is 310 kilometers (190 miles) from Halifax via the South Shore (Highway 103) and 330 kilometers (205 miles) via the Annapolis Valley (Highway 101); allow at least four hours for either route.

Ferries from Portland, Maine, dock downtown in Yarmouth. The **CAT** (877/762-7245, www.ferries.ca) operates this service between mid-June and October, charging adult $107, senior $102, child $65, vehicle under 6.6 feet $199. The crossing takes 5.5 hours, with departures from Portland daily at 2:30pm and departures from Yarmouth daily at 8:30am.

sunset over Cape Forchu

Fundy Coast

The natural beauty of Nova Scotia's Fundy

Coast is sublime. Sea breezes bathe the shore in crisp salt air, and the sun illuminates the seascape colors with a clarity that defies a painter's palette.

Wildflowers bloom with abandon, nourished by the moist coastal air. And fog, thick as cotton, sometimes envelops the region during the summer. This is the Fundy Coast, which stretches from Yarmouth in the west to the farthest reaches of the Bay of Fundy in the east. Quietly and relentlessly, twice a day, a tidal surge that has its beginnings far away pours into the bay, creating the highest tides on the planet. Fishing boats are lifted from the muddy seafloor, and whales in pursuit of silvery herring hurry along the summertime currents,

Highlights

Look for ★ to find recommended sights, activities, dining, and lodging.

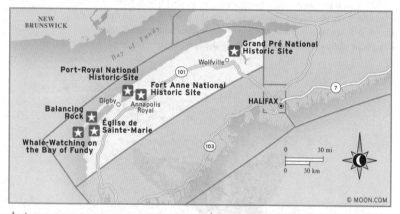

★ **Église de Sainte-Marie:** You may strain your neck viewing the tallest wooden church in North America, located on the charming Acadian Coast (page 112).

★ **Balancing Rock:** Out on Digby Neck, a short trail suddenly emerges at the Bay of Fundy—and this stunning pillar balanced precariously over the water (page 117).

★ **Whale-Watching on the Bay of Fundy:** Use Digby Neck and the adjacent islands as a base for whale-watching trips into the Bay of Fundy (page 117).

★ **Fort Anne National Historic Site:** After centuries of changing hands between the British and the French, this onetime capital of Nova Scotia is now managed by the government as a tourist attraction (page 119).

★ **Port-Royal National Historic Site:** The oldest European settlement north of St. Augustine, Florida, has been re-created here (page 120).

★ **Grand Pré National Historic Site:** This outdoor museum brings to life Longfellow's story of Evangeline, a young girl caught up in the Acadian deportation (page 132).

their mammoth bulks buoyed by the 100 billion tons of seawater that gush into the long bay between Nova Scotia and New Brunswick. The cycle from low to high tide takes a mere six hours. The tide peaks, in places high enough to swamp a four-story building, and then begins to retreat. As the sea level drops, coastal peninsulas and rocky islets emerge from the froth, veiled in seaweed. The seafloor reappears, shiny as shellac and littered with sea urchins, periwinkles, and shells. Where no one walked just hours ago, local children run and skip on the beaches, pausing to retrieve tidal treasures. Locals take the Fundy tides for granted. For visitors, it's an astounding show.

To a great extent, the history of the province's Fundy Coast is the story of all of Nova Scotia, and this is reflected in the region's wealth of historic and cultural wonders. France's colonial ambitions began at Port-Royal and clashed head-on with England's quest for New World dominance, and multiple national historic sites along the coast lie in testament to these troubled times. The trim Acadian villages of La Côte Acadienne, the historic streetscape of Annapolis Royal, and the gracious towns of Wolfville and Windsor add to the appeal.

PLANNING YOUR TIME

You can drive between Yarmouth and Halifax in a single day, but you should allow a minimum of two days, which lets you reserve a room at one of Annapolis Royal's many historic inns. This small town is definitely the historic heart of the Fundy Coast, with sights such as **Fort Anne National Historic Site** and **Port-Royal National Historic Site** easily filling out a full day of sightseeing. For this reason, two days and two nights should be allotted for exploring the Fundy Coast. At the western end, the detour through La Côte Acadienne and stops at Acadian icons such as **Église de Sainte-Marie** add only slightly to the length of the drive. The most impressive Acadian attraction, **Grand Pré National Historic Site,** is farther east, and it deserves at least three hours of your time. At some point during your travels through the region you'll want to focus on the Bay of Fundy (digging into a plate of plump Digby scallops doesn't count). Taking the above into consideration, if you have two nights planned for the Fundy Coast and you are traveling east from Yarmouth, spend the first morning meandering along La Côte Acadienne, order scallops for lunch in Digby, and continue to Annapolis Royal. Spend the rest of the afternoon and the first part of the next morning exploring the town before moving on to Wolfville. Spend the night, rise early for a short hike through **Blomidon Provincial Park,** and then move on to Grand Pré National Historic Site. You'll be back in the capital by late afternoon. With an extra day and night, plan on driving along Digby Neck and combining a hike to **Balancing Rock** with **whale-watching.**

Previous: whale-watching off Brier Island; main street in Annapolis Royal; Grand Pré National Historic Site.

Fundy Coast

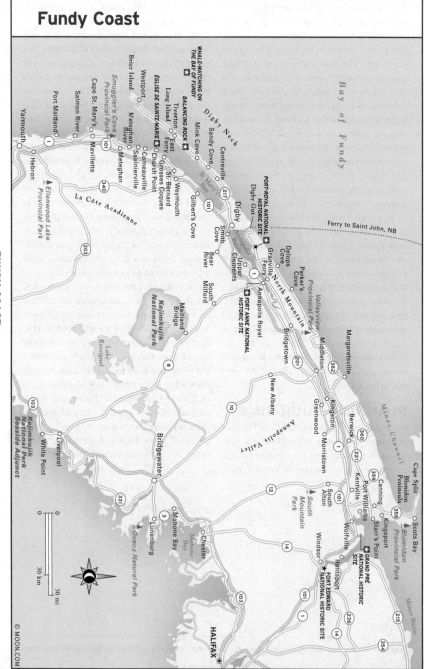

© MOON.COM

La Côte Acadienne

Those who zoom along Highway 101 between Yarmouth and Digby will miss the charming La Côte Acadienne (Acadian Coast), also known as the Municipality of Clare, a 50-kilometer (31-mile) coastal stretch populated by descendants of the French who resettled here after the Acadian expulsion of 1755. The place-names, the soaring Catholic churches, and the proud Acadian flags (a French tricolor with a single yellow star) announce that you're in the largest Francophone enclave in Nova Scotia.

MAVILLETTE AND VICINITY

For a look at the dynamic Fundy, check out **Mavillette Beach Provincial Park,** on the south side of Cap Sainte-Marie (Cape St. Mary's). The sign for Cape View Restaurant signals the turn from Highway 1; the road peels down to the sea and runs alongside high dunes. Boardwalks cross the dunes to the 1.5-kilometer-long (0.9-mile-long) beach, where sandbars trap water in warm pools at low tide. On sunny days, beachcombers walk the expanse and hunt for unusual seashells. Though this is one of the finest beaches in all of Nova Scotia, crowds are nonexistent.

Food and Accommodations

Across the beach access road from the Cape View Motel and with wonderful views of the beach and its stunning sunsets is **Cape View Restaurant** (157 John Doucette Rd., 902/645-2519, mid-May-Oct. daily 11am-8pm, $15-27), which dishes up relatively inexpensive seafood with an Acadian twist.

Along the beach access road you'll find **Cape View Motel and Cottages** (124 John Doucette Rd., 902/645-2258, www.capeviewmotel.ca, May-Oct.). The motel's 10 basic rooms ($90-145 s or d) and five cottages ($110-140) are set on expansive grounds overlooking sand dunes and the provincial park.

Smuggler's Cove Provincial Park

From Mavillette Beach, it's 16 kilometers (9.9 miles) north to **Smuggler's Cove Provincial Park.** Walkways here lead to great bluff-top views of the coast and down steep, tree-lined steps to the rocky shoreline. The coastal cliffs in this area are notched with caves, which were used by Prohibition-era rum runners. Some of the caves can be explored at low tide. The park also holds numerous picnic tables (making it an ideal lunch stop), but no campsites.

Getting There

Mavillette is just over 30 kilometers (19 miles) north of Yarmouth, a 25-minute drive via Highway 1. From Halifax, the quickest way to reach Mavillette is via Highway 101 along the Bay of Fundy (300 km/185 mi, 3.5 hours).

METEGHAN TO POINTE DE L'ÉGLISE

I recommend staying on the coastal route (Highway 1) between Meteghan and Pointe de L'Eglise (20 km/12.4 mi, 20 minutes), rather than the much faster inland Highway 101.

Although the seaport of Meteghan, 15 kilometers (9.3 miles) north of Mavillette, has few tourist facilities, it's worth stopping and taking a look around the dock area, as the main wharf is a hive of activity throughout the day, with local fishermen hauling up mostly lobster and scallops. The area was settled by a number of Acadian families in 1785 and is now the district's commercial hub, although the population still numbers fewer than 1,000. Although currently not open to the public, one of the oldest homes in town is **La Vieille Maison,** built by the founding Robicheau family in the late 1700s.

Food

A seafood cornucopia is brought in daily by

the seaport's scallop draggers, herring seiners, and lobster boats. **Seashore Restaurant** (8467 Hwy. 1, 902/645-3453, daily 9am-7pm, $12-19) is a good place for seafood dining, and on a warm summer evening, enjoying dinner on the outdoor deck overlooking the water is priceless.

Getting There

Meteghan is 45 kilometers (28 miles) north of Yarmouth, a 35-minute drive along Highway 1. It's 280 kilometers (175 miles) west of Halifax, 3.5 hours along Highway 101.

North from Meteghan

The village of **Meteghan River**, about 2 kilometers (1.2 miles) north of Meteghan, is Nova Scotia's largest wooden shipbuilding center. One of the nicest lodgings along La Côte Acadienne is **Au Havre du Capitaine** (9118 Hwy. 1, 902/769-2001, www.havreducapitaine. ca, $115-145 s or d), a country-style inn with hardwood floors and a sitting area set around a large stone fireplace. Choose from rooms with private baths and TVs or larger suites with whirlpool tubs. The inn's licensed dining room is open daily for breakfast, lunch, and dinner.

Also in Meteghan River, lobster lovers should stop in at **Riverside Lobster** (9089 Hwy. 1, 902/769-3340, Mon.-Fri. 8am-5pm), where you can buy live lobsters kept in flow-through crates at the large warehouse—perfect if you're camping or if your accommodation has cooking facilities.

Comeauville

The village of Comeauville, around 8 kilometers (5 miles) north of Meteghan River, is notable for **La Galerie Comeau** (767 Hwy. 1, 902/778-0422, call for hours), where artist Denise Comeau displays and sells her folksy watercolors that reflect the region and its Acadian roots.

POINTE DE L'ÉGLISE (CHURCH POINT)

This aptly named community is the last major Acadian community for northbound travelers, but it's also the most interesting.

★ Église de Sainte-Marie

Built between 1903 and 1905, the enormous **Église de Sainte-Marie** (St. Mary's Church), the largest and tallest wooden church in North America, dominates this village of 490 inhabitants. The building is laid out in the shape of a cross, and its soaring 56-meter (184-foot) steeple has been ballasted with 40 tons of rock to withstand the winter wind. Inside, **Le Musée Sainte-Marie** (902/769-2808, mid-May-mid-Oct. daily 9am-5pm, adult $2, child free) exhibits religious artifacts and historical documents and photos. Mass takes place Sunday at 10:30am.

Food

Through town to the south is ★ **Rapure Acadienne** (1443 Hwy. 1, 902/769-2172, Mon.-Sat. 8am-5:30pm), the most authentic place in all of Nova Scotia to try rappie pie, a traditional Acadian chicken dish with a rather unusually textured potato filling. The pies are massive (and also come with beef and clam fillings) and cost $9, including a side of butter or molasses. Order at the inside window (where you can peek through at the big ovens) and eat at the one indoor table or the picnic tables outside.

Camping

Campers can head to the full-service **Belle Baie Park** (Hwy. 1, 902/769-3160, www. bellebaiepark.ca, May-late Sept., tents $30, hookups $40-55), an oceanfront campground with its own beach, an outdoor pool, a playground, Internet access, and a launderette.

Getting There

Pointe de l'Église is just over 60 kilometers (37 miles) north of Yarmouth on Highway 1.

NORTH TO DIGBY
Grosses Coques

The last of the Acadian communities is **Grosses Coques,** a small village immediately north of Pointe de l'Église that takes its name from the huge bar clams harvested here on the tidal flats, an important food source for early settlers.

Grosses Coques is almost 65 kilometers (40 miles) north of Yarmouth via Highway 1.

Gilbert's Cove

A short, unpaved road leads from Highway 101 to **Gilbert's Cove Lighthouse** (Hwy. 101, www.gilbertscovelighthouse.com, July-Aug. Mon.-Sat. 10am-4pm, Sun. noon-4pm, donation). Built in 1904 to help vessels navigate the upper reaches of St. Mary's Bay, it has been restored and is open to the public in July and August, but the site can be visited any time of the year.

Gilbert's Cove is on Highway 101. It's about 85 kilometers (53 miles) north of Yarmouth via Highway 101. Allow about 70 minutes.

Digby and Vicinity

The port of Digby (pop. 2,100), 105 kilometers (65 miles) northeast of Yarmouth and 235 kilometers (146 miles) west of Halifax, is the terminus for the ferry from Saint John (New Brunswick) and home for the world's largest scallop fleet. The Mi'kmaq name for the area is Te'Wapskik, meaning "flowing between high rocks," a reference to Digby Gut, a narrow opening in the Annapolis Basin to the north of town. Digby derived its English name from Admiral Robert Digby, who sailed up the Fundy in 1793 and settled the place with 1,500 Loyalists from New England. The scallop fleet ties up off Fishermen's Wharf off Water Street; be there at sunset when the pastel-painted draggers lie at anchor in a semicircle, backlit by the intense setting sun.

SIGHTS AND RECREATION

A couple of worthwhile attractions are scattered through town, but the highlights are farther afield—Digby Neck and Kejimkujik National Park, both covered in this section.

Admiral Digby Museum

Digby's place in history is on display at the harbor-front **Admiral Digby Museum** (95 Montague Row, 902/245-6322, mid-June-Aug. Mon.-Sat. 9am-5pm, the rest of the year Wed. and Fri. 9:30am-4:30pm, donation), housed in a trim two-story Georgian-era residence with exhibits of old photographs, interesting maps, and maritime artifacts.

Bear River

Calling itself the "Switzerland of Nova Scotia" may be a stretch, but the small village of **Bear River,** straddling the waterway of the same name, 8 kilometers (5 miles) south of Digby, is nestled in a delightful little valley, where the trees turn glorious colors in late September. Along the main street are a motley collection of wooden buildings in various states of repair, many built on stilts above the river far below. Those that have been restored now hold craft shops.

ENTERTAINMENT AND EVENTS

Montague Row to Water Street is the place for people-watching, especially at sunset. **Club 98** (28 Water St., 902/245-4950, 10am-midnight) in the Fundy Restaurant has a band (cover charge) or disc jockey Friday-Saturday. The lounge at the **Pines Resort** (103 Shore Rd., 902/245-2511, Mon.-Sat.) is known for tamer pursuits, low lighting, a comfortable ambience, and finely tuned mixed drinks.

The port's famed scallops attract

Digby

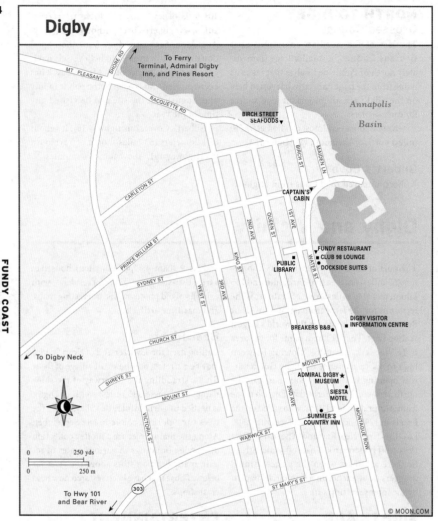

appropriate fanfare the second week of every August during **Digby Scallop Days** (www.digbyscallopdays.com), with a parade, scallop-shucking competitions, scallop barbecues, street vendors, the crowning of the Scallop Queen and Princesses, music, fireworks, and a parade of the scallop fleet.

FOOD

Right downtown, **Fundy Restaurant** (34 Water St., 902/245-4950, daily 10am-10pm,

$13-25) is a large, casual restaurant overlooking the scallop fleet. Seating is inside in a main dining room, in a solarium, or out on the balcony. Digby scallops are the specialty, prepared any way you'd like them or in combination with other seafood—the Fundy (scallop) omelet is an interesting breakfast choice, while the rest of the day, dishes such as scallop chowder and a platter of scallops cooked in various styles are good ways to sample this tasty treat.

One block back from the water, **Captain's Cabin** (2 Birch St., 902/245-4868, daily 11am-9pm, $11-18) is a locals' hangout, but it still specializes in seafood. Dishes are a little less creative, but the scallops are just as fresh and delicious.

Check out ★ **Birch Street Seafoods** (35 Birch St., 902/245-6551, Mon.-Fri. 9am-5:30pm, Sat. 9am-noon) for fresh seafood for those staying somewhere with cooking facilities. Naturally scallops are the main draw, but you can also order seasonal catches such as halibut, haddock, and flounder by the pound, as well as Digby chicks (smoked herring).

ACCOMMODATIONS AND CAMPING

$50-100

Digby has a few motel rooms under $100, including the **Siesta Motel** (81 Montague Row, 902/245-2568, www.siestamotel.org, $75-95 s or d), but there are no real bargains in town. The rooms do have wireless Internet and there is a pleasant garden out front.

$100-150

Two blocks from the waterfront, **Summer's Country Inn** (16 Warwick St., 902/245-2250, www.summerscountryinn.ca, May-Oct., $109-129 s or d) has nine guest rooms in an 1830s home and attached annex. Each room

has a private bath and comfortable bed, although the decorations are bright—in some a little too flowery for my taste. Rates include a delicious cooked breakfast.

The **Admiral Digby Inn** (441 Shore Rd., 902/245-2531 or 800/465-6262, www.digbyhotels.com, early Apr.-Oct., $119-249 s or d) is across the road from the Annapolis Basin, halfway between town and the ferry terminal. Better-than-average motel rooms start at $119 s or d, and for $160 you get a balcony with water views. Cottages with one and two bedrooms are $179 and $249, respectively. All rates include a light breakfast. Amenities include a restaurant, a lounge, an indoor pool, and a laundry.

Breakers Bed and Breakfast (5 Water St., 902/245-4643 or 866/333-5773, www.thebreakersbb.com, May-Oct., $159-179 s or d, including full breakfast) is an 1853 two-story home across from the waterfront. The three guest rooms are extra large and furnished in keeping with a heritage theme. A covered front porch with water views and the book-filled sitting room add to the charm.

Dockside Suites (26 Water St., 902/245-4950, www.fundyrestaurant.com, $119-189 s or d) is part of the Fundy Restaurant complex. Each of the 11 modern units is air-conditioned and has a balcony with harbor views and a separate bedroom. Other in-room

Digby is home to the world's largest fleet of scallop trawlers.

Digging into Digby Scallops

Digby is known for its scallops, so there is no better place to try them than this small Fundy Coast port. Unlike other bivalves (such as clams), scallops do not bury themselves in the sand. Instead, they live on the bottom of the Bay of Fundy and "swim" by quickly opening and closing their shells. The fishermen of Digby harvest scallops by dragging large wire baskets over the seafloor. They are shucked (opened) immediately and put on ice until reaching the shore.

The water temperature in the Bay of Fundy varies only slightly through the year, which, combined with the tides creating lots of nutrient movement, creates ideal conditions for the scallops. The result is the plumpest yet most delicate and succulent meat you could imagine. As a bonus, scallops are low in fat and full of protein.

Across Nova Scotia and beyond, Digby scallops appear on menus by name. In better dining rooms they are sautéed in butter with light spices or combined in seafood casseroles or dishes such as bouillabaisse. Local eateries such as the **Fundy Restaurant** (34 Water St., 902/245-4950, daily 10am-10pm), which has views of the fishing fleet, get creative with scallop omelets, scallop chowder, and scallop fettuccine. At **Birch Street Seafoods** (35 Birch St., 902/245-6551, Mon.-Fri. 9am-5:30pm, Sat. 9am-noon), you can buy them fresh from the trawler (if the weather is bad, the boats don't go out, and they may not have any stock) and prepare them as you please back at your kitchen-equipped accommodation. Expect to pay around $20 per pound.

amenities include a TV/DVD combo and wireless Internet.

Over $200

Appealing to visitors looking for an old-fashioned resort experience, the baronial **Pines Resort** (103 Shore Rd., 902/245-2511 or 800/667-4637, www.digbypines.ca, mid-May-mid-Oct., from $239 s or d) peers down over the port from the brow of a hill on the town's outskirts. The French-Norman manor of stucco and stone was built in 1903 and served as a Canadian Pacific Railway hotel until the province bought it in 1965. The accommodations include more than 80 contemporary rooms in the manor and 30 cottages shaded by spruce, fir, and pine trees. The hotel offers a dining room of provincial renown, an 18-hole golf course (greens fee $69), an outdoor pool, a fitness center, a day spa, tennis courts, hiking trails, and afternoon tea. Most guests stay as part of a package.

Campgrounds

Close to town is **Digby Campground** (Smith's Cove, 230 Victoria St., 902/245-1985, www.digbycampground.ca, mid-May-mid-Oct., $25-40). To get there, take Exit 26 from Highway 101 and follow the signs toward the ferry for 3 kilometers (1.9 miles). Within walking distance of downtown, it has an outdoor pool, a launderette, and hookups.

INFORMATION

Downtown, the **Digby Visitor Information Centre** (110 Montague Row, 902/245-5714) is open June-early October daily 9am-5pm.

GETTING THERE

Lying outside the area's main roads, Digby is easily bypassed. Digby is 105 kilometers (65 miles) northeast of Yarmouth, a 1.5-hour drive via Highway 101. It's 230 kilometers (143 miles) west of Halifax, 2.5-3 hours on Highway 101.

The terminus of the ferry from Saint John, *Princess of Acadia,* is through town near the mouth of the Annapolis Basin. Operated by **Bay Ferries** (902/245-2116 or 888/249-7245, www.ferries.ca), the large vessel plies the Bay of Fundy between Saint John (New Brunswick) and Digby (Nova Scotia) one or two times daily throughout the year. High-season one-way fares are adult $46, senior and youth $36, child under five free, vehicle $92 plus a $20 fuel surcharge. The crossing takes 3.5 hours, and reservations are essential if you're traveling with a vehicle.

DIGBY NECK

The Digby Neck is a long, spindly peninsula reaching like an antenna for almost 80 kilometers (50 miles) back down the Bay of Fundy from Digby. Beyond the end of the peninsula are two small islands. Off the main tourist path, the peninsula will appeal to those interested in nature and spending time in tiny coastal villages where the pace of life is much slower than elsewhere along the Fundy Coast.

From Digby, Highway 217 runs down the center of Digby Neck, through the villages of **Centreville, Sandy Cove,** and **Mink Cove.** At picturesque Sandy Cove, houses cling to the shoreline, while a nearby trail leads to Nova Scotia's highest waterfall. At East Ferry, a ferry departs every 30 minutes on the half hour for **Long Island.** The trip across takes just five minutes and costs $5 per vehicle, including passengers.

★ Balancing Rock

Beyond Tiverton, the main town on Long Island, a 2-kilometer (1.2-mile), 30-minute each way trail leads through a forest dotted with marshes, then descends over 200 stairs to a wooden platform where the natural wonder of **Balancing Rock** presents itself in all its glory. This towering basalt column balances precariously above St. Mary's Bay, looking as if it will topple at any time.

Brier Island

A second ferry (also $5) connects Long Island to Brier Island, Nova Scotia's westernmost extremity. The island has a bustling little fishing port at **Westport** and a tourism business that revolves around spring wildflowers, summer whale-watching, and year-round bird-watching. The island's most famous inhabitant was Joshua Slocum (the two vehicle ferries are named for him and his famous sailing boat, *Spray*), who spent his childhood on the island before taking to the high seas and becoming the first person to sail around the world solo.

A small monument on a headland south of Westport commemorates the feat.

★ Whale-Watching on the Bay of Fundy

Digby Neck is the base for a thriving whale-watching community. Companies generally offer half-day excursions between mid-June and early October, with regular sightings of finback, right, humpback, and minke whales, as well as Atlantic white-sided dolphins and porpoises. **Ocean Explorations,** based on Long Island at Tiverton (902/839-2417 or 877/654-2341, www.oceanexplorations.ca, adult $79, child $55), is notable for guide Tom Goodwin, a well-known biologist who takes interested visitors out into the bay aboard high-speed but stable inflatable Zodiac boats. In addition to the most common species, Goodwin searches out North Atlantic right whales when they gather in the middle of the bay (usually Aug.). Estimated to number fewer than 300, these are the world's rarest whales, so named because they were the "right" whales to hunt. Other operators with similar prices include **Brier Island Whale and Seabird Cruises** (Westport, Brier Island, 902/839-2995 or 800/656-3660, www.brierislandwhalewatch.com) and **Mariner Cruises** (Westport, Brier Island, 902/839-2346 or 800/239-2189, www.novascotiawhalewatching.ca).

Food and Accommodations

Between the ferry and Westport (1 km/0.6 mi from each), **Brier Island Lodge** (Northern Point Rd., 902/839-2300 or 800/662-8355, www.brierisland.com, May-early Oct., $119-169 s or d) sits on a bluff overlooking the sea. The 40 motel-style rooms are spacious and bright; most have water views, and some have king beds. The lodge's homey pine-paneled restaurant (breakfast and dinner daily) is my favorite island dining room. You can order old-fashioned roast turkey dinner or local specialties such as smoked pollock chowder and steamed periwinkles.

Annapolis Royal

The history of Annapolis Royal (pop. 500) spans four centuries, with much of the past preserved along a main street that is lined with the finest collection of pre-1800 buildings in Canada. The town and surrounding area has 150 registered historic buildings, three national historic sites, and Canada's oldest wooden building. Add to the mix one of the world's only tidal power-generating plants, Nova Scotia's largest fun park and its smallest pub, and a selection of gracious accommodations, and you find a town like no other in the province.

History

In 1605, Samuel de Champlain and the survivors of the bitter winter in New Brunswick moved across the Bay of Fundy and established the fortified Port-Royal across Annapolis Basin from modern-day Annapolis Royal. It was the first permanent European settlement north of St. Augustine, Florida. After eight years, the settlement came to an abrupt end when it was attacked and destroyed by New Englanders. In the 1630s, the French governor Charles de Menou d'Aulnay built a new Port-Royal on the south shore of the Annapolis Basin, attracting French settlers who came to be known as Acadians. The site would remain the capital of Acadie for the next eight decades. The British captured the fort in 1710, renaming it Fort Anne and rechristening the town Annapolis Royal, in honor of their queen. It would serve as Nova Scotia's first capital until 1749, when it was succeeded by the new town of Halifax.

SIGHTS

It's easy to spend a half day wandering through Fort Anne National Historic Site and the adjacent St. George Street, which curves

---

1: Balancing Rock; 2: whale-watching; 3: Breakers Bed and Breakfast

downhill to the waterfront. For Annapolis Royal's other attractions, you'll need a vehicle.

Annapolis Tidal Station

It may not be the town's oldest attraction, but it contains the local tourist information center, so it makes a sensible starting place for your visit. Near the head of Annapolis Basin, signposted to the right as you come into town off Highways 1 or 101, the **Annapolis Tidal Station** (236 Prince Albert Rd., 902/532-0502, May-June and Sept.-mid-Oct. daily 9am-5pm, July-Aug. daily 9am-8pm, free) is the only facility in North America that generates electricity from the tides. Originally built as an experiment, the plant still operates and is capable of generating 20 kilowatts of electricity (enough to power 4,000 homes). The facility harnesses the energy of the massive Fundy tides, which fill a head pond twice daily and then pass through a turbine as they flow back out toward the ocean. The plant's top floor is dedicated to describing the process, with windows allowing views of the head pond and down the bay.

★ Fort Anne National Historic Site

An 18th-century fort and grounds and Canada's first national historic site, **Fort Anne** (St. George St., 902/532-2397, June and Sept. Tues.-Sat. 9am-5:30pm, July-Aug. daily 9am-5:30pm, adult $4, senior $3.50, child $2), overlooks Annapolis Basin from the heart of Annapolis Royal. Considered the key stronghold for possession of Nova Scotia, as the British knew the region—it was Acadie to the French—the site had particular importance to both parties. It has been fortified on at least eight occasions since Scots built Fort Charles in 1629. The earliest French fort, dating to 1630, was designed with a star-shaped layout. Earthwork from the French fort of 1702 remains today, impressively banked with sweeping verdant lawns, which are open to the public year-round. Interpretive boards describe features such as a parade ground, chapel site, and restored powder magazine. The British added an officers' garrison in 1797. This whitewashed building now houses a museum that tells the long and colorful story of the fort.

Historic Gardens

The **Historic Gardens** (441 St. George St., 902/532-7018, May-June and Sept.-Oct. daily 9am-5pm, July-Aug. daily 9am-8pm, adult $14.50, senior $12.50, child $6) comprise 4 hectares (9.9 acres) of theme gardens, a restaurant, and a gift shop. The gardens are undeniably beautiful, but they are also interesting. The Acadian Garden, complete with an Acadian house and outdoor oven, replicates that of the earliest European settlers. Vegetables such as beets, carrots, parsnips, onions, and cabbages are surrounded by a hedge to keep out wild animals, and off to one side is a hedge-encircled orchard of apple and pear trees. Other highlights include the Knot Garden, styled after a hedge garden of the Middle Ages; the Governor's Garden, laid out as a formal garden from the 1750s, when Annapolis Royal was the capital; and a striking Rose Garden with more than 200 varieties, including early English and modern hybrids. The gardens are at their most spectacular in summer, with roses peaking mid-July-September.

★ Port-Royal National Historic Site

The first lasting settlement north of Florida, the 1605 fort at the **Port-Royal National Historic Site** (902/532-2898, mid-May-mid-Oct. daily 9am-5:30pm, adult $4, senior $3.50, child $2) has been reconstructed at what is believed to be the original location. The original French settlement has been rebuilt from Samuel de Champlain's plan using 17th-century construction techniques; the rustic buildings—governor's house, priest's dwelling, bakery, guardroom, and others, furnished

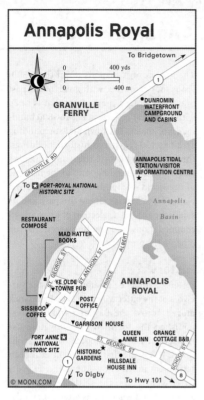

with period reproductions—form a rectangle around a courtyard within the palisaded compound. The original outpost boasted many historic firsts: Canada's first play, *Le Théâtre de Neptune*, was written and produced here by the young Parisian lawyer Marc Lescarbot; the continent's first social club, l'Ordre de Bon Temps (the Order of Good Cheer) was founded here in 1606; and the New World's first grain mill was built here to grind meal from the first cereal crops. The story of all this is brought to life by knowledgeable staff dressed in period costume. To get to Port-Royal, cross Annapolis Basin by the generating station and turn left at Granville Ferry. It's 10 kilometers (6.2 miles) along the road (2 km/1.2 mi beyond Melanson Settlement National Historic Site).

RECREATION
Hiking

Delaps Cove, 24 kilometers (15 miles) west of Annapolis Royal (cross Annapolis Basin, head south toward Port-Royal for 8 kilometers (5 miles), and turn right on the unpaved road that ends at the Bay of Fundy), is a small fishing village that is the start of the **Delap's Cove Wilderness Trail,** one of the few longer hiking trails along this stretch of coast. From the wharf at the end of the road, the trail meanders southwest along the coast for 15 kilometers (9.3 miles). It takes about eight hours round-trip, but you can hike for just an hour or so before turning around if time is an issue.

Amusement Parks

Upper Clements Parks (2931 Hwy. 1, Upper Clements, 902/532-7557, late June-early Sept. daily 11am-7pm, entry $11, $5 per ride) is Nova Scotia's largest theme park. Its style is thoroughly Nova Scotian, featuring a train ride on a historical replica, a mini-golf course designed as a map of the province, and the re-creation of a fishing village. The park also has a roller coaster, a flume ride, a carousel, pedal boats, live entertainment, dinner theater Friday-Saturday evenings, a crafts area with demonstrations and a shop, and dining rooms. The adjacent **Adventure Park,** featuring 14 ziplines, obstacle courses, and suspended bridges, costs $35 for a full-day pass.

FOOD

St. George Street has many dining choices, including diner-style cafés and fine-dining restaurants. For surprisingly good coffee, roasted locally, head to **Sissiboo Coffee** (262 St. George St., 902/286-3010, Mon.-Sat. 7:30am-4pm, Sun. 9pm-5pm), which shares a space in a gallery with a local photographer. In addition to coffee, Sissiboo has locally produced apple cider and a limited menu of cakes and pastries.

Facing Annapolis Basin from behind the main row of shops, **Restaurant Composé** (235 St. George St., 902/532-1251, Mon.-Sat. 11:30am-2:30pm and 5pm-8:30pm, Sun.

5pm-8:30pm, $20-35) is easy to miss. This European-style eatery has evolved from a café into a popular restaurant, with the menu blending local seafood (namely scallops and lobster) with Continental cooking styles. The best place to enjoy the view is in the water-facing solarium. The apple strudel is a great way to finish your meal.

Locals gather for afternoon beer and pub grub on the outdoor patio or for nightcaps in the cozy interior of English-style **Ye Olde Towne Pub** (9 Church St., 902/532-2244, Mon.-Sat. 11am-11pm, Sun. noon-8pm, $11-21), beside the outdoor farmers market at the bottom end of St. George Street. Built in 1884 as a bank and reputed to be the smallest bar in Nova Scotia, its meals are typical pub fare, but the portions are generous. Look to the blackboard for seafood specials.

★ **Garrison Grill** (350 St. George St., 902/532-5501, daily from 6pm, $21-32) is a refined restaurant spread through three connected rooms of an 1854 inn. The chef is renowned for sourcing seasonal produce, while year-round specialties include fish cakes and Acadian jambalaya. With its impressive wine list and professional service, this is the best place in town for fine dining.

If you're staying at a campground or have chosen an accommodation with cooking facilities, head over North Mountain to Parker's Cove and pick up fresh seafood such as scallops, lobsters, mussels, halibut, and haddock from **Nautical Seafoods** (Shore Rd. W., 902/532-2212, summer daily 11am-7pm). You can also order seafood chowder, boiled lobsters, and lobster rolls to eat at the picnic tables out front.

ACCOMMODATIONS AND CAMPING
$50-100

Aside from the cabins at Dunromin Waterfront Campground and Cabins, few places offer rooms for less than $100 in July and August. One option is **Grange Cottage B&B** (102 Richie St., 902/532-7993, $85 s, $95 d), where the two guest rooms share one

bathroom. The rear deck has river views, and the front porch is a relaxing place to cool off on hot afternoons. Rates include a full breakfast.

$100-150

The closest of the historic bed-and-breakfasts to downtown is **Garrison House** (350 St. George St., 902/532-5750 or 866/532-5750, www.garrisonhouse.ca, mid-Apr.-Oct., $109-149 s or d), which is across the road from Fort Anne. Built in 1854 as a hotel, this gracious building holds seven guest rooms of varying configurations, as well as a downstairs restaurant open daily for dinner.

Hillsdale House Inn (519 St. George St., 902/532-2345 or 877/839-2821, www. hillsdalehouseinn.ca, May-Oct., $142-195 s or d) is on a 6-hectare (14.8-acre) estate that has been graced by kings and prime ministers. The main house has 11 air-conditioned guest rooms, and the adjacent coach house another four. Antiques fill public areas, including a cozy lounge. A cooked breakfast is included in the rates.

Set on 2 hectares (4.9 acres) of landscaped grounds, ★ **Queen Anne Inn** (494 Upper St. George St., 902/532-7850 or 877/536-0403, www.queenanneinn.ns.ca, May-Oct., $149-249 s or d) is a restored 1865 Victorian mansion with a grand mahogany staircase that sweeps upstairs to 10 guest rooms outfitted with period furnishings. Room 10 is significantly smaller than the remaining nine, which are extra large. Behind the main house, the carriage house contains two two-bedroom units, perfect for two couples traveling together or a family. Rates include a full three-course breakfast and afternoon tea.

Swimming, hiking, wagon rides, canoeing, and lawn games fill the day at **Mountain Top Cottages** (888 Parker Mountain Rd., 902/532-2564 or 877/885-1185, www. mountaintopcottages.com, May-Oct., $124-154 s or d), in a forested setting atop North Mountain. Seventeen simple cottages with one or two bedrooms overlook a private lake. Each has a microwave and fridge as well as wireless Internet. To get there, cross Annapolis Basin at the tidal power plant, follow Highway 1 through Granville Ferry, and take Parker Mountain Road off to the north.

Campgrounds

Running right down to a private beach on the Annapolis Basin, ★ **Dunromin Waterfront Campground and Cabins** (902/532-2808, www.dunromincampground.ca, mid-May-mid-Oct., campsites $30-46) is the perfect place for families. With a fort-themed playground, an outdoor pool, mini-golf, lawn games, canoe and SUP rentals, and a café, the biggest problem will be dragging the children off for a day of sightseeing. The campground has 165 sites, most of them serviced. The Gypsy Wagon accommodation is $65, and cabins range from $78 with shared bathroom to $125 for a two-bedroom waterfront cottage.

INFORMATION AND SERVICES

Annapolis Royal Visitor Information Centre (Hwy. 1, 902/532-5769, May-June and Sept.-mid-Oct. daily 9am-5pm, July-Aug. daily 9am-8pm, free) is at the tidal power plant, on the north side of downtown. Coming into town from Exit 22 along Highway 101, turn right before the historic main street.

GETTING THERE

Annapolis Royal is 35 kilometers (22 miles) from Digby, a 30-minute drive along Highway 101. It's 200 kilometers (124 miles) west of Halifax, 2.5 hours on Highway 101.

1: cannon at Fort Anne; 2: Historic Gardens;
3: Queen Anne Inn

Kejimkujik National Park

Deep in the interior of southwestern Nova Scotia, Kejimkujik (kedji-muh-KOO-jick, or "Keji" or "Kedge" for short) National Park lies off Highway 8, about midway between Liverpool and Annapolis Royal. Encompassing 381 square kilometers (147 square miles) of drumlins (rounded glacial hills), island-dotted lakes (legacies of the last ice age), and hardwood and conifer forests, the park and the adjacent Tobeatic Game Sanctuary are an important refuge for native wildlife and town-weary Nova Scotians.

Wildlife enthusiasts visit the park for bird-watching (including barred owls, pileated woodpeckers, scarlet tanagers, great crested flycatchers, and loons and other waterfowl) and may also spot black bears, white-tailed deer, bobcats, porcupines, and beavers. The many lakes and connecting rivers attract canoeists and swimmers in warm weather, as well as anglers (particularly for perch and brook trout). Hikers can choose from a network of trails, some leading to backcountry campgrounds; some of the campgrounds are also accessible by canoe. In winter, cross-country skiers take over the hiking trails.

RECREATION

The two most popular park activities are hiking and canoeing. The **Beech Grove Trail,** a 2-kilometer (1.2-mile) loop, starts at the visitors center and wends along the Mersey River, where it climbs a drumlin hilltop swathed in an almost-pure beech grove. The **Farmlands Trail** is another drumlin variation, and the 45-minute hike makes its way up a drumlin to an abandoned farm on the hilltop. A little farther south along the park access road is the trailhead for the 1-kilometer (0.6-mile) **Rogers Brook** loop, which passes through a forest of red maple and hemlock trees.

You can rent canoes, rowboats, and bicycles ($8 per hour, $30 per day) at Jakes Landing, on the northeast side of large Kejimkujik Lake;

the adjacent stretch of the Mersey River is placid and suitable for beginning paddlers.

ACCOMMODATIONS AND CAMPING

Within the park, **Jeremy's Bay Campground** (mid-May-mid-Oct., $27.50-31.50), on the north side of Kejimkujik Lake, has 360 sites, some with power hookups, as well as washrooms and showers, fire pits and firewood ($8), a playground, picnic areas, and an interpretive program. Another 46 wilderness sites ($18) are scattered in the woodlands and offer toilets, tables, grills, and firewood. From mid-January, a percentage of sites can be booked through the **Parks Canada Campground Reservation Service** (519/826-5391 or 877/737-3783, www.reservation.pc.gc.ca) for $12 per reservation.

Milford House (902/532-2617, www.milfordhouse.ca, from $155 s or d) is in South Milford, about 20 kilometers (12.4 miles) north of the park toward Annapolis

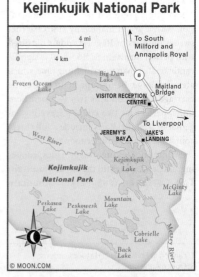

Kejimkujik National Park

© MOON.COM

Royal. The resort features a main lodge (re-built after it was destroyed by fire in 2014) and 28 lakeside cabins. All cabins have separate bedrooms, a wood-burning fireplace, and a full bathroom. Four hiking trails radiate out from the resort, some leading to lakes where canoes are available free of charge. Dinner and breakfast is a very reasonable adult $35, child $25, per day.

INFORMATION

The **Visitor Reception Centre** (902/682-2772, mid-June-Aug. daily 8:30am-8pm, Sept.-mid-June daily 8:30am-4pm) is just be-yond the park entrance. This is the place to buy day passes (adult $6, senior $5, child $3) and fishing licenses ($10 per day, $35 annual) and pick up literature on the park, including hiking trail descriptions.

GETTING THERE

Although the park is just 50 kilometers (31 miles) from Annapolis Royal along Highway 8, allow about an hour to reach the entrance, as the road is narrow and winding.

From Halifax, take Highway 101 along the South Shore to Liverpool and then Highway 8 north. The total distance from Halifax to the park is 170 kilometers (105 miles), a two-hour drive.

Annapolis Valley

The Annapolis Valley, which spreads along the Annapolis River east from Annapolis Royal, is a haze of white when its apple or-chards bloom in late May-early June. The valley, extending northeast from Annapolis Royal, supports more than magnificent apple orchards, however; if you look closely, you'll also see hectares of strawberries, plums, peaches, pears, and cherries, as well as crops of hay, grain, and tobacco.

The Annapolis Valley has a legion of fans, among them the Mi'kmaq, who first settled this region. According to Mi'kmaq legend, Glooscap, a deity taking the form of a giant man, roamed the upper Fundy. He made his home atop the basalt cliffs of the penin-sula—the lofty hook-shaped cape that fin-ishes in sea stacks at Cape Split—and buried jewels on the Fundy beaches. (Today's tides still claw at the coastline to reveal agate, am-ethyst, and zeolite from Hall's Harbour to Cape Split's tip.)

ANNAPOLIS ROYAL TO CANNING

From Annapolis Royal, Highway 101 heads northeast, crossing the Annapolis River near Bridgetown and continuing east for 100 ki-lometers (62 miles) to Wolfville. You don't see a great deal from the highway, so plan to travel Highway 1 (cross the Annapolis Basin at Annapolis Royal to get going). Along this route, you pass through the villages and apple orchards now bypassed by Highway 101.

Bridgetown

This town has wide streets lined with grand old homes and stately trees. **James House Museum** (12 Queen St., 902/665-4530, June-Aug. Tues.-Sat. 10am-5pm, free) is an 1835 residence sandwiched between modern shops along the main street.

Take Church Street north out of town and you reach **Valleyview Provincial Park** after 5 kilometers (3.1 miles). This small park sits atop North Mountain, an ancient ridge of lava that forms a cap over softer shale and sand-stone that has been gouged away to the south, forming the Annapolis Valley. From the park, views extend across the valley to the prov-ince's remote interior. The park campground (mid-June-mid-Oct., $29) has just 30 sites, but it only ever fills on summer weekends. It has toilets and drinking water but no showers.

GETTING THERE

Bridgetown is 24 kilometers (15 miles) northeast of Annapolis Royal, a 20-minute drive along Highway 101. From Halifax, Bridgetown is 170 kilometers (105 miles) west, two hours on Highway 101.

Kentville

The commercial hub of the Annapolis Valley is Kentville (pop. 6,100). The town is on the north side of Highway 101 and at the junction of Highway 12, which cuts south through the Nova Scotia interior to Mahone Bay and Lunenburg. In the historic heart of town is **Kings County Museum** (37 Cornwallis Ave., 902/678-6237, Mon.-Sat. 9am-4pm, free), which contains a predictable collection of pioneer artifacts, as well as many interesting historical photographs within a two-story 1903 red-brick courthouse.

South Mountain Park (Hwy. 12, South Alton, 902/678-0152 or 866/860-6092, www.southmountainparkcampground.com, campsites $41-49, cabins $81) fills with holidaying families through its mid-May-mid-October season. A few kilometers south of Kentville, it's not really set up for quick overnight stays. But if you have children and are looking for a break from touring, it's a great place to kick back for a few days. The activities offered could easily fill a week of fun—everything from fishing to tennis to wagon rides to walking paths. Amenities include a par-3 golf course, a games room, a TV room, a library with wireless Internet access, a large outdoor pool, and lots more. On the downside, campsites offer little privacy.

GETTING THERE

Kentville is about 95 kilometers (59 miles) northeast of Annapolis Royal, just over an hour via Highway 101. It's 100 kilometers (62 miles) northwest of Halifax, 1.5 hours on Highway 101.

Starr's Point

Prescott House Museum (1633 Starr's Point Rd., 902/542-3984, June-Sept. Mon.-Sat. 10am-5pm, Sun. 1pm-5pm, adult $4, senior and child $3) harks back to the valley's orchard beginnings, when horticulturist Charles Ramage Prescott imported species to add to the provincial store of fruit trees. His profits built this Georgian-style homestead. The restored mansion, constructed circa 1812, displays period furnishings and sits amid beautiful gardens. Its special events celebrate the fall harvest. It's along Highway 358, which leads north from Greenwich.

GETTING THERE

Starr's Point is about 110 kilometers (68 miles) northeast from Annapolis Royal, a 1.5-hour drive via Highway 101.

Canning

The east end of the Annapolis Valley has a smattering of emerging boutique wineries, including **Blomidon Estate Winery** (10318 Hwy. 221, 902/582-7565, June-Oct. Mon.-Sat. 10am-6pm, Sun. 11am-5pm). This winery was the first in Nova Scotia to produce classic varietals such as chardonnay, pinot noir, and shiraz. Tours depart daily at 1pm and 3pm, ending with a tasting session ($10 per person). You can also order meat and cheese platters, accompanied by a glass of wine of course, and enjoy them on the patio. The winery is 2 kilometers (1.2 miles) east of Canning along Highway 221.

GETTING THERE

Canning is about 115 kilometers (71 miles) northeast of Annapolis Royal, a 1.5-hour drive along Highway 101. It's 105 kilometers (65 miles) northwest of Halifax on Highway 101.

BLOMIDON PENINSULA

The Blomidon Peninsula is at the northern end of North Mountain. Extending into the Minas Channel and with Minas Basin to its back, it features more fantastic Fundy scenery and a couple of good campgrounds.

The Look-Off

On the north side of Canning, **Look-Off**

Family Camping (Hwy. 358, 902/582-3022, www.lookoffcamping.com, mid-May-late Sept., campsites $30-36, cabins $70-100 s or d) lives up to its name with a long list of activities—think hayrides, bingo, and fitness classes—and workshops such as kite-making and cookie painting. Other facilities include a café open daily at 9am, a playground, a pool, and a launderette. The namesake Look-Off (a Nova Scotian term for a lookout) is across the road and has wonderful views across the bucolic Annapolis Valley.

Blomidon Provincial Park

The dramatically positioned 759-hectare (1,876-acre) **Blomidon Provincial Park** (902/582-7319) is along the eastern side of the Blomidon Peninsula, facing Minas Basin. To get there, turn off Highway 358, 3 kilometers (1.9 miles) north of the Look-Off and follow the secondary road north for 14 kilometers (8.7 miles). The red shale and sandstone that make the park so striking were laid down millions of years ago and then eroded by glacial and water action to form 180-meter-high (591-foot-high) bluffs that are topped by coastal forest. Fundy tides sweep up to the cliff face twice daily, but as the water recedes, you can walk along the red-sand beach, searching for semiprecious stones such as amethyst and agate. The uplands area is covered in forests of sugar maple, beech, and birch, yet also present are alpine plants such as maidenhair.

The best place for a walk is along the beach, but check at the park office or information boards for tide times. Four official trails wind their way through the park. The best views are from the **Look-Off Trail,** an easy 1-kilometer (0.6-mile) walk to a lookout high atop the cliffs. The 5.6-kilometer (3.5-mile) **Jodrey Trail** fringes the cliffs, while the **Interpretive Trail** passes information boards describing the forest and its inhabitants. The main day-use area is where the access road enters the park. It's one of the few places along the Fundy Coast where the water gets warm enough for swimming.

Beyond the day-use area, the access road climbs to the **campground** (early June-early Oct., $27), where sites are spread through the forest on two short loops. Facilities include showers, a playground, and drinking water.

To Cape Split

At the tip of the Blomidon Peninsula is Cape Split. To get there, continue north on Highway 358 from the Look-Off to Scots Bay, where there's a small day-use-only provincial park

Blomidon Provincial Park is notable for its high sea cliffs.

with a pebbly beach fronting Minas Channel. The road ends just beyond Scots Bay, from where it's 13 kilometers (8.1 miles) on foot to Cape Split. It's a long way to walk (and make the return trek) in one day, but there is no elevation gain and the rewards are total wilderness and sweeping views from the cliff top at the end of the trail.

Getting There

The Blomidon Peninsula is about 130 kilometers (81 miles) northeast of Annapolis Royal, a 1.5-hour drive along Highway 101, and about 20 kilometers (12.4 miles) north of Canning, a 20-minute drive.

Wolfville and Vicinity

At the eastern end of the Annapolis Valley, the genteel town of Wolfville (pop. 4,200) began with the name Mud Creek, an ignoble tribute from the founding New England planters who wrestled with the Fundy coastal area once farmed by early Acadians. Now the town sits in the lushest part of the Annapolis Valley, and you won't want to miss it. Highway 1 runs through town as Main Street, where large houses with bay windows and ample porches sit comfortably beneath stately trees. Acadia University's ivy-covered buildings and manicured lawns lie along Main and University Avenue.

The town, just six blocks deep, has an uncomplicated layout alongside Highway 1 and Highway 101.

SIGHTS
Main Street

Wolvelle's refined nature is apparent to anyone walking along Main Street, which is dotted with grand stone buildings and, at the eastern end, stately trees.

Randall House Museum (259 Main St., 902/542-9775, June-late Aug. Tues.-Sat. 10am-5pm, Sun. 1:30pm-5pm, donation) is an 1815 historic home with period furnishings and local artifacts from the 1760s to the 20th century.

Acadia University Art Gallery (Beveridge Arts Centre, 10 Highland Ave., 902/585-1373, Tues.-Sun. noon-4pm, free) has a fine-arts collection of local and regional

works, highlighted by Alex Colville's oils and serigraphs.

Waterfront

Most visitors miss Wolfville's waterfront, but the town does have one, one block north of Main Street across Front Street. Trails and a small park have been developed at the mouth of the Cornwallis River, which was once lined with busy shipyards. Views extend across the Minas Basin to the red cliffs of Blomidon Provincial Park.

Along Front Street to the west is **Robie Tufts Nature Centre,** which is a series of covered interpretive boards describing the flora and fauna native to the area. The main purpose of the structure is to provide a dwelling for chimney swifts, which make their home in the red-brick chimney rising through the roof.

SHOPPING

The **Harvest Gallery** (462 Main St., 902/542-7093, July-Oct. Mon.-Sat. 10am-5pm, Sun. noon-5pm, closed Mon. the rest of the year) displays the work of local artists. Especially eye-catching are the colorful oil paintings of Jeanne Aisthorpe-Smith.

Although apples get most of the glory, lots of other farming happens in the Annapolis Valley. **Gaspereau Valley Fibres** (830 Gaspereau River Rd., 902/542-2656, www.gaspereauvalleyfibres.ca, Tues.-Fri. 10am-5pm, Sat.-Sun. 11am-4pm) highlights the local wool industries, with knitting, weaving,

Wolfville

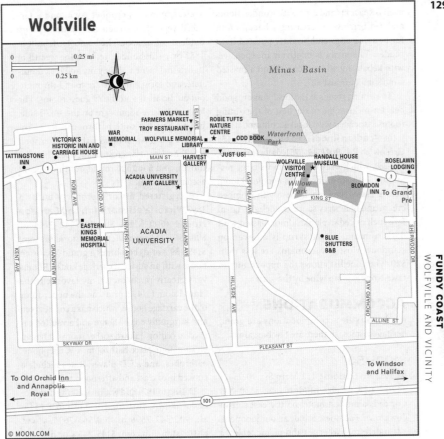

and spinning, as well as raw materials sold as-is. The shop is on a farm on the south side of Highway 101; to get there from town, take Gaspereau Road south.

FOOD

For a small town, Wolfville has a surprising number of eateries, but my suggestion if you're in town on a Wednesday or Saturday is to head to ★ **Wolfville Farmers Market** (24 Elm St., 902/697-3344, May-Dec. Wed. 4pm-7pm, year-round Sat. 8:30am-1pm), which has a mouthwatering selection of choices from local producers, including many cooked on the spot, such as Harbourville Schnitzelhaus, which sells authentic German dishes using

lots of local produce. Many stalls sell items to go, such as baked goods, preserves, smoked meats, and wine.

Just Us! (450 Main St., 902/542-7731, Mon.-Fri. 7am-7pm, Sat. 8am-7pm, Sun. 9am-7pm, lunches $6-9) pours organic coffees and a wide range of teas from the front of a historic theater building, with seating spread through the lobby. Meals are very inexpensive ($7.50 for soup and sandwich), and the muffins are baked fresh daily.

Tucked away between Main Street and the farmers market, ★ **Troy Restaurant** (12 Elm St., 902/542-4425, daily 11am-9pm, $16-28) specializes in Mediterranean cuisine, with the emphasis on Turkish favorites. The room itself is spacious and airy, with wooden floors and red-brick walls creating a background for hanging rugs and brightly painted light shades. The menu is relatively inexpensive, with kebabs mostly under $20 and a roasted lamb shank for just $27.

The dining rooms at the local inns are good bets for meals. One of the best of the dining rooms associated with local accommodations is the **Acadian Room** (Old Orchard Inn, 153 Greenwich Rd., 902/542-5751, daily 7am-9pm, $17-29), which draws diners to its large restaurant with stunning views and good food. Before 11am, the French toast with whipped cream and blueberry sauce is a delight. Local fare such as cedar-plank salmon basted with dark rum and maple syrup is an evening standout. Most dinner mains are less than $20. The wine list allows the opportunity to taste Nova Scotian wine by the glass.

ACCOMMODATIONS

Most Wolfville accommodations are grand heritage homes, so there are few bargains.

$100-150

Roselawn Lodging (32 Main St., 902/542-3420, www.roselawnlodging.ca, $110-200 s or d) is a modest motel on the east side of downtown. Facilities include an outdoor pool, a launderette, barbecues and picnic tables, a tennis court, and a playground. The 28 motel rooms are clean and comfortable, and 12 adjacent cottages come with kitchens.

On the hill behind the information center, **Blue Shutters Bed and Breakfast** (7 Blomidon Terr., 902/542-3363, www.blueshuttersbnb.ns.ca, $110-130 s, $120-145 d) has three well-equipped guest rooms. Each has an en suite bathroom, a TV/DVD combo, wireless Internet, and an electric fireplace. Rates include a full breakfast.

If you're a garden lover, you won't want to leave the expansive grounds of ★ **Blomidon Inn** (195 Main St., 902/542-2291 or 800/565-2291, www.blomidon.ns.ca, $149-269 s or d), which is surrounded by more than 1 hectare (2.5 acres) of cacti, roses, rhododendrons,

azaleas, ponds, a croquet lawn, and a terraced vegetable garden that doubles as an outdoor eating area. The home itself, built in 1882 by a shipbuilder, reflects the wealth of its original owner. Mahogany and teak dominate, and local antiques are found throughout public areas and the 29 guest rooms. The least expensive rooms are on the small side, but all have en suite bathrooms. Rates include a continental breakfast and afternoon tea. Tennis courts, a restaurant open daily for dinner, and a lounge round out this elegant accommodation.

A registered historic property built in 1893, **Victoria's Historic Inn and Carriage House** (600 Main St., 902/542-5744 or 800/556-5744, www.victoriashistoricinn.com, $149-189 s or d) combines a grand Victorian house with an adjacent carriage house. Rooms vary greatly in character; my favorite is the Hunt Room ($149 s or d), on the upper floor of the carriage house, which has a smart green and burgundy color theme and a vaulted cathedral ceiling. Like the other rooms, it has an en suite four-piece bathroom, TV, telephone, bathrobes, and a CD player. Rates include a cooked breakfast and afternoon tea.

Dating to 1874 and within walking distance of downtown, **Tattingstone Inn** (630 Main St., 902/542-7696 or 800/565-7696, www.tattingstoneinn.com, $145-245 s or d) is casually formal, with nine guest rooms spread through the main house and adjacent carriage house. All are decorated with antiques, and some have whirlpool tubs. The inn also offers a music room, a dining room, a steam room and heated outdoor pool, and a tennis court. Rates include a cooked breakfast.

The **Old Orchard Inn** (153 Greenwich Rd., 902/542-5751 or 800/561-8090, www.oldorchardinn.com) is a sprawling resort near Exit 11 of Highway 101. It comprises more than 100 motel-style guest rooms ($145-195 s or d) and 29 cabins (May-Oct., $175-245 s or d) spread through the forest. Tennis courts, an indoor pool, saunas, spa services, hiking

---

1: Wolfville Farmers Market; 2: Blomidon Inn

trails, and a stone patio with sweeping valley views add to the appeal. The resort also has a dining room and lounge.

INFORMATION AND SERVICES

In Willow Park at the east end of town is the **Wolfville Visitor Centre** (11 Willow Ave., 902-542-7000, www.wolfville.ca, May-Oct. daily 9am-6pm).

Eastern Kings Memorial Hospital (902-542-2266) is at 23 Earnscliffe Avenue. Call the **police** at 902-542-3817 or the **RCMP** at 902/679-5555.

GETTING THERE

Wolfville is 120 kilometers (74 miles) east of Annapolis Royal, a 1.5-hour drive along Highway 101. It's 90 kilometers (56 miles) northwest of Halifax, just over an hour on Highway 101.

GRAND PRÉ

This small village was the epicenter of one of the most tragic events in Canadian history, the expulsion of the Acadians from their homeland. First settled in 1680 by an Acadian family who moved from the confines of nearby Port-Royal, Grand Pré grew to become the largest Acadian settlement in Nova Scotia. The main attraction is Grand Pré National Historic Site, but also worth visiting is **Grand Pré Wines** (Hwy. 1, 902-542-1753, July-mid-Oct. Mon.-Sat. 10am-6pm, Sun. 11am-6pm, mid-Oct.-Dec. Wed.-Sun. 11am-5pm), where grapes are grown on 60 hectares (148 acres) of former Acadian farmland. In the main building you'll find a restaurant (summer Mon.-Sat. 10am-6pm, Sun. 11am-6pm), wine shop, and crafts corner. Free winery tours are offered through summer (daily 11am, 3pm, and 5pm).

★ Grand Pré National Historic Site

Commemorating the Acadian deportation, the **Grand Pré National Historic Site** (2242 Grand Pré Rd., 902/542-3631, mid-May-mid-Oct. daily 9am-5pm, adult $7.80, senior $6.60, child $4) brings Acadian history and the deportation to life. It wasn't until Henry Wadsworth Longfellow wrote the poem *Evangeline* in 1847 that the English-speaking world became aware of the expulsion, but by then nothing remained of Grand-Pré (Great Meadow), the setting for the story of the Acadian heroine separated from her lover by the deportation.

In 1922, an interested benefactor with Acadian roots built a small stone church on the presumed site of Grand Pré, and this became the foundation for the historic site of today. Visitors enter through a large museum complex, where there's a bookstore and gift shop, along with information panels describing Acadian life, the deportation, and the return of Acadians to Nova Scotia. Outside are sprawling grounds crisscrossed by pathways that lead to vegetable gardens, a blacksmith shop, an orchard, a lookout over the diked farmland, and a statue of Henry Wadsworth Longfellow. In the middle of the site is a statue of Evangeline. Directly behind the statue is the 1922 church. It houses an exhibit of paintings that showcase the history of the people and a copy of the original expulsion order that was read to a congregation within the original church, as well as stained-glass windows with a story to tell. Guided tours of the grounds (included with admission) are highly recommended. A guide is also stationed within Église Saint-Charles to lead you through the story of each painting.

Food and Accommodations

Stop at the headquarters of locally owned **Just Us!** (11865 Hwy. 1, 902/697-4225, Mon.-Wed. 7am-5pm, Thurs.-Fri. 7am-6pm, Sat. 8am-6pm, Sun. 9am-6pm). Here, on the north side of the historic site, you'll find a roaster, a shop selling a thoughtful collection of coffee-related items, and a small museum (free) explaining the owners' dedication to free trade coffee and why it's important. Out back is a garden that visitors are free to wander through.

The best choice of accommodations are in nearby Wolfville, but the centrally located **Evangeline Inn and Motel** (11668 Hwy. 1, 902/542-2703 or 888/542-2703, www.evangelineinncafe.com, May-Oct., $115-145 s or d) provides comfortable accommodations right at the turnoff to the historic site. Choose from motel units or five guest rooms in the adjacent boyhood home of Sir Robert Borden, prime minister of Canada for nine years in the early 20th century. All guests have use of the swimming pool. Also on the grounds is a modern **restaurant** (May-Oct. daily 8am-8pm), where cooked breakfasts are less than $10, and dishes such as haddock chowder with a warmed scone on the side are $6-10.

Getting There

To get to Grand Pré from Wolfville, head east on Highway 1 for about 5 kilometers (3.1 miles), or take Exit 10 from Highway 101. From Halifax, head north on Highway 101 for 85 kilometers (53 miles), a one-hour drive.

WINDSOR

If you've toured along the South Shore and then traveled along the Fundy Coast, the temptation may be to stay on the highway and give Windsor, just 60 kilometers (37 miles) northwest of Halifax, a miss. But this gracious town on the banks of the Avon River is worth the short detour from busy Highway 101. To get there from the main highway, take Exit 6, which leads into downtown. Before town is a small **information center** (902/798-2690, mid-May-mid-Oct. daily 9am-5pm).

Fort Edward National Historic Site

Dating to 1750, the **Fort Edward National Historic Site** (King St., 902/542-3631, mid-June-late Sept. daily 10am-6pm, free) preserves the last 18th-century blockhouse in Nova Scotia. Fort Edward was one of the main assembly points for the deportation of the Acadians from the province in 1755. Although the building is open only during summer, touring the grounds will give a good feel for the location of the fort and the chance to see earthen mounds where the rest of the fort once stood.

Historic Homes

Sprawling **Haliburton House** (414 Clifton Ave., 902/798-5619, June-Sept. Mon.-Sat. 10am-5pm, Sun. 1pm-5pm, adult $4, senior and student $3) was owned by 19th-century author, humorist, historian, and judge

FUNDY COAST
WOLFVILLE AND VICINITY

Grand Pré National Historic Site

Holy Pumpkins!

Windsor may be famous as the birthplace of hockey, but no attraction is bigger than the pumpkins grown on the south side of town at **Howard Dill Enterprises** (400 College Rd., 902/798-2728, summer Mon.-Fri. 9am-5pm, Sept.-Oct. daily 9am-6pm, free). The Dill family is renowned in the giant pumpkin-growing business for developing seeds that go on to produce some of the world's largest pumpkins, some of which swell to over 700 kilograms (1,543 pounds).

You won't find the pumpkins grown from Dill's seeds on grocery store shelves. They are used for fall fairs and pumpkin-growing competitions, and as jack-o-lanterns by folks with strong porches. Most of the company's business is done online; at www.howarddill.com you can order the precious seeds and books such as *How to Grow World Class Giant Pumpkins,* as well as download growing tips. At the Dill farm, visitors are encouraged to drop by and see Dill's own pumpkin patch, where even the smallest pumpkins are in the 180- to 230-kilogram (397- to 507-pound) range leading up to the late September-early October harvest.

Thomas Chandler Haliburton, who was born in Windsor in 1796. Among the sayings that originated in Haliburton's writings are "It's raining cats and dogs," "barking up the wrong tree," "facts are stranger than fiction," and "quick as a wink." The Victorian mansion on 10 hectares (24.7 acres) is open to the public, as are the surrounding gardens. For hockey fans, Haliburton's written memories of childhood have special meaning. In them, he reminisced about children "playing ball on ice" behind Haliburton House, which is the earliest mention of the game of ice hockey.

On Ferry Hill, **Shand House** (389 Avon St.) is another vintage beauty and marks the wealthy Shand family's prominence in Windsor. When it was built in the early 1890s, the Queen Anne-style mansion was one of the first residences in the area fitted with electric lights and indoor plumbing. Currently, there is no public access, but the grandeur can be admired from the grounds.

Getting There

Windsor is southeast of Wolfville, about 30 kilometers (19 miles) away, a 25-minute drive via Highway 1 or Highway 101. Windsor is about 60 kilometers (37 miles) northwest of Halifax, 45 minutes via Highway 101.

Central Nova Scotia

Perfect for those looking for low-key attractions as varied as ancient fossils, beautiful beaches, and remote park, Central Nova Scotia extends north from Halifax to Truro (the geographical center of the province) and then west to the New Brunswick border and east to the causeway leading to Cape Breton Island.

The region can be divided roughly into manageable sections—each very different in look and feel. The Trans-Canada Highway slices through the region's northwest corner and extends to Cape Breton Island in the east. But this route promises little besides uninterrupted speed. Detour south to explore an area that was once the realm of Glooscap, the mythical Mi'kmaq god who roamed this part of Nova Scotia in the form of a man as large as Gulliver among the

Highlights

Look for ★ to find recommended sights, activities, dining, and lodging.

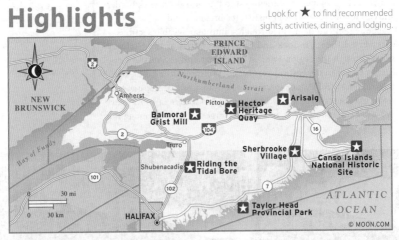

© MOON.COM

★ **Riding the Tidal Bore:** This phenomenon occurs in only a few places in the world. Locals call it the Total Bore, and while admittedly it's not exactly exciting to watch from the sidelines, riding the wave on a raft is a once-in-a-lifetime experience (page 139).

★ **Balmoral Grist Mill:** The reflection of this bright red building in an adjacent pond creates a scene of tranquility (page 149).

★ **Hector Heritage Quay:** Step aboard a full-size replica of the *Hector*, upon which Pictou's first settlers arrived, to get a taste of the hardships that they endured crossing the Atlantic Ocean (page 150).

★ **Arisaig:** Unassuming cliffs are filled with fossils that have helped scientists understand the evolution of life on earth 400 million years ago (page 153).

★ **Taylor Head Provincial Park:** Marine Drive passes dozens of protected areas, but Taylor Head stands out for its ease of access and interesting geology (page 157).

★ **Sherbrooke Village:** History comes alive at this living museum. For the full effect, join the Hands on History program and dress up in period costume (page 159).

★ **Canso Islands National Historic Site:** The focus of this attraction is Grassy Island, once home to a thriving fishing community in the early 1700s. But the best part for budget-conscious travelers is the price—which includes a boat trip (page 161).

Lilliputians. According to legend, Glooscap slept stretched out over the region's northern portion and used Prince Edward Island as his pillow. While the Northumberland Strait has long been the domain of vacationing locals—attracted by warm water and long stretches of beautiful beach—other visitors on a fast track often see the region as a flash of landscape from the Trans-Canada Highway. The other option for reaching Cape Breton Island from Halifax is to drive along the Eastern Shore, which is as rugged as the Northumberland Strait shore is tame. This super-scenic road unfurls itself at a leisurely pace, and it's worth slowing down and taking two or three days to travel its length. Passing tiny fishing ports reminiscent of the seafaring life of decades ago, and rock-bound coves where the forest grows right down to the sea, the road's services are few and far between (Canso, with a population of 950, is the largest town), so plan ahead by making accommodations reservations and keeping your gas tank full.

PLANNING YOUR TIME

Central Nova Scotia is not a destination like Cape Breton Island, where you would plan your visit around an itinerary that lasted a certain length of time. Instead, you will surely find yourself passing through central Nova Scotia on more than one occasion—for example, driving from New Brunswick through to Halifax and then again on the way to Cape Breton Island. If you've been touring through New Brunswick, you'll already be well aware of the massive Fundy tides. In central Nova

Scotia, you can **ride the tidal bore** on the Shubenacadie River. Along Northumberland Strait, beaches lapped by warm water will tempt you to linger, while historic attractions such as **Balmoral Grist Mill** and Pictou's **Hector Heritage Quay Museum** keep the past alive. From Halifax, you could plan on spending two days reaching Cape Breton Island via the above-mentioned attractions, which would also allow time for a detour to **Arisaig,** a fossil hot spot protected by a small provincial park. If you have an extra day or two, consider taking Marine Drive to or from Cape Breton Island. The distance (320 km/200 mi from Dartmouth to Canso) is deceiving when planning how long the drive will take. Add a ferry trip to a winding, often narrow road that passes through dozens of small townships, and you should expect the journey to take six hours, without stops. From Canso, it will take another 90 minutes to reach Port Hastings, the gateway to Cape Breton Island. But of course, this estimate of 7.5 hours to complete the Marine Drive is sans stops, and if you're only interested in reaching Cape Breton Island from Halifax, the Highway 102/104 route via Truro takes about half as long. Leaving Halifax in the morning, an ideal scenario would be to spend one night en route and to plan on reaching Cape Breton Island later the following day. This would allow time to explore **Taylor Head Provincial Park,** to step back in time at **Sherbrooke Village,** and to take the boat trip to **Canso Islands National Historic Site.**

Previous: historic boat at dock; Balmoral Grist Mill; Salmon River beach.

Central Nova Scotia

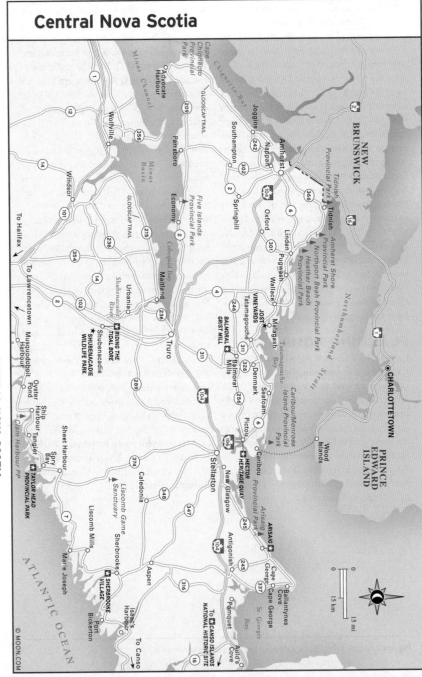

© MOON.COM

Halifax to Truro

As you head north from Halifax, suburbia is quickly left behind, as divided Highway 102 speeds north to Truro, which is easily reached in an hour from downtown. Highway 2, the original route between these two cities, may look appealing on the map, but the scenery is no different from what you'll see from Highway 102—it simply takes around 30 minutes longer.

SHUBENACADIE

If you're willing to try something new, or you have an animal-loving family, there are two good reasons to visit Shubenacadie.

★ Riding the Tidal Bore

The **Shubenacadie River,** which drains into the Bay of Fundy at Cobequid Bay, is not just a good place to view the tidal bore but also to *ride* it. **Tidal Bore Rafting Resort** (Hwy. 215, Urbania, 902/758-4032 or 800/565-7238, www.raftingcanada.ca) operates two- and four-hour Zodiac raft excursions May-October. You board the rafts at low tide and head downstream, just in time to catch the tidal bore back upriver. The driver rides the wave, then doubles back to blast through its face, finding rapids along the way to keep the adrenaline pumping. Rates for the two-hour tour range $60-70 depending on the extremity of the tide. Departures are dependent on the tides; check the website for times.

Shubenacadie Wildlife Park

Families will enjoy **Shubenacadie Wildlife Park** (149 Creighton Rd., 902/758-2040, mid-May-mid-Oct. daily 9am-6:30pm, mid-Oct.-mid-May Sat.-Sun. 9am-3pm, adult $4.75, child $2), a provincially operated zoo well signposted from Highway 102 (take Exit 10 or 11). Throughout the spacious grounds are Canadian animals you are unlikely to see in the wild (fishers, otters, and more), ones that you don't want to meet face to face (bears,

cougars, wolves, and lynx), and those you'll see only at Christmas (reindeer). The Sable Island horses may look like regular horses, but they are one of the world's few wild horse populations.

Accommodations and Camping

★ **Rafters Ridge Cottages** (Hwy. 215, Urbania, 902/758-4032 or 800/565-7238, www.raftingcanada.ca, $160-203 s or d) is part of the Tidal Bore Rafting Resort complex, so it's no surprise that many guests come for the rafting (rooms are discounted when a rafting package is purchased). In the riverside location, you can also rent canoes or hang out around the outdoor pool. Lodging is in one- and two-bedroom cottages. The cottages have decks, barbecues, and pleasant views across a tree-sprinkled hillside. The facility also has a restaurant open daily for breakfast and dinner.

In the vicinity of the rafting park and also right on the Shubenacadie River is **Wide Open Wilderness Campground** (Urbania, 902/261-2228 or 866/811-2267, www.wowcamping.com, mid-May-Sept., campsites $31-44, cabins $80 s or d). You can watch the tidal bore, walk marked hiking trails, relax around the pool, try your hand at the horseshoe pits, or join in the many scheduled activities.

Getting There

To get to Shubenacadie from Halifax, take Exit 10 from Highway 102. It's a 60-kilometer (37-mile), 45-minute drive.

MAITLAND

Maitland, at the mouth of the Shubenacadie River, was where Canada's largest wooden ship, the three-masted *William D. Lawrence*, was built. Documentaries, ship portraits, and memorabilia are kept at the shipbuilder's

Truro

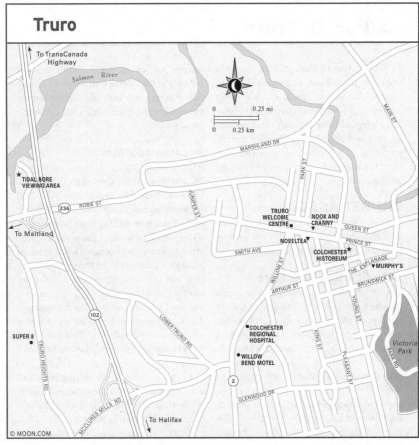

To TransCanada Highway

Salmon River

TIDAL BORE VIEWING AREA

ROBIE ST
236

To Maitland

MARSHLAND DR

PARK ST

MAIN ST

JUNIPER ST

TRURO WELCOME CENTRE
NOOK AND CRANNY

QUEEN ST

NOVELTEA
PRINCE ST

COLCHESTER HISTOREUM

SMITH AVE

WILLOW ST

THE ESPLANADE
MURPHY'S

BRUNSWICK ST

ARTHUR ST

YOUNG ST

102

LOWER TRURO RD

COLCHESTER REGIONAL HOSPITAL

WILLOW BEND MOTEL

KING ST

PLEASANT ST

PARK RD

Victoria Park

SUPER 8

TRURO HEIGHTS RD

2

GLENWOOD DR

MCCLURES MILLS RD

To Halifax

© MOON.COM

0   0.25 mi
0   0.25 km

CENTRAL NOVA SCOTIA
HALIFAX TO TRURO

former homestead, the **Lawrence House Museum** (8660 Hwy. 215, 902/261-2628, June-Sept. Tues.-Sat. 10am-5pm, adult $3.90, senior and child $2.80), which overlooks Cobequid Bay. The actual 1874 launching is commemorated on the middle Saturday of each September with a parade of period-dressed locals, a symbolic launch, and seafood suppers hosted throughout the village.

Getting There

To get to Maitland from Halifax, it's a 90-kilo-meter (56-mile), 70-minute drive starting with Highway 118 and ending with Highway 215.

If you've been moseying eastbound along the Bay of Fundy and don't particularly want to detour back through Halifax, turn at Windsor (take Exit 5 from Highway 101) and follow Highway 215 along the edge of Minas Basin to Maitland, crossing the Shubenacadie River to meet busy Highway 102 at Truro. Between Windsor and Truro it's 90 kilometers (56 miles), 1.5 hours—you won't save any time, but the scenery is better than via Halifax (120 km/74 mi, 1.5 hours).

TRURO

Situated at the convergence of the province's major expressways and served by VIA Rail, Truro (pop. 12,000) is called the hub of Nova Scotia. It is the province's third-largest population center, with an economy based on shipping, dairy products, and the manufacture of clothing, carpets, plastic products, and wines. Truro's academic side includes a teachers' college in town and an agricultural college on the outskirts.

Sights

The access road leading into 400-hectare (988-acre) **Victoria Park** (corner of Brunswick St. and Park Rd.) ends at a wide-open day-use area where beds of tulips flower through June, a colorful highlight of the town. At other times of the year, the park is still worth visiting—forests of spruce, hemlock, and white pine are spliced with hiking trails that lead along a deep canyon and past two waterfalls.

In a quiet residential area, the **Colchester Historeum** (29 Young St., 902/895-6284, June-Aug. Mon.-Sat. 10am-5pm, shorter hours Sept.-May, adult $5, senior $4, child $1) does a fine job entwining exhibits on Fundy eccentricities and the area's natural history.

WATCHING THE TIDAL BORE

Tidal bores only occur in a few places in the world, and one of the most accessible is at the **Salmon River,** which flows through Truro. Best described as a small wave, the bore is particularly high along the Salmon River, as it is at the head of Cobequid Bay, where the incoming tide pushing up the Bay of Fundy is forced into a narrow funnel. At Truro, the lead wave travels up the river as it pushes toward town beneath the Highway 102 overpass. If you want a close-up look at the tidal bore, take Robie Street west out of town beyond Highway 102 (or, from Hwy. 102 take Exit 14) and take the signed road that leads to the Tidal Bore Observation Deck. Tidal bore arrival times are listed at the deck, in the *Truro Daily News*, and at the Truro Welcome Centre (Commercial St.).

Food

NovelTea (622 Prince St., 902/895-8329, Mon.-Fri. 7:30am-8pm, Sat. 9am-7pm, Sun. 9:30am-5pm, lunches $8-11) combines a wide selection of teas, excellent coffee, and a secondhand bookstore. Part of the appeal is the setting—a surprisingly bright space filled with comfortable couches and colorful local artwork.

In a nondescript strip mall near the heart of downtown, ★ **Murphy's** (88 Esplanade, 902/895-1275, Mon.-Sat. 11am-7pm, $9-18) serves some of the best-priced seafood anywhere in this part of the province. I had the deep-fried haddock and chips—cooked to

looking out from the Tidal Bore Observation Deck

perfection—for just $11. A variety of fish is offered—pan-fried, poached, or "Texas style"—amid bright nautical-themed decor.

Another favorite is **Nook and Cranny** (627 Prince St., 902/895-0779, Sun.-Mon. 11am-9pm, Tues.-Wed. 11am-10pm, Thurs.-Sat. 11am-midnight, $12-28). While locals often stop by just for a craft beer on the outdoor tables, the lunch and dinner menu provides good value (I've yet to find another place in Nova Scotia where a striploin steak is under $20), with most dishes featuring local produce and game.

Accommodations

Lodgings in Truro are plentiful and reasonably priced. Motels line all the main routes into town, and you shouldn't have a problem finding a room at short notice.

The standout for value is the **Willow Bend Motel** (277 Willow St., 902/895-5325 or 888/594-5569, www.willowbendmotel. com, $105-149 s or d) along Highway 2, which feeds into downtown from the south. From the highway, it doesn't look that impressive, but the guest rooms have been given a major modern overhaul, creating the impression that you are spending a lot more money than you really are. The beds are super comfortable and the bathrooms a delight. Adding to the appeal is a heated outdoor pool and landscaped surrounds.

As usual, the **Super 8** (85 Treaty Trail, 902/895-8884 or 877/508-7666, www. wyndhamhotels.com, $155 s or d) is close to a main artery and filled with clean, comfortable, air-conditioned rooms packed with amenities. Here you also get an indoor pool with a waterslide and hot tub. A light breakfast is included, and you are within walking distance of restaurants for dinner. Call for last-minute specials.

Information

The **Truro Welcome Centre** (493 Prince St., 902/893-2922, mid-May-June and Sept.-mid-Oct. daily 9am-5pm, July-Aug. daily 8:30am-7:30pm) is at the heart of downtown overlooking Victoria Square; ask for a map of the tree-trunk sculptures scattered through town, and check your email using the free wireless Internet.

Getting There

True to its nickname, the "Hub of Nova Scotia," Truro is centrally located within the province at the junction of Highways 102 and 104. It's an easy one-hour run between Halifax and Truro (100 km/62 mi apart), and even less from Halifax Airport (66 km/41 mi south). Baddeck on Cape Breton Island is 252 kilometers (155 miles) to the northeast (allow three hours), and Moncton, New Brunswick, is 172 kilometers (107 miles), a 90-minute drive to the west.

Glooscap Trail

Named for the mighty Glooscap, a mythical Mi'kmaq figure who controlled the tides, this region is far enough from the main highway that it is missed by most visitors. It's a shame, because it is dotted with interesting seaside villages, has beaches that occasionally give up precious gemstones, and has been the site of some amazing dinosaur discoveries. The Glooscap Trail extends along the Bay of Fundy from as far west as Windsor; this section covers the best of Highway 2, which follows the coast west from Truro to Cape Chignecto and then north to Amherst.

TRURO TO PARRSBORO

Take Exit 14A from Highway 102 and you'll quickly find yourself on Highway 2, heading west along Cobequid Bay. En route to Parrsboro are a string of small fishing villages,

Glooscap Trail

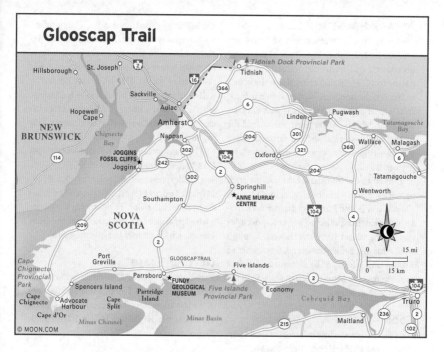

lookout points, and a couple of spots where beach access is possible at low tide.

Five Islands Provincial Park

As the name suggests, **Five Islands Provincial Park** does protect five islands, but it also encompasses more than 600 hectares (1,483 acres) of the mainland between Economy and Parrsboro. Among the park's coastal extremes are high cliffs and beaches, the latter revealing gems such as agate, amethyst, and jasper as the huge Fundy tides sweep across the bay. The 5-kilometer (3.1 mile) round-trip **Red Head Trail** reaches almost a dozen lookouts, including the Old Wife, a point of land that enjoys views across to the five islands. Allow 90 minutes for the hike.

PARRSBORO

The sea's erosive force has opened a window on the ancient world here along the coastlines of Chignecto Bay and Minas Basin. Archaeological digs have yielded 100,000 fossilized bone fragments of ancient dinosaurs, crocodiles, lizards, sharks, and primitive fish.

Sights
FUNDY GEOLOGICAL MUSEUM

Cross the bridge from downtown via Two Islands Road to reach **Fundy Geological Museum** (162 Two Islands Rd., 902/254-3814, mid-May-mid-Oct. daily 10am-5pm, adult $9, senior $7.50, child $5.25). It highlights the Bay of Fundy, with displays describing how the tides have eroded the bedrock to expose numerous geological wonders, such as precious gemstones and the fossilized remains of dinosaurs. It also holds the collection of Eldon George, a local man who spent 60 years collecting fossils from around the world, including some of the world's smallest dinosaur tracks, which he uncovered in the Parrsboro region.

OTTAWA HOUSE MUSEUM

Through town is **Ottawa House Museum** (902/254-2376, June-Sept. daily 10am-6pm, donation), a 21-bedroom waterfront home dating to 1775. All that remains on the beach in front of the home are broken-down pylons, so it's hard to believe that this was once an important shipbuilding port. Now cared for by the local historical society, Ottawa House has two floors of historical displays and a tearoom.

Linked to the mainland by a narrow strip of rocky beach that begins below Ottawa House, you'll find Partridge Island; archaeological evidence points to Mi'kmaq occupation of the island 10,000 years ago. A rough road ends just before the island, from where a hiking trail winds to the summit and allows views across the Minas Basin to Cape Split (30 minutes round-trip).

Food

As you cruise the main street, **Glooscap Restaurant** (758 Upper Main St., 902/254-3488, daily 11:30am-8pm, $12-19) is obvious, but a better choice is the **Harbour View Restaurant** (476 Pier Rd., 902/254-3507, summer daily 7am-9pm, $14-27), which has uninterrupted water views off Two Island Road. It's a friendly place, with all the usual seafood choices, including daily specials that are sourced from seasonal catches. The lobster dinner is a favorite.

Accommodations

Riverview Cottages (3575 Eastern Ave., 902/254-2388 or 877/254-2388, www.riverviewcottages.ca, mid-May-mid-Oct., $60-105 s or d) lies along the Farrells River on the east side of town. The cabins are older, and only a few have cooking facilities such as funky woodstoves, but canoes are available for guest use, and the price is right.

Within walking distance of downtown, the ★ **Maple Inn** (2358 Western Ave., 902/254-3735, www.mapleinn.ca, $129-169 s or d) smoothly combines two historic homes into an accommodation with 11 regular rooms and a spacious two-bedroom suite. The building was originally a hospital, so the inn has special meaning to those visitors returning to the town where they were born (Room 1 was the delivery room). The inn is surrounded by well-tended gardens, while inside is a lounge with a TV and a library of books. Rates include a full breakfast served in a cheery dining room.

The guest rooms at **Gillespie House Inn** (358 Main St., 902/254-3196 or 877/901-3196, www.gillespiehouseinn.com, May-Oct., $129-149 s or d) ooze old-world charm, and each has an en suite bathroom. The Elderkin Room has a wooden sleigh bed and looks over the front garden, which catches the morning sun.

Getting There

Parrsboro is just over 90 kilometers (56 miles) west from Truro, a 1.5-hour drive via Highway 2. It's 180 kilometers (112 miles) from Halifax, 2.5 hours via Highways 102 and 2 through Truro.

WEST TO CAPE CHIGNECTO

At Parrsboro, most travelers head north to Springhill on Highway 2, but Highway 209 along Minas Channel makes for a pleasant drive. It's 50 kilometers (31 miles) to the last village of any consequence, Advocate Harbour. At the halfway mark is Port Greville, once home to four shipbuilding companies. Today, you can take Wagstaff Street to the cliff edge and peer down at the river mouth that 100 years ago would have been filled with ships in various stages of construction. Across the water, Cape Split is plainly visible.

Advocate Harbour

At Spencers Island, Highway 209 turns inland to **Advocate Harbour,** a quiet corner of the province first visited by Europeans in 1604, when Samuel de Champlain came ashore. Just before town, take the signposted road to Cape d'Or, where a light-keeper's residence has been converted into ★ **The Lighthouse on Cape d'Or** (902/670-8314, www.capedor.ca,

May-mid-Oct., $125 s or d). Perched on high cliffs overlooking the Bay of Fundy, this four-room lodge is a wonderful place to kick back and do absolutely nothing at all. One room has an en suite bathroom, while the other three share two bathrooms, and the common room is stocked with books and board games. The attached restaurant is open for breakfast, lunch, and dinner (mains $15-30), but call ahead to confirm hours.

Cape Chignecto Provincial Park

As the crow flies, **Cape Chignecto Provincial Park** isn't far from the Trans-Canada Highway or the city of Saint John (New Brunswick), but it is a world away from civilization, protecting an arrow-shaped headland jutting into the Bay of Fundy. Cliffs up to 185 meters (607 feet) high are lapped by the world's highest tides, which pour into Chignecto Bay on one side and Minas Basin on the other. No roads penetrate the park. Instead, from the end of the road at Red Rocks, just beyond the village of West Advocate and 46 kilometers (29 miles) from Parrsboro, a hiking trail leads around the cape and loops back through the forested interior. Most backpackers complete the circuit in three days, packing their own food and water and pitching their tents at backcountry campgrounds. Cabins along the way at Arch Gulch and Eatonville provide an alternative to camping (call 902/392-2085 for reservations). All hikers should be experienced in backcountry travel and totally self-sufficient.

JOGGINS

This town on the Chignecto Bay coast is 40 kilometers (25 miles) southwest of Amherst.

Joggins Fossil Cliffs

Declared a UNESCO World Heritage Site in 2008, **Joggins Fossil Cliffs** have yielded thousands of fossils from the Carboniferous period (350-280 million years ago). Plants are most common, but a forest of upright petrified tree stumps is what the site is best known for. First noted in the 1850s, the hollow stumps contained the fossilized remains of *Hylonomus*, the earliest reptile ever discovered. It is supposed that these 30-centimeter-long (11.8-inch-long) critters fell inside and were unable to escape. The site has also revealed a two-meter-long (6.6-foot-long) arthropod with 30 sets of legs, as well as dinosaur footprints.

In conjunction with the UNESCO designation, the location of the **Joggins Fossil Centre** (100 Main St., off Hwy. 302, 902/251-2727, mid-Apr.-June and Sept.-Oct. daily 10am-4pm, July-Aug. daily 9:30am-5:30pm, adult $10.50, senior and child $8) on the site of an abandoned coal mine at the top of the cliffs provides the perfect setting to learn about the importance of the site. In addition to displays of ferns, fish scales, reptile footprints, and gastropods, visitors can watch lab technicians at work. To fully immerse yourself in the experience, plan on joining a guided tour. Departing daily from the interpretive center, they are tide-dependent; options include an easy 30-minute stroll ($10.50 per person), a more in-depth two-hour tour ($25 per person), and a more strenuous four-hour outing ($75 per person). All tours include admission to the center, and guests joining the four-hour tour are supplied with a picnic lunch.

Getting There

From Parrsboro, take Highway 2 north to Southampton and then follow Highways 302 and 242 north and then west for 40 kilometers (25 miles), a 40-minute drive, until you reach Joggins. From Halifax, take Highway 102 north to Truro, then Highway 104 west to Amherst, where Highways 302 and 242 lead to Joggins. Allow 2.5 hours for the 225-kilometer (140-mile) drive from Halifax.

SPRINGHILL

The sultry voice of crooner Anne Murray is known the world over, but the folks in the small town of Springhill, on a slight rise just off Highway 104, take special pride in this local girl who has gone on to sell 50 million albums and win more awards than any other female vocalist.

Anne Murray Centre

You probably already guessed that Springhill would provide a home for the **Anne Murray Centre** (36 Main St., 902/597-8614, mid-May-mid-Oct. daily 9am-4:30pm, adult $9, senior and student $8). The museum pays tribute to the beloved local warbler who hit the Top 40 in the 1970s with "Snow Bird" and is still going strong. Exhibits include photos, clothing, and other memorabilia, and an audiovisual display catalogs Murray's career.

Getting There

Springhill is 45 kilometers (28 miles) northeast of Parrsboro, a 45-minute drive via Highway 2. It's 180 kilometers (112 miles) north then west of Halifax, two hours via Highways 102 and 104.

AMHERST AND VICINITY

Amherst (pop. 9,500) is built on high ground above Amherst Marsh—part of the larger 200-square-kilometer (77-square-mile) Tantramar Marshes—on the isthmus joining Nova Scotia to the mainland of Canada. The fertile marshes were first diked and farmed by the Acadians in the 1600s and are still productive today, mainly as hayfields.

Sights

Amherst is at its architectural best along Victoria Street, where the profits of industry and trade were translated into gracious houses, commercial buildings, and churches garnished in Tudor, Gothic, and Queen Anne Revival styles (the red sandstone **First Baptist Church** on Victoria Street in the heart of downtown is particularly impressive). A few blocks south of the historic district, **Cumberland County Museum** (150 Church St., 902/667-2561, Feb.-Dec. Tues.-Fri. 9am-5pm, also Sat. noon-5pm in summer, adult $3) is in an 1838 residence. The museum does an impressive job of tracking the past, with exhibits on early Acadian settlements, Amherst's Anglo background, and spicy tidbits relating to Russian revolutionary Leon Trotsky, who was interned in an Amherst POW camp in 1917.

Amherst Point Migratory Bird Sanctuary, a few kilometers from town at the end of Victoria Street, spreads out over 190 hectares (470 acres) with trails through woodlands, fields, and marshes and around ponds. The sediment-rich Cumberland Basin lures

First Baptist Church

200 bird species, including Eurasian kestrels, bald eagles, hawks, and snowy owls.

Information

The **Nova Scotia Visitor Information Centre** (90 Cumberland Loop, 902/667-8429, July-Aug. daily 8am-8pm, Sept.-June daily 8:30am-4:30pm) is a large complex well signposted from Highway 102 as you enter the province from New Brunswick to the west. Adjacent is a promenade describing driving routes through the province, with picnic tables overlooking Tantramar Marshes.

Getting There

Staying on Highway 2, Amherst is 25 kilometers (15.5 miles) northwest of Springhill, a 20-minute drive. Taking Highway 102 then Highway 104, Amherst is 200 kilometers (124 miles) northwest of Halifax. Allow two hours for the drive.

Sunrise Coast to Pictou

The quickest way to reach Pictou from Amherst is to take Highway 104 via Truro, but Highway 6 is more scenic. Throughout the region, the land dips and sweeps in manicured farmlands extending to the red beaches and cliffs of Northumberland Strait. The villages are small, and the backcountry roads are scenic. This is rural Nova Scotia at its best. Allow three hours, plus stops.

TIDNISH AND VICINITY

Highway 366 branches off Highway 6 a few kilometers northeast of Amherst and reaches the Northumberland Strait at Tidnish, which lies right on the provincial border between Nova Scotia and New Brunswick.

Tidnish Dock Provincial Park

Across the Tidnish River from town is **Tidnish Dock Provincial Park.** This small day-use park protects the northern terminus of an ambitious railway construction project that was designed to transport vessels across the isthmus between the Bay of Fundy and Northumberland Strait. The initial proposal had been for a canal link, but the government decided that constructing a rail line would be easier. The plan called for the construction of hydraulic presses at either end to lift the boats into cradles that were to be pulled across the 28-kilometer (17-mile) rail line by locomotives. In 1891, nearing completion, the entire project was abandoned; the dock and a short length of the rail bed remain.

Continuing East Along Highway 366

Head east from Tidnish to **Amherst Shore Provincial Park.** From the day-use area, a short trail follows Annebelles Brook to a short beach, while on the other side of the highway is a **campground** (mid-May-mid-Sept., $29) with flush toilets, showers, and fire pits. Continue east for 7 kilometers (4.3 miles) to **Northport Beach Provincial Park,** renowned for its excellent beach and water warmed by shallow sandbars. Next up, and equally popular for swimming, is **Heather Beach Provincial Park.**

Getting There

Tidnish is about 30 kilometers (19 miles) northeast of Amherst, a 30-minute drive. From Highway 6, take Highway 366 until you reach Tidnish. From Halifax, Tidnish is 215 kilometers (133 miles) northwest, 2.5 hours via Highways 102, 104, 6, then 366.

PUGWASH

Recognized mostly for its delightful name, Pugwash (from the Mi'kmaq word *pagweak,* meaning "shallow water") lies at the mouth of Pugwash Basin, 50 kilometers (31 miles) east of Amherst. Durham Street (Hwy. 6) is

Thinker's Lodge

Recognized mostly for its delightful name, Pugwash (from the Mi'kmaq word *pagweak*, meaning "shallow water"), 50 kilometers (31 miles) east of Amherst, is best known as the origin of the Pugwash Conferences on Science and World Affairs (www.pugwash.org). The first of these took place in 1955 in Pugwash after Albert Einstein called for a meeting to discuss the dangers of a nuclear war. Cyrus Eaton, who had made his fortune in the United States as an industrialist, offered to sponsor the event on the condition it was held in his hometown. And so in 1957 it came to be that 13 Cold War nuclear scientists, including three from the USSR, met at what became known as the Thinker's Lodge, a large but otherwise unremarkable residence on the Pugwash foreshore. It was the first of many such gatherings, which now take place annually in major cities around the world, as well as occasionally still at Pugwash. Weapons of mass destruction are still discussed, but topics have broadened to include breaking down international borders, the environment, and economic prosperity. To get to Thinker's Lodge (249 Water St., www.thinkerslodge.org, tours June-mid-Aug. Mon.-Fri. 10am-4:30pm, free), follow Durham Street to its eastern end and turn right down Water Street.

the main drag. Here you'll find a summer-only information center and the usual array of small-town businesses. Across the water to the south of downtown is a salt mine. Current production is 1.2 million tons annually. The best opportunity to get an idea of the operation's scope is to watch the freighters being loaded at the downtown dock.

Food and Accommodations

Sheryl's Bakery & Café (10480 Durham St., 902/243-2156, Mon.-Fri. 7am-4:30pm, Sat. 8am-2pm, lunches $6-9) is a friendly little place where you are guaranteed soup made in-house each day and the sweetest, stickiest, most delicious cinnamon buns imaginable.

Downtown, the vaguely Irish-themed **Inn the Elms** (10340 Durham St., 902/243-2885, www.inntheelms.com, June-mid-Oct., $98 s or d) has a distinctive green and red exterior and four guest rooms with older furnishings. The dining room is open Wed.-Sun. 9am-2:30pm; a cooked breakfast is included for all paying guests.

Getting There

Pugwash is 50 kilometers (31 miles) east of Amherst, a 45-minute drive via Highway 6. It's 40 kilometers (25 miles) from Tidnish to Pugwash, 40 minutes for those traveling along Highway 366. From Halifax, it's a 200-kilometer (124-mile), 2.5-hour drive northwest.

PUGWASH TO PICTOU

It's 110 kilometers (68 miles) between Pugwash and Pictou, a 1.5-hour drive along Highway 6, but there are many worthwhile detours; the first, Gulf Shore Road, starts from downtown Pugwash.

Along Gulf Shore Road

From downtown's Durham Street, Gulf Shore Road spurs north and then follows the edge of Northumberland Strait in an easterly direction before rejoining Highway 6 at Wallace. About 4 kilometers (2.5 miles) from Pugwash is **Gulf Shore Picnic Park,** a day-use area with fireplaces and picnic tables spread across a grassed area that slopes to a red-sand beach.

Near where Gulf Shore Road loops south to Wallace is **Fox Harb'r Golf Resort and Spa** (1337 Fox Harbour Rd., 902/257-1801 or 866/257-1801, www.foxharbr.com). While the resort and its facilities wouldn't look out of place in Arizona or on the Atlantic Coast, it's certainly unique in rural Nova Scotia. At $230 for a round of golf, the greens fee is high, but it's a beautiful course. Other facilities include an Olympic-size indoor pool, spa services, guided kayaking, and formal dining (jacket required) in the Great Room. Guests soak up pure luxury in suites (from $475 s or d) contained within chalets that line the fairways and look out over Northumberland Strait.

Jost Vineyards

About 34 kilometers (21 miles) west of Pugwash, **Jost Vineyards** (48 Vintage Ln., 902/257-2636, Apr.-Dec. daily 10am-5pm, extended to 6pm mid-June-mid-Sept.) is signposted off Highway 6. The creation of the Jost (pronounced yost) family from Europe's Rhineland and now part of Devonian Coast Wineries, this 40-hectare (99-acre) vineyard produces fine white wines that are sold throughout the province, including at many better restaurants. The best-known blends are the Jost ice wines. To produce this style, grapes are left on the vines until after the first frost, then gently pressed to produce just a few drops of concentrated juice from each grape. The result is an intensely sweet wine that is perfect as an after-dinner treat. The winery café is open daily 11am-5pm.

★ Balmoral Grist Mill

Best known for its 1864 gristmill, the town of Balmoral Mills lies along Highway 311, 10 kilometers (6.2 miles) south of Tatamagouche and 38 kilometers (24 miles) north of Truro. Nestled at the base of a wooded vale, bright red **Balmoral Grist Mill** (660 Matheson Brook Rd., 902/657-3016, June-early Oct. Mon.-Sat. 10am-5pm, Sun. 1pm-5pm, adult $4, senior and child $2.80) is a photographer's ideal setting. Wheat, oats, and barley are still ground using 19th-century methods at this historic gristmill-cum-museum built in 1874. Milling demonstrations are at 10am and 2pm. The mill is busiest the first Sunday in October—an Open Day drawing a crowd of hundreds with activities such as milling demonstrations and popular taste-testing of oatmeal cakes.

Seafoam

At the coastal village of **Seafoam,** 24 kilometers (15 miles) east of Tatamagouche, you'll find the ★ **Seafoam Campground** (Harris Ave., 902/351-3122, www. seafoamcampground.ca, mid-May-Sept., $32-43.50), a large facility with direct access to the beach and warm swimming water. Amenities include lawn games, a playground, showers, and a laundry. On the west side of the campground, a side road leads to an abandoned dock, where a concrete wall has created a barrier for shifting sand. The result is a wide stretch of beach, perfect for lazing away a few hours on a warm summer day.

Pictou

Pictou (PIC-toe), 160 kilometers (99 miles) east of Amherst and 14 kilometers (8.7 miles) north of Exit 22 from Highway 104, is a historic port town of 3,500 on Northumberland Strait. It is also the ferry gateway to Prince Edward Island, meaning plenty of traffic passes through.

Nearly everything in Pictou happens at the waterfront, which is home to the main museum, restaurants, and historic accommodations. Some of the older buildings have a distinct Scottish vernacular style, designed to reflect local lineage. The residential streets also have numerous fancier styles; you'll see examples of stone Gothic and Second Empire designs along Water, Front, and Church Streets.

History

In 1773, 33 families and 25 unmarried men arrived from the Scottish Highlands aboard the *Hector,* and Pictou quickly became known as the "birthplace of New Scotland." The flamboyant Presbyterian minister and doctor Thomas McCulloch, en route to ministerial duties on Prince Edward Island, arrived

Pictou

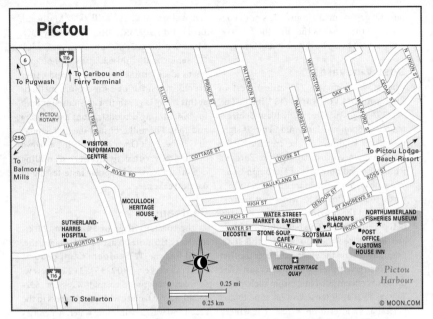

Map labels: To Pugwash; To Caribou and Ferry Terminal; PICTOU ROTARY; 6; 116; 256; To Balmoral Mills; PINE TREE RD; VISITOR INFORMATION CENTRE; W RIVER RD; ELLIOT ST; PRINCE ST; PATTERSON ST; WELLINGTON ST; OAK ST; CEDAR ST; N UNION ST; WELSFORD ST; COTTAGE ST; LOUISE ST; PALMERSTON ST; To Pictou Lodge Beach Resort; ROSS ST; FAULKLAND ST; HIGH ST; DENOON ST; ST ANDREWS ST; MCCULLOCH HERITAGE HOUSE; SUTHERLAND-HARRIS HOSPITAL; HALIBURTON RD; CHURCH ST; WATER ST; WATER STREET MARKET & BAKERY; DECOSTE; STONE SOUP CAFE; SCOTSMAN INN; CALADH AVE; SHARON'S PLACE; FRONT ST; NORTHUMBERLAND FISHERIES MUSEUM; POST OFFICE; CUSTOMS HOUSE INN; HECTOR HERITAGE QUAY; Pictou Harbour; To Stellarton; 116; 0 0.25 mi; 0 0.25 km; © MOON.COM

here with his family by accident in 1803 when a storm blew his ship into Pictou Harbour. Local immigrants asked him to stay, and McCulloch agreed. In addition to providing medical care to the immigrants, McCulloch tried to reform the province's backward educational system.

SIGHTS

★ Hector Heritage Quay

At the heart of the downtown waterfront, **Hector Heritage Quay** (33 Caladh Ave., 902/485-4371, June-Sept. daily 10am-4pm, adult $8, senior and student $6, child $3) is home to a three-floor interpretive center detailing the Scottish immigrants' arrival and early years. An elevated outdoor walkway overlooks the harbor. Admission includes access to the *Hector*, a replica of the sailing ship that transported Scottish settlers from across the Atlantic.

Take time to look over the *Hector*. The three-masted black-and-off-white replica is a splendid vessel, wide-hulled and round-ended. From the shape of the ship, though, you'll easily see that the voyage from Scotland

was not so splendid. The ship's hull is unusually wide, and indeed the *Hector*, owned by the Dutch and chartered by the Scots for the voyage, was built as a freighter and modified only slightly to carry human cargo. Remarkably, the 200-plus immigrants from the Highlands survived, and Nova Scotia owes its Scottish heritage to those seaworthy voyagers.

Northumberland Fisheries Museum

The fascinating **Northumberland Fisheries Museum** (21 Caladh Ave., 902/485-8925, mid-June-Sept. daily 10am-6pm, adult $8, senior $6, child $3) is within a red-brick railway station, away from the redeveloped waterfront precinct and easy to miss. Displays tell the story of the local fishing industry through a vintage lobster boat, an aquarium holding local marine species, a mock fisherman's bunkhouse, period photos, and other memorabilia.

McCulloch Heritage Centre

The next worthwhile attraction is east of downtown along Old Haliburton Road. The main building at **McCulloch Heritage Centre** (86 Old Haliburton Rd., 902/485-4563, June-mid-Oct. Mon.-Sat. 9am-5pm, Sun. 10am-5pm, adult $5, senior and child $3) showcases fine arts as part of the national arts exhibit circuit. The site is also one of the province's best genealogical libraries. A path leads uphill from the main building to McCulloch House, the early 1800s home of Thomas McCulloch. With distant water views, it holds period antiques and a small library. The print of a Labrador falcon downstairs was a gift to McCulloch from artist-naturalist John James Audubon.

ENTERTAINMENT

The local performing arts scene is based at **deCoste** (85 Water St., 902/485-8848, https://decostecentre.ca), a modern waterfront entertainment complex that puts on upwards of 100 shows each year. In July and August, the center hosts the Summer Sounds of Nova Scotia series. These concerts highlight top Celtic dancers, singers, and fiddlers, who hit the stage Tuesday-Thursday at 8pm. Tickets are generally under $20.

FOOD

Pictou doesn't have any standout coffee joints, although **Stone Soup Cafe** (41 Water St., 902/485-4949, Mon. 7:30am-3pm, Tues.-Sat. 7am-8pm, Sun. 8am-8pm, $12-19) is a popular hangout for locals and visitors alike for delicious breakfasts made with mostly local ingredients—including lobster (the lobster Benedict is a real winner). The rest of the day is more of the same, with healthy sandwiches and simple dishes. The small patio is the place to be on a warm day. A few doors down, **Water Street Market and Bakery** (50 Water St., 902/485-8454, mid-May-Dec. Thurs.-Sun. 9am-4pm) combines a local arts and crafts market with breads and pastries baked on-site.

The vibe at **Sharon's Place** (12 Front St., 902/485-4669, Mon.-Fri. 10am-7pm, Sat.-Sun. 9am-6pm, $8-16) is also local and low-key, with simple, inexpensive cooking (think burgers or fish-and-chips). Friendly staff and delicious desserts add to the appeal.

Across the road from the harbor, **Lobster Bar Restaurant** (50 Caladh Ave., 902/382-8527, Tues. 4:30pm-8pm, Wed.-Sun. 11:30am-8pm, $15-24) is owned and operated by a longtime local family. As the name suggests, the menu is inspired by the ocean, with lots of

Climbing aboard this replica of the *Hector* is a highlight of visiting Pictou.

traditional choices such as haddock cakes and, of course, lobster dinners.

Five kilometers (3.1 miles) out of town, the dining room at the ★ **Pictou Lodge Beach Resort** (172 Braeshore Rd., 902/485-4322, mid-May-mid-Oct. daily 7am-9pm, $18-31) is a woodsy, old-fashioned space. You'll enjoy strait views from an intimate setting, with tables centered around a massive stone fireplace. The menu features entrées such as Indian-spiced lamb shank, cedar-planked salmon, and smoked maple pork belly with grilled scallops. Sunday brunch (11am-2pm) attracts locals for a buffet that includes everything from sushi to smoothies.

ACCOMMODATIONS AND CAMPING

Pictou has a wonderful choice of historic lodgings, many within walking distance of the waterfront and all well priced.

$100-150

In the heart of downtown and close to the waterfront, the 1865 **Scotsman Inn** (78 Coleraine St., 902/485-1433, www.scotsmaninn.com, $115-125 s or d) has 10 comfortable guest rooms, each with an en suite, and some offer harbor views. Downstairs is a dining room where guests gather for a light breakfast each morning, while at the back of the building is a private balcony for all guests to enjoy.

Right on the water and within walking distance of downtown, the **Customs House Inn** (38 Depot St., 902/485-4546, www.customshouseinn.ca, $135-165 s or d) dates to 1870. It's a historic building overlooking the harbor constructed of red brick and sandstone that was, as the name suggests, originally a customs house. The restored inn has eight guest rooms, all air-conditioned and some with exposed brickwork and water views. Rates include a light breakfast.

Dating to the 1920s, **Pictou Lodge Beach Resort** (172 Braeshore Rd., 5 km/3.1 mi east of town, 902/485-4322 or 800/495-6343, www.pictoulodge.com, mid-May-mid-Oct.,

$145-445 s or d) sits on a 67-hectare (166-acre) oceanfront estate overlooking Northumberland Strait. The roomy lodge has been restored with rustic comforts and features a long outside porch, dining in the high-ceilinged rotunda, and a nearby pond with canoes. Lodging choices include oceanfront villas, three-bedroom chalets, suites of various sizes and configurations, and standard motel rooms. All units have private baths, and many have fireplaces, kitchens, and separate living rooms. Resort amenities include canoe rentals, an outdoor pool, and a playground.

Camping

Caribou/Munroes Island Provincial Park (mid-June-mid-Oct., $29) has 87 campsites (Loop B is closest to the beach), cooking shelters, flush toilets, and fire pits. It fronts a long red-sand beach, which at low tide links Munroes Island to the mainland. The park is 6 kilometers (3.7 miles) west of town, signposted from Highway 6.

INFORMATION AND SERVICES

Pictou's **Destination Eastern and Northumberland Shores Visitor Information Centre** (902/485-8540, June-Sept. daily 9am-6pm) is west of downtown beside the Rotary (where Highway 106 meets Highway 6).

Sutherland-Harris Hospital is at 1059 Haliburton Road (902/485-4324). Locals do their banking in style at the architecturally resplendent **Bank of Nova Scotia,** in a Second Empire-style building at the corner of Front and Colerain Streets (902/485-4378). The **post office** is at 49 Front Street.

GETTING THERE

If you're combining your travels through Nova Scotia with a visit to Prince Edward Island, you have the choice of driving across the Confederation Bridge or catching the ferry. From Caribou, a short drive north of Pictou, **Northumberland Ferries** (902/566-3838 or 800/565-0201, www.ferries.ca) operates

5-9 sailings May-mid-December daily to the eastern side of Prince Edward Island. The trip takes just over an hour, and the fare is $78 round-trip per vehicle, regardless of the number of passengers (you pay when leaving the island).

From the west, it's 110 kilometers (68 miles), a 1.5-hour drive along Highway 6 to Pictou from Pugwash. Heading north from Halifax, Pictou is 165 kilometers (102 miles), two hours along Highways 102, 104, and 106.

Pictou to Cape Breton Island

The Trans-Canada Highway promises little besides uninterrupted speed on its route across the northeastern mainland. The best vistas, beaches, camping, and other attractions lie off the expressway, along the strait's coastal roads between Tatamagouche and Cape Breton. Shallow pools of seawater among sandbars turn warm in the sun, making for comfortable wading and swimming at Rushton's Beach Provincial Park, Tatamagouche Bay, and Melmerby Beach Provincial Park, east of Pictou.

CAPE GEORGE SCENIC DRIVE

The route to fossil hunting at Arisaig and Cape George's ruggedly beautiful eastern coastline lies along Highways 245 and 337 between New Glasgow and Antigonish via a 110-kilometer (68-mile), two-hour drive. From Exit 27 east of New Glasgow, allow half a day to reach Antigonish, which is enough time to visit the sights detailed here.

This is a sparsely populated region—there are no tourist services, such as accommodations or restaurants, so plan accordingly.

★ Arisaig

Like many other places in Nova Scotia, Arisaig, 57 kilometers (35 miles) northeast of New Glasgow, is an unassuming place that is much more interesting than the casual visitor might imagine. The cliffs on the west side of the village tell the story of a 4-million-year period of life on earth 400 million years ago—one of the only places in the world where such a long period of time is exposed in a single layered cliff line. This area was a shallow sea 400 million years ago, and as the layers of sediment built up on its floor, brachiopods (shells), nautiloids (related to squid), trilobites (ancient crabs), crinoids (filter-feeders that attached themselves to the seabed), and bryozoans (coral) were buried. As ocean levels dropped, cliffs were formed along the shoreline, and as erosion broke the sediment down further, fossils from the Silurian period were exposed, perfectly preserved in bands of rock that represent specific time periods all those millions of years ago. Added to the mix is the upper cliff face, which is topped with up to 4 meters (13.1 feet) of sand and gravel left behind when glaciers retreated across the area at the end of the last ice age. Geologists have studied the site since the mid-1800s, and as the erosion process continues and more fossils are uncovered, interest continues.

You can walk to the cliffs from the harbor at Arisaig, but the official access is from **Arisaig Provincial Park,** on the west side of the town. The advantage of using the park access is that there are interpretive panels beside the parking lot, which help visitors appreciate the geology down at sea level. From these panels, steps descend to the beach far below, from where it's a short stroll westward along the beach to Arisaig Brook, where the largest concentration of fossils is found. It is illegal to dig at the cliff face, but scavenging through fallen rock is permitted.

Cape George

At Malignant Cove, Highway 337 branches north from Highway 245 and climbs steadily before peaking at an elevation of 190 meters (623 feet) at Cape George. The setting is a bicyclist's favorite scene and a just reward after the steep coastal climb. The panorama from the lighthouse at the cape's tip takes in the manicured farmlands of the Pictou-Antigonish highlands to the south as well as the misty vision of Prince Edward Island across the strait.

Along Cape George's eastern side, Highway 337 peels down from the peak alongside St. George's Bay. Nestled below the cape is **Ballantynes Cove.** From the town wharf, a rough walking trail climbs back to the lighthouse. The 1.8-kilometer (1.1-mile) route takes less than an hour each way and makes reaching the cape more satisfying than simply driving to its summit.

ANTIGONISH

First impressions of Antigonish (an-tee-guh-NISH), from a Mi'kmaq name meaning "place where the branches are torn off by bears gathering beechnuts," are not promising. As it passes through town, the highway is a thicket of fast-food restaurants and service stations—but the town is not without its charms. Dig deeper and you'll find a bustling university town with nearby beaches and hiking trails, a

good choice of places to stay and eat, and two popular festivals.

Sights

In a 1908 red-brick railway building on the north side of downtown, the **Antigonish Heritage Museum** (20 E. Main St., 902/863-6160, July-Aug. Mon.-Sat. 10am-5pm, Sept.-June. Mon.-Fri. 10am-noon and 1pm-5pm, free) tells the town's story through donated items and historical photographs. Back toward the historic heart of town is the **County Courthouse** (168 Main St.), still in use even though it has been designated a national historic site. Although no tours are offered, the landscaped grounds of gracious **St. Francis Xavier University** (take Exit 32 north from Highway 104) are pleasant for a stroll, especially in summer when the campus is deserted.

Festivals and Events

The first week of July, the town hosts the **Antigonish Highland Games** (902/863-4275, www.antigonishhighlandgames.ca)— the longest-running in North America, celebrated since 1863. Highlights include Celtic music, pipe bands, dancing, heavy sports such as caber tossing, and a kilted golf tournament. Throughout July and August,

These rocks at Arisaig are filled with fossils.

the **Festival Antigonish** (902/867-3333 or 800/563-7529, www.festivalantigonish.com), Nova Scotia's largest and most successful professional summer theater program, features a variety of drama, musicals, comedies, cutting-edge improv, and children's entertainment at the university campus.

Food

Antigonish offers a surprising number of good dining options along the main street. If you're looking for good coffee or a quick bite to eat, search out **Tall and Small** (342 Main St., 902/863-4682, Mon.-Wed. 7am-6pm, Thurs.-Sat. 8am-9pm, lunches $6-10), a modern space brightened by local artwork on the walls. It has the usual array of soup and sandwiches, as well as muffins and pastries.

At first glance, **Little Christo's** (332 Main St., 902/867-4992, Mon.-Thurs. 11am-9:30pm, Fri. 11am-10pm, Sat. 9:30am-10pm, Sun. 9:30am-9pm, $11-19) may look like just another pizza joint, but the food is made from scratch each morning, very creative, and most importantly, well priced. The pizzas are the highlight, but there are also Mediterranean-inspired platters to share, vegetarian and gluten-free options, and entrées such as a lamb burger topped with pomegranate yoghurt sauce. The attached patio is in high demand on warmer evenings.

Being close to the university, **Piper's Pub** (33 College St., 902/863-2590, Mon.-Sat. 10am-2am, Sun. noon-1am, $14-21) is a popular student hangout. The typical pub grub is well priced, and bands play Saturday night.

Accommodations

Maritime Inn Antigonish (158 Main St., 902/863-4001 or 888/662-7484, www.maritimeinns.com, $135-185) is open year-round. It has 32 modern units, free Internet, free daily newspapers, and a restaurant open daily for breakfast, lunch, and dinner. Directly across the road, **Antigonish Victorian Inn** (149 Main St., 902/863-1103 or 800/706-5558, www.antigonishvictorianinn.ca, $130-175 s or d) is a splendid bed-and-breakfast occupying a dark burgundy-colored William Critchlow Harris-designed Queen Anne-style mansion. Each of the 12 guest rooms has a private bath and TV. Rates include a full cooked breakfast.

Getting There

The most direct route to Antigonish from New Glasgow is along Highway 104, about 60 kilometers (37 miles), a 40-minute drive. Via the Cape George scenic drive, it's about 110 kilometers (68 miles) and two hours from New Glasgow to Antigonish. Antigonish is 215 kilometers (133 miles) north then east from Halifax, 2.5 hours via Highways 102 and 104.

Marine Drive

Marine Drive extends 320 kilometers (200 miles) along the Eastern Shore from Dartmouth to Canso, at the eastern tip of mainland Nova Scotia. From Canso, it's another 80 kilometers (50 miles) to the Canso Causeway, gateway to Cape Breton Island. The Marine Drive is a scenic alternative to Highways 102 and 104 via Truro. It's longer (allow 5-6 hours, not counting stops) and beyond the main tourist path, but it features delightful bays, sandy beaches, and interesting fishing villages around every bend.

LAWRENCETOWN

Begin the Marine Drive by following Cole Harbour Road from Exit 7 of Highway 111 in Dartmouth to **Lawrencetown Beach,** one of Canada's best-known surf spots. Easily reached in 30 minutes from Dartmouth, this long stretch of sand backed by high dunes is an enjoyable stop even if you don't plan to take to the water.

Surfing at Lawrencetown Beach

The waves of "L-town," as it's known to locals, break along the length of the beach and off a rocky headland that breaks the main beach in two. They are best November-May, when winter swells provide large and consistent waves. These waves also coincide with the coldest ocean temperatures. But even with water temperatures of 0°C (32°F) and air temperatures that drop to -20°C (-4°F), it's not unusual to see footprints leading down a snow-covered beach to the breakers beyond. Summer is not devoid of waves. They are just likely to be smaller and less consistent. Hardy locals swim in the ocean in the warmer months, when water temperatures rise to 15°C (59°F), but for surfing, be prepared with a wetsuit. The beach's southern headland provides an ideal vantage point for watching the action.

Kannon Beach Surf Shop (4144 Lawrencetown Rd., 902/434-3040, Mon.-Sat. 9am-6pm, Sun. 10am-4pm) is a full-service surf shop in a renovated house on the hill between Lawrencetown and Stoney Beaches. Surfboard and wetsuit rental packages (complete with gloves and booties) are $40 per day, and stand-up paddleboard rentals cost $50 per day. **East Coast Surf School** (902/434-3040, www.ecsurfschool.com, July-early Sept. daily 9am-6pm), which bases itself at the beach itself each summer day, offers lessons for $75 per day, which includes a rental board and wetsuit.

Accommodations

Ocean views from ★ **Moonlight Beach Suites** (Hwy. 207, north end of Lawrencetown Beach, 902/827-2712, www. moonlightbeachinn.com, $139-169 s or d) are nothing short of stunning. The four guest rooms are decorated in a nautical theme, and each has a private deck, jetted tub, and TV/DVD combo, while thoughtful extras include binoculars and beach towels. The largest of the three rooms is massive and has a huge private deck with sweeping water views. Rates include a full breakfast.

Getting There

Lawrencetown is about 15 kilometers (9.3 miles) east of Dartmouth (a suburb of Halifax), a 20-minute drive via Highway 207.

MUSQUODOBOIT HARBOUR TO SHERBROOKE

From Musquodoboit Harbour, 50 kilometers (31 miles) from Halifax, a 40-minute drive via Highway 107, it's a further 150 kilometers (93 miles) east along the Marine Drive to Sherbrooke. The journey takes around two hours, but there are many worthwhile stops and a couple of good accommodations options, which I've recommended below.

Musquodoboit Harbour

With just 900 people, Musquodoboit Harbour is nevertheless the largest community between Dartmouth and Canso. The only real attraction in town is the **Musquodoboit Harbour Railway Museum** (7897 Hwy. 7, 902/889-2689, June-Aug. daily 9am-4pm, free), housed within a 1918 railway station and three vintage rail cars. The **tourist information center** is in the same building. Ten kilometers (6.2 miles) south of Musquodoboit Harbour on East Petpeswick Road, **Martinique Beach Provincial Park** protects the southern end of Nova Scotia's longest beach. The beach is often windy, but it's still a relaxing place for a long, easy walk.

Salmon River Bridge

Cross the bridge for which the village of Salmon River Bridge, 13 kilometers (8.1 miles) east of Musquodoboit Harbour, is named and you'll reach a neat little lodge nestled between a forested hill and the river. Dating to 1850 and operating as a guesthouse since 1920, **Salmon River Country Inn** (9931 Hwy. 7, 902/889-3353, www.salmonrivercountryinn. ca, $95-130 s or d) has seven guest rooms, all with en suite bathrooms and some with water views, and a riverfront cottage with a fireplace. Part of the inn is the seafood-oriented **Mermaid Eatery** (Apr.-mid-Oct. daily noon-3pm and 5pm-8pm, $13-30), with seats that spill outside to a large riverfront deck. Lobsters kept in the tank are often larger than three pounds, but there's a wide choice of less-expensive seafood, including delicious fish-and-chips.

Drive 3 kilometers (1.9 miles) beyond Salmon River Bridge and then 4 kilometers (2.5 miles) north to reach ★ **Webber's Lakeside Park** (738 Upper Lakeville Rd., 902/845-2340 or 800/589-2282, www. webberslakesideresort.com), which is filled with opportunities for activities that include lake swimming with a floating dock, canoe and boat rentals, a playground, and a games room with table tennis. The two-bedroom cottages ($150 s or d) have kitchens and wide decks, and the campground (mid-May-mid-Oct., $36-43) has full hookups and hot showers. Being just an hour's drive from Halifax, this place fills up every summer weekend, so you'll need reservations.

Oyster Pond

Turn south off Highway 7 just beyond Salmon River Bridge to visit the small but interesting **Fisherman's Life Museum** (58 Navy Pool Loop, 902/889-4209, June-Sept. Mon.-Fri. 8am-4pm, adult $4, senior and child $2.80). Rather than a collection of artifacts, this museum within a small homestead re-creates the simple, self-sufficient lifestyle of a fisherman, his wife, and their 13 children.

Clam Harbour Provincial Park and Vicinity

Clam Harbour Provincial Park, along the south-facing side of Clam Bay, protects a long stretch of hard white sand. The beach has supervised swimming in summer, as well as changing rooms and picnic areas, but no camping. (From the end of the access road, turn right to reach the nicest picnic area, where tables are nestled in windswept coastal forest.)

Members of the Murphy family have lived in Murphy Cove for seven generations, and have been involved through time in everything from rum running to fishing. Now they operate ★ **Murphy's Camping on the Ocean** (308 Murphy's Rd., 902/772-2700, www.murphyscamping.ca, mid-May-mid-Oct., $30-69), which sprawls across a grassy headland. The campground has all the usual facilities—showers, boat and kayak rentals, a laundry, a playground, and more—but it's Brian's evening storytelling, boat tours (two hours for $23), clam-digging trips, and complimentary mussel bakes that make this place stand apart.

Kayaking at Tangier

Tangier, 85 kilometers (53 miles) east of Dartmouth, a 1.5-hour drive via Highway 7, is the base for **Coastal Adventures** (84 Mason's Point Rd., 902/772-2774, www. coastaladventures.com), which pushes off into the cove on full-day kayak excursions ($110 pp, including lunch) that include a visit to uninhabited islands. Kayak rentals are $70 per day for a single and $90 for a double. The same people operate ★ **Paddler's Retreat Bed and Breakfast** ($65-95 s or d), which is an excellent spot to spend one or more nights. Most guests staying in this restored 1860s fisherman's home do so as part of a kayaking instruction package or before or after participating in a day trip. Three of the four rooms share bathrooms, while the fourth has an en suite bathroom and private entrance. Rates include a full breakfast.

★ Taylor Head Provincial Park

Turn off at Spry Bay, 15 kilometers (9.3 miles) beyond Tangier, to reach the interesting oceanside **Taylor Head Provincial Park,** which protects a narrow peninsula extending 6 kilometers (3.7 miles) to Taylor Head. The west-facing side of the spit is rugged and windswept, with stunted white spruce trees clinging precariously to the rocky ground, while the east side is characterized by sandy coves lapped by calm waters. A 5-kilometer (3.1-mile) unpaved road from Highway 7 hugs the west side of the peninsula before crossing to protected **Psyche Cove.** At the

Fabled Sable Island

Just under 200 kilometers (124 miles) off Nova Scotia's eastern coastline is a 40-kilometer-long (25-mile-long) sliver of sand that was known to generations of seafarers as the "Graveyard of the Atlantic." Protected today as a national park, Sable Island is inhabited by a herd of horses that have taken on almost mythical proportions.

The island is made up entirely of sand. The sand is part of a terminal moraine left behind by the receding ice cap at the end of the last ice age 11,000 years ago. Hardy marram grass stabilizes the central part of the island, and seals and birds are also native. The island's most famous residents are horses; they were introduced in the late 1700s. Some say it was to feed shipwreck victims, while others claim they were aboard ships that came to grief. Today, Sable Island is home to about 400 horses. They are of special interest since they are one of the world's few truly wild horse populations, without feral intruders (such as domestic horses gone wild), and they are free to roam, feed, and reproduce without human interference.

Since Sable Island was first mapped in the late 1500s, more than 350 vessels have been wrecked along its fog-shrouded shore (the last was a small yacht, the *Merrimac*, in 1999). In 1801 a station manned with a lifesaving crew was established on the island. This government-operated service soon expanded to five stations and continued until 1958. Today the island has a year-round population of fewer than 20 people—mostly scientists who study the weather and monitor the island's environment.

Only about 200 intrepid travelers visit Sable Island each year, most arriving by air charter or private vessel and staying for just the day. The season runs June-October, but June and July are often foggy. If you'd like to visit, the first step is to register with Parks Canada (902/426-5080, www.pc.gc.ca/sable). You will then need to arrange fixed-wing air charters from Halifax through Sable Aviation (902/860-3994, www.sableaviation.ca), which charges $6,900 for the round-trip, inclusive of taxes and the $500 Parks Canada landing fee. These flights take up to seven passengers, so the best way to reduce costs is to check directly with the company or visit their Facebook page for cost-sharing opportunities. The best source of island information is the website of the Friends of Sable Island Society (www.sableislandfriends.ca).

end of the road is a series of small parking lots with beach access. You can walk along the beach back toward the mainland to Bob Bluff, or head in the opposite direction to a headland with sweeping views up and down the peninsula and of island-dotted Mushaboom Harbour. Taylor Head itself is 4 kilometers (2.5 miles) by hiking trail from the end of the road. If you return via rocky Spry Bay, you'll have walked 10 kilometers (6.2 miles); allow four hours.

Spry Bay to Liscomb Mills

Marine Drive between Spry Bay and Liscomb Mills passes a string of fishing villages with delightful names such as Ecum Secum (a Mi'kmaq word of unknown origin) and Spanish Ship Bay (named for a nearby headland that resembles a Spanish galleon). Linked to Highway 7 by a short bridge, Sober Island's name has a more cynical origin (the first residents bemoaned the lack of alcohol).

In Liscomb Mills, Liscombe Lodge Resort (2884 Hwy. 7, 902/779-2307 or 877/375-6343, www.liscombelodge.ca, mid-May-mid-Oct., from $180 s or d) boasts an idyllic setting along the Liscomb River. Amenities include an indoor pool, a sauna, hot tubs, a fitness center, hiking trails, tennis courts, a small marina with boat, canoe, and fishing-equipment rentals, and a comfortable dining room overlooking the river (where children eat free).

SHERBROOKE

Highway 7 leaves the coast at Liscomb, turning north to Sherbrooke, from which it continues north to Antigonish; the Marine Drive spurs east, continuing along the Eastern Shore as Highway 316. Sherbrooke (pop. 400) was founded at the farthest navigable point of the St. Mary's River in the early 1800s. By 1869 gold had been discovered in the area, and the town was booming. In addition to mining, mills were established to process lumber for export, and local farms depended on the town for services. By 1890 the gold rush was over, and the population began slipping away.

★ Sherbrooke Village

By the late 1960s, Sherbrooke was a shadow of its former self. Gold rush-era buildings remained in varying states of disrepair, but the only visitors were anglers chasing salmon along the river. At this point, a local trust stepped in, and under the guidance of the Nova Scotia Museum, an ambitious restoration project took place. Today, **Sherbrooke Village** (42 Main St., 902/522-2400, early June-late Sept. daily 9:30am-5pm, adult $16, senior $11, child $5) comprises more than 80 restored buildings that are integrated with the town itself. About 20 buildings are open to the

Sherbrooke Village

public, including an ambrotype photography studio, the colonnaded courthouse, a jail, a water-powered sawmill, the Sherbrooke Hotel, a drugstore, a blacksmith shop, a church, and a farmyard. The site is brought alive by costumed interpreters who wander the village streets, tend to their crops, and go about operating each business as folks would have done in the late 1800s.

To fully immerse yourself in the experience, consider participating in the Hands on History program (July-Aug. only, $190 per family), where the costume department will dress you in period clothing and you can spend the day helping in the kitchens, trying your hand at pottery, or learning skills from the blacksmith. The Courthouse Concert Series ($10 per person) takes place 2-3 nights a week through the summer season; entertainment varies from traditional Celtic ceilidhs to musical comedies. Starting time is usually around 7pm. The main parking lot and entrance are off Court Street (turn left at the end of the modern-day main street).

Food and Accommodations

In the Sherbrooke Hotel, within the historical village, the ★ **What Cheer Tea Room** (June-mid-Oct. daily 9:30am-5pm, lunches $7-14) is a countrified restaurant with friendly staff and basic but tasty dishes that will set you up for more historical sightseeing. You can try traditional rural dishes such as fish cakes with a side of homemade baked beans. **Sherbrooke Village Inn Restaurant** (7975 Hwy. 7, 902/522-2235, May-Oct. daily 7am-7pm, $15-26) is a small wood-paneled restaurant on the east (Halifax) side of town. The emphasis is on simple presentations of local seafood. You could start with fish chowder and then choose between dishes such as deep-fried scallops and strip loin or a lobster from the tank. Save room for the homemade pie with ice cream.

On the east side of town, a 10-minute walk from the village, is **Sherbrooke Village Inn** (7975 Hwy. 7, 902/522-2235 or 866/522-3818,

www.sherbrookevillageinn.ca, May-Oct., $125-159 s or d). The medium-size motel rooms are plain but comfortable, the pine-paneled cabins have kitchens, and the on-site restaurant is open daily 7am-7pm.

GETTING THERE

Sherbrooke is about 200 kilometers (124 miles) east of Dartmouth, a three-hour drive along Highway 7.

SHERBROOKE TO CANSO

It's only a little more than 100 kilometers (62 miles) between Sherbrooke and Canso, but the drive will take at least two hours, plus any time you wait for the ferry at Country Harbour.

Port Bickerton Lighthouse

There could be no better location for a lighthouse display than in a restored light-keeper's home at the end of a windswept, often fog-enshrouded peninsula—which is exactly where the **Port Bickerton Lighthouse** (Lighthouse Rd., Port Bickerton, 902/364-2000, July-Sept. daily 9am-5pm, adult $3) is situated. Built in 1901 and deactivated in 1962, the two-building complex now holds a display describing the lonely life of Nova Scotian light-keepers and their families, the original foghorn, and a directory of Nova Scotia's lighthouses. Stairs lead to an observation tower. Outside, a trail leads past clumps of tasty blueberries and cranberries to a sandy beach. From the turnoff in Port Bickerton, 25 kilometers (15.5 miles) beyond Sherbrooke and 7 kilometers (4.3 miles) before the ferry across Country Harbour, it's 3 kilometers (1.9 miles) to the interpretive center, the last 2 kilometers (1.2 miles) along an unpaved road.

Country Harbour

The **Country Harbour ferry,** along Highway 316, 7 kilometers (4.3 miles) north of Port Bickerton, departs from the east (Halifax) side of the bay on the half hour and the west side on the hour. During the laughably named "rush hour" (9am-10am and 5pm-6pm), ferries operate more frequently. The ferry has room for just 12 passenger vehicles or a limited number of trucks and RVs, and the fare is $7 (cash only), which is paid to the attendant upon loading. From the west side of the bay, it's 86 kilometers (53 miles) to Canso. Aside from the short detour to Tor Bay, it's worth slowing down to admire the village of Isaacs Harbour, which on a calm day is reflected across the bay of the same name from Goldboro.

Tor Bay

Named for granite knolls that dot the region, Tor Bay is lined by three small communities established by Acadians after their deportation by the English in 1755. For visitors, the highlight is **Tor Bay Provincial Park,** on an isthmus along a peninsula that forms the southern boundary of the bay. This small day-use park has one of the few sandy beaches this far east along the Marine Drive. A boardwalk leads to the beach, from where a short trail leads to a rocky headland where covered interpretive boards describe the geology that led to the creation of the beach.

CANSO

The remote town of Canso, 320 kilometers (200 miles) along Marine Drive from Halifax, is the jumping-off point to an interesting historic site that protects Canada's oldest fishing village. In more recent times, Canso was an important link in trans-Atlantic communications. The most striking reminder of this era is the 1884 **Hazel Hill Cable Station,** just outside town. It was from here that the distress signal from the sinking *Titanic* and news of the 1929 stock market crash were transmitted to the rest of the world.

★ Canso Islands National Historic Site

Archaeological digs point to European settlement as early as the 1500s on the small island that comprises the **Canso Islands National Historic Site,** one kilometer (0.6 mile) offshore from Canso. These visitors' time on the island was only temporary, and no obvious signs of this era remain today. Two hundred years later, the French and British were fighting for control of North America, with ownership of the Canso Islands in dispute even after the signing of the Treaty of Utrecht in 1713. In 1718 the French were displaced, and the same year, fearing a reprisal attack by the French, the British built a small fort on Grassy Island to protect access to cod stocks that were being harvested at the amazing rate of 10 million pounds per year. Grassy Island grew into a prosperous community, complete with wealthy merchants who built solid stone homes. The village was destroyed by a French invasion from Louisbourg in 1744 and was never rebuilt.

The site comprises a **visitors center** (Union St., 902/366-3136, July-Aug. daily 10am-6pm, $5 donation) on the Canso waterfront and the island itself. Mainland exhibits include a scale model of the settlement, fragments of French pottery dated to the early 1700s, and a short documentary film. Boats run on demand between the visitors center and the island. Once safety regulations are described, the small craft is off, and you'll be on the island within 15 minutes. A mowed trail passes eight information boards describing the settlement and what remains—cellar pits, mounds of rubble from residences, and terraced vegetable plots—before looping back down to the dock. Allow about 30 minutes to walk the trail. If visitation is slow, the boat will be waiting at the wharf for your return; otherwise, expect a wait of up to 30 minutes while it transports more visitors across. The only services on the island are pit toilets and a shelter, so bring warm clothes and water. The suggested donation at the visitors center includes the boat ride to the island.

Stan Rogers Folk Festival

On the last weekend of July, the population

of Canso increases 10 times as music fans descend on the town for *"Stanfest"* (888/554-7826, www.stanfest.com), a folk-music festival of 50 acts from around the world performing on six stages. In addition to the music, the festival features a food fair, craft show, and beer garden. Most visitors camp at the Acoustic Campground, set up by the organizers within walking distance of the main stage. Other temporary campgrounds take the overflow, with shuttle buses running to the grounds and to showers at the local high school. A camping pass is $70-90, and entry to the concert is $125 for the entire weekend.

Accommodations and Camping

Canso is most definitely not a tourist town. The **Last Port Motel** (Hwy. 16, 902/366-2400, www.lastportmotel.com, $90-110 s,

$95-110 d) is just before town. It offers 13 basic rooms with wireless Internet access, as well as a restaurant open daily 7am-8pm. A better option for those looking for a memorable stay is ★ **DesBarres Manor Inn** (90 Church St., 902/533-2099, www.desbarresmanor.com, $189-259 s or d), 56 kilometers (35 miles) east in Guysborough. Dating to 1837, the three-story inn has been beautifully restored, and the grounds remain in immaculate shape. The 10 guest rooms are stylish and come with niceties like 600-thread-count sheets on super-comfortable mattresses, plus luxurious bathrooms. Rates include a gourmet cooked breakfast, with dinner available with many of the packages offered online.

Ten kilometers (6.2 miles) west of Canso along Highway 16 is **Seabreeze Campground and Cottages** (230 Fox Island Rd., Fox Island, 902/366-2352, www.

Canso Islands National Historic Site

seabreezecampground.com, mid-May-mid-Oct., campsites $27-37, cottages $100-110 s or d), where modern facilities, full hookups, and views across Chedabucto Bay keep the 51 campsites full through July and August. One- and two-bedroom cottages have basic cooking facilities, a lounge area with TV, and separate bedrooms. Other resort amenities include coin-operated showers, a laundry, firewood sales, a playground, canoe rentals, and even a lobster pound where you can buy live lobsters.

Information
Whitman House (1297 Union St., 902/366-2170, June-Sept. daily 9am-5pm, donation), a handsome three-story 1885 house with displays illustrating local history, doubles as an information center.

Getting There
Canso is about 320 kilometers (200 miles) east of Dartmouth, a suburb of Halifax, 5-6 hours via Highway 7.

Cape Breton Island

Alexander Graham Bell, perhaps Cape Breton

Island's most renowned transplant, once wrote, "I have seen the Canadian and American Rockies, the Andes and the Alps, and the Highlands of Scotland; but for simple beauty, Cape Breton outrivals them all."

Linked to the mainland by a two-lane causeway, nearly every coastal and inland backcountry road on the western half of the island leads eventually to the Cabot Trail, the scenic highway rimming the unforgettable landscape of northwestern Cape Breton. The dramatic coastal scenery alone qualifies the Cabot Trail as one of the world's great drives, but you can also spend time soaking up local Acadian culture, hiking through pristine forests of the Cape Breton Highlands,

Highlights

Look for ★ to find recommended sights, activities, dining, and lodging.

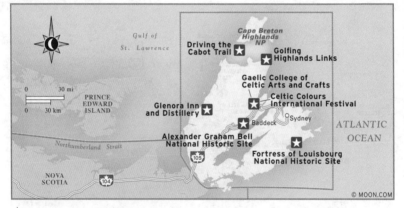

★ **Glenora Inn and Distillery:** Tucked into a quiet glen along the remote west coast is North America's only single-malt whiskey distillery, complete with a restaurant and guest rooms (page 170).

★ **Alexander Graham Bell National Historic Site:** Dedicated to one of the world's most prolific inventors, this museum will interest all ages (page 172).

★ **Driving the Cabot Trail:** This 311-kilometer (190-mile) circuit traversing varying landscapes—including Cape Breton Highlands National Park—is one of the world's great scenic drives (page 180).

★ **Golfing Highlands Links:** Walk the fairways of one of the world's finest golf courses,

knowing that what you've paid to play is less than at many regular city courses (page 183).

★ **Gaelic College of Celtic Arts and Crafts:** No, you don't need to sign up for a course. Instead, take in music recitals and demonstrations such as weaving (page 186).

★ **Celtic Colours International Festival:** This October festival draws crowds who enjoy traditional music while soaking up the colors of fall (page 186).

★ **Fortress of Louisbourg National Historic Site:** Sprawling across 10 hectares (24.7 acres) of a remote headland is this reconstruction of a French town destroyed by the British 250 years ago (page 189).

Cape Breton Island

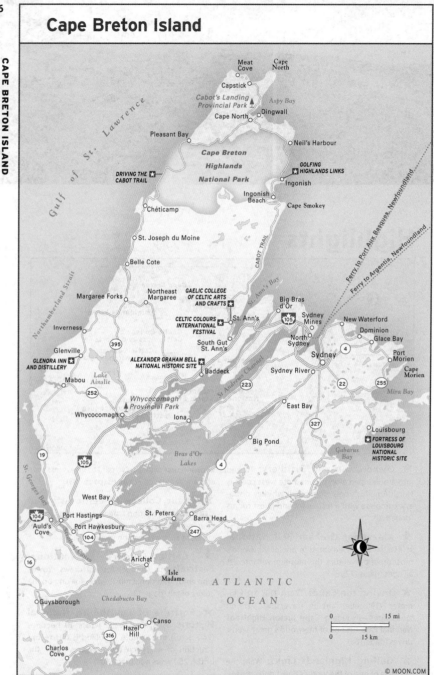

Meat Cove
Cape North
Capstick
Cabot's Landing Provincial Park
Aspy Bay
Dingwall
Cape North
Pleasant Bay
Neil's Harbour
Cape Breton Highlands National Park
GOLFING HIGHLANDS LINKS
DRIVING THE CABOT TRAIL
Ingonish
Ingonish Beach
Cape Smokey
Chéticamp
St. Joseph du Moine
Belle Cote
CABOT TRAIL
Gulf of St. Lawrence
St. Ann's Bay
Margaree Forks
Northeast Margaree
GAELIC COLLEGE OF CELTIC ARTS AND CRAFTS
Big Bras d'Or
Sydney Mines
New Waterford
CELTIC COLOURS INTERNATIONAL FESTIVAL
St. Ann's
105
Dominion
Glace Bay
Inverness
South Gut St. Ann's
North Sydney
Sydney
4
Port Morien
Glenville
395
ALEXANDER GRAHAM BELL NATIONAL HISTORIC SITE
Baddeck
223
Sydney River
Cape Morien
GLENORA INN AND DISTILLERY
Mabou
252
Lake Ainslie
St Andrews Channel
22
255
Mira Bay
Whycocomagh Provincial Park
East Bay
Whycocomagh
Iona
327
19
105
Bras d'Or Lakes
4
Big Pond
Gabarus Bay
Louisbourg
FORTRESS OF LOUISBOURG NATIONAL HISTORIC SITE
St. Georges Bay
West Bay
104
Port Hastings
St. Peters
Barra Head
247
Auld's Cove
Port Hawkesbury
104
16
Arichat
Isle Madame
Guysborough
Chedabucto Bay
ATLANTIC OCEAN
Canso
Hazel Hill
316
Charlos Cove
Northumberland Strait

Ferry to Port Aux Basques, Newfoundland
Ferry to Argentia, Newfoundland

0   15 mi
0   15 km

© MOON.COM

or simply relaxing on white-sand beaches. The most spectacular section of the route is in the far northern part of the island, through magnificent Cape Breton Highlands National Park, which stretches from coast to coast and is as wild and remote as the Highlands of Scotland. Green, steeply pitched highlands begin at the sea in the south and sweep north, cut by salmon-filled rivers. As the elevation increases, the Acadian and boreal forests give way to a taiga tableland of stunted, windswept trees.

The Northumberland Strait opens into the Gulf of St. Lawrence on the western coast, while the Atlantic washes the opposite shore. The 1,098-square-kilometer (424-square-mile) Bras d'Or Lakes forms the island's heart. The saltwater "Arm of Gold," though barely influenced by tidal cycles, is an inland arm of the Atlantic consisting of a sapphire-blue main lake with numerous peripheral channels, straits, and bays.

PLANNING YOUR TIME

Although you can fly into the airport at Sydney, most visitors drive to Cape Breton from Halifax, reaching the causeway linking the island to the mainland in less than four hours. From the causeway, a choice of routes present themselves, including the little-traveled route up the west coast, which passes the **Glenora Inn and Distillery.** The geographic and tourist hub is Baddeck. Plan to spend at least one full day at this resort town, which is enough time to visit the **Alexander Graham Bell National Historic Site** and take to the waters of Bras d'Or Lakes. Baddeck is also a good starting point for beginning the **Cabot Trail,** a 311-kilometer (190-mile) highway that loops through the wilderness of **Cape Breton Highlands National Park.** The park scenery is the highlight of the drive, but along the way, plan on browsing the **arts and crafts of Chéticamp** and **golfing** at Cabot Links and Highlands Links. If your travels correspond with the October **Celtic Colours International Festival,** plan on taking in as many concerts as you can. At other times of the year, St. Ann's **Gaelic College of Celtic Arts and Crafts** is the place to immerse yourself in Celtic culture. To hit all the highlights mentioned above, you should allow yourself at the very least three days from Halifax, but preferably four or five. The main reason for veering from the Cabot Trail is to visit the **Fortress of Louisbourg,** a lesser-known but impressive attraction that re-creates a French town from the mid-1700s.

Port Hastings to Baddeck

Canso Causeway, easily reached in four hours from Halifax, links Cape Breton to the mainland. From this point, Highways 104 and 105 (the Trans-Canada) and Highway 19 fan out across the island. Highway 19 follows the west coast up to Mabou and Inverness, and then links up with the Cabot Trail in the Margaree Valley. The Trans-Canada Highway lies straight ahead, leading through the center of the island to Baddeck and on to Sydney. The endless stream of buses packed with tourists makes a beeline along this route, connecting with the Cabot Trail at Baddeck. Highway 4 branches off to the east (or take the more direct Highway 104 for the first 28 km/17 mi), passing the turnoff to Isle Madame and then following Bras d'Or Lakes, en route to Sydney.

PORT HASTINGS

The main reason to stop in Port Hastings, the gateway town to Cape Breton Island, is to load up with brochures at the well-stocked

---

Previous: Keltic Lodge in Ingonish; Cabot Links in Inverness; beach in Cape Breton Highlands National Park.

Nova Scotia Visitor Information Centre (902/625-4201, May-June and Sept.-Dec. daily 9am-5pm, July-Aug. daily 9am-8:30pm), on the right as the Trans-Canada Highway crosses to the island. Behind the center, views extend back across to the mainland, and information boards describe the processes involved in constructing the causeway.

Accommodations

Through town toward Port Hawkesbury, **Hearthstone Inn** (388 Hwy. 4, 902/625-0621 or 800/867-2212, www.hearthstonehospitality. ca, Apr.-late Dec., $115-165 s or d) has air-conditioned rooms, each with comfortable beds, coffeemaker, and wireless Internet. Bonuses include a small indoor pool and a small onsite restaurant.

Getting There

Port Hastings is 60 kilometers (37 miles) east of Antigonish, a 45-minute drive via Highway 104. It's 275 kilometers (170 miles) north then east from Halifax, three hours via Highways 102 and 104.

ISLE MADAME

Settled by French fishermen in the early 1700s, this was one of the first parts of the province to be settled, and it's one of the oldest fishing ports in North America. Isle Madame has four main communities—Arichat, West Arichat, Petit Grat, and D'Escousse.

The wooded island is a popular weekend getaway, with two provincial parks (**Lennox Passage** to the north and **Pondville Beach** on the east side) and plenty of picnicking, swimming, and vista spots. In Arichat, on the waterfront, **LeNoir Forge Museum** (708 Veteran's Memorial Dr., 902/226-9364, June-Aug. Tues.-Sun. 10am-5pm, donation) is a restored working 18th-century forge open to visitors.

The Clairestone Inn (2375 Hwy. 206, Arichat, 902/226-2200, www. theclairestoneinn.com) is designed as a 19th-century Acadian-style inn, with eight inviting rooms, one with a jetted tub, in the main

building ($130-145 s or d) and nine adjacent comfortable motel units ($120-130 s or d). Rates include a light breakfast.

Getting There

Take Highway 104 for 30 kilometers (19 miles) east from Port Hastings, a 30-minute drive, and then Highway 320 south over Lennox Passage Bridge to reach this 43-square-kilometer (16.6-square-mile) island.

BRAS D'OR LAKES SCENIC DRIVE

The most direct route between the Canso Causeway and Sydney is Highway 105 through Baddeck, a total distance of 130 kilometers (81 miles); allow 90 minutes. This route hugs the northwestern shore of Bras d'Or Lakes, but I recommend the slightly longer **Bras d'Or Lakes scenic drive,** which traces the southern shore, passing through the villages of St. Peters and Big Pond, a total distance of 148 kilometers (92 miles), a two-hour drive via Highway 4.

Highway 4 steers away from the water until passing St. Peters, but a short detour to West Bay and then east along West Bay Road will bring you to **Dundee Resort** (368 Shore Rd., Baddeck, 902/295-3500 or 800/565-5660, www.dundeeresort.com, May-Oct.), a destination in itself. The resort, 12 kilometers (7.5 miles) from Highway 4, is set on 223 hectares (551 acres) overlooking Bras d'Or Lakes. It features an 18-hole golf course (greens fee $68), an outdoor pool, a marina with all manner of watercraft for rent, an arcade activities center, summer programs for the kids, and a restaurant. Motel rooms, most with balconies, range $159-219 s or d, while cottages with limited cooking facilities and up to three bedrooms are $159-259.

St. Peters and Vicinity

The first town reached along the Bras d'Or scenic drive is St. Peters, where photography buffs should check out the **MacAskill House Museum** (7 MacAskill Dr., 902/535-2531, mid-June-Aug. daily 9:30am-5:30pm,

Fiddling the Night Away

A ceilidh (KAY-lee) was originally an informal gathering, usually on a Friday or Saturday night, that would bring together young people to dance the night away to lively Celtic music in a local hall. These social gatherings originated in Gaelic-speaking regions of Scotland and Ireland, with the tradition introduced to the New World by immigrants in the 1700s. Although nightclubs and pubs may have replaced the ceilidh in popularity in the city, along the west coast of Cape Breton Island and in other rural areas they remain an important part of the social scene. Most important, the music has retained its original roots, with progressive dancing in which the woman moves along a ring from man to man or everyone dancing in formation (similar to line dancing). The most skilled dancers break away from the formations to step dance.

Highway 19 is known as the Ceilidh Trail, and for good reason, as ceilidhs take place in towns and villages along the route year-round. Everyone is welcome, with many of the summer events especially tailored for visitors. At Mabou, the Mabou Community Hall (11538 Hwy. 19, Mabou) fills with the sound of fiddle music every Tuesday through summer, while the following night, the foot-stomping fun happens down the road at the local museum. Passing through on Thursday? Plan for a lively evening of entertainment at the Inverness Fire Hall (15797 Central Ave., Inverness) ceilidh.

donation), in the restored childhood home of Wallace MacAskill, one of the world's preeminent marine photographers. The museum exhibits a collection of his most memorable photographs as well as historic cameras.

Overlooking Bras d'Or Lakes, 1.5 kilometers (0.9 mile) east of St. Peters, **Joyce's Motel and Cottages** (902/535-2404, www.joycesmotel.com, mid-May-Oct., $79-105 s or d) offers the choice of regular motel rooms or larger but dated one-bedroom cottages. The motel offers extensive landscaped grounds, water views, an outdoor swimming pool, and a laundry. **Battery Provincial Park** (off Hwy. 4, 1 km/0.6 mi east of town, 902/535-3094, mid-June-early Sept.) has hiking trails and ocean views. The 52 open, wooded, unserviced campsites rent for $29.

GETTING THERE

The village of St. Peters lies along the Bras d'Or Lakes scenic drive, 12 kilometers (7.5 miles), a 10-minute drive, beyond the turnoff to Isle Madame and 55 kilometers (34 miles), 40 minutes, from the Canso Causeway. St. Peters is 320 kilometers (200 miles) from Halifax, 3.5 hours via Highways 102 and 104.

Big Pond

From St. Peters, the run to Sydney takes a little more than an hour, with Highway 4 paralleling Bras d'Or Lakes for much of the way. A good halfway-point lunch stop is **Rita's Tea Room** (902/828-2667, summer daily 10am-5pm, lunch $8-12), in a converted schoolhouse at Big Pond. Opened by well-known folk singer Rita MacNeil, who grew up in Big Pond and who continued to promote Cape Breton Island around the world until her death in 2013, the café serves specially blended teas, sandwiches, and salads in a country setting. An adjacent room is devoted to her distinguished career.

GETTING THERE

Big Pond is 50 kilometers (31 miles) northeast of St. Peters, a 45-minute drive along Highway 4, and 370 kilometers (230 miles) from Halifax, four hours via Highways 102, 104, and 4.

HIGHWAY 19: THE CEILIDH TRAIL

The least traveled of the three routes north from the Canso Causeway, Highway 19 hugs the coastline and passes many small villages that haven't changed much in decades.

This stretch of coastline is a bastion of Celtic music, hence the nickname Ceilidh Trail. Natalie MacMaster and the Rankins, as well as a new generation of stars headed by Chrissy Crowley, were all born and raised in the area.

Mabou

The town of Mabou (pop. 400) is the center of Gaelic education in Nova Scotia (the language is taught in the local school) and the location of Our Lady of Seven Sorrows Pioneers Shrine. The Mabou Gaelic and Historical Society Museum, or **An Drochaid** (902/945-2311, July-Aug. Tues.-Sun. 9am-5pm, donation), housed in a former general store, focuses on crafts, local music and poetry, genealogical research, and Gaelic culture.

The Mabou Mines area, near the coast, has some excellent hiking trails into a roadless section of the **Mabou Highlands.**

GETTING THERE

Mabou is a 60-kilometer (37-mile), 40-minute drive north up Highway 19 from the Canso Causeway. It's 335 kilometers (210 miles) from Halifax, 3.5 hours via Highways 102, 104, and 19.

★ Glenora Inn and Distillery

The **Glenora Inn and Distillery** (Hwy. 19, Glenville, 902/258-2662 or 800/839-0491, www.glenoradistillery.com, tours May-Oct. daily 9am-5pm, adult $7) is North America's only single-malt whiskey distillery. (It can't be called Scotch whiskey, as it's not from Scotland.) The final product is marketed as Glen Breton Rare, with 250,000 liters distilled annually. Built in 1990 using impressive post-and-beam construction and traditional copper pots for the distilling process, the complex is open for 25-minute tours daily on the hour 9am-5pm. Better still, it's also a country inn with 28 units ($145-345 s or d) in various buildings scattered across the property, including spacious log chalets that sleep up to six people. Also at the distillery is **Glenora Dining Room and Washback Pub** (May-Oct. daily 11am-11pm, $17-39), which serves hearty lunches and dinners accompanied by live Celtic music.

GETTING THERE

Glenville is 12 kilometers (7.5 miles) north of Mabou on Highway 19.

Inverness

Golfers know this Scottish settlement (pop.

Glenora Inn and Distillery

1,300), the largest town along Highway 19, for **Cabot Links** (Beach Rd. #2, 902/258-4653, mid-May-Oct., greens fee $295), one of North America's few links courses and rated one of the world's top 100 golf courses, and the equally spectacular **Cabot Cliffs,** which opened to rave reviews in 2016 (same contact information and greens fee). Located between the town and the ocean, the location alone makes the effort to reach Inverness worthwhile. Overlooking the original course, **Cabot Links Lodge** (Beach Rd. #2, 902/258-4653, www.cabotlinks.com, May-Oct., $295-435 s or d) features 72 modern hotel-style rooms in five configurations, as well as a restaurant and lounge. If you're not a golfer, spend your time beyond the course, walking along the seemingly endless sandy beach below the golf course. Back up the hill in town, the **Ned Macdonald Museum** (62 Lower Railway St., 902/258-3291, June-Oct. daily 10am-6pm, adult $1) focuses on the region's mining history and pioneer families.

Ten kilometers (6.2 miles) north of Inverness on Highway 19 is ★ **MacLeod's Beach Campsite** (Dunvegan, 902/258-2433, www.macleods.com, June 15-Oct. 15, campsites $38-50, cottages $180-210 s or d), which slopes down to a delightful beach that rarely gets crowded. Amenities include washrooms, showers, fire pits, a store, a launderette, a games room, volleyball, basketball, horseshoes, and more.

GETTING THERE
Inverness is about 20 kilometers (12.4 miles) north of Mabou on Highway 19.

HIGHWAY 105 TO BADDECK
From the Canso Causeway, it's 90 kilometers (56 miles) to Baddeck along Highway 105 (the Trans-Canada Highway). This is the main route north to Sydney and the Cabot Trail.

Iona
Where it intersects with Highway 105, Highway 223 crosses Little Narrows to Iona, then follows the shoreline of St. Andrews Channel all the way to Sydney. It's the least traveled of the many up-island highways, but no less interesting than the other options. The route is posted as Bras d'Or Lakes Drive.

Set on 16 hectares (39.5 acres) overlooking the narrow body of water between Bras d'Or Lakes and St. Andrews Channel, Iona's **Highland Village** (Hwy. 223, 902/725-2272, June-mid-Oct. daily 10am-5pm, adult $11, senior $9, child $5) tells the story of the island's Gaelic heritage through features such as 10 historic buildings, as well as many examples of working farm equipment.

GETTING THERE
From the intersection of Highway 105 and Highway 223, it's 25 kilometers (15.5 miles) to Iona along Highway 223.

Baddeck and Vicinity

Baddeck (from *abadak*, or "place near an island," as the Mi'kmaq called it, referring to Kidston Island just offshore) is a picturesque town of 800 that lies on the misty wooded shore of St. Patrick's Channel, a long inlet of Bras d'Or Lakes. Baddeck also marks the traditional beginning and ending point for the Cabot Trail.

SIGHTS AND RECREATION

Many visitors plan a stop in Baddeck for its heritage accommodations and fine dining, but there are also a few things to see and do, including a national historic site that everyone should visit.

★ Alexander Graham Bell National Historic Site

At the east end of Baddeck (within walking distance of downtown) is the **Alexander Graham Bell National Historic Site** (902/295-2069, late May-Oct. daily 9am-5pm, adult $7.80, senior $6.55, child $3.90), a tremendously satisfying museum with displays on Bell's life, his family, and his seemingly inexhaustible curiosity about science. The multimedia exhibits include working models of Bell's first telephones and a full-size reproduction of his speed-record-setting HD-4 hydrofoil, but some of the most interesting displays are information panels describing how Bell's interest in teaching the deaf to speak led to the invention of the telephone. The inventor always had a soft spot for children, and his love of the younger generation is reflected in the museum's Children's Corner, a large space where kids of all ages can make and decorate kites, do experiments, and generally have fun in an educational environment. Allow at least two hours, more if you have children.

Kidston Island

A free ferry runs from Government Wharf (Jones St.) out to **Kidston Island,** just 200 meters (656 feet) from the mainland, which has a beach with supervised swimming. The wooded island also has numerous short walking trails, including one that leads to a lighthouse that has been guiding vessels on Bras d'Or Lakes for more than a century. The ferry operates every 20 minutes July-August (Mon.-Fri. 10am-6pm, Sat.-Sun. noon-6pm). The trip takes less than five minutes.

Boat Tours

The *Amoeba* (902/295-7780, June-mid-Oct., adult $30, child $15), a 67-foot concrete-hulled yacht built by the owner's father during a 10-year period, provides an inexpensive way to enjoy the Bras d'Or Lakes. Ninety-minute trips depart from Government Wharf at the end of Jones Street three or four times daily through the summer season. In addition to enjoying the lake, you'll pass Alexander Graham Bell's estate and can often spot bald eagles perched atop shoreline trees.

FOOD

Cafés and restaurants line Baddeck's main street, but most are open only through the warmer months, and by mid-October, choices become very limited.

Lobster Supper

Lobster suppers originated as local gatherings held in church basements and community halls. Today, they have become a little more commercialized, but they are still a fun and inexpensive way to enjoy this succulent seafood treat. One of the few regularly scheduled in Nova Scotia (Prince Edward Island is a hotbed of lobster suppers) is **Baddeck Lobster Suppers** (17 Ross St., 902/295-3307, early June-mid-Oct. daily 4pm-9pm), held in a community hall just off Main Street. A 1- to 1.5-pound lobster with all-you-can-eat chowder, mussels, trimmings, dessert, and

Baddeck

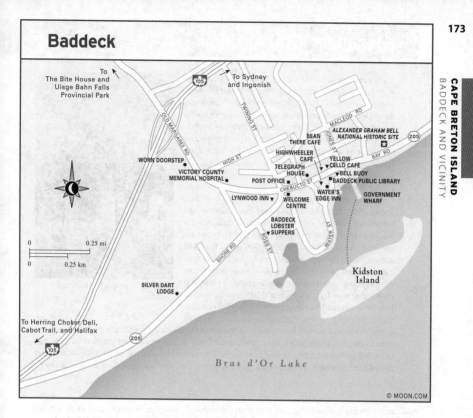

To
The Bite House and
Uisge Bahn Falls
Provincial Park

To Sydney
and Ingonish

TWINING ST

OLD MARGAREE RD

105

MACLEOD RD

JONES ST

ALEXANDER GRAHAM BELL
NATIONAL HISTORIC SITE

205

BAY RD

BEAN
THERE CAFÉ

HIGHWHEELER
CAFÉ

HIGH ST

WORN DOORSTEP

VICTORY COUNTY
MEMORIAL HOSPITAL

TELEGRAPH
HOUSE

POST OFFICE

CHEBUCTO ST

YELLOW
CELLO CAFÉ

BELL BUOY
BADDECK PUBLIC LIBRARY

WATER'S
EDGE INN

GOVERNMENT
WHARF

LYNWOOD INN

WELCOME
CENTRE

WATER ST

BADDECK
LOBSTER
SUPPERS

ROSS ST

SHORE RD

Kidston
Island

0   0.25 mi

0   0.25 km

SILVER DART
LODGE

To Herring Choker Deli,
Cabot Trail, and Halifax

105

205

Bras d'Or Lake

© MOON.COM

nonalcoholic drinks costs $45 per person. If you're not a lobster fan, substitute salmon, crab, or steak at the same price.

Casual Dining

For breakfast, sandwiches, pizzas, and light meals, the **Yellow Cello Cafe** (525 Chebucto St., 902/295-2303, May-mid-Oct. daily 8am-9pm, $13-22) is centrally located and well priced, with an indoor dining room and veranda in front. The calzones are delicious, the beer selection is good, and the people-watching can't be beat.

For the best coffee in town, head to the **Highwheeler Café** (484 Chebucto St., 902/295-3006, May-mid-Oct. Tues.-Sun. 6am-6pm, lunches $8-12). This café has an in-house bakery, so you know everything is fresh, including daily soup specials and healthy sandwiches made to order.

Across the road from the Highwheeler, **Bean There Cafe** (503 Chebucto St., 902/295-1634, Mon.-Sat. 6:30am-5pm, Sun. 7am-5pm) is another decent place for coffee, with a few outdoor tables good for watching the world of Baddeck pass by.

With a welcoming, woodsy ambience, ★ **Herring Choker Deli** (Hwy. 105, 902/295-2275, daily 8am-5pm, lunches $9-18) overlooks the water from 11 kilometers (6.8 miles) west of town. Instead of greasy cooked breakfasts, tuck into homemade granola or freshly made breakfast wraps. The lunchtime highlight: thick gourmet sandwiches packed with goodies on bread baked each morning. The coffee is also excellent, and there is a wide selection of meats and cheeses to go.

Other Restaurants

The most unique dining experience in

Alexander Graham Bell

Once a major shipbuilding center, Baddeck claims as its most famous resident not a sailor but an inventor—Alexander Graham Bell. The landscape, language, and people all reminded the Scotsman of his native land. He built a grand summer home, Beinn Bhreagh (pronounced Ben Vreeah), across the inlet from Baddeck (it is still owned by his descendants and is not open to the public). While the telephone is his most famous invention, Bell possessed an intellectual curiosity that is almost impossible to comprehend in today's world.

At Beinn Bhreagh, he studied heredity by breeding sheep and seeking to increase twin births. Even when separated from the rest of the world at Baddeck, he maintained friendships in high places—after the attempted assassination of President Garfield in 1881, Bell was hastily commissioned to invent an electromagnetic device to find the bullet. When his son died after experiencing breathing problems, he developed a breathing device that was the prototype of the iron lungs used to help polio victims. More than anything else, Bell was captivated by flight. He tested propeller-driven kits as early

Alexander Graham Bell National Historic Site

as the 1890s, and in 1909, four years after the Wright brothers' famous flight, the great inventor took to the air over Bras d'Or Lakes in the Silver Dart. But he wasn't done yet: In 1919, at the age of 72, Bell and his estate manager, Casey Baldwin, invented the hydrofoil, which set a water-speed record of more than 70 miles per hour. Bell died three years later and was buried at Beinn Bhreagh.

Baddeck—and arguably one of the most unique in all of Nova Scotia—can be enjoyed at ★ The Bite House (1471 Westside Rd., eat@thebitehouse.com, May-Dec. Thurs.-Sat. 6pm-9pm, $70). Here, in a century-old farmhouse, Chef Bryan Picard cooks for 12 lucky diners each night. The five-course tasting menu he offers comprises solely locally grown, sourced, and even foraged ingredients, all prepared simply yet presented perfectly. Wine and beer are available. Reservations many months in advance are a must, and can be made by email starting in January for the following summer season.

Watching the sun set over Bras d'Or Lakes from a window table at the Bell Buoy Restaurant (536 Chebucto St., 902/295-2581, mid-May-June daily 4pm-9pm, July-mid-Oct. daily 11:30am-9pm, $16-30) is worth the price of dinner alone. A menu highlight is the seafood chowder, which comes chock-full of

haddock, salmon, mussels, and even lobster, as well as a slab of homemade oatmeal bread as a side. Mains vary from pastas to whole lobsters, with a number of vegetarian and gluten-free options also offered.

Of many local lodges with dining rooms that welcome nonguests, none is better than the Lynwood Inn (24 Shore Rd., 902/295-1995, mid-May-mid-Oct. daily noon-8:30pm, $16-32), a grand 1868 home that has been converted into an inn and restaurant. The smallish dining room is tastefully decorated in Victorian-era style. The menu is less expensive than you might imagine.

ACCOMMODATIONS AND CAMPING
$50-100

A 10-minute walk from town and the Alexander Graham Bell National Historic Site, the ★ Worn Doorstep (43 Old

Margaree Rd., 902/295-1997, $95 s or d) has four delightful en suite rooms, each with its own private entrance, air-conditioning, basic cooking facilities such as a microwave and toaster, and a TV. All guests share a rooftop patio with sweeping views across Bras d'Or Lakes.

Over $100

Owned by the same family for five generations, **Telegraph House** (479 Chebucto St., 902/295-1100, www.baddeckhotel.com, $110-140 s or d) combines 18 basic rooms in the grandly historic original 1861 home with a row of 13 modern motel units. The lodge has two historic links of note—it was once home to a telegraph office that sent some of the first transatlantic messages, and Alexander Graham Bell was a frequent guest. The room that Bell called his own looks exactly like it would have in the 1880s; others have been given a modern look while retaining the historical feel through antique furnishings. Amenities include a library, a sitting room, and a dining room open daily for breakfast, lunch, and dinner. Telegraph House is also one of the few downtown accommodations open year-round.

Named for Alexander Graham Bell's famous airplane, **Silver Dart Lodge** (257 Shore Rd., 902/295-2340 or 888/662-7484, www.maritimeinns.com, mid-May-mid-Oct., $165-250 s or d) sits on a 40-hectare (99-acre) hillside overlooking the lake. Amenities include a heated outdoor pool and playground, as well as free use of bikes, a small stretch of private beach, and hiking trails. Large windows in the restaurant allow diners to take full advantage of the water views, but the food is also good, including a large buffet breakfast (daily 7am-10am, $16 pp), prepacked picnic lunches, and dinner mains (5:30pm-9pm, $21-30) such as maple whiskey salmon.

★ **Water's Edge Inn** (22 Water St., 902/295-3600 or 866/439-2528, www.thewatersedgeinn.com, June-mid-Oct., $185-195 s or d) is across the road from the lake and also within easy walking distance of downtown restaurants. Four of the six rooms have lake views and private balconies. All six are heritage-themed yet stylishly outfitted with modern touches such as air-conditioning and TV/DVD combos. A nice touch is the downstairs gallery, which is filled with regional art.

Campgrounds

Bras d'Or Lakes Campground (5 km/3.1 mi west of Baddeck on Hwy. 105, 902/295-2329, www.brasdorlakescampground.com, mid-June-Sept., campsites $40-65, cabins $67-95 s or d) has almost 100 unserviced and hookup sites. The only local campground actually on the lake, it has showers, washrooms, a launderette, wireless Internet throughout, an outdoor swimming pool, a book exchange, and free coffee each morning. You'll need to bring your own linens for the cabins, and they do share bathrooms, but for families they provide excellent value.

In the vicinity, **Adventures East Campground** (between Exits 7 and 8 of Hwy. 105, 902/295-2417 or 800/507-2228, www.adventureseast.ca, early June-mid-Oct., campsites $32.50-42, cabins $165-185 s or d) also has all the necessary amenities for an overnight or longer stay—showers, a laundry, and an outdoor pool.

INFORMATION AND SERVICES

At the east end of the main street, the **Baddeck Welcome Centre** (corner of Chebucto St. and Shore Rd., 902/295-1911, www.visitbaddeck.com, June-Sept. daily 9am-5pm) is indeed welcoming. Friendly staff will help out with finding accommodations and, as always, love handing out maps and brochures.

For emergencies, dial 911 or **Victoria County Memorial Hospital** (902/295-2112).

GETTING THERE

Halfway between the Canso Causeway and Sydney, Baddeck is 350 kilometers (215 miles) northeast from Halifax (allow at least four hours driving time).

Cabot Trail: Planning Your Drive

Looping around the northern end of Cape Breton Island by driving the 311-kilometer (190-mile) Cabot Trail is always a highlight of my travels through Nova Scotia, but understanding the route is key to making the most of your travel time. It is possible to drive the entire Cabot Trail in less than five hours—but don't. Instead, plan on immersing yourself in the destination for at least two full days. Offering a mix of historic and resort-style accommodations and dining options, Baddeck is an ideal base. Those equipped for camping will appreciate the numerous campgrounds through Cape Breton Highlands National Park, or for unequalled historical ambience, make reservations at the Keltic Lodge, which is perched high above the ocean overlooking Ingonish Beach.

Unlike every other highway in the province, the Cabot Trail does not have a specific number designation; instead it is a combination of numbered highways (also called "routes" by the locals). Nor does the Cabot Trail have an official start or finish point, although many start their journey by veering off Highway 105 at Whycocomagh, 50 kilometers (31 miles) north of the Canso Causeway, and heading north on Highway 395. From Whycocomagh, key driving distances (and minimum driving times) are:

- **Whycocomagh to Margaree Forks:** 48 kilometers (30 miles), 50 minutes. Highway 395 from Whycocomagh leads north through lush valleys and prime angling territory.

- **Margaree Forks to Chéticamp:** 39 kilometers (24 miles), 30 minutes. Heading north from Margaree Forks, the Cabot Trail follows the Margaree River to the Gulf of St. Lawrence, then hugs the ocean to the Acadian village of Chéticamp.

- **Chéticamp to Ingonish:** 110 kilometers (68 miles), 80 minutes. This section through Cape Breton Highlands National Park is the highlight of the Cabot Trail, with seemingly endless ocean views before crossing the rugged interior to emerge at the white-sand beaches of Ingonish.

- **Ingonish to St. Ann's:** 73 kilometers (45 miles), 90 minutes. It's only 73 kilometers (45 miles) from Ingonish south to St. Ann's, but the road is narrow and there are many tight corners, so allow at least 90 minutes, plus any time spent at the numerous lookouts en route.

- **St. Ann's to Baddeck:** 21 kilometers (13 miles), 30 minutes. Heading south from St. Ann's, the Cabot Trail is extremely narrow and winding. At South Haven, you reach the main island highway and can head south to Baddeck or north to Sydney.

- **Baddeck to Whycocomagh:** 25 kilometers (15.5 miles), 20 minutes. The final leg of the Cabot Trail is along Highway 105, the main route up-island to Sydney.

MARGAREE RIVER VALLEY

Eight kilometers (5 miles) west of Baddeck, the Cabot Trail branches off the Trans-Canada Highway northwest through the hills and into the valley of the Margaree River, a renowned salmon-fishing stream and the namesake of seven small communities.

The peak time for fishing is mid-June–mid-July and September–mid-October; many guides are available locally. Near North East Margaree, the **Margaree Salmon Museum** (60 E. Big Intervale Rd., 902/248-2848, mid-June–mid-Oct. daily 9am-5pm, adult $2, child $1) tells the story of the river and its fishy inhabitants.

Accommodations

Even though it's away from the ocean, the Margaree River Valley is a popular spot to get away from it all. Near the village of Margaree Valley, **Normaway Inn** (691 Egypt Rd., 902/248-2987 or 800/565-9463, www.thenormawayinn.com, $99-229 s or d) is typical of the many accommodations options. This elegantly rustic 1920s resort is nestled on 100 hectares (247 acres) in the hills. The main lodge has eight guest rooms, and the grounds hold 19 one- and two-bedroom cabins. Activities include nightly films or traditional musical entertainment, tennis, walking trails, bicycling, weekly barn dances, and fiddling contests. The dining room (daily 7:30am-9:30am and 6pm-8pm) serves dishes of Atlantic salmon, lamb, scallops, and fresh fruits and vegetables. The Normaway is about 30 kilometers (19 miles) along the Cabot Trail from Highway 105, and then 3 kilometers (1.9 miles) along Egypt Road.

On Lake O'Law, **The Lakes Resort** (902/248-2360 or 888/722-2112, www.thelakesresort.com, May-Oct., campsites $26-35, cottages $125-145 s or d) comprises treed campsites and eight two-bedroom cottages overlooking the lake. Each cottage has a bathroom, microwave, living area, and outdoor barbecue. Recreational opportunities include boating, fishing, canoeing, mini-golf, and go-karting, while the resort restaurant offers well-priced, simple cooking, including lobster dinners. To get there, turn off the Cabot Trail at North East Margaree.

Getting There

The Margaree River Valley is about 50 kilometers (31 miles) northwest of Baddeck via the southern portion of the Cabot Trail.

Chéticamp

Along the Cabot Trail, Chéticamp is an Acadian fishing village (pop. 1,000) set along a protected waterway that opens to the Gulf of St. Lawrence. Deep-sea fishing and whale-watching charter boats leave from the central Government Wharf, and the entrance to Cape Breton Highlands National Park is 5 kilometers (3.1 miles) north of town.

The village was first settled by Acadians expelled from the Nova Scotia mainland in the 18th century. Today, the weeklong **Festival de l'Escaouette,** in early August, celebrates aspects of Acadian culture with a parade, arts and crafts, and music.

SIGHTS

The first stones for **St. Pierre Catholic Church** were laid in 1893, but it took almost 20 years to finish. Its tower pierces the sky at a height of more than 50 meters (164 feet) and can be seen from far up and down the coast.

One of the major cottage industries of this area is the production of **hooked rugs,** a craft developed by Acadians centuries ago. In the late 1930s, a group of Chéticamp women formed a rug-hooking cooperative that still thrives. The Co-op Artisanale de Chéticamp gives demonstrations and displays its wares at the Acadian Museum. You can also see beautiful hooked rugs and tapestries at **Les Trois Pignons** (15584 Main St., 902/224-2642, mid-May-mid-Oct. daily 8:30am-5pm, adult $5, senior and child $4), in a striking red-roofed building at the northern end of Chéticamp. The building also houses the visitor information center.

A number of galleries and shops hereabouts also sell locally produced **folk arts**—brightly colored, whimsical carvings and paintings of fish, seabirds, fishermen, boats, or whatever strikes the artists' fancy. One kilometer (0.6 mile) north of the visitors center, the **Sunset Art Gallery** (15856 Cabot Trail, 902/224-1831, mid-May-mid-Oct. daily 9am-5:30pm) features the colorfully painted woodcarvings of William Roach.

RECREATION

Along the boardwalk opposite the Irving gas station, **Seaside Whale & Nature Cruises** (902/224-2899, adult $55, child $32.50) takes guests out on two-hour whale-watching trips two or three times daily mid-June-September.

FOOD

On a warm day, you'll love relaxing with a coffee on the outdoor tables at the **Frog Pond Café** (15856 Cabot Trail, 902/224-1831, mid-May-mid-Oct. daily 9am-5:30pm), which is affiliated with the Sunset Art Gallery. Cakes and pastries are made in-house daily, and if you're lucky local musicians will be performing.

At the north end of town, **Happy Clam Café & Grill** (15559 Main St., 902/224-3888, summer daily 7am- 9pm, $11-24) has a few outdoor tables with water views. The food is simple but tasty, ranging from burgers to lobster-stuffed chicken.

Evangeline (15150 Main St., 902/224-2044, daily 6:30am-9pm, $12-20) is a family restaurant specializing in homemade soups and meat pies.

ACCOMMODATIONS

If you're traveling on a budget, a choice of older, inexpensive motels along the main street makes Chéticamp a good base for day trips into Cape Breton Highlands National Park. Best of the bunch is **Albert's Motel** (15086 Cabot Trail, 902/224-2077, www.albertsmotelcheticamp.com, May-Oct., $80-125 s or d), which has remarkably comfortable rooms for the price.

Overlooking the ocean a few kilometers south of town, ★ **Chéticamp Outfitters Inn B&B** (13938 Cabot Trail, Point Cross, 902/224-2776, www.cheticampoutfitters.com, Apr.-mid-Dec., $100-150 s or d) is a large, modern home with six guest rooms and common areas that include a deck with sweeping ocean views. The less-expensive rooms share two bathrooms, while all rates include a full

breakfast. The hosts operate a charter fishing business, so this is a good base for anglers.

At the north end of the main street, ★ **Ocean View Chalets** (15569 Cabot Trail, 902/224-2313 or 877/743-4404, www.oceanviewchalets.com, motel rooms $135-150 s or d, cabins $150-190 s or d) has a delightful oceanfront setting, with a wide strip of green space separating the cabins from the water. Each unit has a kitchen, a separate bedroom, and a wood barbecue out front.

Behind the main street and linked to the local golf course by a short trail, **Cabot Trail Sea and Golf Chalets** (902/224-1777 or 877/244-1777, www.seagolfchalets.com, mid-May-mid-Oct., $159-299 for up to four people) is a complex of spacious and modern freestanding units, each with a bathroom, kitchen, deck, and barbecue.

INFORMATION

On the north side of town, **Chéticamp Visitor Information Centre** (15584 Main St., 902/224-2642, mid-May-mid-Oct. daily 8:30am-5pm) has information on tours, accommodations, and campgrounds. For national park information, continue north through town to the large visitors center complex.

GETTING THERE

Chéticamp is 90 kilometers (56 miles) northwest of Baddeck, just over an hour via the Cabot Trail. The trip northeast from Halifax is 400 kilometers (250 miles) and takes five hours.

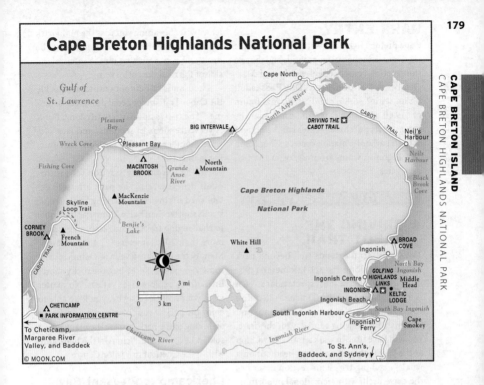

Cape Breton Highlands National Park

Protecting a swath of wilderness at the northern tip of Cape Breton Island, this national park is one of the finest in Canada. While outdoor enthusiasts are attracted by opportunities to hike and bike, anyone can enjoy the most spectacular scenery simply by driving the Cabot Trail, which spans the length of the park from Chéticamp in the west to Ingonish in the east.

THE LANDSCAPE

Heath bogs, a dry rocky plateau, and a high taiga 400 meters (1,312 feet) above sea level mark the interior of the 950-square-kilometer (367-square-mile) park. Rugged cliffs characterize the seacoast on the west side, where the mountains kneel into the Gulf of St. Lawrence, and gentler but still wildly beautiful shores define the eastern side. Nova Scotia's highest point, 532-meter (1,745-foot) White Hill, is simply a windswept hump, far from the nearest road and with no formal access trail reaching it.

Typical Acadian forest, a combination of hardwoods and conifers, carpets much of the region. Wild orchids bloom under the shade of thick spruce, balsam fir, and paper birch. The **Grand Anse River** gorge near MacKenzie Mountain is the Acadian forest's showpiece. Its terrain—with sugar maples, yellow birches, and rare alpine-arctic plants—has been designated an international biological preserve. The park is also a wildlife sanctuary for white-tailed deer, black bears, beavers, lynx, mink, red foxes, snowshoe hares, and more than 200 bird species, including eagles and red-tailed hawks.

PARK ENTRY

Cape Breton Highlands National Park is open year-round, though campgrounds and the two information centers operate only mid-May-October. A **National Parks Day Pass** (adult $7.80, senior $6.80, child $3.90, maximum of $19.60 per vehicle) is valid until 4pm the day after its purchase. Passes can be bought at both park information centers, Chéticamp and Ingonish Campgrounds, or at the two park gates.

TOP EXPERIENCE

★ DRIVING THE CABOT TRAIL

The Cabot Trail extends well beyond park boundaries along its 311-kilometer (190-mile) length, but the most spectacular stretch is undoubtedly the 110 kilometers (68 miles) through the park between Chéticamp and Ingonish. By allowing a full day for the drive, you will have time to walk a trail or two, stop at the best lookouts, and even head out on a whale-watching trip. This section describes the drive itself, with recreational opportunities discussed next. You can of course follow the Cabot Trail in either direction, but I've laid out the drive from Chéticamp to Ingonish (clockwise), meaning you pass the main park information center at the beginning of the drive and you're driving on the safer inland side of the road the entire way.

Thousands of outdoor enthusiasts tackle the Cabot Trail under pedal power each summer. The trip is not particularly long, but it is very strenuous in sections, and lack of a wide shoulder can make for some hair-raising moments.

Hiking is a major attraction for visitors of all fitness levels. The park offers 26 established hiking trails, varying from simple strolls shorter than half a kilometer (0.3 mile) to challenging treks leading to campgrounds more than 20 kilometers (12.4 miles) away. Many of the trails are level; a few climb to awesome viewpoints. Some hug the rocky shoreline; others explore river valleys. No matter what your abilities may be, you'll be able to enjoy the park at your own speed. For details on hiking in the park, browse the many books sold at Les Amis du Plein Air, the bookstore within the Chéticamp Visitor Centre.

Chéticamp to Pleasant Bay

Make your first stop inside the park at the **Chéticamp Visitor Centre** (902/224-2306, mid-May-June and Sept.-Oct. daily 9am-5pm,

The Cabot Trail is one of the world's great scenic drives.

July-Aug. daily 8:30am-7pm). Pick up a map, ask about hiking opportunities, browse the natural history displays, and hit the highway. You can pay for park entry here or at the tollgate a little farther up the road.

This is the most impressive stretch of one of the world's most spectacular drives, with the highway clinging to the shoreline and then climbing steeply along oceanfront cliffs to a viewpoint 18 kilometers (11.2 miles) north of the visitors center.

HIKING

On the light side, the self-guiding **Le Buttereau Trail** leads 1.9 kilometers (1.2 miles) to wildflowers and good bird-watching opportunities. The trailhead is just north of the park gate north of Chéticamp.

Serious backpackers gravitate to the **Fishing Cove Trail** (16 km/9.9 mi round-trip), a rugged journey to a campground and beach. You can reach the end of the trail in two hours, but allow at least three for the strenuous return trip back up to the highway. The trailhead is just south of Pleasant Bay.

WHALE-WATCHING

From Pleasant Bay, one of two whale-watching spots in Nova Scotia (the other is the Bay of Fundy), a number of operators depart daily through summer. The region boasts a high success rate when it comes to spotting pilot, humpback, and minke whales, simply because of the high numbers close to the coastline. **Captain Mark's** (902/224-1316 or 888/754-5112) is easily recognized down at the harbor by his booth shaped like a lighthouse. This company offers the option of stable ex-fishing boats (adult $50, senior $45, child $30) or rigid-hulled Zodiacs (adult $60, senior $55, child $40). The advantage with the latter is that the whales are reached much more quickly. You should book by phone in advance for July and August sailings.

Continuing Around the Cape

From Pleasant Bay, the park's northwestern corner, the highway turns inland and wraps

upward to 455-meter-high (1,493-foot-high) **French Mountain.** From this point, a level stretch barrels across a narrow ridge overlooking deeply scooped valleys. The road climbs again, this time to **MacKenzie Mountain,** at 372 meters (1,220 feet), and then switchbacks down a 10-12 percent grade. Another ascent, to **North Mountain,** formed more than a billion years ago, peaks at 445 meters (1,460 feet) on a 3-kilometer (1.9-mile) summit. The lookout opens up views of a deep gorge and the North Aspy River.

HIKING

For fit and energetic visitors, the 7-kilometer (4.3-mile), two hours one-way **Skyline Loop Trail** climbs a headland, from which the lucky can spot pilot whales; along the way, look for bald eagles, deer, and bears. The trail begins where the Cabot Trail heads inland at French Mountain.

On overcast or wet days, the much easier **Benjie's Lake Trail** provides an ideal break from driving. From a trailhead 6 kilometers (3.7 miles) east of the start of the Skyline Loop Trail, this easy walk takes about 30 minutes each way.

Cape North and Vicinity

The northernmost point on the Cabot Trail is Cape North, the name of a small service town (as well as a geographical feature to the north). Here a spur road leads 22 kilometers (13.7 miles) north to Meat Cove. Although outside the park, this road traverses complete wilderness before reaching the open ocean at St. Lawrence Bay. En route, **Cabot's Landing Provincial Park,** the supposed landing site of English explorer John Cabot, offers a sandy beach on Aspy Bay (good for clam digging) and a picnic area, and marks the starting point for hikes up 442-meter-high (1,450-foot-high) Sugar Loaf Mountain.

The East Coast to Ingonish

From Cape North, it's 45 kilometers (28 miles) east and then south to the resort town of Ingonish. Aside from tucking into a seafood feast at Neil's Harbour, you should make time for a stop at **Black Brook Cove.** Backed by a short stretch of beach, the cove is an extremely popular spot for picnicking and swimming. To escape the summertime crowd, walk to the north end of the beach and follow the Jack Pine Loop through open coastal forest.

ACCOMMODATIONS AND CAMPING

Since it's a national park, there are no hotel accommodations within the park boundary. Instead, visitors stay at Chéticamp for its Acadian heritage, at Ingonish for its beaches and golfing, or at one of the following choices in between the two.

Under $50

HI-Cabot Trail Hostel (23349 Cabot Trail, 902/224-1976, www.cabottrailhostel.com, dorm $26, $60 s or d) is within walking distance of Pleasant Bay, 38 kilometers (24 miles) north of Chéticamp on the park's western side. The facility is small but friendly and comfortable, with 18 dorm beds in two rooms and an adjacent bunkhouse. Guests have use of communal washrooms, two kitchens, a deck with a barbecue, and wireless Internet access.

$100-150

Just more than 40 kilometers (25 miles) north of Chéticamp, the Cabot Trail exits the park for a short distance at Pleasant Bay. Here, the distinctively salmon-pink **Midtrail Motel & Inn** (23475 Cabot Trail, 902/224-2529 or 800/215-0411, mid-May-Oct., $115-135 s or d) offers 20 bright but basic motel rooms, some with ocean views, as well as a family-friendly seafood restaurant, a launderette, and a couple of Adirondack chairs perched high above the motel on a knob of land offering sweeping ocean views.

Over $150

Set on 25 hectares (62 acres) of oceanfront property, **Markland Beach Cottages** (802 Dingwall Rd., Dingwall, 902/383-2246, www.themarkland.com, May-mid-Oct., $189-319

s or d) is 52 kilometers (32 miles) north of Ingonish (signposted off the Cabot Trail between Cape North and South Harbour). Although it is a resort, the emphasis is on the outdoors, with most guests spending their time on the adjacent beach or lazing around the outdoor pool. The cottages (from $219 s or d) are an excellent value. The resort restaurant features the freshest of fresh seafood combined with seasonal produce such as fiddleheads and wild mint.

Campgrounds

Cape Breton Highlands National Park is the most popular camping destination in Nova Scotia. Parks Canada operates six auto-accessible campgrounds within the park. Sites at three of those listed below—Chéticamp, Corney Brook, and Broad Cove—can be reserved through the **Parks Canada Campground Reservation Service** (519/826-5391 or 877/737-3783, www.pccamping.ca) for $12 per reservation beginning in January every year. If you're traveling in the height of summer and require hookups, this booking system is highly recommended.

Chéticamp Campground (5 km/3.1 mi north of Chéticamp, mid-May-late Oct.) is behind the main park visitors center. Amenities include showers, flush toilets, kitchen shelters, playgrounds, and an outdoor theater hosting a summer interpretive program. Only some sites have fire pits. Tent sites are $25.50 per night, serviced sites $38.20. Continue north from the park gate for 10 kilometers (6.2 miles) to ★ **Corney Brook Campground** (mid-May-early Oct., $23.50), which is not much more than a parking lot with 20 designated sites, but incredible ocean views more than make up for a lack of facilities. Beyond Pleasant Bay, the 10 sites at **MacIntosh Brook Campground** (mid-May-early Oct., $21.50) fill quickly. Ten kilometers (6.2 miles) farther east is **Big Intervale Campground** (mid-May-early Oct., $18), also with 10 sites. Neither of these two campgrounds has drinking water. With over 200 sites, **Broad Cove Campground** (mid-May-late Oct., $25.50), on the ocean just north of Ingonish, is the park's largest campground. Campers have use of showers, flush toilets, kitchen shelters, playgrounds, and an outdoor theater. **Ingonish Beach Campground** (mid-May-late Oct., $25.50) is within a finger of the park that extends to the ocean along the Ingonish coastline. Although it's close to the resort town of Ingonish, the wooded setting is quiet and private and within walking distance of a sandy beach with safe swimming. It has showers, flush toilets, and kitchen shelters.

INFORMATION

Turn right as soon as you cross into the park north of Chéticamp for the excellent **Chéticamp Visitor Centre** (902/224-2306, mid-May-June and Sept.-Oct. daily 9am-5pm, July-Aug. daily 8:30am-7pm). It features natural-history exhibits, weather reports, an activities schedule, and helpful staff.

Parks Canada also operates a smaller information center in Ingonish (mid-May-June and Sept.-Oct. daily 9am-5pm, July-Aug. daily 8:30am-7pm) for those entering the park from the east. It's located along the Cabot Trail beside Freshwater Lake.

Ingonish and Vicinity

Ingonish (pop. 1,100), 110 kilometers (68 miles) east of Chéticamp and 100 kilometers (62 miles) north of Baddeck, is a busy resort center at the eastern entrance to Cape Breton Highlands National Park. The town is a lot more than somewhere simply to rest your head: It is fringed by beautiful beaches, has one of Canada's premier golf courses, and offers a delightful choice of seafood restaurants. If you are allowing yourself some rest time on your Nova Scotia travels, this is the place to book two or more nights in the same accommodation.

SIGHTS AND RECREATION

Ingonish has no official attractions as such. Instead, beach lovers gather on **Ingonish Beach,** where a lifeguard watches over swimmers splashing around in the shallow water that reaches enjoyable temperatures July-August.

Drag yourself away from one of Canada's finest beaches and you'll find the **Freshwater Lake Loop,** a 2-kilometer (1.2-mile) circuit that encircles a shallow lake where beavers can often be seen hard at work in the evening. The trailhead is the parking lot at Ingonish Beach.

Even if you're not a guest at the **Keltic**

Lodge, the grounds are a pleasant place for a stroll. Beyond the end of the lodge access road, a walking trail leads 2 kilometers (1.2 miles) to the end of Middle Head Peninsula.

★ Highlands Links

Highlands Links (3 km/1.9 mi north of Ingonish Beach, 902/285-2600 or 800/441-1118) is generally regarded as one of the world's top 100 golf courses, and relative to other courses of similar reputation, the greens fees are a steal—$130 in high season, with twilight rates from just $70. Power carts are an additional $35. The course, which opened in 1939, was designed by Stanley Thompson, the same architect commissioned to design famous courses in Banff and Jasper National Parks.

FOOD

Occupying a weathered wooden building on the high headland at Neil's Harbour is the ★ **Chowder House** (90 Lighthouse Rd., 902/336-2463, June-Sept. Tues.-Sun. noon-7:45pm, $12-22). Order at the inside window and wait for your number to be called. Then tuck into creamy clam chowder ($6), fish-and-chips ($10), a lobster burger ($12), or a full crab ($22). Dollar for dollar, you're doing well if you find better value than the food at this always-busy establishment.

Keltic Lodge

The **Keltic Lodge** (Middle Head Peninsula, 902/285-2880) is home to two very different restaurants. Along the access road is the **Atlantic Restaurant** (mid-May-mid-Oct. daily 11am-9pm, $16-34), a big family-style restaurant with seafood for all tastes and budgets: beer-battered fish-and-chips, grilled salmon, and lobster. An excellent add-on is the salad bar ($12). The tables along the east side have stunning ocean views. The smart-casual **Purple Thistle Dining Room** (late May-mid-Oct. daily 7am-10am and 6pm-9pm) has one of Nova Scotia's finest reputations, especially in seafood. Meals are four courses (about $70 per person) rather than à la carte, with an emphasis on lobster in varied creations and other seafood. If you're tooling along Cabot Trail and hope to stop here for dinner, reservations are very wise.

ACCOMMODATIONS

Accommodations are spread along the Ingonish coastline, but demand is high in July and August, so book well ahead. Also note the given open dates, as very few places are open year-round.

$100-150

Sea Breeze Cottages and Motel (8 km/5 mi north of the east park gate, 902/285-2879 or 888/743-4443, www.seabreezecottagesandmotel.com, mid-Apr.-mid-Dec.) overlooks the ocean and boasts a playground that children will love. Accommodations options include basic motel rooms ($115 s or d) or cottages scattered through a forested area ($135-185 s or d).

Open year-round, **Ingonish Chalets** (36784 Cabot Trail, Ingonish Beach, 902/285-2008 or 888/505-0552, www.ingonishchalets.com, $125-205 s or d) has access to the beach and hiking trails. Nine two-bedroom log chalets are $240 for up to four guests, while five motel-style rooms cost $150 s or d. The rooms

are furnished in a very woodsy way, with pine paneling extending from the handcrafted furniture to the wall linings. These units also come with basic cooking facilities—microwave, kettle, and so on.

It would be difficult to claim boredom at ★ **Glenghorm Beach Resort** (36743 Cabot Trail, Ingonish, 902/285-2049 or 855/285-4631, www.glenghorm.net, May-Oct., $155-410 s or d), a sprawling complex that extends from the Cabot Trail to a long arc of sandy beach. Things to do include walking along the beach, relaxing around the outdoor pool, renting kayaks and paddling through calm offshore waters, or working out in the fitness room. There are also lawn games, tennis, volleyball, and bike rentals. At the end of the day, you can relax with a glass of wine in one of the shoreline Adirondack chairs or try a Nova Scotian brew at the resort pub. Accommodations options are motel rooms up by the highway, older-style cottages (some right by the ocean), and my favorite rooms in all of Cape Breton Island—casual but stylish kitchen-equipped suites with private balconies.

Over $200

The Cabot Trail has its devoted fans, and so does the **Keltic Lodge** (902/285-2880 or 800/565-0444, www.kelticlodge.ca, mid-May-mid-Oct., from $275 s or d), on Middle Head Peninsula. The access lane from the Cabot Trail meanders through thick stands of white birches and finishes at the lodge. The long, low, wood-sided lodge—painted bright white and topped with a bright red roof—is as picturesque as a lord's manor in the Highlands of Scotland. The main lodge has 32 rustic rooms off a comfortable lobby that is furnished with overstuffed chairs and sofas arranged before a massive stone fireplace. Another 40 rooms are in the adjacent newer White Birch Inn. In addition, nine cottages with suite-style layouts (nice for families) are scattered across the grounds. Well-marked hiking trails meander through the adjacent national park woodlands and ribbon the coastal peninsula. An outdoor pool, tennis courts, and a spa facility are also available.

Affiliated with one of the region's finest restaurants, ★ **Seascape Coastal Retreat** (36083 Cabot Trail, Ingonish, 902/285-3003 or 866/385-3003, www.seascapecoastalretreat.com, Apr.-Oct., $279 s or d) is suited to couples looking for a quiet getaway in romantic surroundings. Within the walls of this very private resort are 10 wooden cottages, each air-conditioned and with a private deck overlooking the ocean and a separate bedroom. Bathrobes, jetted tubs, and TV/DVD combos add to the appeal. Outside, paths lead through landscaped gardens to an herb garden and courtyard where guests gather in the evening. Rates include use of bikes and kayaks and a full breakfast in a smart, stylish dining room overlooking the ocean.

GETTING THERE

Ingonish lies on the Cabot Trail 110 kilometers (68 miles) east of Chéticamp, a 1.5-hour drive, and 100 kilometers (62 miles) north of Baddeck, 1.5 hours. To get to Ingonish from Halifax, it's 440 kilometers (275 miles) northeast, a five-hour drive.

SOUTH FROM INGONISH

South of Ingonish Beach, the Cabot Trail descends hairpin turns. Stop at 366-meter-high (1,201-foot-high) **Cape Smokey** for a picnic or hiking along the cliff top, which has wonderful views. The steep and twisting road finishes in a coastal glide with views of the offshore Bird Islands. Lying off the northwest side of the cape at the mouth of St. Ann's Bay, these two islands are the nesting site of a multitude of seabird species.

ST. ANN'S

During the 1850s, about 900 of St. Ann's residents, dissatisfied with Cape Breton, sailed away to Australia and eventually settled in New Zealand, where their descendants today make up a good part of the Scottish population. Despite this loss of nearly half its population, St. Ann's, 73 kilometers (45 miles) south of Ingonish and 30 kilometers (19 miles) north of Baddeck, is today the center of Cape Breton's Gaelic culture.

A good place to eat in this area is the **Lobster Galley** (51943 Cabot Trail, 902/295-3100, daily 9am-8pm, $13-30), at the head of St. Ann's Harbour. Fish cakes and Caesar salad are just $14, a filled lobster roll $18, or try the full lobster dinner for $30.

Gaelic College of Celtic Arts and Crafts

★ Gaelic College of Celtic Arts and Crafts

The only institution of its kind in North America, the **Gaelic College of Celtic Arts and Crafts** (51779 Cabot Trail, 902/295-3411) was established in 1938. Programs include Highland dancing, fiddling, piping, Gaelic language, weaving, and other subjects. The summer session attracts Gaelophiles from around the world. The **Great Hall of the Clans** (July-Aug. daily 9am-5pm, free), on the campus, examines the course of Scottish culture and history, including the migrations that brought Highlanders to Cape Breton. Activities include weaving and instrument-making demonstrations, as well as music and dance performances (July-Aug. Mon.-Fri.). The campus gift shop sells a predictable collection of kilts and tartans.

★ Celtic Colours International Festival

The popular **Celtic Colours International Festival** (902/567-3000 or 888/355-7744, www.celtic-colours.com) takes place the second full week of October. It celebrates Cape Breton's Gaelic heritage through concerts held at venues around the island, but the Gaelic College of Celtic Arts and Crafts is a focal point, especially for its nightly Festival Club, where musicians get together for an unofficial jam after performing elsewhere. The festival proper features six or seven concerts nightly, usually in small town halls, with visitors enjoying the brilliant colors of fall as they travel from venue to venue.

Getting There

St. Ann's is 73 kilometers (45 miles), over an hour's drive, south of Ingonish and 30 kilometers (19 miles) north of Baddeck, 25 minutes. To get to St. Ann's from Halifax, it's 400 kilometers (250 miles) northeast, a five-hour drive.

The Northeast

SYDNEY

Cape Breton Island's only city is Sydney (pop. 31,000), set around a large harbor on the island's northeast corner. In the early 1800s, it was the capital of the colony of Cape Breton. At the turn of the 20th century the Sydney area boomed, ranking as one of Canada's major steel production centers.

Sights

Historic buildings constructed of stone quarried at nearby Louisbourg dot the streets north of downtown. One of these, the 1828 **St. Patrick's Church Museum** (87 Esplanade, July-Aug. Tues.-Sat. 9am-5pm, donation), is Cape Breton's oldest Roman Catholic sanctuary. **Cossit House** (75 Charlotte St., 902/539-7973, mid-June-Oct. Mon.-Sat. 9am-4pm, adult $2, senior and child $1) is almost as old as Sydney itself. The 1787 manse has been restored to its original condition.

Food

The best coffee in town is poured at **Dillan's at Wentworth** (697 George St., 902/563-7590, Mon.-Fri. 7am-7pm, Sat. 9am-7pm, Sun. 11am-5pm, lunches $7-10), a modern café with the usual range of drink choices as well as a changing menu of lunches such as wraps and sandwiches using top-notch ingredients. It's located in a converted residence on the south side of downtown.

★ **Trio** (Cambridge Suites Hotel, 380 Esplanade, 902/563-7009, daily 6:30am-10am and 5pm-10pm, $16-28) stands out as the best place in town for a healthy, well-priced meal in contemporary surroundings. Breakfast is served buffet-style, while in the evening tasty

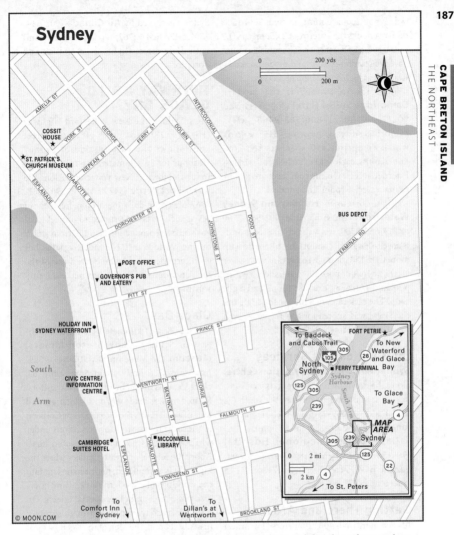

Sydney

temptations include blackened haddock, an East Coast hot pot, and beef tenderloin.

Away from the hotel dining scene, **Governor's Pub & Eatery** (233 Esplanade, 902/562-7646, daily 11am-11pm, $14-30) has two bustling patios, a pub-style room, and a restaurant. The food is surprisingly good, with seafood and steak the specialties. You could start with maple mandarin salad and then choose from mains such as beer-battered

fish-and-chips with hand-cut fries or slow-cooked pork back ribs.

Accommodations

Motel rooms in Sydney are generally more expensive than they should be. Use the websites to search out package rates or wait until the last minute and start calling around for deals.

Comfort Inn Sydney (368 Kings Rd., 902/562-0200, www.

sydneynovascotiacomfortinn.com, $130-150 s or d) overlooks the waterfront 2 kilometers (1.2 miles) south of downtown. The midsize rooms have contemporary style and modern necessities such as high-speed Internet access.

My pick in Sydney is the modern **Cambridge Suites Hotel** (380 Esplanade, 902/562-6500 or 800/565-9466, www.cambridgesuitessydney.com, $155 s or d), which comprises 150 spacious self-contained units, each with a kitchen and wireless Internet access. On the roof level are a pool, sauna, exercise room, and sundeck.

Right downtown, **Holiday Inn Sydney Waterfront** (300 Esplanade, 902/562-7500 or 877/660-8550, www.ihg.com, $160 s or d) is a well-designed, comfortable high-rise with more than 150 rooms, a restaurant with water views, an indoor pool and waterslide, a whirlpool and sauna, an exercise room, and a gift shop. The rack rates of $200 are too high, but the $150 I was quoted for a water-view room in early June seemed about right.

Information and Services

Sydney Port Visitor Information Centre, along the downtown waterfront, is well signposted as you enter town from the south (74 Esplanade, 902/539-9876, www.cbisland.com, June-mid-Oct. daily 8:30am-4:30pm).

Cape Breton Regional Hospital (902/567-8000) is at 1482 George Street. For the **RCMP,** call 902/564-7171, or 911 in emergencies.

Getting There and Around

It's just more than 400 kilometers (250 miles) between Halifax and Sydney—easily driven in under five hours.

The main reason to fly in would be the ease of getting to Cape Breton Highlands National Park, a two-hour drive northeast of town. **Sydney Airport** (YQY, 280 Silver Dart Way, 902/564-7720, http://sydneyairport.ca) is 14 kilometers (8.7 miles) northeast of the city center. A taxi to town costs $25, or rent a car through Avis, Budget, Hertz, or National, all of which have rental desks at the airport.

Sydney is served by **Air Canada** (902/539-7501 or 888/247-2262, www.aircanada.com) with daily direct flights from Halifax and Toronto.

HIGHWAY 28 TO GLACE BAY

From Sydney, the New Waterford Highway (Highway 28) spurs north off Prince Street and follows the eastern side of Sydney Harbour for 26 kilometers (16 miles) to the industrial town of New Waterford. Along the way is **Fort Petrie** (3479 Hwy. 28, 902/862-8367, May-Nov. daily 10am-6pm, free), one of seven such forts constructed to protect local coal and steel production facilities from attack during World War II. Not much remains, but an interpretive display tells the story of the fort, and views of the harbor make the stop worthwhile.

Glace Bay

At Glace Bay, 21 kilometers (13 miles) northeast of Sydney, **Cape Breton Miners' Museum** (17 Museum St., 902/849-4522, June-mid-Oct. daily 10am-6pm, adult $7, child $5.50) is the main attraction for visitors. Retired miners guide you on an underground tour of a real mine, the Ocean Deeps Colliery, to show the rough working conditions under which workers manually extracted coal. Above the mine is an exhibit gallery where the highlight is a simulated, multimedia trip into the workings of a modern mine, using laserdisc projection and other special effects. On selected Tuesday evenings through summer (usually at 8pm), the Men of the Deeps, a local singing group composed of miners dressed in their coveralls, gives concerts at the museum. Also in the main building is **Miners' Village Restaurant** (May-Sept. daily 11am-8pm), where the food is both tasty and well priced.

LOUISBOURG

This small fishing town (pop. 1,200), 32 kilometers (20 miles) southeast of Sydney, is famous for its historic links to France and for its reconstruction of an entire walled town.

Louisbourg may be well off the main Baddeck-Cape Breton Highlands National Park itinerary of many visitors, but it gets a steady flow of visitors through summer and has limited accommodations, so plan accordingly.

★ Fortress of Louisbourg National Historic Site

The **Fortress of Louisbourg National Historic Site** (259 Park Service Rd., 902/733-3552, mid-May-Oct. daily 9:30am-5pm, adult $17.60, senior $15, child $8.80) is a fantastic re-creation of the original French fort. Parks Canada has reconstructed 50 of the original 80 buildings, right down to the last window, nail, and shingle, based on historical records.

Louisbourg reveals itself slowly. The seaport covers 10 hectares (24.7 acres), and you can spend the better part of a day exploring. From the Visitor Reception Centre, it's a brief bus ride across fields and marsh to the back of the fortress. The reconstructed fortress and town open a window on New France; they are designed to reflect Louisbourg on a spring day in 1744, the year preceding England's first attack, when the seaport hummed with activity. The houses, fortifications, ramparts, and other structures—as authentically 18th-century French as anything you will find in France—were conceived as a statement of grandeur and power in the New World. The fancy houses lining cobbled lanes belonged to the elite, who ate sumptuous meals on fine china and drank the finest French wines. The simpler houses are the rustic cottages of the working class. Guides and reenactors—portraying soldiers, merchants, workers, and craftspeople—are on hand to answer questions and demonstrate military exercises, blacksmithing, lace making, and other skills. The historical feel flows through to three dining rooms. Hungry visitors can feast on a slice of heavy bread and a chunk of cheese at the **King's Bakery;** at **Hotel de la Marine** servers dish up simple fare in big wooden bowls; while over in **Grandchamps Inn** the "wealthy" can dine on exquisite European cuisine served up on the finest china.

The site is open and fully staffed June-mid-October. In May and through the last two weeks of October, access is by guided tour only (departs daily 10am and 2pm). There are no services during these periods, and so admission is reduced (adult $7.50, senior $6.25, child $4.25). The grounds are closed the rest of the year.

Be prepared for walking, and bring a sweater or jacket in case of breezy or wet

Fortress of Louisbourg National Historic Site

weather. Louisbourg's reconstructed buildings stretch from the bus stop to the harbor. Remaining ruins lying beyond the re-creation are marked by trails. You can wander on your own or join a tour—usually 10am and 2pm for English tours and 1pm for the French-language tour.

Food

Wander Louisbourg's main street and you'll find numerous dining choices. My favorite is ★ **Grubstake Restaurant** (7499 Main St., 902/733-2308, daily noon-9pm, $13-25), which has been open since the 1970s but offers an up-to-date menu of seafood, with such offerings as linguine topped with shrimp, scallops, haddock, and salmon in a cream sauce. If you want to take a break from seafood, this is the place to do so—the meatloaf with mashed potatoes and vegetables is delicious.

Accommodations and Camping

Accommodations in Louisbourg are limited, so it's wise to make reservations.

Overlooking the harbor is **Stacey House** (7438 Main St., 902/733-2317 or 866/924-2242, www.thestaceyhouse.com, June-mid-Oct., $75-105 s or d). It offers four rooms, two with private baths, and an antiques-filled parlor, all within walking distance of town. Rates include a cooked breakfast.

Perfectly situated on a headland with sweeping views of the fortress, ★ **Point of View Suites** (15 Commercial St., 902/733-2080 or 888/374-8439, www.louisbourgpointofview.com, mid-May-Oct., $125-199 s or d) is Louisbourg's finest accommodation. The sun-filled suites (some with ocean views) and much larger apartments look as if they are straight out of a glossy architectural magazine with their crisp color schemes, hardwood floors, and sliding doors that open to balconies with ocean views. At the edge of the property is a private beach, and each evening at 6pm guests are invited to a Beggar's Banquet in the adjacent restaurant.

Riverdale RV Park (9 Riverdale St., 902/733-2531, mid-May-mid-Oct., campsites $27-35, cottages $110) enjoys a quiet setting within walking distance of the fort. Amenities include showers, 30-amp hookups, and a laundry.

The wilderness camping nearest to Louisbourg is at **Mira River Provincial Park** (mid-June-early Sept., $29), 17 kilometers (10.6 miles) before town off Highway 22. The park has showers, fire pits and firewood sales, and canoe rentals. Sites are scattered through the forest or along the river.

Getting There

Louisbourg is 30 kilometers (19 miles) southeast of Sydney, a 25-minute drive along Highway 22. It's 440 kilometers (275 miles) northeast from Halifax.

New Brunswick

Saint John and the Fundy Coast

Imagine the scene: A pervasive unearthly stillness. Seabirds wheel and dart across the horizon. Suddenly, the birds cry out in a chorus as the incoming tide approaches. The tidal surge, which began halfway around the world in the southern Indian Ocean, quietly and relentlessly pours into the Fundy's mouth, creating the highest tides on the planet. Fishing boats are lifted from the muddy seafloor, and whales in pursuit of silvery herring hurry along the summertime currents, their mammoth hulks buoyed by the 100 billion tons of seawater that gush into the long bay between New Brunswick and Nova Scotia.

The cycle from low to high tide takes a mere six hours. The tide peaks, in places high enough to swamp a four-story building, and

Highlights

Look for ★ to find recommended sights, activities, dining, and lodging.

★ **Prince William and Germain Streets:** Downtown Saint John oozes history at every corner, but nowhere is it as concentrated as along these two streets (page 198).

★ **Irving Nature Park:** Nature is left to its own devices within this oceanfront park, but what makes it remarkable is its vicinity to a major shipping port (page 203).

★ **St. Andrews National Historic District:** Yes, wandering along the main street of St. Andrews seems to be all about shopping and dining, but there is a wealth of history behind the bright facades (page 211).

★ **Kingsbrae Garden:** Blending formal gardens with trails through Acadian coastal forest, Kingsbrae will soothe your senses (page 212).

★ **Grand Manan Island:** Catch the ferry over to this Bay of Fundy island to watch the abundance of seabirds that gather each spring and fall (page 218).

★ **Fundy National Park:** Protecting a huge swath of coastline, this park offers plenty of chances to get back to nature—or, if you prefer, to go golfing and feast on fresh seafood (page 221).

★ **Hopewell Rocks:** This attraction, where you can "walk on the ocean floor," is a wonderful natural phenomenon helped along by the massive Fundy tides (page 224).

Saint John and the Fundy Coast

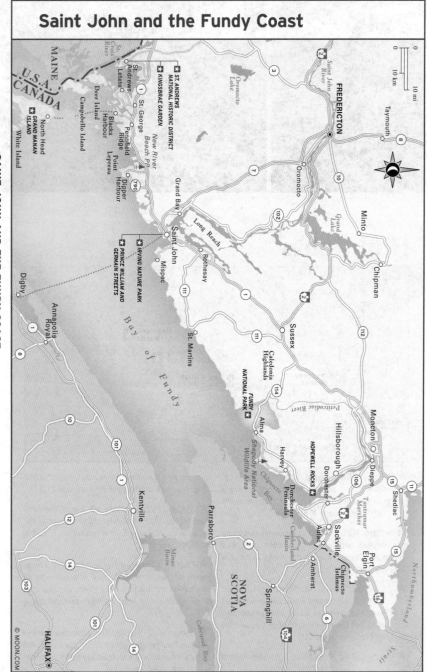

MAINE
U.S.A.
CANADA

St. Croix River
Chamcook

St. Andrews
Letete
St. George
★ ST. ANDREWS NATIONAL HISTORIC DISTRICT
★ KINGSBRAE GARDEN

Deer Island
Campobello Island
North Head
★ GRAND MANAN ISLAND
White Island
Blacks Harbour
Pennfield Ridge
Point Lepreau
Dipper Harbour

New River Beach P.P.
Grand Bay

Saint John
★ PRINCE WILLIAM AND GERMAIN STREETS
★ IRVING NATURE PARK

Mispec
Rothesay
Long Reach

FREDERICTON
Taymouth
Oromocto Lake
Oromocto
Minto
Chipman
Grand Lake

Bay of Fundy

Digby
Annapolis Royal
Kentville
Parrsboro
St. Martins
Sussex
Caledonia Highlands
FUNDY NATIONAL PARK ★
Alma
Harvey
Shepody National Wildlife Area
Chignecto Bay
Cumberland Basin
HOPEWELL ROCKS ★
Hillsborough
Dorchester
Dorchester Peninsula
Petitcodiac River
Moncton
Dieppe
Shediac
Aulac
Sackville
Tantramar Marshes
Port Elgin
Chignecto Isthmus
Northumberland Strait

NOVA SCOTIA
Springhill
Amherst
Minas Basin
Cobequid Bay
HALIFAX

0   10 mi
0   10 km

© MOON.COM

then begins to retreat. As the sea level drops, coastal peninsulas and rocky islets emerge from the froth, veiled in seaweed. The seafloor reappears, shiny as shellac and littered with sea urchins, periwinkles, and shells. Where no one walked just hours ago, local children run and skip on the beaches, pausing to retrieve tidal treasures. New Brunswickers take the Fundy tides for granted. For visitors, it's an astounding show.

The Fundy Coast is a paradox: It's at once the most- and least-developed part of the province. Saint John—the province's largest city and major port—sits at the midpoint. To either side, the coastline is remotely settled and wonderfully wild. The region is best considered as two distinct areas, with Saint John interposed between them. The Lower Fundy, situated at the bay's southwestern end, includes St. Andrews—the province's definitive resort town on sheltered Passamaquoddy Bay—and the Fundy Isles, the archipelago (made up of Grand Manan, Deer, Campobello, and White Islands) that dangles into the sea alongside Maine's northernmost coast. The Upper Fundy area, situated at the coast's northeastern end, takes in Fundy National Park and several coastal bird sanctuaries.

PLANNING YOUR TIME

New Brunswick's 250-kilometer-long (155-mile-long) Fundy coastline is central to all of mainland Atlantic Canada, with the port city of Saint John roughly halfway between the U.S. border and the head of the bay. This is the place to explore historic **Prince William and Germain Streets,** get a taste of nature at **Irving Nature Park,** and take advantage of fine lodgings and restaurants. Everywhere else is within day-tripping distance of Saint John, but then you'd miss out on soaking up the old-fashioned resort atmosphere of **St. Andrews.** So plan on spending at least one night there, which will also allow time to wander through the **St. Andrews National Historic District** and visit **Kingsbrae Garden.** If you're driving up through Maine to Atlantic Canada, St. Andrews makes an ideal first stop. If you've rented a vehicle in Halifax, St. Andrews marks your turnaround point on a loop that incorporates a ferry trip from Digby to Saint John. Either way, on the north side of Saint John, plan on stops at **Fundy National Park** and **Hopewell Rocks** as you follow the Fundy Coast north to Moncton. By virtue of their location, the Fundy Isles require some extra time to reach, especially **Grand Manan Island,** but nature lovers will be rewarded with a magnificent display of birds, whales, and seals.

Saint John and Vicinity

Saint John (pop. 70,000), 110 kilometers (68 miles) south of Fredericton and 155 kilometers (96 miles) southwest of Moncton, ranks as New Brunswick's largest city, its major port, and its principal industrial center. It is also Canada's largest city in terms of area, sprawling across 321 square kilometers (124 square miles). The city perches on steep hills, laid out southwest to northeast across two peninsulas

that almost mesh, like two hands about to meet in a handshake. The setting is among Atlantic Canada's most unusual—Saint John looks east across the spacious Saint John Harbour to the Bay of Fundy and is backed on the west by the confluence of the Saint John River and Kennebecasis Bay.

. Saint John began as a collection of small Loyalist settlements. Today these settlements

Previous: Grand Manan Island; St. Andrews Harbour; a great blue heron; Swallowtail Lighthouse on Grand Manan Island.

maintain their identities in the form of neighborhoods within greater Saint John. This accounts for numerous street-name duplications, a confusing fact of life when sightseeing across the oddly laid-out city. One Charlotte Street, for example, runs through the city's historic part, while another Charlotte Street is found in western Saint John. It helps to keep a map handy, or to just ask: The locals are sympathetic to the visitor's confusion.

Locals and visitors alike take full advantage of a revitalized waterfront precinct that includes the provincial museum, dining and shopping in Market Square, live outdoor entertainment, and the 2.3-kilometer (1.4-mile) Harbour Passage, a walking and biking trail that rims the waterfront.

HISTORY

Saint John's history as an Anglo settlement began with 14,000 Loyalists, who arrived by ship in 1783. The refugees quickly settled the fledgling town and spread out to found Carleton west of the harbor and Parrtown to the east. The city was incorporated in 1785, making it Canada's oldest. The city's next great wave of immigrants brought the Irish, who were fleeing poverty and persecution at home. Saint John's reputation as Canada's

most Irish city began with a trickle of Irish in 1815; before the wave subsided in 1850, the city's 150,000 Irish outnumbered the Loyalists, and Saint John's religious complexion changed from Protestant to Roman Catholic.

Despite its early social woes, Saint John strode ahead economically, and by the 1850s was ranked third worldwide as a wooden ship builder. After steel-hulled steam vessels began to replace the great sailing ships in the 1860s, the city plunged into a decline, which was deepened by the Great Fire of 1877. Undaunted, Saint John replaced the damage with more elaborate, sturdier brick and stone buildings designed in the ornate Victorian style, which remain in place to this day.

ORIENTATION

On a map, Saint John looks large and somewhat unmanageable, almost intimidating. Forget about Saint John's unusual shape and the soaring bridges that connect the city's parts. Instead, concentrate on the main highways: The closely aligned Highway 1 and Highway 100, which parallel each other in most parts, are often the best routes for getting from one section of the city to another.

Tackle Saint John by areas. Most sightseeing

Saint John skyline

Saint John

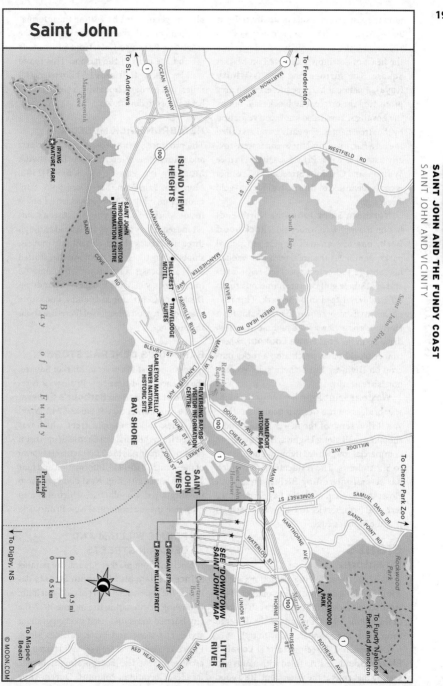

To St. Andrews

To Fredericton

OCEAN WESTWAY

MARITION BYPASS

Managuagomish Cove

IRVING NATURE PARK

WESTFIELD RD

ISLAND VIEW HEIGHTS

BAY ST

South Bay

Saint John River

SAINT JOHN THROUGHWAY VISITOR INFORMATION CENTRE

MANAWAGONISH AVE

MANCHESTER

DEVER RD

GREEN HEAD RD

HILLCREST MOTEL

FAIRVILLE BLVD

MAIN ST W

TRAVELODGE SUITES

B a y   o f   F u n d y

BLEURY ST

LANCASTER AVE

Reversing Rapids

CARLETON MARTELLO TOWER NATIONAL HISTORIC SITE

BAY SHORE

DUKE ST W

MARKET PL

REVERSING RAPIDS VISITOR INFORMATION CENTRE

DOUGLAS AVE

CHESLEY DR

HOMEPORT HISTORIC B&B

MAIN ST

MILLIDGE AVE

To Cherry Park Zoo

Partridge Island

SAINT JOHN WEST

MARKET ST

Saint John Harbour

SAMUEL DAVIS DR

SOMERSET ST

HAWTHORNE AVE

SANDY POINT RD

Rockwood Park

To Digby, NS

PRINCE WILLIAM STREET

GERMAN STREET

WATERLOO ST

SEE "DOWNTOWN SAINT JOHN" MAP

UNION ST

THORNE AVE

Marsh Creek

ROCKWOOD PARK

To Fundy National Park and Moncton

0   0.5 mi

0   0.5 km

N

Courtenay Bay

BAYSIDE DR

LITTLE RIVER

RED HEAD RD

RUSSELL ST

ROTHESAY AVE

To Mispec Beach

© MOON.COM

is on the eastern peninsula in **uptown Saint John.** Access is easiest from Highway 1's Exits 121 or 125; the access roads peel down into the heart of downtown, centered on Market Square. The surrounding area is **Trinity Royal,** a national heritage preservation area protecting the original 20 blocks laid out by the Loyalists. You'll also know you've arrived by the street names: The early Loyalists called the area Parrtown, and the avenues were royally named as King, Princess, Queen, Prince William, and Charlotte Streets. This precinct is easily identified by distinctive blue and gold street signs.

Northern Saint John (the North End) lies on the highways' other side. **Rockwood Park,** one of Canada's largest municipal parks, dominates the area, with 870 wooded hectares (2,150 acres) speckled with lakes and an 18-hole golf course; numerous roads off Highway 1 feed into the park. This part of the city is also known to offer Saint John Harbour's best views; for a sublime overview, drive up to the **Fort Howe Lookout,** where timber blockhouses perch atop a rocky outcrop on Highway 1's northern side. Worthy hotels are nearby.

Western Saint John lies across the highway bridges on the western peninsula. Here you'll find some of the newer motels and a shopping mall along Highway 100, the area's commercial row, while Highway 1 heads west to St. Andrews. The residential area, which has several interesting B&Bs, spreads out closer to the water, while the Bay Ferries ferry terminal (with service to Digby, Nova Scotia) is at the harbor's edge.

SIGHTS
Downtown
Hills aside, the following attractions are all within walking distance of one another. If the steep streets look daunting, flag a cab in front of the Hilton Saint John and ask the driver to drop you at King's Square ($5 with tip).

Downtown sightseeing starts at **Loyalist Plaza,** an outdoor strip filled with plants and seating that ends at the waterfront. It's a good place to get oriented by visiting the information center (in Market Square) and taking the **Harbour Passage** waterfront promenade around the head of the harbor. This paved walking/biking trail leads 2.3 kilometers (1.4 miles) to a pavilion, from which views extend back across to downtown.

NEW BRUNSWICK MUSEUM
The province's prime resource for fine arts and natural history lore, the **New Brunswick Museum** (St. Patrick St., 506/643-2300, Mon.-Fri. 9am-5pm, Sat. 10am-5pm, Sun. noon-5pm, adult $10, senior $8, child $6) is inside Market Square. One of Canada's oldest museums, its displays are spread through three floors packed with elegant ship models, shipbuilding tools, war memorabilia, stuffed birds and beasts, agricultural and domestic implements, you name it. There's a hands-on Discovery Centre for kids and a bookstore that stocks a good selection of literature about the province.

BARBOUR'S GENERAL STORE
Across Loyalist Plaza from Market Square, the essence of old-time New Brunswick is recreated at the restored **Barbour's General Store** (10 Market Sq., 506/642-2242, May-Oct. Tues.-Sat. 10am-6pm, free), which was moved from the village of Sheffield, upstream of Saint John. Inside are 2,000 artifacts typical of the period 1840-1940, information and tour services, and a gift shop. Next door, peek into the bright red schoolhouse, which was also moved to the site from rural New Brunswick.

★ PRINCE WILLIAM AND GERMAIN STREETS
A block up from Market Square, the parallel **Prince William and Germain Streets** delineate the commercial heart of old Saint John. Following a devastating fire in June 1877, the city hurried to rebuild itself in even grander style. The stone and brick edifices along Prince William Street are a splendid farrago of architectural styles, incorporating Italianate facades, Corinthian columns, Queen Anne

Downtown Saint John

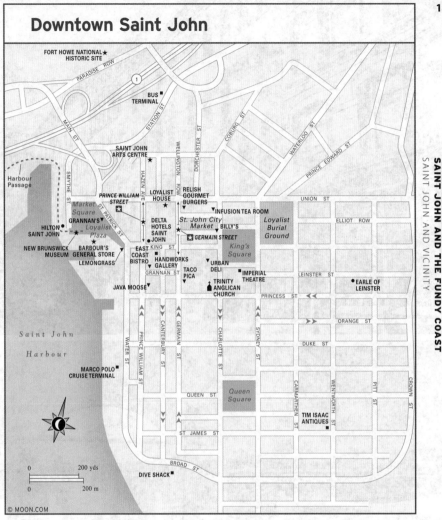

Revival elements, scowling gargoyles, and other decorative details. One of the country's finest surviving examples of 19th-century streetscape, this was the first "national historic street" in Canada. Some good art galleries and craft shops are ensconced here among other businesses. Two blocks east, Germain Street is the more residential counterpart, proffering a number of opulent townhouses.

LOYALIST HOUSE NATIONAL HISTORIC SITE

The simple, white clapboard, Georgian-style **Loyalist House National Historic Site** (120 Union St., 506/652-3590, mid-May-June Mon.-Fri. 10am-5pm, July-mid-Sept. daily 10am-5pm, adult $5, child $2) was built between 1810 and 1817 by pioneer David Merritt, and it remained in his family for five generations. Having survived the 1877 fire and now meticulously restored, it's the oldest unaltered

building in the city. The original front door with brass knocker opens into an authentic evocation of the early Loyalist years, furnished with Sheraton, Empire, and Duncan Phyfe antiques.

SAINT JOHN ARTS CENTRE

One block west of the Jewish museum, the grandiose former Carnegie Library is now a cultural complex, the **Saint John Arts Centre** (20 Hazen Ave., 506/633-4870, June-early Sept. daily 10am-5pm, early Sept.-May Tues.-Sat. 9am-5pm, free). Inside, six galleries (including the City of Saint John Gallery) hold frequently changing fine arts and photography exhibits.

SAINT JOHN CITY MARKET

For a visual and culinary treat, spend some time at **Saint John City Market** (47 Charlotte St., 506/658-2820, Mon.-Fri. 7:30am-6pm, Sat. 7:30am-5pm, free), spanning a whole city block between Charlotte and Germain Streets. The setting is impressive. The original ornate iron gates stand at each entrance, and there's usually a busker or two working the crowd. Inside the airy stone building, local shipbuilders framed the expansive ceiling in the form of an inverted ship's hull. "Market Street," the market's central, widest aisle, divides the space in half; alongside the adjacent aisles, the bustling stalls stand cheek-by-jowl, their tables groaning with wares. Notice the building's pitched floor, a convenient arrangement on the slanted hillside that makes hosing the floor easier after the market closes each day.

The market is a great venue for people-watching and for sampling freshly baked goods, cheeses, seafood, meat, and produce. If you haven't yet tried dulse, a leather-tough purple seaweed that's harvested from the Bay of Fundy, then dried and sold in little packages for a dollar or two, here's your chance. Splendid, reasonably priced crafts have a sizable niche here, too.

1: historic downtown buildings; **2:** the Harbour Passage

KING'S SQUARE AND THE LOYALIST BURIAL GROUND

Across Charlotte Street from the City Market are two maple-shaded, vest-pocket green spaces situated on separate kitty-corner blocks. At **King's Square,** the walkways are laid out like the stripes on the British Union Jack, radiating from the 1908 bandstand, the site of summertime concerts.

Across Sydney Street is the **Loyalist Burial Ground,** a surprisingly cheerful place with benches and flower gardens, scattered with old-style headstones dating back to 1784.

As busy as the square and burial ground are—alive with schoolchildren on field trips, bantering seniors, and moms with strollers—**Queen's Square,** three blocks south, is virtually deserted.

TRINITY ANGLICAN CHURCH

A victim of the city's historic fires, the handsome Loyalist **Trinity Anglican Church** (115 Charlotte St., 506/693-8558, Mon.-Fri. 9am-3pm, free) was built in 1791, rebuilt in 1856, and rebuilt again in 1880 after the Great Fire. The sanctuary's famed treasure is the House of Hanover Royal Coat of Arms from the reign of George I, which was rescued by fleeing Loyalists from the Boston Council Chamber in 1783 and rescued again from the 1877 runaway fire.

West of Downtown

FORT HOWE NATIONAL HISTORIC SITE LOOKOUT

Fort Howe, the blockhouse of 1777, did double duty as harbor defense and city jail. The structure itself is a replica, but the rocky promontory **lookout site** on Magazine Street nonetheless offers an excellent panoramic view of the city and harbor. To get there from downtown, cross the highway along Main Street.

REVERSING RAPIDS

If ever there were a contest for Most Overhyped Tourist Attraction, **Reversing Rapids** would win the grand prize. Tour buses and out-of-province license plates pack the parking lot, disgorging gaggles of camera-toting visitors to see . . . what? At low tide, the Bay of Fundy lies 4.4 meters (14.4 feet) below the Saint John River, and the river flows out to sea across a small falls (more like a rapids) here. During the slack tide, the sea and the river levels are equal and the rapids disappear. Then, as the slack tide grows to high tide, the waters of the rising sea enter Saint John Harbour, muscling the river inland for 100 kilometers (62 miles) and creating some turbulent rapids. It's an unspectacular sight, and even the minimal physical science interest can't be appreciated unless you're willing to hang around for 12 hours and watch the tide go through a full cycle. Nevertheless, throngs of visitors line up here for the requisite photo opportunity. To get there from downtown, cross Highway 1 via Main Street and turn left on Clesley Drive. The complex is on the far side of the bridge spanning the river.

For a reverse angle on Reversing Rapids, go to **Fallsview Park,** which overlooks the spectacle from the east side of the river, off Douglas Avenue.

CARLETON MARTELLO TOWER NATIONAL HISTORIC SITE

The massive circular stone **Carleton Martello Tower** (Fundy Dr. at Whipple St., Saint John West, 506/636-4011, June-early Oct. daily 10am-5pm, adult $4, senior $3.50, child $2) served as a harbor defense outpost from 1812 and was declared a national historic site in 1924. The superstructure above it was a military intelligence center during World War II. Within, stone staircases connect the restored quarters and powder magazine. The observation decks provide splendid views of the harbor.

PARTRIDGE ISLAND

Near the mouth of Saint John Harbour, a national and provincial historic site and now a coast guard light station, **Partridge Island** was a quarantine station for almost a million arriving immigrants during the 19th and

20th centuries, many of whom arrived sick with cholera, typhus, and smallpox. Some 2,000 newcomers who never made it any farther are buried here in six graveyards. A Celtic cross was erected for the Irish refugees, and a memorial stone commemorates Jewish immigrants. From the early 1800s up to 1947, the island was used as a military fortification. Most of the old wooden buildings have now been destroyed. Although the island had been off-limits to the public for decades, **River Bay Adventures** (506/658-8435, from $70 pp) is now licensed to take visitors to the island by kayak. If you're catching the ferry to Digby (Nova Scotia), stand on the starboard (right) side as the vessel pulls away from the terminal and you'll get a great view of the island.

RECREATION

A visit to Saint John is about soaking up history and enjoying the services affiliated with a city, but there are a few things to keep you busy beyond sightseeing. The two parks detailed below have good walking trails, **Rockwood Park Golf Course** (1255 Sandy Point Rd., 506/634-0090, greens fee $48) offers a challenging tree-lined layout, and there are water sports to try.

Parks
ROCKWOOD PARK

The huge woodland **Rockwood Park** (506/658-2883, daily dawn-dusk), speckled with 13 lakes and laced with foot and horse trails, is across Highway 1 from downtown, with access from Exits 123, 125, and 128. In spring, yellow lady's slipper and colorful wild orchid varieties bloom on the forest floor, and the gardens and arboretum are in their full glory. Activities in summer include fishing, boating, swimming, bird-watching, hiking, horseback riding, golfing at the 18-hole course, picnicking at lakeside tables, and camping. In winter, the ice skaters come out and the trails are taken over by cross-country skiers.

Cherry Brook Zoo (901 Foster Thurston Rd., 506/634-1440, daily 10am-7pm, adult

$10.50, senior $8.50, child $5.50), at the park's northern end, off Sandy Point Road, is stocked with lions, leopards, zebras, and other exotic animals. The zoo includes Vanished Kingdom Park, where you'll find replicas of extinct animals.

★ IRVING NATURE PARK

Irving Nature Park occupies an unlikely setting. The forested reserve encompasses an entire peninsula dangling into Saint John Harbour, the province's busiest port. At the harbor's northeastern corner rises the skyline of New Brunswick's largest city. Across the harbor's center, oceangoing vessels enter and leave the port. Yet at the harbor's western corner, this expanse of natural terrain remains as undeveloped as it was when the city's founding Loyalists arrived centuries ago.

To get there, take Highway 1 out of the city to western Saint John and watch for the Catherwood Street turnoff (Exit 119). The narrow road angles south off the highway, takes a jog to the right (west), descends through a residential area, and then lopes across an undeveloped marshland to the 225-hectare (556-acre) reserve. A long beach backed by the Saints Rest Marsh is near the park's entrance. Many visitors park at the bottom of the

hill and continue on foot. It is also possible to continue by road into the park, to a parking lot 500 meters (0.3 mile) from the beach, or to follow a one-way road that encircles the entire headland. Trails probe the park's interior and also wander off to parallel the water.

The reserve's mixed ecosystem offers interesting trekking terrain and draws songbirds, waterfowl, and migratory seabirds. More than 240 bird species are seen regularly; 365 species have been sighted over the past 20 years. Rare red crossbills and peregrine falcons are occasionally spotted in the marsh. Eastern North America's largest cormorant colony lies offshore on Manawagonish Island. Semipalmated plovers like the reserve's quiet beaches and tidal flats. You can count on sandpiper varieties on the beach in July, greater shearwaters and Wilson's stormy petrels gliding across the water during summer, and a spectacular show of loons, grebes, and scoters during the autumn migration along the Atlantic flyway. Birds are the most noticeable but by no means the only wildlife to be found here. Deer, porcupines, red squirrels, and snowshoe hares inhabit the reserve, and starfish and sea urchins laze in the tidal pools.

Irving Nature Park

Water Sports

The **Dive Shack** (9 Lower Cove Loop, 506/634-8265, Mon.-Tues. and Thurs.-Fri. 10am-5pm, Wed. noon-5pm, Sat. 10am-3pm) is the city's prime source for dive trips to the Bay of Fundy. The shop also rents equipment, runs courses, and offers weekend charters. Lower Cove Loop is an extension of Water Street south through downtown.

The top-notch facilities at the **Canada Games Aquatic Centre** (50 Union St., 506/658-4715, Mon.-Fri. 6am-9pm, Sat. 6am-midnight, pool access adult $9, senior and child $6.50) include a 50-meter pool with five diving boards, two shallower pools, two waterslides, whirlpools, saunas, a fitness room, and a cafeteria.

You'll find supervised swimming at Fisher Lake in **Rockwood Park,** at **Dominion Park** in Saint John West, and at **Little River Reservoir** off Loch Lomond Road in the city's eastern area. **Mispec Beach** at Saint John Harbour's eastern edge is unsupervised, and the water is cold, but it's a nice spot on a warm day and provides close-up views of ships from around the world entering and leaving the harbor. To get there, take Union Street and make a sharp right turn to Bayside Drive, and then turn onto Red Head Road.

ENTERTAINMENT AND EVENTS

Nightlife

Saint John may seem historic and charming during the day, but remember that it's primarily an international port. Be careful after dark, especially at the south end of downtown. That said, bars and restaurants along Market Square have a beautiful outlook, with lots of outdoor tables that stay full with locals and visitors well into the night on summer weekends, when musicians take to an outdoor stage. **Grannan's** (1 Market Sq., 506/634-1555, daily from 11:30am) forms a hub for the many nearby bars of many moods, and its indoor lounge has an inviting pub ambience. Adjacent **McGill's** (1 Market Sq., 506/693-6666, daily 11am-2am) and **Saint John Ale**

House (1 Market Sq., 506/657-2337, Mon.-Fri. 11:30am-midnight, Sat.-Sun. noon-2am) also have wide portions of Loyalist Plaza packed with outdoor furniture, with the former offering a dance party on Friday night. Toward the water, **York Bistro & Pub** (Hilton Saint John, Market Sq., 506/632-8564, daily 11:30am-1am) is less pretentious than you might expect and has outside tables facing the harbor.

The historic Trinity Royal area, bounded by Prince William, Princess, King, and Germain Streets, is another nightlife center, with nightclubs, pubs, lounges, and sports bars. One of the more welcoming places is **O'Leary's** (46 Princess St., 506/634-7135, Mon.-Tues. 11:30am-11pm, Wed.-Fri. 11:30am-2am, Sat. 3pm-2am), a convivial Irish pub with the obligatory Guinness on tap and the sound of Celtic musicians filling the room Thursday-Saturday.

Performing Arts

The city's pride and joy is the immaculately restored 1913 **Imperial Theatre** (12 King Sq. S., 506/674-4100, www.imperialtheatre.nb.ca). In its heyday, the theater hosted performances by the likes of Ethel Barrymore, John Philip Sousa, and Harry Houdini. After closing in the 1950s, it was reopened and used by the Full Gospel Assembly Pentecostal Church for 25 years. In 1994, decade-long renovations to restore the theater to its former glory were completed. Today it's once again the star venue of Saint John's performing arts scene, hosting concerts by Symphony New Brunswick, stage productions of Theatre New Brunswick, and a variety of touring performers.

Festivals and Events

On the second Saturday in May, the Marco Polo Cruise Terminal (111 Water St.) fills with the smells of the best in local cooking for the **Taste of the Maritimes** (www. tasteofthemaritimes.ca). Admission is $75, which includes a book of tickets that can be redeemed for food and drink from over 30 local pubs and restaurants.

In addition to free evening entertainment

in Loyalist Plaza, summer brings the **Buskers on the Bay** (www.marketsquaresj.com) festival to Market Square and the boardwalk during the second weekend of July.

Saint John Ex finishes the summer with a super-size county fair geared to families. It runs for five days in late August at the Exhibition Grounds (McAllister Dr., 506/633-2020, www.exhibitionparksj.com). Expect all the usual carnival rides as well as agricultural demonstrations and musical performances.

SHOPPING

The city's main shopping district—along Charlotte, Union, Princess, Germain, and Prince William Streets—is filled with interesting outlets selling everything from Inuit art to Irish tartan. The local penchant for high-quality weaving and handmade apparel is particularly evident at **Handworks Gallery** (12 King St., 506/631-7626, Mon.-Sat. 10am-5:30pm). In the vicinity is one of Atlantic Canada's preeminent antiques dealers, **Tim Isaac Antiques** (213 Wentworth St., 506/652-3222, Mon.-Fri. 10am-4pm).

FOOD

Market Square is the most obvious and convenient choice for visitors looking for a meal, but head uphill into the heart of downtown and you'll come across restaurants that trade on good food and prices alone.

Market and Deli

You won't know which way to turn once you've walked through the doors of the ★ **Saint John City Market** (47 Charlotte St., 506/658-2820, Mon.-Fri. 7:30am-6pm, Sat. 7:30am-5pm), a city institution. Choose from a couple of old-fashioned cafés, a seafood market with live lobsters (they'll box them for you) and mussels for just $3 per pound, a delicatessen with sliced meats and gourmet cheeses, and Wild Carrot Café, boasting healthy juices and muffins.

If you're looking for something a little more sophisticated for lunch than the offerings at Saint John City Market, head over to **Urban Deli** (68 King St., 506/652-3354, Mon.-Sat. 11:45am-3pm, lunches around $12), where lunches such as Montreal-style smoked meat sandwiches and quinoa salads cost under $15.

Seafood

Grannan's (1 Market Sq., 506/634-1555, Mon.-Wed. 11am-11pm, Thurs.-Sat. 11am-midnight, Sun. noon-10pm, $19-38) is one of the Market Square restaurants with as many tables outside as in. The specialty is seafood, and everything is good. The chowder is expensive but delicious, while mains include blackened Creole salmon, seafood casserole, and snow crab.

★ **Billy's Seafood Company** (49 Charlotte St., 506/672-3474, Mon.-Fri. 11am-10pm, Sat. 9am-10pm, Sun. 4pm-10pm, $16-33) is tucked away at the back of the Saint John City Market. It's part fish market, part restaurant, so you know everything will be fresh. Everything is good—Atlantic Canada delicacies include Malpeque oysters served raw in their shells, fish cakes, seafood chowder, lobster-stuffed haddock, Digby scallops sautéed in a pesto sauce, blackened salmon with an apple-cinnamon glaze, and a creamy shrimp risotto.

Other Restaurants

If you have only one night in Saint John, my pick for eating out is ★ **East Coast Bistro** (60 Prince William St., 506/696-3278, Mon. 11am-2pm, Tues.-Fri. 11am-9pm, Sat. noon-10pm, $16-29), in the heart of downtown one block uphill from the waterfront in a long, narrow space with exposed brick on one side and local artwork and a bar on the other. Ingredients are sourced locally, which leads to an ever-changing menu of simple yet tasty dishes.

Saint John proves it's up on restaurant trends at **Lemongrass** (1 Market Sq., 506/657-8424, daily 11:30am-10pm, $19-26), a warmly decorated Thai-influenced dining room in the bustling Market Square complex. You can't miss with *tod mun pla* (fish cakes infused with red curry and coriander) and either

phad yum (seafood curry with lime leaves) or *hor neing pla* (steamed haddock with lemongrass and other herbs wrapped in a banana leaf) as a main.

Just a block off King Street, the city hustle and bustle drops off dramatically. Small, bright, and casual ★ **Taco Pica** (96 Germain St., 506/633-8492, Mon.-Sat. 10am-10pm, $18-24) is a real find on a quiet side street in the Trinity Royal historic area, away from the tourist traffic. The Guatemalan proprietor offers a mouthwatering menu of recipes from his homeland, as well as dishes from Mexico and Spain. Try the *pepian* (a spicy Guatemalan beef stew) or Spanish paella, washed down with a Mexican beer.

The dining rooms in the major hotels are also safe bets, though pricier. Contemporary **Mix Resto Bar** (Delta Hotels Saint John, 39 King St., 506/649-0731, daily 7am-midnight, $15-34) offers tempting selections such as a Fundy Bay salmon fillet grilled on a cedar plank.

The sleek **York Bistro + Pub** (Hilton Saint John, Market Sq., 506/693-8484, daily 6:30am-midnight, $16-32) opens to a dockside patio. Menu highlights include thin-crust pizzas, mussels steamed in wheat beer, and mushroom-crusted rack of lamb.

Coffee and Tea

For gourmet coffee-lovers, Saint John doesn't have a great number of choices, but the owners of **Java Moose** (84 Prince William St., 506/657-7283, Mon.-Fri. 7am-5pm, Sat.-Sun. 8am-3pm) do an excellent job of sourcing high-quality beans to roast. Java Moose also has an outlet in the Saint John City Market. Looking for gourmet teas? Try **Infusion Tea Room** (41 Charlotte St., 506/613-8327, daily 8am-6pm, lunches $7-10), which also has simple soup and sandwich offerings.

1: waterside dining at the York Bistro + Pub; **2:** Market Square

ACCOMMODATIONS AND CAMPING

Ideally, you'll want to be within walking distance of historic old Saint John and the harbor. The area's B&Bs often provide sumptuous accommodations for lower cost than many hotels. Lodgings beyond walking distance include the Fort Howe-area hotels, with great harbor vistas at reasonable prices, and the many budget choices on Manawagonish Avenue in Saint John West.

$50-100

Of the B&B lodgings clustered near King's Square, none are better value than **Earle of Leinster** (96 Leinster St., 506/652-3275, www. earleofleinster.com, $95-160 s or d), with congenial hosts and a very central location. This gracious brick Victorian townhouse has 12 rooms with private baths. All have Wi-Fi and TVs, and some have basic cooking facilities. Other amenities include laundry facilities, a game room with a pool table, and a courtyard. Rates include a full breakfast.

Around 5 kilometers (3.1 miles) from downtown, Manawagonish Avenue is lined with inexpensive motels—a reminder of the time when this was the main route west out of the city. To get there from the west, take Exit 100 from Highway 1 and follow Ocean Westway toward the city; from downtown, take Exit 119 and follow Catherwood Street north. Best choice under $100 is the **Hillcrest Motel** (1315 Manawagonish Ave., 506/672-5310, $60-80 s or d), around 7 kilometers (4.3 miles) from downtown, which has views of the Bay of Fundy.

$100-150

★ **Homeport Historic Bed & Breakfast** (80 Douglas Ave., 506/672-7255 or 888/678-7678, www.homeport.nb.ca, $109-175 s or d) is arguably the best B&B in Saint John. Set high on the hill overlooking the harbor and city, this lodging combines two mansions dating from the mid-1800s. From the impressive collection of antiques to the super-comfortable beds to the decanter of port left in the lobby for guests returning from dinner, it is obvious hosts Ralph and Karen Holyoke know how to make their guests feel like they're paying a lot more than they really are. Standard rooms are $109 s or d, but the luxury rooms from $149 are well worth the extra money. Rates include a full breakfast.

Travelodge Suites (1011 Fairville Blvd., 506/635-0400 or 800/578-7878, www.wyndhamhotels.com, from $130 s or d) is your typical midrange roadside motel, with clean, comfortable, and practical guest rooms that were last renovated in 2013. Standard rooms are $130 s or d, but the much larger suites, with separate bedrooms and king beds, are a good value at $160. A complimentary light breakfast is laid out for guests. Take Exit 117 from Highway 1.

Over $200

Occupying a prime waterfront locale and linked to Market Square by an elevated walkway is ★ **Hilton Saint John** (1 Market Sq., 506/693-8484 or 800/561-8282, www.hilton.com, $225 s or d), a 12-story high-rise dating to the mid-1980s. Most of its 200 rooms have water views and windows that open. They come with all the usual niceties—daily newspaper, coffeemaker, hair dryer, and more—while a waterfront restaurant, a fitness room, and an indoor pool are downstairs. Check online for packages that include a buffet breakfast.

Rack rates at the **Delta Hotels Saint John** (39 King St., 506/648-1981 or 888/890-3222, www.marriott.com, $235 s or d) may be on the high side, but reserve online and you'll pay less. Part of the Brunswick Square Mall and one block back from the harbor, this modern hotel has 254 elegant rooms, as well as an indoor pool, a fitness room, and a restaurant and lounge.

Campgrounds

A five-minute drive from downtown, **Rockwood Park Campground** (142 Lake Dr. S., 506/652-4050, www.rockwoodparkcampground.com, May-Oct.,

$32-42) has more than 200 sites, most with electricity and water. Amenities include big communal bathrooms, kitchen shelters, fireplaces, and a campers' canteen. Available recreation includes golfing at the nearby course, swimming, boating at the lake, and hiking on trails around the lake. The easiest way to get to the campground is to take Exit 121 or 125 from Highway 1 and follow the signs north. No reservations are taken, but the sites rarely fill.

INFORMATION AND SERVICES

Tourism Saint John (506/658-2855 or 866/463-8639, www.discoversaintjohn.com) does a great job of promoting the city, and its helpful website should be your first point of contact in planning your trip. It operates the city's main **Visitor Information Centre** (15 Market Sq., daily 9am-6pm, in summer daily until 8pm) at the eastern entrance to Market Square; it faces the corner of St. Patrick and King Streets. If you are coming into the city from the west along Highway 1, stop at the **Saint John Throughway Visitor Information Centre** (1509 Saint John Throughway W., 506/658-2940, May-Oct. daily 10am-5pm, longer hours in summer).

Saint John Regional Hospital (400 University Ave., 506/648-6000) is on the university campus near Rockwood Park. For the police or other emergencies, call 911. A convenient downtown pharmacy is **Lawton's Drugs** (Brunswick Sq., 39 King St., 506/634-1422, Mon.-Sat. 9am-6pm).

GETTING THERE
Car

From Bangor, Maine, Saint John is a 170-kilometer (105-mile) east along Highway 9 to the New Brunswick border, and then via Highway 1 into the city. The drive takes around three hours.

Saint John is 110 kilometers (68 miles) south of Fredericton, a more than one-hour drive, and 155 kilometers (96 miles) southwest of Moncton, 1.5 hours.

Air

Saint John Airport (YSJ, www. saintjohnairport.com) is 16 kilometers (9.9 miles) east of downtown. The airport is served by **Air Canada** (888/247-2262, www. aircanada.com) from Halifax, Toronto, and Montréal. Car rental companies represented are Avis, Budget, Hertz, and National, while other airport services include a restaurant and gift shop.

Taxis wait outside the airport for flight arrivals; the 25-minute cab ride to Market Square costs about $40.

Bus

Saint John Bus Terminal (125 Station St., 506/672-2055) is the arrival and departure point for **Maritime Bus** (www.maritimebus. com) service to and from Fredericton (three buses daily, 1.5 hours, $31) and Moncton (three buses daily, two hours, $39).

Ferry

Bay Ferries (902/245-2116 or 888/249-7245, www.ferries.ca) sails the *Princess of Acadia* between Saint John and Digby (Nova Scotia) year-round, up to three times daily in summer. It's a good option if you've driven through New Brunswick and want to explore Nova Scotia's Fundy Coast. The crossing is 3.5 hours (adult $46, senior and youth $36, child $31, vehicle $92 plus a $20 fuel surcharge). To get to the terminal from Highway 1, take Exit 120 and follow the signs south along Market Street. The terminal has no café, so if you're looking for a snack while waiting in line, stop at the Tim Hortons along Market Street.

GETTING AROUND

Saint John is a walking town in the historic area, but beyond there you'll need wheels. Highway 1 serves as the city's high-speed expressway and routes east-west traffic through Saint John from St. Stephen and Moncton. Highway 100 is the city's local traffic route, and it serves as a feeder route for Highway 7 to and from Fredericton. Driving is slow going most everywhere in Saint John, but it's worst during the 7am-9am and 4:30pm-6pm rush hours.

Parking garages and lots in the historic area are plentiful and inexpensive. Outdoor lots cost $1 an hour; indoor lots are slightly higher. Coming off Highway 1 at Exit 122, take the first right and you'll pass outdoor pay parking on your right, or continue to the bottom of the hill and turn left for underground parking.

Bus

Saint John Transit (506/658-4700, $2.50-3.50 per sector) buses run throughout the city (Mon.-Fri. 6am-midnight, with limited service on weekends). The company also offers two-hour guided bus tours (adult $20, child $5) of Saint John twice daily (10am and 12:30pm) late June-September.

Taxi

Cabs wait in front of the Delta and Hilton hotels, or call **Saint John Taxi** (506/693-0000), **Diamond Taxi** (506/648-8888), or **Royal Taxi** (506/652-5050). Fares are based on 14 city zones; expect to pay around $10 from Market Square to Fort Howe and $40 to the airport.

SAINT JOHN TO ST. ANDREWS

In addition to the intrinsic beauty of the coast—with thick forests growing right down to the rocky shoreline—several detours spice up the 90-kilometer (56-mile) drive west to St. Andrews. For the first 40 kilometers (25 miles) out of Saint John there is little reason to detour from Highway 1, but at Lepreau the original coastal route (now known as Highway 175) spurs south to **Lepreau Falls,** a picturesque stop with a few picnic tables set on their own personal decks overlooking the falls.

Lepreau and Vicinity

From Lepreau Falls, Highway 175 continues west, although there is the option to head south on Highway 790 to **Point Lepreau Nuclear Generating Station.** It opened in 1980 as Canada's first nuclear power station and currently supplies 30 percent of New Brunswick's power needs.

Backtracking to Lepreau Falls, Highway 175 heading west quickly reaches **New River Beach Provincial Park** (506/755-4046, mid-May-late Sept.), one of the best beaches along the entire Fundy Coast. Walk along the beach back toward Saint John to explore rock pools, laze on the sand, or have a picnic high above the ocean in the cliff-top day-use area. Unfortunately, there is a downside: Access costs $10 per vehicle per day. Across the road from the beach is a large provincial park campground (506/755-4046, mid-May-late Sept., $28-43) with forested sites, many with power hookups.

A good-value accommodation along this stretch of highway is the **Clipper Shipp Beach Motel** (1312 Hwy. 175, Pocologan, 506/755-2211, www.clippershipp.com, Mar.-Nov., $95-150 s or d). The rooms are very basic—you're paying for a stunning waterfront location.

GETTING THERE

Lepreau is about 40 kilometers (25 miles) southwest of Saint John on Highway 1 (take Exit 86).

St. George

The most impressive sight at St. George, 32 kilometers (20 miles) before reaching St. Andrews, is the thundering granite gorge of **Magaguadavic Falls.** Visitors can park and walk down a staircase beside the falls to watch salmon swimming upstream past a viewing window. The specialty at **Oven Head Salmon Smokers** (101 Ovenhead Rd., 506/755-2507, daily 8am-7pm) is, of course, Atlantic salmon, cold-smoked to perfection over hickory and oak chips. The smokehouse wholesales to upscale restaurants throughout the province, although it's much cheaper if purchased directly from the on-site shop.

St. George is also the place to turn off Highway 1 for the short drive to the Deer Island ferry terminus at Letete. Highways 772 and 776 lead to Black Bay, picturesque **Blacks Harbour** (terminus for the Grand Manan Island ferry), and a welter of other islets.

GETTING THERE

St. George is 70 kilometers (43 miles) west of Saint John, a one-hour drive on Highway 1.

Lepreau Falls

St. Andrews and Vicinity

St. Andrews by the Sea, as it is marketed by the local tourism authority, is an immensely attractive seaside town (pop. 1,800) 90 kilometers (56 miles) west of Saint John. New Brunswick's first—and now definitive—resort town, St. Andrews sits at the end of a peninsula dangling into tranquil Passamaquoddy Bay, sheltered from the tumultuous Fundy by Deer Island and Letang Peninsula. The resort crowd revels in St. Andrews's version of old-time velvet-glove Canadiana, especially visible at the many upscale lodgings.

HISTORY

The town has a special, almost sacred historic status among New Brunswickers. It was founded by Loyalists who sailed into the Fundy and followed the coastal curve to the peninsula's tip in 1783. The courageous journey was a technical wonder. The settlers, originally from England's former colonies farther south, had moved to what they believed was Canada at Castine, Maine. But a subsequent international boundary decision forced them to relocate once again. The pro-Crown settlers reloaded convoys with all their possessions, disassembling houses and reloading the structures on barges, and set sail for a safe homeland. St. Andrews was their creation. Most every street is named for George III or one of his kin. A few Loyalist houses remain and sit cheek-by-jowl with similar New England-style houses fronting narrow residential streets.

SIGHTS

For a town that encourages relaxation, there's a lot to see and do. Many historic attractions are within walking distance of downtown accommodations, while others are just a short drive away. You could easily spend two days in town and still not have time to golf the hallowed fairways of the Algonquin Golf Course or go whale-watching. One of the most interesting things to do in St. Andrews is to watch the effect of the tide. I'm not suggesting you sit at the end of the Town Wharf for six hours, but take a peek at low or high tide, and then return six hours later—the difference is amazing.

TOP EXPERIENCE

★ St. Andrews National Historic District

As one of the best-preserved Colonial towns in North America (nearly half the buildings in the town core date back more than 100 years), the heart of **St. Andrews** is preserved as a national historic site. Adding to the charm, most buildings have been restored to their original condition. Those along Water Street, the main downtown thoroughfare that follows the shoreline for five blocks, have been brightened up with a variety of pastel-colored paints, creating a resort vibe that extends into the many boutiques and restaurants.

One block back from Water Street, **Sheriff Andrews House** (63 King St., 506/529-5080, late June-early Sept. Mon.-Sat. 9:30am-4:30pm, Sun. 1pm-4:30pm, donation) offers an attractive visual insight into the early Loyalist era. Costumed guides will show you around the county sheriff's neoclassical-style 1820 house, which is simply but elegantly furnished in local period style.

The whitewashed **Charlotte County Court House** (Frederick St., 506/529-3843, July-Aug. Mon.-Sat. 9:30am-noon and 1pm-4:30pm, free) dates to 1840 and is thought to be the country's oldest courthouse in continuous use.

Ross Memorial Museum (188 Montague St., 506/529-5124, early June-early Oct. Tues.-Sat. 10am-4:30pm, donation), in an early 19th-century neoclassical brick home, preserves the furniture, porcelains, rugs, mirrors, paintings, and other items of Henry and

St. Andrews

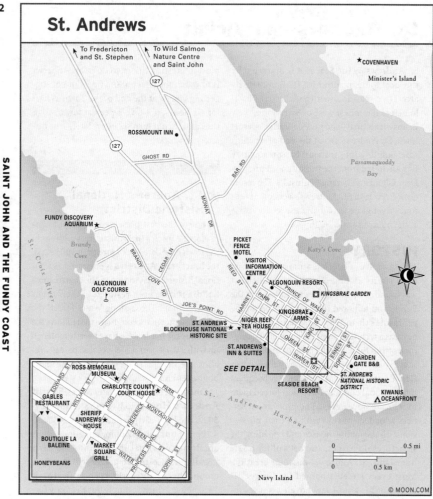

© MOON.COM

Sarah Ross, discerning collectors of antiques and objets d'art.

★ Kingsbrae Garden

Kingsbrae Garden (220 King St., 506/529-3335, mid-May-mid-Oct. daily 9am-6pm, adult $16, senior and child $12) incorporates gardens that were once part of the Kingsbrae Arms estate, as well as additional land, to create 11 hectares (27 acres) of tranquility on the hill above downtown. It is home to more than 2,000 species—a place to feast your eyes on rhododendrons, roses, an orchard, a working windmill, an Acadian coastal forest, and a children's garden featuring miniature houses. The complex also includes a shop selling floral-themed gifts and a **café** (mid-May-mid-Oct. daily 10am-4:30pm) overlooking the garden.

St. Andrews Blockhouse National Historic Site

A pleasant walk along Water Street from downtown will lead you to **St. Andrews**

St. Croix Island

In 1604, a French exploration party of 79 led by Samuel de Champlain sailed into the Bay of Fundy and named the Saint John River. After rejecting the site of the present city of Saint John as an improper spot for a settlement, the group spent the bitterly cold winter of 1604-1605 on Douchet's Island in the St. Croix River. The settlement marked the beginning of a French presence in North America. After the bitter winter in which hunger and scurvy claimed 35 lives, the remaining settlers packed up and headed for Nova Scotia's more agreeable side of the Fundy. There they established Port-Royal, the early hub of "Acadia," the name they gave this part of eastern Canada.

The St. Croix River, which drains into the Bay of Fundy at St. Andrews, forms the international border, and the site of the settlement is now protected as **St. Croix Island International Historic Site.** Beside Highway 127, 9 kilometers (5.6 miles) north of St. Andrews, where views extend over the island, interpretive boards tell the story of the settlement. On the U.S. side, there's a viewing platform 13 kilometers (8.1 miles) south of Calais.

Blockhouse National Historic Site (23 Joes Point Rd., 506/529-4270, June-Aug. daily 10am-6pm, adult $1, child $0.40). The fortification, the last survivor of 12 similar structures, was intended to protect the town from attack in the War of 1812, but nary a shot was fired in battle at this site. The interior depicts the War of 1812 era with re-created soldiers' quarters.

Even if you're not hot on history, the site is worth exploring for the wide grassy expanse out front, which edges the St. Croix River. Time your visit for the ebb (receding) tide, and you'll watch the revealing of a rocky peninsula and pools that are fully submerged at high tide.

Minister's Island Historic Site

The 200-hectare (494-acre) **Minister's Island Historic Site** in Passamaquoddy Bay was where Canadian Pacific Railway magnate William Van Horne built his summer retreat, **Covenhoven** (506/529-5081, $10 pp over age eight, cash only). Completed in 1903, the 50-room home was built of locally quarried sandstone, and it, a windmill, a tidal swimming pool, and a barn remain. The island is only accessible at low tide, so the two daily tours depart at different times each day (ask at the St. Andrews Visitor Information Centre for times or check the website at www.ministersisland. net). You will be asked to meet at the end of Bar Road, 2 kilometers (1.2 miles) northeast of town, from where you follow a lead vehicle across a strip of sand that is exposed only at low tide. The entry fee includes a guided tour.

Fundy Discovery Aquarium

Beyond the golf course, **Fundy Discovery Aquarium** (Brandy Cove Rd., 506/529-1200, mid-May-mid-Oct. daily 10am-5pm, adult $14.25, senior $11.75, child $10) is part of the Huntsman Marine Science Centre, a nonprofit marine biology study facility drawing researchers from far and wide. The aquarium is stocked with hundreds of local fish, crustaceans, mollusks, and marine plant species. A touch tank gives children gentle access to intertidal critters, while seals cavort in the outdoor pool. The center also offers environmental classes with guest lecturers and field and lab work (around $1,000 per week).

Wild Salmon Nature Centre

On the road back to Saint John, the **Wild Salmon Nature Centre** (24 Chamcook Lake Rd., 506/529-1384, mid-May-mid-Oct. daily 9am-5pm, adult $7, senior $6, child $3.50) is part of a much larger research facility. Displays describe the life cycle of Atlantic salmon and breeding techniques. From the sun-filled room, paths lead upstream to Chamcook Lake and downstream to Passamaquoddy Bay.

SHOPPING

Craft and gift shops abound here. Whether you're looking for sweaters, souvenir T-shirts, locally produced pottery, or what have you, one of the de rigueur activities in St. Andrews is strolling along Water Street and drifting in and out of the shops. One of the nicest is **Boutique la Baleine** (173 Water St., 506/529-3926, Mon.-Sat. 10am-5pm, Sun. noon-5pm), which has a wide range of whale- and nautical-oriented souvenirs.

RECREATION
On the Water

Whale-watching is a popular activity here, and several companies offer cruises in search of finback, minke, and humpback whales. In addition to whales, you'll see harbor seals and lots of seabirds. All tours depart from the wharf at the foot of King Street.

Quoddy Link Marine (6 King St., 506/529-2600, www.quoddylinkmarine.com) has a stable covered boat that takes visitors on three-hour naturalist-narrated cruises. Light snacks and beverages and the use of binoculars and foul-weather gear are included in the price (adult $60, senior $54, child $30). For the more adventurous, **Fundy Tide Runners** (16 King St., 506/529-4481, www.fundytiderunners.com, June-Sept., adult $70, child $55) runs out to the whale-watching area in large inflatable Zodiacs, which reach the area more quickly than Quoddy Link's boat.

Eastern Outdoors (165 Water St., 506/529-4662, www.easternoutdoors.com) offers a 2.5-hour kayak paddle around Passamaquoddy Bay from the St. Andrews waterfront, with an emphasis on wildlife and human history. The cost is a reasonable $69 per person.

Golf

St. Andrews may not have the history of its Scottish namesake, but golfers have been drawn to the scenic fairways of the **Algonquin Golf Course** (Brandy Cove Rd., 506/529-8165, Apr.-Oct.) for more than 100 years. The course was thoroughly modernized in 2000, with a complete redesign that highlights the sparkling Bay of Fundy at every turn, and then redesigned again in 2017. Summer greens fees are an excellent value at $125, with discounts early and late in the season. Rates include access to the driving range and a power cart.

FOOD

While St. Andrews has cafés and restaurants to suit all tastes and budgets, seafood dominates local menus.

Toward the entrance to town, **Honeybeans** (157 Water St., 506/529-4888, Wed.-Mon. 7:30am-5pm) is a small space serving up great coffee as well as muffins and other pastries. Free Wi-Fi and a few outdoor tables are a bonus.

Overlooking the Blockhouse National Historic Site, **Niger Reef Tea House** (1 Joe's Point Rd., 506/529-8005, May daily 11am-3pm, June-Sept. daily 11am-8pm, lunches $12-17) is in a small waterfront cabin built in 1926 as a chapter house for the Imperial Order of the Daughters of the Empire, a Canadian women's organization that dedicated itself to charity work. Today the setting is almost folksy, with views out across green space to the water of St. Andrews Harbour. The seafood chowder is an excellent choice, or go for the richness of a lobster salad sandwich. Still hungry? Try the strawberry rhubarb crumble.

If you're after casual seafood dining with water views, look no farther than ★ **Gables Restaurant** (143 Water St., 506/529-3440, Wed.-Mon. 11:30am-9pm, $16-30), which occupies a choice spot right on the bay. The waterfront wooden deck out back is a great place for lunch, and couldn't be more romantic in the evening—a great spot for sipping an after-dinner cognac and watching the lights shimmer across the water. The menu stays the same for lunch and dinner, with blackboard specials your best bet. Last time I was through, the seafood pie was delicious. The entrance is down an alleyway (if you pass a massive lobster wood carving, you've found the right spot).

You don't need to be a guest at The Algonquin Resort (184 Adolphus St., 506/529-8823) to take advantage of the in-house restaurant **Braxton's** (summer daily 7am-9pm, the rest of the year Sun.-Wed. 7am-11am, Thurs.-Sat. 7am-11am and 5pm-9pm, $22-48), which specializes in modern presentations of regional game and produce. It's also a good place to come for breakfast, with hot dishes such as eggs Benedict on a lobster cake.

ACCOMMODATIONS AND CAMPING

St. Andrews has a wealth of options, ranging from the family-friendly (Seaside Beach Resort) to the extravagant (take your pick). Always make reservations for July and August.

$50-100

A couple of inexpensive but clean and comfortable motels are along the road into town, including the **Picket Fence Motel** (102 Reed St., 506/529-8985, www.picketfencenb.com, $90-110 s or d), where the pricier units have basic cooking facilities.

$100-150

Views from the sweeping lawns of **Rossmount Inn** (4599 Hwy. 127, 506/529-3351 or 877/529-3351, www.rossmountinn.com, Apr.-Dec., $135-145 s or d) extend unimpeded across Passamaquoddy Bay. The three-story mansion holds a dining room, a lounge, an outdoor pool, and 18 guest rooms decorated in soothing cream colors and furnished with Victorian antiques. Outdoors, guests congregate on the patio or use the walking trails to explore the expansive 35-hectare (86.5-acre) grounds. The lodge is 6 kilometers (3.7 miles) northeast of town along the highway to Saint John.

$150-200

Garden Gate Bed and Breakfast (364 Montague St., 506/529-4453, www.bbgardengate.com, $160 s or d) is a lovely late 19th-century home surrounded by mature gardens. Each of the three guest rooms has an en suite or private bathroom, and rates include a cooked breakfast.

For no-frills waterfront accommodations, it's difficult to recommend anywhere but ★ **Seaside Beach Resort** (339 Water St., 506/529-3846 or 800/506-8677, www.seaside.nb.ca, $165-285 s or d). Within walking distance of downtown, this complex comprises a collection of buildings dating back to the mid-1800s. There are over 20 units, some of which are self-contained cabins; others are larger structures complete with slanted floors and handmade windows. My favorite is Harbourview Two, which is right on the water and has two bedrooms and a small deck with a barbecue. All units have kitchens and older televisions.

Right on the edge of the bay and 200 meters (656 feet) from the heart of the village, **St. Andrews Inn & Suites** (111 Water St., 506/529-4571, www.standrewsmotorinn.com, $170-240 s or d) is a modern three-story motel with a small indoor pool. The rates are high for a reason—most rooms have balconies with magnificent water views.

Over $200

The Algonquin Resort (184 Adolphus St., 506/529-8823 or 855/529-8693, www.algonquinresort.com, $240-455 s or d) is a classy Canadian resort with manicured grounds dominating the hill above St. Andrews. Everything about it bespeaks gentility and class—verdant lawns dotted with flowerbeds, gardens, young couples in tennis whites leisurely sipping cool drinks on the veranda—and the tinkling of crystal is the loudest noise you'll hear in the upscale dining room. The original resort opened as a Canadian Pacific Railway hotel in 1889, but burned down in 1914. The Tudor-style replacement that opened the following year is what remains to this day, although it has undergone many expansions and improvements, most recently during 2012-2014, when it was closed for two years for a massive renovation that included giving all guest rooms a modern yet elegant makeover. Amenities include

Braxton's Restaurant and Bar, a large outdoor pool complex, an indoor pool and waterslide, tennis courts, day spa services, and a fitness center.

A member of the prestigious Relais & Chateaux group, the Kingsbrae Arms (219 King St., 506/529-1897, www.kingsbrae.com, $329-699 s or d) features eight of the most luxurious guest rooms you'll find anywhere in Atlantic Canada. From the marble bathrooms to the refined room service, this is the place for a serious splurge.

Campgrounds

Through town to the east, and a 10-minute walk to downtown, ★ **Kiwanis Oceanfront Camping** (550 Water St., 506/529-3439 or 877/393-7070, www.kiwanisoceanfrontcamping.com, May-mid-Oct., $38-53) lives up to its name, with a front row of campsites that enjoy unimpeded water views. Amenities include showers, a playground, a grocery store, a kitchen shelter, wireless Internet access, and a laundry.

INFORMATION

As you enter town from the west, the **St. Andrews Visitor Information Centre** (24 Reed St., 506/529-3556, www.standrewsbythesea.ca, early May-early Oct. daily 9am-6pm) is tucked away in the trees on the left side of the road beyond the Picket Fence Motel.

GETTING THERE

To get to St. Andrews, head west on Highway 1 out of Saint John for just over 80 kilometers (50 miles), then go south on Highway 127 for about 20 kilometers (12.4 miles). Allow 1.5 hours without stops for this drive.

Fundy Isles

The Fundy Isles are a world away from mainland living, an archipelago of islands spread across the New Brunswick side of the Bay of Fundy. Four islands—Deer, Campobello, Grand Manan, and White Head—are populated and are linked to the mainland by ferry. They make an interesting diversion from coastal cruising and are little known outside Atlantic Canada.

DEER ISLAND

The sea swirls mightily around Grand Manan but diminishes in intensity as the currents spin off around the coast of Maine to Deer Island, which lies closer to the United States than to the Canadian mainland. Sovereignty of Deer and Campobello Islands was disputed for decades after the American Revolution; a treaty gave the islands to New Brunswick in the 1840s.

Sights and Recreation

Wilder and with a lower profile than Campobello, Deer Island is nevertheless reached first from the New Brunswick mainland. It's devoted to fishing and is encircled with herring weirs (stabilized seine nets); other nets create the "world's largest lobster pounds." The **Old Sow,** the largest tidal whirlpool in the Western Hemisphere, can be viewed three hours before high tide from **Deer Island Point Park,** at the island's south end.

Accommodations

A great place to stay is **Deer Island Inn** (272 Rte. 772, 506/747-1998, www.deerislandinn.com, $85-105 s or d), a grand Victorian-era residence overlooking the village of Lord's Cove. The five rooms have en suite bathrooms, and rates include breakfast.

Getting There

Ferries to Deer Island depart year-round

1: Algonquin Golf Course 2: The Algonquin Resort

from Letete, 15 kilometers (9.3 miles) from Highway 1 (turn off at Exit 56, 4 km/2.5 mi west of St. George). Ferries depart up to 20 times daily from 7am. The government-run service is free, and no reservations are taken.

CAMPOBELLO ISLAND

Linked by a bridge to Lubec, Maine, Campobello is inextricably linked to the United States, but in summer a ferry links the island to Deer Island, making it a natural extension of your travels through the Fundy Isles.

Campobello, cloaked in granite, slate, and sandstone, was a favorite retreat of U.S. president Franklin Delano Roosevelt. The shingled green and bell-pepper-red family vacation home is now the main attraction at the **Roosevelt Campobello International Park** (459 Rte. 774, Welshpool, 506/752-2922, mid-May-mid-Oct. daily 10am-6pm, free). The 34-room interior is furnished with authentic family trappings, made somehow all the more poignant because FDR was stricken with polio while on vacation here.

East-facing, 425-hectare (1,050-acre) **Herring Cove Provincial Park** (136 Herring Cove Rd., 506/752-7010, late May-late Sept., $28-43) has a long stretch of beach, six hiking trails, and a nine-hole golf course (506/752-7041, greens fee $35). Around half of the campground's 88 sites come with electricity, and all have picnic tables and fire pits.

Getting There

Aside from driving to the island from Maine, between mid-June and September you can reach Campobello by ferry from Deer Island in about 20 minutes. **East Coast Ferries** (506/747-2159, www.eastcoastferriesltd.com, vehicle and driver $16, $3 per extra passenger) schedules hourly crossings daily 9am-6pm.

★ GRAND MANAN ISLAND

As the Fundy Isles' largest and most southerly island, Grand Manan (pop. 2,700) gets the brunt of the mighty Fundy high tide. Pity the

centuries of ships that have been caught in the currents during malevolent storms. Near the island, shipwrecks litter the seafloor and pay homage to the tide's merciless power.

The most photogenic of the island's four lighthouses is **Swallowtail Lighthouse,** which can be seen atop North Head as you approach the island by ferry. Illuminating the sea lanes and warning ships off the island's shoals since 1860, Swallowtail and its surrounding grassy headland provide a wonderful introduction to the island.

Apart from the surging tide, Grand Manan is blissfully peaceful. White, pink, and purple lupines and dusty-pink wild roses nod with the summer breezes. Windswept spruce, fir, and birch shade the woodland pockets. Amethyst and agate are mixed with pebbles on the beaches at **Whale Cove, Red Point,** and **White Head Island** offshore. Dulse, a nutritious purple seaweed rich in iodine and iron, washes in at **Dark Harbour** on the western coast, and islanders dry and package the briny snack for worldwide consumption.

Offshore, every species of marine life known to the Bay of Fundy congregates in the bay's nutrient-rich mouth. Whales in pursuit of herring schools swim in on incoming currents, cavorting in the tempestuous seas—the right, finback, humpback, and minke whales are at their most numerous when the plankton blooms, mid-July-September.

Bird-Watching

Birds of almost 350 species flutter everywhere in season, and each species has a place on this rock in the sea. Seabirds and waterfowl nest at the **Castalia Marsh** on the island's eastern side. Ducks and geese by the thousands inhabit the **Anchorage Beach** area, where a wet-heath bird sanctuary is speckled with ponds that attract many other species, including great blue herons. Expect to see bald eagles and other raptors on the southern cliffs mid-August-November. The eider, storm petrel, and Atlantic puffin prefer offshore islets.

Bird populations are thickest early April-June and late summer-autumn. A great way

Fundy Birding

In the Upper Fundy, where the tides are at their most dramatic, the setting belongs to a few remote villages and one of North America's most spectacular shows of migratory birds. The American bittern, Virginia rail, short-eared owl, marsh wren, and hundreds of other species soar across the wide stage. The bird-watching season varies according to species, but it generally runs late March-late May and August-September.

One of the best bird-watching spots is **Grand Manan Island.** On the mainland, bird sanctuaries are scattered from upper Chignecto Bay's western coast across Shepody Bay to the Dorchester Peninsula and the Chignecto Isthmus. They are easily missed—signs are often obscure, and numbered roads may be the only landmarks. Many are managed by **Ducks Unlimited Canada** (506/458-8848), a nonprofit environmental group that manages around 20,000 hectares (49,421 acres) of wetlands in New Brunswick alone. Another good source of information is the **Canadian Wildlife Service,** which has its Atlantic head office at **Sackville Waterfowl Park** (17 Waterfowl Ln., Sackville, 506/364-5044, Mon.-Fri. 8am-4pm). At this location, there is a display room with details of species you're likely to spot in the adjacent wetland as well as down the road at the **Tintamarre Sanctuary,** a national wildlife area. A similar reserve is **Shepody National Wildlife Area** between Alma and Hopewell Cape.

to see the birds is by hiking one of the 18 trails (totaling 70 km/43 mi) that crisscross the headland. Many wind through bird sanctuaries. Another incredible place for bird-watching is **Machias Seal Island,** the outermost bird sanctuary island. Boat tours, restricted to a limited number of passengers, depart Grand Manan to see the archipelago's highest concentration of exotic bird species, including razorbill auks, arctic terns, and 900 pairs of nesting Atlantic puffins.

Tours

While you can take whale- and bird-watching trips from St. Andrews, Grand Manan is where serious nature lovers base themselves. Space is limited and always in demand on the following tours, so make reservations.

One of the finest, most well-established sightseeing outfits in town is **Sea Watch Tours** (North Head, 506/662-8552, www.seawatchtours.com), which runs tour boats ($115 for a six-hour trip) to Machias Seal Island late June-early August. Whale-watching tours ($66) are scheduled July-September.

Food

North Head Bakery (199 Rte. 776, North Head, 506/662-8862, May-Oct. Tues.-Sat.

7:30am-5:30pm) has a great selection of cookies and cakes, plus bread baked daily from organic ingredients. Also along the main road through North Head, **Harbour Grille** (1140 Rte. 776, North Head, 506/662-3103, Mon.-Sat. 7am-9pm, Sun. noon-9pm, $11-21) is a small restaurant that is a popular gathering spot for locals. Don't expect anything too creative—come here for simple meals such as burgers, pizza, and fish-and-chips at reasonable prices.

Accommodations and Camping

Though lodgings can be found across the island, it's smart to book ahead. **Compass Rose** (83 Rte. 776, North Head, 506/662-3563, www.adventurehigh.com, mid-Apr.-Oct., $99-165 s or d) sits atop a headland in the village of North Head, at the island's north end. Its six comfortable guest rooms are spread through two buildings, one of which was the island's original post office. Breakfast (included in the rates) is served in a sunny dining room, and seafood-oriented dinners are available with advance notice. The inn is operated by a local tour company, so this is the place to stay if you are planning on kayaking or biking while on the island.

Also recommended at North Head is **Inn at Whale Cove Cottages** (120 Whistle Rd., 506/662-3181, www.whalecovecottages.ca, June-mid-Oct., $140-180 s, $150-180 d), which combines three guest rooms in a renovated 1816 residence and five cabins with a restaurant open daily for dinner through the summer season. The rooms each have private bathrooms and frilly fabrics and wallpaper, while the cottages (rented weekly) are self-contained, including the Willa Cather Cottage, in a private location perched on an oceanfront cliff.

You'll need a vehicle to get to **Anchorage Provincial Park** (Seal Cove, 506/662-7022, May-Oct., $25-39), at the south end of the island. The park contains 100 unserviced or serviced campsites with toilets, hot showers, and kitchen shelters. Reservations are not accepted, so it's wise to call ahead to check on availability.

Getting There

Coastal Transport Ltd. (506/662-3724, www.coastaltransport.ca) operates ferries between Blacks Harbour (11 km/6.8 mi south of Exit 60 from Highway 1) and North Head. The 27-kilometer (17-mile) crossing takes about 90 minutes. The car/passenger ferries sail daily year-round, with up to seven departures scheduled daily July-early September. The round-trip fare (adult $12, child $6, vehicle from $36) is collected when leaving the island. Reservations are by phone or online; you can also check online for real-time sailing information, including how full each ferry is.

Upper Fundy Coast

The impact of tidal action is extraordinarily dramatic on the Upper Fundy's coastline. The sea floods into the bay and piles up on itself, ravaging the shore at Mispec—where it has clawed into the land's edge to reveal gold veins—and pocking the coastline with spectacular caves at St. Martins. St. Martins also marks the starting point for the region's most challenging trek, to Fundy National Park. The backpacking trip involves just 40 kilometers (25 miles), but expect to spend 3-5 days. In places the high tide washes out all beach access and forces hikers back inland.

Beyond the national park, the tide's strength increases as the bay forks into the narrow Chignecto Bay and Cumberland Basin. No place is safe during an incoming tide, especially the stretch of coast from Saint John to Hopewell Cape. At Alma, the village at the park's eastern edge, the sea rises waist-high in a half hour and continues rising to a height of 14 meters (46 feet).

The Fundy orchestrates its final swan song at Hopewell Cape. Beyond the cape, its tidal impact is exhausted; some of the sea moves inland as a tidal bore and flows up the Petitcodiac River to Moncton, and the remainder washes Dorchester Peninsula's coastal marsh edges.

SAINT JOHN TO FUNDY NATIONAL PARK

From Saint John, it's about 90 kilometers (56 miles) northeast along Highway 1 to Exit 211, from which the boundary of Fundy National Park is 22 kilometers (13.7 miles) southeast.

St. Martins

St. Martins, founded in 1783 as Quaco, became one of the busiest shipbuilding centers in the Maritimes in the 1800s, turning out more than 500 ships over the course of the 19th century. Today the handsome little village is a fishing port, as evidenced by the stacks of lobster traps on the quay. At the harbor, two covered wooden bridges stand within a stone's throw of one another. The local tourist information office is housed in the lighthouse close by.

Some of the great attractions in the vicinity

are the **seaside caves** scooped out of the red sandstone cliffs by the Fundy tides. The caves can be explored at low tide.

ACCOMMODATIONS

The village has two excellent accommodations, and being just a 40-minute drive from downtown Saint John, it's worth considering staying an extra night and using St. Martins as a base for a day trip to the city. The historic **Tidal Watch Inn** (16 Beach St., 506/833-4772 or 888/833-4772, www.tidalwatchinn.ca, $110-200 s or d) has comfortable beach house quarters with 15 guest rooms, a dining room open daily for dinner, and a hot tub housed outdoors in a gazebo. Overlooking the Bay of Fundy, the Victorian Gothic ★ **St. Martins Country Inn** (303 Main St., 506/833-4534 or 800/565-5257, www.stmartinscountryinn. ca, $139-249 s or d), former home of one of the seaport's most prosperous shipbuilding families, has aptly been dubbed "the Castle" by locals. The beautifully restored mansion has 16 antiques-furnished rooms, each with a private bath and some with canopied beds. Rates include a cooked breakfast; the in-house restaurant is also open for dinner daily.

GETTING THERE

The Highway 1 route to Fundy National Park misses St. Martins. Reach St. Martins from Saint John by following Highway 111 east from the Saint John Airport for 30 kilometers (19 miles). To continue on to Fundy National Park, take Highway 111 north until you rejoin Highway 1 about 50 kilometers (31 miles) later.

★ FUNDY NATIONAL PARK

The magnificent **Fundy National Park** is a bit out of the way, but well worth the effort to get to. The 206-square-kilometer (79.5-square-mile) park encompasses a cross section of Fundy environments and landforms: highlands; deeply cut valleys; swampy lowlands; dense forests of red and sugar maple, yellow birch, beech, red spruce, and balsam fir; and a shoreline of dizzying cliffs and sand and shingle beaches. For all its wilderness, though, Fundy National Park has a surprising number of civilized comforts, including rustic housekeeping chalets, a motel, a restaurant, and a golf course.

From Saint John, Highway 1 feeds into the Trans-Canada Highway, and the backcountry Highway 114 branches off east of Sussex, peels over the Caledonia Highlands, and plummets through woodlands to sea level. Thick woods rise on one side and conceal the park's deep valleys sown with rivers and waterfalls. Glimpses of the sea, cradled by beaches, appear on the road's other side; most of the 13-kilometer (8.1-mile) shoreline is wrapped with formidably steep sandstone cliffs.

Park Entry

The park is open year-round, though full services operate and entry fees are charged only mid-May-mid-October. A one-day pass (adult $8, senior $7, child $4) is valid until 4pm the following day.

Hiking

Two dozen hiking trails wander the coastline or reach up into the highlands. The highlands hikes are easy-to-moderate treks, while the toughest trails lie along the coast, impeded by cliffs, ridges, fern glades, and thick forests.

Shorter, easier trails include the **Caribou Plain**, a 3.4-kilometer (2.1-mile) loop on flat terrain through forest and bog, and **Dickson Falls**, a 1.5-kilometer (0.9-mile) loop that offers views above and below the waterfall via a system of boardwalks and stairs. The moderately difficult **Goose River Trail** is 7.9 kilometers (4.9 miles) each way, along an old cart track to a wilderness campground at the mouth of the Goose River in the park's southwestern corner. The 10-kilometer (6.2-mile) each way **Coastal Trail** is graded as difficult, but the rewards include lush fern glades and forest and great ridgetop views over the bay and coastal sea stacks. You can get more detailed information at park headquarters or the Wolfe Lake information center, both of

which sell the useful *Fundy National Park Trail Guide.*

Other Recreation

Beyond the grassed meadow below the Visitor Reception Centre is the **Saltwater Pool** (Point Wolfe Rd., late June-early Sept., 11am-7pm, adult $4, senior $3.50, child $2), which is filled with heated saltwater piped in from the Bay of Fundy. If you prefer to be on the water rather than in it, head to **Bennett Lake,** where canoe, kayak, and rowboat rentals are $10 per hour.

Fishing is good for the plentiful trout found in the lakes and rivers; a national park fishing license, available at either visitors center, is required ($10 per day, $35 for an annual pass valid in all national parks).

Fundy National Park Golf Course (506/887-2970, mid-May-mid-Oct.) is a fun, old-fashioned nine-hole layout that tumbles down the hillside near the administration building and slices through the coastal forest like a green velvet glove whose fingers reach into the woodlands. The greens fee is $19 for nine holes, or you can play all day for $34. Adjacent to the golf course are **tennis courts** and **lawn bowling;** rental equipment is available at the pro shop.

Food

For locally harvested seafood to take back and cook at your campsite, head for ★ **Collins Lobster Shop** (20 Ocean Dr., Alma, 506/887-2054, daily 10am-8pm), which sells live and cooked lobsters, delicious lobster sandwiches, mussels, and scallops. Also in Alma is **Tides** (Parkland Village Inn, 8601 Main St., 506/887-2313, daily 8am-9pm, $15-28), a casual dining room overlooking the Bay of Fundy that not surprisingly serves lots of local seafood; it's best sampled on the Seafood Platter.

Accommodations

Lodging within the park and in the adjacent

1: Swallowtail Lighthouse on Grand Manan Island; 2: a quiet pond in Fundy National Park; 3: Fundy National Park; 4: Parkland Village Inn

fishing village of **Alma** is well priced. The best deal is at **Vista Ridge Cottages** (41 Foster Rd., 506/887-2808, www.fundyparkchalets.com, $150 s or d), which are within walking distance of most park attractions. Each cabin has three bedrooms, a small kitchen, an electric fireplace, and satellite TV.

Fundy Highlands Inn and Chalets (8714 Hwy. 114, 506/887-2930 or 888/883-8639, www.fundyhighlandchalets.com, $95-125 s or d) is 2 kilometers (1.2 miles) from the main facility area and enjoys a lofty location high above the bay in the Caledonia Highlands. Choose between comfortable rooms in the main lodge or chalets with water views. All units have cooking facilities.

Parkland Village Inn (8601 Main St., 506/887-2313 or 866/668-4337, www.parklandvillageinn.com, Apr.-Oct., $135-165 s or d) is an older three-story motel with a waterfront location along Alma's main street. The rooms are simple but regularly revamped, and most have water views. The two-bedroom suites ($165) are a steal.

Camping

The park has four campgrounds. Reservations can be made through the **Parks Canada Campground Reservation Service** (450/505-8302 or 877/737-3783, www.pccamping.ca) for $11 per booking, but they are only really necessary for July and August.

Headquarters Campground (mid-May-Oct., $26-36) is within walking distance of the Visitor Reception Centre, the swimming pool, the golf course, and Seawinds Dining Room. Facilities include showers, playgrounds, and full hookups. Back up Highway 114 a little way is **Chignecto North Campground** (mid-May-mid-Oct., $26-36), with similar facilities.

At the end of Point Wolfe Road, 6 kilometers (3.7 miles) southwest of the Visitor Reception Centre, ★ **Point Wolfe Campground** (late June-Aug., $26) has a delightful beachside location and is linked to coastal hiking trails. It has showers but no hookups.

In the park's northwest corner, **Wolfe**

Lake Campground (mid-May-mid-Oct., $17) has basic facilities such as pit toilets and fire pits.

Information

The main **Visitor Reception Centre** (506/887-6000, www.pc.gc.ca, spring and fall daily 10am-5:45pm, mid-June-early Sept. daily 8am-9:45pm) is on the park's eastern edge, just across the river from the village of Alma. In addition to handing out general park information, the center is home to various natural history displays and holds a bookstore.

Entering from the northwest, you'll find a small **visitors center** (Hwy. 114, late May-early Oct. daily 10am-5:45pm) beside picturesque Wolfe Lake.

Getting There

Fundy National Park is about 130 kilometers (81 miles) from Saint John, a 1.5-hour drive via Highway 1, then Highway 114.

ALMA TO HOPEWELL CAPE

It's 40 kilometers (25 miles) from Alma, the town just east of Fundy National Park, to Hopewell Cape. For bird-watchers there is one important detour, to New Horton Marsh.

Shepody National Wildlife Area

Shepody National Wildlife Area—New Brunswick's stellar bird-watching sanctuary—is made up of three different habitat areas. **Germantown/Beaver Brook Marshes,** 14.7 kilometers (9.1 miles) northeast of Alma, is the reserve's only inland area and spreads out on 686 hectares (1,695 acres) on Highway 114's east side. As you approach the area, look for Midway Road, the reserve's southern boundary. Turn right on Midway, cross the covered bridge, and park beyond it at the second path. The 9-kilometer (5.6-mile) trail follows the marsh's edge alongside woodlands and fields rich with ducks and herons.

The 185-hectare (457-acre) **New Horton Marsh** attracts ducks and herons to a coastal

setting. At Alma, take coastal Highway 915 for a 30-kilometer (19-mile) drive to the mudflats. The reserve's northern tip is situated where the road divides; one branch leads to inland Riverside-Albert, the other to Mary's Point Road farther out on the coast. A 4-kilometer (2.5-mile) trek through the marsh starts on a dike off the latter road. Be wary of the tides: The mudflats reach almost to the sea and quickly flood.

A few kilometers beyond New Horton Marsh, Mary's Point Road leads to **Mary's Point,** Canada's only shorebird reserve. Shorebirds by the hundreds of thousands set down on the 109-hectare (269-acre) coastal reserve, their numbers peaking mid-July-mid-August. Among the onslaught are about 9,000 blue herons and an uncountable number of cormorants, all of which swarm over the intertidal zone.

GETTING THERE

Shepody National Wildlife Area is about 20 kilometers (12.4 miles) north of Alma, a 15-minute drive via Highway 114.

HOPEWELL CAPE

The great Fundy tides have created a curiously compelling scene at Hopewell Cape, 45 kilometers (28 miles) northeast of Alma and 35 kilometers (22 miles) south of Moncton.

★ Hopewell Rocks

Hopewell Cape is the place-name, and **Hopewell Rocks** (Hwy. 114, 506/734-3534, mid-May-June and Sept.-mid-Oct. daily 9am-5pm, July-Aug. daily 9am-8pm, adult $10, senior $8, child $7.25) is the name of the natural attraction. You pay the entry fee at the tollgate and then are directed to the main Interpretive Centre, where interesting displays describe the geology of the cape and its relationship to the Fundy tides.

Trails lead to a number of cliff-top lookouts, but the vast majority of visitors make a beeline for the **Flowerpot Rocks.** The walking trail takes around 20 minutes, or you can pay $2 each way to ride the oversized golf cart shuttle. Either way, next up is a steep descent down a stairway to the ocean floor. At the staircase's first landing, you overlook an otherworldly collection of giant natural arches and mushroom-shaped pillars jutting up from the seafloor. Known as "flowerpots," these sea-sculpted red shale and conglomerate sea stacks have been separated from the mainland cliffs by the abrasive tide. Many of the flowerpots are "planted" with stunted black spruce and balsam fir, looking somewhat like clipped haircuts stuck atop the stacks. At low tide, sightseers—dwarfed by the enormous pillars—roam the beach and retrieve seashells left by the tide. Be wary of falling rocks; the pillars and cliffs are continually eroding, and there's always a chance that rocks will loosen and tumble, as happened in March 2016, when one of the best known of the formations, Elephant Rock, collapsed.

It's only possible to "walk on the ocean floor" (as it's promoted) around the flowerpots from three hours before low tide to two hours after. Catch the scene again at high tide and you'll understand why. The tide rises 16 meters (52.5 feet) here, fully flooding the area. All you'll see are the pillars' tree-covered crowns. Information centers in Fundy National Park and Moncton can tell you when the tide is low at Hopewell Rocks, or check the website (www.thehopewellrocks. ca). When low tide falls during the middle of the day in July and August, the "ocean floor" gets extremely crowded.

Food and Accommodations

Near the access road is **Hopewell Rocks Motel** (Hwy. 114, 506/734-2975 or 888/759-7070, www.hopewellrocksmotel.com, May-mid-Oct., $120-140 s or d), which has 33 rooms with water views, an outdoor swimming pool, and a restaurant with lots of seafood and dishes such as roast beef dinners.

Getting There

Hopewell Cape is 45 kilometers (28 miles) northeast of Alma, a 40-minute drive on Highway 114. To get to Hopewell Cape from Moncton, it's a 35-kilometer (22-mile) drive, 30 minutes south along Highway 114.

Flowerpot Rocks

Saint John River Valley

Tumbling along, over riverbed boulders and

through glistening pools frequented by moose and white-tailed deer, the Saint John River originates in remote northern Maine near the Québec border.

It flows through Edmundston and then curves southeast through the French-flavored towns and villages of Madawaska until it's squeezed into a spuming torrent at the stony gorge at Grand Falls. The rest of the river's journey grows increasingly placid. It's tamed by hydro dams at Beechwood and Mactaquac, and it flows under the world's longest covered bridge at Hartland before draining into the Bay of Fundy at Saint John. The river's interior course splits the inland provincial capital of Fredericton in two. This city of just 58,000 is a sightseer's

Highlights

Look for ★ to find recommended sights, activities, dining, and lodging.

★ **Historic Garrison District:** Filling two blocks of downtown Fredericton, this wide-open attraction lets visitors step back in time—while surprising them with quirky attractions, including a 17-kilogram (37.5-pound) frog (page 230).

★ **Beaverbrook Art Gallery:** Atlantic Canada's finest art gallery holds an impressive collection of Canadian work, as well as paintings by notables like Salvador Dalí (page 231).

★ **Christ Church Cathedral:** In a land of grandiose churches, this is one of the most impressive. Come for summer music recitals, or simply wander through the gardens (page 233).

★ **Kings Landing Historical Settlement:** Loyalist history comes alive at this outdoor museum that will easily fill a full day (page 240).

★ **Hartland Covered Bridge:** The most memorable way to reach the quiet village of Hartland is by crossing the Saint John River via the world's longest covered bridge (page 242).

★ **Mount Carleton Provincial Park:** This remote park takes some effort to reach, but hardy travelers will be rewarded with empty hiking trails leading to beautiful lakes, mountaintops, and waterfalls (page 244).

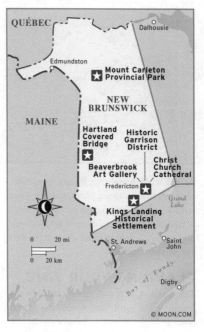

Saint John River Valley

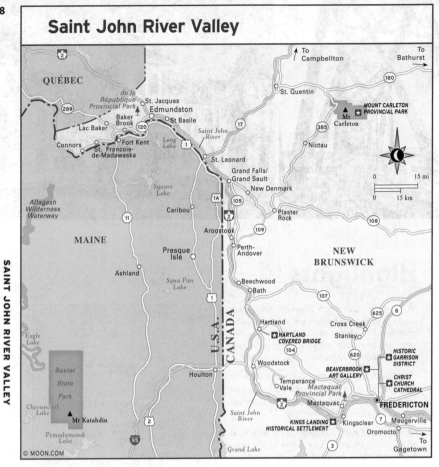

© MOON.COM

delight, with an appealing historic downtown core, riverfront walking paths, and tree-lined streets feeding back to quiet residential areas of historic homes with open porches, bay windows, and gardens of pearl-colored peonies and scarlet poppies.

PLANNING YOUR TIME

The majority of travelers who traverse the length of the Saint John River arrive overland through Québec and make the northwestern region of New Brunswick their first stop, with the more adventurous visitors detouring to the remote lakes and forests of **Mount Carleton Provincial Park**. If you've flown into Halifax and caught the ferry across the Bay of Fundy, it will take a little over an hour to reach Fredericton, which should be your focus for a day of sightseeing. This will give you enough time to explore the **Historic Garrison District,** walk through **Beaverbrook Art Gallery,** and marvel at **Christ Church Cathedral. Kings Landing Historical Settlement** is only a short drive

---

Previous: Saint John River; a bridge over the Saint John River; Legislative Assembly Building in Fredericton.

from the capital, but it would make for a long day to lump it in with the other city attractions in a single day. Besides, you'll want to continue upriver beyond Kings Landing to **Hartland** to drive across the world's longest covered bridge.

Fredericton and Vicinity

Fredericton (pop. 58,000), in the southwestern heart of the province, is New Brunswick's legislative, cultural, and educational center, and it's one of the country's oldest settlements. The city is the exception to the usual rule of thumb that a province's busiest and largest city is the logical choice for the capital. Fredericton is hardly a metropolis. Rather, it's of modest size, elegant, picture-book pretty, and very Anglo in tone and shape. "There is something subtle and elusive about it," Michael Collie wrote of Fredericton, "like a person who has had long sessions of psychoanalysis and has become more sophisticated and charming in the course of them."

Visitors flying to New Brunswick will find Fredericton makes a good introduction to the province and a good sightseeing base. Roads lead from here to every part of the province. St. Andrews and Saint John on the Fundy are each just over an hour's drive south, and Moncton is 180 kilometers (112 miles) east. And it's always nice to return to Fredericton, the province's quintessential hometown.

HISTORY

In 1783, the British created a settlement beside the Saint John River and named it Frederick's Town, in honor of King George III's second son. Two years later the little river town was designated the colonial capital—the government had grand plans for Fredericton. Surveyor Charles Morris drew up the first street grid between University Avenue and Wilsey Road. By 1786 the population center had shifted, and central Fredericton as you see it today was redrawn by another surveyor and extended from the riverfront to George Street, bounded by University Avenue and Smythe Street. Space was set aside for the Church of

England sanctuary and King's College, now the University of New Brunswick. Public commons were marked off between the riverfront and Queen Street, except for two blocks earmarked for the British Army garrison. By 1800, wharves lined the riverfront from Waterloo Row to Smythe Street, and sloops, schooners, and brigantines sped between the capital and Saint John. Shipping lumber was a profitable early business, and Fredericton added foundry products, processed leather, carriages, and wagons to its economy in the 1800s. The city was incorporated in 1848, and in 1873 the city limits were extended to nearby towns, doubling the population.

England's plan for Fredericton as a

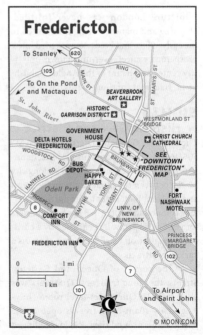

Downtown Fredericton

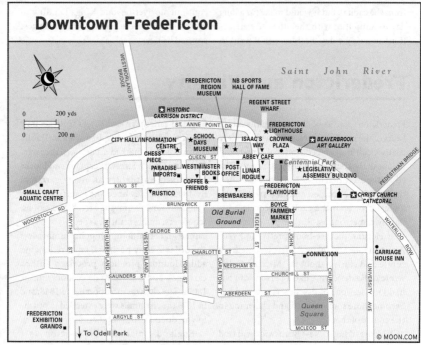

miniature London was never fulfilled. Shipping and manufacturing diminished in the early 1900s, and Fredericton settled into a prosperous, genteel government town, university center, and haunt of the Anglo establishment, roles that continue to this day.

SIGHTS

★ Historic Garrison District

The **Historic Garrison District** (Queen St., 506/460-2129), a national historic site, dominates downtown, encompassing two long city blocks between the modern city to the south and the Saint John River to the north. A military compound built in 1784 as headquarters for the British army, it is enclosed by a curlicue wrought-iron black fence that contains a variety of attractions.

At the corner of Queen and Carleton Streets, the stone **Officers' Quarters** was built in 1827. One street-level room (July-Aug. daily 10am-6pm, free) is open to the public, while around the back, low-ceilinged rooms once used to store ammunition now provide a home for vendors selling arts and crafts. Across the courtyard is the **Guard House** (July-Aug. daily 10am-6pm, free), a simple stone building that looks much like it would have in the mid-1800s, complete with costumed guards out front in summer.

FREDERICTON REGION MUSEUM

Facing the Parade Square at the east end of the Historic Garrison District, the **Fredericton Region Museum** (571 Queen St., 506/455-6041, May and Sept. Tues.-Sat. 1pm-4pm, June-Aug. daily 10am-5pm, adult $6, child $3) is housed within the former Officers' Quarters (1825), a three-story stone building designed by the Royal Engineers and unusually styled with a ground-level colonnade of white pillars and an iron handrail. The museum is devoted to provincial history from early Malecite and Mi'kmaq to contemporary events. The unlikely surprise is the Coleman Frog, a 17-kilogram (37.5-pound), 1.6-meter-long

(5.2-foot-long) amphibian stuffed for posterity and squatting inside a glass showcase on the second floor. The believe-it-or-not frog was found a century ago by local Fred Coleman, who developed a friendship with the frog and fattened it up by feeding it rum pudding and June bugs in honey sauce—or so the story goes.

SCHOOL DAYS MUSEUM

Step back into the classroom at the **School Days Museum** (corner of Queen and York Sts., 506/459-3738, mid-June-Aug. Mon.-Fri. 10am-4pm, Sat. 1pm-4pm, free), across York Street from City Hall. In addition to a reconstructed classroom, you'll find an interesting display on one-room schools, textbooks and training manuals, and furniture from as early as the mid-1800s.

NEW BRUNSWICK SPORTS HALL OF FAME

The John Thurston Clark Memorial Building is an impressive 1881 Second Empire French Revival edifice that once served as customs house and post office. The building now provides a home for the **New Brunswick Sports Hall of Fame** (503 Queen St., 506/453-3747, June-early Sept. Tues.-Fri. noon-5pm, Sat. 10am-5pm, adult $3, child $2), with exhibits highlighting the province's best sporting men and women.

City Hall

The red-brick **City Hall**, at the corner of Queen and York Streets and across from the Historic Garrison District, is central to everywhere downtown. The elegant 1876 building has housed city offices, a jail, a farmers market, and an opera house. Its high tower showcases the city's copper clock, and the decorative fountain in front—crowned by the figurine that Frederictonians have dubbed "Freddie, the little nude dude"—was added in 1885.

Inside, the **Council Chamber** is adorned with a series of 27 locally produced tapestries depicting the city's history. The **Fredericton**

Visitor Information Centre (397 Queen St., 506/460-2129), in the building's front vestibule, conducts chamber tours (mid-May-early Oct. daily 8:15am-7:30pm, early Oct.-mid-May Mon.-Fri. by appointment 8:15am-4:30pm).

Fredericton Lighthouse

Cross Regent Street from the Historic Garrison District to reach the privately operated **Lighthouse on the Green** (659 Queen St., 506/455-3371, mid-June-mid-Sept. daily 10am-10pm, adult $2). The interior consists of 13 separate landings exhibiting shipping and river-sailing artifacts. The top level commands a magnificent riverfront view. At ground level, you'll find a gift shop and outdoor café serving light lunches and delicious ice cream.

★ Beaverbrook Art Gallery

On the east side of downtown is **Beaverbrook Art Gallery** (703 Queen St., 506/458-2028, Mon.-Sat. 10am-5pm, Sun. noon-5pm, adult $10, senior $8, child $5), which was donated to the city by New Brunswick art maven Lord Beaverbrook, also known as William Maxwell Aitken. The gallery boasts an impressive 2,000-piece collection—the most extensive British fine arts collection in Atlantic Canada, if not the nation. Among the British painters represented are Thomas Gainsborough, Sir Joshua Reynolds, John Constable, and Walter Richard Sickert. You'll find Graham Sutherland's sketches of Winston Churchill—drawn in preparation for Churchill's official portrait—and works by Atlantic Canada's Miller Brittain, Alex Colville, and Jack Humphrey. Also central to the collection are the oils of Cornelius Krieghoff, depicting social and domestic scenes of early life in Acadia. Lord Beaverbrook could not resist the European masters—Salvador Dalí's large-scale *Santiago El Grande* and Botticelli's *Resurrection* are prominently displayed.

Legislative Assembly Building

The splendidly regal **Legislative Assembly**

Building (706 Queen St., 506/453-2527, mid-June-Aug. daily 9am-5pm, Sept.-mid-June Mon.-Fri. 8:30am-4pm, free) lies kitty-corner from the Beaverbrook Art Gallery. The sandstone French Revival building spreads across a manicured lawn, its massive wings pierced with high arched windows, and the upper floor and tower rotunda are washed in glistening white. The building was completed in 1882 at a cost of $120,000, including construction and furnishings. The front portico entrance opens into an interior decorated in high Victorian style—the apex of expensive taste at the time. Glinting Waterford prisms are set in brass chandeliers, and the spacious rooms are wallpapered in an Oriental design. The interior's pièce de résistance is the **Assembly Chamber,** centered around an ornate throne set on a dais and sheltered with a canopy.

John James Audubon's *Birds of America* is kept in the **Legislative Library.** One of four volumes is on display in a climate-controlled exhibit, and pages are periodically turned to show the meticulous paintings.

★ Christ Church Cathedral

Gothic-styled cathedrals were designed to soar grandiosely toward heaven, and this storied stone cathedral is no exception. With a lofty copper-clad central spire and elegant linear stone tracery, **Christ Church Cathedral** (506/450-8500) rises from a grassy city block at Church and Brunswick Streets. Begun in 1845 and consecrated in 1853, this was the first entirely new cathedral founded on British soil since the Norman Conquest way back in 1066. It was rebuilt after a fire in 1911 and is still the place where the city's nabobs go to pay their respects to the benevolent powers that be. It's open year-round, with recitals taking place in summer on Friday 12:10pm-12:50pm.

Historic Cemeteries

The **Old Burial Ground** is bounded by

1: Historic Garrison District; 2: Christ Church Cathedral

Regent, Brunswick, George, and Sunbury Streets. The site—spliced with walkways beneath tall trees—is one of two historic burial grounds in town. This spread of greenery was the final resting place for Loyalist notables.

The **Loyalist Cemetery** (formerly the Salamanca graveyard), on an unmarked gravel road off Waterloo Row at the riverfront, is simpler and marks the final resting place of the founding Loyalists who died in the town's first winter of 1783-1784.

Odell Park

Of the 355 hectares (877 acres) of lush parkland throughout the city, **Odell Park** (Rockwood Ave., 506/460-2038) is the choice spread, holding 16 kilometers (9.9 miles) of trails, formal lawns, duck ponds, a deer pen, barbecue pits, and picnic tables. The park is Fredericton's largest, covering 175 hectares (432 acres). It is best known for an arboretum holding every tree species in the province; a 2.8-kilometer (1.7-mile) walking trail divided into three loops wanders through the shady expanse. To get there from downtown, head south on Rockwood Avenue.

RECREATION

The riverfront **Small Craft Aquatic Centre** (83 Brunswick St., 506/460-2260, July-Aug. daily 6:30am-9am and noon-8:30pm, shorter hours in spring and fall) rents recreational rowing shells, canoes, and kayaks; gives lessons; and leads kayak tours.

ENTERTAINMENT AND EVENTS
Nightlife

Locals love their low-key pubs, and you will find many around the downtown core. The **Lunar Rogue** (625 King St., 506/450-2065, Mon.-Sat. 11am-1am, Sun. 11am-10pm) heads the list with English pub ambience, Canadian and British draft beer, and live music—usually with a Celtic flavor—several nights a week. A cluster of pubs surrounds Pipers Lane, an alley that connects the 300 blocks of King and Queen Streets. **Dolan's Pub** (349 King

St., 506/454-7474, Mon.-Tues. 11:30am-11pm, Wed.-Sat. 11:30am-2am) offers an excellent menu of pub grub and slightly fancier fare, as well as live entertainment Thursday-Saturday.

Performing Arts

Fredericton specializes in entertaining summertime visitors. Outdoor festivities center around the Garrison Historic District, where **Theatre in the Park** (www.calithumpians.com) takes to the boards July-early September. Its humorous and historical productions take place daily at 12:15pm and on weekends at 2pm. Best of all, this entire program is presented free of charge.

Theatre New Brunswick (55 Whiting Rd., 506/460-1381, www.tnb.nb.ca), the province's only professional English-speaking theater company, operates full-tilt during the autumn-spring theater season. **The Playhouse Fredericton** (686 Queen St., 506/458-8344, theplayhouse.ca), right downtown, is a stylish venue that hosts touring artists and local theater companies year-round.

Festivals and Events

Festival Francophone, for three days late in May, celebrates Acadian language and culture with concerts, dancing, and children's activities. The festivities take place at **Centre Communautaire Sainte-Anne** (715 Priestman St., 506/453-2731, www.centre-sainte-anne.nb.ca).

The **New Brunswick Highland Games** (506/452-9244, www.highlandgames.ca), a three-day Celtic tribute featuring pipe bands, highland dancing, Gaelic singing, heavy sports, clan booths, and more, takes over the city the last weekend of July.

Fredericton had its first fall fair in 1825, and the tradition continues at the **New Brunswick Provincial Exhibition** (361 Smythe St., 506/458-8819, www.nbex.ca, adult $10, senior $9, child $5), with six days of country fair trappings, including harness racing, lawn mower races, tractor pulls, chainsaw carving, and stage shows. It's held at the Fredericton Exhibition Grounds during early September.

The summer season finishes in a clamor of music as the outdoor **Harvest Jazz and Blues Festival** (506/454-2583, www.harvestjazzandblues.com) takes over the downtown streets for five days the second week of September. It's billed as the biggest jazz and blues fest east of Montréal, and it features musicians from all over North America.

the Old Burial Ground

By Any Other Name

Fredericton is known by many names. New Brunswickers have dubbed the city "North America's Last Surviving Hometown." You could debate the claim, perhaps, but it nonetheless does sum up local priorities.

The naming trend goes back to the 1800s, when locals ruefully joked that the city had a fire every Saturday night and dubbed it the "City of Fires." In 1911, one such fire destroyed the Christ Church Cathedral. The sanctuary was quickly rebuilt, its grandiose silhouette on the skyline leading to the moniker "Cathedral City."

Another Fredericton nickname, "City of Stately Elms," is a testament to Fredericton's leafy ambience. The quiet streets are lined mainly with elms, a choice that goes back to founding Loyalist times. They've survived centuries, even beating Dutch elm disease, which the city quelled in the 1960s and 1970s.

Fredericton's reputation as "Canada's Poets' Corner" is a tribute to native sons Bliss Carmen, Sir Charles G. D. Roberts, and Francis Joseph Sherman. And finally, the nickname "Canada's Pewtersmith Capital" singles out the city's preeminent craft, developed here first by pewtersmith Ivan Crowell in the 18th century.

SHOPPING

Shopping areas are concentrated downtown, mainly along Regent, Queen, York, and King Streets as well as the adjacent side streets, plus on Woodstock Road and at the malls.

Arts and Crafts

Several shops are known for craft specialties. **Aitkens Pewter** (408 Queen St., 506/453-9474, Mon.-Fri. 9am-6pm, Sat. 10am-5pm) stocks handcrafted pewter holloware, jewelry, and decorative pieces. **Cultures Boutique** (383 Mazzuca Ln., 506/462-3088, Mon.-Thurs. and Sat. 10am-5pm, Fri. 10am-7pm) is a nonprofit operation featuring crafts produced by third-world artisans. It is located off York Street between King and Queen Streets.

Connexion (732 Charlotte St., 506/478-4484, Tues.-Fri. noon-4pm or check www.connexionarc.org for special events) is a nonprofit artists' outlet with an eminent reputation for the province's arts. In a stylishly renovated residence, **Gallery 78** (796 Queen St., 506/454-5192, Tues.-Fri. 10am-5pm, Sat. 10am-3pm, Sun. 1pm-4pm) is a stylish space within a grand residence on the east side of downtown that represents the province's very best artists.

FOOD

Fredericton has a reputation for so-so dining. Don't believe it. True, you won't find tony dining rooms by the dozens, and aside from at a few fine restaurants, the cooking is less than fancy. Nonetheless, you can sample virtually all the capital's fare without a qualm, and your dining dollar will go a long way, too.

Contemporary

Enthusiastic local owners, a funky ambience in an 1855 courthouse, and well-priced meals make ★ **Isaac's Way** (649 Queen St., 506/474-7222, Mon. 4pm-10pm, Tues.-Fri. 11:30am-10pm, Sat.-Sun. 10am-10pm, $19-31) a solid choice for lunch or dinner. Game and produce are sourced from within the province, and everything is made from scratch—right down to the sauces and desserts. Sample dinner mains include maple curry salmon (using local maple syrup, of course) and chicken breast stuffed with goat cheese and cranberries.

Pubs

The **Lunar Rogue** (625 King St., 506/450-2065, Mon.-Sat. 11am-1am, Sun. 11am-10pm, $12-24), one of Fredericton's most popular pubs, offers dining indoors or alfresco. The same menu is offered throughout the day and has something to suit everyone—sandwiches, salads, soups, stir-fries, pastas, and a decent selection of seafood such as haddock fish cakes for $12 and a seafood platter for $24.

Hotel Dining

The dining rooms at the major hotels are good bets for fancier fare. At the Crowne Plaza Fredericton Lord Beaverbrook (659 Queen St., 506/451-1804), **Maxwell's** (daily 6:30am-11pm, $18-34), with city and river views, offers breakfast and lunch at moderate prices and dinner items using regional produce.

At the Delta Hotels Fredericton, **Catch Urban Grill** (225 Woodstock Rd., 506/457-7000, Mon.-Sat. 7am-2pm and 5pm-9pm, Sun. 7am-2pm, $25-38) lures crowds for fare such as chicken saltimbocca—a sautéed stuffed chicken breast basted with white wine and served on linguine—and seafood, beef, and pasta. Look for cooked breakfasts under $15 and the ever-popular Sunday brunch buffet ($29). Also at the Delta is **The Dip** (June-Aug. daily 11am-11pm), an outdoor poolside restaurant with tables and chairs spread across a terrace where the views extend across the river. The menu covers all bases, from simple sandwiches to a lobster boil.

Although it's not actually within a hotel, **Diplomat Restaurant** (253 Woodstock Rd., 506/454-2400, 24 hours daily, $13-24) is across the parking lot from the Delta Hotels Fredericton on the west side of downtown. This family-style restaurant has well-priced breakfasts served throughout the day and a mix of Canadian and Chinese dishes that aren't a bargain, but portions are generous. The lunch buffet is $18 and the dinner buffet $22 ($27 on weekends); children 10 and under eat for half price.

Mediterranean

RustiCo. (304 King St., 506/451-3473, daily 11:30am-midnight, $15-30) is a large space with an almost equally large patio that fills every night with a mix of locals and visitors. The highlight is pizza from a wood-fired oven, but the menu is wide-ranging, with a few vegetarian choices and an abundance of local produce and game.

Pizza

Anyone hankering for pizza can step into **BrewBakers** (546 King St., 506/459-0067, Mon. 11:30am-9pm, Tues.-Thurs. 11:30am-10pm, Fri. 11:30am-11pm, Sat. 5pm-11pm, Sun. 5pm-9pm, $15-29), where the pizzas are baked in a wood-fired oven and accompanied by pastas and salads in a contemporary setting.

Cafés and Cheap Eats

Beside City Hall in the heart of downtown, **Chess Piece** (361 Queen St., 506/459-1969, Mon.-Fri. 7am-9pm, Sat. 8am-9pm, Sun. 10am-4pm) is a handy location to pick up freshly made croissants, sandwiches to go, and European-inspired cakes and pastries.

★ **Happy Baker** (520 King St., 506/455-7551, Mon.-Fri. 7am-3pm, lunches $7-10) is worth searching out in the bowels of the HSBC Building. In addition to the usual array of coffee concoctions, you can purchase a wide array of European-style breads, pastries, and desserts. Continental breakfasts and lunches, including the very best sandwiches I've found in the city, round out this excellent little spot. In the vicinity, **Coffee & Friends** (415 King St., 506/455-4554, Mon. 11am-4pm, Tues.-Fri. 7am-5pm, Sat. 10am-5pm, lunches $6-10) has a smaller selection of similar lunches, but it also has a wide selection of teas, as well as a few outdoor tables.

Coffee-loving locals will tell you that the best coffee is poured at **Paradise Imports** (95 York St., 506/455-1711, Mon.-Fri. 10am-7pm, Sat. 9am-6pm), a funky jewelry store with an espresso bar in one corner. The coffee is roasted in-house daily and served with muffins and cakes.

Year-round, the **Boyce Farmers' Market** (665 George St., between Regent St. and Saint John St., 506/451-1815, Sat. 6am-1pm) lures everybody with stalls heaped with baked goods, homemade German sausage, other local delicacies, and crafts.

Abbey Cafe (546 Queen St., 506/455-6368, Mon. 11am-6pm, Tues.-Fri. 9am-9pm, Sat. 11am-9pm, Sun. noon-6pm, $9-16) is a small restaurant offering simple vegetarian and vegan cooking in a casual atmosphere. Local art on the walls brightens up the room.

ACCOMMODATIONS AND CAMPING

In keeping with its status as a provincial capital, Fredericton has a choice of downtown chain hotels, each offering a wide range of modern services aimed at business travelers. Other options are historic inns dotted around the outskirts of downtown and regular motels along major arteries. The main concentration of the latter is 3 kilometers (1.9 miles) south of downtown at the junction of Regent and Prospect Streets (Exits 6A and 6B off Hwy. 8).

$50-100

Across the river from downtown, the **Fort Nashwaak Motel** (15 Riverside Dr., 506/472-4411 or 800/684-8999, www.fortnashwaak.com, $85-100 s or d) and, 4 kilometers (2.5 miles) downstream, the **Norfolk Motel** (815 Riverside Dr., 506/472-3278 or 800/686-8555, $80-100 s or d) are basic cheapies with wireless Internet and a number of kitchenettes.

$100-150

The three-story Queen Anne Revival **Carriage House Inn** (230 University Ave., 506/452-9924 or 800/267-6068, www.carriagehouse-inn.net, $130 s, $140 d) is a restored 1875 home southeast of downtown but still within walking distance. The 10 guest rooms are furnished with antiques; guests have use of a solarium and laundry. Breakfasts are a real treat.

None of the motels around the junction of Regent and Prospect Streets offer anything extraordinary. Instead, you get the reliability of chains such as the **Comfort Inn** (797 Prospect St., 506/453-0800 or 800/228-5150, www.choicehotels.ca, $120 s, $135 d). In the vicinity, and one of the largest motels in the city, is the four-story **Fredericton Inn** (1315

Regent St., 506/455-1430 or 800/561-8777, www.frederictoninn.nb.ca, $135 s or d), between the Regent and Fredericton shopping malls. It has 200 guest rooms, two restaurants (one open for dinner buffets and summer lobster suppers), a lounge, and an indoor pool.

Around 20 kilometers (12.4 miles) west of downtown along Highway 102 (at Exit 274), **Riverside Resort** (35 Mactaquac Rd., 506/363-5111 or 800/561-5111, www.riversidefredericton.com, from $150 s or d) has a very un-city-like location within striking distance of Kings Landing. It's a sprawling property with a restaurant and lounge and a fitness center with a heated indoor pool, a hot tub, and an exercise deck. It features 85 motel-like rooms in the three-story main building, and six two-bedroom chalets ($280 s or d) are also on the manicured grounds.

$150-200

★ **On the Pond** (Rte. 615, Mactaquac, 506/363-3420 or 800/984-2555, www.onthepond.com, from $175 s or d) is a grandiose country inn where the emphasis is on being pampered in a back-to-nature environment. Guests enjoy a wide variety of spa services, proximity to Mactaquac Provincial Park and its golf course, and a fitness center. The eight guest rooms have an earthy old-world charm, with little niceties such as plush robes and inviting living areas. Bed-and-breakfast rates start at $170 per person, but also check the website for spa and golf packages.

Along the river, within striking distance of downtown attractions, is the ★ **Delta Hotels Fredericton** (225 Woodstock Rd., 506/457-7000 or 888/890-3222, www.marriott.com, from $199 s or d), which has an agreeable resort-style atmosphere centering on a large outdoor pool complex, complete with resort furniture and a poolside bar. It also has an indoor pool, a fitness room, two restaurants, and a lounge. Check the website for discounted rooms, and maybe consider a splurge on a suite that will cost the same as a regular room in a big-city hotel.

Over $200

One of Fredericton's better lodgings is the **Crowne Plaza Fredericton Lord Beaverbrook** (659 Queen St., 506/455-3371 or 866/444-1946, www.crowneplaza.com, $230-460 s or d), aimed squarely at those in town on government business. Don't let the dowdy exterior of this bulky hotel put you off—the 165 guest rooms are thoroughly modernized. Amenities include an indoor pool and fitness complex, two dining rooms, and a lounge.

Campgrounds

The closest camping to Fredericton is at **Hartt Island RV Resort,** 7 kilometers (4.3 miles) west of town on the Trans-Canada Highway (2475 Woodstock Rd., 506/462-9400, www.harttisland.ca, May-Oct., $45-75), which is a great spot to enjoy river sports like canoeing and kayaking. Amenities include a huge outdoor pool complex, mini-golf, and kayak tours.

On the same side of the city, but on the north side of the river, **Mactaquac Provincial Park Campground** (Hwy. 105, 506/363-4747, mid-May-mid-Oct., $33-40) is a huge facility 24 kilometers (15 miles) from downtown. In addition to 305 campsites, there's a golf course, hiking, biking, swimming, and fishing.

INFORMATION AND SERVICES

The main **Visitor Information Centre** (397 Queen St., 506/460-2129, mid-May-late June and Sept.-mid-Oct. daily 8am-5pm, late June-Aug. daily 8am-8pm) is right downtown, inside the lobby of City Hall. For advance information, contact **Fredericton Tourism** (506/460-2041 or 888/888-4768, www.tourismfredericton.ca).

In an emergency, call 911 or the **RCMP** (1445 Regent St., 506/452-3400). For medical emergencies, contact the **Dr. Everett Chalmers Hospital** (700 Priestman St., 506/452-5400) or **Regent Street After Hours Clinic** (1015 Regent St., 506/458-0200, Mon.-Fri. 5:30pm-9:45pm).

GETTING THERE

Fredericton is in the south-central portion of New Brunswick along the Trans-Canada Highway (Highway 2). From Bangor, Maine, it's around three hours via Highway 95, then Highway 2 to Fredericton. It's 110 kilometers (68 miles) to Fredericton from Saint John, over an hour via Highway 7, and 180 kilometers (112 miles) from Moncton, two hours via Highway 2. If you are driving from Halifax to Fredericton, allow around 4.5 hours for the 440-kilometer (275-mile) drive via Moncton.

Fredericton Airport (2570 Hwy. 102, 506/460-0920, www.frederictonairport.ca), 14 kilometers (8.7 miles) southeast of downtown off Highway 102, is served by daily **Air Canada** (506/458-8561 or 888/247-2262, www.aircanada.com) flights from Montréal, Toronto, Ottawa, and Halifax. Avis, Hertz, Budget, and National have counters near the baggage carousels. Other airport facilities include a café, a gift shop, free wireless Internet, and a business center. A cab to downtown costs $22.

Maritime Bus (105 Dundonald St., 506/455-2049, www.maritimebus.com) has daily bus service from Fredericton to Saint John, Moncton, and Edmundston. The small terminal is open daily 8am-8:30pm.

GETTING AROUND

Fredericton Transit (506/460-2200) has a web of nine bus routes connecting downtown with outlying areas (Mon.-Sat.). Fare is $2.75 per sector.

Look for cabs cruising downtown streets and waiting at major hotels, or call **Trius Taxi** (506/454-4444).

Car rental firms are plentiful. Chains in town include **Avis** (506/446-6006), **Budget** (506/452-1107), **Hertz** (506/446-9079), and **National** (506/453-1700).

Metered parking is plentiful in parking lots behind sights and curbside on Queen, King, upper York, Carleton, Regent, and Saint John Streets. The city provides free three-day parking passes for out-of-province visitors; the passes are available at City Hall and the

Legislative Assembly Building, both on Queen Street.

GAGETOWN AND VICINITY

The Saint John River downstream of Fredericton is dotted with islands, around which a skein of twisting channels is braided. It's beautiful countryside, and a delightful drive, with Gagetown, 60 kilometers (37 miles) from the capital, a good turnaround point. Quite a bit goes on in this little town of 600 over the course of the season. Look for the four-day **Queens County Fair** (www.queenscountyfair.com) in mid-September, which features lots of agricultural attractions and competitions.

Sir Leonard Tilley House (69 Front St., 506/488-2966, mid-June-mid-Sept. daily 10am-5pm, adult $3) is a handsome white wooden house that was the birthplace of Sir Leonard Tilley, one of the "Fathers of Confederation." The first floor is dutifully furnished with Loyalist antiques, and upstairs holds vintage county exhibits.

The riverfront town of **Oromocto,** halfway to Gagetown, is built around Canadian Forces Base Gagetown, a military training installation located near the town center off Broad Road. On the base itself, the **New Brunswick Military History Museum** (506/422-1304, Mon.-Fri. 8am-4pm, $2) has exhibits on the past and present of the Canadian armed forces since the late 18th century, with weapons, uniforms, and other memorabilia.

Getting There

To get to Oromocto from Fredericton, follow Highway 102 east along the river for just over 20 kilometers (12.4 miles). Continue on to Gagetown on Highway 102, cross divided Highway 2 (the Trans-Canada Highway), and, 60 kilometers (37 miles) later, you'll find yourself in the pretty riverfront town of Gagetown.

Up the Saint John River

From Fredericton, Highway 2 (the Trans-Canada Highway) wends north along the Saint John River, crossing it numerous times before reaching Edmundston after 270 kilometers (165 miles). As part of the transcontinental highway, it's easy, smooth driving, but leave the main route and you'll find beautiful rural scenery and a region dotted with small towns. The region's highlights are within daytripping distance of Fredericton, so you could travel as far as Hartland to see the world's longest covered bridge and then spend the afternoon at Kings Landing.

MACTAQUAC AND VICINITY

Stemming the flow of the Saint John River is **Mactaquac Dam,** part of a massive hydroelectric scheme 20 kilometers (12.4 miles) west of Fredericton that supplies power to 10 percent of New Brunswick residences. Completed in 1968, the dam rerouted the river and raised the water level 60 meters (197 feet), flooding the valley and creating the Mactaquac Lake Basin. Historic buildings from the flooded area found a new home at the Kings Landing Historical Settlement, a provincial heritage park that opened in 1974.

Mactaquac Provincial Park

Not all New Brunswickers were pleased with this massive river alteration, but the creation of 525-hectare (1,297-acre) **Mactaquac Provincial Park,** which opened the following year, was a sweetener. It's beside Highway 105 on the north side of the river, 24 kilometers (15 miles) upriver from Fredericton.

The park ($10 per vehicle per day) offers hiking trails, supervised beaches, bike rentals, picnic areas, and bass fishing, but its pièce de résistance is the 18-hole **Mactaquac Golf Course** (506/363-4926, greens fee $55), a challenging tree-lined layout considered one of Atlantic Canada's top public courses.

The wooded campground has more than 300 sites ($28 unserviced, $38 with electrical hookups) with kitchen shelters, hot showers, a launderette, and a campers' store fronting the Mactaquac Lake Basin. The park and campground are open mid-May-mid-October.

Getting There

Mactaquac is 25 kilometers (15.5 miles) west of Fredericton, a 20-minute drive via Highway 102. You can also reach Mactaquac from Fredericton by using Highway 105, making for a 30-kilometer (19-mile) drive that takes 30 minutes.

★ KINGS LANDING HISTORICAL SETTLEMENT

A marvelous counterpoint to Caraquet's Village Historique Acadien, the Kings Landing Historical Settlement (5804 Rte. 102, 506/363-4999, mid-June-early Oct. daily 10am-5pm, adult $18, senior $16, child $13)—a grand-scale living museum—is in a beautiful setting alongside the Saint John River, 35 kilometers (22 miles) west of Fredericton. The river valley was settled by Loyalists who arrived in New Brunswick in 1783, and it is this era through to the early 1900s that the village represents. Bring comfortable walking shoes, since the site spreads across 120 hectares (296 acres) with 70 houses and buildings—among them a sawmill, farmhouses, a school, a forge, and a printing office. Informative costumed "residents" depict rural New Brunswick life as it was lived in the 1800s. One of many interesting links to the past is an orchard where hybrid apples developed by Francis Peabody Sharp in the mid-1800s are grown. Demonstrations include horseshoeing, metal forging, cloth spinning and weaving, and farming. Special events include live theater, an agricultural fair in late August, the Provincial Town Criers' Competition in early September, and a Harvest Festival in early October to close out the season.

No one ever leaves the Kings Head Inn (506/363-4950, late May-mid-Oct. daily 11:30am-4:30pm, lunches $7-14) complaining about being hungry. At the riverside end of the village, this restaurant serves up hearty fare like salmon chowder, crunchy almond fish cakes, and divine desserts that include maple-brandy squash pie.

Getting There

Kings Landing is about 35 kilometers (22 miles) west of Fredericton, a 30-minute drive via Highway 2 (take Exit 253).

TO GRAND FALLS

West from Kings Landing, the Trans-Canada Highway follows the Saint John River along one of its loveliest stretches. Tourism New Brunswick refers to this stretch of highway, the 200 kilometers (124 miles) between Fredericton and Grand Falls, as the River Valley Scenic Drive. To fully appreciate the forested scenery and the wide and blue river, bounded by green fields and forests of maple and hemlock, detour from the Trans-Canada Highway and take secondary roads such as Highway 105 through the riverside communities of Woodstock and Hartland. Allow four hours to travel between Fredericton and Grand Falls along these roads.

Woodstock

Around 100 kilometers (62 miles) west then north from Fredericton, Woodstock is a charming riverside town with paths and parkland along the Saint John River. The gracious 1884 red-brick courthouse is a dominant feature of the main street, but The River Restaurant (558 Main St., 506/325-2829, Mon.-Sat. 11am-midnight, Sun. 11am-10pm, $11-21) is where you'll find the law-abiding locals. The most sought after tables on a warm day are those out on the riverside deck, but inside is also welcoming at this part pub, part restaurant. The food is typical pub fare, with a

---

1: Saint John River; 2: Kings Landing Historical Settlement

few Irish favorites thrown in—cottage pie and meatloaf are both reasonably priced.

GETTING THERE
Following Highway 2, it's 100 kilometers (62 miles) from Fredericton to Woodstock, a one-hour drive.

★ Hartland Covered Bridge

North from Woodstock, give the Trans-Canada Highway a miss and stick to Highway 103, which hugs the west bank of the Saint John River for 30 kilometers (19 miles), from where it makes a sharp right turn and crosses the world's longest covered bridge before emerging in the village of Hartland. The **Hartland Covered Bridge** is only wide enough for one-way traffic, so make sure no one else is driving toward you before entering the bridge. Built in 1901, covered in 1921, and now protected as a national historic site, it stretches 391 meters (nearly a quarter mile) over the Saint John River. On the east side is an information center (summer daily 9am-6pm) with displays on the bridge's history and on other covered bridges in New Brunswick. From this point, a walking trail leads upstream and then along the Becaguimac Stream.

Grand Falls (Grand-Sault)

The otherwise placid Saint John River becomes a frothing white torrent when it plunges 23 meters (75.5 feet) over the stony cataract that gave Grand Falls, or Grand-Sault, its name. Below the falls, which have been harnessed to produce hydroelectric power, the tremendous force of the river has worn a 2-kilometer-long (1.2-mile-long), horseshoe-shaped gorge through 70-meter-high (230-foot-high) rock walls. Here the river is at its narrowest, and the gorge's bottleneck impedes the water's force. The river pushes through the narrows in tumultuous rapids, like pent-up champagne bursting from the bottle.

Grand Falls Visitor Information Centre (25 Madawaska Rd., 506/475-7788, early May-June and Sept.-mid-Oct. daily 9am-6pm, July-Aug. daily 9am-9pm) makes a convenient starting point for exploring the area. From the center's rear windows, you'll see the thundering cataracts tumbling through the gorge. A 2-kilometer-long (1.2-mile-long) path leads along the gorge to **La Rochelle.** From there, a rock staircase leads down to the cataract edge, where the agitated river swirls in the rocky wells. The river is most spectacular during spring runoff.

Hartland Covered Bridge

Several well-priced lodgings in Grand Falls make the town all the more appealing for overnight stays. The best choice is the **Quality Inn** (10039 Rte. 144, 506/473-1300, www.choicehotels.ca, $120-175 s or d), on the north side of town. It has 100 well-appointed rooms, an indoor pool, and a small fitness room, and a light breakfast is included.

GETTING THERE

It's nearly 200 kilometers (124 miles) from Fredericton to Grand Falls, less than a two-hour drive via Highway 2.

EDMUNDSTON AND VICINITY

Originally settled by Acadian refugees on the site of a Malecite village, Edmundston boasts 16,000 residents, over 90 percent of whom are French speakers, a higher percentage than any other North American city outside Québec.

Sights and Recreation

For an insight into the area's checkered history and "mythical Madawaska," stop in at the **Madawaska Museum** (195 Blvd. Hébert, 506/737-5282, July-Aug. Mon.-Fri. 10am-5pm, Sat.-Sun. 1pm-5pm, Sept.-June Mon.-Thurs. 10am-3pm, Sat.-Sun. 1pm-5pm, adult $5, child $3). But to truly experience the local Acadian-flavored culture, come for the five-day **Foire Brayonne** (506/739-6608, www.foirebrayonne.com), on the weekend closest to August 1. More than 100,000 people show up for the celebration of Brayon foods, music, dance, sports, and other entertainment.

Accommodations

Edmundston's ritziest lodging is the large **Four Points by Sheraton Edmundston** (100 Rice St., 506/739-7321 or 800/576-4656, www.marriott.com, from $135 s or d), which has over 100 spacious and elegantly decorated guest rooms, an indoor pool, hot tub, and sauna, a restaurant, a lounge, and free wireless Internet throughout. With similar facilities is **Quality Travelodge by Wyndham Edmundston** (919 Canada Rd., 506/735-5525 or 800/407-9832, www.wyndhamhotels.com, $135-145 s or d). Both are accessed from Exit 18 of the Trans-Canada Highway.

Getting There

From Fredericton, it's 270 kilometers (165 miles) northwest, less than three hours along Highway 2, to Edmundston.

Saint-Jacques

North of Edmundston, about halfway to the Québec border, is the town of Saint-Jacques, home of **République Provincial Park,** where the highlight is the **New Brunswick Botanical Garden** (Exit 8 of the Trans-Canada Hwy., 506/737-5383, May-June and Sept. daily 9am-5pm, July-Aug. daily 9am-8pm, adult $18, senior $15, child $8). The formal garden complex on 17 hectares (42 acres) was designed by the skilled Michel Marceau (who also designed the famous Montreal Botanical Garden). It brims with 60,000 plants of 1,500 species. Roses, perennials, and rhododendrons bloom among the prolific posies in nine gardens, all orchestrated with classical music in a romantic vein. **Butterflies of the World** (included in admission fee) is a glass pavilion filled with butterflies from Central and South America. Other park facilities include an outdoor heated swimming pool ($2.50 pp), tennis courts, and a **campground** (506/735-2541, May-Sept., $28-36) beside the Madawaska River.

Targeted at visitors entering New Brunswick from Québec, the **Provincial Visitor Information Centre** (17412 Rte. 2, 506/735-2747, late May-June and Sept.-early Oct. daily 9am-6pm, July-Aug. daily 9am-7pm) is alongside the Trans-Canada Highway, 9 kilometers (5.6 miles) south of the border.

GETTING THERE

Saint-Jacques is about 10 kilometers (6.2 miles) north of Edmundston, a 10-minute drive via Highway 2. It's 280 kilometers (175 miles) northwest from Fredericton, three hours, also along Highway 2.

Lac-Baker

Lac-Baker is in New Brunswick's remote northwestern corner, near where the Saint John River flows into the province from the northern reaches of Maine. Here you'll find all the quiet woodlands you could ever want, as well as the rustic **Camping Plein Air Lac Baker** (510 Church Rd., 506/992-2136, www. campinglacbaker.com, mid-May-mid-Sept.). The lakeshore complex lies several kilometers north of the river and has eight cabins ($85-105 s or d), campsites ($28-40), a dining room and canteen, and swimming, canoeing, and kayaking.

GETTING THERE

Lac-Baker is about 35 kilometers (22 miles) west of Edmundston, a 30-minute drive via Highway 120. From Fredericton, head northwest on Highway 2, then west from Edmundston on Highway 120, for a total of 300 kilometers (185 miles), over three hours.

★ Mount Carleton Provincial Park

The 17,000-hectare (42,008-acre) **Mount Carleton Provincial Park,** in the remote interior of New Brunswick, is far from the normal tourist route but well worth searching out if you are looking for a true wilderness experience. The park centers around a string of unspoiled lakes surrounded by dense forest and the province's highest peaks. Wildlife such as deer, moose, lynx, porcupines, and over 100 species of birds are present. Access to the park costs $10 per vehicle per day.

Get a feeling for the park by driving around the road that encircles Big and Little Nictau Lakes, although be warned that the gravel road is narrow and very winding in places. Along the way are numerous lake access points, including short stretches of beach. Hiking trails leading from the road are as short as a 300-meter (984-foot) path to photogenic **Williams Falls,** but keen hikers will want to reach the summit of the Maritimes' highest point of land, **Mount Carleton** (820 meters/2,690 feet). If you go, wear sturdy shoes and bring a jacket to combat the winds. The easiest, marked ascent goes up a 4.4-kilometer (2.7-mile) trail through a spruce, fir, and yellow birch forest. The mountain's peak rises above the tree line, and the view is marvelous, overlooking the adjacent mountains

Williams Falls

and lakes from a summit strewn with mountain cranberries and wild blueberries.

Within the park are three auto-accessible campgrounds (506/235-0793, mid-May-mid-Sept., $28-36), of which only one, **Armstrong Campground,** is suitable for RVs and campers. It has 88 campsites, flush toilets, showers, kitchen shelters, a playground, a small beach, and a concession (July and Aug. only). Another option are older cabins on the south side of Nictau Lake and the southeast side of Bathurst Lake ($60-120 s or d). They require guests to supply their own sleeping bags and cooking utensils, but are otherwise a great way to experience the park. Along with campsites, the cabins can be booked online (https://parcsnbparks.ca).

The entrance to the park is 50 kilometers (31 miles) east of Saint-Quentin along Highway 180. Saint-Quentin is roughly halfway between Grand Falls and Campbellton, so if you're looping around the province by road, you'll pass within 50 kilometers (31 miles) of the park. For travelers northbound along Highway 2, take Exit 115 at Perth-Andover (halfway between Hartland and Grand Falls) and follow Highway 109 and the Mamazekel River through Plaster Rock to reach the park via a more direct route than continuing north to Grand Falls.

GETTING THERE

Mount Carleton is about 150 kilometers (93 miles) east of Edmundston, a two-hour drive. To get there, take Highway 2 east, Highway 17 northeast, and Highway 180 east, then follow signs for the park. To get there from Fredericton, allow at least 3.5 hours for the 245-kilometer (152-mile) journey northwest via Highways 2, 17, and 180.

Acadian Coast

Along the eastern edge of New Brunswick is the
Acadian Coast—a French-flavored realm of seaports, barrier beaches, sand dunes, salt marshes, sandy pine-clad shores, and rocky coastline.

Northumberland Strait is the shallow, narrow sea strip between New Brunswick's southeastern coast and Prince Edward Island. Here the coastline attracts summertime sunbathers, swimmers, and windsurfers to welcoming beaches and waters warmed by the Gulf Stream. Farther north, the warm sea mixes with the cooler Gulf of St. Lawrence. Here the Labrador Current swirls in the open gulf, and the swift currents arrive ashore with low rolls of surf. Offshore, barrier islands hold sheltered seaports. Farthest north, the Baie des Chaleurs ("Bay of

Highlights

Look for ★ to find recommended sights, activities, dining, and lodging.

★ **Bore Park:** This is a good place to watch the tidal bore, and it's home to the region's main information center (page 250).

★ **Sackville Waterfowl Park:** Bird-watchers will be enthralled with the many and varied bird species that call this reserve home (page 258).

★ **Parlee Beach:** Buff—and not so buff—bods flock to Parlee Beach for its long expanse of sand, warm swimming water, and holiday vibe. Long after the crowds have left, the evening sunset is sublime (page 261).

★ **Le Pays de la Sagouine:** The literary world learned about Acadian life from the novels of Antonine Maillet. This energetic historical park in her hometown brings her writing to life (page 262).

★ **Kouchibouguac National Park:** This coastal park is laced by hiking trails leading through wetlands, across coastal bays via boardwalk, and along extended stretches of sand (page 263).

★ **Village Historique Acadien:** Experience Acadian life up close and personal at this outdoor museum (page 270).

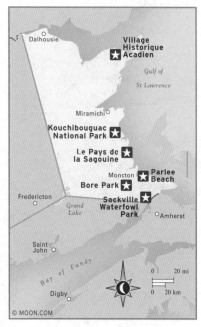

Acadian Coast

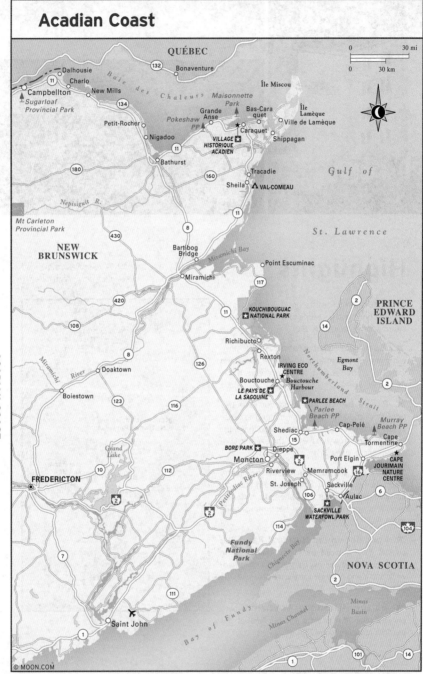

QUÉBEC

0   30 mi
0   30 km

Dalhousie
Charlo
Campbellton
New Mills
Sugarloaf
Provincial Park
11
134
Baie des Chaleurs
132
Bonaventure
Île Miscou
Maisonnette
Park
Grande
Anse
Pokeshaw
PP
Bas-Cara
quet
Île
Lamèque
Ville de Lamèque
Petit-Rocher
Nigadoo
VILLAGE
HISTORIQUE
ACADIEN
Caraquet
Shippagan
11
Bathurst
180
160
Tracadie
Sheila
VAL-COMEAU
Gulf of
Nepisiguit R.
11
St. Lawrence
Mt Carleton
Provincial Park
430
8
Bartibog
Bridge
Miramichi Bay
NEW
BRUNSWICK
Miramichi
Point Escuminac
117
2
PRINCE
EDWARD
ISLAND
420
11
KOUCHIBOUGUAC
NATIONAL PARK
14
108
8
Richibucto
Egmont
Bay
Northumberland
Doaktown
126
Rexton
IRVING ECO
CENTRE
2
Boiestown
123
116
Bouctouche
LE PAYS DE
LA SAGOUINE
Bouctouche
Harbour
Miramichi River
PARLEE BEACH
Parlee
Beach PP
Strait
Cap-Pelé
Murray
Beach PP
Cape
Tormentine
Shediac
15
Grand
Lake
BORE PARK
Dieppe
Moncton
Riverview
St. Joseph
Memramcook
Port Elgin
CAPE
JOURIMAIN
NATURE
CENTRE
10
112
2
Petitcodiac River
FREDERICTON
2
106
Sackville
Aulac
16
6
114
SACKVILLE
WATERFOWL PARK
104
7
Fundy
National
Park
Chignecto Bay
NOVA SCOTIA
111
2
Minas
Basin
1
Saint John
Bay of Fundy
Minas Channel
1
101
14

© MOON.COM

Warmth") is the shallow sea pocket between northern New Brunswick and Québec's Gaspé Peninsula.

The essence of French-speaking Acadia is entwined in its dining and festivals. To understand the region's cultural roots, visit the Village Historique Acadien at Caraquet, where early Acadian life has been re-created with authentic buildings and costumed re-enactors. In the south, Moncton, northern New Brunswick's trendy urban commercial and educational center, is Caraquet's bustling modern counterpoint—a very successful Acadia of the new millennium. Acadian pride runs high, and everywhere in the region the Acadian flag—the red, white, and blue French tricolor with a single gold star—is displayed prominently. But other ethnic groups are represented here as well, most notably the Irish.

Stretched-out distances notwithstanding, getting around is easy and very manageable. Highway 11 lopes along most of the three coasts from seaport to seaport, with the sea almost always within view. End to end, it's an easygoing 10-hour one-way drive between Campbellton and Shediac, if you take your time. But by all means, take the side roads branching off the main route and amble even closer to the water to explore the seaports and scenery. For example, Highway 11 diverges from the coast and cuts an uninteresting bee-line between Miramichi and Bouctouche. Coastal Highway 117 is far more scenic, running through Kouchibouguac National Park and curling out to remote Point Escuminac—a lofty shale plateau at Miramichi Bay's southeastern tip, frequented, in season, by thousands of migratory seabirds.

PLANNING YOUR TIME

Moncton, at the south end of the Acadian Coast, is central to the entire Maritimes region, so you'll probably pass through at least once on your Atlantic Canada vacation. The bustling downtown core is well worth exploring, with **Bore Park** a good starting point. (If you're traveling with children, they'll definitely want you to stop at the city's **Magnetic Hill** commercial attractions.) Getting back to nature, a nearby highlight for bird-watchers is **Sackville Waterfowl Park.**

If you look at a map of New Brunswick, you'll see that the Acadian Coast extends the entire length of the province (it's 320 km/200 mi) from Moncton to Campbellton), so to avoid returning along the coastal highway, plan on combining time along the Acadian Coast with the drive down the Saint John River valley to Fredericton—in effect, two of three legs of a loop around the entire province. This circuit will take four days at an absolute minimum, and preferably six. If the weather is warm, factor in some beach time, and there's no better place for this than **Parlee Beach,** just a short drive from Moncton. As you drive north, passing the coastal wilderness of **Kouchibouguac National Park,** it is impossible not to be intrigued by the pockets of Acadian culture. The best places to learn more about this culture's tragic history and revitalized present are **Le Pays de la Sagouine** and **Village Historique Acadien.**

Previous: the world's largest lobster is a sculpture in Shediac; Chateau Moncton in downtown Moncton; Kelly's Beach in Kouchibouguac National Park.

Moncton

With a population of 72,000 (135,000 in Greater Moncton), this bustling city is the geographic center of the Maritimes. It does an admirable job of promoting its many and varied attractions, and it exudes a vitality and energy unlike anywhere else in the province. Visitors can take in two very different natural attractions—one related to the colossal Fundy tides, the other to a quirk of nature—while children will be attracted to Atlantic Canada's largest theme park. The bustling downtown core is packed with well-priced accommodations, good restaurants, and a lively nightlife.

The city is officially bilingual. About 30 percent of the population speaks French as a first language. So while most everyone also speaks English, knowledge of French will help the visitor.

DOWNTOWN SIGHTS

Downtown Moncton is centered on the north side of "The Bend," a sharp turn in the Petitcodiac River. The busy and bustling **Main Street,** a block in from the river, has brick sidewalks, old-time lampposts, and park benches beneath sapling trees. The following sights are ordered by distance from the water, starting at the riverfront and moving outward. There's no parking on Main Street. Instead, use one of the adjacent side streets and deposit a loonie ($1 coin) for an hour in a metered parking slot, or park in one of the nearby lots.

★ Bore Park

The huge Bay of Fundy tides reach Moncton twice daily, when the tidal bore, a lead wave up to 60 centimeters (24 inches) high, pulses up the Petitcodiac River. Within an hour or so, the muddy bed of the Petitcodiac—locally dubbed the "Chocolate River"—will be drowned under some 7.5 meters (24.6 feet) of water. The tourist information center at Resurgo Place can provide a tidal schedule. While the Moncton tourism folks put

watching the tidal bore on their list of must-see attractions, many locals call it the "Total Bore." In any case, the sight is most impressive at those times of the month when the tides are highest—around the full and new moons.

The best place to witness the tidal phenomenon is off Main Street at **Bore Park,** which is dotted with shade trees and park benches, and even has tiered seating overlooking the river. This is also the site of a riverside boardwalk.

Resurgo Place

Artifacts from the city's history—from the age of the Mi'kmaq to World War II—and touring national exhibits are displayed in the modern, architecturally stunning **Resurgo Place** (20 Mountain Rd., 506/856-4383, Tues.-Sat. 10am-5pm, Sun. noon-5pm, adult $10, senior $8, child $5), which opened in 2014. Although the building is new, the architect concocted an interesting arrangement that combined the original native sandstone facade of the original city hall, which stood on the site, inside the building. Also within the building are the Transportation Discovery Centre, where the focus is on interactive displays; the Moncton Museum, telling the city's story; Moncton's main visitors center; and a gift shop.

Adjacent to Resurgo Place, the tidy, small **Free Meeting House**—Moncton's oldest building—dates to 1821 and served as a sanctuary for religious groups as diverse as Anglicans, Adventists, Jews, and Christian Scientists.

Thomas Williams House

A century ago, the Intercolonial Railroad brought the movers and shakers to town. Among them was Thomas Williams, the railroad's former treasurer. His 12-room Second Empire-style mansion, the **Thomas Williams House** (103 Park St., 506/857-0590, late June-late Aug. Wed.-Sun. 10am-4:30pm, donation) was built in 1883 and is now open

Moncton

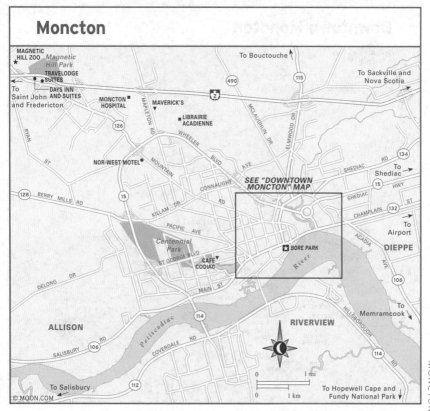

to the public. Elegantly furnished with period pieces, it's a showpiece of the good old days. The Tea Room serves tea, coffee, and muffins in summer.

Galerie d'Art et Musée Acadien

The Acadian region is as creatively avant-garde as it is historic. At the Université de Moncton in the Clément Cormier Building, the **Galerie d'Art et Musée Acadien** (off Wheeler Blvd., 506/858-4088, June-Sept. Mon.-Fri. 10am-5pm, Sat.-Sun. 1pm-5pm, the rest of the year Sat.-Sun. 1pm-4pm, adult $2), a gallery and museum, touches upon numerous aspects of Acadian culture in the combined exhibits. The university itself spreads across a large campus north of downtown. It is Atlantic Canada's sole French-speaking university and grants degrees in business, fine arts, science, education, nursing, and law.

MAGNETIC HILL

Magnetic Hill is an attraction in itself, but the surrounding area (generally also called Magnetic Hill) is dotted with commercial attractions, and if you're traveling with children, this part of the city will be the focus of your time in Moncton.

The namesake **Magnetic Hill** (506/853-3540, mid-May-early Sept. daily 8am-8pm) is just a hill, but if you believe your eyes, you'll agree it's one of the world's oddest. Is Magnetic Hill magnetic? It must be. The unassuming dirt road, which seems to defy the rules of logic, is said to be Canada's third most popular natural tourist attraction, behind Niagara Falls and the Canadian Rockies.

Downtown Moncton

The hill's slope plays tricks on anything with wheels. Set your car at the hill's "bottom," shift into neutral, and release the brake. The car appears to coast backward *up* the hill. Cars aren't the only things that defy gravity here. A stream alongside the road seems to flow uphill, too.

The illusion baffled Monctonians for decades. Before the 1900s, the local farmers fought the incline when they tried to haul wagons "down" the hill. Several decades later, reporters from Saint John discovered Magnetic Hill. Their newspaper coverage of the "natural phenomenon" brought a slew of spectators, and the stream of nonbelievers hasn't stopped since.

If you think a strange and otherworldly force powers Magnetic Hill, think again. For the record, the whole countryside hereabouts

is tilted. Magnetic Hill forms the southern flank of 150-meter-high (492-foot-high) Lutes Mountain, northwest of Moncton. The hill is an optical illusion, and believe it or not, the hill's top crest is lower than the hill's "bottom." Try to walk the hill with your eyes closed. Your other senses will tell you that you are traveling down rather than up. To get there from downtown, follow Mountain Road northwest; from the Trans-Canada Highway, take Exit 488.

Attractions

So many tourists arrived to observe the illogical hill that an adjacent gift shop was opened in the 1970s, and the area quickly grew into a concentration of family-oriented attractions.

1: Bore Park; **2:** Resurgo Place

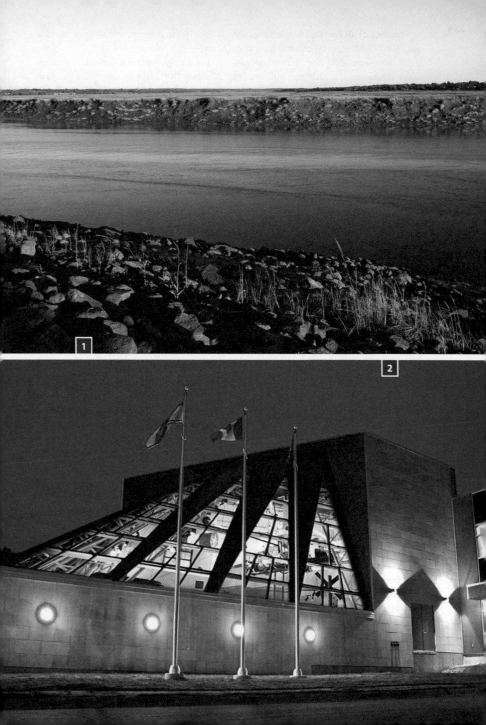

Magnetic Hill Zoo (125 Magic Mountain Rd., 506/877-7718, Apr.-June and Sept.-Nov. daily 10am-4pm, July-Aug. daily 9am-7pm, adult $15, senior $13, child $11) bills itself as the largest zoo in Atlantic Canada. It houses some 100 animal species, including zebras, reindeer, tigers, camels, wolves, and gibbons. A petting zoo entertains the wee ones, and the crowds gather daily at 2:30pm for Meet the Ranger.

Magic Mountain Splash Zone (150 Magic Mountain Rd., 506/857-9283, late June-mid-Aug. daily 10am-7pm, mid-Aug.-end of Aug. daily 10am-6pm, $47 for those over 48 inches tall, $38 for between 42 and 48 inches, and $30 for under 30 inches) has an outdoor wave pool, numerous chutes, tube rides, and mini-golf.

The Boardwalk (506/852-9406, summer daily 9am-dusk) offers go-kart rides, mini-golf, batting cages, a driving range, and a playground. The adjacent **Wharf Village** (506/858-8841, summer daily 8am-9pm) is a shopping area featuring arts and crafts and a family-style restaurant overlooking an artificial pond.

ENTERTAINMENT AND EVENTS
Nightlife

Most of the drinking and dancing action happens along Main Street, where the college crowds gather at bars and nightclubs and tables spill onto the streets. The **Pump House Brewpub** (5 Orange Ln., 506/855-2337, Mon.-Wed. 11am-midnight, Thurs. 11am-1am, Fri.-Sat. 11am-2am, Sun. noon-midnight) is a little quieter than most and has a sun-drenched patio out front. It brews its own beer, which is available on draught and in bottles.

Live music at the **Tide and Boar** (700 Main St., 506/857-9118, Sun.-Wed. 11am-midnight, Thurs.-Sat. 11am-2am) every Friday and Saturday night could be anything from up-and-coming Halifax bands to the most popular Canadian indie groups. At any time, it's a good place to sample craft beers from

across North America and some of the most creative pub cooking in town.

For a quiet drink, **Le Galion,** in Château Moncton (100 Main St., 506/870-4444, daily from 11am) is a good choice. With seating inside and out, you get to enjoy the river scenery up close and can sip a beer while waiting for the tidal bore in a bright, contemporary setting. In the Crowne Plaza Moncton Downtown, **Bin 1005** (1005 Main St., 506/854-6340, daily from 11am) is a typical upscale hotel lounge, with the bonus of an excellent wine list.

Theater
The Capitol (811 Main St., 506/856-4379, www.capitol.nb.ca) has been transformed from a 1920s vaudeville theater to a gracious symbol of the past. Today this lovely old grande dame, ornately decorated with frescoes and murals, glitters with concerts, ballets, shows, and film festivals.

Festivals and Events
Moncton hosts the **World Wine & Food Expo** (506/531-5102, www.wineexpo.ca) over the first week of November. It brings together wine representatives from around the world with celebrity chefs, but the ambience is anything but pompous as the general public gathers to soak up the worldly atmosphere at seminars, tastings, and dinners.

The mid-November **Festival International du Cinéma Francophone en Acadie** (506/855-6050, www.ficfa.com) is a major French-language film festival.

RECREATION
Centennial Park
At the western side of town, the 180-hectare (445-acre) **Centennial Park** (St. George Blvd., 506/853-3516, daily 9am-11pm) makes a pleasant place to picnic and relax amid woodlands, and offers hiking trails and a lake with a sandy beach. Summer activities include lawn bowling, swimming, tennis, and canoeing and paddling on the lake. In winter, lighted

trails invite cross-country skiers, skaters, and hockey players to take to the frozen lake.

SHOPPING

Major shopping malls in the area include Dieppe's **Champlain Place** (corner of Paul St. and Champlain St., Mon.-Sat. 10am-9pm, Sun. noon-5pm), Atlantic Canada's largest mall, and **Northwest Centre Plaza** (1380 Mountain Rd.), a typical North American strip mall, but to sample the local flair for arts and crafts, you'll need to look elsewhere.

If you're in town on the weekend, head to **Moncton Market** (120 Westmorland St., www.marchemonctonmarket.ca, Sat. 7am-2pm) for local arts and crafts, as well as delicious foods from local farmers and suppliers. It's difficult to miss the bright pink facade of **Gifts Galore** (569 Main St., 506/857-9179, Mon.-Sat. 10am-5pm, Sun. noon-5pm), which carries a little bit of everything—glass, pottery, pewter, T-shirts, and more. It helps to speak French at some shops, such as **Galerie Sans Nom** (140 Botsford St., 506/854-5381, Tues.-Wed. 10am-5pm, Thurs.-Fri. 11am-7pm), a cooperative where the emphasis is on contemporary arts and crafts.

FOOD

You might stumble on a few Acadian dishes, but most local restaurants keep it simple and straightforward, appealing to the college crowd with cheap food and energetic service.

Downtown
PUBS

Most of the pubs along Main Street serve food, but the offerings at **Tide and Boar** (700 Main St., 506/857-9118, Sun.-Wed. 11am-midnight, Thurs.-Sat. 11am-2am, $14-24) are a notch above the rest. The platters to share are a good way to start (or the Boar Poutine for the brave), before moving on to parmesan-crusted haddock, beer-battered cod, or pizza with caramelized plums and goat cheese. Wash your meal down with a beer from the long list of choices or a house-made ginger beer and rum.

Pump House Brewpub (5 Orange Ln.,

506/855-2337, Mon.-Wed. 11am-midnight, Thurs. 11am-1am, Fri.-Sat. 11am-2am, Sun. noon-midnight, $12-22) has been around since the late 1990s, and it remains popular both for its handcrafted beer and well-priced food. Highlights are the wood-fired pizzas, including such varieties as roast vegetable and bacon cheeseburger.

STEAK AND SEAFOOD

T-bones (Crowne Plaza Moncton, 1005 Main St., 506/854-6340, daily 6am-11pm, $18-40) has a predictable wide-ranging menu that doesn't offend anyone, with choices that include everything from vegetarian fettuccine to 16-ounce namesake T-bone steaks.

VEGETARIAN

Along the main street, ★ **Calactus** (125 Church St., 506/388-4833, daily 11am-10pm, $11-18) is a cheery little vegetarian restaurant with a few outdoor tables on a patio. Ingredients are sourced locally, but cooking styles are taken from around the world, including in the selection of delicious pizzas (Indian, Greek, Mexican, and more). One of the favorites is the veggie burger with roasted potatoes and Caesar salad for just $15. House-made desserts and a drink list that varies from organic wines to fruit smoothies and great coffee round out this excellent choice for lunch or dinner.

CAFÉS

Main Street is the place to head for a coffee at a street-side table, and no one pours better drinks than **Cafe C'est la Vie** (785 Main St., 506/854-0994, Mon.-Fri. 7:30am-5pm, Sat.-Sun. 9am-5pm, lunches under $10), where, in addition to the usual choices, the menu includes a mint latte and a caramelized macchiato brule. The food is also delicious and inexpensive, including soups, salads, and sandwiches.

In a red-brick heritage building two blocks east of Café C'est la Vie, **Café Cognito** (700 Main St., 506/854-4888, Mon.-Fri. 7:30am-4:30pm, Sat. 10am-4pm, lunches $7-10) also has excellent coffee, along with chai lattes, daily-made soups, grilled sandwiches made to order, and baked pastries and treats. Outdoor tables add to the appeal.

Outside Downtown

To the northwest of downtown toward Magnetic Hill, **Café Codiac** (666 St. George Blvd., 506/854-7100, Mon.-Fri. 7am-6pm, Sat. 8am-5pm, Sun. 9am-5pm, lunches $6-9) is worth searching out for excellent coffee, delicious soups made daily, hearty sandwiches, and a wide range of baked goodies.

The stylish steakhouse ★ **Maverick's** (Four Points by Sheraton, 40 Lady Ada Blvd., 506/855-3346, Mon.-Thurs. 6:30am-10pm, Fri. 6:30am-11pm, Sat. 7:30am-11pm, Sun. 7:30am-9pm, $23-36) is out on the main highway through town. All the favorites are offered—an extra-thick cut of prime rib, tender rib eye, and a variety of strip loins—and they all come exactly how you ordered them. The menu also offers top-notch seafood, including boiled lobster. A well-rounded wine list adds to the appeal.

Overlooking the pond at Wharf Village is **Wharf Village Restaurant** (50 Magic Mountain Rd., 506/859-1812, May-Oct. daily 11am-9pm, lunches $8-13), which does a fine job feeding Magnetic Hill visitors familiar family fare at good value for the dollar. Seating is outside on a covered deck or inside with basic decor and air-conditioning. On the right side of the restaurant is a self-service counter hawking soup and sandwiches to go.

ACCOMMODATIONS AND CAMPING

Lodgings are conveniently concentrated in two main areas—downtown and at the city's northwestern corner, near Magnetic Hill. Overall, prices are reasonable, especially for the larger downtown properties.

$100-150

The three-story **Rodd Moncton** (434 Main St., 506/382-1664 or 800/565-7633, www. roddvacations.com, $135 s or d, extra for

river views) overlooks Bore Park with 97 guest rooms and an outdoor pool (summer only). The rooms aren't particularly large but are clean and comfortable, and the location still makes this place a good value, especially since a light breakfast is included.

The motels clustered around Magnetic Mountain (take Exit 488 from the Trans-Canada Highway) are mostly within this price range. **Days Inn & Suites Moncton** (2515 Mountain Rd., 506/384-1050, www. wyndhamhotels.com, $135 s or d) has the most facilities, with an indoor pool, hot tub, sauna, restaurant, lounge, business center, and family suites with bunk beds.

The folks at **Nor-West Motel** (1325 Mountain Rd., 506/384-1222 or 800/561-7904, www.norwestmotel.com, from $120 s or d) have done a great job of upgrading an older motel out near Magnetic Hill, with colorful flower arrangements out front adding to the appeal. A hot breakfast is included in the rates.

Travelodge Suites (2475 Mountain Rd., 506/852-7000, www.wyndhamhotels.com, from $145 s or d) has 77 spacious, nicely appointed guest rooms with free in-room movies, work desks, and small fridges. A daily newspaper, wireless Internet access, and a hot buffet breakfast are included in the rates.

$150-200

On the eastern edge of downtown, ★ **Château Moncton** (100 Main St., 506/870-4444 or 800/576-4040, www. chateaumoncton.ca, $170-250 s or d) is a distinctive red-roofed chateau-style lodging overlooking the tidal bore. Guests enjoy 97 modern and spacious rooms and suites with wireless Internet access, an exercise room, voice mail, free local calls, and daily newspapers. Rates include a cooked breakfast. The hotel also has a riverside deck and a pleasant lounge.

My pick for downtown accommodations is the ★ **Residence Inn** (600 Main St., 506/854-7100 or 888/236-2427, www.marriott. com, from $170 s or d), with 133 modern and spacious guest rooms in the heart of the city. Many units have one or two bedrooms, and all have kitchens. Other amenities include a surprisingly large indoor pool and a fitness room. Adding to the appeal, rates include a hot breakfast buffet.

Crowne Plaza Moncton (1005 Main St., 506/854-6340 or 866/854-4656, www.ihg. com, $189 s or d) comes complete with contemporary decor, the best beds in town, CD clock radios, and many other niceties. The in-house steakhouse and lounge save leaving the property in the evening. Other amenities include an indoor pool and a large fitness room.

Delta Hotels by Marriott Beauséjour (750 Main St., 506/854-4344 or 888/236-2427, www.marriott.com, from $189 s or d) is equal to the Crowne Plaza in style, service, and facilities, but everything is a little less new. On the plus side, the 310 guest rooms are very spacious. Other facilities include a café, two restaurants, a lounge, and an indoor pool with a waterslide.

INFORMATION AND SERVICES

The city's main **Tourist Information Centre** (20 Mountain Rd., 506/8564383, www.moncton.ca, mid-May-early Sept. daily 8:30am-5:30pm) is in Resurgo Place, on the north side of downtown.

Both the **Moncton Hospital** (135 Macbeath Ave., 506/857-5111) and **Dr. Georges-L.-Dumont University Hospital Centre** (330 University Ave., 506/862-4000) are between Magnetic Hill and downtown. For the **RCMP,** call 911 or 506/857-2400.

GETTING THERE

Moncton lies in the geographic heart of the three Maritimes provinces, so even if you don't make the city a destination in itself, you will probably pass through on your travels.

Car

Driving time to Moncton from Saint John (155 km/96 mi to the southwest) is around 80 or 90 minutes. From the provincial capital of Fredericton (180 km/112 mi west), the drive is slightly longer. For those continuing to Prince Edward Island, allow an hour to reach the Confederation Bridge, 92 kilometers (57 miles) to the east.

Air

Greater Moncton Airport (777 Aviation Ave., Dieppe, 506/856-5444, www.cyqm.ca) is 10 kilometers (6.2 miles) from downtown Moncton on Champlain Street/Highway 132 (a continuation of Main Street in Moncton) in adjacent Dieppe. The airport has a food court, a lounge, wireless Internet, and car rental desks (Avis, Budget, Hertz, and National). A metered taxi ride with **Air Cab** (506/857-2000) to Main Street in Moncton costs about $20 one-way.

The airport is served by **Air Canada** (888/247-2262, www.aircanada.com) from Halifax, Montréal, and Toronto and by **WestJet** (800/538-5696, www.westjet.com) from Toronto, Hamilton, and Calgary.

From **Halifax International Airport,** allow around two hours for the 230-kilometer (143-mile) trip north along Highway 102 and then west along the Trans-Canada Highway to Moncton (without a single traffic light en route).

Train and Bus

Moncton is served by **VIA Rail** (1240 Main St., 506/857-9830 or 800/561-3952, www.viarail. ca) on its route between Montréal and Halifax (four hours, $30). The railway station is behind Highfield Square on Main Street.

By virtue of its central location, Moncton is a hub for **Maritime Bus** (1240 Main St., 506/854-2023, www.maritimebus.com). Services run to Saint John, Fredericton, Charlottetown, Halifax, and along the Acadian Coast to Campbellton from the Maritime Bus Terminal, which is part of the main railway station on the west side of downtown. Buses depart three times daily for Saint John (two hours, $34). From Halifax, the thrice-daily service takes around four hours to reach Moncton ($49).

GETTING AROUND

Codiac Transit (506/857-2008) operates local bus service (Mon.-Wed. and Sat. 6:20am-7pm, Thurs.-Fri. 6:20am-10:15pm). Fare is $2.50 per sector.

Air Cab (506/857-2000) charges $4 to start and about $1.75 per kilometer.

Major car rental companies with downtown and airport desks are **Avis** (506/855-7212), **Budget** (506/857-3993), **Hertz** (506/858-8525), and **National** (506/382-6114).

Southeast from Moncton

Geologically, the area southeast of Moncton is related to the Bay of Fundy, but as it is separated from the rest of the Fundy Coast, it is covered here. Driving nonstop, you'll cross over to Nova Scotia in a little over 30 minutes and be in Halifax in three hours.

MEMRAMCOOK

Take Highway 106 southeast from Moncton for 20 kilometers (12.4 miles) to reach the village of Memramcook and **Monument-Lefebvre National Historic Site** (488 Centrale St., 506/758-9808, June-mid-Oct. daily 9am-5pm, mid-Oct.-May Mon.-Sat. 9am-5pm, adult $4, senior $3.50, child $2), which is dedicated to the memory of Father Camille Lefebvre, founder of Canada's first French-language university. Within the historic Monument-Lefebvre building on the Memramcook Institute campus, the **Acadian Odyssey** exhibit explains Acadian survival with a series of displays.

Getting There

Memramcock is just over 20 kilometers (12.4 miles) southeast of Moncton, a 20-minute drive via Highway 106. To get there from Fredericton, take Highway 2 east for 180 kilometers (112 miles), then Highway 106 southeast for 20 kilometers (12.4 miles), 2.5 hours total.

SACKVILLE

The 17th-century settlers who founded Sackville, 50 kilometers (31 miles) southeast of Moncton, emigrated from around the estuaries of western France, so they were experienced in wresting tidelands from the sea. By creating an extensive system of dikes called *aboideaux*, they reclaimed thousands of acres of Chignecto Isthmus marsh and brought the extremely fertile alluvial lands into agricultural production. Their raised dikes can be seen around Sackville and into Nova Scotia.

Mount Allison Academy (later University) was founded here in 1843; a "Female Branch" was opened 11 years later. In 1875, the university gained the distinction of being the first in the British Empire to grant a college degree to a woman.

The beautiful campus, surrounded by stately houses and tree-shaded streets, is still at the heart of this town. A number of artists have chosen Sackville as their home, and one of the best places to see their work is at Mount Allison University's **Owens Art Gallery** (61 York St., 506/364-2574, Mon.-Fri. 10am-5pm, Sat.-Sun. 1pm-5pm, free). The Owens ranks as one of the major galleries in the province and emphasizes avant-garde work by local, regional, and national artists.

★ Sackville Waterfowl Park

If you're short on time and can stop at only one of the area's several wildlife sanctuaries, make it the **Sackville Waterfowl Park** (daily dawn-dusk, free), a 22-hectare (54.4-acre) reserve where more than 150 bird species have been recorded. The main entrance, just a few blocks north of downtown, is easy to miss but offers interesting park displays. From this point, the sanctuary spreads out, with trails routed through bush and over

ity of Aulac, on the Bay of Fundy side of

bleached wooden walkways crossing wetlands. Ducks, great blue herons, teals, and bitterns are common, while spotting loons, Canada geese, sandpipers, and peregrine falcons is possible. At the entrance to the park is **Sackville Visitor Information Centre** (34 Mallard Dr., 506/364-4967, May-mid-Oct. daily 9am-5pm, until 7pm in summer), with displays related to the surrounding bird-rich environment.

Food and Accommodations

For a place to stay, consider ★ **Marshlands Inn** (55 Bridge St., 506/536-0170, www.marshlands.nb.ca, $145-165 s or d), among the province's best-value historic lodgings. The inn, built in the 1850s, got its name from an early owner, who christened the mansion in honor of the adjacent Tantramar Marshes. The resplendent white wooden heritage inn sits back from the road under shady trees and offers 20 guest rooms furnished with antiques and a dining room of local renown. Open daily for guests and nonguests, the dining room is smart and elegant, with many steak and seafood choices ($18-33), including crepes filled with lobster, shrimp, and scallops.

Getting There

To get to Sackville from Moncton, take Highway 2 southeast for about 50 kilometers (31 miles), a 30-minute drive. From Fredericton, take Highway 2 east for 230 kilometers (143 miles), a 2.5-hour drive.

Dorchester Peninsula

Another prime birding site is not far from Sackville. From Dorchester, 14 kilometers (8.7 miles) west of Sackville on Highway 106, turn off on Highway 935. The backcountry gravel road loops south around the **Dorchester Peninsula**—the digit of land separating Shepody Bay from the Cumberland Basin. Some 50,000 semipalmated sandpipers nest mid-July-mid-September between Johnson Mills and Upper Rockport, where the road loops back toward Sackville. Roosting sites lie along pebble beaches and mudflats, and the birds are most lively at feeding time (low tide). Smaller flocks of dunlins, white-rumped sandpipers, and sanderlings inhabit the area late September-October.

AULAC AND VICINITY

The last town before crossing into Nova Scotia is Aulac, on the Bay of Fundy side of

Sackville Waterfowl Park

the Trans-Canada Highway at the turnoff to the Confederation Bridge.

Fort Beauséjour

Eight kilometers (5 miles) east of Sackville, a signpost marks the turnoff from the Trans-Canada Highway to the **Fort Beauséjour National Historic Site** (111 Fort Beauséjour Rd., 506/364-5080, June-mid-Oct. daily 9am-5pm, adult $4, senior $3.50, child $2), overlooking the Cumberland Basin just west of the Nova Scotia border. Continue on the road to the fort ruins, which mark France's last-ditch military struggle against the British, who threatened Acadia centuries ago. France lost the fort in 1755 after a two-week siege. The Brits renamed it Fort Cumberland and used it in 1776 to repel an attack by American revolutionaries. The fort stood ready for action in the War of 1812, though no enemy appeared. Fort Cumberland was abandoned in the 1830s, and nature soon reclaimed the site. Some of the ruins have since been restored. Facilities include a picnic area and a museum-visitors center with exhibits on life in the old days.

Tintamarre Sanctuary

Tintamarre National Wildlife Area fans out beyond the fort ruins. Continue on Highway 16 for about 10 kilometers (6.2 miles) to Jolicure, a village at the reserve's edge. No trails penetrate the 1,990-hectare (4,917-acre) mix of marshes, uplands, old fields, forests, and lakes. A few dikes provide steady ground through some of the terrain, but you are asked to stay on the roads encircling the area to do your bird-watching. Amid the cattails, sedges, and bulrushes, sightings include migratory mallards, grebes, red-winged blackbirds, yellow warblers, swamp swallows, common snipes, black ducks, Virginia rails, and bitterns; short-eared owls take wing at dusk. Bring binoculars—and insect repellent. The area can be thick with mosquitoes.

Getting There

Aulac is 55 kilometers (34 miles) southeast of Moncton, a 30-minute drive via Highway 2. From Fredericton, take Highway 2 east for 235 kilometers (146 miles), 2.5 hours.

Strait Coast

The Strait Coast runs from Cape Tormentine, New Brunswick's easternmost extremity, to Miramichi, 143 kilometers (89 miles) northwest of Moncton. It fronts Northumberland Strait, the narrow body of water separating New Brunswick from Prince Edward Island, and so it's no surprise that the main towns and attractions are focused on the water.

CAPE TORMENTINE

Most travelers drive, literally, over the top of Cape Tormentine on their way to Prince Edward Island via the Confederation Bridge.

Cape Jourimain Nature Centre

Nestled below the southern end of the Confederation Bridge, the large, modern wooden **Cape Jourimain Nature Centre** (5039 Hwy. 16, 506/538-2220, mid-May-mid-Oct. daily 9am-5pm, donation) fits in well with the surrounding coastal environment. It is the gateway to linked walking trails that lead into and through a 675-hectare (1,668-acre) wildlife reserve, home to a reported 170 species of birds. Before heading out into the park, visit the Exhibit Hall to learn about local natural and human history, and then climb the observation tower to get a lay of the land. When you're done at the main building, wander down to the sandy beach, where views of the Confederation Bridge are front and center. Other trails lead along boardwalks, through coastal forest, and to an 1870 lighthouse. Back at the main building,

Iceberg Landing Restaurant (5039 Hwy. 16, 506/538-2220, mid-May-mid-Oct. Wed.-Sun. 9am-4pm, lunches $10-18) has views across to Northumberland Strait and free Wi-Fi Internet access. It's okay to stop in for just a coffee, but the menu is surprisingly good, with an emphasis on local produce; the Sunday brunch buffet (10am-2pm, $18) is especially popular.

The nearest camping is at **Murray Beach Provincial Park** (Hwy. 955, 506/538-2628, May-Sept., $29-33), 13 kilometers (8.1 miles) west toward Shediac. In addition to a good sandy beach with warm water, amenities include more than 100 campsites on a wooded bluff, showers, a laundry, and a playground.

Getting There

Cape Tormentine is just over 50 kilometers (31 miles) northeast of Aulac, a 45-minute drive via Highway 16. From Fredericton, it's 280 kilometers (175 miles), 3.5 hours via Highways 2 and 16.

West to Shediac

A few fine, quiet beaches dot the Cap-Pelé area, farther west on Highway 15. At Gagnon Beach, **Camping Gagnon Beach** (506/577-2519 or 800/658-2828, www.gagnonbeach. com, late May-mid-Sept., $30-45) has 208 sites with full hookups plus a separate wooded tenting area.

SHEDIAC

The self-proclaimed "Lobster Capital of the World," 20 kilometers (12.4 miles) northeast of Moncton, Shediac backs up its claim with the **world's largest lobster**—an 11-meter-long (36-foot-long) cast-iron sculpture by Winston Bronnum sitting beside the road into town. For the real stuff, head for the town's restaurants, which have a reputation for some of the province's best lobster dinners.

★ Parlee Beach

This is *the* beach getaway for Moncton residents, and it can be crowded on weekends. **Parlee Beach Provincial Park** (506/533-3363) protects one of many beaches strung out to the east. This placid 3-kilometer-long (1.9-mile-long) beach is popular for the warmth of the water, which reaches 24°C (75°F) in summer. The entrance is from the eastern edge of Shediac, along an access road that ends at a massive parking lot behind low sand dunes. Behind the beach are changing rooms, a café, and a restaurant, while down on the beach swimming is supervised by trained

looking out across Cape Jourimain

lifeguards. Access is $13 per vehicle per day (collected in summer only).

Food

Overlooking the water near the end of the road out to Pointe-de-Chene Marina (turn off the highway on the east side of town), you'll find ★ **Captain Dan's** (506/533-2855, daily 11am-10pm, $12-27), a super-casual, perennially crowded bar and grill with a beachin' atmosphere and great food. Hang loose, watch the boats, and feel your blood pressure drop.

Accommodations and Camping

Most visitors holidaying at Parlee Beach either camp or stay in privately owned cottages. Many of these are marketed through **Parlee Beach Chalets and Cottages** (506/756-9049, www.parleebeach.com). The only downside is that most rentals are weekly. For a shorter stay, make reservations at **Parlee Beach Motel** (691 Hwy. 133, 506/756-9099, www.parleebeachmotel.com, $84-165 s or d), a 15-minute walk (or two-minute drive) from the beach. The 35 rooms are air-conditioned, and most are very spacious.

In the heart of Shediac, ★ **Tait House** (293 Main St., 506/532-4233 or 888/532-4233, www.maisontaithouse.com, $99-149 s or d) is a beautifully restored 1911 mansion with historical guest rooms complemented by contemporary features, such as polished hardwood floors and plush mattresses topped with white linens. The in-house restaurant offers a menu of local ingredients prepared with cooking styles from throughout Europe. Rates include a continental breakfast.

Parlee Beach Provincial Park (45 Parlee Beach Rd., 506/533-3363, June-Aug., $28-38) is within walking distance of the beach. It has hot showers, a playground, and more than 165 sites. It's also very popular, so make reservations as far ahead as possible through the government website https://parcsnbparks.ca.

Getting There

Shediac is a little more than 20 kilometers (12.4 miles) northeast of Moncton, a 25-minute drive via Highway 11/Highway 15. To get there from Fredericton, head east on Highway 2 for 180 kilometers (112 miles), then northeast for 20 kilometers (12.4 miles) on Highway 11/Highway 15. Allow just over two hours.

BOUCTOUCHE

North of Shediac, Highway 11 zips through a wooded corridor, sacrificing scenery for efficiency. For a taste of the slower pace of rural coastal Acadia, strike out on any of the local highways (such as 530, 475, or 505) to the east, which hug the coast and lead to quiet beaches at Saint-Thomas, Saint-Edouard-de-Kent, and Cap-Lumière. Along the way, the routes come together at Bouctouche, 30 kilometers (19 miles) north of Shediac. You can learn about two centuries of Acadian culture at **Le Musée de Kent** (150 Chemin du Couvent, 506/743-5005, July-early Sept. Mon.-Sat. 9am-5:30pm, Sun. noon-6pm, adult $4, senior $3, child $2), in a restored 1880 convent 2 kilometers (1.2 miles) east of downtown, but the two main local attractions are Le Pays de la Sagouine and Irving Eco-Centre.

★ Le Pays de la Sagouine

Author Antonine Maillet is renowned in the literary world for her colorful descriptions of Acadian life, and so there is no better place to re-create the ambience of her work than this lively outdoor theme park in her hometown of Bouctouche. **Le Pays de la Sagouine** (57 Acadie St., 506/743-1400, late June-early Sept. daily 10am-5:30pm, adult $20, senior and child $15) is on a peninsula and islet with a hamlet of houses and other buildings, a reception center, and a craft shop. The highly recommended guided tour (included in admission) leaves daily at 11am and 3pm. Evening dinner theater (in French) is the site's big draw; you'll have a choice of seafood, Canadian, or—the best bet—traditional Acadian fare. And your meal will be accompanied by Acadian music, which might be in any number of styles. The show only is adult $60, child $30, or pay $70 and $40, respectively, for park admission, dinner, and show.

Irving Eco-Centre

Continue through town beyond Le Musée de Kent and turn north up the coast to reach **Irving Eco-Centre** (Hwy. 475, 506/743-2600, June and Sept. daily 10am-5pm, July-Aug. daily 10am-6pm, free), which preserves the ecosystem surrounding a 12-kilometer-long (7.5-mile-long) sand dune along Bouctouche Bay. The ecosystem was created as a public relations gesture by New Brunswick megacorporation J. D. Irving Ltd. (which is involved in petroleum, logging, you name it). A 2-kilometer-long (1.2-mile-long) wheelchair-accessible boardwalk leads from an interpretive center through the dunes. Other trails traverse forest and marshland. Naturalists work on-site May-November, doing ecology research and leading school field trips. Bird-watchers will spot great blue herons, piping plovers, and long-winged terns, among other species.

Getting There

Bouctouche is about 35 kilometers (22 miles) north of Shediac, a 25-minute drive along Highway 11. To get there from Fredericton, drive east on Highway 2 for 180 kilometers (112 miles), northeast on Highway 11/Highway 15 for 20 kilometers (12.4 miles), then northwest on Highway 11 for 35 kilometers (22 miles). Allow 2.5 hours.

★ KOUCHIBOUGUAC NATIONAL PARK

The Northumberland Strait coast ends at **Kouchibouguac National Park,** a 238-square-kilometer (91.9-square-mile) gem of a park that takes its name from the Mi'kmaq word for "river of the long tides"— a reference to the waterway that meanders through the midsection of the low-lying park. Some pronounce it KOOSH-ee-buh-gwack, others say kee-gee-boo-QUACK, and Parks Canada says it's kou-she-boo-gwack. You'll hear many other variations.

Slender barrier islands and sandy beaches and dunes, laced with marram grass and false heather, face the gulf along a 25-kilometer (15.5-mile) front. A gray seal colony occupies one of the offshore islands. In the park's interior, boardwalks ribbon the mudflats, freshwater marshes, and bogs, and nature trails probe the woodlands and fields.

Park Entry

Entry fees are charged mid-May-mid-October. A one-day pass is adult $8, senior $7, child $4 (to a maximum of $20 per vehicle).

Recreation

The land and coast are environmentally sensitive; park officials prefer that you stay on the trails and boardwalks or use a bike to get around on the 30 kilometers (19 miles) of biking and hiking trails. Naturalist-led programs and outings are organized throughout summer. Check at the Visitor Reception Centre and campgrounds for a schedule.

If time is limited, my suggestion is to head straight for the **Kelly's Beach Boardwalk** trail, which leads from a large parking lot over shallow channels and across sand dunes to a beautiful stretch of beach, from where you can take off your shoes and head in either direction for as long as you like. Other trails that explore the park's varied ecosystems include the **Pines** and **Salt Marsh** trails, and the 1.8-kilometer (1.1-mile) **Bog** trail. You can take longer hikes on the **Clair-Fontaine** (3.4 km/2.1 mi), **Osprey** (5.1 km/3.2 mi), and **Kouchibouguac** (14 km/8.7 mi; allow five hours) trails.

The Black, St. Louis, Kouchibouguac, and other rivers that weave through the park are wonderful to explore by canoe, kayak, rowboat, or pedal boat. Those watercraft, as well as fishing equipment and bicycles, are available at **Ryan's Rental Centre** (506/876-3733, mid-June-early Sept. daily 8am-9pm). Fishing in the national park also requires a license: $10 per day or $35 for an annual license. Swimming is supervised at **Kelly's Beach** in summer, while swimming at Callander's and other beaches is unsupervised.

Camping

Within the park are two campgrounds. Finding a site shouldn't be a problem, except in July and August. At these times, reservations through the **Parks Canada Campground Reservation Service** (877/737-3783, www.pccamping.ca) are wise. The cost is $12 per booking plus the campsite fee.

South Kouchibouguac Campground (mid-May-mid-Oct., $28-33) offers 265 unserviced sites and 46 sites with power hookups. Civilized comforts include showers, flush toilets, kitchen shelters, firewood ($7 per bundle), launderettes, and a campers' store near the beach.

Côte-à-Fabien Campground (mid-June-early Sept., $16) has 32 primitive campsites but few facilities and no hookups.

Information

Make your first stop the **Visitor Reception Centre** (1 km/0.6 mi inside the main entrance off Hwy. 134, 506/876-2443, www.pc.gc.ca, mid-May-mid-June and early Sept.-mid-Oct. daily 9am-5pm, mid-June-early Sept. daily 8am-8pm). For a memorable introduction, be sure to see the 20-minute slide presentation, *Kouchibouguac*. Campsite registration is handled at the center, and information on activities, outdoor presentations, and evening programs is posted here, too.

Getting There

Kouchibouguac National Park is nearly 100 kilometers (62 miles) north of Shediac, a one-hour drive via Highway 11. From Fredericton, drive east on Highway 2 for 180 kilometers (112 miles), northeast on Highway 11/Highway 15 for 20 kilometers (12.4 miles), then northwest for 100 kilometers (62 miles) on Highway 11. Allow at least three hours.

Miramichi River

The gorgeous Miramichi (meer-ma-SHEE) River and its myriad tributaries drain much of the interior of eastern New Brunswick. The river enjoys a wide reputation as one of the best (if not *the* best) Atlantic salmon waters in the world.

Leaving the conurbation of Miramichi near the river's mouth, Highway 8 follows the river valley southwest for most of its length. Most of the valley is lightly populated.

MIRAMICHI

Don't get too confused if that old road map of New Brunswick you're using doesn't seem to jibe with the signs you're seeing out the car window. No, the cities of Chatham and Newcastle didn't disappear; in 1995 they amalgamated into a single municipal entity called Miramichi. The former Chatham is now Miramichi East, and the former Newcastle is Miramichi West.

Old French maps of this area show the Miramichi River as the Rivière des Barques, the "River of Ships." From as early as the last quarter of the 18th century, the locally abundant timber and the deepwater estuary made this an excellent location for the shipbuilding industry. The Cunard brothers began their lucrative shipbuilding empire at Chatham in 1826 and built some of the finest vessels of their day. The industry thrived for half a century and then faltered and faded, leaving no physical evidence—outside of museums—that it ever existed.

Sights

At Miramichi East, before Highway 11 crosses to the north side of the river, **St. Michael's Basilica** (10 Howard St., 506/778-5150, daily 8am-4pm, free) is a distinctive 1920 sandstone church overlooking the river.

1: Le Pays de la Sagouine; **2:** Kouchibouguac National Park

Across the river and farther southwest along Highway 8 is **Miramichi West** (formerly Newcastle), a pleasant river town with lots of old buildings that center on a small square hosting a memorial to Lord Beaverbrook. One of the most powerful newspapermen in British history, he was raised at what is now known as **Beaverbrook House** (518 King George Hwy., 506/622-5572, June-early Sept. Mon.-Sat. 9am-5pm, Sun. noon-5pm), where a tour and entry to a small museum dedicated to his life and links to New Brunswick is included in the $5 admission charge. If it's a warm sunny day, head down to **Ritchie Wharf Park** (Ledden St.), a former shipbuilding yard that has been spruced up with riverfront shops and cafés, a nautically themed playground, and a gazebo where live music is performed on most summer evenings and Sunday afternoons.

Festivals and Events

In the mid-19th century, Middle Island, a river island just east of town, was the destination of thousands of Irish emigrants, many of them fleeing the catastrophic potato famine of the 1840s. Their descendants are still in the region, and since 1984 the area has celebrated its Irish heritage with **Canada's Irish Festival** (506/778-8810, www.canadasirishfest.com). The three-day event in mid-July includes concerts, dances, a parade, lectures and music workshops, booths selling Irish mementos and books, and the consumption of a good deal of beer.

The first week of August is the five-day **Miramichi Folksong Festival** (506/622-1780, www.miramichifolksongfestival.com), which opens with an outdoor gospel concert and continues with a shindig of traditional and contemporary singing, dancing, and fiddling.

Food

1809 Restaurant (Rodd Miramichi River, 1809 Water St., Miramichi East, 506/773-3111, Sun.-Thurs. 7am-10pm, Fri.-Sat. 7am-11pm, $15-29), on the south side of the river, has a dependable breakfast, lunch, and dinner menu, with lots of outdoor riverside seating in summer and an indoor log fireplace to keep diners warm during winter. Salmon is the specialty, and it is offered in a number of different ways, including blackened with mango chutney for a reasonable $25.

some of the oldest buildings in Miramichi

Salmon Fishing on the Miramichi

Fly-fishing is the only method allowed for taking Atlantic salmon. Fish in the 13- to 18-kilogram (28.7- to 39.7-pound) range are not unusual; occasionally, anglers land specimens weighing up to 22 kilograms (48.5 pounds). The salmon season runs mid-May–mid-October. Nonresidents are required to hire guides, who are plentiful hereabouts.

Riverside fishing resorts, which let you drop a line in rustic elegance, are a popular way to enjoy the piscatorial experience. They're not cheap, however. One of the best and most historic is **Upper Oxbow Adventures** (2260 Rte. 420, near Trout Brook, 506/622-8834, www. upperoxbow.com), which has been in operation since 1823 through five generations of the same family. The company offers day trips ($250 pp, guides and equipment included), but most anglers stay overnight on packages that typically cost from $400 per person per day, including meals, accommodations, and guiding.

A more luxurious option is **Pond's Resort** (Porter Cove Rd., Sillikers, 506/369-2612 or 877/971-7663, www.pondsresort.com), which charges $475 per person per day for lodging in a riverside log cabin, meals, and guided fishing.

Accommodations and Camping

Step back in time at the **Governor's Mansion Inn** (62 St. Patrick's Dr., 506/622-3036 or 877/647-2642, www.governorsmansion.ca, $109-159 d), which dates to the 1860s and was once used as the official residence of New Brunswick's lieutenant governor. This historic home is in a quiet out-of-town setting across the road from the Miramichi River. The four rooms have en suite bathrooms, and two have river views and king beds. Breakfast is extra, and dinner is available on weekends.

At the upper end of the price range is the **Rodd Miramichi River** (1809 Water St., Miramichi East, 506/773-3111 or 800/565-7633, www.roddvacations.com, $135-165 s or d), a modern riverside complex where rooms are painted in warm heritage colors. Amenities include a restaurant and an indoor pool.

Enclosure Campground (8 Enclosure Rd., 506/622-0680, www. enclosurecampground.ca, $28-35) is in a pleasant riverside location 10 kilometers (6.2 miles) south of town along Highway 8. It offers over 100 campsites, hiking trails, a heated outdoor pool and hot tub, kitchen shelters, a café with Wi-Fi Internet access, and a playground.

Information

Miramichi Visitor Information Centre (199 King St., 506/778-8444, www. discovermiramichi.com, June-Aug. daily 10am-5pm) is beside Highway 11 as it enters town from the south. Wi-Fi Internet access is free, and there's a short trail for walking your dog.

Getting There

Miramichi is 130 kilometers (81 miles) north of Shediac, a 1.5-hour drive via Highway 11. From Fredericton, Mirimichi is 175 kilometers (109 miles) northeast, 2-2.5 hours on Highway 8.

MIRAMICHI TO FREDERICTON

From Miramichi, it's 175 kilometers (109 miles) southwest along the Miramichi River to Fredericton, the capital of New Brunswick. The route is a handy highway if you're planning to drive a loop around the province, but aside from the rural scenery, the drive's biggest draw is salmon fishing.

Doaktown

Crossing through the deep interior of the province, Highway 8 runs alongside the famed salmon-rich Miramichi River to

Doaktown, 86 kilometers (53 miles) southwest of Miramichi. Squire Robert Doak from Scotland founded the town and gave it a boom start with gristmills and paper mills in the early 1800s. The squire's white wooden house (with some original furnishings) and nearby barn have been set aside as **Doak Historic Site** (386 Main St., 506/365-2026, July-Sept. Mon.-Sat. 9am-5pm, Sun. noon-5pm, adult $5).

Also in town, the **Atlantic Salmon Museum** (263 Main St., 506/365-7787, June-Sept. Mon.-Sat. 9am-5pm, Sun. noon-5pm, adult $8, senior $6, child $5) will be especially interesting to anglers. Exhibits depict the life cycle and habitat of this king of game fish, as well as the history of the art of catching it (including a collection of rods, reels, and gaudily attractive flies). Live salmon specimens at various stages of development swim in the aquariums.

GETTING THERE
Doaktown is about 86 kilometers (53 miles) southwest of Miramichi, a 1.5-hour drive via Highway 8. Coming from Fredericton, it's a 50-kilometer (31-mile) drive northeast, 45 minutes along Highway 8.

Boiestown
Another well-conceived museum is the **Central New Brunswick Woodmen's Museum** (6342 Hwy. 8, 506/369-7214, June-early Sept. daily 9:30am-5pm, adult $10, senior $8, child $5), which spreads over 6 hectares (15 acres) along Highway 8 near Boiestown. The museum's exhibits explain forestry's past and present. Among the buildings are replicas of a sawmill and a blacksmith shop, wheelwright shop, trapper's cabin, bunkhouse, and cookhouse. A Forestry Hall of Fame remembers the Paul Bunyans of New Brunswick's timber industry, and a miniature train makes a 15-minute loop through the grounds.

GETTING THERE
Boiestown is about 110 kilometers (68 miles) southwest of Miramichi, a 1.5-hour drive via Highway 8, and 65 kilometers (40 miles) northeast of Fredericton, one hour on Highway 8.

Baie des Chaleurs

North of Miramichi Bay, the Acadian peninsula juts northeast into the Gulf of St. Lawrence. One side of the peninsula faces the Gulf of St. Lawrence, while the other side fronts the Baie des Chaleurs. In contrast to the wild Gulf of St. Lawrence, the shallower Baie des Chaleurs is warm and calm. Busy seaports dot the eastern coast of the bay—the region's commercial fishing fleets lie anchored at Bas-Caraquet, Caraquet, and Grande-Anse. Interspersed between the picturesque harbors are equally beautiful peninsulas, coves, and beaches. Swimming is especially pleasant along the sheltered beaches, where the shallow sea heats up to bathtub warmth in summer. Across the bay, Québec's Gaspé Peninsula is usually visible, sometimes with startling clarity when conditions are right. From Bathurst west, the fishing villages give way to industrial towns.

ACADIAN PENINSULA
Bartibog Bridge
It's a 10-minute drive on Highway 11 from Miramichi to this bayside town, where **MacDonald Farm Heritage Site** (600 Hwy. 11, 506/778-6085, late June-early Sept. Tues.-Sun. 10am-4pm, adult $4, senior $3, child $2) re-creates a Scottish settler's life in 1784. Guides take visitors through the two-story 1820s stone farmhouse, fields, orchards, and outbuildings.

Acadian Deportation

After the signing of the Treaty of Utrecht in 1713, England had demanded but not enforced an oath of allegiance from the Acadians who lived under its jurisdiction. By the 1750s, however, the British decided to demand loyalty. Those who refused to sign the oath of allegiance were rounded up and deported, and their villages and farmlands burned.

The Acadians being deported were herded onto ships bound for the English colonies on the Eastern seaboard or any place that would accept them. Some ships docked in England, others in France, and still others in France's colonies in the Caribbean. As the ports wearied of the human cargo, many of them refused the vessels entry, and the ships returned to the high seas to search for other ports willing to accept the Acadians.

In one of the period's few favorable events, the Spanish government offered the refugees free land in Louisiana, and many settled there in 1784, where they became known as Cajuns. Many Acadians fought the British in guerrilla warfare or fled to the hinterlands of Cape Breton Island, Prince Edward Island, New Brunswick, and Québec.

Exact deportation numbers are unknown. Historians speculate that 10,000 French inhabitants lived in Acadia in 1755; by the time the deportation had run its course in 1816, only 25 percent of them remained. The poet Longfellow distilled the tragedy in his *Evangeline*, a fictional story of two lovers divided by the events.

Val-Comeau

Farther north on Highway 11, straddling a narrow peninsula jutting into the Gulf of St. Lawrence, **Camping Val-Comeau** (506/393-7150, June-mid-Sept., $30-40) is a 190-site campground with spacious sites, beach swimming, and a playground. The peninsula itself is interesting for lush sphagnum bogs, formed when the last ice sheet melted and pooled without a place to drain on the flat terrain. Seabirds inhabit the surrounding nutrient-rich marshes, and birdlife is prolific.

Shippagan

New Brunswick's largest commercial fishing fleet is based in this sheltered bay at the tip of the Acadian Peninsula, 110 kilometers (68 miles) northeast of Miramichi (allow at least 90 minutes). **New Brunswick Aquarium and Marine Centre** (100 Aquarium St., 506/336-3013, June-late Sept. daily 10am-6pm, adult $9.15, senior and child $7) opens up the world of gulf fishing with exhibits and viewing and touch tanks holding over 100 native fish species.

Camping Shippagan (4 km/2.5 mi west of town, 506/336-3960, www.camping.shippagan.com, June-Sept., $27.50-36.50) enjoys a great location, right on the water with a nice beach. Amenities include firewood, showers and washrooms, kitchen shelters, a picnic area, a launderette, and organized activities through July and August.

Getting There

Continuing north from Miramichi, the options are to take Highway 8 directly north to Bathurst (75 km/47 mi, well under one hour) or detour along the Acadian Peninsula (via Highway 11) to Shippagan and rejoin the main highway at Bathurst. Total distance for this second option is around 200 kilometers (124 miles), but you should allow at least three hours since the road passes through many towns.

ÎLE LAMÈQUE

Offshore of Shippagan, Île Lamèque noses into the gulf at the brow of the Acadian Peninsula. Connected to the mainland by a bridge, the island changes with the seasons: Spring brings a splendid show of wildflowers; summer brings wild blueberries ripening on the barrens; autumn transforms the landscape to a burnished red. The spruce trees here are bent and dwarfed by the relentless sea winds, but oysters, moon snails, blue mussels, and jackknife clams thrive along the beautiful white-sand beaches.

Lamèque International Baroque Music Festival

Île Lamèque is best known for the late July **Lamèque International Baroque Music Festival** (506/344-3261, www.festivalbaroque.com), as unlikely as that may seem out here among the peat bogs and fishing villages. It is the only festival in North America dedicated to the celebration of music from the baroque period (1600-1760) and has been attracting the world's best early music performers since the early 1970s. The setting is superb—almost divine—within the acoustically perfect 1913 Church Sainte-Cecile.

Accommodations

The fanciest digs on the island are at **Auberge des Compagnons** (11 rue Principale, Lamèque, 506/344-7766 or 866/344-7762, $135-190), a modern 16-room lodge with sweeping water views. The restaurant serves a buffet-style breakfast, which is extra.

Getting There

Île Lamèque is 125 kilometers (78 miles) north of Miramichi, a two-hour drive via Highway 11, then Highway 113 into and through Shippagan. From Fredericton, head 175 kilometers (109 miles) northeast on Highway 8 to Mirimichi and on to Île Lamèque, for a 300-kilometer (185-mile), four-hour drive.

CARAQUET

From the south, Highway 11 lopes into town and turns into a boulevard lined with shops, lodgings, and sights. Established in 1758, picturesque Caraquet (pop. 4,200), 32 kilometers (20 miles) west of Shippagan, is northern New Brunswick's oldest French settlement and is known as Acadia's cultural heart.

Sights and Recreation

★ VILLAGE HISTORIQUE ACADIEN

Ten kilometers (6.2 miles) west of Caraquet, **Village Historique Acadien** (14311 Rte. 11, Rivière du Nord, 506/726-2600, mid-June-late Sept. daily 10am-6pm, adult $20, senior $16, families $45) provides a sensory journey through early Acadia. To re-create the period 1780-1890, more than 40 rustic houses and other authentic buildings were transported to this 1,133-hectare (2,800-acre) site and restored. The buildings—including a church, smithy, school, printing shop, carpenter's

Village Historique Acadien

shop, gristmill, farmhouses, and others—are spread across woods and fields along the North River. You walk the dusty lanes or hop aboard a horse-drawn wagon to get from one building to the next, where costumed "residents" describe their daily lives, jobs, and surroundings in French and English. Out in the park, two "post houses" serve sandwiches, snacks, and drinks. The site also holds **La Table des Ancetres,** which serves typical hearty Acadian dishes at reasonable prices.

THE ACADIAN MUSEUM

The **Acadian Museum** (15 St-Pierre Blvd., 506/726-2682, June-mid-Sept. Mon.-Sat. 10am-6pm, Sun. 1pm-6pm, adult $4, child $1.50) is a less ambitious look at local history than the waterfront Village Historique Acadien, but it's still a worthwhile stop. The adjacent **Carrefour de la Mer** (51 St-Pierre Blvd., 506/726-2688), whose name translates to "Crossroads of the Sea," encompasses the local information center, an art gallery, a playground, and a restaurant.

Festivals and Events

Caraquet is the place to be for early August's 12-day **Festival Acadien** (www.festivalacadien.ca), one of the province's best-attended events. It includes the blessing of the huge fishing fleet by the local Roman Catholic clergy; jazz, pop, and classical music concerts; live theater; food and drink; and the Tintamarre, a massive street celebration on Acadia Day (Aug. 15).

Food and Accommodations

The distinctive three-story, crisply colored red-and-green ★ **Hotel Paulin** (134 St-Pierre Blvd. W., 506/727-9981 or 866/727-9981, www.hotelpaulin.com, $195-315 s or d) is a family-run boutique hotel that has been entertaining guests since 1901. The 12 guest rooms have hardwood floors, comfortable beds, and a low-key but stylish decor. The top-floor Waterfront Suites are huge. The downstairs restaurant oozes charm and opens nightly for creative table d'hôte dining.

Getting There

Caraquet is about 110 kilometers (68 miles) north of Miramichi, a 1.5-hour drive via Highway 11. From Fredericton, head 175 kilometers (109 miles) northeast on Highway 8 to Mirimichi and on to Caraquet for a 285-kilometer (175-mile), four-hour drive.

GRANDE-ANSE AND VICINITY

From Caraquet, Highway 11 heads west, then jogs north at Bertrand to reach the shoreline of Baie des Chaleurs. For a swim in the warm bay, take Highway 320, the narrow road that diverges to the right, to **Maisonnette Park,** an exquisite spread of beach overlooking Caraquet across Baie Caraquet. The warm-water beach is a favorite, especially when the tide retreats to reveal sand dune fingers washed by shallow, sun-heated waters.

Take a left turn where Highway 11 hits the coast and you'll quickly reach Grand-Anse, where **Musée des cultures fondatrices** (184 Acadie St., 506/732-3003, mid-June-Sept. daily 10am-5pm, adult $6, senior and child $3) commemorates the visit of Pope John Paul II to New Brunswick in 1985. Exhibits include vestments, chalices, and other ecclesiastical paraphernalia, plus a detailed scale replica of St. Peter's Basilica.

Getting There

Grande-Anse is about 20 kilometers (12.4 miles) west of Caraquet, a 20-minute drive along Highway 11. From Fredericton, head northeast on Highway 8 for 260 kilometers (160 miles), then northeast on Highway 11 for 50 kilometers (31 miles). Allow four hours.

BATHURST AND VICINITY

The town of Bathurst (pop. 12,300) sits by its own fine natural harbor at the vertex of Nepisiguit Bay, a broad gulf on the Baie des Chaleurs. It's 75 kilometers (47 miles) west of Caraquet, or 75 kilometers (47 miles) north of Miramichi as you shoot up Highway 8. All routes into town converge downtown at the pleasant **La Promenade Waterfront,** where you'll find a boardwalk, local **visitors center** (86 Douglas Ave., 506/548-0418, summer daily 9am-5pm), shops selling local arts and crafts, cafés, an ice cream shop, and a gazebo that hosts musicians throughout summer.

Daly Point Nature Reserve spreads across 40 hectares (99 acres) of salt marshes, woodlands, and fields northeast of town; an observation tower provides views of nesting ospreys, various seabirds, and songbirds. To get there, take Bridge Street (the Acadian Coastal Drive) east from Bathurst, then turn left on Carron Drive. Bring insect repellent.

Getting There

Bathurst is about 75 kilometers (47 miles) north of Miramichi, less than an hour's drive via Highway 8. To get there from Fredericton, head northeast on Highway 8 for 260 kilometers (160 miles), three hours.

Bathurst to Campbellton

Highway 11 stays inland for the scenically dull 85-kilometer (53-mile) stretch between Bathurst and Charlo. Far preferable is coastal Highway 134, which runs through the fishing villages of Nigadoo, Petit-Rocher, Pointe-Verte, and Jacquet River. The coast between Bathurst and Dalhousie is famed for sightings of a phantom ship. Numerous witnesses over the years have described a ship under full sail engulfed in flames on the bay; sometimes the vision includes a crew frantically scurrying across the deck. Some say the vision dates from the Battle of Restigouche (1760)—the last naval engagement between France and England in this part of eastern Canada—when France's fleet was destroyed by the British.

At the end of a narrow, private wooded road, ★ **La Fine Grobe Sur-Mer** (289 Rue Principale, Nigadoo, 506/783-3138, daily 4:30pm-9:30pm, $20-50) enjoys a delightful setting overlooking Chaleur Bay. One of the region's finest and most respected restaurants, La Fine Grobe Sur-Mer has been in the business of serving French-inspired dishes like chateaubriand, herb-crusted rack of lamb, and seafood pancakes for decades. For a memorable splurge, order the seafood casserole.

CAMPBELLTON

At the head of the Baie des Chaleurs, the New Brunswick and Gaspé coastlines meet near Campbellton (pop. 7,400), the area's largest town. A bridge here spans the broad mouth of the Restigouche River to connect with Québec's Highway 132. Highway 17 plunges

La Fine Grobe Sur-Mer

deep into the unpopulated interior of New Brunswick, across the Restigouche Uplands. Along this route, it's 92 kilometers (57 miles) to Saint-Quentin, where you can veer east to Mount Carleton Provincial Park or continue another 80 kilometers (50 miles) to join the Saint John River valley at Saint-Léonard.

Sights and Recreation

Restigouche Gallery (39 Andrew St., 506/753-5750, summer Mon.-Sat. 9am-5pm, the rest of the year Tues.-Sat. 10am-4pm, adult $2) is a public art gallery displaying works by local, national, and international artists, as well as natural history and science exhibits.

Sugarloaf Park (Exit 415 off Hwy. 11, 506/789-2366) overlooks the whole region. A year-round chairlift offers views to the 305-meter (1,001-foot) gumdrop-shaped peak of Sugarloaf Mountain. The park also has hiking trails, chairlift-assisted mountain biking ($25 per day), tennis courts, and supervised swimming. In winter, the park is popular for snowmobiling, skating, and cross-country skiing. The park campground is open mid-May-mid-October and has 76 wooded sites for $28-36.

Accommodations

The centrally located **Super 8** (26 Duke St., 506/753-7606 or 877/582-7666, www.super8campbellton.com, $115-145 s or d) has a small indoor swimming pool and a complimentary breakfast.

Getting There

Campbellton is 115 kilometers (71 miles) northwest of Bathurst, a 1.5-hour drive via Highway 11. The most direct route to Campbellton from Fredericton is to follow Highway 2 then Highway 17 from Saint-Léonard. The drive is 390 kilometers (240 miles), four hours.

Prince Edward Island

Charlottetown and Queens County

As Canada's smallest provincial capital,
Charlottetown (pop. 36,000)—the island's governmental, economic, cultural, and shopping center—makes no pretense of being a big city. Rather, this attractive town is walkable, comfortable, and friendly. Its major attractions include a beautiful harborside location, handsome public and residential architecture, sophisticated art and cultural happenings, and plentiful lodgings and appealing restaurants.

The city also makes a good sightseeing base for exploring surrounding Queens County, which is the definitive Prince Edward Island as you imagined the province would be. The region is temptingly photogenic, a meld of small seaports with brightly colored craft at anchor and farmland settings with limpid ponds and weathered barns.

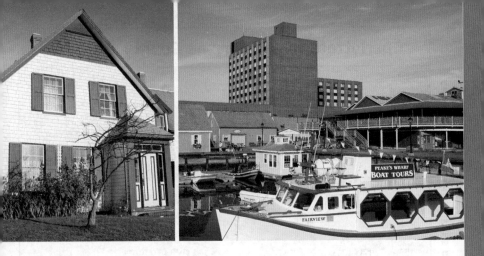

Highlights

Look for ★ to find recommended sights, activities, dining, and lodging.

★ **Province House:** This historic sandstone building in the heart of Charlottetown hosted the Fathers of Confederation in 1864 and continues today as the provincial seat of government (page 281).

★ **Victoria Park:** Take a break from the relative bustle of downtown with a walk through this waterfront park, home to the impressive Fanningbank residence (page 282).

★ **International Shellfish Festival:** You can feast on seafood year-round in Charlottetown, but this late-September festival is the place to try all your favorites at once (page 286).

★ **Prince Edward Island National Park:** Stretching along the Gulf of St. Lawrence, this park is one of the island's few undeveloped tracts of land. Warm water, beaches, and red cliffs are the main draws (page 296).

★ **North Rustico Harbour:** It's just a dot on the map, but this small fishing village is particularly photogenic. A lighthouse, kayak tours, and an excellent restaurant add to the appeal (page 300).

★ **Green Gables Heritage Place:** Northern Queens County is lovingly known as "Anne's Land," for Anne of Green Gables, one of the world's best-known literary characters (page 302).

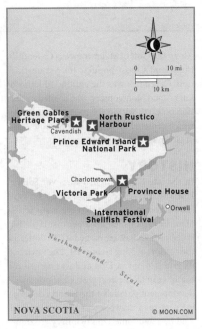

Charlottetown and Queens County

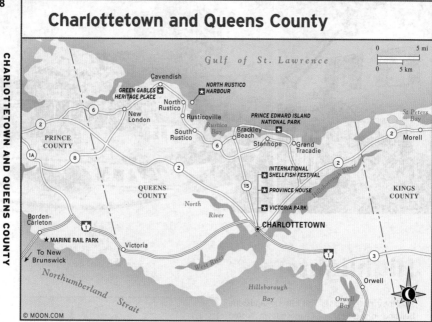

Along the Gulf of St. Lawrence is Cavendish, the island's most popular tourist destination. Cavendish was the childhood home of Lucy Maud Montgomery, who created perfection on earth within the pages of her books, which centered on the spunky heroine Anne of Green Gables.

HISTORY

In the late 1750s, English surveyor Samuel Holland surveyed all of Prince Edward Island, recommending that the main settlement be established on a peninsula within Hillsborough Bay. He named it Charlotte, for the consort of King George III. The town had its grid laid out in 1764 and was named the island's capital the next year. Charlottetown's development paralleled the island's development. A road network was laid out by 1850. And by 1860, some 176 sawmills were transforming forests into lumber, greasing the

island's economy and providing the raw materials for a thriving shipbuilding industry. As the center of government and commerce, the town was enriched with splendid stone churches and public buildings, many of which date to the mid-1800s and stand to this day.

PLANNING YOUR TIME

For many visitors, Queens County *is* Prince Edward Island. A typical itinerary would be to catch the ferry to Wood Islands, spend one day in the capital, Charlottetown, and another in Cavendish before driving off the island via the Confederation Bridge. This is enough time in the capital to visit major attractions such as **Province House** while having enough time to end the day with an evening walk through **Victoria Park.** If your travels coincide with the late September **International Shellfish Festival,** you may want to stay longer.

Cavendish, the most popular destination

Previous: lobster traps in front of oyster barns in New London; Borden-Carleton lighthouse; Green Gables Heritage Place; Peake's Wharf in Charlottetown.

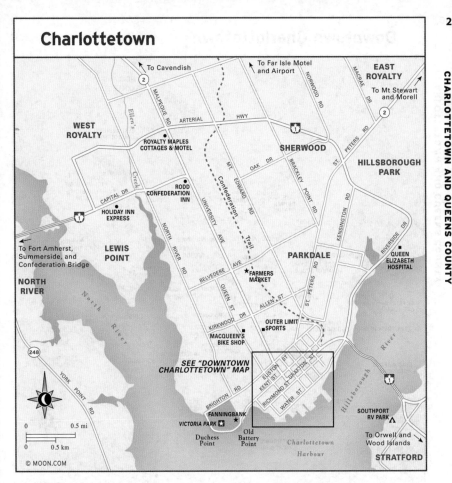

Charlottetown

on all of Prince Edward Island, is just an hour's drive from the capital. This makes a day trip possible and means you can settle yourself into Charlottetown for two or more nights, taking advantage of the theater and many restaurants. Cavendish does have many accommodations, but good dining rooms are severely lacking. Regardless of where you stay, your trip to Cavendish should include a drive through **Prince Edward Island National Park,** the short detour to **North Rustico Harbour,** and a visit to **Green Gables Heritage Place.**

ORIENTATION

The city, small as it is, may be baffling for a new visitor because of the way historic and newer streets converge. The town began with a handful of harbor-front blocks. The centuries have contributed a confusing jumble of other roads that feed into the historic area from all sorts of angles.

From either direction, the **Trans-Canada Highway** (Route 1) will take you right into the heart of town. From the west, it crosses the North River, turns south at the University of Prince Edward Island campus, and becomes University Avenue. From the east, take the

Downtown Charlottetown

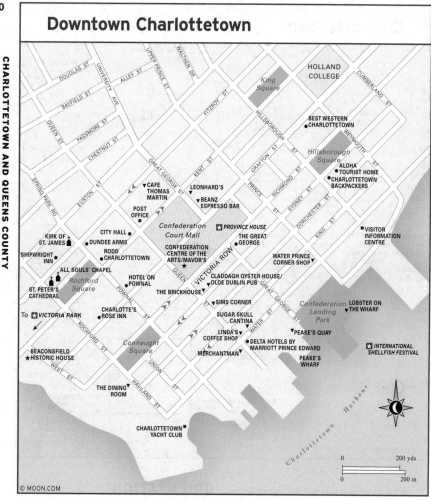

© MOON.COM

Water Street exit to reach the visitors information center.

Extending from the harbor to Euston Street, the commercial area is pleasantly compact, attractive, and easily covered on foot. **Old Charlottetown** (or Old Charlotte Town, depending on who's describing the area) has been restored with rejuvenated buildings and brick walkways, lighted at night with gas lamps.

The most sought after residential areas, with large stately houses, rim Victoria Park and North River Road. Working-class neighborhoods fan out farther north beyond Grafton Street and are marked with small, pastel-painted houses set close to the streets.

Sights and Recreation

Downtown Charlottetown is compact; plan on parking and exploring on foot. The waterfront area is the best place to leave your vehicle. Not only is it central, but you can make the provincial **Visitor Information Centre** (6 Prince St., 902/368-4444, www.discovercharlottetown.com, May daily 9am-5pm, June daily 9am-6pm, July-Aug. daily 8am-7pm, Sept. daily 8:30am-5pm, Oct. daily 9am-4pm) your first stop.

DOWNTOWN

Most visitors to Prince Edward Island arrive by road, traveling either across the Confederation Bridge or on the ferry. You can also fly to Charlottetown.

Confederation Players

The **Confederation Players** are keen local historians who dress in period costume to conduct walking tours ($10-15 pp) of downtown Charlottetown July-mid-August. The Great George Street walking tour departs Tuesday-Saturday at 10:30am and 3:30pm from the Visitor Information Centre at 178 Water Street, taking in all the historical highlights along one of Canada's best known boulevards. The Historic Queen Square tour departs from its namesake in the heart of downtown Tuesday-Saturday at 2:30pm, focusing on Province House and the Confederation Centre of the Arts.

Downtown Waterfront

A rejuvenation project has resulted in much improvement in the downtown waterfront precinct. The adjacent **Confederation Landing Park** is rimmed by a seaside boardwalk and filled with pleasant gardens and well-trimmed grass. The park is integrated with **Peake's Wharf**, where the Fathers of Confederation arrived on the island. This is now a tourist hub of sorts, with restaurants and shops, and tour boats line the docks waiting to take interested visitors on sightseeing trips.

★ Province House

The nation of Canada began at **Province House** (corner of Grafton St. and Great George St., 902/566-7626, June-Sept. daily 9am-5pm, Oct.-May Mon.-Fri. 9am-5pm, free), four blocks up Great George Street from the harbor. Now protected as a national historic site, the buff sandstone neoclassical edifice at the high point of downtown was erected in 1847 to house the island's colonial legislature. It quickly became the center of public life on the island. It was the site of lavish balls and state functions, including the historic 1864 conference on federal union. The provincial legislature still convenes here; meetings are in session between mid-February and early May for 5-17 weeks, depending on how much provincial government haggling is under way.

In the late 1970s, Parks Canada undertook restoration of the age-begrimed building, a five-year task completed in 1983. Layers of paint came off the front columns. The double-hung windows throughout were refitted with glass panes from an old greenhouse in New Brunswick. About 10 percent of the original furnishings remained in the building before restoration and were retained. Most of the rest were replaced by period antiques obtained in the other provinces and the northeastern United States. A flowered rug was woven for Confederation Chamber, where the Fathers of Confederation convened. Every nook and corner was refurbished and polished until the interior gleamed. Today, Province House is one of Atlantic Canada's most significant public buildings.

Confederation Centre of the Arts

Confederation Centre of the Arts (145 Richmond St., 902/628-1864, www.

confederationcentre.com) is the other half of the imposing complex shared by Province House. The promenades, edged with places to sit, are great places for people-watching, and kids like to skateboard on the walkways.

The center opened in 1964 to mark the centennial of the Charlottetown Conference, as the confederation meeting became known in Canadian history. It's a great hulk of a place, compatible with its historic neighbor in its design and coloring. The center houses an art gallery, the provincial library, four theaters, and a café. The emphasis at the **Confederation Centre Art Gallery** (902/628-6142, mid-May-early Oct. daily 9am-5pm, early Oct.-mid-May Wed.-Sat. 11am-5pm, Sun. 1pm-5pm, free) is the work of Canadian artists—expect to see some of island artist Robert Harris's paintings and Lucy Maud Montgomery's original manuscripts. A gift shop stocks wares by the cream of PEI's artisans.

All Souls' Chapel

A few blocks west of Queen Street, the remarkable **All Souls' Chapel** next to **St. Peter's Cathedral** (Rochford St., 902/566-2102, daily 8am-6pm, free) was a joint Harris family creation. The architect William Harris styled it in island sandstone with a dark walnut interior. His brother Robert painted the murals and deftly mixed family members and friends among the religious figures.

Beaconsfield Historic House

A bright yellow, 25-room mansion, **Beaconsfield Historic House** (2 Kent St., 902/368-6603, tours summer daily 10am-4pm, spring and fall Mon.-Fri. 10am-4pm, adult $5, senior and child $4) was built in 1877 from a William Critchlow Harris design. The building has survived more than a century of varied use as a family home, a shelter for "friendless women," a YWCA, and a nurses' residence. It was rescued in 1973 by the PEI Museum and Heritage Foundation, which turned it into foundation headquarters and a heritage museum. A good bookstore is on the first level, and genealogical archives are kept across the hall and upstairs. The wide front porch overlooking the harbor across a long lawn is a great place to have tea and scones.

★ Victoria Park

Victoria Park, adjacent to Beaconsfield House, reigns as one of Charlottetown's prettiest settings, with 16 wooded and grassy hectares (39.5 acres) overlooking the bay at Battery

Province House

Getting to Prince Edward Island

CONFEDERATION BRIDGE

The impressive **Confederation Bridge** (902/437-7300 or 888/437-6565, www.confederationbridge.com) is Prince Edward Island's most important transportation link to the rest of Canada. From Cape Jourimain (New Brunswick), 80 kilometers (50 miles) east of Moncton, the bridge stretches across Northumberland Strait to Borden-Carleton, which is in Prince County, 60 kilometers (37 miles) west of Charlottetown. Driving across the impressive 12.9-kilometer (8-mile) span takes about 10 minutes (views are blocked by concrete barriers erected as a windbreak).

The round-trip bridge toll is $47 per vehicle, including passengers. Payment (credit card, debit card, or cash) is collected at Borden-Carleton upon leaving the island.

Confederation Bridge

BY FERRY

Prince Edward Island is also linked to the rest of Atlantic Canada by ferry. The mainland departure point is Caribou (Nova Scotia), near Pictou, a two-hour drive from Halifax. The ferry docks at Wood Islands, a scenic 62-kilometer (38-mile) drive southeast from Charlottetown. The 75-minute crossing is operated by **Northumberland Ferries** (902/566-3838 or 800/565-0201, www.ferries.ca) May-mid-December, with up to nine crossings in each direction daily during peak summer season. The round-trip fare is $78 per vehicle, regardless of the number of passengers. As with the bridge crossing, payment is made upon leaving the island, so to save a few bucks, take the ferry to PEI and return on the Confederation Bridge.

BY AIR

Air Canada (888/247-2262, www.aircanada.com) has direct flights to Charlottetown from Halifax, Montréal, Ottawa, and Toronto. **WestJet** (403/250-5839 or 888/937-8538, www.westjet.com) flies in from Toronto.

Point. The greenery spreads out across the peninsula tip; to get there, follow Kent Street as it turns into Park Roadway. The park's rolling terrain is built of moraines, heaps of gravelly deposits left behind by ice-age glaciers.

Joggers like the park's winding paths, and birders find abundant yellow warblers, purple finches, and downy woodpeckers nesting in the maples, firs, oaks, pines, and birches. The white palatial mansion overlooking the water is **Fanningbank** (Government House), the lieutenant governor's private residence—nice to look at, but it's closed to the public.

BEYOND DOWNTOWN

Charlottetown Farmers Market

The **Charlottetown Farmers Market** (100 Belvedere Ave., 902/626-3373, Sat. 9am-2pm and summer Wed. 9am-2pm) is across from the university campus. The indoor market holds about 40 vendors selling everything from flowers and crafts to baked goods, produce, and fish.

Fort Amherst-Port-la-Joye National Historic Site

Just 4 kilometers (2.5 miles) across the harbor

from downtown but a 35-minute drive via Routes 1 and 19, **Fort Amherst-Port-la-Joye National Historic Site** protects the island's first European settlement. It all began in 1720, when three French ships sailed into Port-la-Joye (today's Charlottetown Harbour) carrying some 300 settlers. Most of them moved to the north shore and established fishing villages, but the rest remained here at the military outpost.

Within just four years, adverse conditions had driven out most of the French. The British burned Port-la-Joye in 1745 and took control of the island. The French later returned to rebuild their capital, but were compelled to surrender Port-la-Joye to a superior British force in 1758. The British renamed the post Fort Amherst. After the British established a new capital at Charlottetown, Fort Amherst fell quickly into disrepair, and now no buildings remain. The grounds, which have picnic tables, are open June-August.

RECREATION

Those looking for easy walking gravitate to the waterfront at the southwestern end of downtown. This is the starting point for a **paved trail** that extends to Old Battery Point and Victoria Park. While this area is also popular for biking, cyclists looking for longer rides will be impressed at how easy it is to reach the rural landscape beyond city limits. From downtown, the ride out to Brackley Beach (45 km/28 mi) is a good full-day ride.

MacQueen's Bike Shop (430 Queen St., 902-368-2453, Mon.-Sat. 8:30am-5:30pm, Sun. 10am-2pm) provides complete bike and accessory rental and repairs and can also arrange island cycle-touring packages. **Outer Limit Sports** (330 University Ave., 902/569-5690, Mon.-Sat. 9am-6pm, Sun. 9am-4pm) also offers rentals and repairs, as well as drop-offs for the Confederation Trail. Both companies charge from $30 per day for a road bike.

Entertainment and Events

Charlottetown once rolled up the sidewalks at night, but in recent years a rousing nightlife and pub scene has emerged centered on drinking and dancing. Last call for drinks is at 1:30am; the doors lock at 2am. For complete listings of all that's happening around the city, check out *The Buzz* (www.buzzon.com) or the weekend editions of *The Guardian* (www.theguardian.pe.ca).

NIGHTLIFE

Peake's Quay (11 Great George St., 902/368-1330, Mon.-Thurs. 11am-10pm, Fri.-Sat. 11am-2am, Sun. 9am-10pm) has a prime waterfront location, making it popular with both locals and visitors. While the service is often indifferent, it's a good family-friendly environment with inexpensive food and lots of outdoor seating. Look for live music most weekends after 9pm. **Olde Dublin Pub** (131 Sydney St., 902/892-6992, Mon.-Wed.

11am-midnight, Thurs.-Sat. 11am-2am, Sun. 4pm-11pm) has a popular deck and offers Celtic and Irish music Thursday-Saturday for a small cover charge.

Mavor's (145 Richmond St., 902/628-6107, Mon.-Wed. 11am-9pm, Thurs.-Sat. 11am-midnight), in the Confederation Centre of the Arts, is a colorful space with more than 40 wines by the glass, top-notch martinis, and a thoughtful menu of light meals under $25.

Water's Edge Bar (Delta Hotels by Marriott, 18 Queen St., 902/894-1208, daily 7am-10pm) is a sophisticated space within one of the city's top hotels. The highlight for beer-lovers is a long list of regional brews.

The Brickhouse (125 Sydney St., 902/566-4620, Sun.-Thurs. 11am-10pm, Fri.-Sat. 11am-11pm) is another good choice for a quiet drink and conversation. Located in an 1850s building where the timber-frame and red brick is exposed, it's a stylish space that is best known as a restaurant, but there's no problem stopping by for a quiet drink at the bar or heading upstairs to the more private lounge (Thurs. 5pm-11pm, Fri.-Sat. 5pm-1am).

A mainstay of the live music scene is **Baba's Lounge** (upstairs at 81 University Ave., 902/892-7377, Mon.-Sat. noon-2am, Sun. 5pm-2am), a popular hangout with the younger set since the earlier 1990s. "Intimate" is an understatement here; bodies writhe to the rhythm on a dance floor about the size of a postage stamp. Expect live music ranging from slightly alternative to modern rock.

PERFORMING ARTS

The **Confederation Centre of the Arts** (145 Richmond St., 902/566-1267) is the performing arts capital of the province and the site of the **Charlottetown Festival** (www. confederationcentre.com), which runs mid-June-mid-September. The festival is best known for the *Anne of Green Gables* musical (July and Aug. daily at 1:30pm and 7:30pm); tickets cost $50-70. Also on the bill are repertory productions in the center's main theater and cabaret-style productions at the **MacKenzie Theatre**, the festival's second stage (University Ave. and Grafton St.).

FESTIVALS AND EVENTS

June

The mid-June-mid-September **Charlottetown Festival** (902/566-1267, www. confederationcentre.com) presents musical theater and cabaret at the Confederation Centre of the Arts and the nearby MacKenzie Theatre. Two musicals are presented, including one centering on *Anne of Green Gables*.

July

The **Canada Day** long weekend (first weekend in July) is celebrated on the waterfront with a food fair, nationalistic displays, buskers, and island music.

Organized by the Charlottetown Yacht Club, **Race Week** (902/892-9065, www. cyc.pe.ca) runs Wednesday-Saturday in the middle of July. The program revolves around yacht races for various classes of boats, with other scheduled activities including shore games and nightly entertainment. Even if you're not involved in the event, watching the yachts racing across the harbor is a sight to behold.

August

The mid-August **Old Home Week**

judging at the International Shellfish Festival

(902/629-6623, www.oldhomeweekpei.com), Atlantic Canada's largest agricultural exposition, centers on Charlottetown Driving Park, northeast of downtown along Kensington Road. The city unofficially shuts down for the festival-ending **Gold Cup Parade** (www.goldcupparade.ca) through the streets of Charlottetown—said to be Atlantic Canada's biggest and best-attended parade. Daily grounds admission is a reasonable adult $12, child $5.

September
★ INTERNATIONAL
   SHELLFISH FESTIVAL

Summer ends with the **International Shellfish Festival** (866/955-2003, www.peishellfish.com), over the third weekend of September. Festivities along the waterfront include an oyster-shucking contest, a Chowder Challenge, "touch tanks," cooking classes, the World Is Your Oyster children's program, sock-hanging, and chefs from the local culinary institute sharing their cooking skills with the public.

Shopping

Centrally located and PEI's largest city by far, Charlottetown is the island's shopping hub. Downtown is a pleasant blend of old and new shopping experiences, although the main concentration of shopping malls is north of downtown along University Avenue. Stores catering to islanders are normally open Monday-Saturday about 9am-5pm, while touristy ones stay open later in July and August and also operate on Sunday.

ARTS AND CRAFTS

Local artists capture the island in masterful watercolors, acrylics, oils, and sculpture. Local crafts include finely made quilts, knits and woolens, stained glass, jewelry, pewter, pottery, and handsome furniture. The Anne doll is the most popular souvenir, and it's produced in innumerable variations for as little as $20 to as much as $800.

An exquisite handmade quilt costs $400-800—seldom a bargain. But well-crafted quilts are sturdily constructed and will last a lifetime with good care. Sweaters ($75-300) are especially high quality. One of the best sources is **Northern Watters Knitwear,** which operates a downtown factory outlet (150 Richmond St., 902/566-5850, www.nwknitwear.com, Mon.-Fri. 9am-8pm, Sat. 9am-6pm, Sun. 11am-5pm).

The **PEI Crafts Council** (www.peicraftscouncil.com) is a driving force behind local arts and crafts. It counts about 100 provincial craftspeople among its esteemed ranks. A visit to its website shows all members and the variety of their products (quilts, glassware, sculpture, clothing, knitted apparel, and jewelry ad infinitum), and provides a list of markets and craft shows they attend.

Food

Island fare is *good*, and while it centers on homegrown produce and seafood from the surrounding ocean, everything comes together in the capital, where you'll find an excellent array of dining opportunities for all budgets. The center of the eating action is **Victoria Row,** a block of vintage buildings along Richmond Street between Queen and Great George Streets. The street is pedestrian-only through summer. The restaurants set up outdoor tables while musicians play to the assembled crowd of diners.

Even if you're not in town for the **International Shellfish Festival** (third weekend of Sept.), you'll find local delicacies such as lobster and Malpeque oysters on menus throughout the city. Local produce and dairy products are delicious. Chefs make the most of island-grown succulent berries, locally produced maple syrup, and thick, sweet honey.

SEAFOOD

★ **Water Prince Corner Shop** (141 Water St., 902/368-3212, May-Oct. Mon.-Sat. 9am-10pm, Sun. 11am-10pm, $18-35) looks like a regular convenience store from the outside, but inside the ocean-blue clapboard building is a casual dining space where the emphasis is on fresh seafood at reasonable prices. It's all good—lobster burgers, lobster dinners with potato salad and mussels, Malpeque oysters, seafood chowder, steamed clams, and more.

Taking full advantage of its harbor-front locale is the upstairs **Peake's Quay** (11 Great George St., 902/368-1330, Mon.-Thurs. 11am-10pm, Fri.-Sat. 11am-2am, Sun. 9am-10pm, $13-24), with informal indoor and outdoor dining and an enviable seafood selection; try the scallops sauced with honey butter. Peake's Quay is also arguably the hottest nightspot in town, drawing locals, landlubber tourists, and yachties (who tie up at the adjacent marina)

alike to see and be seen while listening or dancing to top touring bands, so plan on dining early.

Northeast along the waterfront, **Lobster on the Wharf** (2 Prince St., 902/368-2888, May-Oct. 11:30am-10pm, $17-36) is a longtime favorite with visitors and locals alike. It has well over 300 seats, with more than 100 of these outside on multi-tiered decks built over the water. As the name suggests, lobster is the specialty (the two-person Lobster Feed is a local favorite), but the fish-and-chips and baked halibut are also excellent.

Fishbones (136 Richmond St., 902/628-6569, May-Oct. daily 11am-midnight, $16-31) is a fresh, casual restaurant along pedestrian-only Victoria Row. Start at the oyster bar before moving on to a set menu of contemporary creations, such as butter salmon curry. Other highlights include lobster mac and cheese, grilled halibut with mango salsa, and a wide selection of local beers and creative cocktails.

The ★ **Claddagh Oyster House** (131 Sydney St., 902/892-9661, Mon.-Sat. 5pm-10pm, Sun. 5pm-9pm, $27-34) is authentically Irish. Local oysters dominate the menu and come in many forms (including a tasting platter of 10 for $29). Seafood is the specialty on the main menu, with choices such as lobster risotto—a rich-tasting splurge.

Merchantman (23 Queen St., 902/892-9150, Sun.-Wed. 11am-9pm, Thurs.-Sat. 11am-10pm, $19-34) has a casual atmosphere and a menu dominated by local seafood, including steamed clams, calamari salad, and live lobster.

CANADIAN

The Dining Room (4 Sydney St., 902/894-6868, summer Mon.-Sat. 5pm-9pm, the rest of the year Tues.-Fri. 11:30am-1pm and 5:30pm-8:30pm, Sat. 5:30pm-8:30pm, $29-36) is the training restaurant for the culinary program at Holland College, a respected school that attracts students from across the country. Turn a blind eye to the rather institutional room, concentrate on the water views, and sit back to enjoy enthusiastic service and well-priced meals that blend contemporary and Continental cuisine.

Take a break from seafood by making reservations at ★ **Sims Corner** (86 Queen St., 902/894-7467, Mon.-Thurs. 11am-10pm, Fri. 11am-10:30pm, Sat. 10am-10:30pm, Sun. 10am-10pm, $18-38), the island's only true steakhouse. Ensconced in a historic 1860s red-brick building, the subtle setting is the perfect place to indulge in island-raised beef cooked exactly as ordered. For the full effect, choose a robust red from the extensive wine list and end your meal with a slab of dark chocolate brownie parfait.

If you want to dine in one of the city's best restaurants, but don't want to pay for an expensive dinner, eat breakfast at **Water's Edge** (Delta Hotels by Marriott Prince Edward, 18 Queen St., 902/894-1208, daily 7am-10pm, $24-39). Try dishes as traditional as blueberry muffins or as creative as lobster eggs Benedict. Things go upscale in the evening: That's when you can order beet salad or seafood chowder, followed by pan-seared halibut with a side of curried mussels.

The **Griffon Dining Room** (Dundee Arms, 200 Pownal St., 902/892-2496, daily for breakfast, lunch, and dinner, $26-38) is away from the tourist crush within a restored three-story manor that combines an old-fashioned setting with elegantly conceived fine cuisine emphasizing red meats and seafood. If you feel like a break from seafood, you won't regret the mint-rubbed rack of lamb.

MEXICAN

Sugar Skull Cantina (83 Water St., 902/370-2149, Mon.-Sat. 11am-10pm, Sun. noon-10pm, $10-18) serves up inexpensive Mexican food in a bright, casual setting, with picnic tables out front filling every warm evening. Adding to the appeal is a range of Mexican drinks, including build-your-own margaritas.

CAFÉS

What began with a German couple selling homemade bread to a local farmers market has morphed into **Leonhard's** (142 Great George St., 902/367-3621, daily 9am-5pm, lunches $6.50-13), a cozy café where the emphasis is on hearty yet healthy European-style cooking. Look for mouthwatering French toast and Bavarian-style omelets for breakfast; at lunch, the delicious gluten-free soups

Beanz Espresso Bar

are made from scratch, or choose the smoked turkey focaccia.

A couple of doors down from Leonhard's, **Beanz Espresso Bar** (138 Great George St., 902/892-8797, Mon.-Fri. 6:30am-5pm, Sat. 8am-4pm, lunches $7-12) gets rave reviews for its coffee, but the soups, salads, sandwiches, and old-fashioned pastries draw me back every time I'm in Charlottetown.

One block northwest of the two places recommended above, **Cafe Thomas Martin** (98 Fitzroy St., 902/892-0809, Mon.-Fri. 7:30am-2pm, lunches $6-10) is a friendly place far enough away from the main tourist attractions that it is missed by most tourists. On the menu are dozens of hot drink choices, light lunches such as chowders and sandwiches, and a tempting array of sweet treats.

At the Confederation Centre of the Arts, ★ **Mavor's** (145 Richmond St., 902/628-6107, daily 8am-8pm, lunches $8-15) is a striking room where you can get your fill of Starbucks coffee. The kitchen opens daily (except Sun.) at 11am, serving up fresh and wholesome food, with ethnic influences showing through in dishes such as blue mussels steamed in Thai curry broth. Also good: the thin-crust smoked salmon pizza and sweet potato wedges with a side of sour cream.

If you like old-fashioned diners with menus to match the era, sidle up to a booth or the counter at **Linda's Coffee Shop** (32 Queen St., 902/892-7292, daily 7am-3pm, lunches $6-11).

ICE CREAM

Dairy fanciers whoop it up at ★ **Cow's,** a local ice cream company that is renowned as much for its creamy treats wrapped in handmade waffle cones as for its colorful merchandise. Downtown outlets include one opposite the Confederation Centre (corner of Queen St. and Grafton St., 902/892-6969, summer daily 10am-11pm, until 6pm the rest of the year) and at Peake's Quay (902/566-4886, May-Oct. daily 10am-10pm).

Accommodations and Camping

You'll find every kind of lodging, from plain budget places to sumptuous expensive rooms, in Charlottetown's 100-plus lodgings. Also, unlike elsewhere in the province, most are open year-round.

Unless noted otherwise, prices given are for a double room; sales tax is not included.

DOWNTOWN
Under $50

The city's lone hostel is the HI-affiliated **Charlottetown Backpackers** (60 Hillsborough St., 902/367-5749, www. charlottetownbackpackers.com, dorm beds $29-33, $72-80 d), a converted residential home two blocks east of Province House. Facilities include a living room with a fireplace, bike rentals, a recreation room, and wireless Internet.

$50-100

In the vicinity of the hostel is another cheapie—**Aloha Tourist Home** (234 Sydney St., 902/892-5642 or 855/892-5642, www. alohaamigo.com, $95-225 s or d), an inexpensive downtown accommodation for those looking for private rooms. The renovated home has six guest rooms with single or double beds, two shared bathrooms, a shared kitchen, a lounge area, and free wireless Internet throughout. The least expensive rooms share bathrooms, while the others have en suites.

$100-150

Best Western Charlottetown (238 Grafton St., 902/892-2461 or 800/565-6589, www. bestwestern.com, $145-185 s or d including a hot breakfast) is a three-block jaunt from Province House. It has 143 midsize rooms fronting both sides of the street. Facilities include an indoor pool, fitness center, hot tub, and launderette.

$150-200

The elegant 1860s ★ **Shipwright Inn** (51 Fitzroy St., 902/368-1905 or 888/306-9966, www.shipwrightinn.com, $169-299 s or d) was originally the home of shipbuilder James Douse. The inn has eight rooms and suites, all with private baths and furnished in richly colored nautical themes (my favorite is the Chart Room, with an 1830s four-poster walnut bed, heavy drapes, and historic sea charts on the walls). Rates include a full breakfast.

What makes **Elmwood Heritage Inn** (121 N. River Rd., 902/368-3310 or 877/933-3310, www.elmwoodinn.pe.ca, $185-295 s or d including breakfast) stand out is the setting. Still within easy walking distance of downtown, its parklike grounds are surrounded by mature gardens; a row of stately elm trees leads up from the wrought-iron entry gates to the front door. Built for the grandson of Samuel Cunard in 1889, the mansion boasts 28 very Victorian guest rooms, many with jetted tubs and fireplaces.

A restored Queen Anne Revival mansion awash with antiques, **Dundee Arms** (200 Pownal St., 902/892-2496 or 877/638-6333, www.dundeearmspei.com, $175-230 s, $185-240 d) has been taking in guests since the early 1970s. Conveniently located between downtown and Victoria Park, its other pluses include a good restaurant and comfortable beds. Note that half of the 22 rooms are in a modern addition behind the original home, but these are still stylishly decorated and come with wireless Internet, bathrobes, and more.

Charlotte's Rose Inn (11 Grafton St., 902/892-3699 or 888/237-3699, www.charlottesrose.com, Apr.-Oct., $199-249 s or d) is a three-story 1884 home on a quiet residential street. Original hardwood floors, high ceilings, and Victorian-era furnishings add to the charm of guest rooms in the main house. Rates include a hot breakfast, wireless Internet, and use of bikes.

Over $200

A few steps from Province House, ★ **The Great George** (58 Great George St., 902/892-0606 or 800/361-1118, www.thegreatgeorge.com, $235-385 s or d) comprises 60 guest rooms spread through 15 beautifully restored buildings from as early as 1811. The lobby is in a building that was originally known as the Pavilion Hotel, at the corner of Great George and Sydney Streets. It was here that the Fathers of Confederation stayed during the 1864 Charlottetown Conference. This building also has a large lounge area and a fine-dining restaurant. Rooms in this building and others running up Great George Street and beyond have been beautifully restored, with the addition of modern amenities like air-conditioning and wireless Internet.

Extensive renovations have transformed the old Islander motel into the ★ **Hotel on Pownal** (146 Pownal St., 902/892-1217 or 800/268-6261, www.thehotelonpownal.com, from $240 s or d), offering chic boutique lodging. The 45 guest rooms are smartly decorated and filled with modern amenities, including extra-large wall-mounted TVs, iPod docking stations, and wireless Internet. Comfortable beds, luxurious bathrooms, and a free continental breakfast round out this popular downtown lodging.

Rodd Charlottetown (75 Kent St., 902/894-7371 or 800/565-7633, www.roddvacations.com, from $245 s or d) is a grand red-brick 1931 Georgian gem with magnificent woodwork and furnishings made by island craftspeople. It offers 115 rooms and suites and a restaurant, whirlpool, indoor pool, and rooftop patio. As always with these top-end properties, check the website for the best deals.

Like the nearby Confederation Centre of the Arts, the **Delta Hotels by Marriott Prince Edward** (18 Queen St., 902/566-2222, www.marriott.com, $250 s or d) stands out for its boxy look amid the gracious buildings of downtown. Inside are 211 well-decorated rooms. The more expensive Delta Rooms have king beds and water views. It offers all the amenities of a full-service hotel, including underground valet parking, a day spa, a fitness room, an indoor pool, a lounge, and a restaurant. Disregard the rack rates and check online—you should find packages that include accommodations and either theater tickets or greens fees for around $200 d.

NORTH OF DOWNTOWN

Staying downtown has its perks, but if you're looking for a well-priced motel room or are traveling with a family, staying on the north side is a good alternative.

$50-100

Out near the airport, **Fair Isle Motel** (Rte. 2, 902/368-8259 or 800/309-8259, www. fairislepei.com, Apr.-Nov., $85-125 s or d) is an old roadside motel where rooms overlook landscaped gardens and a small playground. All rooms have wireless Internet and basic cooking facilities. If you've picked up fresh seafood at Lobster on the Wharf, take advantage of this motel's barbecues for a great outdoor dinner.

I doubt too many Canadian capitals boast a cottage complex surrounded by expansive lawns within city limits, but Charlottetown does, in the form of ★ **Royalty Maples Cottages & Motel** (Rte. 2, 902/368-1030 or 800/831-7829, www.royaltymaples.com, May-Nov., $109-149 s or d), which is 1 kilometer (0.6 mile) north of the junction of Routes 1 and 2. The 10 one- and two-bedroom cottages each have a full kitchen, living area, and

air-conditioning. Six motel rooms also go for $80-120 s or d per night.

$150-200

At the busy intersection of Routes 1 and 2, north of downtown along University Avenue, is **Rodd Royalty** (14 Capital Dr., 902/894-8566 or 800/565-7633, www.roddvacations. com, $165-210 s or d). This spread-out property features 119 standard rooms and suites (the latter are a better value). Other facilities include an indoor pool with a long waterslide, a fitness room, and a restaurant.

The **Holiday Inn Express** (200 Capital Dr., 902/892-1201 or 877/660-8550, www. ihg.com, $165-210 s or d) maintains the same standards and facilities expected of this worldwide chain. The modern rooms have air-conditioning and high-speed Internet access, and rates include a continental breakfast. Families can take advantage of children's suites, complete with Nintendo systems and bunk beds separate from the main bedroom. Other amenities include an indoor pool and a sundeck.

CAMPGROUNDS

★ **Cornwall/Charlottetown KOA** (208 Ferry Rd., off Rte. 248, 2 km/1.2 mi east of Cornwall, 902/566-2421, www.koa.com, mid-May-early Oct., $35-45) spreads across 25 beautiful hectares (62 acres) along the West River. Amenities include an outdoor swimming pool, a playground, hayrides, showers, a launderette, and a kitchen shelter.

Transportation and Services

Charlottetown Visitor Information Centre (6 Prince St., 902/368-4444, May daily 9am-5pm, June daily 9am-6pm, July-Aug. daily 8am-7pm, Sept. daily 8:30am-5pm, Oct. daily 9am-4pm) is along the waterfront. The staff answers questions and stocks a good supply of literature about the city, as well as the province.

Queen Elizabeth Hospital is on Riverside Drive (902/894-2200). For **police** call 902/566-7112.

GETTING THERE

Air

Charlottetown Airport (250 Maple Hills Ave., 902/566-7997, www.flypei.com) is 8 kilometers (5 miles) north of downtown along Brackley Point Road. The airport has a restaurant, gift shop, seasonal visitors center, and wireless Internet (for a fee). Taxis wait outside during flight arrivals and charge $12 for one person or $16 for two for the 15-minute drive to town. Avis, Budget, Hertz, and National rent vehicles at the airport, but their counters are not staffed between flights. **Air Canada** (888/247-2262, www.aircanada.com) has direct flights from Toronto, Montréal, Ottawa, and Halifax, while **WestJet** (888/937-8538, www.westjet.com) flies in from Toronto.

Car

From Moncton, it's a little more than 160 kilometers (99 miles) to Charlottetown, a two-hour drive via Route 15 and the Confederation Bridge.

Ferry

From Caribou, a short drive north of Pictou,

Northumberland Ferries (902/566-3838 or 800/565-0201, www.ferries.ca) operates 5-9 sailings May-mid-December daily to the eastern side of Prince Edward Island. The trip takes just over an hour, and the fare is $78 round-trip per vehicle, regardless of the number of passengers (you pay when leaving the island).

GETTING AROUND

Use **Charlottetown Transit** (902/566-9962) to get anywhere in Greater Charlottetown for adult $2.50, child $1.25; buses run weekdays only.

Charlottetown taxis are plentiful; you'll pay $8-10 to get almost anywhere downtown. Taxis cruise the streets or wait at major downtown hotels. Taxi companies include **City Cab** (902/892-6567), **Co-op** (902/892-1111), and **Yellow Cab** (902/566-6666).

Local car rental agencies include **Avis** (902/892-3706), **Budget** (902/566-5525), **Hertz** (902/966-5566), and **National** (902/628-6990).

Boat Tours

Peake's Wharf Boat Tours (1 Great George St., 902/394-2222, www.charlottetownboattours.com) operates a covered 42-foot boat from Peake's Wharf, at the foot of Great George Street. Options include a 2.5-hour seal-watching cruise (2:30pm, adult $48) and 70-minute evening and sunset cruises (6:30pm and 8pm, both adult $34). The tours run June-early September, with children half the adult price.

The South Shore

From Charlottetown, Route 1 (Trans-Canada Highway) whisks travelers 56 kilometers (35 miles) southwest to Borden-Carleton, where the Confederation Bridge provides a link to the rest of Canada. If you're arriving on the island via the bridge, consider veering off Route 1 at DeSable and following scenic Route 19 along the South Shore to Rocky Point and Fort Amherst-Port-la-Joye National Historic Site for views of the city skyline across sparkling Charlottetown Harbour.

VICTORIA

Victoria (pop. 200), 35 kilometers (22 miles) west of Charlottetown, marks Queens County's southwestern corner. The village owed its start to shipbuilding, and by 1870 Victoria ranked as one of the island's busiest ports. As the demand for wooden ships faded, the seaport turned to cattle shipping—herds of cattle were driven down the coastal slopes to water's edge, where they were hoisted with slings onto waiting ships.

Today Victoria shows just a spark of its former luster. The seaport slipped off the commercial circuit decades ago, and the settlement shrank to a handful of waterfront blocks. Happily, island craftspeople discovered the serene setting. It's still a quiet place where the fishing fleet puts out to sea early in the morning as the mist rises off the strait. But now the peaceful seaport also holds a modest arts colony, with outlets along the main street.

Victoria Playhouse

If an evening at the theater sounds good, make plans to attend the **Victoria Playhouse** (Howard St., 902/658-2025, www.victoriaplayhouse.com, adult $32.50, senior $30.50, child $20.50), a repertory theater that showcases historically themed comedy and drama, as well as concerts of jazz and folk music.

Food and Accommodations

Enterprising locals remodeled the old general store and post office and opened ★ **Landmark Café** (12 Main St., 902/658-2286, June-Sept. daily 11:30am-2:45pm and 5pm-9:30pm, $16-32). You can't go wrong with any of the fresh seasonal cooking, but the soups and meat pies are especially good.

Kitty-corner to the theater, the **Orient Hotel** (34 Main St., 902/658-2503 or 800/565-6743, www.theorienthotel.com, mid-May-mid-Oct., $100-164 s or d) has been taking in guests since 1900. It features a few smallish guest rooms and three larger suites (from $125). Rates include a delicious breakfast and tea and coffee throughout the day.

Getting There

To get to Victoria from Charlottetown, it's 35 kilometers (22 miles), a 25-minute drive along Route 1.

BORDEN-CARLETON

The twin villages of Borden-Carleton, 55 kilometers (34 miles) west of Charlottetown, are the closest point of the island to mainland Canada, and so have always been an important transportation hub. Back in the late 1700s, iceboats carrying mail and passengers crossed Northumberland Strait when the island was icebound from December to early spring. The voyages generated hair-raising tales of survival, and the iceboats—rigged with fragile sails and runners—were often trapped in the strait's ice. It wasn't until 1916 that the first vehicle ferry made the crossing. In 1997, the Confederation Bridge opened and the ferry service was discontinued. Since the opening of the bridge, Borden-Carleton has seen much development, as thousands of travelers peeling off the bridge come looking for food and information, and those leaving stop to stock up on last-minute souvenirs.

Gateway Village

As you descend the final span of Confederation Bridge, 12-hectare (29.7-acre) **Gateway Village** soon comes into view down on the right. It is designed especially for bridge travelers, but it's worth visiting even if you're on your way back to the mainland. Designed on the theme of an island streetscape of the early 1900s, the shops are filled with island souvenirs, some tacky (T-shirts, Christmas decorations), some tasty (fresh lobster), and some trendy (wine from Rossignol Estate Winery). The epicenter for new arrivals is the cavernous **Gateway Village Visitor Information Centre** (902/437-8570, winter daily 9am-6pm, spring and fall daily 9am-8pm, summer daily 9am-10pm), where friendly staff will help sort out the best way to spend your time on the island. Displays focus on various island experiences. Outside, amid the café tables and wandering visitors, free musical performances and crafts demonstrations add to the appeal.

Marine Rail Park

From the heart of Gateway Village, head south toward Northumberland Strait on Carleton Street and turn right on Borden Avenue to reach **Marine Rail Park.** Until the bridge was completed in 1997, this was where ferries from the mainland docked, and today the area has been converted to a green space. Interpretive boards tell the story of the former ferry service, but the best reason to visit the park is for unobstructed views of the Confederation Bridge.

Accommodations

A few kilometers east of Borden-Carleton toward Charlottetown, **Carleton Motel** (Trans-Canada Hwy., 902/437-3030, www.carletonmotelpei.com, $89-119 s or d) offers 22 basic rooms, some with cooking facilities; a small adjacent café is open daily 7am-3pm.

★ **Lord's Seaside Cottages** (Bells Point Rd., off Rte. 10, 902/437-2426 or 888/228-6765, www.lordsseasidecottages.com, June-Sept., $155-185 s or d per night in spring and fall, $950-1,250 per week in July-Aug.) is well worth the extra money. Sitting on Bells Point, a few kilometers west of Borden-Carleton, the eight simple cottages each have 1-3 bedrooms, a TV, and a deck with a barbecue—an excellent deal for families or couples traveling together.

Getting There

From Charlottetown, it's 55 kilometers (34 miles) to Borden-Carleton, a 40-minute drive via Route 1.

CROSSING THE CONFEDERATION BRIDGE

If you arrived in Borden-Carleton via the Confederation Bridge, you enjoyed a free ride. If you're leaving the island, it's time to pay. The toll is $47 per departing vehicle, including passengers. Payment is collected at toll booths on the island side of the bridge. Have cash, a credit card, or a debit card ready.

Charlottetown to Cavendish

The most direct route between Charlottetown and Cavendish is to take Route 2 west from the capital for 25 kilometers (15.5 miles), and then head north from Hunter River on Route 13. It takes less than one hour to reach the coast. A more leisurely alternative (1.5 hours) begins by taking Route 2 northeast from Charlottetown to Grand Tracadie and then following Route 6 west along the coast to Cavendish. If you've been traveling through Kings County (on eastern Prince Edward Island), Tracadie Cross, the turnoff for the coastal route, is just 7 kilometers (4.3 miles) west of Mount Stewart.

GRAND TRACADIE

Grand Tracadie is about 20 minutes from Charlottetown. It is the eastern gateway to Prince Edward Island National Park, but it is best known for a historic inn that lies within the park, 2 kilometers (1.2 miles) from the town center.

Food and Accommodations

Elegant green-roofed ★ **Dalvay by the Sea** (16 Cottage Ln., 902/672-2048 or 888/366-2955, www.dalvaybythesea.com, mid-June-early Oct., $220-420 s or d, including breakfast) appeals to guests who like an old-money ambience. The rustic mansion was built in 1895 by millionaire American oil industrialist Alexander MacDonald, who used the lodging as a summer retreat. Today the hotel, its antiques, and its spacious grounds are painstakingly maintained by the national park staff. Eight three-bedroom cottages on the grounds ($400-420 d, including breakfast) are most popular with families.

The hotel's dining room is locally renowned, and nonguests are welcome with advance reservations. Entrées ($24-42) feature formal Canadian cuisine prepared with a French flair. The emphasis is on the freshest produce, best seafood, and finest beef cuts.

Mains include rack of lamb crusted with hazelnut and grainy mustard; the sticky date pudding topped with toffee sauce is an easy choice for dessert. Other hotel facilities include a well-stocked gift shop, a nearby beach, a tennis court, bike rentals, a lake with canoes, and nature trails.

Getting There

Grand Tracadie is a little over 25 kilometers (15.5 miles) northeast of Charlottetown, a 20-minute drive via Route 2 and Route 6.

BRACKLEY BEACH

With its proximity to the national park, excellent beaches, golf, deep-sea fishing, and other attractions, Brackley Beach is a popular base.

Just south of town is **Dunes Studio Gallery and Cafe** (Brackley Point Rd., 902/672-2586, June-Oct. daily 9am-9pm), an architecturally distinctive building with the ocean-facing wall composed almost entirely of windows. Inside, a wide spiral walkway passes the work of some 70 artists, including island craftspeople who create stoneware, framed photography, gold jewelry, pottery, watercolors, woodcarvings, oils, and sculptures. It's worth browsing just for porcelains crafted by owner Peter Jansons. Make sure you find your way up to the rooftop garden.

Food

For its stylish setting, sweeping views, and creative dishes, the restaurant within the ★ **Dunes Cafe** (Brackley Point Rd., 902/672-2586, June-Sept. daily 11:30am-9pm, Oct. daily 11:30am-2:30pm, $29-42) is one of the best places to eat on Prince Edward Island. Seating choices are in a sunken area at the rear of the gallery or on a higher level overlooking the garden. No reservations are taken for lunch, but you will most definitely need reservations for dinner any time through July and August. Lunches are priced $10-18 and include a seafood stew and a grilled lamb burger. In the evening, both the seafood chowder and brie and pear pizza can't be faulted as starters, while for a main, the banana breadcrumbed halibut is hard to pass up.

Accommodations and Camping

Distinctive red-and-white ★ **Shaw's Hotel** (99 Apple Tree Rd., 902/672-2022, www. shawshotel.ca, June-mid-Oct., $145-240 s or d) overlooks the bay from a 30-hectare (74-acre) peninsula at the edge of Prince Edward Island National Park. This was the Shaw family's homestead in the 1860s, and it's still in the family, now protected as a national historic site. The property has 16 antiques-furnished guest rooms in the main house, 25 adjacent historic cottages, and 15 newer upscale waterfront chalets. In high season, rates start at $145 s or d for a room only; in the off-season, you can pay from $120 per person to include breakfast and dinner. The ambience is informal and friendly—a nice place for meeting islanders and other visitors. The hotel dining room (June-mid-Oct., daily 8am-10am and 6pm-9pm, $24-36) is consistently good; start with a chowder appetizer and stick to the chef's daily choices, prepared from whatever seafood is in season.

Camping is available nearby at the 12-hectare (29.7-acre) **Vacationland Travel Park** (east of Rte. 15, overlooking Brackley Bay, 902/672-2317 or 800/529-0066, www. vacationlandrvcampground.com, mid-May-mid-Sept., $40-62). Facilities include a convenience store, a launderette, a heated pool, hot showers, mini-golf, and other recreational activities.

Getting There

Brackley Beach is about 15 kilometers (9.3 miles) west of Grand Tracadie, a 10-minute drive via Route 6. To get there directly from Charlottetown, take Route 15 north from the Charlottetown Airport for about 15 kilometers (9.3 miles), 10 minutes.

★ PRINCE EDWARD ISLAND NATIONAL PARK

The sandy beaches, dunes, sandstone cliffs, marshes, and forestlands of **Prince Edward Island National Park** represent the island as it once was, unspoiled by 20th-century development.

The park protects a slender 40-kilometer-long (25-mile-long) coastal slice of natural perfection, extending almost the full length of Queens County, as well as a 6-square-kilometer (2.3-square-mile) spit of land farther east, near Greenwich on the North Shore of eastern Prince Edward Island. The park also extends inland at Cavendish to include Green Gables Heritage Place and Green Gables Golf Course. The main body of the park is bookended by two large bays. At the eastern end, Tracadie Bay spreads out like an oversized pond with shimmering waters. Forty kilometers (25 miles) to the west, New London Bay forms almost a mirror image of the eastern end. In between, long barrier islands define Rustico and Covehead Bays, and sand dunes webbed with marram grass, rushes, fragrant bayberry, and wild roses front the coastline.

Sunrise and sunset here are cast in glowing colors. All along the gulf at sunrise, the beaches have a sense of primeval peacefulness, their sands textured like herringbone by the overnight sea breezes.

Getting around is easy. Route 6 lies on the park's inland side, connecting numerous park entrances, and the Gulf Shore Parkway runs along the coast nearly the park's entire length. You can drive through the park year-round. Cyclists will appreciate the smooth wide shoulders and light traffic along the Gulf Shore Parkway.

Park Entry

Between early June and mid-September, a

1: Dalvay by the Sea; 2: Prince Edward Island National Park

one-day pass is adult $8, senior $7, child $4, to a maximum of $16 per vehicle. Before purchasing a pass, check with your Cavendish accommodation, as some local lodgings include a park pass in their rates.

Environmental Factors

The national park was established in 1937 to protect the fragile dunes along the Gulf of St. Lawrence and cultural features such as Green Gables Heritage Place. Parks Canada walks a fine line, balancing environmental concerns with the responsibilities of hosting half a million park visitors a year. Boardwalks route visitors through dunes to the beaches and preserve the fragile landscape.

Bird-watchers will be amply rewarded with sightings of some of the more than 100 species known to frequent the park. Brackley Marsh, Orby Head, and the Rustico Island Causeway are good places to start. The park preserves nesting habitat for some 25 pairs of endangered piping plovers—small, shy shorebirds that arrive in early April to breed in flat, sandy areas near the high-tide line. Some beaches may be closed in spring and summer when the plovers are nesting; it's vital to the birds' survival that visitors stay clear of these areas.

Recreation

The park's unbroken stretches of sandy beaches—some white, others tinted pink by iron oxide—are among the best in Atlantic Canada. On warm summer days, droves of sunbathers laze on the shore and swim in the usually gentle surf. The busier beaches have a lifeguard on duty, but always be aware of undertows.

Stanhope Beach, opposite the Stanhope Campground, is wide and flat and remains relatively busy throughout summer. Next up to the east, **Brackley Beach** is backed by higher sand dunes. The adjacent visitors center has changing rooms and a snack bar. **Cavendish Beach** is the busiest of all; those toward Orby Head are backed by steep red-sandstone cliffs.

Established **hiking trails** range from the 0.5-kilometer (0.3-mile) wheelchair-accessible **Reeds and Rushes Trail,** beginning at the Dalvay Administration Building near Grand Tracadie, to the 8-kilometer (5-mile) **Homestead Trail** beginning near the entrance to Cavendish Campground. The latter wends inland alongside freshwater ponds and through woods and marshes, and is open to both hikers and bikers. Be wary of potentially hazardous cliff edges and of the poison ivy and ticks that lurk in the ground cover.

If you'd like to learn more about the park's ecology, join one of the **nature walks** led by Parks Canada rangers. The treks lead through white spruce stunted by winter storms and winds, to freshwater ponds, and into the habitats of such native animal species as red fox, northern phalarope, Swainson's thrush, and junco.

Camping

The park's two campgrounds are distinctly different from one another. A percentage of sites can be reserved through the **Parks Canada Campground Reservation Service** (877/737-3783, www.pccamping.ca) for $12 per reservation. During July and August, especially for weekends, reservations are recommended. The remaining sites are offered on a first-come, first-served basis.

Stanhope Campground (north of Stanhope, early June-early Oct.) is across the road from the ocean and has 95 unserviced sites ($28), 16 sites with two-way hookups ($33), and 14 sites with full hookups ($36). Amenities include showers, a playground, a grocery store, laundry facilities, and wooded tent sites.

Closest to Cavendish and the center of the park's summer interpretive program is **Cavendish Campground** (early June-early Oct.). This, the most popular of the two campgrounds, has 230 unserviced sites ($28) and 78 hookup sites ($36). Campground facilities include a grocery store, kitchen shelters, launderettes, flush toilets, and hot showers.

Information

The main **Cavendish Visitor Information Centre** (7591 Cawnpore Ln., 902/963-7830, mid-May-June and Sept.-mid-Oct. daily 9am-5pm, July-Aug. daily 8am-9pm) is combined with the province's Visitor Information Centre, 50 meters (164 feet) north of the Route 6 and Route 13 intersection in Cavendish. As well as offering general park information, displays depict the park's natural history, and a small shop sells park-related literature and souvenirs. Another source of information is Parks Canada (www.pc.gc.ca).

Getting There

The Gulf Shore Parkway runs along the coast nearly the park's entire length, with four access points along a 12-kilometer (7.5-mile) stretch of Route 6 between Cavendish and North Rustico. You can drive through the park year-round.

The closest entrance to Charlottetown is at North Rustico, 30 kilometers (19 miles) north of the capital along Routes 2, 7, and 6, a 30-minute drive. Continuing north for 4 kilometers (2.5 miles) from North Rustico, you can access the park along Cape Road. This access point is 34 kilometers (21 miles) north of Charlottetown, 32 minutes via Routes 2, 7, and then 6. The main park entrance is at Cavendish, 40 kilometers (25 miles) north of Charlottetown, a 40-minute drive via Routes 2 and 13. Less than 1 kilometer (0.6 mile) west of this entrance is Grahams Lane, which leads to the park's most popular beach. This access point is 41 kilometers (25 miles) north of Charlottetown, 40 minutes via Routes 2 and 13 to Cavendish and then west on Route 6.

RUSTICO BAY

A decade after the French began Port-la-Joye near Charlottetown, French settlers cut through the inland forest and settled Rustico Bay's coastline. England's Acadian deportation in 1755 emptied the villages, but not for long. The Acadians returned, and the five revived Rusticos—Rusticoville, Rustico, Anglo Rustico, North Rustico, and North Rustico Harbour—still thrive and encircle Rustico Bay's western shore.

Sights and Recreation

For a glimpse at Acadian culture, check out the imposing two-story **Farmers' Bank of Rustico Museum** (Church Rd., Hunter River, 902/963-3168, June-Sept. Mon.-Sat. 9:30am-5:30pm, Sun. 1pm-5pm, adult $6, senior $4.50, child $3.50). Built in 1864 as Canada's first chartered people's bank (the precursor to today's credit unions), the building served as the early Acadian banking connection, then as a library. Exhibits at this national historic site include heritage displays plus artifacts from the life of the Reverend Georges-Antoine Belcourt, the founder.

Half a dozen charter fishing operators tie up at Rustico Harbour (along the wharf behind Fisherman's Wharf Lobster Suppers). The average cost is a remarkably low $50 per person for a three-hour outing or $200 for a full day's charter; the catch includes cod, mackerel, flounder, and tuna. Most charters operate July-mid-September. The crew will outfit you in rain gear if needed, provide tackle and bait, and clean and fillet your catch. **Aiden's Deep Sea Fishing Trips** (902/963-3522, www.peifishing.com) has been in business for decades and has three excursions (adult $50, child $40) scheduled daily mid-June-mid-September.

Food

Fisherman's Wharf Lobster Suppers (7230 Rustico Rd., North Rustico, 902/963-2669, mid-May-mid-Oct. daily noon-8pm) is a cavernous 500-seat restaurant that attracts the tour bus crowd from Cavendish and Charlottetown. Although it's open for lunch, the lobster supper doesn't start until 4pm. Choose from three different sizes of lobster ($34-42), pay your money, and join the fray. The cost includes one full lobster and unlimited trips to the super-long buffet counter, including chowder, mussels, hot entrées, salad, dessert, and hot drinks.

If your accommodation has cooking

Lucy Maud Montgomery

Lucy Maud Montgomery, known and beloved around the world as the creator of *Anne of Green Gables*, was born at New London, Prince Edward Island, in 1874, a decade after the Charlottetown Conference. When she was only two, her mother died and her father moved to western Canada. Maud, as she preferred to be called, was left in the care of her maternal grandparents, who brought her to Cavendish.

Cavendish, in northern Queens County, was idyllic in those days, and Montgomery wrote fondly about the ornate Victorian sweetness of the setting of her early years. As a young woman, she studied first at the island's Prince of Wales College and later at Dalhousie University in Halifax. She then returned to the island as a teacher at Bideford, Lower Bedeque, Belmont, and Lot 15. In 1898, her grandfather's death brought her back to Cavendish to help her grandmother.

The idea for *Anne of Green Gables* dated to her second Cavendish stay, and the book was published in 1908. In 1911, Montgomery married the Reverend Ewen MacDonald at her Campbell relatives' Silver Bush homestead overlooking the Lake of Shining Waters. (The Campbell descendants still live in the pretty farmhouse and have turned their home into a museum.) The couple moved to Ontario, where Montgomery spent the rest of her life, returning to PEI only for short visits. But Maud never forgot Prince Edward Island. Those brief revisitations with her beloved island must have been painful; after one trip, she wistfully recalled in her journal:

facilities, head to **Doiron Fisheries** (56 Harbourview Dr., 902/963-2442, May-early Oct. daily 8am-7pm) for lobsters, mussels, clams, fish, and delicious Malpeque oysters.

Accommodations and Camping

Accommodations at **Rustico Resort** (corner of Rte. 6 and Rte. 242, Rustico, 902/963-2357, www.rusticoresort.com, May-Oct., from $215 s or d) are usually filled with golfers, who stay in the cottages as part of a package that includes greens fees on the resort's 18-hole course. Other amenities include motel-style rooms, grass tennis courts, a heated pool, paddleboard rentals and lessons, and a restaurant with tasty pizzas from $14.

The 1870 **Barachois Inn** (2193 Church Rd., Rustico, 902/963-2194 or 800/963-2194, www.barachoisinn.com, May-Oct., $185-315 s or d) overlooks Rustico Bay from just off Route 243. The main house holds four historically themed guest rooms, while the adjacent McDonald House contains four larger, more modern rooms. Rates include a full breakfast.

Cymbria Campground and RV Park (729 Grand Pere Point Rd., Cambria, 902/963-2458, www.cymbria.ca, June-early Sept., tent sites $32, hookups $36-42) occupies a quiet 12-hectare (29.7-acre) location close to the beach, 4 kilometers (2.5 miles) east of Rustico. Facilities include a store, game room, playground, dump station, and hot showers.

Getting There

Rustico is 10 kilometers (6.2 miles) west of Brackley Beach along Route 6, a 10-minute drive. To get to Rustico Bay directly from Charlottetown, go north on Routes 2 and 7, then west on Route 6, for a total of 30 kilometers (19 miles), 30 minutes.

★ NORTH RUSTICO HARBOUR

The tiny village of North Rustico Harbour, on the north side of Rustico Bay, is one of my favorite spots on Prince Edward Island. It's around 1.5 kilometers (0.9 mile) east of North Rustico by road, but a more enjoyable way to get there is to walk along the harbor-front boardwalk from North Rustico. The village itself has only a few homes, built on a slight rise sloping down to the water. At the end of the road you'll find a restored wharf with shops and cafés, sea kayak rentals, and a few shops. Add to the scene an old wooden lighthouse, a

This evening I spent in Lover's Lane. How beautiful it was—green and alluring and beckoning! I had been tired and discouraged and sick at heart before I went to it—and it rested me and cheered me and stole away the heartsickness, giving peace and newness of life.

Montgomery died in 1942 and was buried in Cavendish Cemetery. She left 20 juvenile books and myriad other writings. Her works have been published worldwide, translated into 16 languages. In Japan, Montgomery's writings are required reading in the school system, which accounts for the island's many Japanese visitors.

Montgomery wrote for children, and she viewed Cavendish and Prince Edward Island with all the clarity and innocence that a child possesses. Her books are as timeless today as they were decades ago. Some critics have described Montgomery's writings as mawkish. Contemporary scholars, however, have taken a new look at the author's works and have begun to discern a far more complex style. The academic community may debate her literary prowess, but no matter—the honest essence of Montgomery's writings has inspired decades of zealous pilgrims to pay their respects to her native Cavendish. To islanders, she is Lucy Maud, their literary genius, on a first-name basis.

beach that is used as a parking lot at low tide, and one of the region's best restaurants, and you have a destination as far removed from nearby commercial Cavendish as you could imagine. Although it's out of sight from the harbor, make sure to wander across the dunes behind the lighthouse to **North Rustico Beach** (which is within Prince Edward Island National Park).

North Rustico Harbour is the push-off point for kayak tours operated by **Outside Expeditions** (370 Harbourview Dr., 902/963-3366, www.getoutside.com, mid-May-mid-Oct.). A 90-minute paddle around the bay is $45 per person; a three-hour trip, with the chance of seeing abundant birdlife, is $65; and a six-hour trip across to Robinsons Island is $125, including lunch.

North Rustico Harbour

Food

A shack on the main dock has been converted to the ★ **Blue Mussel Café** (Harbourview Dr., 902/963-2152, mid-June-mid-Sept. daily 11:30am-8pm, $15-28), where many of the tables are outside on a private corner of the wharf. The menu reads like a list of what fisherfolk haul in from local waters—salmon, haddock, mackerel, oysters, mussels, and lobster—and unlike at most other island restaurants, there's not a deep fryer in sight.

Getting There

To get to North Rustico Harbour from North Rustico, go east on Harbourview Drive for 2 kilometers (1.2 miles). North Rustico Harbour is about 30 kilometers (19 miles) northwest of Charlottetown, a 30-minute drive via Routes 2, 7, and 6.

Cavendish

Thanks to Lucy Maud Montgomery and a certain fictional character named Anne, Cavendish, 40 kilometers (25 miles) northeast of Charlottetown, is Prince Edward Island's most popular tourist destination. Unfortunately, those who come here expecting to find a bucolic little oasis of tranquility will be sorely disappointed. The once rural Cavendish area has become a maze of theme parks, fast-food outlets, and souvenir shops in parts, and the village has repositioned itself as an official resort municipality to try to grapple with fame. To dedicated readers of Montgomery's sentimental books, the village's lure is emotional. For others—those who don't know Anne of Green Gables from Anne Frank—it might best be avoided. Still, if you end up here and are looking for something to do, you'll have a multitude of choices—including heading into adjacent Prince Edward Island National Park, golfing at Green Gables Golf Course, or browsing through craft shops.

Montgomery portrayed rural Cavendish as an idyllic "neverland" called Avonlea, imbued with innocence and harmony. Beyond the crass commercialism, as you drive the rambling red-clay lanes and walk the quiet woods, meadows, and gulf shore, you'll have to agree that the lady did not overstate her case. The most pastoral and historic places are preserved as part of **Prince Edward Island National Park.** Cavendish itself is home to two important Anne attractions, while others dot the surrounding countryside.

★ GREEN GABLES HERITAGE PLACE

Located on the west side of the Route 6 and Route 13 intersection, **Green Gables Heritage Place** (902/963-7874, May-Oct. daily 9am-5pm, adult $8, senior $7, child $4) reigns as the idyllic hub of a Montgomery sightseeing circuit. The restored 19th-century farmhouse, once home to Montgomery's elderly cousins and the setting for her most famous book, *Anne of Green Gables*, is furnished simply and stolidly, just as it was described in the novel. A fire in 1997 badly damaged portions of the house, but repairs commenced immediately, and within a couple of weeks the landmark was back in perfect condition. Among other memorabilia in the pretty vintage setting are artifacts such as the author's archaic typewriter, on which she composed many well-loved passages. Period-style gardens, farm buildings, and an interpretive center and gift shop complete the complex. From the grounds, the Balsam Hollow and Haunted Woods trails feature some of Montgomery's favorite woodland haunts, including Lover's Lane.

Cavendish and Vicinity

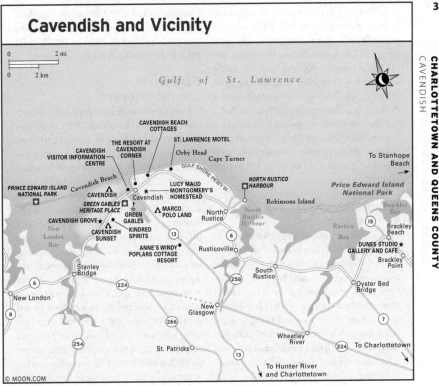

0   2 mi

0   2 km

Gulf   of   St. Lawrence

CAVENDISH BEACH COTTAGES

THE RESORT AT CAVENDISH CORNER

ST. LAWRENCE MOTEL

CAVENDISH VISITOR INFORMATION CENTRE

Orby Head   Cape Turner

GULF SHORE PKWY W

NORTH RUSTICO
★ HARBOUR

To Stanhope Beach

Price Edward Island National Park

PRINCE EDWARD ISLAND NATIONAL PARK   Cavendish Beach

Cavendish

LUCY MAUD MONTGOMERY'S HOMESTEAD

Robinsons Island

Brackley Bay

GREEN GABLES HERITAGE PLACE

GREEN GABLES

MARCO POLO LAND

North Rustico   *North Rustico Harbour*

Rustico Bay

15   Brackley Beach

CAVENDISH GROVE ★

New London Bay

CAVENDISH SUNSET

KINDRED SPIRITS

DUNES STUDIO ★ GALLERY AND CAFE

Brackley Point

ANNE'S WINDY POPLARS COTTAGE RESORT   13

Rusticoville

Stanley Bridge   6

224   258   South Rustico   Oyster Bed Bridge

New London   8

266   New Glasgow   7

254   Wheatley River   224   To Charlottetown

St. Patricks   13

To Hunter River and Charlottetown

© MOON.COM

LUCY MAUD MONTGOMERY HOMESTEAD

Montgomery spent much of her childhood living with her grandparents in a small home 1 kilometer (0.6 mile) east of Green Gables Heritage Place. "I wrote it in the evenings after my regular day's work was done," she recalled of her most famous novel, "wrote most of it at the window of the little gable room that had been mine for many years." While the main building is long gone, the stone cellar remains. Surrounded by a white picket fence and apple trees, it has been converted to a **small museum and bookstore** (Rte. 6, 902/963-2231, mid-May-June and Sept.-mid-Oct. daily 9am-5pm, July-Aug. daily 9am-6pm, adult $3, child $1) operated by Montgomery's descendants, who live at the end of the road.

Montgomery is buried in the nearby **Cavendish Cemetery,** at the corner of Route 6 and Route 13.

RECREATION

The focus of most visitors to Cavendish are the beaches of **Prince Edward Island National Park,** which parallel the main highway through town and are within easy walking and biking distance of many accommodations. In the heart of the commercial strip, **Cavendish Grove** was once the site of a fun park, but upon its closing, the land was incorporated into the national park. Today, it's a pleasant green space with artificial ponds, manicured lawns, and paths leading to the beach.

Golf

Little known outside Canada, Stanley Thompson was one of the world's great

20th-century golf course architects. His best-known courses are those within the country's national park system. **Green Gables Golf Course** (Rte. 6, 902/963-4653 (greens fees $105 including cart, $60 after 3pm) may not be as revered as Thompson-designed Highland Links (Cape Breton Highlands National Park) or Banff Springs (Banff National Park), but this old-fashioned layout within Prince Edward Island National Park is a gem of composition defined by water views and deep bunkers. Twilight rates are as low as $50 in high season.

Amusement Parks and Museums

The only theme park with any relationship to Anne of Green Gables is **Avonlea Village** (8779 Cavendish Rd., 902/963-3050, www.avonlea.ca, mid-June-early Sept. daily 10am-6pm, free), which used to be a full-blown amusement park, but now offers free admission. Instead of Anne's world being brought to life through musical shows and costumed interpreters, you'll find a number of cafés and restaurants, as well as occasional live music performances.

You'll see the rides of **Sandspit Amusement Park** (8986 Cavendish Rd., 902/963-3939, www.sandspit.com, mid-June daily 10am-6pm, July-Aug. daily 10am-10pm), east of the junction of Routes 6 and 13, long before arriving at the front gate. The huge park, a magnet for kids on vacation, features a roller coaster (The Cyclone, billed as the largest in the Maritimes), a carousel, and other rides, rides, rides. It's free to get in, but each ride costs a small amount. All-day ride packages cost $13.50-25, depending on your height.

And what tourist town would be complete without a **Ripley's Believe It or Not! Museum** (8863 Cavendish Rd., 902/963-2242, June and Sept. daily 10am-6pm, July-Aug. daily 9am-9pm, adult $15, senior $11.50, child $9) or a wax museum—in this case, the adjacent **Wax World of the Stars** (8863

Cavendish Rd., 902/963-3444, mid-May-June and Sept. daily 10am-4:30pm, July-Aug. daily 9am-7:30pm, adult $15, senior $11.50, child $9), which is exactly as the name suggests.

FOOD

Lobster Supper

Lobster suppers are casual good-value gatherings held across the island. They can be very commercial or simply an annual gathering of locals in a church basement. A great compromise is the ★ **New Glasgow Lobster Suppers** (604 Rte. 258, 902/964-2870, June-mid-Oct. 4pm-8:30pm), 8 kilometers (5 miles) southeast of Cavendish along Route 13. In operation since 1958, this one fills a cavernous hall with up to 500 diners at a time. It even has its own lobster holding pond, allowing the tradition to continue beyond lobster fishing season. Choose the size of lobster and pay at the front desk, then feast on limitless mussels, clam chowder, salad, and bread until your lobster is brought to your table. Options range from a one-pound lobster ($37) to a four pounder ($78), or share a four-pound lobster for $102. If lobster isn't your thing, many other options are offered, ranging from vegetarian to scallops ($25-36).

Other Dining Options

Man cannot live on lobster alone, so if you're in town more than one night, you'll need to find somewhere else to eat. If you have cooking facilities at your accommodation (even just a barbecue), pick up fresh seafood at **Doiron Fisheries** (56 Harbourview Dr., 902/963-2442, May-early Oct. daily 8am-7pm) at North Rustico Harbour.

For do-it-yourself meals, take your choice of markets along major highways; shops at **Cavendish Beach Shopping Plaza** answer most needs. The main excuse to stop at **Cavendish Boardwalk,** another mall, is for an ice cream at **Cow's** (9139 Rte. 6, 902/963-2692, mid-June-mid-Sept. daily 10am-6pm).

1: Green Gables Heritage Place; 2: Green Gables Golf Course

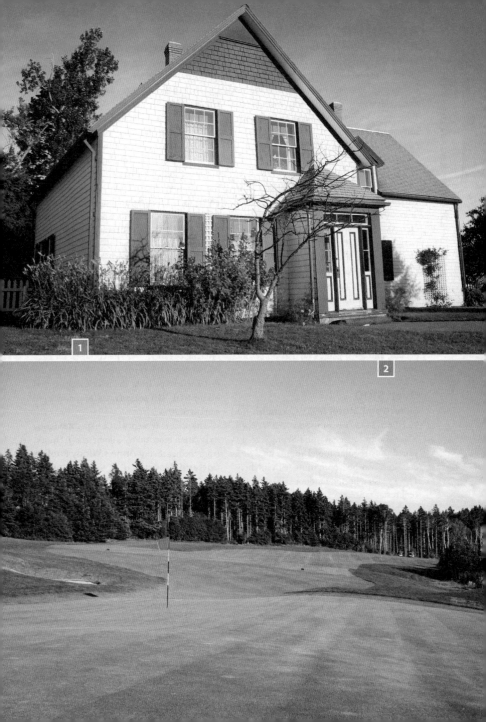

ACCOMMODATIONS AND CAMPING

While accommodations in Cavendish are plentiful, they book up well in advance for July and August. No place in Atlantic Canada sees a more dramatic drop in room rates for the shoulder seasons (mid-May-June and Sept.-mid-Oct.), while the rest of the year, most accommodations close completely.

$50-100

The **St. Lawrence Motel** (351 Gulf Shore Parkway W., 902/963-2053 or 800/387-2053, www.stlawrencemotel.com, mid-May-early Oct., $85-185 s or d) is within Prince Edward Island National Park between Cavendish and North Rustico. Set on 8 hectares (19.8 acres), this 16-room property overlooks the gulf, a short walk from the water. All but one of the units has a kitchen, and the largest have three bedrooms. The beach is a short walk down the road, and on-site amenities include an outdoor swimming pool, a recreation room, barbecues, and lawn games such as horseshoes and croquet.

Over $100

Silverwood Motel (8933 Cavendish Rd., 902/963-2439 or 800/565-4753, www.silverwoodmotel.com, June-Sept., $125-175 s or d) has regular motel rooms as well as one- and two-bedroom units with kitchens. There's also a heated outdoor pool and adjacent restaurant.

At the corner of Routes 6 and 13, near the entrance to the national park, **The Resort at Cavendish Corner** (7600 Cawnpore Ln., 902/963-2251 or 877/963-2251, www.resortatcavendishcorner.com, May-Oct., $120-320 s or d) offers more than 100 rooms and cottages spread across a 3-hectare (7.4-acre) site, across from the main visitors center and within walking distance of the beach. Amenities include barbecues, two outdoor heated pools, two playgrounds, a restaurant, and wireless Internet throughout.

From ★ **Kindred Spirits Country Inn and Cottages** (46 Memory Ln., off Rte. 6, 902/963-2434 or 800/461-1755, www.kindredspirits.ca, mid-May-mid-Oct., $155-395 s or d), guests can stroll along Lover's Lane to Green Gables Heritage Place, just the way Lucy Maud Montgomery described in *Anne of Green Gables*. This grandly Victorian estate is handy to the golf course as well, but it's also very private and far removed from busy Route 6. Bed-and-breakfast rooms in the main inn ($135-180 s or d) are decorated with stylish antiques. Some have balconies and fireplaces. Surrounding the inn are 14 kitchen-equipped cottages, each surrounded by green space. Rates range from $205 for a one-bedroom unit to $375 for a three-bedroom cottage with a whirlpool bath.

Overlooking the Gulf of St. Lawrence from within Prince Edward Island National Park is **Cavendish Beach Cottages** (1445 Gulf Shore Parkway W., 902/963-2025, www.cavendishbeachcottages.com, early May-Sept., $180-245 s or d), a complex of 13 simply furnished yet modern cottages, each with a deck offering ocean views. The cottages, set back 200 meters (219 yards) from the beach, are just a few steps from the park's jogging and hiking trails. Off-season rates (May and Sept.) start at $120.

The price may seem a little high considering its location more than 2 kilometers (1.2 miles) from the beach, but **Anne's Windy Poplars Cottage Resort** (Rte. 1, 902/963-2888 or 800/363-5888, www.anneswindypoplars.com, late Apr.-mid-Oct., $200-380 s or d) has many things going for it—spacious and immaculate cottages, a pleasant pool complex with a hot tub and sauna, and well-tended gardens dotted with playgrounds. The cottages all come with kitchens, decks, up to three bedrooms, and wireless Internet.

Campgrounds

What ★ **Cavendish Campground** (late May-early Oct., $28-36) lacks in facilities it makes up for in location, close to the ocean within Prince Edward Island National Park and just a few kilometers from downtown Cavendish. Amenities include showers, kitchen shelters, and fire pits (firewood $8 per bundle). Even with more than 300 campsites, it fills most summer days, so plan on arriving before noon or booking a site in advance. These can be made through the **Parks Canada Campground Reservation Service** (877/737-3783, www.pccamping.ca) for $12 per reservation.

Marco Polo Land (7406 Rte. 13, 902/963-2352 or 800/665-2352, www.marcopololand. com, late May-mid-Sept., $36.50-47.50) is the island's definitive commercial campground, replete with resort trappings. Facilities at the 40-hectare (99-acre) park include more than 400 campsites, tennis courts, mini-golf, a full-size outdoor pool, a street hockey rink, a petting zoo, a wading pool, a restaurant, and a grocery store.

The 465-site **Sunset Campground** (9095 Cavendish Rd., 902/963-2440 or 800/715-2440, www.cavendishsunsetcampground. com, June-early Sept., $34.50-48.50, cabins $170-240 s or d) is big, bold, and very family-friendly. It has many of the same amenities as Marco Polo Land, although on a smaller scale. Its selling point is its location within walking distance of Cavendish's many commercial attractions.

INFORMATION AND SERVICES

Cavendish has no downtown. Instead, services such as restaurants and gas stations are scattered along a 5-kilometer (3.1-mile) stretch of Route 6 southeast from the junction with Route 13. Plan on doing chores such as grocery shopping, banking, and posting mail back in Charlottetown.

Cavendish Visitor Information Centre (7591 Cawnpore Ln., 902/963-7830, mid-May-June and Sept.-mid-Oct. daily 9am-5pm, July-Aug. daily 8am-9pm) is combined with the provincial Visitor Information Centre, 50 meters (164 feet) north of the Route 6 and Route 13 intersection, and represents local operators and accommodations. Tourism Prince Edward Island shares the building with Parks Canada, which hands out national park information.

GETTING THERE

From North Rustico Harbour, it's about 15 kilometers (9.3 miles) northwest to Cavendish, a 10-minute drive via Route 6. To get to Cavendish directly from Charlottetown, go north on Route 2 and Route 13. The trip is about 40 kilometers (25 miles) and takes 40 minutes.

VICINITY OF CAVENDISH

Hamlets encircle Cavendish. The rural scenery is lovely, and exploring the beaches and back roads should help you sharpen your appetite for a night at one of PEI's famed lobster-supper community halls, which are scattered hereabouts.

Stanley Bridge

Craft lovers will enjoy **Stanley Bridge Studios** (10095 Rte. 6, 902/886-2800, daily 10am-5pm), where shelves and floor space overflow with woolen sweaters, quilts, apparel, stoneware, porcelain, jewelry, and Anne dolls.

GETTING THERE

It's 7 kilometers (4.3 miles) to Stanley Bridge west from Cavendish along Route 6. From Charlottetown, take Route 2 west, then Route 230 north, then Route 254 north, for a total distance of 45 kilometers (28 miles), a 50-minute drive.

New London

The **Lucy Maud Montgomery Birthplace** (corner of Rte. 6 and Rte. 20, 902/886-2099, mid-May-mid-Oct. daily 9am-5pm, adult $4, child $2) lies 10 minutes from Cavendish, at what was once Clifton. The author was born in the unassuming house in 1874. The exhibits include her wedding dress, scrapbooks, and other personal items.

Old-fashioned tearooms dot the countryside around Cavendish, and none are more welcoming than ★ **Blue Winds Tea Room**

(10746 New London Rd., 902/886-2860, late May-mid-Oct. Fri.-Wed. 11:30am-5pm, Thurs. 2pm-5pm), on the south side of the village. Here the soups are made from scratch, breads and pastries are baked daily, and recipes for treats such as New Moon Pudding are taken from historic cookbooks. On Thursday, afternoon tea is served for $14 per person.

GETTING THERE

New London is about 12 kilometers (7.5 miles) west of Cavendish via Route 6. From Charlottetown, take Route 2 west, then Route 8 north, a total distance of 45 kilometers (28 miles), a 50-minute drive.

Park Corner

Anne of Green Gables Museum (Rte. 20, 902/436-7329, www.annemuseum.com, mid-May-June and Sept.-mid-Oct. daily 11am-4pm, July-Aug. daily 9am-5pm, adult $6, child $2), 8 kilometers (5 miles) northwest of New London, is another Montgomery landmark and the ancestral home of the author's Campbell relatives. The estate spreads out in a farmhouse setting in the pastoral rolling countryside, with the Lake of Shining Waters, described in *Anne of Green Gables*, in front of the main buildings. Montgomery described the house as "the big beautiful home that was the wonder castle of my dreams," and here she was married in 1911. The museum's exhibits include Montgomery's personal correspondence and first editions of her works.

GETTING THERE

Park Corner is 22 kilometers (13.7 miles) northwest of Cavendish, a 25-minute drive. Get there by taking Route 6 west, then Route 20 north. The village is 70 kilometers (43 miles) northwest of Charlottetown, a one-hour drive via Routes 2, 8, and 20.

1: Kindred Spirits Country Inn and Cottages;
2: Lucy Maud Montgomery Birthplace

Prince County

Prince County encompasses the western third

of Prince Edward Island. Like Kings County in the east, it is well off the main tourist path.

Along the southern portion of Prince County, the land is level, and the pastoral farmlands flow in gentle, serene sweeps to the strait coastline. Thick woodlands span the county's midsection, and you'll see fields of potatoes that blossom in July and green carpets of wheat nodding in the summer breezes. The northern tip is a remote and barren plain with a windswept coast, where farmers known as "mossers" use stout draft horses to reap Irish moss (a seaweed) from the surf.

Summerside, the province's second-largest town, boasts an ample supply of lodgings, restaurants, and nightlife. Just west of there is the

Highlights

Look for ★ to find recommended sights, activities, dining, and lodging.

★ **College of Piping:** Students from around the world gather at this school to learn the art of bagpiping and Highland dancing. Visitors are more than welcome to watch (page 314).

★ **Green Park Shipbuilding Museum and Yeo House:** An attraction that is as scenic as it is historic, this waterfront estate was once the center of a thriving shipbuilding industry (page 318).

★ **Our Lady of Mont-Carmel Acadian Church:** This magnificent church rises high above the trim Acadian homes of Mont-Carmel (page 319).

★ **Canadian Potato Museum:** Learn about the province's main agricultural crop at this museum; it is more interesting than the name might suggest (page 322).

★ **North Cape:** Drive to the end of the road on Prince Edward Island and you'll find yourself in the middle of a wind farm with panoramic ocean views in all directions (page 325).

North Cape ★
Tignish

Canadian Potato Museum ★
O'Leary

Green Park Shipbuilding ★
Museum and Yeo House

Cavendish

Mont-Carmel ★
Summerside
Our Lady ★ College of Piping
of Mont-Carmel
Acadian Church
Northumberland
Borden-
Carleton

NEW BRUNSWICK
Strait

0   10 mi
0   10 km

© MOON.COM

Prince County

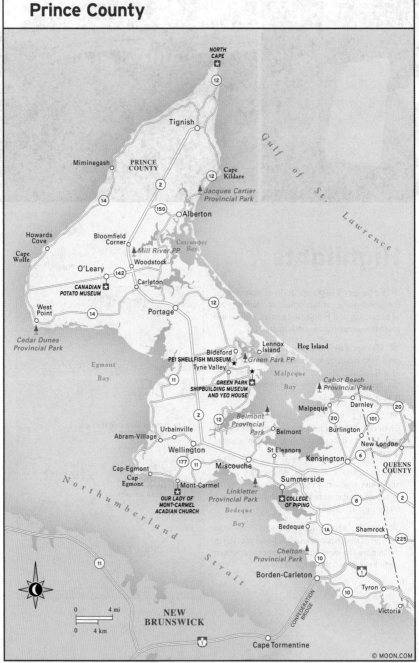

NORTH CAPE

12

Tignish

Miminegash

PRINCE COUNTY

2

Cape Kildare

12

Jacques Cartier Provincial Park

150

Alberton

Gulf of St. Lawrence

Howards Cove

Cape Wolfe

Bloomfield Corner

Mill River PP

Cascumpec Bay

Woodstock

O'Leary

142

CANADIAN POTATO MUSEUM

Carleton

West Point

14

Portage

12

Cedar Dunes Provincial Park

Egmont Bay

11

Lennox Island

Hog Island

Bideford

PEI SHELLFISH MUSEUM

Tyne Valley

Green Park PP

Malpeque Bay

GREEN PARK SHIPBUILDING MUSEUM AND YEO HOUSE

Cabot Beach Provincial Park

2

12

Belmont Provincial Park

Belmont

Malpeque

Darnley

20

Abram-Village

Urbainville

20

101

Burlington

Wellington

177

11

Miscouche

St Eleanors

6

New London

Kensington

QUEENS COUNTY

Cap-Egmont

Cap Egmont

Mont-Carmel

OUR LADY OF MONT-CARMEL ACADIAN CHURCH

Linkletter Provincial Park

Bedeque Bay

Summerside

COLLEGE OF PIPING

8

2

Bedeque

1A

Shamrock

225

Chelton Provincial Park

10

Northumberland Strait

11

Borden-Carleton

10

Tyron

Victoria

NEW BRUNSWICK

CONFEDERATION BRIDGE

0   4 mi

0   4 km

Cape Tormentine

© MOON.COM

province's largest Acadian area, the Région Évangéline. Count on high-quality crafts and wares at town boutiques and outlying shops throughout the region; the region's craftspeople are renowned for quilts, knitted apparel, Acadian shirts, and blankets.

Route 2, PEI's main expressway, enters Prince County at the town of Kensington, glides past the seaport of Summerside on a narrow isthmus, and leads inland for 100 kilometers (62 miles) to finish at the village of Tignish, near the island's northwestern tip. The highways up and down the east and west coasts come together as Lady Slipper Scenic Drive, one of the provincial scenic sightseeing routes (it's signposted with a red symbol of the orchid-like flower). The county's most idyllic scenery—and some of the island's most spectacular sea views—lie along this route, at the sea's edges of Northumberland Strait and the Gulf of St. Lawrence. About 50 meandering side roads lead off the coastal route to connect with Route 2 and others. You may become temporarily lost on the roads, but not for long—the blue sea invariably looms around the next bend.

PLANNING YOUR TIME

It's possible to reach the northern tip of Prince County on a day trip from Charlottetown, but a more sensible option if you have just one day would be to concentrate on the southern half of the county. A suggested route would be to stop in Summerside to visit the **College of Piping,** drive through Région Évangéline past the spectacular **Our Lady of Mont-Carmel Acadian Church,** and jog north to the **Green Park Shipbuilding Museum and Yeo House.** The main reason to explore further is for the coastal scenery, especially along the Northumberland Strait. Other attractions include the **Canadian Potato Museum,** golfing at Mill River, and the feeling of accomplishment of driving to the end of the road at **North Cape.**

Tourist services are more limited in Prince County than elsewhere in the province. You should be able to find somewhere to stay with a few days' notice, but for top picks such as **West Point Lighthouse** (West Point), plan on being disappointed if you arrive without reservations.

Summerside

Summerside (pop. 14,800), 60 kilometers (37 miles) west of Charlottetown and 30 kilometers (19 miles) northwest of the Confederation Bridge, is Prince Edward Island's second-largest town and its main shipping port. It's got all the bustle yet none of the seaminess usually associated with seaports. Stately old homes anchor wide lawns, and quiet streets are edged with verdant canopies.

SIGHTS AND RECREATION
Along the Harbor
The tourist's Summerside lies along Heather Moyse Drive, where **Spinnakers' Landing** was developed after a military base was phased out. The complex comprises numerous shops and restaurants, an outdoor stage built over the water, a nautical-themed playground, and a lighthouse.

Taking its name from the Mi'kmaq word for "hot spot," **Eptek Art & Cultural Centre** (130 Heather Moyse Dr., 902/888-8373, July-Aug. Mon.-Sat. 9am-5pm, Sun. noon-5pm, the rest of the year Tues.-Fri. 10am-4pm, admission varies) has a spacious main gallery hosting touring national fine arts and historical exhibits.

Previous: Summerside harbor; the Acadian flag painted on a rock in Région Évangéline; Spinnakers' Landing in Summerside.

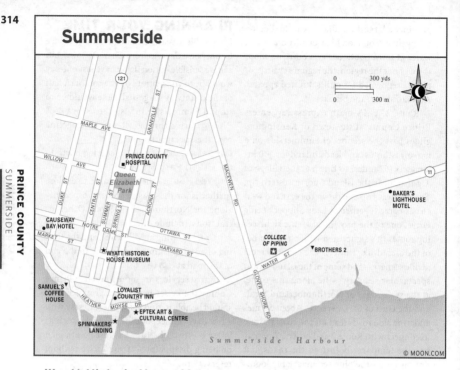

Summerside

Wyatt Historic House Museum

The home of Wanda Lefurgey Wyatt until her death at 102 in 1998, the grandly restored **Wyatt Historic House** (85 Spring St., 902/432-1332, July-Aug. Mon.-Sat. 10am-5pm, adult $6, child $4.50) allows you to step back into the lives of a well-to-do family with long ties to the Summerside community. Adding to the charm are guided tours of the 1867 home led by costumed guides.

★ College of Piping

The **College of Piping** (619 Water St. E., 902/436-5377, www.collegeofpiping.com), affiliated with Scotland's College of Piping in Glasgow, attracts students from around the world to its teaching programs of Highland dancing, step dancing, fiddling, and bagpiping. Students perform for the public at a series of summer concerts that take place weekdays on the hour between 11am and 3pm in July and August ($7 pp). For other summer

programing open to the public, check the college's website.

FOOD

At the west end of the original main street (uphill from the waterfront), **Samuel's Coffee House** (4 Queen St., 902/724-2300, Mon.-Fri. 7:30am-8pm, Sat.-Sun. 8am-5pm, lunches $7-10) pours the best coffee in town within a stylish room at street level of a historic red-brick bank building. A coffee and muffin before 9am is just $3, but the breakfast sandwiches are also good. The rest of the day, expect soups, sandwiches, and muffins, all freshly made and delicious.

Away from the water, **Brothers 2** (618 Water St. E., 902/436-9654, Mon.-Tues. 4pm-9pm, Wed. 4pm-10pm, Thurs.-Fri. 11:30am-10pm, Sat. 4pm-10pm, Sun. 4pm-8pm, $16-26) has been Summerside's social hub for decades. It's no-frills family-style seafood dining at its best. Mains come as simple as meatloaf and as fancy as scallops poached in white wine. If it's a warm evening, talk your way into a table on the rooftop patio.

ACCOMMODATIONS AND CAMPING

Summerside's least expensive motel is **Baker's Lighthouse Motel** (802 Water St., 902/436-2992, $70 s, $80-90 d), 2 kilometers (1.2 miles) east of downtown. The rooms are plain but clean and comfortable. There's also wireless Internet access and air-conditioning.

The 108-room **Causeway Bay Hotel** (311 Market St., 902/436-2157 or 800/565-7829, www.causewaybayhotels.ca, $135-195) is centrally located and offers large rooms (some with kitchenettes), an indoor pool, a restaurant, a lounge, and amenities for the physically challenged.

Across the road from Spinnakers' Landing, **Loyalist Country Inn** (195 Heather Moyse Dr., 902/436-3333, $155-205 s or d) features 103 spacious motel rooms decorated with a distinct country inn-style decor. It offers a good range of amenities—tennis, an indoor pool, a fitness room, bike rentals, a pub, and a restaurant—making it a good choice for those looking for city-type accommodations.

Summerside's closest campground is in beachside **Linkletter Provincial Park** (Rte. 11, 902/888-8366, early June-late Sept., $27-36), 8 kilometers (5 miles) west of town. This 30-hectare (74-acre) park on Bedeque Bay has 84 serviced and unserviced sites, hot showers, and a launderette, dump station, kitchen shelter, and nearby store.

INFORMATION

In the heart of harbor-front Spinnakers' Landing, the **Visitor Information Centre** (124 Heather Moyse Dr., 902/888-8364, www. exploresummerside.com, late June-early Sept. daily 9:30am-9:30pm) is well signposted as you come into town.

GETTING THERE

Summerside is 60 kilometers (37 miles) west of Charlottetown, a 45-minute drive via Route 2. To get to Summerside from the Confederation Bridge, take Route 10 north from Borden-Carleton, then go west on Route 11, for a total of 30 kilometers (19 miles), 20 minutes.

Malpeque Bay

Sheltered from the open gulf by the long, narrow sandbar of Hog Island, the shallow waters of broad Malpeque Bay are tranquil and unpolluted. The bay's long fretted coastline is deserted, nearly bereft of development apart from three small provincial parks. Conditions are perfect for the large oyster fishery that thrives here. Ten million Malpeque oysters—Canada's largest source of the shellfish—are harvested each year. The purity of the bay water in part accounts for the excellent flavor of the oysters, which has made them famed worldwide as a gustatory treat. You'll find them served in a variety of ways at restaurants in the region.

KENSINGTON

Kensington lies at the intersection of five roads, including the trans-island Route 2. Summerside is 15 kilometers (9.3 miles) to the southwest, Charlottetown is 48 kilometers (30 miles) to the east, and Cavendish is 38 kilometers (24 miles) to the northeast.

Sights

Make your first stop **Kensington Railyards,** where you'll find the **Kensington Welcome Centre** (902/836-3031, www.kensington. ca, mid-May-Sept. daily 9am-9pm) and a **farmers market** (July-Sept. Sat. 10am-2pm), a good place to come for fresh produce, baked goods, snacks, and crafts.

On the main road through town, **Haunted**

Mansion (81 Victoria St. W., 902/836-3336, mid-June and early Sept. daily 10am-5pm, July-Aug. daily 9am-7pm, adult $15, senior $13, child $9) is a popular spot with children. This imposing Tudor-style mansion was built in the 1890s by a homesick Englishman and has been reinvented as a tourist attraction, with access to the labyrinth of underground rooms and extensive gardens.

Getting There

Kensington is about 15 kilometers (9.3 miles) northeast of Summerside, a 15-minute drive via Route 2. It's 48 kilometers (30 miles) northwest of Charlottetown, 40 minutes via Route 2.

CABOT BEACH PROVINCIAL PARK

From Kensington, Route 2 loops around the head of Malpeque Bay to the Tyne Valley, but Cabot Beach Provincial Park (902/836-8945, late June-early Sept.) is worth the 10-minute detour.

This 140-hectare (346-acre) park, 30 kilometers (19 miles) north of Summerside on Route 20, is the most worthwhile attraction along the east side of Malpeque Bay. It occupies a gorgeous setting on a peninsula tip just inside the bay, including a coastline of sandy beaches broken by rocky headlands. At the park's day-use area is Fanning School (mid-June-mid-Sept. daily 10am-dusk, free), a schoolhouse built in 1794 and unique (for the time) for having two stories. Finally closed in 1969, it's now open to the public. Facilities at the park campground include more than 150 sites (unserviced sites $27, hookups $33), a supervised ocean beach, a launderette, hot showers, kitchen shelters, and a nearby general store.

Getting There

Cabot Beach is 15 kilometers (9.3 miles) north of Kensington, a 15-minute drive via Route 20. It's 60 kilometers (37 miles) northwest of Charlottetown, one hour via Routes 2 and 20.

WEST SIDE OF MALPEQUE BAY
Tyne Valley

Quiet and bucolic, the crossroads hamlet of Tyne Valley (pop. 200), at the intersection of backcountry Routes 12, 178, and 167, lies on the west side of Malpeque Bay, a 30-minute drive from Summerside and uncountable kilometers from the rest of the modern world.

In the 1800s, Tyne Valley began as a Green Park suburb. Two generations of the Yeo family dominated the island's economy with their shipbuilding yards on Malpeque Bay, and the empire begun by James Yeo—the feisty, entrepreneurial English merchant who arrived in the 1830s—spawned the next generation's landed gentry.

The empire's riches are gone, but the lovely landscape remains, like a slice of Lucy Maud Montgomery's utopian Avonlea, transplanted from Cavendish to this corner of Prince County. To get there, follow Route 12 around Malpeque Bay, or from Route 2, turn east on Route 132 or 133. The paved and red-clay roads ripple across the farmlands like velvet ribbons on plump quilts.

The quiet village stirs to life in the first weekend of August with the Tyne Valley Oyster Festival (www.peioysterfest.com), a three-day tribute to Malpeque oysters. Daytime oyster-farming exhibits and evening oyster and lobster dinners are accompanied by talent shows, oyster-shucking demonstrations, fiddling and step-dancing contests, a parade, and a dance.

GREEN PARK PROVINCIAL PARK

Take Route 12 east from Tyne Valley and continue north through the hamlet of Port Hill to reach the beautiful Green Park Provincial Park, protecting a peninsula that juts into Malpeque Bay. From the end of the road (at the Shipbuilding Museum), a 3-kilometer (1.9-mile) hiking trail brings you as deep into the bay as you can go without getting your feet

1: Tyne Valley; 2: artifacts at the Green Park Shipbuilding Museum and Yeo House

wet. (Wear sneakers anyway, and bring insect repellent; mosquitoes flourish in the marsh pools.) The trail starts among white birches, short and stunted because of the bay's winter winds and salt. Beyond there, the path wends through hardwood groves, brightened with a ground cover of pink wild roses, bayberries, and goldenrod. Eventually the trail gives way to marshes at the peninsula's tip. The small inland ponds at the bay's edge are all that remain of a local effort to start oyster aquaculture decades ago. Marsh hay and wild grasses bend with the sea winds. Minnows streak in tidal pools, and razor clams exude continuous streams of bubbles from their invisible burrows beneath the soggy sand.

Green Park Campground (902/859-1508, www.greenparkcampground.com, late June-early Sept., $25-35) is a privately operated facility within the provincial park that fronts the bay beneath tree canopies on a sheltered coastal notch. It offers a launderette, kitchen shelters, hot showers, and a riverside beach.

★ GREEN PARK SHIPBUILDING MUSEUM AND YEO HOUSE

Green Park Shipbuilding Museum and Yeo House (902/831-7947, June Mon.-Fri. 9am-4:30pm, July-Aug. daily 9am-4:30pm, adult $6, senior $5, child $4) lies on the edge of the provincial park. The Yeo House sits back on a sweep of verdant lawn. It's a gorgeous estate, fronted by a fence that rims the curving road. Inside, rooms are furnished with period antiques. Up four flights of stairs, the cupola—from which James Yeo would survey his shipyard—overlooks the grounds and sparkling Malpeque Bay. Behind the house, the museum has exhibits explaining the history and methods of wooden shipbuilding, Prince Edward Island's main industry in the 19th century. From these buildings, it's a short walk through a meadow to the water, where outdoor displays include a partially finished vessel cradled on a frame, plus historic shipbuilding equipment.

PEI SHELLFISH MUSEUM

North of Tyne Valley, turn onto Route 166 to reach the modest **PEI Shellfish Museum** (166 Bideford Rd., Bideford, 902/831-3374, late June-early Sept. Mon.-Sat. 9am-5pm, Sun. 1pm-5pm, adult $5, child $2.50). Everything you could ever want to know about oysters and mussels is explained. A small aquarium contains mollusks, lobsters, snails, and inshore fish; outside, experimental farming methods are underway in the bay.

GETTING THERE

Tyne Valley is about 45 kilometers (28 miles) northwest of Kensington, a 40-minute drive via Routes 2, 132, then 178. It's 90 kilometers (56 miles) northwest of Charlottetown, 1.5 hours via Routes 2, 132, then 178.

Lennox Island

A causeway off Route 163 brings you to this small island, home to 250 people of Mi'kmaq ancestry intent on cultivating oysters, spearing eels, trapping, and hunting while pursuing recognition of the 18th-century treaties with England that entitled them to their land. The province's Mi'kmaq are said to have been the first native Canadians converted to Christianity. Their history is kept alive at the **Mi'kmaq Cultural Centre** (8 Eagle Feather Trail, 902/831-3109, summer Mon.-Sat. 10am-7pm, Sun. noon-6pm, donation). The 1895 **St. Anne's Roman Catholic Church,** a sacred tribute to their patron saint, grips the island's coastline and faces the sea. A craft shop just north of the church markets Mi'kmaq baskets, silver jewelry, pottery, and other wares.

GETTING THERE

Lennox Island is about 15 kilometers (9.3 miles) northeast of Tyne Valley, a 15-minute drive via Route 12 and Route 163. It's 100 kilometers (62 miles) northwest of Charlottetown, 1.5 hours via Routes 2, 133, 12, then 163.

Région Évangéline

The bilingual inhabitants of the Région Évangéline, the province's largest Acadian area, date their ancestry to France's earliest settlement efforts. The region offers French-flavored culture at more than a dozen villages spread west of Summerside between Route 2 and the strait seacoast. Miscouche, the commercial center, is a 10-minute drive west of Summerside on Route 2, and Mont-Carmel, the region's seaside social and tourist hub, is 30 minutes from the seaport along coastal Route 11.

MISCOUCHE

As you approach from the east, the high double spires of **St. John the Baptist Church** announce from miles away that you've left Protestant, Anglo Prince Edward Island behind and are arriving in Catholic territory.

The village of 700 inhabitants at the intersection of Routes 2 and 12 began with French farmers from Port-la-Joye in the 1720s, augmented by Acadians who fled England's Acadian deportation in 1755. The settlement commands a major historical niche among Atlantic Canada's Acadian communities and was the site of the 1884 Acadian Convention, which adopted the French tricolor flag, with the single gold star symbolizing Mary.

Musée Acadien

On the east side of town, **Musée Acadien** (Rte. 2, 902/432-2880, July-Aug. daily 9:30am-5pm, Sept.-June Mon.-Fri. 9:30am-5pm, Sun. 1pm-4pm, adult $4.50, student $3.50) is a genealogical resource center and also has exhibits of early photographs, papers, and artifacts, as well as a book corner (mainly in French) with volumes about Acadian history and culture on Prince Edward Island since 1720. Don't miss the documentary on events leading up to the 1755 Acadian deportation; it's screened on demand.

Getting There

Miscouche is 20 kilometers (12.4 miles) west of Kensington via Route 2, a 15-minute drive. It's 65 kilometers (40 miles) northwest of Charlottetown, also via Route 2, a one-hour drive.

MONT-CARMEL

Two kilometers (1.2 miles) south of Miscouche and 10 kilometers (6.2 miles) west of Summerside, the backcountry Route 12 meets the coastal Route 11 (Lady Slipper Scenic Drive), which lopes south and west across Acadian farmlands to this hamlet, best known for Le Village, a complex of lodgings with a restaurant. Mont-Carmel, 16 kilometers (9.9 miles) from Miscouche, makes a handy sightseeing base for touring the Région Évangéline.

★ Our Lady of Mont-Carmel Acadian Church

The magnificent **Our Lady of Mont-Carmel Acadian Church,** between Route 11 and the red cliffs fronting Northumberland Strait, reflects the cathedral style of France's Poitou region, which is renowned for its Romanesque churches featuring elaborate exteriors. The cathedral is open Sunday during Mass, but public access to the grounds is allowed at any time.

Getting There

Mont-Carmel is 25 kilometers (15.5 miles) west of Summerside, a 30-minute drive along Route 11. Head northwest from Charlottetown to Summerside on Route 2, then west on Route 11, for a total distance of 85 kilometers (53 miles), 1.5 hours.

CONTINUING ALONG ROUTE 11
Cap-Egmont

A few kilometers west of Mont-Carmel is the village of Cap-Egmont, best known for the very un-Acadian **Bottle Houses** (Rte. 11, 902/854-2987, mid-May-June and Sept.-early Oct. daily 9am-6pm, July-Aug. daily 9am-8pm, adult $8, senior $7.50, child $3). They are the work of Edouard Arsenault, who in the 1970s mortared together 25,000 glass bottles of all colors, shapes, and sizes to form three astonishing buildings—a chapel with an altar and pews, a tavern, and a six-gabled house. The structures qualified for inclusion in *Ripley's Believe It or Not.*

Turn off on the west side of the village to reach **Cape Egmont Lighthouse.** Although it's not open to the public, this light sits in a commanding position overlooking Northumberland Strait. Built in 1884, it is the same design as the one at Wood Islands (where the ferry from Nova Scotia docks), and like other lighthouses around the island, it has been moved back from the ocean edge as erosion has taken its toll on surrounding cliffs.

GETTING THERE
Cap-Egmont is about 5 kilometers (3.1 miles) west of Mont-Carmel via Route 11. From Charlottetown, head northwest on Route 2 to Summerside, then west on Route 11, for a total distance of 90 kilometers (56 miles), a 1.5-hour drive.

Abram-Village
From Cap-Egmont, the scenic coastal Route 11 wends north for 10 kilometers (6.2 miles) and turns inland to this hamlet known for crafts. **La Co-op d'Artisanat d'Abram Village** (2181 Cannontown Rd., 902/854-2096, mid-June-Sept. Mon.-Sat. 9:30am-5:30pm), at the intersection of Routes 11 and 124, is the area's definitive craft source, with weavings, rugs, Acadian shirts, pottery, and dolls.

GETTING THERE
To get to Abram-Village from Mont-Carmel, take Route 11 west, then north, for a total of 15 kilometers (9.3 miles), a 15-minute drive. From Charlottetown, it's 90 kilometers (56 miles) northwest on Route 2, then west on Route 124, 1.5 hours.

Our Lady of Mont-Carmel Acadian Church

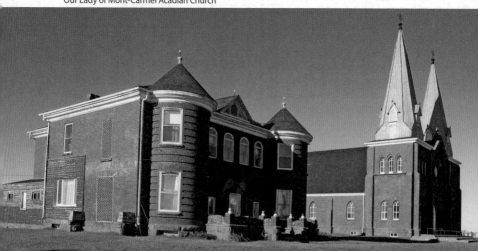

Western Prince County

Beyond Summerside and the Région Évangéline, Route 2 cuts into the interior, out of sight of the seas. Nonetheless, most backcountry roads off the main route eventually finish at the water. To the west, the Northumberland Strait is the pussycat of summer seas, and the warm surf laps peacefully along the southern and western coastlines. The Gulf of St. Lawrence, however, is more temperamental, with a welter of rolling waves breaking onto the north shore.

For sightseeing information, stop at the provincial Visitor Information Centre (Rte. 2, 902/831-7930, June and Sept. daily 9am-4:30pm, July-Aug. daily 9am-7pm) in Portage, which is 43 kilometers (27 miles) north of Summerside.

MILL RIVER PROVINCIAL PARK

As you exit Route 2 at Woodstock, you enter a wooded realm on a ribbon of a road into Mill River Provincial Park. The park meshes lush landscapes with contemporary resort trappings and full recreation facilities, including the championship-quality Mill River Golf Course.

Recreation

The 18-hole, par-72 Mill River Golf Course (902/859-8873 or 800/377-8339, greens fees $70) is generally regarded as one of Canada's top 100 courses and has hosted many national events through the years. The course spans 6,747 yards and is open May-October. During July and August, you'd be wise to make reservations 48 hours in advance.

Food and Accommodations

The three-story Mill River Resort (180 Mill River Resort Rd., 902/859-3555 or 844/375-3555, www.millriver.ca, Jan.-Oct., $155-295 s or d) is a sleek wood-sided hotel with 90 spacious and modern rooms and suites. Guests are attracted to the resort-style activities—golf, tennis, canoeing, biking, swimming in the indoor pool, and more. The resort's Callaghan's Restaurant (daily 7am-midnight, $20-38) boasts regionally renowned dining that draws an appreciative clientele from Summerside; expect a reasonably priced menu featuring seafood specialties, with a dish-of-the-day emphasis on salmon, halibut, or lobster. It also features a large outdoor dining area overlooking the golf course.

The park's riverfront campground (902/859-3555 or 844/375-3555, www.millriver.ca, mid-June-late Sept.) has 72 sites: 18 unserviced ($30) and 54 hookups ($33-38). Amenities include kitchen shelters, hot showers, and a launderette, and campers can purchase access to the resort's recreational facilities for a small fee.

Getting There

Mill River Provincial Park is 60 kilometers (37 miles) northwest of Summerside, a 50-minute drive along Route 2. It's 120 kilometers (74 miles) northwest of Charlottetown, 1.5 hours via Route 2.

O'LEARY

On Prince Edward Island, O'Leary is synonymous with potatoes. Legend has it that the hamlet took its name from an Irish farmer who settled here in the 1830s. By 1872, rail service connected the hamlet with the rest of the island, and with that link in place, O'Leary was on its way to becoming Canada's largest potato producer.

O'Leary straddles backcountry Route 142, a five-minute drive from Route 2 and 50 minutes from Summerside. You might expect mountains of potatoes; rather, O'Leary (pop. 900) is a tidy place, nestled in the midst of surprisingly attractive fields of low-growing potato plants. If you're in the area during the autumn harvest, you'll see the fields lighted by tractor headlights as the farmers work late at night to harvest the valuable crop before the frost.

★ Canadian Potato Museum

Don't be put off by the name; the **Canadian Potato Museum** (1 Dewar Ln., off Rte. 142, 902/859-2039, mid-May-mid-Oct. daily 9:30am-5:30pm, adult $10, senior $9, family $25) is an interesting stop that depicts the history of Prince Edward Island's most famous crop. The museum explains the story of the potato's humble beginnings in South America, the way the crop is grown and harvested, and how science has played a hand in the potatoes we eat today. A barn, a schoolhouse, and a chapel are out back. Within the museum is the **Potato Country Kitchen** (mid-May-mid-Oct. daily 11am-5pm), with rotating daily specials such as potato oyster stew and cottage pie. You can order a loaded potato (including one topped with a lobster hollandaise sauce), potato soup, and poutine (fries topped with gravy and cheese curds). Save room for a slice of seaweed pie, which is actually a slice of cake made with locally harvested seaweed and topped with strawberry sauce and whipped cream.

Getting There

O'Leary is 60 kilometers (37 miles) northwest of Summerside, a 50-minute drive via Routes 2 and 142. It's 120 kilometers (74 miles) northwest of Charlottetown, 1.5 hours via Routes 2 and 142.

WEST POINT AND VICINITY

Route 14 exits Route 2 at Carleton, 8 kilometers (5 miles) west of Portage, doglegs west across the verdant farmlands, and heads to West Point at the island's western tip. From there, the scenic coastal route hugs the strait shore and brings some of the island's most magnificent sea views—a total distance of 80 kilometers (50 miles) to Tignish. Potato fields peter out at the strait coastline, which is definitely off the beaten tourist route. The coast's long stretches of beach are interspersed with craggy red cliffs.

Cedar Dunes Provincial Park

Cedar Dunes Provincial Park fronts Northumberland Strait 30 kilometers (19 miles) from Route 2. It's only a small park, but it has a sandy beach backed by sand dunes and a small campground (902/859-8785, late June-early Sept., $28-37) with around 60 campsites, a supervised beach, an activities program, a nature trail, kitchen shelters, a nearby store, and hot showers.

Within the park is one-of-a-kind ★ **West Point Lighthouse** (Cedar Dunes Park Rd., 902/859-3605, www.westpointharmony.ca, mid-June-mid-Sept., $169-189 s or d), the only place in Canada where you can stay overnight in a lighthouse. There's just one guest room in the actual lighthouse ($189 s or d), but others are spread through adjacent buildings. The complex also has a small museum and a gift shop.

West Point to Miminegash

Beyond West Point, Route 14 cleaves to the coastline and heads north, first to **Cape Wolfe** (where British general James Wolfe is said to have stepped ashore on the way to battle the French in 1759) and then to **Howards Cove,** fronted with precipitous cliffs of burnished red. The distance from West Point to Miminegash is 36 kilometers (22 miles).

Getting There

To get to West Point from Summerside, take Route 2 west and north, then Route 14 west, for a total of 75 kilometers (47 miles), just over an hour. To get there from Charlottetown, take Route 2 west and north and then Route 14 west for 135 kilometers (84 miles), a 1.5-hour drive.

1: Canadian Potato Museum; **2:** the beach at Miminegash

MIMINEGASH

Nestled beside a body of water protected from the winds of Northumberland Strait by low dunes, Miminegash is renowned as the home of people who earn a living from collecting seaweed. Storm winds whip the sea on this side of the island into a frenzy, churning sea-floor plants into a webbed fabric that floats to the surface and washes to shore. This seaweed, known as **Irish moss,** was traditionally used as a stabilizer in ice cream and toothpaste (a practice that continues, though to a much smaller degree than in years past). It is harvested from the sea by boat, as well as from along the shore—after a storm you may see locals raking the beach north of the harbor, reaping the Irish moss and hauling it away with the help of draft horses.

Getting There

Miminegash is 36 kilometers (22 miles) north of West Point, a 40-minute drive via Route 14. To get to Miminegash from Charlottetown, head west then north on Route 2, northwest on Route 145, then north on Route 14. Total driving time for this 140-kilometer (87-mile) trip is 1.5 hours.

ROUTE 12 NORTH TO TIGNISH

None of the three highways that lead north through Prince County to Tignish are particularly busy, but Route 12, along the Gulf of St. Lawrence, is the least traveled. It branches off Route 2 just beyond the village of Portage, 42 kilometers (26 miles) from Summerside.

Alberton

The seaport of Alberton (pop. 1,200) is the northern area's largest town. Named for Albert, Prince of Wales, the town began in 1820 with 40 families who worked at the shipyards in nearby Northport. Deep-sea fishing aficionados will readily find charter boats here. The **Alberton Museum** (457 Church St., 902/853-4048, June-Sept. Mon.-Sat. 9:30am-5:30pm, donation) is in a historic 1878 stone building that was originally

Rail to Trail

A joy for hiking and biking, the **Confederation Trail** spans Prince Edward Island, extending from Tignish in the west to Elmira in the east, a distance of 279 kilometers (175 miles). Spur trails, including those leading to Charlottetown's downtown waterfront and the Confederation Bridge, add an additional 80 kilometers (50 miles).

The trail was developed on a decommissioned rail line. The advantages of creating the trail on a rail line were twofold—there are no hilly sections, and the route passes through dozens of towns and villages. Add a base of finely crushed gravel, extensive signage, picnic tables, benches, and lookouts, and you get one of the finest opportunities for outdoor recreation in all of Atlantic Canada.

The Confederation Trail is well promoted by both the provincial tourism authority and **Island Trails** (www.islandtrails.ca), a nonprofit organization that manages the system. Accommodations in villages along the route provide a handy base for traversing sections of the trail or as an overnight stop for those traveling longer distances. Some, such as the **Trailside Café & Inn** (Mount Stewart, 902/394-3626, www.trailside.ca), have been specifically developed for trail travelers, offering beds and meals.

a courthouse and jail. Exhibits delve into the town's history with antiques, clothing, and farm tools. The fox farming display is particularly interesting.

JACQUES CARTIER PROVINCIAL PARK

It's only a short hop from Alberton back to Route 2, then 16 kilometers (9.9 miles) north to Tignish, but a worthwhile detour is to continue north on Route 12 to the coastal **Jacques Cartier Provincial Park** (902/853-8632, mid-June-early Sept., $28-37), occupying the site where explorer Cartier is believed to have stepped ashore in 1534. The campground rims the gulf. It offers a sandy beach, over 50 campsites (many with water views), hot showers, a launderette, and a summer interpretive program.

GETTING THERE

Alberton is about 65 kilometers (40 miles) north of Summerside, a one-hour drive via Route 2 and Route 12. From Charlottetown, head west then north on Route 2, then take Route 150 east, for a total distance of 125 kilometers (78 miles), 1.5 hours.

TIGNISH AND VICINITY

Tignish (pop. 700) is simply laid out, with Church Street/Route 2 as the main street. The town is 20 minutes from Alberton, a half hour from O'Leary, and 70 minutes from Summerside. Stories of legendary riches and the fur that created a haute-couture sensation over a century ago embellish the lore of Tignish and the northern peninsula. The world's first successful silver fox breeding began in the Tignish area in 1887. Charles Dalton—later knighted by the queen—was the innovator; he joined with Robert Oulton from New Brunswick to breed the foxes. The pelts sold for thousands of dollars in fashion salons worldwide. From 1890 to 1912, the Dalton and Oulton partnership kept a keen eye on the venture and the number of silver fox breeding pairs. As luck would have it, generosity was their downfall: Their empire fell apart when one of the partners gave a pair of the breeding foxes to a relative. The cat—the fox, that is—was out of the bag. That single pair begat innumerable descendants that were sold worldwide, and breeding became an international business.

Sights

Make your first stop the **Tignish Cultural Centre** (Maple St., 902/882-1999, mid-June-mid-Sept. daily 10am-4pm, free), which offers a small display on the natural and human history of the area, holds the usual array of tourism brochures, and offers public Internet access. Nearby, the **St. Simon and St. Jude Church** (902/882-2049, daily 8am-7pm) is

the town's stellar attraction (and the island's largest church), notable for its frescoes of the apostles and its mighty pipe organ. The organ, built by Louis Mitchell of Montréal, features 1,118 pipes, from six inches to 16 feet in length. It was installed in 1882, and until the 1950s the organ was pumped by hand.

Food and Accommodations

M.J.'s Bakery (300 Church St., 902/882-2454, Mon.-Sat. 11am-5pm, lunches $5-9) has a small but tasty selection of sandwiches, bread baked daily, and sweet treats like blueberry pinwheels. The bakery has a small dining area, or purchase to go.

Right in town, an old red-brick convent has been converted to the **Tignish Heritage Inn** (Maple St., 902/882-2491, www.tignishheritageinn.ca, mid-June-mid-Oct, $110-155 s or d). The 17 guest rooms are basic but adequate, and the inn has amenities such as a lounge area, a laundry, wireless Internet, and a kitchen, as well as continental breakfast. A highlight is relaxing in the extensive garden out front. The inn is set back from Route 14, the main road through town; access it from Church Street or down beside St. Simon and St. Jude Church.

Getting There

Tignish is 85 kilometers (53 miles) north of Summerside, a 70-minute drive via Route 2. To get to Tignish from Alberton, it's a 20-kilometer (12.4-mile), 20-minute drive along either Route 2 or Route 12. From Charlottetown, head west then north on Route 2 for 140 kilometers (87 miles), two hours.

★ North Cape

Some 15 kilometers (9.3 miles) north of Tignish, Route 12 ends at **North Cape,** the northern tip of Prince County. The dominant artificial feature, the **Wind Energy Institute of Canada,** juts up from the windy headland with a federal project complex that tests and evaluates wind turbines. There's no access to the main site, although interpretive panels along its fence set the scene. Better still, make time to visit the adjacent **North Cape Wind Energy Interpretive Centre** (21817 Rte. 12, 902/882-2991, May-June and Sept.-Oct. daily 10am-6pm, July-Aug. daily 9am-8pm, adult $6, senior and child $3), which describes the science behind the wind turbines and also has a small aquarium. The center is also the starting point for the **Black Marsh Nature Trail.** This easy path (5.5 km/3.4 mi round-trip) passes under a windmill, over marshland, and along the rugged coastline.

When you've finished exploring the cape, head back to the interpretive center, where the **Wind and Reef Restaurant** (21817 Rte. 12, 902/882-3535, May-June and Sept.-Oct. daily 10am-6pm, July-Aug. daily 9am-8pm, lunches $9-16) has priceless views across the Gulf of St. Lawrence. Seafood dominates the menu of this casual eatery, but there's also salads and burgers.

Four kilometers (2.5 miles) before the cape, the low-slung **Island's End Motel** (42 Doyle Rd., Sea Cow Pond, 902/882-3554, www. islandsendmotel.com, $95-115 s or d) overlooks the Gulf of St. Lawrence and is within walking distance of a beach. Some units have full kitchens.

GETTING THERE

North Cape is about 15 kilometers (9.3 miles) north of Tignish along Route 12, a 15-minute drive. To get there from Charlottetown, head west then north on Route 2 to Tignish, then north on Route 12, for a total of 155 kilometers (96 miles), just over two hours.

Eastern Prince Edward Island

The eastern third of Prince Edward Island, much of it within Kings County, is cut off geographically from the rest of the province by the Hillsborough River. One of this region's main attractions is the lack of crowds.

It has none of the hype of Cavendish, and its activities and sights are more limited. If you're looking for sightseeing and recreation combined with natural attractions—coastal windswept peninsula beaches, seal colonies, sand dunes, and, inland, an improbable herd of provincial bison—you'll find that and more.

A two-lane highway circumnavigates the entire region, with farmland laid out on the intensely red earth on one side, and the sea and sapphire-blue sky on the other. The eastern shore, from Cardigan through

Highlights

Look for ★ to find recommended sights, activities, dining, and lodging.

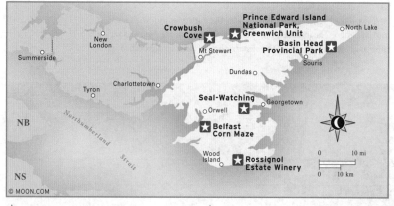

© MOON.COM

★ **Belfast Corn Maze:** If you can drag your children away from the coastline, encourage them to get lost in this country-style attraction that will (hopefully) keep them busy for hours (page 331).

★ **Rossignol Estate Winery:** The vineyard at Rossignol is perched atop red cliffs high above Northumberland Strait—and the wine isn't bad either (page 333).

★ **Seal-Watching:** Seal colonies inhabit islands along the southeast coast, but none are more accessible than those near Montague (page 336).

★ **Basin Head Provincial Park:** The unlikely combination of a fascinating fisheries museum and silica-filled sand that "sings" as you walk across it makes for a stop that all ages will enjoy (page 339).

★ **Prince Edward Island National Park, Greenwich Unit:** The Greenwich Unit of the island's only national park protects a moving sand dune system that is slowly burying a coastal forest (page 342).

★ **Crowbush Cove:** Prince Edward Island is dotted with golf courses, but the best is the oceanfront Links at Crowbush Cove (page 342).

Eastern Prince Edward Island

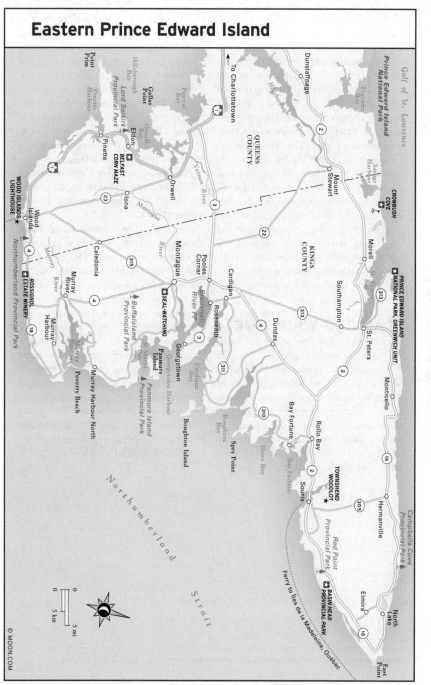

Gulf of St. Lawrence

Prince Edward Island National Park

Point Prim

Point Pim

Hillsborough Bay

Pinette Harbour

Gallas Point

Orwell Bay

Penmal Bay

To Charlottetown

Dunstaffnage

Hillsborough River

Trucadie Bay

QUEENS COUNTY

Vernon River

Mount Stewart

Surge Harbour

St. Peters Bay

CROWBUSH COVE

KINGS COUNTY

PRINCE EDWARD ISLAND NATIONAL PARK, GREENWICH UNIT

Eldon

BELFAST CORN MAZE

Pinette

Orwell

Iona

WOOD ISLANDS LIGHTHOUSE

Wood Islands

Northumberland Provincial Park

Caledonia

Montague River

Montague

Pooles Corner

Cardigan

Southampton

Morell

St. Peters

Monticello

Murray River

ROSSIGNOL ESTATE WINERY

Murray River

Murray Harbour

Buffaloland Provincial Park

SEAL-WATCHING

Brudenell River P.P.

Roseneath

Georgetown

Georgetown Harbour

Dundas

Bay Fortune

Rollo Bay

Hermanville

Campbells Cove Provincial Park

Panmure Island

Panmure Island Provincial Park

St. Marys Bay

Cardigan Bay

Boughton Bay

Spry Point

Boughton Island

Bay Fortune

Howe Bay

Souris

TOWNSHEND WOODLOT

Red Point Provincial Park

Murray Harbour North

Poverty Beach

Northumberland Strait

Ferry to Îles de la Madeleine, Quebec

BASIN HEAD PROVINCIAL PARK

Elmira

North Lake

East Point

0   5 mi
0   5 km

© MOON.COM

to Murray Harbour, is tattered with little off-shore islands and dozens of deeply indented bays and river estuaries. The southern region's climate is warm, humid, and almost tropical; islanders refer to this region as the "banana belt," and even such crops as wine grapes and tobacco thrive here. The long northern coast is nearly straight and uninterrupted, except at large St. Peters Bay, where a tract of coast is protected as part of Prince Edward Island National Park. The northeast area is relatively remote, lightly populated and developed, and, inland, thickly wooded. As any islander will tell you, the county's northern portion is "far out"; that is, far out of sight and out of mind from mainstream Prince Edward Island. But the pastoral inland countryside is beautiful. It is cultivated in farms of corn, berries, grains, potatoes, and tobacco and rimmed on the north by forests and tracts of provincial woodlot plantations.

PLANNING YOUR TIME

Distances throughout the eastern portion of the island are much shorter than they may first appear when poring over the provincial road map. It is possible to drive around the entire region (under 400 km/250 mi) in one day from Charlottetown, and you can reach Souris, in the far eastern corner, in one hour from the capital. Visitors arriving on the island by ferry land at Wood Islands. Most make a beeline for the capital, less than an hour's drive to the west (unless you have children that demand a stop at the **Belfast Corn Maze**), but this is also a good starting point for exploring the region by heading in the opposite direction, to Murray Harbour, and beginning the convoluted coastal route north and then west along the North Shore. Aside from exploring the provincial parks and admiring the coast-meets-farmland scenery, the three highlights of the drive are taking a **seal-watching trip** from Montague, visiting the beach and museum at **Basin Head Provincial Park,** and admiring the coastal wilderness of **Prince Edward Island National Park.**

Even though Prince Edward Island is tiny, the eastern portion of the province is well off the main tourist route. This means you will find well-priced accommodations. For this reason, it's a good place to take a break from touring. An ideal scenario would be to book a cabin for a couple of days and plan on spending time exploring the surrounding area, relaxing on the beach, strolling through the surrounding towns, golfing at one of the top-notch golf courses such as **Crowbush Cove,** or doing nothing at all. Larger villages have seafood markets, so plan on doing your own cooking, then kick back in the evening with a glass of wine from **Rossignol Estate Winery,** which you pass right near the Wood Islands ferry terminal.

Previous: sunset over St. Peters Bay; the beach at Basin Head Provincial Park; Souris lighthouse.

Along Northumberland Strait

The Trans-Canada Highway (Highway 1) extends southeast from Charlottetown for 62 kilometers (38 miles) to Wood Islands. This small village is the termination point for ferries from Nova Scotia, and also the starting point for touring through Kings County.

ORWELL

The small village of Orwell, 27 kilometers (17 miles) east of Charlottetown, has a couple of interesting historical attractions; it is also the turnoff for those cutting across Kings County to Montague.

Sights

Orwell Corner Historic Village (98 Macphail Park Rd., 902/651-8515, June and Sept.-Oct. Mon.-Fri. 8:30am-4:30pm, July-Aug. daily 8:30am-4:30pm, adult $10, senior $9, child $5) is a restored Scottish village representing the 1890s. Buildings include a farmhouse, general store, dressmaker's shop, blacksmith's shop, church, and barns. In summer, there's a ceilidh (Celtic music and dancing) Wednesday at 8pm.

Beyond the historic village is the **Sir Andrew Macphail Homestead** (271 Macphail Park Rd., 902/651-2789, July-mid-Sept. daily 9am-5pm, donation), the summer home of a doctor of national renown who was involved in developing the island's potato industry. Three walking trails lead through the 57-hectare (141-acre) grounds, and afternoon tea is served Wednesday-Sunday 11:30am-2:30pm.

Getting There

Orwell is 27 kilometers (17 miles) southeast of Charlottetown, a 25-minute drive via Route 1.

ORWELL TO WOOD ISLANDS

Eldon

★ **BELFAST CORN MAZE**

When the corn reaches a height of 1.8 meters (6 feet), the 4-hectare (9.9-acre) **Belfast Corn Maze** (5265 Trans-Canada Hwy., Eldon, 902/659-2246, Aug. daily 10am-7pm, Sept.-Oct. Sat.-Sun. 10am-7pm, $13 pp) fills with children and adults trying to find their way

lost in Belfast Corn Maze

out. Cut into a different design each year, it's one of the few such mazes in Atlantic Canada, and takes at least an hour to get through. The destination is more than a maze, with a petting zoo, a giant sandbox, "corn cannons," a jumping pillow, and a rope climbing wall adding to the appeal.

The maze is part of the family-operated **Chuck Wagon Farm Market** (Aug.-early Sept. daily 10am-7pm, early Sept.-Oct. Sat.-Sun. 10am-7pm), where produce is picked daily for the public. In addition to locally grown fruit and vegetables, you can buy jams and preserves, treat the kids to an ice cream (if they make it out of the maze), or enjoy a barbecue lunch at an outdoor table.

LORD SELKIRK PROVINCIAL PARK

Tucked on the eastern shore of Orwell Bay, an inlet off the larger Hillsborough Bay, is beachfront **Lord Selkirk Provincial Park** (142 Selkirk Park Rd., 902/659-2794, late June-early Sept.). The park, named for the Scottish leader of one of the early immigrant groups, is right off the Trans-Canada Highway, a stone's throw west of Eldon, 10 kilometers (6.2 miles) south of Orwell. Although the beach here isn't good for swimming, it's great for walking, beachcombing, and clam digging. The park's campground has unserviced sites ($26) and hookups ($33), an outdoor swimming pool, a nine-hole golf course, mini-golf, laundry, kitchen shelters, fireplaces, and a nearby campers' store.

A naturalist program runs throughout summer, and the first weekend of August, the park is the site of the annual **Highland Games,** which include piping, dancing competitions, Scottish athletic competitions, and lobster suppers.

GETTING THERE

Eldon is 9 kilometers (5.6 miles) south of Orwell along Highway 1. It's 35 kilometers (22 miles) southeast of Charlottetown on Route 1.

Point Prim

Point Prim Lighthouse (2147 Point Prim Rd., 902/659-2768, July-Sept. daily 10am-6pm, adult $5, child $3.50) is at the end of Route 209, which peels off the Trans-Canada Highway and runs 10 kilometers (6.2 miles) down the long, slender peninsula jutting into Hillsborough Bay. Built in 1845, it's Prince Edward Island's oldest lighthouse and Canada's only circular brick lighthouse tower. The view overlooking the strait from the octagonal lantern house at the top is gorgeous.

Beside the lighthouse and with a large oceanside deck, the **Chowder House** (2150 Point Prim Rd., 902/659-2187, summer daily 11:30am-3pm and 4:30pm-8pm, lunches $9-17) serves fresh local clams and mussels, chowder, sandwiches, and homemade breads and pastries.

GETTING THERE

Point Prim is about 20 kilometers (12.4 miles) southwest of Orwell, a 20-minute drive via Routes 1 and 209. To get there from Charlottetown, head east then south on Routes 1 and 209, for a total distance of 45 kilometers (28 miles), 45 minutes.

WOOD ISLANDS

Not an archipelago of islands at all, but a little village 62 kilometers (38 miles) southeast of the capital, this is where the ferry service from Nova Scotia unloads its cargo of vehicles and people.

Along the main highway through town is the **Plough the Waves Centre** (13056 Shore Rd., 902/962-3761, mid-May-mid-Oct. daily 9am-6pm), which holds the local information center.

Wood Islands Lighthouse

Ferry travelers will spot the traditional red-and-white **Wood Islands Lighthouse** (173 Lighthouse Rd., 902/962-3110, early June-late Sept. daily 9:30am-6pm, adult $6, senior $5, child $4) long before arriving at Wood Islands (stand on the starboard side for the best views). Dating to 1876, it is part of a small provincial park right beside the ferry dock. You can climb to the top of the lighthouse and admire displays that tell the story of the ferry service and rum running.

Getting There
CAR
Wood Islands is about 35 kilometers (22 miles) south of Orwell, a 30-minute drive, and 60 kilometers (37 miles) southeast of Charlottetown, one hour via Route 1.

FERRY
Between May and mid-December (the rest of the year, ice in Northumberland Strait restricts shipping), ferries depart Wood Islands 5-9 times daily for Caribou, Nova Scotia. The crossing takes 75 minutes, but expect to wait at least that long during peak travel periods (July and Aug. weekends). The round-trip fare is $78 per vehicle, including passengers. For a schedule, contact **Northumberland Ferries** (902/566-3838 or 877/635-7245, www.ferries. ca).

WOOD ISLANDS TO MURRAY HARBOUR
From Wood Islands, Route 4 continues into Kings County, making a sharp left inland to Murray River. Route 18 sticks to the coast, wrapping around Murray Head before leading into the town of Murray Harbour and then into Murray River.

Northumberland Provincial Park
Just 3 kilometers (1.9 miles) from Wood Islands, **Northumberland Provincial Park** (Rte. 4, 902/962-7418, late June-late Aug.) fronts the ocean, near enough to the terminal to see the ferries coming and going to Caribou. The park offers rental bikes, hayrides, a nature trail, a stream for fishing, an ocean beach with clam digging, and mini-golf. Facilities at the well-equipped campground include 60 sites (tent sites $28, hookups $33-36), a launderette, kitchen shelters, a nearby campers' store, and hot showers.

★ Rossignol Estate Winery
Beyond Northumberland Provincial Park, the highway crosses into Kings County and quickly reaches Prince Edward Island's only commercial winery, **Rossignol Estate Winery** (11147 Shore Rd., 902/962-4193, www.rossignolwinery.com, May-Oct. Mon.-Sat. 9:30am-5pm, Sun. noon-5pm, tastings free). Try not to let the glorious ocean views distract you from the task at hand—tasting a wide range of reds and whites (including

tending grapes at Rossignol Estate Winery

chardonnay and pinot cabernet), along with fruit wines and deliciously sweet blackberry mead. The winery produces 45,000 bottles annually and does everything right, including using oak barrels for aging. No tours are offered, but you are free to wander down the red-dirt path leading to the ocean cliffs.

Murray Harbour to Souris

From Wood Islands, you'll pass through tiny hamlets like Little Sands and White Sands, marked more by road signs than clusters of houses, as Route 18 approaches Murray Harbour. An enormous number of seals live in this well-sheltered harbor, and they love to loll about on offshore islands.

The Murray family settled the area and has namesakes everywhere: The Murray River flows into Murray Harbour, whose entrance is marked by Murray Head; seal colonies cluster on the harbor's Murray Islands; and the three seaport villages are Murray Harbour, Murray River, and Murray Harbour North.

MURRAY HARBOUR

On the south side of the bay is the small village of Murray Harbour. Beyond town to the east is **Beach Point Lighthouse,** from where seals are often visible.

Set on a waterfront property between Murray Harbour and the Murray River, ★ **Ocean Acres** (247 Fox River Rd., 902/962-3913, www.oceanacres.ca, cottages $160 s or d, camping $25-40) offers five two-bedroom cottages. Each unit has modern furnishings, a flat-screen TV, wireless Internet, and a deck with private barbecue. The property also has an outdoor pool, bike and kayak rentals, and a small café. In Murray Harbour itself, **Harbour Motel** (174 Mill Rd., www.harbourmotelpei.com, 902/962-3660, $95 s or d) has seven kitchen-equipped units within walking distance of town.

Easily the best place to eat in town, **Harbourview Restaurant** (7 Mariners Ln., 902/962-3141, Apr.-late Sept. daily 10am-8pm, $14-21) has a big deck overlooking the river.

The menu is strong on seafood, simply prepared and well priced.

Getting There

To get to Murray Harbour from Wood Islands, take Route 4 east then Route 18A north for 20 kilometers (12.4 miles), a 20-minute drive. From Charlottetown, take Route 1 west to Wood Islands, then Routes 4 and 18A, for a total distance of 80 kilometers (50 miles), 1.5 hours.

MURRAY RIVER

The oval-shaped harbor is centered on the town of Murray River, hub of the island's southeast corner.

Sights and Recreation

Children will love **King's Castle Provincial Park** (1887 Gladstone Rd., 902/962-7422, mid-June-mid-Sept. daily 9am-9pm, free), on the banks of the Murray River east of town. A grassy meadow is filled with concrete storybook characters, trails lead through the woods, and there's a riverside beach (complete with hot showers). A covered picnic shelter is the perfect spot for lunch.

If you like woodland walking, stretch your legs at **Murray River Pines,** a provincial woodlot near town. The site, off Route 4, is remote. Look for an abandoned mill, the former provincial Northumberland Mill and Museum, now closed; the woodlot is inland behind the site. A 30-minute hike on the red-clay road leads to dense groves of red and white pines abutted by stands of balsam, red maple, and red spruce. The largest pines date to the 1870s, when England's Royal Navy cut down most of the forest for masts. Somehow these trees survived, and they have become havens for birds of all kinds, including blue herons, kingfishers, swallows, blue jays, and chickadees.

The **Old General Store** (9387 Main St., 902/962-2459, July-Aug. Mon.-Sat. 10:30am-5:30pm, Sun. noon-5pm, shorter hours in spring and fall) ranks as one of the island's best crafts sources, and stocks folk art, linens, and domestic wares.

Accommodations and Camping

On a small lake east of town, **Forest and Stream Cottages** (446 Fox River Rd., 902/962-3537 or 800/227-9943, www.forestandstreamcottages.com, mid-June-Oct., $120-235 s or d) comprises simple but tidy cottages, each with a kitchen, a bedroom, and a covered porch. Rowboats are supplied, and there's a playground.

Continue through town to the northeast to reach ★ **Seal Cove Campground** (87 Mink River Rd., 902/962-2745, www.sealcovecampground.ca, mid-May-Sept., $29-49, cabins $120 s or d), which overlooks offshore seal colonies. When you're done watching seals, there's a nine-hole golf course ($20 greens fee for a full day), an outdoor pool, kayak rentals, and a playground to keep everyone busy.

Getting There

Murray River is 10 kilometers (6.2 miles) northwest of Murray Harbour via Route 18. From Charlottetown, take Route 1 west to Wood Islands and then Route 4 east and north, for a total of 80 kilometers (50 miles), 1.5 hours.

MURRAY RIVER TO MONTAGUE

Route 4 is the most direct road between Murray River and Montague, but Route 17 is more scenic.

Through the village of Murray Harbour North, **Poverty Beach,** at the end of a spur off Route 17, is a long, narrow sandbar that separates the sea from the harbor. It's quiet, remote, and wrapped in a sense of primeval peacefulness. The peninsula is worth a trek, but think twice about swimming in the surf; powerful sea currents here can be dangerous, and no lifeguards are around to rescue foundering bathers.

Panmure Island

Panmure Island, a remote and windswept wilderness, lies 15 kilometers (9.3 miles) north of Poverty Beach. It is linked to the mainland by a narrow strip of land, traversed by Route 347, which rambles out along the flag-shaped peninsula that wags between St. Mary's Bay, Georgetown Harbour, and the sea. A supervised beach fronts the strait, and a wisp of a road angles into the interior and emerges at the waterfront with views of Georgetown across the harbor. Back on the mainland is **Panmure Island Provincial Park** (902/838-0668, late June-early Sept.). A campground here has 22 unserviced sites and 16 two-way hookup sites ($27-33), supervised ocean swimming off a beautiful white-sand beach, a launderette, a campers' canteen, fireplaces, and hot showers.

GETTING THERE

Via Route 17, Panmure Island is about 25 kilometers (15.5 miles) north of Murray River, a 25-minute drive. To get there from Charlottetown, take Route 1 southwest to Wood Islands, then Route 4 east and north, then Route 17 east and north, then Route 347 north, for a total of 105 kilometers (65 miles), 1.5 hours.

Buffalo Park

Halfway between Murray River and Montague along Route 4, the 40-hectare (99-acre) **Buffalo Provincial Park** (year-round, free) may seem deserted at first glance. If you look closely, though, you'll spot bison (historically known as buffalo) and white-tailed deer roaming the woodlands. The namesake herd began with 14 bison imported from Alberta in 1970 as part of a federal experiment to help preserve the almost-extinct species. There's still no population explosion, but the herd numbers around 25 bison now. No guarantees, but in mid-afternoon the bison herd often emerges to feed near the Route 4 fence.

MONTAGUE

Montague, 46 kilometers (29 miles) east of Charlottetown and 25 kilometers (15.5 miles) north of Wood Islands, is the largest town in Kings County, yet the population is under 2,000. The town is defined by the Main Street bridge over the Montague River. In fact, the town began as Montague Bridge in 1825, when the bridge was made of logs and the area had just four farms. Shipbuilding brought riches to the town, and many a schooner or other sailing craft was launched here on the broad river.

The town is uncomplicated, pretty, clean, and friendly. Everything important lies along Main Street, which slices through town and proceeds up, over, and down the bridge.

Sights and Recreation
GARDEN OF THE GULF MUSEUM
The **Garden of the Gulf Museum** (564 Main St., 902/838-2467, mid-June-late Sept. Mon.-Sat. 9am-5pm, adult $5, cash only) is housed in an old post office overlooking the Montague River at the bridge. The building is an impressive hulk of red brick with a steeply pitched roof, showing its French architectural influence. The collection includes exhibits on local history, including the colorful story of Trois Rivières, which was established nearby in 1732 by French entrepreneur Jean Pierre de Roma.

★ SEAL-WATCHING
Tightline Tours (1 Station St., 902/969-0412, adult $60, child $40) offers two-hour seal-watching tours from the town's marina just off Route 4. Departure times are tide-dependent (so call ahead), but typically head downstream toward the ocean. The experienced captain knows the most likely places harbor seals will be sunning themselves along the shoreline, but you may also see them swimming near the boat. Birdlife includes great blue herons, gulls, and ospreys. On the return journey, freshly harvested mussels are boiled up on board for a memorable feast.

Accommodations
Overlooking the water, **Lanes Riverhouse Inn** (33 Brook St., 902/838-2433 or 800/268-7532, www.lanesriverhouseinn.com, $111-189

Harbor seals are often sighted on boat tours from Montague.

s or d) combines a newer 30-room hotel with a pleasant cluster of older cottages that have basic cooking facilities. The hotel rooms are spacious and have river-facing balconies, air-conditioning, and the most comfortable beds in this part of the province.

Getting There

Via Route 315, Montague is 25 kilometers (15.5 miles) north of Wood Islands, a 25-minute drive. Via Routes 1 and 3, then Route 4 south, Montague is 46 kilometers (29 miles) east of Charlottetown, 50 minutes.

VICINITY OF MONTAGUE

Brudenell River Provincial Park

The 30-hectare (74-acre) park-cum-resort called **Brudenell River Provincial Park** occupies a gorgeous pastoral setting on the peninsula that juts out into Cardigan Bay between the Brudenell and Cardigan Rivers. You enter the park from Route 3, 5 kilometers (3.1 miles) north of Montague and then 3 kilometers (1.9 miles) east of Pooles Corner, and the road winds through manicured grounds to Brudenell River Resort.

RECREATION

Golfers enjoy walking the fairways of two golf courses, **Brudenell River** and the newer **Dundarave** (902/652-8965 or 800/377-8336, May-Oct., greens fees $85-95), which plays to a challenging 7,300 yards from the back tees. The courses both rank among Atlantic Canada's superior golf greens and have been the site of various national and Canadian Professional Golfers' Association tournaments.

Other park activities include canoeing (rentals $42 per day), horseback riding (902/652-2396, $40 for a one-hour beach ride), indoor and outdoor pools, tennis, and boat tours. All park activities are open to campers, resort guests, and day visitors alike.

FOOD AND ACCOMMODATIONS

The epicenter of the resort complex is **Rodd Brudenell River Resort** (902/652-2332 or 800/565-7633, www.roddvacations.com, May-mid-Oct., $180-280 s or d). Dating from the early 1990s, the resort holds two distinct types of rooms: contemporary and spacious hotel rooms in the main lodge and two-bedroom Echelon Gold Cottages with kitchens and fireplaces. Check the website for deals and packages. The resort's **Club 19 Restaurant** (daily 6:30am-9pm, $14-29) is a casual space with something for everyone and in every price range.

The 15 modern units at ★ **Brudenell Chalets** (Rte. 3, 902/652-2900 or 866/652-2900, www.brudenellchalets.com, $225-350 s or d) are more like mini houses than chalets. Each has 2-4 bedrooms, a well-designed kitchen, a lounge room with TV, washer and dryer, and a deck with a barbecue. On the edge of the park, the place is close to the golf courses and also has its own outdoor swimming pool and playground.

CAMPING

The park isn't all resort. Continue beyond the main entrance to reach **Brudenell River Provincial Park Campground** (902/652-8966, mid-May-late Sept.). Tent sites are spread through a wooded area ($27), while hookup sites ($31-36) have plenty of room to maneuver big rigs. Amenities include hot showers, kitchen shelters, a launderette, interpretive programs, a riverfront beach, and a walking trail that links the campground to the resort.

Georgetown

Located at the end of Route 3, beyond Brudenell River Provincial Park, Georgetown was once a major shipbuilding center. The naming of Georgetown was surveyor Samuel Holland's tribute to George III of England. The port boasted one of the island's most perfectly created deepwater harbors. Its early economy was built with British money, however, and when England's economy had a short-lived collapse, Georgetown lost its economic edge and never regained it. The town slid into the shadows, replaced by Montague first as a shipbuilding and shipping center and then as the area's principal market town. Georgetown is now best known for the King's Playhouse (65 Grafton St., 902/652-2053, www.kingsplayhouse.com, June-mid-Sept., $15-20), a repertory company that stages dramas and comedies in a downtown theater year-round.

Cardigan

At the hamlet of Cardigan, 5 kilometers (3.1 miles) north of Brudenell River Provincial Park, Cardigan Lobster Suppers (4557 Wharf Rd., 902/583-2020, late June-early Oct. Tues.-Sun. 4pm-9pm) are well worth partaking in. Seating is inside, or outside on a deck with sweeping water views. The full lobster supper is $43 per person (including all-you-can-eat seafood chowder), or there's other choices aimed at children.

TOP EXPERIENCE

BAY FORTUNE

About 30 kilometers (19 miles) northeast of Cardigan, the Fortune River flows into Bay Fortune, which was named long before the fortunes of Broadway fueled the local retreats of producer David Belasco and playwright Elmer Harris. Upriver 6 kilometers (3.7 miles) is the hamlet of Dingwells Mills, where *Johnny Belinda*, one of Harris's most successful Broadway plays and later a movie, was set.

Food and Accommodations

The ★ Inn at Bay Fortune (Rte. 310, 902/687-3745, www.innatbayfortune.com, late May-mid-Oct., $275-475 s or d) has earned an international reputation, thanks to the care lavished on the property by innkeepers Michael and Chastity Smith. The estate was once the summer home of renowned playwright Elmer Harris, who designed the 19th-century version of a motel to house the entourage of thespians who traveled with him. The 16 guest rooms are impeccably furnished and filled with natural light. The most sought-after is the two-level Tower Suite, which has sweeping water views from the upstairs lounge. Rates include a cooked breakfast.

One of Atlantic Canada's most memorable dining experiences is ★ FireWorks Feast, hosted by the inn's co-owner, who is also one of Canada's best-known celebrity chefs. It is a multi-course, farm-to-table dinner with every course cooked over an open fire. The evening begins with a tour of the property and its farm, which grows over 200 fruits and vegetables—or you can wander around yourself. It then moves on to Oyster Hour, with oysters harvested from the adjacent bay shucked on demand at an outdoor food station. Other food stations serve up local delicacies cooked over fire pits and in the smokehouse. All this happens before the main meal is served—which is always an extravagant offering. The dinner is $145 per person (drinks extra), and you'll need reservations well in advance. Although you don't need to be a guest to dine here, many are, staying as part of a package. It is offered nightly through the inn's operating season and starts at 6pm.

Getting There

Bay Fortune is 30 kilometers (19 miles) northeast of Cardigan, a 30-minute drive via Routes 4 and 332. To get there from Charlottetown, head east and northeast on Routes 1, 3, 4, and 332 for 70 kilometers (43 miles), 1.5 hours.

Souris and Vicinity

Any islander will tell you that the fishing town of Souris is "far out," the end of the line on the beaten tourist track. The town (pop. 1,800), notched on the strait seacoast 80 kilometers (50 miles) northeast of Charlottetown and 45 kilometers (28 miles) northeast of Montague, garners unqualified raves for its setting. Consider Souris as a base for touring throughout the northeast. The location translates as good value for the dollar in lodgings and dining. The restaurants are plainly furnished and specialize in seafood platters, ranked by islanders as among the province's best and freshest.

SIGHTS AND RECREATION

The town overlooks Northumberland Strait from sloping headlands, bounded in part by grasslands that sweep down to the water and in other parts by steeply pitched red cliffs. On the southern boundary, the Souris River rushes toward the sea in a gush of red water and pours into the blue strait, like a palette of blended watercolor pigments.

Townshend Woodlot

Townshend Woodlot is a 106-hectare (262-acre) spread that closely resembles the island's original Acadian forest. In 1970, the International Biological Program designated the setting as one of the island's finest examples of old-growth hardwood groves. To get there, take Route 305 for 3 kilometers (1.9 miles) north to the hamlet of Souris Line Road. The woodlot plantation lies off the road, fairly well hidden and obscurely marked—you may want to ask for directions in Souris. Acquired by the province in 1978, the woodlot lacks a clear hiking route, but it's easily walkable on a level grade of sandy loam. The groves meld beech trees—a species that once dominated half the island's forests—with yellow birch, red maple, and sugar maple, whose dark brown trunks stretch up as high as 32 meters (105 feet). Eastern chipmunks nest in underground tunnels. Dwarf ginseng—rare on the island—and nodding trillium thrive.

★ Basin Head Provincial Park

Formed by the winds, most sand dunes grow and creep along, albeit at a snail's pace. At **Basin Head Provincial Park,** off Route 16, 13 kilometers (8.1 miles) east of Souris, the dunes are known as "walking" dunes for their windblown mobility. The high silica content of the sand here and at nearby Red Point Provincial Park causes it to squeak audibly when crunched underfoot; islanders poetically describe the phenomenon as "singing sands." At Basin Head, the dunes are high and environmentally fragile; visitors should stay off the dunes and tread instead along the beach near the water's edge. But the beach is most popular simply for being somewhere to sunbathe and swim throughout summer, and it can get very busy.

Access to the beach is from the end of Basin Head Road, which is also home to the **Basin Head Fisheries Museum** (Rte. 16, 902/357-7233, mid-June-late Sept. daily 9am-5pm, adult $4, child $3.50), which sits high on the headland overlooking the beach and an inlet you must cross to reach the sand. Here you'll find boats, nets, and a museum with expertly conceived exhibits detailing the historic inshore fishing industry and local coastal ecology.

FESTIVALS AND EVENTS

In early July, musicians from across the island and beyond gather southeast of town at Rollo Bay for the **Prince Edward Island Bluegrass & Old Time Music Festival,** where a weekend ticket costs $65. The highlight of the local event calendar is the late July **Mermaid Tears Sea Glass Festival** (www.

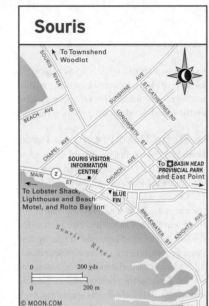

Souris

To Townshend Woodlot

SOURIS RIVER

BEACH AVE

CHAPEL AVE

SUNSHINE AVE

ST. CATHERINES RD

LONGWORTH ST

MAIN ST

SOURIS VISITOR INFORMATION CENTRE

CHURCH AVE

To ★ BASIN HEAD PROVINCIAL PARK and East Point

← To Lobster Shack, Lighthouse and Beach Motel, and Rollo Bay Inn

BLUE FIN

Souris River

BREAKWATER ST

KNIGHTS AVE

0   200 yds
0   200 m

© MOON.COM

peiseaglassfestival.com), which, as the name suggests, features sea glass art in a variety of forms, as well as family-friendly events throughout the town.

FOOD

If it's a warm, sunny day, plan on eating at the ★ **Lobster Shack** (8 Main St., 902/743-3347, June daily 10am-6pm, July-mid-Sept. daily 10am-7pm, $12-18), beautifully located along the boardwalk overlooking the beach and ocean. Choices are very simple: shucked oysters or lobster rolls; seating is on adjacent picnic tables.

The **Blue Fin** (10 Federal Ave., 902/687-3271, Mon.-Sat. 6am-10pm, Sun. 7pm-10pm, $11-19) is partly protected from the tourist crowd by its tucked-away location off the main street. But for well-priced, simple seafood dishes, it's well worth searching out. The

seafood chowder and the fish-and-chips are both excellent.

ACCOMMODATIONS AND CAMPING

Fronting the ocean and within walking distance of a beach, **Lighthouse and Beach Motel** (51 Sheep Pond Rd., off Rte. 2, 902/687-2339 or 800/689-2339, www.lighthouseandbeachmotel.ca, mid-June-mid-Sept., $110-195 s or d) offers 20 regular motel rooms with a light breakfast included in the rates. New self-contained units are $150-195 s or d, including a two-story cottage built in the shape of a lighthouse. This lodging is 2 kilometers (1.2 miles) west of town.

A farther 6 kilometers (3.7 miles) west is **Rollo Bay Inn** (Rte. 2, 902/687-3550 or 877/687-3550, www.therollobayinn.com, $125 s or d). This lodging combines a re-created Georgian setting with 15 rooms, housekeeping units, and suites on spacious grounds with a restaurant serving basic island cuisine.

Red Point Provincial Park (13 km/8.1 mi east of Souris, off Rte. 16, 902/357-2463, late June-early Sept.) has a campground with 32 tent sites ($29) and 58 powered sites ($33). Amenities include kitchen shelters, fireplaces, and hot showers.

INFORMATION

Souris Visitor Information Centre (95 Main St., 902/687-7030, June-Sept. daily 9am-6pm) is in a two-story wooden blue building in the middle of town.

GETTING THERE

Souris is 45 kilometers (28 miles) northeast of Montague, a 40-minute drive via Routes 4 and 2. From Charlottetown, it's an 80-kilometer (50-mile), 1.5-hour drive northeast to Souris along Routes 5 and 4, then Route 2.

North Shore

If you like photogenic landscapes, windy seacoasts washed with tossing surf, and weathered seaports, consider northeastern Kings County for a revealing glimpse of this seafaring island as it once was. Beyond Souris, the strait seacoast stretches 25 kilometers (15.5 miles) to windswept East Point, the island's easternmost point. On the equally remote gulf coast in this region, you'll find few tourists, a dozen tiny seaports, and a handful of lonesome lighthouses that stand as sentinels along the 75-kilometer-long (47-mile-long) coastline, strewn with centuries of shipwrecks.

FAR EAST
East Point

At the northeastern tip of Prince Edward Island, 25 kilometers (15.5 miles) northeast of Souris, Northumberland Strait and the Gulf of St. Lawrence meet in a lathered flush of cresting seas, sometimes colored blue and often tinged with red from oxide-colored silt. Here stands the 20-meter-high (66-foot-high) octagonal tower of **East Point Lighthouse** (404 Lighthouse Rd., off Rte. 16, 902/357-2106, June-Sept. daily 9am-6pm, guided tours adult $6, senior $5, child $3), which is still in use. The first lighthouse at this spot was built in 1867, but erosion has forced subsequent structures to be moved farther back from the cliff edge.

GETTING THERE

East Point is 100 kilometers (62 miles) northeast of Charlottetown, a two-hour drive via Routes 5, 4, and 2, then Route 16. From Souris, it's about 25 kilometers (15.5 miles) northeast on Route 16 to East Point, 25 minutes.

Elmira
Elmira Railway Museum (Rte. 16A, 902/357-7234, June-late Sept. Mon.-Fri. 9am-5pm, daily in July-Aug., adult $5, child $4) is the end of the line—literally. This is where a rail line that once spanned Prince Edward Island came to an end. The original station now serves as a testament to the island railroad's halcyon years, with the province's only exhibits and documentation on rail service. The museum is on the **Confederation Trail,** the old rail bed, which has been converted to a walking and bike path that extends 279 kilometers (175 miles) to the west end of the island.

GETTING THERE

Elmira is about 20 kilometers (12.4 miles) northeast of Souris, just off Route 16, a 20-minute drive. From Charlottetown, it's about 95 kilometers (59 miles), 1.5 hours via Souris on Routes 5, 4, and 2, then Route 16.

North Lake and Vicinity

North Lake harbor is one of four departure points for deep-sea fishing; anglers try for trophy catches of giant bluefin tuna, which can grow to 500 kilograms (1,102 pounds). Expect to pay up to $1,300 for a full-day charter for up to six anglers. Trips depart daily during the July-early October season from the North Lake, Naufrage, Launching, and Red Head harbors. **Tony's Tuna Fishing** (902/357-2055, www.tonystunafishing.com), at North Lake harbor, is among the most respected operators.

Points East Beach Motel (7 Cape Rd., 902/357-2228, www.peimotel.com, July-Sept., $120-140 s or d) has 10 above-average motel rooms right on the beach.

Campbells Cove Campground (Rte. 16, 3 km/1.9 mi west of North Lake, 902/357-3080, www.campbellscovecampground.com, late June-early Sept., campsites $27-42, cabins $55-90 s or d) fronts the gulf and a long stretch of beautiful sandy beach that is rarely crowded. In addition to campsites and basic cabins, facilities include kitchen shelters, a launderette, and a convenience store.

North Lake is about 8 kilometers (5 miles) west of East Point, a 10-minute drive via Route 16. It's about 100 kilometers (62 miles), 80 minutes, to get to North Lake via the northern route (northeast on Routes 2 and 16) from Charlottetown. Or use the southern route (east on Route 5, northeast on Route 4, east on Route 2 and then 16), also 100 kilometers (62 miles) but a slightly longer driving time (1.5 hours).

GULF SHORE

St. Peters Bay

If you're in the area the first week of August, check out the port's **Wild Blueberry Festival** (www.stpetersblueberryfestival. com), an islander favorite with concerts, entertainment, blueberry dishes, a lobster and beef barbecue, and a pancake brunch.

At **St. Peters Bay Campground** (5890 St. Peters Rd., 902/961-2786, www.stpeterspark. ca, mid-June-late Sept., $27-36), you have a choice of 11 unserviced sites and more than 70 full-hookup sites. Amenities include a launderette, kitchen shelters, free firewood, an outdoor swimming pool, and hot showers.

GETTING THERE

St. Peters Bay is about 30 kilometers (19 miles) northwest of Souris, a 25-minute drive via Route 2. It's 50 kilometers (31 miles) northeast of Charlottetown, 50 minutes, also on Route 2.

★ Prince Edward Island National Park, Greenwich Unit

Take Route 313 west from St. Peters along the north side of St. Peters Bay to reach the easternmost of three units that comprise **Price Edward Island National Park.** Known as the **Greenwich Unit,** this 6-square-kilometer (2.3-square-mile) tract of land encompasses a fragile dune system and wetlands. Near the end of the park access road is **Greenwich Interpretation Centre** (902/963-2391, mid-June-mid-Sept. daily 10am-4pm, until 6pm July-Aug., adult $8, senior $7, child $4). From the interpretive center, a boardwalk leads across the dunes to the beach, but the hiking trails starting from the very end of the road are the highlight. The 4.8-kilometer (3-mile) round-trip **Greenwich Dunes Trail,** which leads through a coastal forest and across the dunes, typifies the coastal habitat best. Wind is slowly pushing the dunes here back into the forest, burying trees that over time become bleached skeletons—an intriguing and unique sight.

MORELL AND VICINITY

Berries are the focus at Morell, 40 minutes from Charlottetown. The St. Peters Bay seaport makes much of the harvest at mid-July's six-day **Morell River Run Festival,** with a parade, concerts, dances, barbecues, strawberry desserts, and other community events.

★ Crowbush Cove

Along the coast just west of Morell is the **Links at Crowbush Cove** (902/368-5761, May-Oct., greens fees $95-115), a highly acclaimed, 18-hole, par-73 golf course. A links course in the Scottish tradition, Crowbush challenges players with nine water holes and nine holes surrounded by dunes. Overlooking the golf course is ★ **Rodd Crowbush Golf & Beach Resort** (902/961-5600, www. roddvacations.com, mid-May-mid-Oct.), comprising contemporary rooms in the main lodge and two-bedroom cottages spread along the course. Amenities include spa services, a fitness center, an indoor pool, tennis courts, and a restaurant overlooking the course. Most guests stay as part of golf packages, from $230 per person per night.

Getting There

Morell is about 40 kilometers (25 miles) northwest of Souris, a 40-minute drive via Route 2, and about 40 kilometers (25 miles) northeast of Charlottetown, 40 minutes, also via Route 2.

1: a hiking trail in Prince Edward Island National Park; **2:** Links at Crowbush Cove

Îles de la Madeleine

Souris is the departure point for ferries to Québec's Îles de la Madeleine (Magdalen Islands), in the Gulf of St. Lawrence, 105 kilometers (65 miles) from the northern tip of Prince Edward Island and 215 kilometers (133 miles) from the closest point of Québec. This remote archipelago comprises 12 islands, 6 of which are linked by rolling sand dunes, and totals 200 square kilometers (77 square miles). The islands are renowned as a remote wilderness destination, featuring great beaches and abundant birdlife. Villages dot the islands, and each has basic tourist services.

CTMA Ferry (418/986-3278 or 888/986-3278, www.ctmatraversier.ca/en) operates a vehicle/passenger ferry between Souris and the islands year-round. The 134-kilometer (83-mile) crossing takes five hours, with a schedule that includes 6-8 sailings weekly in each direction. Most runs leave Souris at 2pm and leave Cap-aux-Meules for the return at 8am. One-way passenger fares are adult $53, senior $43, child $26, vehicle from $100.

For information on the Magdalens, contact the local **tourism office** (128 Chemin Débarcadère, Cap-aux-Meules, 418/986-2245). This office also maintains an excellent website, www.tourismeilesdelamadeleine.com/en, with detailed island information and links to accommodations.

MOUNT STEWART

Located on the Hillsborough River, 30 kilometers (19 miles) northeast of Charlottetown, Mount Stewart grew as a shipbuilding center in the second half of the 19th century. Today, instead of shipyards, the draw is the **Confederation Trail,** a rail bed that has been converted to a hiking and biking trail that spans the entire island. Mount Stewart is a good place to base yourself for a day or overnight trip along a short section of the trail.

The main attraction in town is the **Hillsborough River Eco-Centre** (104 Main St., 902/676-2050, July-Aug. daily 10am-6pm, free), which has displays on the river and its ecosystem, public Internet access, and a gift shop. Make sure to climb the tower out back for sweeping views up and down Prince Edward Island's major river.

The ★ **Trailside Music Café & Inn** (109 Main St., 902/394-3626, www.trailside. ca, Apr.-Nov., $115 s or d) is named for the Confederation Trail, which passes through town. Located in a restored general store, the four rooms have private bathrooms, hardwood floors, and televisions. For those looking at traveling the trail, this is a handy place to base yourself. The in-house café is renowned across the island for musical performances (check the website for a schedule). The Trailside often hosts local musicians, including every Sunday at 10am and 12:15pm (two seatings) through summer, when brunch and live gospel music costs just $22 per person.

Getting There

Mount Stewart is on Route 2, 15 kilometers (9.3 miles) southwest of Morell, a 10-minute drive, and 30 kilometers (19 miles) northeast of Charlottetown, 35 minutes.

Newfoundland and Labrador

St. John's and the Avalon Peninsula

St. John's, the provincial capital, is a colorful and

comfortable city. Situated on the steep inland side of St. John's Harbour, the city's rooftops form a tapestry: Some are gracefully drawn with swooping mansard curves, some are pancake-flat or starkly pitched, and others are pyramidal with clay pots placed atop the central chimneys. Against this otherwise picture-perfect tapestry, the tangle of electrical wires strung up and down the hillside is a visual offense.

Contrasts of color are everywhere. House windows are framed in deep turquoise, red, bright yellow, or pale pink and are covered with starched white lace curtains. Window boxes are stuffed to overflowing with red geraniums and purple and pink petunias. Along the streets, cement walls brace the hillside, and any blank surface serves as an

Highlights

Look for ★ to find recommended sights, activities, dining, and lodging.

★ **The Rooms:** With a museum, an art gallery, and spectacular harbor views, this magnificent complex showcases the very best of everything in Newfoundland and Labrador (page 352).

★ **Signal Hill:** The sweeping ocean and city views alone make the drive to the top of Signal Hill worthwhile (page 355).

★ **Johnson Geo Centre:** Descend underground in a glass-sided elevator to see the ancient geological world of the province come to life (page 355).

★ **Quidi Vidi:** With its charming fishing shacks and rugged shoreline, this lake feels remote—but downtown is just over the hill (page 355).

★ **Witless Bay Ecological Reserve:** Jump aboard a tour boat and head out to this reserve, where you're almost guaranteed whale, puffin, and seal sightings (page 373).

★ **Colony of Avalon:** This ongoing archaeological dig is slowly uncovering one of North America's oldest European settlements (page 374).

★ **Cape St. Mary's Ecological Reserve:** Even if you have no real interest in birds, the sights and sounds of thousands of gannets on this offshore rock stack are a spectacle to remember (page 377).

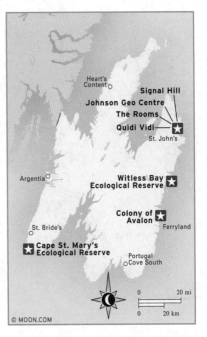

St. John's and the Avalon Peninsula

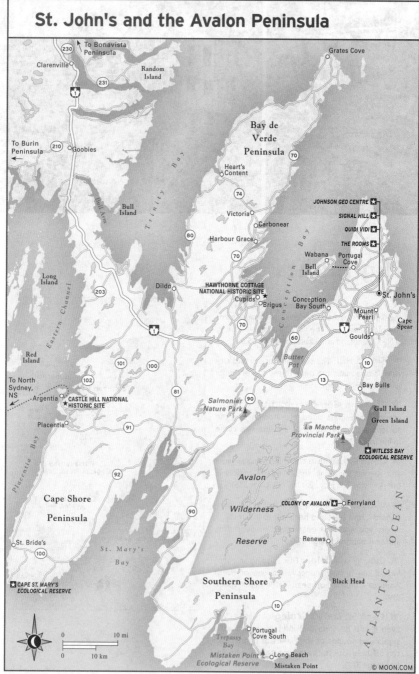

To Bonavista Peninsula

230

Clarenville

Random Island

231

1

Goobies

210

To Burin Peninsula

Bull Island

Bell Arm

Trinity Bay

Bay de Verde Peninsula

70

Heart's Content

74

Victoria

Carbonear

80

Harbour Grace

70

JOHNSON GEO CENTRE ★

SIGNAL HILL ★

QUIDI VIDI ★

THE ROOMS ★

Wabana

Portugal Cove

Bell Island

Long Island

203

Conception Bay

Dildo

HAWTHORNE COTTAGE NATIONAL HISTORIC SITE ★

Cupids

Brigus

70

St. John's

Red Island

1

Conception Bay South

60

Mount Pearl

Cape Spear

101

100

Butter Pot

Goulds

1

Eastern Channel

81

13

10

102

To North Sydney, NS

Argentia

CASTLE HILL NATIONAL ★ HISTORIC SITE

Salmonier Nature Park

90

Bay Bulls

Gull Island

Green Island

Placentia

91

La Manche Provincial Park

★ WITLESS BAY ECOLOGICAL RESERVE

Placentia Bay

92

Cape Shore Peninsula

90

Avalon

Wilderness

Reserve

COLONY OF AVALON ★ Ferryland

St. Bride's

100

St. Mary's Bay

Renews

Black Head

★ CAPE ST. MARY'S ECOLOGICAL RESERVE

Southern Shore Peninsula

10

ATLANTIC OCEAN

0   10 mi

0   10 km

Trepassy Bay

Portugal Cove South

Long Beach

Mistaken Point Ecological Reserve

Mistaken Point

© MOON.COM

St. John's

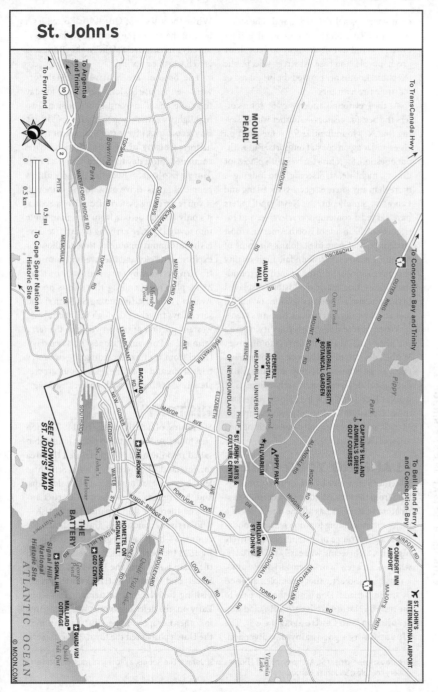

To Argentia and Trinity

To Ferryland

To Cape Spear National Historic Site

0   0.5 mi
0   0.5 km

MOUNT PEARL

To TransCanada Hwy

To Conception Bay and Trinity

ST. JOHN'S AND THE AVALON PENINSULA

To Bell Island Ferry and Conception Bay

Bowring Park

WATERFORD BRIDGE RD

PITTS
MEMORIAL DR

TOPSAIL RD

BLACKMARSH RD

COLUMBUS DR

DR

MUNDY POND RD

Mundy Pond

EMPIRE AVE

LEMARCHANT

NEW GOWER ST

GEORGE ST

WATER ST

SOUTHSIDE RD

BACALAO ▼

MAYOR AVE

FRESHWATER RD

ELIZABETH AVE

PRINCE OF NEWFOUNDLAND DR

PHILIP

MEMORIAL UNIVERSITY

AVALON MALL ■

KENMOUNT RD

THORBURN RD

OUTER RING RD

MOUNT SCIO RD

Oxen Pond

Long Pond

GENERAL HOSPITAL ■

MEMORIAL UNIVERSITY BOTANICAL GARDEN ★

Pippy Park

ALLANDALE RD

RIDGE RD

HIGGINS LN

CAPTAIN'S HILL AND ADMIRAL'S GREEN GOLF COURSES

★ FLUVARIUM

▲ PIPPY PARK

■ ST. JOHN'S ARTS & CULTURE CENTRE

PORTUGAL COVE RD

KINGS' BRIDGE RD

SEE "DOWNTOWN ST. JOHN'S" MAP

■ THE ROOMS

St. John's Harbour

The Narrows

THE BATTERY

ATLANTIC OCEAN

Signal Hill National Historic Site

RD

Georges Pond

★ SIGNAL HILL NATIONAL HISTORIC SITE

● ON SIGNAL HILL

✚ HOMETEL ON SIGNAL HILL

✚ JOHNSON GEO CENTRE

FOREST RD

Quidi Vidi Lake

THE BOULEVARD

LOGY BAY RD

● HOLIDAY INN ST. JOHN'S

MACDONALD DR

NEWFOUNDLAND DR

TORBAY RD

DR

✚ MALLARD COTTAGE

■ QUIDI VIDI

Quidi Vidi Gut

Virginia Lake

AIRPORT RD

MAJOR'S PATH

● COMFORT INN

✈ ST. JOHN'S INTERNATIONAL AIRPORT

© MOON.COM

excuse for a pastel-painted mural. The store-fronts on Water Street, as individual as their owners, stand out in Wedgwood blue, lime green, purple, and rose. At street-side, public telephone booths are painted the bright red of old-time fire hydrants.

As the Newfoundlanders say, St. John's offers the best for visitors—another way of saying that Newfoundland is for some short on cities and long on coastal outports. But without question, St. John's thrives with places for dining, nightlife, sightseeing, and lodging—more than anywhere else across the island and Labrador. Simply put, the Newfoundlanders have carved a contemporary, livable, and intriguing niche in one of North America's most ancient ports. Come to St. John's for some of Atlantic Canada's most abundant high-quality shopping, unusual dining in lush surroundings, interesting maritime history displayed in fine museums, rousing nightlife and music, and an emerging and eclectic fine-arts scene.

When you're done with the city, there's the rest of the Avalon Peninsula to discover. Within day-tripping distance of downtown, you can go whale-watching at Witless Bay Ecological Reserve, watch archaeologists at work at Ferryland, walk in to North America's most accessible bird sanctuary at Cape St. Mary's, and drive through delightfully named villages like Heart's Desire.

PLANNING YOUR TIME

Whether you arrive by air, by ferry, or overland from the west, St. John's is a definite destination in itself. It has all the amenities of a major city, including top-notch accommodations, a good range of restaurants, and lively nightlife. Sightseeing will easily fill two days, with at least a few hours spent at **The Rooms,** a museum and art gallery complex as good as any in Canada. Don't miss the drive up to **Signal Hill National Historic Site,** and stop at **Johnson Geo Centre** along the way. The **Fluvarium** is a good rainy-day diversion.

While the village of **Quidi Vidi** provides a taste of the rest of the province without leaving city limits, the rest of the Avalon Peninsula is well worth exploring.

The options are relatively straightforward—either use St. John's as a base for day trips or plan on an overnight excursion. Two highlights—a whale-watching trip to **Witless Bay Ecological Reserve** and a visit to the historic **Colony of Avalon**—can easily be combined into a day trip. Bird-rich **Cape St. Mary's Ecological Reserve** is also within a couple of hours' drive of St. John's, although if you're arriving by ferry from Nova Scotia, it's only a short detour from the main route into town. If you're arriving by air, five days is the minimum amount of time to allow for exploring the city and the Avalon Peninsula. If you're arriving by ferry with your own vehicle, plan on spending three days on the Avalon Peninsula (including St. John's) and seven days traveling through the central and western portion of the province to the ferry terminal at Port-aux-Basques. Add two days' travel from Halifax (including the two ferry trips from and to Sydney) and you can create a 12-day itinerary with no backtracking.

HISTORY

St. John's officially dates to 1497, when Newfoundlanders say the explorer John Cabot sailed into the harbor and claimed the area for England. By the early 1540s, St. John's Harbour was a major port on old-world maps, and the French explorer Jacques Cartier anchored there for ship repairs. The British—who arrived, conquered, and remained for centuries—have had the greatest impact here. By 1528 the port had its first residence, and the main lanes were the Lower Path (Water Street) and Upper Path (Duckworth Street). Fishing thrived, but settlement was slow. Early on, the defenseless port was easy game for other European imperialists, and in 1665 the Dutch plundered the town. Nevertheless,

---

Previous: iceberg near St. Anthony; colorful homes in St. John's; The Rooms, a provincial museum and art gallery complex; St. John's Harbour.

The Newfoundland Dog and Labrador Retriever

statues of a Labrador retriever and a Newfoundland dog located in Harbourside Park

The large, long-haired Newfoundland dog is believed to have originated with the early Portuguese, who brought mountain sheepdogs across the Atlantic with them. Considered one of North America's finest show dogs, the Newfoundland is better known locally as a working dog. Its swimming prowess, used to rescue shipwrecked fishers and sailors from stormy seas, has inspired local legends.

Contrary to the name, the Labrador retriever originated on the island of Newfoundland as a descendant of the Newfoundland dog. The retriever was known as the "lesser Newfoundland," "St. John's dog," or "St. John's water dog" until its debut in London at the English Kennel Club in 1903.

by 1675, St. John's had a population of 185, as well as 155 cattle and 48 boats anchored at 23 piers. By 1696, the French emerged as England's persistent adversary. The French launched destructive attacks on St. John's in 1696, 1705, and 1709.

St. John's was a seamy port through most of its early years. In a town bereft of permanent settlement and social constraints, 80 taverns and innumerable brothels flourished on Water Street, with a few stores on Duckworth Street and Buckleys Lane (George Street). The port's inhabitants were a motley mix of Spaniards, Portuguese, French, and British; as the latter gained dominance, Anglo immigration was encouraged. In 1892, a huge fire destroyed the city from Water Street to the East End, leveling 1,572 houses and 150 stores and leaving 1,900 families homeless. The stores, commercial buildings, and merchant mansions were re-created in Gothic Revival and Second Empire styles.

Sights

Most of St. John's best sightseeing revolves around the city's long and colorful history. In addition to traditional sights such as The Rooms (the provincial museum) and national historic sites, go beyond the ordinary and plan on sipping a pint of beer at the Crow's Nest and joining a guided walking tour of downtown—both excellent ways to soak up the seafaring ambience of this historic city.

DOWNTOWN

Although adding to the charm in many ways, the layout of downtown defies modern logic. The streets follow footpaths laid out by European fishermen and sailors centuries ago, when towns were not planned but simply evolved for everyone's convenience. Water Street (one of North America's oldest streets) and the other main streets rise parallel to the waterfront and are intersected by roads meandering across the hillside. Historic stone staircases climb grades too steep for paved roads.

★ The Rooms

One of Canada's finest cultural facilities, **The Rooms** (9 Bonaventure Ave., 709/757-8000, June-mid-Sept. Mon.-Sat. 10am-5pm, Sun. noon-5pm, mid-Sept.-May Wed.-Sat. 10am-5pm, Sun. noon-5pm, adult $10, senior $6.50, child $5) combines a provincial museum, art gallery, and archives under one roof. Styled on the simple oceanfront "fishing rooms" where Newfoundlanders would process their catch, this complex setting on the site of a 1750s fort is anything but basic. From a distance, it is nothing short of spectacular to see the ultramodern "rooms" rising above the rest of the city like a mirage. The interior is no less impressive, with huge windows allowing uninterrupted views across the city and harbor. Displays in the museum component encompass the entire natural and human history of Newfoundland and Labrador, from glaciation

to modern-day cultural diversity. The art gallery spreads across two floors. More than 7,000 works of art are displayed, with touring exhibits adding to the artistic mix. If you're a history buff with time to spare, include a visit to the archives, which contain more than 500,000 historical photos, plus government and shipping records, maps and atlases, family histories, and personal diaries.

Basilica Cathedral Museum

The early Roman Catholics aimed to make an impact on the skyline of St. John's, and did so in the mid-1800s with the **Basilica Cathedral of St. John the Baptist** (200 Military Rd., 709/754-2170, http://thebasilica.ca, June-Sept. Sun.-Fri. 8am-4pm, Sat. 9am-5pm, free), one block toward downtown from The Rooms. The Romanesque cathedral, built of stone and shaped like a Latin cross with twin 43-meter-high (141-foot-high) towers, is now a national historic site. In addition to the museum, guided tours point out the ornate ceilings embellished with gold leaf, numerous statues, and other features.

Anglican Cathedral of St. John the Baptist

The **Anglican Cathedral of St. John the Baptist** (16 Church Hill, 709/726-5677, June Mon.-Fri. 10am-noon and 2pm-4pm, July-Sept. Mon.-Fri. 10am-4pm, Sat. 10am-noon, free) is a national historic site revered by locals (and said to be haunted by a resident ghost). English architect Sir George Gilbert Scott designed the impressive Gothic Revival edifice in Newfoundland bluestone. The cornerstone was laid in 1847, and the Great Fire of 1892 almost gutted the structure. Reconstruction within the walls started the next year. Of special interest are the carved furnishings and sculpted arches, and a gold communion service presented by King William IV.

Downtown St. John's

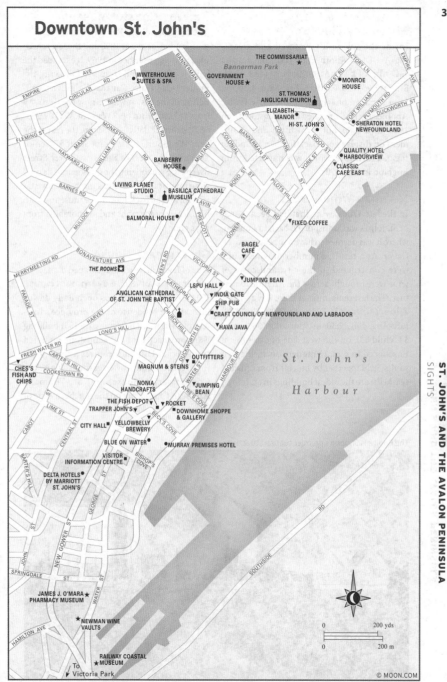

THE COMMISSARIAT ★
Bannerman Park
WINTERHOLME SUITES & SPA ●
GOVERNMENT HOUSE ★
MONROE HOUSE ●
ST. THOMAS' ANGLICAN CHURCH
ELIZABETH MANOR ●
HI-ST. JOHN'S ●
SHERATON HOTEL NEWFOUNDLAND ●
BANBERRY HOUSE ●
QUALITY HOTEL HARBOURVIEW ●
CLASSIC CAFÉ EAST ●
LIVING PLANET STUDIO ■
BASILICA CATHEDRAL MUSEUM ✝
BALMORAL HOUSE ●
FIXED COFFEE ▼
THE ROOMS ✚
BAGEL CAFÉ ●
JUMPING BEAN ▼
LSPU HALL ■
ANGLICAN CATHEDRAL OF ST. JOHN THE BAPTIST ✝
INDIA GATE ▼
SHIP PUB ▼
CRAFT COUNCIL OF NEWFOUNDLAND AND LABRADOR ■
HAVA JAVA ▼
St. John's Harbour
OUTFITTERS ▼
MAGNUM & STEINS ●
NONIA HANDCRAFTS ●
JUMPING BEAN ▼
THE FISH DEPOT ▼
TRAPPER JOHN'S ▼
ROCKET ●
DOWNHOME SHOPPE & GALLERY ●
CITY HALL ■
YELLOWBELLY BREWERY ■
BLUE ON WATER ●
MURRAY PREMISES HOTEL ●
VISITOR INFORMATION CENTRE ■
DELTA HOTELS BY MARRIOTT ST. JOHN'S ●
CHES'S FISH AND CHIPS ▼
JAMES J. O'MARA ★ PHARMACY MUSEUM
NEWMAN WINE VAULTS ★
RAILWAY COASTAL MUSEUM ★
To Victoria Park

0   200 yds
0   200 m

© MOON.COM

James J. O'Mara Pharmacy Museum

Inside the splendidly restored and gleaming Art Deco Apothecary Hall, the **James J. O'Mara Pharmacy Museum** (488 Water St., 709/753-5877, Mon.-Fri. 8am-4:30pm, free) recalls a pharmacy of the early 1900s. Apothecary Hall operated as a drugstore from 1922 until 1986, but furnishings and equipment on display goes back further, including the oak furniture, which was imported from England in the 1870s.

Newman Wine Vaults

In the late 1700s, wine that had been stored in St. John's was transported back to London, where it was deemed to have a much improved flavor. As a result, a number of wine vaults were constructed in the city, and cases of wine were brought across the Atlantic to mature. The last remaining of these is **Newman Wine Vaults** (436 Water St., 709/739-7870, July-Aug. daily 9:30am-5pm, adult $6, senior $4, child $3), on the west side of downtown. Ensconced in a more modern shell, the two vaults, held together by mortar from crushed seashells, are the oldest buildings in St. John's.

Railway Coastal Museum

The Newfoundland Railway was a vital link for islanders between 1898 and the last scheduled passenger service in 1969. It extended the length of the island (roughly following the modern-day Trans-Canada Highway), terminating in the east at what is now the **Railway Coastal Museum** (495 Water St. W., 709/753-5877, summer daily 10am-5pm, the rest of the year Wed.-Sun. 10am-5pm, adult $7, senior $6, child $5), west of the New Gower Street overpass. Symbolizing the grandeur of its one-time importance, the city's main railway station forms the backbone of the museum, with historical photographs and memorabilia from days gone by.

Government House

One of few structures that escaped damage in the Great Fire of 1892, **Government House** (50 Military Rd., grounds open daily dawn-dusk) is the residence of the province's lieutenant governor. The impressive 1831 building was constructed of red sandstone quarried from Signal Hill and features a moat, ceiling frescoes, and flower gardens. This, the Commissariat House, and St. Thomas's Anglican Church are on the northern edge of

The Rooms is St. John's premier cultural attraction.

downtown, a steep five-block walk from the waterfront.

The Commissariat

Now protected as a provincial historic site, **The Commissariat** (11 King's Bridge Rd., 709/729-6370, mid-May-June and Sept.-early Oct. Wed.-Sun. 9:30am-5pm, July-Aug. daily 9:30am-5pm, adult $6, senior $4, child $3) began in 1818 as a residence and office for Fort William's assistant commissary general. Over the years, the three-story building was used as the St. Thomas's Anglican Church rectory, a nursing home, and a hospital. The interior, furnished with antiques, has been restored in the style of the 1830s.

St. Thomas's Anglican Church

St. Thomas's Anglican Church (corner of King's Bridge Rd. and Military Rd., 709/576-6632, free) is known as the Old Garrison Church. Dating to the 1830s, the city's oldest church houses a cast-iron Hanoverian coat of arms over the door, attesting to the royal lineage. Call for details of summer sanctuary tours.

★ SIGNAL HILL

The distinct geological feature of the **Signal Hill National Historic Site** rises high above the Narrows, at the mouth of St. John's Harbour. On a clear day, it's plainly visible from throughout town, but more importantly, it offers stunning views back across the city, down the coast, and out into the Atlantic Ocean. Although Signal Hill is only a little more than 2 kilometers (1.2 miles) from the city center, it's a steep walk, so plan on driving.

★ Johnson Geo Centre

What better place for a geology museum than underground? Access to the **Johnson Geo Centre** (175 Signal Hill Rd., 709/724-7625, daily 9:30am-5pm, adult $12, senior $9, child $6), almost at the top of Signal Hill, is a glass-sided elevator that descends below the rocky landscape to a cavernous room where one entire wall exposes the 550-million-year-old bedrock. Displays describe the entire geological history of the province, from the oldest rocks on earth to modern oil and gas exploration. Highlights include a *Titanic* room, where you can watch footage from exploration of the famous wreck.

Signal Hill National Historic Site

In the 1700s, this hill, once known as the Lookout, served as part of a British signaling system; news of friendly or hostile ships was flagged from Cape Spear to Signal Hill, where the message was conveyed to Fort William in town. In 1762 the Battle of Signal Hill marked the Seven Years' War's final North American land battle, with England victorious and France the loser.

On the road up to the hilltop is the **Visitor Interpretation Centre** (709/772-5367, mid-May-mid-June and Sept.-mid-Oct. Wed.-Sun. 10am-5pm, mid-June-Aug. daily 10am-5pm, adult $4, senior $3.50, child $2), which tells the long and colorful story of Signal Hill through modern and interactive exhibits.

Continuing upward by road or on foot, **Cabot Tower** (mid-Apr.-mid-Nov. daily 9am-5pm, Interpretation Centre admission includes Cabot Tower) is at the very top of Signal Hill. This is where Guglielmo Marconi received the first transatlantic wireless message. The hilltop is pocked with historical remnants. England's Imperial Powder Magazine stored gunpowder during the Napoleonic Wars, and the Queen's Battery—an authentic outpost tucked beneath the cliff—guarded the harbor Narrows from 1833.

For hiking, the **North Head Trail** peels off the top of the hill and follows the cliffs to Fort Chain Rock. The **Cuckold's Cove Trail** wends across Signal Hill's leeward side to Quidi Vidi Village.

★ QUIDI VIDI

The Atlantic's watery inroads permeate the St. John's area. Aside from the city's famed harbor, another sizable pocket of the sea—**Quidi**

Vidi Lake—lies nearby. Its azure-blue waters meet a boulder-bound coastline, all within the bustling city limits. Quidi Vidi Lake ("kiddie viddie" is the local pronunciation) is best known as the site of the Royal St. John's Regatta, held on the first Wednesday in August. The lake's choppy water also lures windsurfers. Locals enjoy strolls along the grassy banks. To get there, follow Water Street west under Pitts Memorial Drive and turn left onto Route 11 (Blackhead Road).

Beyond the lake is picturesque **Quidi Vidi Village.** Wander the narrow, winding streets of this fishing village and you'll never believe a provincial capital lies just over the hill.

Quidi Vidi Battery

Quidi Vidi Battery (Cuckhold's Cove Rd., 709/729-2977, mid-May-Sept. daily 10am-5:30pm, adult $3) sits high on a hill above Quidi Vidi, overlooking the lake and village. The site owes its origin to the French, who built the battery in their effort to capture St. John's in 1762. France lost, and the British took the battery and rebuilt it in 1780. The site has been restored to its War of 1812 glory years, when England fortified the battery in anticipation of an attack by the United States that never materialized. The battery is now staffed by guides dressed in period uniforms of the Royal Artillery.

SOUTH OF DOWNTOWN
Bowring Park

Arguably the city's prettiest, **Bowring Park** has hosted significant guests for many tree-planting ceremonies, including a visit from Queen Elizabeth for the Cabot celebrations in 1997. Crocus and hyacinth beds make a colorful impact during spring, swans glide across the tranquil ponds in summer, and the setting is transformed into a canvas of dappled oranges and reds during autumn. Statues are everywhere, the most famous being of Peter Pan. It's a replica of the original in England's Kensington Gardens, and it serves as a

---

1: the view from Signal Hill; **2:** Quidi Vidi

memorial to Sir Edgar Bowring's godchild, who died in an offshore shipwreck.

To get there, stay south on Water Street until the road splits into Waterford Bridge and Topsail Roads; continue on Waterford Bridge Road for 3 kilometers (1.9 miles) to the park's entrance.

Cape Spear National Historic Site

The eminently photogenic **Cape Spear National Historic Site lighthouse** (off Rte. 11, 709/772-5367, mid-May-mid-June Wed.-Sun. 10am-6pm, mid-June-early Sept. daily 10am-6pm, early Sept.-mid-Oct. Sat.-Wed. 9am-5pm, adult $4, senior $3.50, child $2) crowns a windy 75-meter-high (246-foot-high) promontory above the Atlantic Ocean. Built in 1839, the lighthouse ranks as the province's oldest extant beacon and was used until 1955, when the original lighting apparatus was moved to a more efficient building nearby. The keeper's living quarters have been restored, while the adjacent visitors center displays antiques and maritime artifacts.

Outside the lighthouse, the precipitous slopes hold the rusting remains of World War II gun batteries. Hiking trails fan out from the peak. The 10-kilometer (6.2-mile) trail to Maddox Cove starts here and winds south along the coast, through gullies, bakeapple bogs, and berry patches. If you're lucky, you'll see a family of shy foxes in the high grasses.

The cape, North America's most easterly point, lies 6 kilometers (3.7 miles) southeast of St. John's Harbour as the crow flies and 15 kilometers (9.3 miles) around Route 11's coastal curve. To get there, follow Water Street to the exit for Pitts Memorial Parkway and turn left to Route 11 (Blackhead Road).

PIPPY PARK

Civilization ends and wilderness begins at the **Pippy Park** preserve, which covers 1,343 hectares (3,319 acres) of woodlands, grasslands, and rolling hills on the steep hilltop plateau overlooking St. John's. In addition to the Fluvarium and the botanical garden, the park is laced with hiking trails and is home to two golf courses. Developed along the rim of the hill, the park fronts Confederation Parkway/Prince Philip Drive and encompasses Memorial University's campus and the government Confederation Building complex. Barrens, marshes, woodlands, ponds, and streams make for a splendid landscape. Moose, muskrats, mink, snowshoe hares, meadow voles, and common shrews roam the hilly terrain, which is studded with balsam fir, spruce, and juniper. The green-winged teal, black and pintail duck, sora rail, American bittern, gyrfalcon, and pied-billed grebe are among the birds lured to Long Pond, the oval lake near the park's edge. Long Pond marks the start of the 7-kilometer (4.3-mile) **Rennies River Trail** across the city's hillside to Quidi Vidi Lake.

Fluvarium

The eco-attraction **Fluvarium** (5 Nagle's Pl., 709/754-3474, July-Aug. Mon.-Fri. 9am-5pm, Sat.-Sun. 10am-5pm, Sept.-June Mon.-Fri. 9am-4:30pm, Sat.-Sun. noon-4:30pm, adult $8, senior $6, child $5) overlooks Long Pond from just north of Prince Philip Drive. It's contained in a handsome eight-sided wooden building wrapped with an open porch; you enter on the second floor, a spacious room with ecological exhibits depicting Atlantic salmon and other fish species, marsh birds, and carnivorous plants. The center's pièce de résistance is down a winding stairway. Nine windows pierce the walls and provide spectators a below-water-level look at the brook and brown trout, arctic char, and salmon in Nagle's Hill Brook. It's an innovative variation on the traditional aquarium.

Memorial University Botanical Garden

The 38-hectare (94-acre) **Memorial University Botanical Garden** (306 Mt. Scio Rd., 709/737-8590, May-Aug. daily 10am-5pm, Sept.-Nov. daily 10am-4pm, adult $9, senior and child $6) is the province's only botanical garden. Garden environments include heather beds, a cottage garden, a rock garden, and a wildflower garden. Hiking trails wind through a boreal forest and a fen, both resplendent with native flowers, shrubs, and trees. The gardens feature a medley of soft colors. Blue forget-me-not, white turtlehead and rhododendron, and pink joe-pye weed bloom among spirea, northern wild raisin, dogwood, and high-bush cranberry. White birch, chokecherry, trembling aspen, ash, willow, and

Cape Spear

maple surround the botanical medley. To get to the gardens, follow Allandale Road north past Prince Philip Drive and turn west on Mt. Scio Road.

WEST OF DOWNTOWN
Bell Island

One of many islands in Conception Bay, west of St. John's, 9-kilometer-long (5.6-mile-long) **Bell Island** has a long history of mining. **No. 2 Mine** (709/488-2880, June-Sept. 10am-6pm, adult $12, senior $10, child $5), which stopped operating in 1949, remains one of the world's most productive submarine (underground) iron ore mines. The striking black-and-white photography of Yousuf Karsh is a highlight of the aboveground museum, while underground the main shaft has been restored and is open for inspection. Guided one-hour tours include the use of a hard hat, but you should bring your own sweater.

Newfoundlanders boast an incredible flair for artistic expression, an ability displayed in the **Bell Island murals.** Large-scale scenes painted on the sides of buildings depict the community's life and people during the ore-mining decades. Look for the half-dozen murals in different locations across the tiny island's northeastern corner, mainly in and near **Wabana,** the largest settlement. One assumes the murals were painted from historical photographs, yet there's a sense of real life to each painting—from a car's black luster to the animated figures and even the clear gleam of a miner's eyes.

To get to Bell Island, follow Route 40 west to Portugal Cove, 15 kilometers (9.3 miles) from downtown. The ferry (709/895-6931) operates year-round. In summer, sailings are daily every 20-40 minutes 7am-11:30pm. The fare is $11 per vehicle and driver, plus $5 per additional passenger.

TOURS
Sightseeing Tours

McCarthy's Party (709/579-4480, www.mccarthysparty.com) has been on the sightseeing tour scene for decades. June-August the company offers daily three-hour guided tours to Signal Hill, Cape Spear, the cathedrals, and other major sites for $60 per person.

Walking Tours

One of many informal walking tours of downtown St. John's is **Boyle's Walking Tours** (709/364-6845, www.boyletours.com, mid-June-mid-Sept.), led by the very prim and proper Sir Cavendish Boyle. The Where They Once Stood tour ($30, cash only) departs Tuesday and Friday at 10am from the lobby of the Sheraton Hotel Newfoundland.

The **Haunted Hike** (709/685-3444, www.hauntedhike.com, June-mid-Sept., $10) departs Sunday-Thursday at 9:30pm from the west entrance to the Anglican church at the corner of Duckworth Street and Church Hill. With the Reverend Thomas Wyckham Jarvis leading the way, you'll explore the darkened backstreets learning of murders, mysteries, and ghosts. It's an experience you won't forget in a hurry.

Recreation

Don't let bad weather prevent you from enjoying the outdoors—the locals certainly don't. Sure, it may be foggy or raining, but in many ways this adds to the St. John's experience when you're out hiking or striding the local fairways.

HIKING AND BIKING

The hilly streets of downtown St. John's aren't conducive to walking and biking, but if you're looking for wilderness, you don't need to travel too far from the city. A five-minute drive from downtown is **Pippy Park.** Follow Allendale Road north over the Trans-Canada Highway and look for the parking area beyond the golf course entrance. From this point, hiking trails loop past numerous lakes and through native forest.

Alongside the Trans-Canada Highway, 36 kilometers (22 miles) south of downtown, is **Butter Pot Provincial Park** (day pass $5 per vehicle), a 2,800-hectare (6,919-acre) wilderness of forests, bogs, and barrens—a taste of the interior a 30-minute drive from the city. The name "Butter Pot" is a local term for a rounded hill, many of which occur within the park boundary, including along **Butter Pot Hill Trail,** a 3.3-kilometer (2-mile) walk to a 300-meter-high (984-foot-high) summit. Along the way you'll see signs of ancient glacial action, including displaced boulders known as "erratics," while at the summit,

hikers are rewarded with views extending north to Bell Island. This trail starts beside Site 58 of the park campground. With minimal elevation gain, the **Peter's Pond Trail** parallels a small lake from the day-use area; you can turn around after 1 kilometer (0.6 mile) or continue to Butter Pot Hill.

SCUBA DIVING

Situated on Atlantic Canada's oldest shipping routes, the St. John's area is incredibly rich in shipwrecks. What's more, the waters here are as clear as the Caribbean—20- to 30-meter (66- to 98-foot) visibility is common—and reasonably warm summer-autumn, although a wetsuit is advisable. One of the most accessible wreck-diving sites is **Lance Cove,** on Bell Island, where four iron-ore carriers were torpedoed by German U-boats during World War II. Also in Conception Bay are much older whaling boats and a number of wrecks close enough to be accessible for shore diving. Based at Conception Bay South, **Ocean Quest** (40 O'Leary Ave., 709/834-7234, www.oceanquestadventures.com) takes divers to the bay and other dive sites for a full-day boat charter rate of $170 per person (includes rental gear). This company also operates a dive school and a dive shop, and has a number of packages combining diving with other adventures such as snorkeling with humpback whales.

Entertainment and Events

NIGHTLIFE

It's said St. John's has more pubs, taverns, and bars per capita than anyplace else in Atlantic Canada. Spend any time wandering through downtown after dark and you'll probably agree. The city's international port status is partly the reason. Even better, these watering holes serve double duty as venues for music of various styles, including traditional Newfoundland, folk, Irish, country, rock, and jazz. The website www.georgestreetlive.ca has entertainment listings.

A local band of note is **Great Big Sea,** which combines modern rock and traditional Newfoundland folk to create a sound and atmosphere that draws sellout crowds throughout Canada.

Pubs

The energetic pub scene centers on a one-block stretch of George Street off Water Street. The weekend starts late Friday evening, picks up again on Saturday afternoon, and lasts until 2am (and at some places keeps up through Sunday).

On the corner of George and Water Streets, **YellowBelly Brewery** (288 Water St., 709/757-3780, daily 11:30am-2am) is ensconced in a five-story building that dates to 1725—one of the city's oldest buildings and one of the few to escape the Great Fire of 1892. A faithful renovation creates an authentic atmosphere for enjoying beers brewed on-site, including unique choices such as Hard Tack Ale, which is made from day-old bread sourced from a local bakery. Ask at the restaurant for a tour of the building.

Among George Street's abundance of pubs and eating establishments, **Trapper John's** (2 George St., 709/579-9630, daily noon-2am) ranks as a city entertainment mainstay, hosting notable provincial folk groups and bands. The patrons will gladly initiate visitors to Newfoundland with a "screech-in" ceremony

for free. **Green Sleeves Pub** (14 George St., 709/579-1070, daily noon-2am) doubles as a weekend hub for traditional, rock, and Irish concerts and jam sessions. **Fat Cat Blues Bar** (5 George St., 709/739-5554, Tues.-Sun. 8pm-2am) presents concerts, open mic, blues rock, and women's jam sessions.

The **Ship Pub** (265 Duckworth St., 709/753-3870, Mon.-Sat. noon-2am, Sun. noon-midnight) is a dimly lit room that has been a venue for local and provincial recording acts for years, and it continues to draw Newfoundland's hottest up-and-coming jazz, blues, and folk musicians each weekend night. These same artists, as well as literary types, are the main customers—you just never know who might be on stage or in the audience.

In the vicinity of the Ship Inn, the **Crow's Nest** (709/753-6927, Tues.-Thurs. 4:30pm-7:30pm, Fri. noon-8pm, Sat. 2pm-8pm) opened in 1942 as a retreat for naval officers, but this once-exclusive club is now open to interested visitors (dress code is "smart casual"). The old-fashioned room is a treasure trove of naval memorabilia, which includes a periscope from a German U-boat that was captured off St. John's during World War II. The club is on the fourth floor of an old brick warehouse between Water and Duckworth Streets; the entrance is opposite the war memorial.

PERFORMING ARTS

The **Resource Centre for the Arts** (LSPU Hall, 3 Victoria St., 709/753-4531, www.rca.nf.ca) stages productions by the resident RCA Theatre Company and also hosts professional touring groups throughout the year. Ticket prices vary depending on the event, but are always reasonable.

The **Arts and Culture Centre** (corner of Allandale Rd. and Prince Philip Dr., 709/729-3900) presents a wide range of theater, music, and dance on its Main Stage, with artists and

"Screeched In"

Newfoundlanders dote on the codfish, and visitors are invited to pledge piscatorial loyalty to King Cod in hilarious induction ceremonies conducted on tours and in touristy restaurants. The tradition dates to the early 1900s, when a visiting U.S. naval officer followed the lead of his St. John's host by downing a glass of rum in one gulp. His reaction to swallowing the unlabeled rum was an undignified screech. And so the tradition was born, as U.S. servicemen docked in St. John's came ashore to sample the "screech."

To be "screeched in" in proper style, a visitor dons fishing garb, downs several quick shots of Screech rum, kisses a cod, joins in singing a local ditty, poses for a photograph, and receives an official certificate. It's strictly tourist nonsense, but visitors love it. Mostly because of its authentic atmosphere, Trapper John's (2 George St., 709/579-9630, daily noon-2am) in downtown St. John's is one of the best places to be "screeched in."

troupes from across Canada. The center is also home to the **Newfoundland Symphony Orchestra** (709/722-4441, www.nsomusic.ca), which has a September-April season.

FESTIVALS AND EVENTS
Summer

Shakespeare by the Sea Festival (709/722-7287, www.shakespearebytheseafestival.com) takes place for three weeks in July, Friday-Sunday at 6pm. Expect outdoor productions of the Bard's best by the acclaimed Loyal Shakespearean Company. The venues change annually, but may be as dramatic as Cape Spear National Historic Site or as intimate as the Newman Wine Vault.

The **Signal Hill Tattoo** is a tribute to the landmark Battle of Signal Hill that ended the war between the English and French in North America. The military event is staged dramatically, with military drills by foot soldiers, artillery detachments, fife and drum bands, and more. It all takes place up at Signal Hill National Historic Site early July-mid-August on Wednesday, Thursday, Saturday, and Sunday at 11am and 3pm.

Beginning in late July or early August,

Prince Edward Plaza on George Street is the outdoor setting for the weeklong **George Street Festival** (www.georgestreetlive.ca), which offers performances by top entertainers. Crowds begin gathering in the afternoon, and by midnight there may be upwards of 8,000 revelers on the street.

The **Royal St. John's Regatta** (709/576-8921, www.stjohnsregatta.org) is a city tradition that officially dates back to 1818 (making it North America's oldest organized sporting event), although it was probably contested as early as the late 1700s. What began as a rowing contest between visiting sailors has morphed into a world-class event drawing rowers from around the world. Held at Quidi Vidi Lake on the first Wednesday in August, the event draws up to 50,000 spectators and is so popular that the city long ago declared the day a civic holiday.

Winter

Most of the winter action centers on **Mile One Centre** (50 New Gower St., 709/576-7657, www.mileonecentre.com), where the St. John's IceCaps hockey franchise competes in the American Hockey League.

Shopping

An abundance of arts and crafts stores can be found in downtown St. John's. Aside from these, east along Duckworth Street beyond downtown is a string of interesting shops specializing in Newfoundland music, pet paraphernalia, and the like. My favorite is **Living Planet Studio** (20 Barnes Rd., 709/739-6811, Mon.-Thurs. 9am-3pm, Fri. 8am-4pm), which stocks locally printed shirts that feature a politically incorrect Newfoundland slant.

ARTS AND CRAFTS

Craft shops downtown offer every conceivable craft available, and new developments continually increase the variety. One of the best places to start is the **Craft Council of Newfoundland and Labrador** (275 Duckworth St., 709/753-2749, Mon.-Wed. and Sat. 10am-6pm, Thurs.-Fri. 10am-8pm, Sun. 1pm-5pm), in the heart of downtown, which displays and sells an excellent sampling of traditional and contemporary wares.

Nonia Handcrafts (286 Water St., 709/753-8062, June-Sept. Mon.-Sat. 10am-5:30pm, Sun. 12:30pm-4pm, the rest of the year Tues.-Sat. 10am-5:30pm) is among the best craft shops, carrying handwoven apparel, weavings, parkas, jewelry, hooked mats, domestic wares, and handmade toys.

Other shops sell a variety of wares: Grenfell parkas from St. Anthony, books about Newfoundland, local Purity-brand candies, tinned biscuits or seafood, bottles of savory spices, pottery and porcelain, handmade copper and tin kettles, model ships, soapstone and stone carvings, fur pelts and rugs, apparel, folk art, and handwoven silk, wool, cotton, and linen. Expect to find most of these goods at the **Downhome Shoppe & Gallery** (303 Water St., 709/722-2970, Mon.-Sat. 10am-6:30pm, Sun. noon-5:30pm).

Top-notch private galleries are plentiful. **Christina Parker Gallery** (50 Water St., 709/753-0580, Mon.-Fri. 10am-5:30pm, Sat. 11am-5pm) showcases Newfoundland's avant-garde spectrum; for more traditional art, plan on visiting the **Emma Butler Gallery** (111 George St., 709/739-7111, Tues.-Sat. 11am-5pm).

OUTDOOR GEAR

The Outfitters (220 Water St., 709/579-4453, Mon.-Sat. 10am-6pm, Sun. noon-5pm) sells an excellent range of outdoor wear, including winter jackets. It also has canoes, kayaks, and skis and is a clearinghouse for information about outdoor recreation around the island.

Food

No one would describe the St. John's dining scene as sophisticated, but it is better—by far—than anywhere else in the province. As you might imagine, seafood features prominently on most menus. Cod is a staple, while in better restaurants you'll find Atlantic salmon, mussels, scallops, halibut, and lobster.

REGIONAL CUISINE

"Newfoundland cuisine" revolves around seafood, and traditionally it's been deep-fried, which is often bemoaned by outsiders not used to this style of cooking. That said, it's worth trying fish-and-chips at least once—and not at a regular family restaurant, but somewhere it is a specialty, such as **Ches's Fish and Chips** (9 Freshwater Rd., 709/726-2373, daily 11am-6pm, $9-16). Here, tender deep-fried fillets and crisp french fries are served in an atmosphere of Formica and bright lights.

Walk a few blocks east of downtown to reach **Classic Café East** (73 Duckworth St., 709/579-4444, Sun.-Tues. 8am-2:30pm, Wed.-Sat. 8am-9pm, $13-21), a popular spot that gets crowded with all types who come seeking delicious seafood chowder, cod tongues with scrunchions, and other traditional Newfoundland fare at moderate prices in a cozy atmosphere. For dessert, try the spotted dick (a traditional steamed pudding) or the cheesecake with partridgeberry sauce.

A huge step up in style and price, but still rooted in traditional cooking, is **Bacalao** (65 LeMarchant Rd., 709/579-6565, Tues. 6pm-9:30pm, Wed.-Sun. noon-2:30pm and 6pm-9:30pm, $19-33), which means "salt cod" in Spanish. Within a stylish setting, top chefs serve up Newfoundland's best-known export, cod, in a number of creative ways, using local, organic ingredients whenever possible. The local theme extends through many dishes—mussels are steamed open in Quidi Vidi beer, and the caribou salad is drizzled with blueberry wine from the province's only winery. As an entrée, the salted cod poached in olive oil and accompanied by smoked and braised pork belly is hard to fault, or choose dishes such as seafood risotto and Game of the Day (it was caribou with partridgeberry sauce last time I visited). Save room for a slice of patriotic Republic Mousse, which is decorated in the three colors of the Newfoundland flag.

I've saved the best for last. If you are looking for the combination of creative local cooking within one of North America's oldest wooden buildings, plan on dining at ★ **Mallard Cottage** (8 Barrows Rd., Quidi Vidi, 709/237-7314, Mon. 5pm-7pm, Tues. 5pm-9pm, Wed.-Sat. 10am-9pm, Sun. 10am-6:30pm, $22-34). Located in the fishing village of Quidi Vidi, a five-minute drive north of downtown, the national historic site-protected building has undergone extensive renovations to create a homey and welcoming ambience. But it is the food itself that is the main draw. The menu changes daily (check their website www.mallardcottage.ca) and is always filled with local, seasonal game, seafood, and produce. Generally, seafood and pork dishes dominate the menu; the restaurant also has regular special events, such as lobster boils, outdoor barbecues, live music on Sunday afternoons, and one dish in particular that garners international attention each spring—seal burgers.

CONTEMPORARY

The chic industrial-style signage out front is a giveaway—**Magnum & Steins** (329 Duckworth St., 709/576-6500, Sun.-Thurs. 5:30pm-10pm, Fri.-Sat. 5:30pm-11pm, $28-45) is clearly unlike any other restaurant in the city. If you're looking for a traditional Newfoundland experience, eat elsewhere. If you're looking for creative city-style cooking and top-notch presentation, this place is a welcome break from deep-fried seafood. Sunday-Wednesday, a three-course dinner is $55 per person.

Blue on Water (319 Water St., 709/754-2583, daily for breakfast, lunch, and dinner, $30-46) is a smallish modern space with a bright atmosphere. Modern cooking is combined with traditional foods in dishes such as kippered mackerel baked with cream and shallots. Lunches include gourmet sandwiches and a delicious seafood bouillabaisse. In the evening, things get serious (and expensive) with starters like shrimp in a coconut tempura and spicy pineapple chutney, and mains like salmon stuffed with roasted red peppers and spinach. The wine list covers all bases.

DELIS

Along downtown's busiest street, ★ **Rocket** (272 Water St., 709/738-2011, daily 7:30am-9pm, lunches $8-11) is a deli with a difference. It stocks all the goodies you would expect to find in a Newfoundland deli, as well as bakery and lunch items, soups and sandwiches, and a huge selection of teas and coffees. Many customers pick up their orders and move on to the adjacent room, which is not really a restaurant but somewhere to simply sit down and eat lunch.

Head to **The Fish Depot** (369 Duckworth St., 709/722-9692, Mon.-Fri. 9am-6pm, Sat. 9am-5pm) for a huge variety of fresh and frozen seafood such as cod, shrimp, halibut, mussels, lobsters, and scallops. You'll need cooking facilities for much of the product, but steamed lobster and delicacies such as smoked arctic char from Labrador can be enjoyed as is.

For a tantalizing overview of Newfoundland cuisine, head to ★ **Bidgoods** (355 Main Rd., Goulds, 709/368-3125, Mon.-Sat. 9am-7pm, Sun. 10am-6pm), on the south side of the city. Dating to 1963, this much-loved grocery store stocks every taste sensation known to the province, including seal flipper pie, caribou, salted fish, salmon, and cod tongues and cheeks. Not much is prepackaged here, but the produce (especially west coast strawberries), berry preserves, shellfish, smoked and pickled fish, and sweet tea biscuits make delicious picnic additions.

PUB GRUB

In the heart of downtown, **YellowBelly Brewery** (288 Water St., 709/757-3780, daily 11:30am-2am, $15-28) is best known as one of Canada's best brewpubs, but it also serves up excellent food, with dishes such as Drunken Salmon using beer brewed in-house as a prime ingredient. The menu of wood-fired pizzas includes choices such as the Costa Rican—ham, pineapple, coconut, and banana peppers.

The **Ship Pub** (265 Duckworth St., 709/753-3870, food service daily noon-3pm, lunches $7.50-13) is a cozy neighborhood pub best known for its live music, but you can order simple lunches from the inexpensive blackboard menu.

EAST INDIAN

Fine East Indian cuisine can be found at **India Gate** (286 Duckworth St., 709/753-6006, Tues.-Sun. 11:30am-1:30pm and 5pm-9:30pm, $13-22). The extensive menu includes tandoori dishes; prawns, lamb, beef, and chicken cooked in the masala, korma, and vindaloo styles; and a wide array of vegetarian entrées. Prices are inexpensive to moderate, portions are generous, and the atmosphere is quiet and relaxed.

CAFÉS AND CHEAP EATS

★ **Jumping Bean** (140 Water St., 709/754-2762, Mon.-Fri. 7:30am-5pm, $7-11) is at street level of TD Place in the heart of downtown.

Head to Rocket for delicious cooking in a casual atmosphere.

Disregard the official street address and enter from Duckworth Street, where tables are scattered across the courtyard. The owners are primarily coffee-roasters, so you know you'll be getting the very freshest coffee, but you can also try the most unique flavor in the province—Screech Coffee, which is infused with Newfoundland rum. Jumping Bean also has a downtown location in the **Atlantic Place building** (215 Water St., 709/754-4627, Mon.-Fri. 7am-6pm, Sat.-Sun. 9am-5pm), which is notable for sweeping harbor views and outdoor tables that become prime real estate for coffee-lovers on warm summer days.

The **Bagel Café** (246 Duckworth St., 709/739-4470, daily 7am-10pm, lunches $7-11) feels more like a restaurant than a coffeehouse. All breakfasts are under $10, including heart-smart options like poached eggs and cereal with low-fat yogurt. Potato bakes make a tasty treat, or order something more substantial, like lasagna.

Continuing along Duckworth away from downtown, you soon come to **Fixed Coffee** (183 Duckworth St., 709/576-7797, Mon.-Fri. 7:30am-8pm, Sat.-Sun. 8am-8pm, lunches $8-14), with a distinct artsy feel. The coffee is as good as anywhere in the province, but it also has delicious chai lattes and hot chocolate. The food menu is ever-changing, but generally includes breakfast sandwiches and wraps, as well as lunchtime salads made from produce sourced from a local farm.

Accommodations and Camping

While St. John's may not have a huge selection of budget accommodations, it does provide an excellent choice of historic B&Bs that offer excellent value. A few major chains are represented downtown (and are also well priced), while you'll find all the familiar chains along major arteries. As elsewhere in Atlantic Canada, demand for rooms is highest in summer, and you should make reservations far in advance. While the larger downtown properties supply parking, at smaller properties you may be expected to use metered street parking.

DOWNTOWN
Under $50

Ensconced in one of the city's famously photogenic pastel-colored townhouses is **HI-St. John's** (8 Gower St., 709/754-4789, www.hihostels.ca), an affiliate of Hostelling International. Within walking distance of downtown, dorm rooms are spacious and come with a maximum of four beds. Other facilities include a well-equipped kitchen, a small backyard with a barbecue, and wireless Internet. Rates are $30 for members and $35 nonmembers. The double rooms are $75-85 and $85-89, respectively.

$100-150

Opposite Bannerman Park, **Elizabeth Manor** (21 Military Rd., 709/753-7733 or 888/263-3786, www.elizabethmanor.nl.ca, $109-195 s or d) was built in 1894, following the Great Fire of 1892. Completely revamped, it now offers nine spacious en suite guest rooms, a sundeck, and a library with art and books about the province. Rates include a full breakfast.

A restored Queen Anne-style townhouse, the **Balmoral House** (38 Queen's Rd., 709/754-5721 or 877/428-1055, www.balmoralhouse.com, $139-179 s or d) offers four large guest rooms, each with a fireplace, a private bath, antique furnishings, a TV, Internet access, and an expansive view of the harbor. Rates include a full breakfast and use of off-street parking.

If you're traveling with children and want to stay downtown, **Quality Hotel-Harbourview** (2 Hill O'Chips, 709/754-7788 or 800/228-5151, www.choicehotels.ca, from

$149 s or d) is a good choice. It has 162 midsize rooms, a popular restaurant overlooking the harbor, free outdoor parking, and free local calls. Rooms with harbor views start at $165, but check online for deals.

$150-200

Take a break from the city's abundant historic accommodations by reserving one of the spacious rooms at ★ **Hometel on Signal Hill** (10 St. Joseph's Ln., 709/739-7799 or 866/739-7799, www.hometels.ca, $159-219 s or d). Located near the base of Signal Hill but still an easy stroll to downtown, this newer lodging fills a row of modern townhouses, each containing up to eight guest rooms. The styling is contemporary throughout, with comfortable beds and large bathrooms adding to the appeal. A light breakfast is included in the rates, with guests congregating in a dining room above the lobby to fill themselves with toast, cereal, and fresh muffins.

Instead of a hotel with a restaurant, **Blue on Water** (319 Water St., 709/754-2583 or 877/431-2583, www.blueonwater.com, from $189 s or d) is a restaurant with 12 upstairs rooms. Like the Hometel on Signal Hill, it offers a modern ambience but is more centrally located. The decor is slick and

contemporary—think 400-thread-count sheets, high-speed Internet connections, and flat-screen TVs. On the downside, the nearest parking is a public lot behind the property, there is no elevator, and check-in is within the restaurant. But once you're in your room, you'll think you're paying a lot more than you really are.

Backing onto Bannerman Park and with a beautiful rear garden, ★ **Banberry House** (116 Military Rd., 709/579-8006 or 877/579-8226, www.banberryhouse.com, $159 s or d) oozes style throughout. My favorite of five guest rooms is the Labrador Room, which is filled with stylish mahogany furniture (including a work desk) and has a super-comfortable bed, a four-piece bath, and garden views. Rates include a full Newfoundland breakfast.

Across the road from the heart of the downtown waterfront, a row of 1846 wooden warehouses has been transformed into **Murray Premises Hotel** (5 Becks Cove, 709/738-7773 or 866/738-7773, www.murraypremiseshotel. com, $199-259 s or d). The 67 rooms fill the top two floors and an adjacent wing. Each is super spacious and features luxurious touches such as maple furniture, heated towel racks and jetted tubs in the oversized bathrooms, and TV/DVD combos. In-room coffee,

Hometel on Signal Hill

complimentary newspapers, and free wireless Internet add to the appeal.

Closer to the airport than to the waterfront, the **Holiday Inn St. John's** (180 Portugal Cove Rd., 709/722-0506 or 800/933-0506, www.ihg.com, $175 s or d) is handy to Pippy Park, Memorial University, and the Confederation Building complex. The hotel offers 256 guest rooms, an indoor pool and waterslide, an up-to-date fitness center, a restaurant and lounge, a laundry, and a business center. Outside of the summer season, check online for rooms around $120.

Over $200

Sheraton Hotel Newfoundland (115 Cavendish Sq., 709/726-4980 or 800/325-3535, www.starwoodhotels.com, from $225 s or d) has an auspicious location, on the former site of Fort William. The first Hotel Newfoundland, one of the Canadian Pacific's deluxe properties, opened in 1925. After many years' service, it was demolished to make room for this handsome hotel. Opened in 1982, the hillside property has more than 300 guest rooms, free parking, and a contemporary restaurant, lounge, fitness center (with an indoor pool, table tennis, squash courts, sauna, and whirlpool), and shopping arcade with a hairdresser.

Delta Hotels by Marriott St. John's (120 New Gower St., 709/739-6404 or 888/890-3222, www.marriott.com, from $260 s or d) is an avant-garde high-rise that offers more than 400 rooms and suites; restaurants and a pub; fitness facilities that include an indoor heated pool, exercise equipment, a whirlpool, a sauna, and squash courts; a shopping arcade; and covered parking.

AIRPORT
$100-150

Comfort Inn Airport (106 Airport Rd., 709/753-3500, www.comfortinnstjohns.com, $129-149 s or d) is conveniently located across from St. John's International Airport and features 100 rooms and suites, a restaurant and lounge, a business center, a fitness center, airport transfers, and free continental breakfast.

CAMPGROUNDS

Pippy Park Campground (Nagle's Pl., 709/737-3669, www.pippypark.com, May-Sept., $24-45), 2.5 kilometers (1.6 miles) northwest of downtown, fills on a first-come, first-served basis. It offers more than 150 sites, most of which are private and well spaced. Amenities include a general store, a playground, wireless Internet (in only one section of the campground), and picnic shelters. The Fluvarium (great for children) is across the road, while trails lead from the campground to all corners of Pippy Park.

Butter Pot Provincial Park, along the Trans-Canada Highway, 36 kilometers (22 miles) south of downtown, has a 126-site campground open late May-late Sept. The cost is $28 per night, with showers and laundry facilities provided. Each private site has a fire pit and picnic table. Activities include hiking and water sports such as lake swimming and canoeing (rentals available). Three playgrounds will keep the young ones occupied.

Farther out, but in a beautiful lakeside location, ★ **La Manche Provincial Park** (Rte. 10, late May-late Sept., $18-28) has 83 campsites spread around two forested loops. Although there are no showers or hookups, the facility fills every summer weekend. In addition to kayaking and fishing, campers take advantage of trails leading along La Manche River and down to an abandoned fishing village. Reservations for Butter Pot Provincial Park and La Manche Provincial Park can be made by calling 877/214-2267 or online at www.nlcamping.ca.

Information and Services

TOURIST INFORMATION

The **provincial tourism office** (709/729-2830 or 800/563-6353, www.newfoundlandlabrador.com) and **Destination St. John's** (709/739-8899 or 877/739-8899, www.destinationstjohns.com) are both good sources of information when planning your trip.

There's an **information booth** at the airport (open whenever flights are arriving) and another just beyond the ferry dock at Argentia (open for all ferry arrivals). When you get downtown, search out the **City of St. John's Visitor Information Centre** (348 Water St., 709/576-8106, www.stjohns.ca, May-early Oct. daily 9am-4:30pm, early Oct.-Apr. Mon.-Fri. 9am-4:30pm), in a three-story red-brick building at the south end of the downtown core.

HEALTH AND SAFETY

Local hospitals under the jurisdiction of Eastern Health include the **General Hospital** (300 Prince Philip Dr., 709/737-6335), **Janeway Children's Health Centre** (also at 300 Prince Phillip Dr., 709/778-4228), and **St. Clare's Mercy Hospital** (154 LeMarchant Rd., 709/777-5501).

The **Royal Newfoundland Constabulary** (911 or 709/729-8333) deals with police matters within city limits, while the **Royal Canadian Mounted Police** (709/772-5400) protect the rest of the province.

Getting There and Around

Even though St. John's sits on the far eastern edge of the North American continent, it is a transportation hub for air travel through the province and for shipping routes across the Atlantic Ocean.

GETTING THERE
Air

St. John's International Airport (www.stjohnsairport.com) is off Portugal Cove Road, a simple 15-minute drive northwest from downtown. The airport is a large modern facility, with ATMs, a currency exchange center, an information booth (open daily until the arrival of the last flight), a restaurant and lounge, a duty-free shop, a newsstand, and car rental desks for all the major companies (Avis, Budget, Discount, Hertz, National, and Thrifty). Taxis charge a flat rate to any of the major downtown hotels: $32 for the first person, $6 each additional person.

St. John's is served by direct **Air Canada** (709/726-7880 or 888/247-2262, www.aircanada.com) flights from Halifax, Montréal, and Toronto, with connections made through these three cities from its worldwide network. **WestJet** (888/937-8538, www.westjet.com) uses Halifax as its eastern hub, from where regular connections can be made to St. John's. Local airlines include **PAL Airlines** (709/576-3943 or 800/563-2800, www.palairlines.com), with flights between Halifax and St. John's, plus onward flights throughout the province, and **Air Saint-Pierre** (902/873-3566, www.airsaintpierre.com), with daily shuttle services to the St-Pierre and Miquelon Islands.

Car

If you are coming by car from the mainland, you need to get to Sydney, Nova Scotia. From here, two ferry routes cross to Newfoundland. The longer and more expensive option is to catch the ferry from Sydney to Argentia.

Taking this route, you are left with a much shorter drive upon reaching Newfoundland. Downtown St. John's is 130 kilometers (81 miles) northeast of Argentia via Route 100 and Route 1.

The alternative is to catch the ferry from Sydney to Port-aux-Basques, a short trip, but one that leaves you with a 900-kilometer (560-mile) drive across the province to St. John's, an 11-hour drive via the Trans-Canada Highway.

From Halifax, it's 430 kilometers (265 miles) to Sydney, so allow around 22 hours, inclusive of either ferry crossing, to reach St. John's.

Ferry

One of two ferry services to Newfoundland from North Sydney (Nova Scotia) docks at **Argentia,** a 134-kilometer (83-mile) drive southwest of St. John's. Ferries are operated by **Marine Atlantic** (709/227-2431 or 800/341-7981, www.marineatlantic.ca, adult $125, senior $115, child $62, from $253 for vehicles) two times weekly mid-June-late September (at other times of year, you will need to use the Sydney to Port-aux-Basques route). The trip over from the mainland takes 14 hours; dorm beds and cabins are available.

Bus

There is no bus service between the ferry terminal at Argentia and St. John's. For those arriving in Newfoundland via the ferry to Port-aux-Basques, **DRL-LR** (709/263-2171, www.drl-lr.com) operates daily long-haul bus service to St. John's (14 hours, $126 one-way).

GETTING AROUND

Locals complain that downtown parking space is scarce. Not so, the city says, countering that there are 1,500 parking slots at the Municipal Parking Garage on Water Street, other downtown garages, and on the streets. Some 800 street spaces are metered for loonies (the $1 coin) and quarters; when the time is up, the cops are quick to ticket expired meters.

Bus

Metrobus (709/570-2020, www.metrobus. com, adult $2.50, child $2 per sector) operates an extensive bus network that leads from downtown to all outer suburbs. Transfers are valid for 90 minutes of travel in one direction.

Taxi

Cabs wait at the airport ($32 to downtown for one person, then $6 each additional) and also out front of major hotels like the Delta St. John's and Sheraton Hotel Newfoundland. Travel within downtown runs $6-10. Major companies include **City Wide** (709/722-0003), **Jiffy** (709/722-2222), and **Co-op** (709/726-6666).

Car and RV Rental

All major car rental companies are represented in St. John's, but check local restrictions, such as bans on traveling to certain parts of the island and along the TransLabrador Highway.

During July and August, **Islander RV** (709/738-7368 or 888/848-2267, www. islanderrv.com, May-Oct.) charges $250 per day for a two-person camper and from $305 for an RV that sleeps six. Per day, 150 free kilometers (93 miles) are included, and a seven-day minimum rental is required during summer. Rental rates drop to $190-215 per day in the shoulder seasons.

Avalon Peninsula

If sightseeing time is short and you must by-pass the rest of Newfoundland, consider the Avalon Peninsula as a manageable stand-in. Although it is known by a single name, it is actually four peninsulas, two jutting southward and two northward. The city of St. John's sprawls across one. The highlights of the remaining three are covered in this section.

BACCALIEU TRAIL

This route hugs the northern Avalon coastline, winding around Conception Bay to the town of Carbonear and then looping south along the east side of Trinity Bay back to the Trans-Canada Highway. The loop makes an ideal full-day trip from St. John's (around 380 km/235 mi), but accommodations en route may tempt you to stay longer.

Brigus

Picturesque Brigus lies across Conception Bay from Conception Bay South, or around a 50 minutes' drive via the Trans-Canada Highway and Route 63. The town's most famous native

son, Captain Robert Bartlett, was an Arctic explorer who accompanied Robert Peary on his 1908 North Pole expedition. Bartlett's 1820 house is now **Hawthorne Cottage National Historic Site** (corner of South St. and Irishtown Rd., 709/528-4004, mid-May-late June and early Sept.-early Oct. Wed.-Sun. 9:30am-5:30pm, late June-early Sept. daily 9am-6pm, adult $5, senior $4.50, child $3). Built in 1830, the cottage is a rare intact example of the *cottage orné* (decorative) style, with interpretive panels dotting the gardens telling the stories of Bartlett's northern exploits.

Numerous small-town cafés dot the Baccalieu Trail, but none is more welcoming than **Country Corner** (14 Water St., 709/528-1099, May-Oct. daily 10am-6pm, lunches $5.50-9), where highlights include a bowl of steaming cod chowder and the blueberry crisp.

GETTING THERE

Brigus is 10 kilometers (6.2 miles) north of Conception Harbour, a 10-minute drive via Route 60 and about 85 kilometers (53 miles)

Hawthorne Cottage National Historic Site

west of St. Johns, one hour via Route 1 and Route 70.

Cupids

Plantation owner John Guy established Cuper's Cove in 1610, making what is now called Cupids the oldest British settlement in Canada. Artifacts can be seen at the worthwhile **Cupids Legacy Centre** (368 Seaforest Dr., 709/528-1610, www.cupidslegacycentre.ca, early June-early Oct. daily 9:30am-5pm, adult $8.50, senior $7.60, child $4.25), with many modern, interactive displays. Down on the waterfront and within walking distance of the Legacy Centre is the **Plantation Site,** an ongoing dig that continues to unearth the remains of Guy's plantation. Visitors are welcome to view the dig on 20-minute guided tours that leave on demand (book through Cupids Legacy Centre, early June-early Oct. daily 9:30am-5pm, adult $6, senior $4, child $3).

GETTING THERE

Cupids is about 3 kilometers (1.9 miles) north of Brigus via Keatings Road.

Harbour Grace

Once the second-largest town in Newfoundland, Harbour Grace suffered a series of setbacks when seven fires besieged the town over the span of a century. Many of its oldest buildings survived and now make up the **Harbour Grace Heritage District.** Named "Havre de Grace" by the French in the early 16th century, the town boasts both pirates and pilots in its heritage. **Conception Bay Museum** (Water St., 709/596-5465, July-Aug. daily 11am-5pm, first two weeks of Sept. daily noon-4pm, adult $2, child $1) occupies the former site of the lair of Peter Easton, a notorious pirate of the early 1600s. It's in a three-story red-brick building along the harbor front. Three centuries later, on May 20, 1932, Harbour Grace gained fame when Amelia Earhart took off from the local airfield to become the first woman to fly solo across the Atlantic. The grassed runway of the Harbour Grace airfield is now a national historic site.

To get there, follow Military Road from the main street through to the north side of town and take the signposted unpaved road under the highway to the top of the hill.

Before her famous flight, Amelia Earhart stayed at the red-brick **Hotel Harbour Grace** (66 Water St., 709/596-5156, www.hotelharbourgrace.ca, $90-120 s or d), but a better option today is the **Rothesay House Inn** (34 Water St., 709/596-2268 or 877/596-2268, www.rothesay.com, $165-185 s or d), where the four guest rooms have a distinct Victorian-era look. Rates include a cooked breakfast; dinner at 7pm is $49 per person by advance reservation.

GETTING THERE

To get to Harbour Grace from Brigus, you can take Route 75 (32 km/20 mi, 30 minutes) or Route 70 (28 km/17 mi, 30 minutes) north. From St. John's, it's about 110 kilometers (68 miles) west and north along Route 1 and Route 70 to Harbour Grace, a 1.5-hour drive.

Grates Cove

The peninsula's northernmost village, Grates Cove retains the look and feel of Ireland perhaps more than any other Irish-settled community, thanks to the hundreds of rock walls erected as livestock and farm enclosures by early settlers.

Off the eastern end of the peninsula's tip, the **Baccalieu Island Ecological Reserve** shelters 11 species of seabirds, including Leach's storm-petrels, black-legged kittiwakes, gannets, fulmars, and puffins.

GETTING THERE

To get to Grates Cove from Harbour Grace, it's a 75-kilometer (47-mile), one-hour drive north on Route 70. From St. John's, it's about 180 kilometers (112 miles), 2.5 hours, to Grates Cove west along Route 1, then north on Route 75 and Route 70.

Heart's Content

The first successful transatlantic telegraph cables came ashore in 1866 at Heart's Content,

23 kilometers (14.3 miles) northwest of Carbonear. One of the original cables, which extended from Valentia Island on the west coast of Ireland, is still visible at the shoreline. Across the road, the restored **Heart's Content Cable Station** (Rte. 80, 709/583-2160, mid-May-early Oct. daily 9:30am-5pm, adult $6, senior $4, child free) displays some of the original equipment.

GETTING THERE

To get to Heart's Content from Grates Cove, take Route 70 south, then Route 80 south. It's a 60-kilometer (37-mile), 50-minute drive. If you're driving directly to Heart's Content from St. John's, it's a 130-kilometer (81-mile), 1.5-hour drive west along Route 1, then north along Route 75 and Route 74.

Dildo

Best known for its risqué name (thought to have been bestowed by Captain Cook in reference to a phallic offshore island), Dildo lies at the head of Trinity Bay, 12 kilometers (7.5 miles) north of the Trans-Canada Highway. The history of the 19th-century codfish hatchery on Dildo Island—the first commercial hatchery in Canada—is depicted at the **Dildo and Area Interpretation Centre** (Rte. 80, 709/582-2687, June-Sept. daily 10am-6pm, adult $2, child $1), along with a display of Dorset Inuit harpoon tips estimated to be 1,700 years old. Out front is a replica of an 8.5-meter-long (27.9-foot-long) squid pulled from local waters.

High above Trinity Bay, ★ **Inn by the Bay** (78 Front Rd., 709/582-3170 or 888/339-7829, www.dildoinns.com, $129-209 s or d) stacks up as equal to the best B&Bs in St. John's in all regards—with sweeping water views as a free extra. No stone has been left unturned in transforming this 1888 home into a six-room inn, right down to super-comfortable beds topped with feather-filled duvets and striking antiques that fill the veranda sunroom. Rates include a full breakfast in the delightful Sea Level Dining Room, which overlooks the bay.

GETTING THERE

To get to Dildo from Heart's Content, drive south on Route 80 for 45 kilometers (28 miles), a 40-minute drive. To get to Dildo directly from St. John's, take Route 1 west, then Route 80 north, for a total of 100 kilometers (62 miles), 1.5 hours.

ST. JOHN'S TO FERRYLAND

From downtown St. John's, it's a little over 70 kilometers (105 miles), a one-hour drive, to Ferryland, the ideal turnaround point for a day trip from the capital—except that there are a couple of stops en route worth as much time as you can afford.

★ Witless Bay Ecological Reserve

Newfoundland's seabird spectacle spreads across three offshore islands near the **Witless Bay Ecological Reserve,** 30 kilometers (19 miles) south of St. John's. Overwhelming displays of more than a million pairs of Atlantic puffins, Leach's storm-petrels, murres, black-legged kittiwakes, herring gulls, Atlantic razorbills, black guillemots, and black-backed and herring gulls are the attraction here. The season spans May-August and peaks mid-June-mid-July. Whale numbers in local waters have increased dramatically in the last two decades, and this is mirrored in the number of operators running whale-watching trips. Between May and September, you are most likely to see humpbacks, but killer, fin, and minke whales are also present throughout the reserve. Seeing icebergs is also a possibility.

The closest tour operators to St. John's are **O'Brien's Whale and Bird Tours** (Lower Rd., 709/753-4850 or 877/639-4253, adult $60, senior $55, child $32) and **Gatherall's Puffin and Whale Watch** (Northside Rd., 709/334-2887 or 800/419-4253), which are both based at Bay Bulls, 31 kilometers (19 miles) south. O'Brien's is a well-organized operation, complete with a choice of vessels and an onshore gift shop and restaurant.

La Manche Provincial Park

La Manche Provincial Park was established in the 1960s to protect a scenic valley 53 kilometers (33 miles) south of St. John's along Route 10. The valley comes to an abrupt end at a cove surrounded by high cliffs, and here lies the most interesting aspect of the park. In 1840 a small village developed at the head of the cove, complete with a school, a general store, and wooden "flakes" for drying fish. In 1966 a wild winter storm destroyed most of the settlement. The government resettled the residents, and today concrete foundations and a reconstructed suspension bridge are all that remains. To get there, drive down the fire road beyond the park campground; from the gate, it's 1.5 kilometers (0.9 mile) to the cove (allow one hour for the round-trip). The campground (late May-late Sept., $18-28) has 69 campsites spread around two loops. There are no showers or hookups.

FERRYLAND

This east coast port, 70 kilometers (105 miles) south of St. John's, is one of Canada's oldest fishing villages, and the site of the colony founded by Sir George Calvert in 1621. To him, the region was akin to King Arthur's heavenly paradise, a haven for the beleaguered Roman Catholics from England. Or so he thought. Once settled at Ferryland, Calvert's colony endured diminishing supplies and harsh winters. His wife and son and a number of other colonists headed south to Maryland, and Calvert followed, leaving the plantation and the name of Avalon. Today, Ferryland is one of the most attractive communities on the Avalon Peninsula, but an archaeological dig in the heart of the community draws most visitors.

TOP EXPERIENCE

★ Colony of Avalon

An ongoing archaeological dig and a sparkling interpretive center combine to make the drive from St. John's worthwhile. The Colony of Avalon Visitor Centre (709/432-3200, mid-June-mid-Sept. daily 10am-6pm, adult $15, senior $12, student $11.50) is a big two-story building where display panels tell of Ferryland's long history, with the help of hundreds of artifacts used by the original settlers. Upstairs is a laboratory where you can watch archaeologists at work documenting the finds. The herb garden out front replicates one from the era of the original Colony of Avalon.

From the interpretive center, it's a short walk through the modern-day village to the dig site, where you can watch archaeologists at work weekdays mid-June-mid-October. Admission to the visitors center includes a 90-minute guided walk around the site, where you can see the remnants of a cobblestone street and the site of Calvert's mansion.

Shamrock Festival

The two-day Shamrock Festival (709/432-2052, www.ssfac.com) crowds the town on the last full weekend in July. Thousands of music fans gather within a roped-off area in the heart of the village (along with a few hundred on a distant hillside) to listen to some of Newfoundland's top musicians. The atmosphere is both welcoming and unforgettable—you'll find yourself surrounded by the lilt of Irish accents, the smells of an outdoor fair mixed with fresh ocean air, and the sounds of foot-stomping Celtic music. A plastic cup of Quidi Vidi beer rounds out the experience.

Food

Ferryland doesn't have a great deal of visitor services, but as most visitors are day-trippers from the capital, this isn't a problem.

Earn your lunch by walking up to the headland, through town, to reach ★ Lighthouse Picnics (709/363-7456, mid-June-mid-Sept. Wed.-Sun. 11:30am-4:30pm, adult $26, child $13), which operates out of the red-and-white 1870 lighthouse. Each picnic consists of a sandwich, salad, a dessert, and freshly squeezed lemonade, with options such as

1: a whale greeting one of O'Brien's Whale and Bird Tours; 2: a guided tour through the Colony of Avalon

crab cakes and baked-daily muffins. Picnic baskets—along with blankets—are supplied. Reservations in summer are a must, so call ahead or visit www.lighthousepicnics.ca for a link to their email.

Getting There

Ferryland is about 70 kilometers (105 miles) south of St. John's, a one-hour drive via Route 10.

CONTINUING ALONG THE IRISH LOOP

From Ferryland, Route 10 continues south for 58 kilometers (36 miles), then heads west and north as Route 90 to St. Catherines. From this point, you can head south to Cape St. Mary's or north past Salmonier Nature Park back to the Trans-Canada Highway. This comprises the Irish Loop. While almost 50 percent of Newfoundlanders are of Irish descent, the strong accents and Celtic traditions are more prevalent here than elsewhere in the province.

Mistaken Point Ecological Reserve

At the southern end of the Avalon Peninsula, **Mistaken Point Ecological Reserve** lies alongside a remote coastline. To explore the area, turn off Route 10 at Portugal Cove South and follow the unmarked gravel road for 16 kilometers (9.9 miles) to Long Beach, where the reserve's gently rolling headland stretches to the sea. Bring a warm jacket to fend off the strong winds, and be ready for thick fog banks June-mid-July. Hikers enjoy the trails that meander across the reserve, and photographers relish the offshore boulders and turbulent surf. The rocks at the ecological reserve, acclaimed as one of Canada's most important fossil sites, contain impressions of 20 different species of multicellular marine creatures that lived 620 million years ago.

Salmonier Nature Park

Salmonier Nature Park, on Route 90 halfway between the Trans-Canada Highway and St. Catherines (709/229-7189, June-Aug. daily 10am-5pm, Sept. daily 10am-3pm, free) is well worth searching out. A 2-kilometer (1.2-mile) boardwalk and wood-chip trail runs through a sample forest and across bogs, which back up to the Avalon Wilderness Reserve. Moose, caribou, lynx, bald eagles, snowy owls, otters, beavers, mink, and other indigenous species are exhibited in natural-habitat enclosures.

CAPE SHORE

The Cape Shore juts into Placentia Bay west of the main body of the Avalon Peninsula. It's 215 kilometers (133 miles) from the Trans-Canada Highway, south through Salmonier to St. Bride's, and back to the Trans-Canada Highway, 33 kilometers (20 miles) west of the starting point. The highlight of the region is the bird colony at Cape St. Mary's.

Argentia

Argentia operated as a U.S. naval base between 1941 and 1994, with up to 20,000 American servicemen stationed there during World War II. Ferries operate out of one of the original ports, but most buildings have been demolished. The entire site is wide open and there are few restrictions to wandering around, with unofficial trails leading to lookouts, abandoned bunkers, and good vantage points for watching seabirds.

Beyond the ferry terminal is **Argentia Provincial Visitor Information Centre** (709/227-5272), which opens in conjunction with ferry arrivals. From Argentia, drive south through Placentia to reach Cape St. Mary's or head northwest along Route 100 to the Trans-Canada Highway, which leads into downtown St. John's.

GETTING THERE

Argentia is 8 kilometers (5 miles) north of Placentia (via Charter Avenue) and 130 kilometers (81 miles) southwest of St. John's, a 1.5-hour drive via the Trans-Canada Highway and Route 100.

One of two ferry services to Newfoundland from North Sydney (Nova Scotia) docks at Argentia. Ferries are operated by **Marine**

Atlantic (709/227-2431 or 800/341-7981, www.marine-atlantic.ca, adult $125, senior $115, child $62, from $253 for vehicles) two times weekly mid-June-late September (at other times of year, you will need to use the Sydney to Port-aux-Basques route). The trip over from the mainland takes 14 hours; dorm beds and cabins are available.

Placentia

France chose the magnificent coastal forest area overlooking Placentia Bay for its early island capital, Plaisance, and colonists and soldiers settled here in 1662. The early military fortification crowned a high hill overlooking the port at what is now Jerseyside. The French launched assaults on St. John's from Le Gaillardin, the first small fort of 1692, and then from Fort Royal, the massive stone fortress built the following year. England gained possession of the settlement in 1713 and renamed it Placentia. The hill on which the fortress stands became known as Castle Hill. Exhibits at the visitors center of **Castle Hill National Historic Site** (709/227-2401, June-Aug. daily 10am-6pm, adult $4, senior $3.50, child $2) document French and English history at Placentia. Guided tours are offered in summer. Picnic tables are available, and trails run along the peak's fortifications and the bay's stone beach.

GETTING THERE

Placentia is 130 kilometers (81 miles) southwest of St. John's, 8 kilometers (5 miles) south of Argentia via Charter Avenue. Get there via the Trans-Canada Highway and Route 100.

★ Cape St. Mary's Ecological Reserve

The **Cape St. Mary's Ecological Reserve** lies at the Cape Shore's southern tip, 16 kilometers (9.9 miles) down an unpaved road off Route 100. If you're traveling down from St. John's, allow at least 2.5 hours; from the ferry terminal at Argentia, head south for 73 kilometers (45 miles); allow at least an hour. At the end of the road is an **interpretive center** (709/277-1666, mid-May-early Oct. daily 9am-5pm, free). From this point, a 1-kilometer (0.6-mile) trail leads across the steeply banked headland to North America's most accessible bird sanctuary. You'll hear the birds long before they come into view. And then all of a sudden, Bird Rock emerges in front of you—a 60-meter-high (197-foot-high) sea stack jammed with some 60,000 seabirds. The rocky pyramid seems to come alive with fluttering, soaring birds, whose noisy calls drift out to sea on the breezes. Expect to see northern gannets in one of North America's largest colonies (10,000 nesting pairs), common and thick-billed murres, and black-legged kittiwakes, along with some razorbills, black guillemots, great black-backed gulls, and herring gulls.

Warning: The trail is often slippery and comes very close to precipitous cliffs, so be very careful. Also, be prepared for bad weather by dressing warmly and in layers.

The closest accommodation to Cape St. Mary's is **Bird Island Resort** (64 Main Rd., 709/337-2450, www.birdislandresort.com, $85-130 s or d), in St. Bride's, 20 kilometers (12.4 miles) north. Overlooking Placentia Bay, the "resort" comprises five motel rooms, 15 kitchen-equipped cottages, lawn games, a convenience store, and a launderette.

GETTING THERE

The reserve is 73 kilometers (45 miles) south of Argentia, a one-hour drive via Route 100. It's 170 kilometers (105 miles) southwest of St. John's, 2.5 hours via Routes 1, 90, and 92.

Central and Western Newfoundland

Visualize the island of Newfoundland as not one island but two, similarly shaped but different in size—a mammoth main island and a smaller one. This chapter covers the former—everything west of the Avalon Peninsula.

The "two islands" are linked by an isthmus that begins an hour's drive west from St. John's. Beyond the turnoff to the delightfully named village of Come by Chance, the Trans-Canada Highway enters the meaty part of the island. Think of this highway as a long Main Street. The horseshoe-shaped route edges the interior and connects the Avalon Peninsula with Channel-Port-aux-Basques—a 905-kilometer (560-mile) journey. Well-marked side roads split off the main highway and whisk drivers onto the peninsulas. Aside from the Burin Peninsula's

Highlights

Look for ★ to find recommended sights, activities, dining, and lodging.

★ **Trinity:** Step back in time at this quintessential Newfoundland village with brightly painted, saltbox-style houses lining its narrow lanes (page 384).

★ **Iceberg-Viewing:** You can see icebergs from various points along the northern Newfoundland coast, but one of the most reliable spots is Twillingate (page 392).

★ **Tablelands:** You'll be lost for words scrambling through the moonlike terrain here (page 405).

★ **Boat Tours in Gros Morne National Park:** Take to Western Brook Pond for neck-straining views of an ancient, glacially carved fjord (page 406).

★ **Thrombolites of Flowers Cove:** Never heard of thrombolites? Most people haven't. But don't blink—even though these rare fossils occur in only two places on Earth, they're not signposted as you drive north along the Viking Trail (page 413).

★ **L'Anse aux Meadows:** Follow in the footsteps of the Vikings by exploring the tip of the Northern Peninsula (page 415).

★ **Burnt Cape Ecological Reserve:** This remote limestone outcrop is home to more rare

and endangered species of plants than anywhere else in Atlantic Canada (page 417).

Central and Western Newfoundland

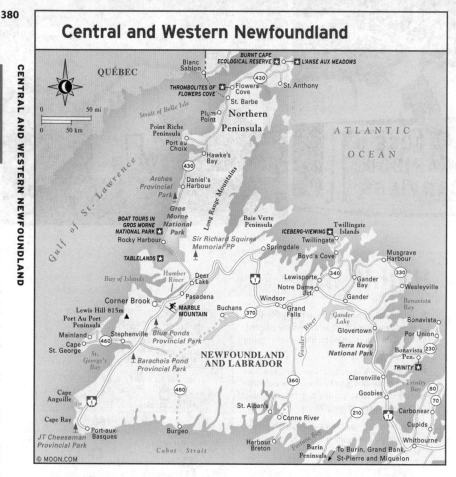

efficient Route 210 and the Northern Peninsula's relatively uncomplicated Route 430, the other side roads to the peninsulas and coastlines meander interminably.

The appeal of raw wilderness aside, this vast part of Newfoundland caters to numerous interests. Majestic icebergs wander into fjords and coves on the northern coastlines. All along the seacoasts, photogenic lighthouses perch atop precipitous cliffs overlooking the surf. Sightseers line up for boat tours led by knowledgeable skippers or academically trained guides, whose vessels nose among whales, seals, and icebergs. If you're interested in a quick trip to France, you can visit a remnant of the long-ago age of exploration: Fortune on the Burin Peninsula is just a two-hour boat ride from St-Pierre, the capital of France's archipelago province of St-Pierre and Miquelon. The ancient world heaved and formed richly diverse landscapes at Gros Morne National Park. A millennium ago, the Vikings arrived and established a coastal camp (North America's first European

Previous: lobster pots; moose and caribou carvings; Lobster Cove Head Lighthouse.

settlement), now re-created at L'Anse aux Meadows National Historic Site.

381

CENTRAL AND WESTERN NEWFOUNDLAND
BURIN PENINSULA AND VICINITY

PLANNING YOUR TIME

While the previous chapter covered a small corner of the province, in this chapter, distances will prove to be important when planning how and where to spend your time. For example, from St. John's, it's 640 kilometers (395 miles) to Deer Lake, 905 kilometers (560 miles) to the ferry terminal at Port-aux-Basques, and almost 1,100 kilometers (680 miles) to St. Anthony at the tip of the Northern Peninsula.

The time you spend in the central and western regions of Newfoundland obviously ties in with your travels to St. John's and the Avalon Peninsula. Traveling to the Bonavista Peninsula and villages like **Trinity** can be a two-day trip from the capital, but travel any farther west and you're committed to driving clear across the island. If you're catching the ferry from Port-aux-Basques, allow at least five days to get there from the capital. This would allow a night at Trinity, a detour from the Trans-Canada Highway to go **iceberg-viewing** at Twillingate, and a couple of days exploring **Gros Morne National Park,** where highlights include hiking through the **Tablelands** and taking a boat tour on **Western Brook Pond.**

What this five-day suggestion doesn't take into consideration is the **Northern Peninsula,** which is one of my favorite places in all of Canada. Its 470 amazing kilometers (290 miles) stretch from Deer Lake to the tip of the peninsula. With time spent exploring the region's beautiful coastline, as well as stops at the **thrombolites of Flowers Cove, L'Anse aux Meadows,** and **Burnt Cape Ecological Reserve,** add at least four days to your cross-province schedule from St. John's to Port-aux-Basques. If you're returning a rental vehicle to St. John's, give the stretch of highway south of Deer Lake a miss, but still add two days to the total trip. By flying in and out of Deer Lake, you can concentrate your time in Gros Morne National Park and the Northern Peninsula—an ideal scenario for outdoors lovers.

Burin Peninsula and Vicinity

The 200-kilometer-long (124-mile-long) Burin Peninsula angles like a kicking boot off Newfoundland's southeastern coastline. The peninsula's interior is a primeval, barren moonscape—if the moon had water, that is, for every hollow and depression in these barrens is filled with bogs, marshes, and ponds. But the coastline rims the edge of the Grand Banks, historically one of the most fertile fishing regions in North America. Along the shore are scattered fishing villages and several burgeoning towns. Marystown, one of the fastest-growing towns in the province, is supported by one of the largest fish-processing plants in eastern Canada, and its shipyard supplies vessels to the booming North Atlantic oil industry. St. Lawrence is the exception to the region; as Canada's only producer of the mineral fluorite, it has relied on mining as much as on marine-related industries. For the most part, however, fishing has been the mainstay of the peninsula's communities since the 1500s.

BOAT HARBOUR

A cottage industry here produces hand-hooked scenic mats made of reused fabric scraps. The mats and other homemade wares are sold at reasonable prices at the **Tea Rose** (Rte. 210, 709/443-2580, summer daily noon-7pm), about 1 kilometer (0.6 mile) south of the Boat Harbour intersection, where you can also get light meals.

Getting There

Boat Harbour is 270 kilometers (165 miles)

west of St. John's, a 3.5-hour drive via the Trans-Canada Highway and Route 210.

BURIN

Near the "heel" of the boot-shaped peninsula, Burin, settled in the early 1700s, lies in the lee of offshore islands. The islands generally protect the town from the open Atlantic, though they weren't enough to stop a destructive tidal wave in 1929. The islands also were a refuge for pirates, who could escape their pursuers among the dangerous channels. During his mapping expeditions of the Newfoundland coast in the 1760s, Captain James Cook used Burin as a seasonal headquarters. A high hill above the town, where watch was kept for smugglers and illegal fishing, still bears his name—Cook's Lookout.

Over the second weekend of July, the **Festival of Folk Song and Dance** (709/891-2655, day pass $8 pp) is a three-day extravaganza of Irish-inspired music making, children's games, seafood meals, and craft shows and sales. The festival ranks among Newfoundland's most popular heritage events.

A comfortable, no-frills accommodation is the **Burin Peninsula Motel** (33 Grandview Blvd., 709/832-2180, www.burinpeninsulamotel.com, $109 s or d). The 10 guest rooms are basic and come with small TVs, but do have wireless Internet.

Getting There

Burin is about 60 kilometers (37 miles) south of Boat Harbour, a one-hour drive via Route 210. It's about 310 kilometers (190 miles) southwest of St. John's, 4-4.5 hours via Route 1 and Route 210.

GRAND BANK

Grand Bank, on the "toe" of the Burin boot, is the best known of the peninsula's towns. Settled in the 1650s by the French and taken over by the British in the early 1700s, Grand Bank (pop. 2,500) has always been associated with the rich fishing grounds of the same name, the Grand Banks to the south and west of Newfoundland.

The **Heritage Walk** visits the province's largest number of Queen Anne-style homes outside of St. John's. The historic district's architectural treasures include the 1905 **Masonic Lodge,** the 1917 **Thorndyke House** (with its Masonic symbolism integrated into the interior design), and the **George C. Harris House** (16 Water St., 709/832-1574, July-Aug. daily 10am-4pm, adult $3). The latter is a 1908 Queen Anne building housing the town's museum. Complementing the Heritage Walk are the Nature Trail, leading to a lookout and salmon spawning beds, and the Marine Trail, which closely follows the shoreline of Fortune Bay to the **Mariners' Memorial.**

After extensive renovations in 2011, the **Provincial Seamen's Museum** (54 Marine Dr., 709/832-1484, May-Sept. Mon.-Sat. 9am-4:30pm, Sun. noon-4:30pm, adult $2.50) is difficult to miss. Styled as an angular white sailing ship, the museum has exhibits on the Grand Banks fisheries and maritime history, with photographs, ship models, and other artifacts.

Getting There

Grand Bank is almost 60 kilometers (37 miles) west of Burin, a one-hour drive via Routes 210 and 222. It's 360 kilometers (225 miles) southwest of St. John's, 4.5 hours via Route 1 and Route 210.

ST-PIERRE AND MIQUELON

Centuries of fierce British and French battles ended in the mid-1700s with Britain's dominance firmly stamped across eastern Canada—*except* on St-Pierre and Miquelon, a trio of islands 25 kilometers (15.5 miles) south of the Newfoundland mainland. Today, this geopolitical oddity is not part of Atlantic Canada, but rather a *département* of France and the last toehold of France's once-vast holdings in North America.

St-Pierre and Miquelon are French in all

regards. Unlike traveling to French regions of Canada, there is a lot more than a foreign language to deal with. Canadians must show photo identification, such as a driver's license or passport. Entry for all other nationalities mirrors entry requirements for France; in other words, a passport is required for U.S. citizens.

Legal tender is the euro (€), but some (not all) businesses accept U.S. and Canadian dollars at fair bank rates. Electrical current throughout St-Pierre and Miquelon is 220 volts, although the bigger hotels have converters.

The islands even have their own time zone—30 minutes ahead of Newfoundland time.

Sights

St-Pierre and Miquelon consists of three islands, with a combined land area of about 242 square kilometers (93 square miles). Tiny **St-Pierre** is the name of the smallest island, as well as a bustling town (pop. 6,300). The topography of this triangular island includes hills, bogs, and ponds in the north, and lowlands in the south. The larger islands are **Miquelon,** which is home to a village of the same name (pop. 600), and uninhabited **Petite Miquelon** (also called Langdale). These two islands are joined by a sand-dune isthmus.

The capital, St-Pierre, is the most popular destination. It dates to the early 1600s, when French fishermen, mainly from Brittany, worked offshore. The port's mood and appearance are pervasively French, with bistros, cafés, bars, brasseries, wrought-iron balconies, and an abundance of Gallic pride. St-Pierre borders a sheltered harbor filled with colorful fishing boats and backed by narrow lanes that radiate uphill from the harbor. The cemetery, two blocks inland from rue du 11 Novembre, has an interesting arrangement of aboveground graves, similar to those in New Orleans.

One of the islands' greatest attractions, of course, is the low duty rates on French wines, and other goods. Visitors may bring back $200 worth of duty-free purchases after a 48-hour visit. You'll find shops with French wines, perfumes, and jewelry.

Food

Make your way through the streets of St-Pierre and it's difficult not to be tempted by the sweet smells coming from the many patisseries and cafés. A favorite is **Les Delices de Josephine** (10 rue du Général Leclerc, 508/41-20-27, Mon.-Sat. 11:30am-6pm, lunches €6.50-11), which has delicious coffee, a great selection of teas, pastries made daily from scratch, and a selection of hot lunch items such as quiche.

One of the best choices for a casual meal is **Le Feu de Braise** (14 rue Albert Briand, 508/41-91-60, daily noon-1:30pm and 7pm-9:30pm, €15-21), a bright room offering a menu dominated by classic French bistro-style dishes.

Accommodations

Because the number of guest rooms is limited, make all lodging arrangements before arriving.

For its beautiful rooms and friendly atmosphere, my favorite island accommodation is **Auberge Saint-Pierre** (16 rue Georges Daguerre, 508/41-40-86, www.aubergesaintpierre.fr, from €131 s or d). A breakfast of hot and cold French specialties is an additional €10.50 per person.

Among the dozen small hotels, pensions, and B&Bs, the largest lodging is the 43-room **Hôtel Robert** (2 rue du 11 Novembre, 508/41-24-19, www.hotelrobert.com, €90-175 s or d), along the harbor front (only the most expensive rooms have water views) and within walking distance of the ferry wharf. Having hosted the American gangster Al Capone in the 1920s, this three-story lodging itself oozes historic charm, yet the renovated rooms have contemporary furnishings.

Information

Once on the island, the best source of

information is the **St-Pierre & Miquelon Tourist Office** (rue Antoine Soucy, 508/41-02-00, www.tourisme-saint-pierre-et-miquelon.com). The website has links to island accommodations as well as tour bundles that include accommodations.

Getting There

Air Saint Pierre (902/873-3566, www.airsaintpierre.com) flies year-round between St-Pierre and St. John's for $360-420 round-trip. The airline also flies into St-Pierre from Halifax and Montréal.

St. Pierre Ferry (709/832-3455 or 855/832-3455; www.saintpierreferry.ca, round-trip adult €73, senior €68, child €49) operates between Fortune, on the Burin Peninsula, and St-Pierre once or twice daily July-August and four days a week April-June and September. The trip takes around 90 minutes each way. In 2018, two new ferries began serving the islands, but at the time of publication there was no vehicle-loading facility in Fortune; this may change, so check the website if you'd like to bring your vehicle to the island.

Bonavista Peninsula

The Bonavista Peninsula rises off the eastern coastline as a broad, bent finger covered with verdant woods, farmlands, and rolling hills. Paved Route 230 runs along the peninsula's length, from the Trans-Canada Highway to the town of Bonavista at the tip; Route 235 returns to Highway 1 along the peninsula's west side.

CLARENVILLE

Founded in 1890, Clarenville, along the Trans-Canada Highway, 190 kilometers (118 miles) from St. John's, serves as the gateway to the Bonavista Peninsula. The town of 6,000 is relatively new compared to the rest of Newfoundland and offers few reasons to stop other than to rest your head for the night.

Along the Trans-Canada Highway are two larger motels. From St. John's, the first of these is the **Clarenville Inn** (134 Trans-Canada Hwy., 709/466-7911 or 877/466-7911, www.clarenvilleinn.ca, from $120 s or d), which fronts the highway, offering 63 rooms with wireless Internet and an outdoor heated pool. One of the best things about this lodging is **Stellar Kitchen,** a restaurant with sweeping views across the town and bay (daily for breakfast, lunch, and dinner, $15-25). In town itself, the **Restland Motel** (Memorial Dr.,

709/466-7636, www.restlandmotel.ca, $130-140 s or d) has a mix of 24 midsize air-conditioned motel rooms and kitchen-equipped units. On-site is a restaurant and pub, and across the road is a shopping mall.

Getting There

Clarenville is 190 kilometers (118 miles) northwest of St. John's, a two-hour drive via Route 1.

★ TRINITY

Just three years after John Cabot bumped into Newfoundland, Portugal commissioned mariners Gaspar and Miguel Côrte-Real to search for a passage to China. That mission failed, but Gaspar accidentally sailed into Trinity Bay on Trinity Sunday in 1501. In 1558, merchants from England's West Country founded a settlement on the same site, making it even older than St. Augustine, Florida.

The attractive village of Trinity (pop. 400) has changed little since the late 1800s. White picket fences, small gardens, and historic homes are everywhere. The best photo vantage point of Trinity is from the Route 239 coastal spur, the narrow road also known as Courthouse Road. The road peels across the headlands, turns a quick corner, and suddenly overlooks the seaport. Ease into the turn so you can savor the view. (To get a photograph, park your car in the village and walk back up the road.) Once down in the village proper, park your car and explore on foot.

Sights

The **Trinity Visitor Centre** (Rte. 239, 709/729-0592, mid-May-mid-Oct. daily 9:30am-5pm), in a handsomely restored building, has historical exhibits about the village. **Mercantile Premises** (West St., 709/464-2042, mid-May-mid-Oct. daily 9:30am-5pm) is a restored 1820s general store. In the 1800s, Emma Hiscock and her two daughters lived in the restored mustard-and-green **Hiscock House** (Church Rd., mid-May-mid-Oct. daily 9:30am-5pm), a block inland from the government wharf. They operated a forge, retail store, and telegraph office in the saltbox-style house. These three attractions are operated by the province; combined admission is adult $6, child $3.

The following buildings, scattered through the village, are looked after by the **Trinity Historical Society** (709/464-3599, www.trinityhistoricalsociety.com, mid-May-mid-Oct. daily 9:30am-5pm, $20 for all four buildings plus the three detailed above, children free). **Lester Garland House** is an imposing Georgian-style red-brick mansion that has been restored to its 1820s appearance and now houses a museum. The **Green Family Forge** (Church Rd.), in a restored 1895 building, is a blacksmith museum displaying more than 1,500 tools, products, and other artifacts of the blacksmith trade. Also on Church Road is an 1880 saltbox-style house that now serves as the **Trinity Society Museum,** displaying more than 2,000 fishing, mercantile, medical, and firefighting artifacts. Although there has been a cooperage (barrel maker) in Trinity since the 1700s, **The Cooperage** is a modern replica of what a similar business would have looked like in times gone by. In summer, you can watch coopers here creating barrels and other wooden objects using traditional techniques.

Entertainment and Events

The summer solstice kicks off Rising Tide Theatre's **Summer in the Bight** (709/464-3232, www.risingtidetheatre.com), presenting original musical and dramatic productions written and performed by some of Newfoundland's best writers and actors. The theater is a re-created fishing shed on Green's Point, at the eastern side of the village. Performances are scheduled 2-3 times

Many of Trinity's historic buildings are open to the public.

a week and cost $28.50 ($43.50 for the dinner theater).

Accommodations

Right on the water, the ★ **Artisan Inn** (57 High St., 709/464-3377 or 877/464-7700, www.trinityvacations.com, May-mid-Oct., $150-220 s or d) is set up as a retreat for artists—if views from the oceanfront studio don't inspire you, nothing will—but everyone is welcome. It offers two en suite rooms and a kitchen-equipped suite. The adjacent Campbell House holds an additional three guest rooms. Rates include breakfast, and dinner is available at the in-house **Twine Loft** with advance notice, with set menus offered at 5:30pm and 7:45pm seatings.

Getting There

Trinity is 70 kilometers (43 miles) northeast of Clarenville along Route 230, a one-hour drive. From St. John's, Trinity is 270 kilometers (165 miles) west, 3.5 hours on Route 1 and north on Route 230.

PORT UNION

The only town in Canada to have been established by a labor union, Port Union lies 30 kilometers (19 miles) past Trinity. The oldest part of town is across the bay from the fish-processing plant. Turn right as you enter the village and you'll soon find yourself in Port Union South, passing through a narrow street of boarded-up company warehouses. Beyond these is **Port Union Historical Museum** (Main St., 709/469-2728, mid-June-Aug. daily 11am-5pm, adult $2, child $1), housed in a waterfront 1917 railway station. Once you've read up on the town's history, backtrack and take a left turn through a narrow rock cleft to Bungalow Hill for sweeping harbor views.

Getting There

From Trinity, it's 30 kilometers (19 miles) northeast on Route 230 to Port Union, a 30-minute drive. To get to Port Union from St. John's, take Highway 1 west and Route 230

north for a total of 290 kilometers (180 miles), four hours.

BONAVISTA

Fifty kilometers (31 miles) up Route 230 from Trinity, Bonavista (pop. 5,000) is a surprisingly large town that sprawls across the far reaches of the Bonavista Peninsula. The town began in the 1600s as a French fishing port, but many believe **Cape Bonavista,** 6 kilometers (3.7 miles) north of town, was the first landfall of Giovanni Caboto (better known as John Cabot), who visited the region in 1497.

Sights

Downtown Bonavista centers on a harbor filled with fishing boats and surrounded by a colorful array of homes and businesses. The historic highlight is **Ryan Premises** (corner of Ryan's Hill and Old Catalina Rd., 709/468-1600, June-Aug. daily 10am-6pm, adult $4, senior $3.50, child $2), where merchant James Ryan established his salt-fish enterprise in the mid-1800s. The site's collection of white clapboard buildings includes a fish store and a re-created retail shop. Across the road is the original manager's residence. All buildings are filled with exhibits and artifacts of the era. In the salt shed, local crafters demonstrate such skills as furniture making; their goods can be purchased in the retail shop.

Signposted through town, the 1871 **Mockbeggar Plantation** (Mockbeggar Rd., 709/468-7300, mid-May-mid-Oct. daily 9:30am-5pm, adult $6, senior $4, child $3) is a whitewashed waterfront building surrounded by a white picket fence. It has been a residence, carpenter's shop, and fish store.

Beyond Mockbeggar Plantation, the photogenic 1843 **Cape Bonavista Lighthouse** (Rte. 230, 709/468-7444, mid-May-early-Oct. daily 9:30am-5pm, adult $6, senior $4, child $3) crowns a steep and rocky headland. The keeper's quarters inside the red-and-white-striped tower have been restored to the 1870

1: a performance by Summer in the Bight;
2: looking down on the Artisan Inn

period. A climb up steep steps leads to the original catoptric light with Argand oil burners and reflectors.

Accommodations

Bonavista makes a pleasant day trip from Trinity, but if you want to stay longer, the best option is one of the four **Oceanside Cabins** (195 Cape Shore Rd., 709/468-7771, $135-155 s or d), with basic kitchens and Wi-Fi.

Getting There

Allow 20 minutes to reach Bonavista from Port Union, which is 20 kilometers (12.4 miles) south via Route 230. To get to Bonavista from St. John's, take Highway 1 west and Route 230 north for a total of 310 kilometers (190 miles), just over four hours.

Clarenville to Deer Lake

It's 450 kilometers (280 miles) from Clarenville to Deer Lake. The Trans-Canada Highway linking these two towns cuts across the interior in a rambling inland path, sometimes angling north to touch a deeply carved bay or reaching into the interior to amble amid the plateau's seemingly endless stretches of tree-blanketed hills. The best chance to get up close and personal with this region is at Terra Nova National Park, but there are also many worthwhile detours, such as to Twillingate, famous for its iceberg-watching tours.

TERRA NOVA NATIONAL PARK

The Trans-Canada Highway enters **Terra Nova National Park** 35 kilometers (22 miles) north of Clarenville, and for the next 50 kilometers (31 miles) it travels within the park boundary. But to really see the park, divert from the highway to remote bodies of fish-filled freshwater, through forests inhabited by moose and bears, and to the rugged coastline where kayakers glide through protected waters and bald eagles soar overhead.

Park Entry

You don't need a pass to drive through the national park, but if you plan on stopping for any reason, you must pay admission (adult $6, senior $5, child $3). Your payment is valid until 4pm the following day.

Park Visitor Centre

Make your first stop the **Park Visitor Centre** (709/533-2942, mid-May-June and Sept.-early-Oct. Thurs.-Mon. 10am-4pm, July-Aug. daily 10am-6pm, free with park admission). Overlooking Newman Sound at Salton's Brook, it is 1 kilometer (0.6 mile) off the Trans-Canada Highway, 35 kilometers (22 miles) north of where it first enters the park. The center features small aquariums, touch tanks, a live feed from an underwater camera, exhibits on the various marine habitats within the park, interactive computer displays, and films, plus a restaurant and gift shop. The center's gift shop sells topographical maps of the park and stocks books about the province's flora, fauna, and attractions.

Hiking

More than a dozen trails thread through the park, providing some 60 kilometers (37 miles) of hiking. Most are uncomplicated loop routes that meander easily for an hour's walk beneath tree canopies. From the Park Visitor Centre, the 1-kilometer (0.6-mile) **Heritage Trail** leads along Salton's Brook, and a 3-kilometer (1.9-mile) one-way trail leads to picturesque and quiet **Blue Hill Pond.** Another 3-kilometer (1.9-mile) trail follows the edge of **Sandy Pond,** starting from 13 kilometers (8.1 miles) south of the Park Visitor Centre. The longest trek, the 55-kilometer (34-mile) **Outport Trail,** requires backcountry camping skills. Most hikers spend one or two nights on the trail, which is notable for the opportunities it affords to see icebergs and whales.

Water Sports

Take a break from the saltwater by planning to spend time at **Sandy Pond,** a shallow body of water 13 kilometers (8.1 miles) south of the Park Visitor Centre and 12 kilometers (7.5 miles) north of the southern park boundary. This day-use area has canoe and kayak rentals (709/677-2221, $10 for 30 minutes), allows swimming, and is encircled by a 3-kilometer (1.9-mile) walking trail (allow one hour).

Food and Accommodations

While there are no accommodations within park boundaries, the following two options lie on the edge of the park.

The village of Charlottetown occupies a pocket of oceanfront land 15 kilometers (9.3 miles) north of the park, outside the official park boundary. Here you'll find the trim **Clode Sound Motel** (709/664-3146, www.clodesound.com, May-Oct., $120-150 s or d). It has 18 rooms and a three-bedroom cottage ($220), an outdoor swimming pool, a playground, a tennis court, a wood-fired barbecue, and wireless Internet. Also on the premises is a highly regarded restaurant (summer daily 8am-10pm) that serves wonderful desserts created with apples from the motel's 90-year-old orchard.

Just beyond the south end of the park is **Terra Nova Resort** (Trans-Canada Hwy., 709/543-2525, www.terranovaresort.ca, May-Oct., from $165 s or d), a full-service resort built alongside the Twin Rivers Golf Course, where golfers get to walk some of Canada's finest fairways for the bargain price of $60 midweek and $69 on weekends. Other amenities include tennis courts, an outdoor heated pool, hiking trails, the **Clode Sound Dining Room** (May-Oct. daily for breakfast, lunch, and dinner, $27-36), and a pub. The 83 guest rooms feature solid furnishings and a contemporary feel. Children are catered to with

a schedule of activities that includes treasure hunts, craft sessions, and picnic lunches.

Camping

Wooded **Newman Sound Campground** (tents $28, hookups $32) has 387 full- and semi-serviced campsites, kitchen shelters, heated washrooms with hot showers, a Nature House (June-Sept. daily 10am-5pm), a launderette, and a daily interpretive program. Reservations are taken for 40 percent of the sites through **Parks Canada** (877/737-3783, www.pccamping.ca). The cost is $11 per reservation, plus the camping fee. The campground turnoff is 30 kilometers (19 miles) north of the southern park boundary. A 4.5-kilometer (2.8-mile) trail along Newman Sound links the campground with the Park Visitor Centre.

From the park's northern edge, head 5 kilometers (3.1 miles) east on Route 310 to reach **Malady Head Campground** ($22.50 per site). The facility has a kitchen/activity area and a playground.

Getting There

The entrance to Terra Nova National Park is 70 kilometers (43 miles) north of Clarenville, a 40-minute drive via Highway 1. To get to the park from St. John's, take Highway 1 west and north for 250 kilometers (155 miles), three hours.

GANDER

The town of Gander (population 11,500) is halfway between Newfoundland's two largest cities (350 km/215 mi from St. John's and 357 km/220 mi from Corner Brook). It was founded in 1951, when the military decided to convert Gander Airport to civilian operations, and so it's fitting that the main attractions today revolve around air travel.

Gateway to North America

When aircraft cross the Atlantic Ocean from Europe, they enter North American airspace somewhere off the coast of Newfoundland. In the early days of aviation, this meant that the planes needed somewhere to refuel, and so

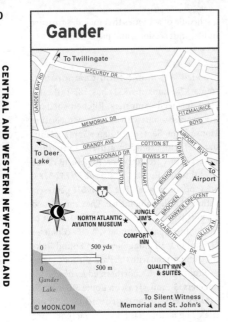

Gander

To Twillingate
MCCURDY DR
GANDER BAY RD
MEMORIAL DR
FITZMAURICE
BOYD
GRANDY AVE
COTTON ST
To Deer Lake
MACDONALD DR
BOWES ST
HAMILTON
EARHART
BISHOP RD
LINDBERGH
AIRPORT BLVD
To Airport
FRASER
BROCHEN
HAWKER CRESCENT
ELIZABETH
SULLIVAN
JUNGLE JIM'S
NORTH ATLANTIC AVIATION MUSEUM
COMFORT INN
0   500 yds
0   500 m
QUALITY INN & SUITES
Gander Lake
To Silent Witness Memorial and St. John's
© MOON.COM

Gander grew as a stopping point for all types of aviation. Although commercial transatlantic flights no longer need to refuel at Gander, the airport retains its importance, such as after the terrorist attacks of September 11, 2001, when 39 commercial planes carrying more than 6,500 crew and passengers were diverted to Gander. Even if you're not departing on one of the scheduled Air Canada or Provincial Airlines flights, it's worth dropping by **Gander International Airport,** on the northeastern side of downtown, to view the many displays and memorabilia through the main terminal.

Gleaming full-size models of World War II Hudson, Voodoo, and Canso water bombers, a Beech 18 aircraft, and a reconstructed De Havilland Tiger Moth greet visitors to the **North Atlantic Aviation Museum** (135 Trans-Canada Hwy., 709/256-2923, summer daily 9am-7pm, the rest of the year Mon.-Fri. 9am-5pm, adult $8, senior and child $7). Inside, exhibits on Gander's strategic role in World War II and the development of transatlantic aviation include early equipment,

uniforms, photographs, and a reconstructed DC-3 cockpit.

The **Silent Witness Memorial,** 4 kilometers (2.5 miles) east of town and 1 kilometer (0.6 mile) south along an unpaved road, marks the site of an aviation disaster. On a cold December day in 1985, the airport was a scheduled refueling stop for a DC-8 flight from the Middle East. The flight carried the U.S. 101st Airborne Division, better known as the Screaming Eagles, who were returning home from a United Nations peacekeeping mission in the Sinai. The plane, with 248 soldiers and an eight-member crew, crashed shortly after takeoff between the highway and Gander Lake, killing all onboard. A group of statues, of an American soldier and two children, backed by Canadian, U.S., and Newfoundland flags, overlooks the lake. The memorial spreads across the rocky hillside, and flower bouquets lie here and there.

Food and Accommodations

Gander is a convenient stop for travelers crossing Newfoundland's interior, and it provides a wide choice of accommodations. The two-story **Comfort Inn** (112 Trans-Canada Hwy., 709/256-3535, www.choicehotels. ca, $115 s, $125 d, including a continental breakfast buffet) has 64 spacious and relatively modern guest rooms. Facilities include wireless Internet and a small fitness room. **Quality Inn & Suites** (100 Trans-Canada Hwy., 709/256-3931 or 800/563-2988, www. qualityhotelgander.com, $120-176 s or d) is older, but it has 152 rooms and suites, a **restaurant** (daily 7am-2pm and 5pm-9pm, $13-27), a lounge with entertainment, an indoor pool, and an exercise room.

Beside the Comfort Inn is **Jungle Jim's** (112 Trans-Canada Hwy., 709/651-3444, Sun.-Tues. 11am-9pm, Wed.-Sat. 11am-11pm, $13-22). If you can get the waitstaff's attention through the vines and bamboo decorations, order dishes such as fish-and-chips or ribs.

Getting There

It's almost 150 kilometers (93 miles) northwest

The Beothuks

Across the island's central area, the arrival of Europeans foretold grave consequences for the Beothuks, who had migrated from Labrador in AD 200 and spread across the Baie Verte Peninsula to Burnside, Twillingate, and the shores of the Exploits River and Red Indian Lake.

In 1769, a law prohibiting murder of the indigenous people was enacted, but the edict came too late. The Beothuks were almost extinct, and in 1819 a small group was ambushed by settlers near Red Indian Lake. In the ensuing struggle, a 23-year-old woman named Demasduit was captured, and her husband and newborn infant were killed. The government attempted to return her to her people when she contracted tuberculosis, but she was too ill, and she died in Botwood. In 1823, her kinswoman, Shanawdithit, was also taken by force. Shanawdithit told a moving tale of the history and demise of her people, punctuating it with drawings, maps, and a sampling of Beothuk vocabulary before she died in 1829, the last of her race.

You'll hear mention of the Beothuks throughout central Newfoundland, but two attractions concentrate on these people—the **Beothuk Interpretation Site** (709/656-3114, mid-May-early Oct. daily 9:30am-5pm, adult $5), 70 kilometers (43 miles) north of Gander on the road to Twillingate, and Grand Falls' **Mary March Provincial Museum** (24 St. Catherine St., 709/292-4522, early May-Sept. Mon.-Sat. 9am-4:30pm, Sun. noon-4:30pm, adult $2.50), which is named for Demasduit's European given name.

to Gander from Clarenville, a 1.5-hour drive via Route 1. From St. John's, it's a 340-kilometer (210-mile), four-hour drive on Route 1.

NORTH TO TWILLINGATE

From Gander, Route 330 heads north to Gander Bay, where Route 331 curves farther northwest and lopes onto the northern archipelago as Route 340, better known as the Road to the Shore.

Boyd's Cove

Boyd's Cove, 70 kilometers (43 miles) north of Gander, at the intersection of Routes 331 and 340, is a small village with a large attraction: **Beothuk Interpretation Site** (709/656-3114, mid-May-early Oct. daily 9:30am-5pm, adult $5). Designed to mimic the shapes of 300-year-old Beothuk dwellings, the center lies at the end of a 2-kilometer (1.2-mile) gravel road. The detour is worth it, though, for the artifacts, dioramas, films, and exquisitely expressive paintings depicting the history of the Beothuk people. Take the 20-minute walk down to the site of the 17th-century Beothuk encampment, excavated in the early 1980s. Eleven house pits, clearly defined by earthen walls, were discovered here,

along with countless artifacts such as beads, stone tools, and iron.

GETTING THERE

From Gander, it's 70 kilometers (43 miles) north to Boyd's Cove, a one-hour drive via Route 330 and Route 331. To get to Boyd's Cove from St. John's, it's a 410-kilometer (255-mile), five-hour drive on Routes 1, 330, and 331.

TWILLINGATE

Beyond Boyd's Cove, causeways link an archipelago of islands lying close to the mainland. Along the way, narrow Route 430 passes farmland (where you might catch a glimpse of the rare Newfoundland pony); gentle, island-filled bays; and tiny outports to finish at South and North Twillingate islands. The archipelago's most northwesterly point, the islands are washed by the Atlantic and shouldered by Notre Dame Bay. The road crosses the southern island and eases into the tiny port at Twillingate Harbour.

Cross the causeway to Twillingate (pop. 2,200) on the northwestern island. Main Street runs alongside the scenic harbor before it zips north and climbs to Long Point.

Sights and Recreation

TWILLINGATE MUSEUM

If you're interested in local lore, stop at **Twillingate Museum** (1 St. Peter's Church Rd., 709/884-2825, mid-May-early Oct. daily 9am-8pm, adult $4, child $2). The whitewashed wooden building sits back from the road and is bordered by a white picket fence—altogether as proper as a former Anglican manse should be. The museum's extensive exhibits include historic fishing gear and tools, antique dolls, and several rare Dorset Inuit artifacts. One room is devoted to the career of Dr. John Olds, Twillingate's famous expatriate surgeon who came from the United States to pioneer medicine in remote Newfoundland. The intriguing medical artifacts include a collection of early 20th-century pharmaceuticals and glass eyes.

★ TOP EXPERIENCE

★ ICEBERG-VIEWING

Icebergs, which wander offshore and sometimes ditch at land's end in Notre Dame Bay, are one of Twillingate's main claims to fame. If you're interested in getting up close, take one of the three daily cruises offered by **Twillingate Island Boat Tours** (50 Main St., 709/884-2242 or 800/611-2374, www.icebergtours.ca, adult $60, child $35), based at the Iceberg Shop, on the south side of the harbor (turn right as you enter town). Tours operate May-September, although the best iceberg viewing is late May-mid-June. Departures are daily at 9:30am, 1pm, and 4pm, and tours last two hours. They are operated by Cecil Stockley, who steers the MV *Iceberg Alley* to wherever icebergs have grounded in the vicinity of Twillingate.

You may also see an offshore iceberg from Back Harbour, a short walk starting from the museum and passing by a cemetery. Otherwise, head for Long Point, the high rocky promontory that juts into the Atlantic Ocean beside Notre Dame Bay. To get there, take Main Street around the harbor (past the museum and Harbour Lights Inn) and follow the road all the way to **Long Point** for the best land-based iceberg viewing in the area. In addition to a photogenic lighthouse, trails lead down through the boulder-strewn point and across to a couple of pebbly beaches.

Accommodations

Visitors to Twillingate often find themselves captivated by the town's charm, and because of this, numerous accommodations can be

icebergs off the coast of Twillingate

The spectacular icebergs that float past Newfoundland and Labrador every summer originate from southwestern Greenland's ice cap, where great chunks of ice calve off the coast and cascade into the bone-chilling Davis Strait. The young bergs eventually drift out to the Labrador Sea, where powerful currents route them south along the watery route known as Iceberg Alley. The parade usually starts in March, peaks in June and July, and in rare cases continues into November.

Although no one actually counts icebergs, an educated guess has 10,000-30,000 of them migrating down from the north annually. Of those, about 1,400-2,000 make it all the way to the Gulf Stream's warm waters, where they finally melt away after a two- to four-year, 3,200-kilometer (1,988-mile) journey.

No two bergs are exactly the same. Some appear distinctly white. Others may be turquoise, green, or blue. Sizes vary too: A "growler" is the smallest, about the size of a dory, and weighs about 1,000 tons. A "bergy bit" weighs more, about 10,000 tons. A typical "small" iceberg looms 5-15 meters (16-49 feet) above water level and weighs about 100,000 tons. A "large" ice mass will be 51-75 meters (167-246 feet) high and weigh 100-300 million tons. Generally, you'll see the largest bergs—looking like magnificent castles embellished with towers and turrets—farther north; the ice mountains diminish in size as they float south and eventually melt. No matter what the size, what you see is just a fraction of the whole—some 90 percent of the iceberg's mass is hidden beneath the water.

Occasionally, a wandering berg may be trapped at land's edge or wedged within coves and slender bays. Should you be tempted to go in for a closer look, approach with caution. As it melts and its equilibrium readjusts, an iceberg may roll over. And melting bergs also often fracture, throwing ice chips and knife-sharp splinters in all directions.

The best website for information and tracking data is www.icebergfinder.com, which includes up-to-date satellite images of where icebergs are located.

found. ★ **Harbour Lights Inn** (189 Main St., 709/884-2763, www.harbourlightsinn.ca, Apr.-late Oct., $120-155 s or d) is a restored early 19th-century home overlooking the harbor. The inn features nine guest rooms decorated in smart colors and appealing furnishings, each with an en suite bathroom and wireless Internet access; two rooms have whirlpool baths. Rates include a cooked breakfast.

If you prefer more privacy, consider **Oceanside Cabins** (130 Main St., 709/884-6489, www.oceansidecabinsinc.com, May-Oct., $149 s or d), comprising a row of cabins built along the harbor foreshore (if the timing is right, you may see icebergs from your cabin). Amenities include comfortable beds, en suites, and basic cooking facilities (fridge, microwave, toaster oven).

Getting There

To get to Twillingate from Boyd's Cove, take Route 340 north for 40 kilometers (25 miles), a 40-minute drive. From St. John's, it's a 445-kilometer (275-mile), six-hour drive west on Route 1, then north on Routes 330, 331, and 340.

GRAND FALLS-WINDSOR

For the sake of government, the two towns of Grand Falls-Windsor have been merged to form one municipality, but keep in mind that Windsor lies north of the Trans-Canada Highway and Grand Falls south. Grand Falls-Windsor lies almost exactly halfway along the Newfoundland leg of the Trans-Canada Highway: St. John's is 428 kilometers (265 miles) to the east, and Port-aux-Basques is 476 kilometers (295 miles) to the west.

Sights

Grand Falls offers the most sightseeing. Turn south off the highway at Cromer Avenue to the **Mary March Provincial Museum** (24 St.

Catherine St., 709/292-4522, early May-Sept. Mon.-Sat. 9am-4:30pm, Sun. noon-4:30pm, adult $2.50), where exhibits about the area's Beothuk people, natural history, geology, and regional industry fill the modern center.

The town is aptly named for its **Grand Falls,** a white-water gush of rapids across the Exploits River as it speeds alongside the town. To see the falls, take Scott Avenue off the Trans-Canada Highway to the south and you'll find yourself in the heart of downtown Grand Falls. Cross the river at a narrow wooden bridge at the now-closed pulp and paper mill and look north for the best views. You can get a close look at the salmon that inhabit the river by continuing beyond the bridge to the **Salmonid Interpretation Centre** (709/489-7350, mid-June-mid-Sept. daily 8am to 8pm, adult $4, child $2.50). The main floor's exhibits explain the salmon's life cycle and habitat, while on the observation level you can watch the migratory salmon through the viewing windows.

Food

On the south side of the highway, the main street of Grand Falls offers a couple of reasonable dining options. Opposite the distinctively arched town hall entrance is **Common Grounds** (12 High St., 709/489-5252, Mon.-Fri. 7:30am-9pm, Sat. 8:30am-9pm, Sun. 10am-6pm, lunches $6-9.50), with a great selection of coffees and teas, as well as light breakfasts and lunches.

Down the hill slightly and across the road from Common Grounds is **Tai Wan Restaurant** (48 High St., 709/489-4222, daily 11am-2:30pm and 4:30pm-9pm, $9-14), filled with bright red-and-gold furnishings and walls decorated in local art. The lunch and dinner buffets are $10 and $13, respectively.

Don't be put off by the look of **Sara's Diner** (7 Church Rd., 709/489-1914, Mon.-Sat. 11am-9pm, $11-16); the food is delicious.

The menu is mostly Indian, with inexpensive build-your-own curries and other traditional delicacies.

Accommodations

On the residential outskirts of Windsor, **Carriage House Inn** (181 Grenfell Heights, 709/489-7185 or 800/563-7133, www.carriagehouseinn.ca, $99-139 s or d) comprises 12 spick-and-span guest rooms, with full breakfast included in the rates. Outside you'll find a covered veranda, a pool, a sundeck, and gardens.

Mount Peyton Resort (214 Lincoln Rd., 709/489-2251 or 800/563-4894, www.mountpeyton.com, $120-170 s or d) is a regular hotel (rather than a resort). It has an array of accommodations on both sides of the Trans-Canada Highway, including 102 hotel rooms, 32 motel rooms, and 16 housekeeping units. The motel's dining room is known locally for its seafood, locally grown vegetables, and dessert, made up of berries in all forms.

★ **Hotel Robin Hood** (78 Lincoln Rd., 709/489-5324, www.hotelrobinhood.com, $140-240 s or d) is Grand Falls-Windsor's most appealing motel. Small and charming, the 14 guest rooms are all air-conditioned, with larger flat-screen TVs, and are comfortable and spacious. Some rooms have jetted tubs. Rates include a continental breakfast.

Information

The best planning tool for visiting the area is the **Town of Grand Falls-Windsor** website (www.grandfallswindsor.com).

Getting There

Grand Falls and Windsor are just shy of 100 kilometers (62 miles) west of Gander, a one-hour drive via Route 1. From St. John's, it's a 440-kilometer (275-mile), five-hour drive northwest on Route 1.

Deer Lake to Port-aux-Basques

It's 270 kilometers (165 miles) from the western hub of Deer Lake south to the ferry terminal at Port-aux-Basques. Along the way is Newfoundland's second-largest city, Corner Brook; Atlantic Canada's premier ski resort; and many interesting provincial parks and scenic detours.

DEER LAKE

Deer Lake (population 5,000), 640 kilometers (395 miles) west of St. John's and 270 kilometers (165 miles) from Port-aux-Basques, is a busy transportation hub at the point where Route 430 spurs north along the Northern Peninsula. The town lies at the north end of its namesake lake, a long body of water that flows into the Humber River. Along the lakeshore is a sandy beach and shallow stretch of water that offers pleasant swimming in July and August. The town's only commercial attraction is the **Newfoundland Insectarium** (2 Bonne Bay Rd., 709/635-4545, mid-May-June and Sept.-mid-Oct. daily 9am-5pm, July-Aug. daily 9am-6pm, adult $12, senior $10, child $8). Inside this converted dairy, displays include active beehives and a collection of butterflies. To get there, take Exit 16 from the Trans-Canada Highway and follow Route 430 for a short distance to Bonne Bay Road.

Sir Richard Squires Provincial Park

Take Route 430 for 8 kilometers (5 miles) to reach the turnoff to the remote **Sir Richard Squires Provincial Park,** which is then a further 47 kilometers (29 miles) from civilization. The park protects a short stretch of the upper reaches of the Humber River; salmon are the main draw. Even if you're not an angler, watching them leap up 3-meter-high (9.8-foot-high) Big Falls in late summer makes the drive worthwhile. Camping is $18 per night.

Accommodations and Camping

Deer Lake Motel (15 Trans-Canada Hwy., 709/635-2108 or 800/563-2144, www.deerlakemotel.com, $130-160 s or d) is your typical low-slung roadside motel; the standard rooms are midsized, but comfortable and regularly revamped. This motel also has a restaurant with dinner mains in the $14-24 range and a small lounge.

Take the Nicholsville Road exit to reach **Deer Lake RV Park** (197 Nicholsville Rd., 709/635-5885, www.dlrvparkandcampground.com, late June-early Sept., $28-35), close to the lake and with showers and a playground.

Information

Along the highway through town (beside the Irving gas station, with its big moose out front) is **Deer Lake Information Centre** (Trans-Canada Hwy., 709/635-2202, May-June and Sept.-Oct. daily 9am-5pm, July-Aug. daily 7am-9pm), which has a number of displays on regional attractions and the Northern Peninsula.

Getting There

Deer Lake Airport (1 Airport Rd., 709/635-5270, www.deerlakeairport.com) is western Newfoundland's air hub. Located on the north side of town, just off the Trans-Canada Highway, it has Avis, Budget, Enterprise, Thrifty, and National car rental desks (make reservations well in advance). The airport is served by **Air Canada** (888/247-2262, www.aircanada.com) from Halifax and Montréal, **WestJet** (888/937-8538, www.westjet.com) to Toronto, and **PAL Airlines** (709/576-3943 or 800/563-2800, www.provincialairlines.ca) from throughout Newfoundland and Labrador.

Deer Lake is about 215 kilometers (133 miles) west of Grand Falls-Windsor, a

2.5-hour drive on Route 1. From the ferry terminal in Port-aux-Basques, it's about 270 kilometers (165 miles) north to Deer Lake on Route 1, three hours.

CORNER BROOK AND VICINITY

Corner Brook, 50 kilometers (31 miles) southwest of Deer Lake and 690 kilometers (430 miles) from the capital, lies at the head of the Humber Arm, 50 kilometers (31 miles) inland from the Gulf of St. Lawrence. The city is picturesquely cupped in a 20-square-kilometer (7.7-square-mile) bowl sloping down to the water, but most of the best natural attractions lie outside city limits, including the area around Marble Mountain and along Route 450 to Lark Harbour. The city ranks as Newfoundland's second largest, combining Corner Brook (pop. 20,000) with outlying settlements on the Humber Arm (another 20,000). It began as a company town, developing around a harbor-front pulp and paper mill that's still in operation, and has grown to become western Newfoundland's commercial, educational, service, and governmental center.

Town Sights

Making your way down to the harbor front from the Trans-Canada Highway is simple enough, but to visit the main downtown sights, orient yourself by stopping at the information center and deciding exactly what you want to see and do.

Captain Cook's Monument is a lofty lookout with views that provide a feeling for the layout of the city. On the road to the monument, you'll be rewarded with glorious views as far as the Bay of Islands. Follow O'Connell Drive across town, turn right (north) on Bliss Street, make another right on Country Road, turn left onto Atlantic Avenue with another left to Mayfair Street, and then right to Crow Hill Road. The monument itself commemorates Cook's Bay of Islands explorations with a plaque and sample chart.

In the wide bowl containing downtown, West Valley Road roughly divides the city in half. Near the bottom end of this thoroughfare and overlooking Remembrance Square is the staid Corner Brook Museum (2 West St., 709/634-2518, July-Aug. Mon.-Fri. 9am-5pm, the rest of the year Mon.-Fri. 10am-noon and 1pm-4:30pm, adult $5, child $3), housed in a historic building that has served as a post office, courthouse, and customs house through the years. Displays center around the various local industries and their impact on the city's growth.

Marble Mountain

Driving south from Deer Lake, you pass Marble Mountain (709/637-7601, www. skimarble.com), 12 kilometers (7.5 miles) east of Corner Brook beside the Trans-Canada Highway. The mountain rises from the south side of the highway, while on the other side of the road is the small community of Steady Brook, which fronts the Humber River. The resort is Atlantic Canada's largest and best-known alpine resort, and although the lifts don't operate in summer, the area is worth a stop during the warmer months. The highlight is Steady Brook Falls, accessible via a steepish trail that begins from the far corner of the main parking lot. The falls are reached in about 15 minutes. From there, a 3.5-kilometer (2.2-mile) one-way unmarked trail continues and brings you nearer to the peak. The views of the Humber Valley and Bay of Islands are splendid.

Between December and April, four chairlifts, including a high-speed detachable quad, whisk skiers from throughout Atlantic Canada and as far away as Toronto up 520 vertical meters (1,706 feet) to access 27 runs, a terrain park, and a half-pipe. The base area is dominated by a magnificent four-story, 6,400-square-meter (68,890-square-foot) day lodge, home to a ski and snowboard school, rental shop, café, restaurant, and bar. Lift tickets are adult $65, senior $48, child $35. Check the website for packages that include accommodations.

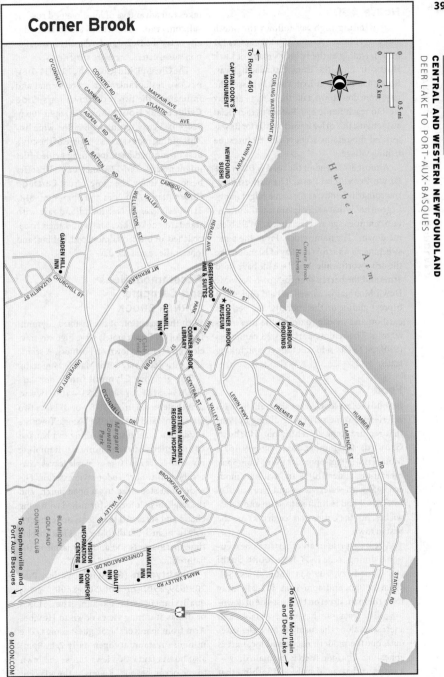

Corner Brook

To Route 450

CAPTAIN COOK'S MONUMENT ★

CURLING WATERFRONT RD

LEWIN PKWY

0   0.5 mi
0   0.5 km

Humber

Arm

O'CONNELL

COUNTRY RD

MAYFAIR AVE

CARMEN
AVE

ATLANTIC
AVE

ASPEN
RD

MT. BATTEN RD

DR

CARIBOU RD

NEWFOUND SUSHI ▼

HERALD AVE

VALLEY RD

WELLINGTON ST

Corner Brook Harbour

GARDEN HILL INN ●

CHURCHILL ST

ELIZABETH ST

MT BERNARD AVE

GREENWOOD INN & SUITES ■

MAIN ST

HARBOUR GROUNDS ▼

GLYNMILL INN ●

CORNER BROOK MUSEUM ★

PARK ST

WEST ST

CORNER BROOK LIBRARY ■

Corner Brook Stream

PREMIER DR

HUMBER RD

UNIVERSITY DR

O'CONNELL DR

Margaret Bowater Park

COBB LN

CENTRAL ST

E VALLEY RD

LEWIN PKWY

CLARENCE ST

WESTERN MEMORIAL REGIONAL HOSPITAL

BROOKFIELD AVE

BLOMIDON GOLF AND COUNTRY CLUB

W VALLEY RD

VISITOR INFORMATION CENTRE ■

CONFEDERATION DR

MAMATEEK INN ●

QUALITY INN ●

● COMFORT INN

MAPLE VALLEY RD

STATION RD

To Stephenville and Port Aux Basques ◄

To Marble Mountain and Deer Lake ►

© MOON.COM

Route 450

This winding highway follows the south shore of Humber Arm for 50 kilometers (31 miles), ending at the fishing village of **Lark Harbour.** From the Trans-Canada Highway, Route 450 begins at Exit 4 and bypasses the city; from downtown, take the Lewin Parkway west to reach Route 450. Rather than official attractions, this drive is worthwhile for its water-and-mountains scenery and picturesque fishing villages.

Almost at the end of the road is **Blow Me Down Provincial Park.** The park isn't extraordinarily windy, as the name might imply. Legend holds that a sea captain saw the mountain centuries ago and exclaimed, "Well, blow me down." The name stuck. From the park, sweeping views across the Bay of Islands make the drive worthwhile. You'll see the bay's fjord arms and the barren orange-brown Blow Me Down Mountains, as well as bald eagles and ospreys gliding on the updrafts, and perhaps caribou and moose roaming the preserve's terrain. The remote park has 28 campsites ($20), pit toilets, a lookout tower, and hiking trails.

Food

Beyond the fast-food places along all the main arteries are some surprising dining options that require some searching out. **Harbour Grounds** (9 Humber Rd., 709/639-1677, Mon.-Fri. 7:30am-6pm, Sat.-Sun. 9am-5pm, everything under $10) is an invitingly modern café with water views and free wireless Internet. Food is limited to soup and sandwiches, but the coffee and tea drinks are the best in town.

A real surprise in an otherwise unexceptional dining scene is ★ **Newfound Sushi** (117 Broadway, 709/634-6666, Tues.-Sat. 11am-2:30pm and 4pm-9pm, $12-24), away from the main street on the west side of downtown. The restaurant has just seven tables and a few seats along the sushi bar (or order takeout), but the modern decor and local art is appealing. The food itself is the main draw— a wonderful array of sushi and sashimi that takes full advantage of local seafood such as salmon, crab, and shrimp. Order individually or try the Dory Load of Sushi for two. For non-sushi eaters, there are stir-fries.

The Glynmill Inn (Cobb Ln., 709/634-5181) has two restaurants. The more formal and intimate of the two is the downstairs **Wine Cellar Steak House** (Mon.-Sat. 6pm-10pm, $24-40), a cozy setting with a fine wine list. This dining room serves up some of the city's best unadorned beef, including grilled filet mignon served in 12-ounce cuts. Upstairs beside the lobby, the more casual **Carriage Room** (daily 7am-2pm and 5pm-9pm, $18-31) specializes in Newfoundland fare with standard cooked breakfasts and then fried, poached, or broiled salmon, cod, halibut, and lobster the rest of the day.

Accommodations and Camping
CORNER BROOK

With the exception of the historic Glynmill Inn, Corner Brook motels serve highway travelers and those in town on business. A scenic alternative is to stay out at Marble Mountain.

The gracious **Glynmill Inn** (Cobb Ln., 709/634-5181 or 800/563-4400, www. steelehotels.com, from $145 s or d) hosts two restaurants and lies near the historic Townsite residential area. It's a charming inn banked with gardens of red geraniums. Rambling ivy, with leaves as large as maple leaves, covers the half-timber Tudor-style exterior. The wide front steps lead to an open porch, and the English-style foyer is furnished with wing chairs and sofas. All the rooms are comfortably furnished, but the older ones feature old-time spaciousness and antique marble in the bathroom.

Quality Inn (64 Maple Valley Rd., 709/639-8901 or 800/563-8600, www. qualityinncornerbrook.com, from $135 s or d) has stunning views down to Humber Arm from many of the 55 guest rooms. The in-house restaurant (open daily 7am-9pm) also boasts fantastic views across the town to the ocean beyond. Rooms at the adjacent

Comfort Inn (41 Maple Valley Rd., 709/639-1980 or 800/228-5150, www.choicehotels.ca, $120 s or d) are not as nice, but are a few dollars cheaper.

Greenwood Inn & Suites (48 West St., 709/634-5381 or 800/399-5381, www.greenwoodcornerbrook.com, from $150 s or d) is right downtown. This full-service hostelry with regularly renovated guest rooms has its own English-style pub with sidewalk tables, an indoor heated pool, wireless Internet access, and underground parking.

MARBLE MOUNTAIN

Across the highway from Marble Mountain, 12 kilometers (7.5 miles) northeast of Corner Brook, is ★ **Marble Inn** (21 Dogwood Dr., Steady Brook, 709/634-2237 or 877/497-5673, www.marbleinn.com), a modern riverside complex that combines regular motel rooms (from $145 s or d) with luxurious two-bedroom suites overlooking the river ($295 s or d). Amenities include an indoor pool, a fitness room, spa services, a café, and a small restaurant open Thursday-Saturday 11:30am-2pm for lunch and Thursday-Monday 4pm-9pm for dinner (mains $18-48).

Also at Steady Brook is **Marble Villa** (709/637-7601 or 800/636-2725, www.skimarble.com, $139-249 s or d), which is right at the base of the alpine resort. Some units have separate bedrooms; all have cooking facilities and wireless Internet. Naturally, winter is high season, when most guests stay as part of a package. In summer, the self-contained units rent from $139 s or d.

George's Mountain Village (709/639-8168) has a limited number of campsites under the shadow of Marble Mountain. It's part of a complex that includes a restaurant, gas station, and sports shop. Powered sites are $35 (although are not really suitable for larger RVs), and cabins with kitchens and separate bedrooms start at $169 s or d.

Information and Services

Take Exit 5 or 6 from the Trans-Canada Highway and follow the signs to the **Visitor Information Centre** (11 Confederation Dr., 709/639-9792, daily 8:30am-4:30pm, longer hours in summer), which is easily recognizable by its lighthouse-shaped design.

Western Memorial Regional Hospital (709/637-5000) is at 1 Brookfield Avenue. For the **RCMP**, call 709/637-4433.

Getting There and Around

Deer Lake, an hour's drive north of Corner Brook, has the region's main airport. **DRL-LR** (709/634-7422, www.drl-lr.com) operates bus service along the Trans-Canada Highway, with daily stops in Corner Brook (at the Confederation Dr. Irving gas station). Departures from St. John's at 8am arrive in Deer Lake at 5:15pm.

If you're coming up from the ferry at Port-aux-Basques, allow around two hours for the 220-kilometer (136-mile) trip north on Route 1. Corner Brook is 50 kilometers (31 miles) southwest of Deer Lake, a one-hour drive on Route 1.

The city has half a dozen cab companies whose cabs wait at lodgings, cruise business streets, and take calls. **City Cabs** (709/634-6565) is among the largest outfits.

STEPHENVILLE AND VICINITY

With a population of more than 6,000, Stephenville, 50 kilometers (31 miles) south of Corner Brook and then 40 kilometers (25 miles) west along Route 460, is the business hub for the Bay St. George-Port au Port region. In the center of town is **Winterhouse** (108 Main St., 709/643-4844), renowned for Winterhouse sweaters ($120-175), designed locally and produced by cottage-industry knitters. The shop is also a source for thrummed mittens ($20-35) and caps. This revived traditional craft combines a knitted woolen facing backed with raw fleece. The shop shelves are stuffed with top-quality wares, including Woof Design sweaters, Random Island Weaving cotton placemats, King's Point Pottery platters and bowls, and handmade birch brooms.

Barachois Pond Provincial Park

One of western Newfoundland's most popular parks, 3,500-hectare (8,650-acre) **Barachois Pond Provincial Park** is beside Route 1 west of Stephenville. It is home to a 3.2-kilometer (2-mile) hiking trail through birch, spruce, and fir trees to Erin Mountain's barren summit (the trailhead is within the campground). Be on the lookout for the rare Newfoundland pine marten along the way. The view at the 340-meter (1,115-foot) summit extends over the Port au Port Peninsula. There's also a summertime interpretive program with guided walks and evening campfires, a lake for swimming and fishing, and 150 unserviced campsites ($18).

Accommodations

Stephenville offers a selection of downtown hotels and restaurants to travelers heading out onto the Port au Port Peninsula. The best of these is **Dreamcatcher Lodge** (14 Main St., 709/643-6655 or 888/373-2668, www.dreamcatcherlodge.ca, $100-120 s or d), at the far end of the main street through downtown. It comprises three buildings filled with a mix of motel rooms and kitchen-equipped units.

Getting There

Stephenville is 170 kilometers (105 miles) north of Port-aux-Basques, a two-hour drive via Route 1.

STEPHENVILLE TO PORT-AUX-BASQUES

Most northbound travelers, having just arrived in Newfoundland (and southbound travelers heading to the ferry) don't plan on lingering along the stretch of highway between Stephenville and Port-aux-Basques, but the detour into the Codroy Valley, 39 kilometers (24 miles) north of Port-aux-Basques, is worthwhile. Near the main highway is the **Wetland Interpretation Centre** (Rte. 406, Upper Ferry, 709/955-2109, June-early Sept. daily 9am-5pm, free), where you can learn about the 300 bird species recorded in the valley, including great blue herons who are at the northern extent of their range. You can also ask for free bird checklists and a map showing the best viewing spots. Continue west to reach **Codroy Valley Provincial Park,** protecting a stretch of coastline including grass-covered sand dunes and a long sandy beach facing Cabot Strait. The highlight for birders is the chance to spot shorebirds such as piping plovers (late spring-midsummer).

sunset along the coast south of the Codroy Valley

Cape Anguille

Continue west beyond the provincial park along Route 406 to reach Cape Anguille, where ★ **Cape Anguille Lighthouse Inn** (Rte. 406, 709/634-2285 or 877/254-6586, www.linkumtours.com, May-Oct., $130-140 s or d) sits high above a rugged shoreline. The lighthouse itself is still in use, but the lighthouse keeper (who was born out here) has opened up a few simple rooms for guests in a trim red-and-white cottage adjacent to the main lighthouse. Breakfast is included, and a highly recommended dinner of local specialties ($35 pp) is available with advance notice.

PORT-AUX-BASQUES

Just over 900 kilometers (560 miles) from its starting point in St. John's, the Trans-Canada Highway reaches its western terminus at Port-aux-Basques, a town of about 5,000 with a deepwater port used by French, Basque, and Portuguese fishing fleets as early as the 1500s. Arriving in town from the north, the main highway continues 2 kilometers (1.2 miles) to the ferry terminal, and a side road branches west, past hotels and fast-food restaurants to the township proper.

Accommodations and Camping

Just over 2 kilometers (1.2 miles) from the ferry terminal is **Shark Cove Suites** (16 Currie Ave., 709/695-3831, $95 s or d), a small complex of simple, slightly rundown units. Each has a kitchen and a lounge with a TV/DVD combo. Originally a Holiday Inn, **Hotel Port aux Basques** (2 Grand Bay Rd., 709/695-2171 or 877/695-2171, www.hotel-port-aux-basques.com, $130-190 s or d) sits on the corner where the highway branches to the ferry terminal. The restaurant has a fair selection of local delicacies at reasonable prices (seafood dishes $14-28), and the hotel also has a lounge.

If you're camping, your best choice is 6 kilometers (3.7 miles) north of town at **J. T. Cheeseman Provincial Park,** where more than 100 sites ($18-27) are spread along a picturesque stream. Facilities are limited, but the park is fronted by a long beach and is a nesting ground for the endangered piping plover.

Information

Housed in a distinctive pyramid-shaped building just north of the turnoff to town is a provincial **Visitor Information Centre** (709/695-2262, May-Oct. daily 9am-8pm and for all ferry arrivals).

Getting There

Port-aux-Basques is 170 kilometers (105 miles) south of Stephenville, a two-hour drive via Route 1.

Continuing to the Mainland by Ferry

Port-aux-Basques is the northern terminus of year-round **Marine Atlantic** (902/794-5254 or 800/341-7981, www.marineatlantic.ca) ferry service from North Sydney (Nova Scotia). It's the shorter and less expensive of the two crossings to Newfoundland from North Sydney. One-way fares and rates for the five- to seven-hour sailing are adult $45, senior $42, child $21, vehicle under 20 feet $120. Extras include reserved chairs in a private lounge ($12-20) and cabins ($130-170).

Gros Morne National Park

UNESCO World Heritage Sites are scattered across the world. Egypt boasts the pyramids. France is known for Chartres Cathedral. Australia has the Great Barrier Reef. And Newfoundland boasts 1,085-square-kilometer (420-square-mile) Gros Morne National Park, a spectacular geological slice of the ancient world.

Gros Morne is on Newfoundland's west coast, 72 kilometers (45 miles) northwest from the town of Deer Lake. While the geological history will amaze you, there's also a wealth of hiking and boating tours and cross-country skiing in winter. Even though the park is remote, it is surrounded by small towns that cater to visitors, with lodging and restaurants to suit all budgets. There's even a dinner theater.

THE LAND

The park fronts the Gulf of St. Lawrence on a coastal plain rimmed with 70 kilometers (43 miles) of coast, edging sandy and cobblestone beaches, sea stacks, caves, forests, peat bogs, and breathtaking saltwater and freshwater fjords. The flattened Long Range Mountains, part of the ancient Appalachian Mountains, rise as an alpine plateau cloaked with black and white spruce, balsam fir, white birch, and stunted tuckamore thickets. Bare patches of peridotite, toxic to most plants, speckle the peaks, and at the highest elevations, the vegetation gives way to lichen, moss, and dwarf willow and birch on the arctic tundra.

Innumerable moose, arctic hares, foxes, weasels, lynx, and a few bears roam the park. Two large herds of woodland caribou inhabit the mountains and migrate to the coastal plain during winter. Bald eagles, ospreys, common and arctic terns, great black-backed gulls, and songbirds nest along the coast, while rock ptarmigans inhabit the mountain peaks. You might see willow ptarmigans on the lower slopes or, especially during the June-early July capelin run, a few pilot, minke, or humpback whales offshore.

PARK ENTRY

Gros Morne National Park is open year-round, although all but one campground and the two information centers operate only in the warmer months. A **National Parks Day Pass** is adult $10, senior $8.50, child $5, to a maximum of $20 per vehicle. It is valid until 4pm the day following its purchase. A **Viking Trail Pass** (adult $45, senior $36, child $24) is valid for park entry and admission to Northern Peninsula national historic sites for seven days from the date of purchase. Passes can be purchased at the information center at Rocky Harbour or the Discovery Centre at Woody Point.

ROUTE 430

This is the main route up the Northern Peninsula. From Wiltondale, it's 86 kilometers (53 miles) to the park's northern extremity; from Rocky Harbour, it's 51 kilometers (32 miles). The highway traverses terrain typical of the island's rocky seacoast and verdant hills and mountains, a distinct contrast to the southern area. Unusual groups of faulted and folded rock layers lie along this coastline.

Lobster Cove Head

The point of land north of Rocky Harbour is **Lobster Cove Head.** Its layers formed as the North American plate slid beneath the eastern Eurasian/African plate 450-500 million years ago. Exhibits inside **Lobster Cove Head Lighthouse** (late May-mid-Oct. daily 10am-5:30pm, free) depict local lore, geological facts, and ancient natural history, but the views from outside are what make a visit worthwhile, especially as the sun sets over Bonne Bay and the Gulf of St. Lawrence beyond.

Gros Morne National Park

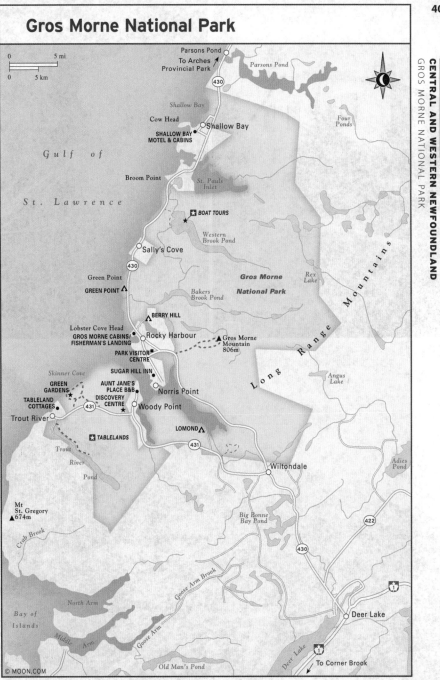

Parsons Pond

To Arches
Provincial Park

430

Parsons Pond

Four
Ponds

Shallow Bay

Cow Head

Shallow Bay

SHALLOW BAY
MOTEL & CABINS

G u l f   o f

Broom Point

*St. Pauls
Inlet*

S t .   L a w r e n c e

★ BOAT TOURS

*Western
Brook Pond*

Sally's Cove

430

Gros Morne

*Rex
Lake*

Green Point

GREEN POINT

*Bakers
Brook Pond*

National Park

BERRY HILL

Lobster Cove Head

Rocky Harbour

Gros Morne
Mountain
806m

GROS MORNE CABINS/
FISHERMAN'S LANDING

PARK VISITOR
CENTRE

L o n g   R a n g e   M o u n t a i n s

SUGAR HILL INN

Skinner Cove

GREEN
GARDENS

AUNT JANE'S
PLACE B&B

Norris Point

*Angus
Lake*

TABLELAND
COTTAGES

DISCOVERY
CENTRE

431

Woody Point

Trout River

★ TABLELANDS

LOMOND

431

Trout

River

Wiltondale

*Adies
Pond*

Mt
St. Gregory
674m

Pond

*Big Bonne
Bay Pond*

422

Crab Brook

430

*Bay of
Islands*

North Arm

Goose Arm Brook

1

Deer Lake

Middle Arm

Goose Arm

Deer Lake

To Corner Brook

Old Man's Pond

© MOON.COM

0   5 mi

0   5 km

Rocky Harbour to Cow Head

More dramatically formed coastal rock lies farther north. **Green Point,** 17 kilometers (10.6 miles) beyond Lobster Cove, presents a tilted, textured surface of ribbon limestone and shale embedded with fossils from the Cambrian and Ordovician periods.

Continuing north, you'll come to the parking lot for the short trail to Western Brook Pond. One kilometer (0.6 mile) farther is where Western Brook drains into the Gulf of St. Lawrence. You'll find a sandy beach and an oceanfront picnic area. The headland immediately to the north is **Broom Point.** Along the access road is a platform and telescope, which you can train on the mountains that rise from Western Brook Pond.

Cow Head

Cow Head, 10 kilometers (6.2 miles) north of Broom Point, features an angled formation similar to that of Green Point, with limestone breccia (jumbled limestone chunks and fossils) spread across a small peninsula. The areas are richly textured. At Cow Head, the breccia looks like light-colored rock pillows scattered across a dark rock surface, while Green Point's surface is a rich green and textured like crushed velvet. The rock layers at both places originated during deepwater avalanches as the Iapetus Ocean formed 460-550 million years ago. In the village itself, beside **St. Mary's Church,** is a small botanical garden.

ROUTE 431

From Wiltondale, 31 kilometers (19 miles) north of Deer Lake, Route 431 leads west, entering the park after 13 kilometers (8.1 miles).

Discovery Centre

If you've entered Gros Morne on Route 431, make your first stop the **Discovery Centre** (709/458-2417, mid-May-June and Sept.-early

Oct. daily 9am-5pm, July-Aug. daily 9am-6pm, included in park entry fee), on the hill above Woody Point. This modern facility showcases everything the national park is renowned for. The main display area holds an impressive 3-D map of the park, geological samples and descriptions, a human history display, and a theater. A gift shop sells park literature, and a café specializes in regional cuisine. Outside, a short trail leads through a garden planted with species native to the park.

★ Tablelands

The **Tablelands,** the park's most prized geological tract, lies along Route 431, halfway between Woody Point and Trout River. It's an odd sight, more resembling Hudson Bay's bleached brown barrens than verdant Newfoundland. The 12-by-7-kilometer (7.5-by-4.3-mile) chunk once lay beneath the ancient Iapetus Ocean. Violent internal upheavals eventually thrust the unearthly landscape to the surface. The parched yellow and tan cliffs and boulders that resulted are formed of peridotite, an igneous rock found in the earth's mantle. You can get a good idea of the landscape from the parking lot, but I encourage you to take a stroll along the easy Tablelands Trail. It's 4 kilometers (2.5 miles) each way, but you only need walk a short way to get a feeling for the starkness of the moon-like terrain.

Trout River

After leaving the Tablelands behind, Route 431 descends to the small fishing village of **Trout River,** on a protected bay 18 kilometers (11.2 miles) from Woody Point. A boardwalk rims the stony beach, leading past weather-worn wooden buildings to the mouth of the Trout River, where wharves are filled with lobster pots and fishing gear. Fronting the boardwalk are historic buildings open to the public, including the bright yellow 1898 Jacob A. Crocker House. Across the river, turn right over the bridge and look for a small sign on the left. This marks the start of a short trail (10

1: Lobster Cove Head Lighthouse; 2: moose, common throughout Gros Morne National Park; 3: the moonlike landscape of the Tablelands

minutes round-trip) leading to the Old Man, a rock stack that is visible from town.

RECREATION

More than 100 kilometers (62 miles) of marked and unmarked hiking trails lead novice to expert trekkers into the park's nooks and crannies. Several privately operated boat tours probe the fjords. A provincial fishing license (available at any sports store) opens up angling for brook trout and arctic char on the fast-flowing streams and rivers.

If you'd like to know more about Gros Morne's natural history and geology, plan on attending a scheduled interpretive program and evening campfire talk; see the information center for a schedule.

Hiking

Even if you're not a keen hiker, you can enjoy short interpretive walks at **Broom Point** (32 km/20 mi north of Rocky Harbour) and the **Tablelands,** as well as the 2-kilometer (1.2-mile) circuit of **Lobster Cove Head.** If you're planning on taking a boat tour on Western Brook Pond, you'll need to lace up your hiking boots for the 3-kilometer (1.9-mile) walk to the dock. But it's the following two longer hikes that get most of the attention.

Between the Tablelands and Trout River are two trailheads for the **Green Gardens.** This feature originated as lava from erupting volcanoes in the Iapetus Ocean. The longer option (16 km/9.9 mi round-trip; allow six hours) begins from Route 431 on the west side of the Tablelands. Four kilometers (2.5 miles) farther west is another trailhead for the Green Gardens. This is a 9-kilometer (5.6-mile) loop; allow four hours. Regardless of which trail you take, the trails emerge on a high headland cloaked in rich green grasses overlooking the gulf. Below the headland, sea stacks and sea caves (accessible only at low tide) rise from the beach floor beside cliffs pocked with pillow lava, the solidified remnants of molten rock from 100 kilometers (62 miles) beneath the ancient seafloor.

Feeling fit? If so, the hike to the 806-meter

(2,644-foot) bald summit of **Gros Morne Mountain** (8 km/5 mi one way; allow eight hours for the round-trip) may be what you're looking for. Beginning from Route 430, just east of the main information center, the first hour's walking is across flat terrain. Tightly packed boulders mark the beginning of the actual ascent, which takes 2-2.5 hours. Unexpectedly, the trail empties at a corner of the flattened peak. The air is clear and exhilarating, but surprisingly chilly. Far below, climbers scramble fitfully up the rocky ascent. To the west rise the Long Range Mountains. Looking south, you'll see a sapphire fjord, laid like an angled ribbon across the green woodlands. The summit is bare shale, limestone, and quartzite rock sprinkled with wild grass tufts. Check weather forecasts before heading out, and carry raingear, a first-aid kit, and extra food, clothing, and drinking water.

If you're not entirely comfortable undertaking longer hikes within the park, consider joining a group organized by **Gros Morne Adventures** (709/458-2722 or 800/685-4624, https://grosmorneadventures.com), which charges $150 per person for a full day of hiking.

★ Boat Tours

Like Scandinavia, Gros Morne National Park is famous for fjords, fringed sea arms carved by the last ice sheet and shouldered by forests and cliffs. Unlike their Scandinavian counterparts, the most spectacular are actually landlocked fjord lakes and are known as "ponds." These ponds—**Trout River, Ten Mile, Bakers Brook,** and **Western Brook**— were carved by the ice sheets. But in each case, when the enormous ice sheet melted out, the coastline—which had been compressed by the sheer weight of the glacier—rebounded like a sponge, rising above sea level and cutting the fjord off from the sea.

Bontours (709/458-2016 or 888/458-2016, www.bontours.ca, adult $65, child $30) offers a cruise on spectacular Western Brook Pond. Tickets can be booked by phone or in person at the Ocean View Motel in Rocky

The Galápagos of Geology

"What the Galápagos are to biology, Gros Morne is to geology," declared Britain's Prince Edward when he visited and dedicated Gros Morne National Park as a UNESCO World Heritage Site in 1987.

Long before Newfoundland was an island, it was a landlocked part of a great supercontinent formed during Precambrian times. When the supercontinent broke apart, the land plates drifted, and a rift formed that filled with water—the Iapetus Ocean. After another 50 million years, give or take, the land plates reversed direction and moved toward each other. As the landmasses were pushed together, Newfoundland, not yet an island, perched high and dry near the center of another supercontinent. At that point, Newfoundland's only distinctive characteristic was a mountain rib—the budding Appalachian Mountains that now rim North America's eastern edge.

Strewn among the mountains now protected by Gros Morne National Park was a colossal geological heritage: remnants from the world's first supercontinent and parts of the Iapetus Ocean's seafloor. East of the mountains, the island's central plateau portion was made up of a great rectangular swatch of the crumpled ancient seabed, 200-250 kilometers (124-155 miles) in width and length.

Between then and now, the eons added a few more topographical touches. The retreating ice sheet uncovered the Labrador Trough, scooped out the Strait of Belle Isle, cut fjords into the coastlines, and pocked the interiors to create myriad lakes, such as spectacular Western Brook Pond.

Harbour. To get to Western Brook Pond, you must drive 30 kilometers (19 miles) north from Rocky Harbour to a marked parking lot. From this point, it's a 3-kilometer (1.9-mile) hike to the boat dock. During July and August, three tours depart daily (10am, 1pm, and 4pm), while in June and September there's just one tour daily (12:30pm). Plan on leaving Rocky Harbour at least 90 minutes before the scheduled departure time. This tour lasts two hours.

Other Tours

Gros Morne Adventures (709/458-2722 or 800/685-4624, https://grosmorneadventures. com) leads geology and natural-history tours through the park late May-September. The four-day backpacking adventure on the Long Range Traverse costs $1,395, inclusive of meals, permits, and camping accommodations. Kayaking is another specialty; a half day with instruction costs $125 per person, and kayak rentals from the company's Norris Point base cost $55-65 per day.

ENTERTAINMENT AND EVENTS

To immerse yourself in the culture of Newfoundland, plan on spending an evening at the **Gros Morne Theatre Festival** (709/639-7238, www.theatrenewfoundland. com, adult $30-45, child $18-25), which runs June-mid-September at Cow Head, 48 kilometers (30 miles) north of Rocky Harbour. The festival comprises two plays enacted by more than 40 professional actors, with performances that tell the story of people and events that have helped shape the province.

In Rocky Harbour, the **Anchor Pub** (Ocean View Hotel, Main St., 709/458-2730, daily 11:30am-close) has traditional Newfoundland music most nights through summer. The cover charge is minimal, and the small space gets surprisingly crowded.

FOOD
Rocky Harbour

If you rise early, head to ★ **Fisherman's Landing** (44 Main St., 709/458-2060, daily 6am-11pm, $13-23), across from the wharf, for a cooked breakfast special that includes juice and coffee. The rest of the day, it's traditional Newfoundland cooking at reasonable prices—grilled pork chops with baked pota-toes and boiled vegetables, poached halibut, pan-fried cod tongues, and more. House wine is sold by the glass, but some bottles are under $30. A few tables have water views.

Cow Bay

Part of the Shallow Bay Motel complex, the **Bay View Family Restaurant** (193 Main St., 709/243-2471, daily 7am-9pm, $13-26) does indeed have bay views, but only from a few of the tables. Dining choices are as simple as a Newfie Mug (tea and molasses bread), but you can also order more recognizable meals, such as blackened salmon with Cajun spices and T-bone steaks.

Woody Point

The best two dining options are along the Woody Point waterfront. **Granite Coffee House** (Water St., 709/451-3236, daily 7am-5pm, breakfasts $8-11) has a wide range of cof-fee drinks, as well as full cooked breakfasts and soup and sandwich specials. Upstairs in a converted warehouse, and with outdoor ta-bles facing the water, **The Old Loft** (Water St., 709/453-2294, May-June and Sept. daily 11am-7pm, July-Aug. daily 11am-9pm, $12-23) is the best choice in town for lunch or dinner. Unlike many other Newfoundland restaurants, The Old Loft dishes up seafood choices that don't require a deep fryer in their preparation. The chowder is an excellent way to start, and if cheesecake is on the dessert menu, go for it.

Trout River

Along the waterfront in this end-of-the-road fishing village, the **Seaside Restaurant** (263 Main St., 709/451-3461, mid-May-mid-Oct. daily noon-9pm, $12-24) enjoys sweeping water views. The restaurant has a reputation for consistently good food. The seafood chow-der is overflowing with goodies, and the fish-and-chips are cooked to perfection.

ACCOMMODATIONS

Rocky Harbour, 72 kilometers (45 miles) from Deer Lake, has the best choice of accommo-dations and is centrally located for exploring the park.

Rocky Harbour

Those not camping will find a variety of ac-commodations in Rocky Harbour, the park's major service area. For B&B accommodations, **Evergreen B&B** (4 Evergreen Ln., 709/458-2692 or 800/905-3494, www.grosmorne.ca/evergreen, $95 s, $105 d) has three guest rooms and a large patio with barbecue facili-ties. It's open year-round, and rates include a full breakfast.

The **Ocean View Hotel** (38 Main St., 709/458-2730 or 800/563-9887, www.theoceanview.ca, mid-Mar.-mid-Dec., from $149-269 s or d) enjoys a prime location across from the water in the heart of Rocky Harbour. Rooms in the older wing are high-quality and spacious, while those in the newer wing offer ocean views (from $169). The motel also has a downstairs bar with nightly entertainment, an upstairs restaurant, a booking desk for Western Brook Pond boat tours, and a super-funky old-fashioned elevator.

A short walk from the harbor, the units at **Mountain Range Cottages** (32 Parsons Ln., 709/458-2199, www.mountainrangecottages.com, mid-May-mid-Oct., $135-165 s or d) are an excellent value. Each of the 10 simple but modern cottages has a full kitchen, a dining table, two separate bedrooms, a bathroom, and a balcony equipped with outdoor furni-ture and a barbecue.

Continue around the southern side of Rocky Harbour to reach ★ **Gros Morne Cabins** (Main St., 709/458-2020 or 888/603-2020, www.grosmornecabins.ca, $149-209 s or d), a modern complex of 22 polished log cabins strung out along the bay. Unfortunately, they don't take full advantage of the wonderful lo-cation (small windows and no balconies), but each has a kitchen, separate bedrooms, a pro-pane barbecue, and wireless Internet. Other amenities include a playground and laundry, while part of the complex is a large general store. These cabins are one of the few accommodations in the park open year-round.

Cow Head

In Cow Head, 48 kilometers (30 miles) north of Rocky Harbour, **Shallow Bay Motel and Cabins** (193 Main St., 709/243-2471 or 800/563-1946, www.shallowbaymotel.com, $105-145 s or d) lies close to long stretches of sandy beach, hiking trails, and Arches Provincial Park. The 68 guest rooms are basic but comfortable, and the 20 cabins have full kitchens. Amenities include a large restaurant and one of the only outdoor pools in western Newfoundland (don't worry, it's heated!).

Along Route 431

A luxurious lodging that seems a little out of place within this remote national park, **Sugar Hill Inn** (115 Sexton Rd., Norris Point, 709/458-2147 or 888/299-2147, www.sugarhillinn.ca, $175-275 s or d) is nevertheless a treat. The 11 guest rooms are accentuated with polished hardwood floors and earthy yet contemporary color schemes. The King Suites each have a vaulted ceiling, jetted tub, and sitting area with a leather couch. Breakfast is included in the rates, while dinner (mains $26-38) is extra. The inn is on the left as you descend to Norris Point.

One block back from the water in the heart of the village of Woody Point is **Aunt Jane's B&B** (1 Water St., 709/453-2485, www.grosmorneescapes.com, mid-May-mid-Oct., $75 s, $85-95 d), a charming 1880s home that contains five guest rooms, four with shared bathrooms. Aunt Jane's is one of numerous other guesthouses in town collectively marketed as **Victorian Manor Heritage Properties** (same contact). Another of these is **Uncle Steve's,** a trim three-bedroom home with a kitchen and a TV lounge. It costs $235 per night for the entire house, with a three-night minimum.

Trout River

At the end of Route 431 and a 10-minute walk along the river from the ocean, **Tableland Cottages** (709/451-2101, www.tablelandcottages.com, May-Oct., $120-150 s or d) has seven two-bedroom cottages, each with a small but workable kitchen.

CAMPING

Almost 300 campsites at five campgrounds lie within Gros Morne National Park. No electrical hookups are available, but each campground has flush toilets, fire pits (firewood costs $8 per bundle), at least one kitchen shelter, and a playground. All campgrounds except Green Point have hot showers.

A percentage of sites at all but Green Point can be reserved through **Parks Canada** (877/737-3783, www.pccamping.ca) for $11 per reservation—reassuring if you're visiting the park in the height of summer. The remaining sites fill on a first-come, first-served basis.

Route 430

Across Route 430 from Rocky Harbour, **Berry Hill Campground** (mid-June-early Sept., $19-26) has 69 sites, showers, kitchen shelters, and a playground. It fills quickly each summer afternoon, mostly with campers that have made advance reservations through Parks Canada, but also because of its central location.

The 31-site ★ **Green Point Campground** ($16), 12 kilometers (7.5 miles) north of Rocky Harbour, is the only park campground open year-round, and it is the only one without showers. The oceanfront setting more than makes up for a lack of facilities.

At the park's northern extremity, **Shallow Bay Campground** (early June-mid-Sept., $19-26) offers full facilities and 62 sites within walking distance of the services of a small town.

Route 431

Lomond Campground (mid-May-early Oct., $19-26) edges Bonne Bay's east arm. It is popular with anglers but also is the start of three short walking trails, including one along the Lomond River.

Turn left at the end of Route 431 to reach **Trout River Pond Campground** (early June-mid-Sept., $19-26), which is close to the Trout River boat tour dock. It's only a small facility (44 sites), but it has a beautiful setting, hot showers, a playground, and wireless Internet.

INFORMATION AND SERVICES

The **Park Visitor Centre** (Rte. 430, 709/458-2417, mid-May-June and early Sept.-mid-Oct. daily 9am-5pm, July-early Sept. daily 8am-8pm) stocks literature, sells field guides, presents slide shows, and has exhibits on the park's geology, landscapes, and history. Outside is a telescope for a close-up view of Gros Morne Mountain. The center is along Route 430, just before the turnoff to Rocky Harbour.

The **Discovery Centre** (Route 431, 709/458-2417, mid-May-June and Sept.-early Oct. daily 9am-5pm, July-Aug. daily 9am-6pm) is another source of park information.

For pre-trip planning, go to the **Parks Canada** website (www.pc.gc.ca) or check out the business links at www.grosmorne.com.

GETTING THERE AND AROUND

The nearest airport is in Deer Lake, 72 kilometers (45 miles) from Rocky Harbour. It is served by **Air Canada** (888/247-2262, www.aircanada.com) from Halifax and Montréal. Car rental companies with airport desks include Avis, Budget, Enterprise, National, and Thrifty. Each allows 200 free kilometers (124 miles) per day, meaning you'll be unlikely to rack up extra charges on a trip to the park.

To get to Rocky Harbour from Deer Lake, head northwest on Route 430 for 72 kilometers (45 miles), a 50-minute drive. From the ferry terminal in Port-aux-Basques, it's about 340 kilometers (210 miles) north to Rocky Harbour, four hours via Route 1 and Route 430.

Northern Peninsula

North of Gros Morne National Park, the Northern Peninsula sweeps northeast across mountainous, flat-topped barrens and ends in tundra strewn with glacial boulders. Route 430 (also known as the **Viking Trail**) runs alongside the gulf on the coastal plain and extends the peninsula's full length, finishing at St. Anthony, 420 kilometers (260 miles) north of Deer Lake.

As you drive this stretch of highway, you'll notice, depending on the time of year, either small black patches of dirt or tiny flourishing vegetable gardens lining the road. These roadside gardens belong to the people of the nearby villages; because of the region's nutrient-poor soil, people plant their gardens wherever they find a patch of fertile ground.

NORTH FROM GROS MORNE

Arches Provincial Park

Right beside the highway, just north of Gros Morne National Park, the intriguing geological feature known as **Arches Provincial Park** is well worth the drive, even if you're not planning on traveling up the Northern Peninsula. Two arches have been eroded into a grassed rock stack that sits along the rocky beach. At low tide you can climb underneath, but most visitors are happy to just stand back and snap a picture.

Daniel's Harbour

About 15 kilometers (9.3 miles) north of Arches Provincial Park is the village of **Daniel's Harbour**. It has an interesting little harbor and historic buildings such as the Nurse Myra Bennett Heritage House, once home to a woman known throughout Newfoundland and Labrador as the "Florence Nightingale of the North" for her medical exploits.

On the south side of town is **Bennett Lodge** (Rte. 430, 709/898-2211, www.bennettlodge.com, May-Oct., $95-105 s or d), nothing more than a modular motel with a restaurant and dimly lit lounge. But it's one of the least expensive motels on the Northern Peninsula and has ocean views through the small guest room windows.

PORT AU CHOIX

About 160 kilometers (99 miles) north of Rocky Harbour, a road spurs west off Route 430 for 10 kilometers (6.2 miles) to Port au Choix, a small fishing village with a human history that dates back more than 4,500 years. The historic site related to these early residents is the town's main attraction, but the local economy revolves around the ocean and cold-water shrimp (those tasty little shrimp you see in salads and the like).

Port au Choix National Historic Site

The Maritime Archaic people and the later Dorset and Groswater Inuit migrated from Labrador, roamed the Northern Peninsula, and then settled on the remote cape beyond the modern-day town of Port au Choix. Today the entire peninsula is protected, with trails leading to the various dig sites. Start your exploration of the **Port au Choix National Historic Site** at the **Visitor Reception Centre** (709/861-3522, mid-June-mid-Sept. daily 9am-5pm, adult $8, senior $6.60, child $4), which is signposted through town. Here, the three cultures are represented by artifacts, exhibits, and a reconstruction of a Dorset Inuit dwelling. Dig sites are scattered over the peninsula, with a 3.5-kilometer (2.2-mile) trail leading from the center to the most interesting site, Phillip's Garden. First discovered in the 1960s, archaeological digs here revealed Dorset dwellings and an incredible wealth of

Maritime Archaic cultural artifacts buried with almost 100 bodies at three nearby burial grounds. The digs continue to this day, and through summer you can watch archaeologists doing their painstaking work (if you're lucky, you may even see them uncover an ancient artifact). Free guided hikes depart daily at 1pm. If you drive through town beyond the shrimp-processing plant, you pass an Archaic cemetery and a parking lot, from which Phillip's Garden is a little closer (2.5 km/1.6 mi one-way).

Museum of Whales and Things

Along the main road into town, the small **Museum of Whales and Things** (709/861-3280, Mon.-Sat. 9am-5pm, donation) is the work of local Ben Ploughman, who has, as the name suggests, collected a 15-meter-long (49-foot-long) sperm whale skeleton, as well as other "things." In an adjacent studio, Ploughman makes and sells driftwood creations.

Food

As you cruise through town, it's difficult to miss the ★ **Anchor Café** (Fisher St., 709/861-3665, daily 11am-8pm, $8-20), with its white ship's bow jutting out into the parking lot. With the cold-water shrimp plant across the road, this is the place to try the local delicacy ($7 for a shrimp burger). You can also eat like locals have done for generations (corned fish with sides of brewis, pork scrunchions, and a slice of molasses bread) or try a Moratorium Dinner (a reference to the cod-fishing ban), such as roast turkey. Also good is the cod and shrimp chowder.

Along the same road, the **Sea Echo Motel** (Fisher St., 709/861-3777, summer daily 7am-9pm, the rest of the year daily 7:30am-7:30pm, $12-24) has a nautically themed restaurant with similar fare, including fish cakes and cod tongues.

Accommodations

As the town of Port au Choix continues to unfold its rich archaeological heritage, it also continues to expand its visitor services. One of these is **Jeannie's Sunrise Bed and Breakfast** (84 Fisher St., 709/861-2254 or 877/639-2789, www.jeanniessunrisebb.com, $99-129 s or d), owned by lifelong Port au Choix resident Jeannie Billard. Each of the five rooms is bright and spacious and has its own TV. The less expensive rooms share a bathroom. Rates include a full breakfast, and dinner is available on request. Jeannie also offers a self-contained two-bedroom cottage for $150 per night.

Sea Echo Motel (Fisher St., 709/861-3777, www.seaechomotel.ca, $125-150 s or d, including breakfast) has 30 fairly standard motel rooms with wireless Internet, three cabins, a few campsites ($20), a restaurant with lots of local seafood, and a lounge.

Getting There

Port au Choix is 160 kilometers (99 miles) north of Rocky Harbour, a two-hour drive on Route 430. From the ferry terminal in Port-aux-Basques, it's 500 kilometers (310 miles) north along Route 1 and Route 430 to Port au Choix, a six-hour drive.

PLUM POINT

Continuing up the Northern Peninsula, the first worthwhile stop north of Port au Choix is Plum Point, where archaeologists have found evidence of human habitation from 4,500 years ago. At Plum Point, 60 kilometers (37 miles) north of Port au Choix, Route 430 continues north and Route 432 spurs east toward Roddickton. The latter is the longer route to St. Anthony, but an abundance of moose makes it an interesting alternative.

Bird Cove

Although visited by Captain Cook in 1764 and settled permanently by Europeans in 1900, Plum Point's first residents made a home for themselves as early as 4,500 years ago. These Maritime Archaic people were prehistoric hunters and gatherers who spent summers on the edge of **Bird Cove.** The two adjacent village sites, discovered as recently as the 1990s, were rare because they presented archaeologists with an undisturbed look at life many thousands of years ago. Shell middens, spear points used to hunt sea mammals, and tools used for woodworking have all been excavated. A boardwalk with interpretive panels leads around the site. To get there, drive to the end of the road, loop left past the grocery store, and take the unpaved road on the right-hand side of the light brown house. The boardwalk is on the left, a little under 1 kilometer (0.6 mile) from the grocery store.

Dog Peninsula

Beyond the general store, stay right as the road loops around, and you soon find yourself at a bridge linking the **Dog Peninsula** to the mainland. The peninsula is laced with walking trails that follow the shoreline and pass through the remains of an 1880s settlement. You can complete the first loop (turn right at the far end of the bridge) in around 30 minutes, even with time spent skimming a few of the super-flat stones into Bird Cove.

Food and Accommodations

Between the highway and the ocean, **Plum Point Motel** (709/247-2533 or 888/663-2533, www.plumpointmotel.com, $110-140 s or d) has 40 motel rooms and 18 basic cabins with kitchenettes. With a few water-view tables, the in-house **restaurant** (daily 7am-9pm, $12-24) serves the usual array of island cooking, including salted cod for breakfast, soups and sandwiches for lunch, and deep-fried seafood for dinner.

Getting There

Plum Point is about 60 kilometers (37 miles) north of Port au Choix, a 50-minute drive via Route 430. From the ferry terminal in Port-aux-Basques, it's about 550 kilometers (340 miles) north to Plum Point, 6.5-7 hours via Route 1 and Route 430.

The main highway up the Northern Peninsula, Route 430, continues north from Plum Point, but an abundance of moose makes Route 432, which spurs east toward

Roddickton, an interesting albeit longer alternative.

ST. BARBE

St. Barbe, 20 kilometers (12.4 miles) north of Plum Point and 300 kilometers (185 miles) north of Deer Lake, is where ferries depart for Labrador. There's little to see or do in town, but accommodations are provided at the **Dockside Motel** (709/877-2444 or 877/677-2444, $99-129 s or d), which isn't at the dock at all. Instead, it's on the road leading down to the waterfront. Rooms are basic but adequate, the 10 cabins have kitchens, and the simple in-house restaurant is open daily for breakfast, lunch, and dinner.

Getting There

St. Barbe is 20 kilometers (12.4 miles) north of Plum Point, a 20-minute drive via Route 430. From the ferry terminal in Port-aux-Basques, it's 580 kilometers (360 miles) north to St. Barbe, seven hours via Route 1 and Route 430.

Catching the Ferry to Labrador

If you are planning on exploring the Labrador Straits region, make ferry reservations long before arriving in St. Barbe. The ticket office is at the Dockside Motel, and even with reservations, you'll need to check in before heading down to the dock. The ferry **MV Apollo** (866/535-2567, www.labradormarine.com) sails from St. Barbe once or twice daily between early May and early January. The crossing takes around two hours. The one-way fare is a reasonable vehicle and driver $36, extra adult $12, senior and child $10. Across the road from the Dockside Motel is a fenced compound with hookups for RVs and a drop-off area for those catching the ferry and not wanting to travel with full rigs.

ST. BARBE TO ST. ANTHONY

It's 110 kilometers (68 miles) between St. Barbe and St. Anthony. For the first 50 kilometers (31 miles), Route 430 hugs the Strait of Belle Isle, passing a string of fishing villages clinging tenuously to the rocky coastline. Tourist services are minimal, but there are a couple of worthwhile stops, and you should take the time to wander through one or more of these outports to get a feeling for the sights, sounds, and smells that go with living along this remote stretch of coastline.

Deep Cove Wintering Interpretation Site

Just beyond the turnoff to the modern-day village of Anchor Cove is **Deep Cove Wintering Interpretation Site,** an observation platform and trail that leads to the site of an 1860s village where residents of Anchor Cove would spend the winter. Only the weathered remains of a few wooden homes are left, but the site is interesting as one of the rare cases of European seasonal migration. It takes about 10 minutes to reach the site from Route 430.

★ Thrombolites of Flowers Cove

The picturesque village of **Flowers Cove,** its low profile of trim homes broken only by the occasional church spire, lies 13 kilometers (8.1 miles) north of St. Barbe. Turn onto Burns Road from Route 430 to reach the red-roofed Marjorie Bridge. Beyond the bridge, a boardwalk leads along the cove to an outcrop of **thrombolites.** Resembling flower-shaped boulders, they are actually the remnants of algae and bacteria that have been dated at 650 million years old, making them among the earliest forms of life on earth. While the actual thrombolites are, of course, interesting, it is the complete lack of surrounding hype for what is one of the world's rarest fossils (the only other place they occur is on the remote west coast of Australia) that makes visiting the site even more unforgettable.

ST. ANTHONY

Although you will want to continue north to L'Anse aux Meadows, St. Anthony (pop. 2,300), 450 kilometers (280 miles) north of

Deer Lake, is the last real town and a service center for the entire Northern Peninsula. Most attractions revolve around Dr. Wilfred Grenfell, a medical missionary from England who established hospitals along both sides of Labrador Straits in the late 1800s. His impact on St. Anthony was especially powerful. It was here, in 1900, that Grenfell built his first year-round hospital and established a medical mission headquarters. St. Anthony still serves as the center of operations for the International Grenfell Association, which continues to build hospitals and orphanages and funds other community endeavors across the country.

The main natural attraction is **Fishing Point Park,** through town. From this lofty point, you have the chance to spy whales or icebergs.

Grenfell Historic Properties

Start your discovery of everything Grenfell at the **Grenfell Interpretation Centre** (West St., 709/454-4010, July-Aug. daily 8am-5pm, Sept.-June Mon.-Fri. 9am-5pm, adult $10, senior $8, child $3). This large facility details Grenfell's many and varied accomplishments, from the establishment of his first hospital at Battle Harbour to the work of the association that carries his name today. Grenfell also

helped foster financial independence for remote outports through profitable organizations such as **Grenfell Handicrafts,** which still produces hand-embroidered cassocks, fox-trimmed parkas, hooked rugs, and jackets that are sold at a gift shop across from the admissions desk of the Grenfell Interpretation Centre.

Exit the museum through the tearoom and you come across the tiny **Dock House Museum** (July-Aug. daily 10am-4pm, free). Displays here describe how Grenfell's ships were pulled from the water for repairs after long voyages to remote communities.

A tribute to the life and works of Dr. Grenfell lives in the **Jordi Bonet Murals,** impressive ceramic panels adorning the walls of the rotunda at the entrance to Curtis Memorial Hospital, which is across the road from the Grenfell Interpretation Centre.

Exhibits at the stately green-and-white **Grenfell House Museum** (July-Aug. daily 8am-5pm, Sept.-June Mon.-Fri. 8am-5pm, free with proof of paid admission to Interpretation Centre), his home for many years, describe Grenfell's home and family life. The home is on the far side of the hospital, a five-minute walk from the Interpretation Centre. A trail starting from behind the home leads to Tea

The thrombolites of Flowers Cove are the world's oldest living organisms.

House Hill, where viewing platforms provide sweeping harbor views.

Tours

As the gateway to Iceberg Alley, St. Anthony is the place to take to the water in a tour boat. **Northland Discovery** (709/454-3092 or 877/632-3747, late May-mid-Sept., adult $61, child $25) departs three times daily from behind the Grenfell Interpretation Centre. When there's a lack of icebergs (mid-June-Aug. is the best viewing period), the captain concentrates on searching out humpback, minke, and fin whales, as well as seabirds. The covered vessel is stable and has washrooms. The 2.5-hour tours include hot drinks.

Food

Drive through town to reach ★ **Lightkeeper's** (Fishing Point Rd., 709/454-4900, summer daily 11:30am-9pm, $19-30), which, true to its name, follows a red-and-white color scheme that extends all the way down to the salt and pepper shakers. Housed in a converted light-keeper's residence overlooking the ocean (you may spot icebergs June-Aug.), this tiered dining room is casual, although a little on the expensive side. Starters include crab claws with garlic butter, while mains are mostly from the ocean, including poached halibut, seafood chowder, and salted cod cakes.

Cartier's Galley (Haven Inn, 14 Goose Cove Rd., 709/454-9100, summer daily 7am-9pm, the rest of the year daily 5pm-8pm, $13-19) is a small, bright dining room that catches the morning sun. Cooked breakfasts are $9-12 and predictable dinners, such as roast beef and mashed potatoes, are all under $20.

Accommodations

Fishing Point B&B (Fishing Point Rd., 709/454-3117 or 866/454-2009, from $120 s or d) is through town and within walking distance of Lightkeeper's, the best place to eat in town. Built in the 1940s, the converted fisherman's home is set right on the harbor and has three guest rooms with either private or en suite bathrooms. Rates include a full breakfast.

Haven Inn (14 Goose Cove Rd., 709/454-9100 or 877/428-3646, www.haveninn.ca, $115-155 s or d) has 30 rooms in various configurations on a slight rise off Route 430. Rooms are fairly standard, but each has a coffeemaker and hair dryer; the more expensive ones have water views and gas fireplaces. The in-house Cartier's Galley restaurant (summer daily 7am-9pm, the rest of the year daily 5pm-8pm) dishes up inexpensive breakfasts.

A converted 1915 nursing residence that has been extensively renovated, **Grenfell Heritage Hotel** (1 McChada Dr., 709/454-8395 or 888/450-8398, www.grenfellheritagehotel.ca, $140-180 s or d) is the town's newest lodging, but it's also the most expensive. Rooms are simple but clean and comfortable. Kitchenettes, a free continental breakfast, and a handy waterfront location are all pluses.

Getting There

It's 110 kilometers (68 miles) from St. Barbe to St. Anthony going north and then east on Route 430, a 1.5-hour drive. From the ferry terminal in Port-aux-Basques, it's about 690 kilometers (430 miles) north to St. Anthony, 9.5 hours via Route 1 and Route 430.

TOP EXPERIENCE

★ L'ANSE AUX MEADOWS

At the very end of Route 436 lies L'Anse aux Meadows, 40 kilometers (25 miles) from St. Anthony and as far as you can drive up the Northern Peninsula. It was here that the Vikings came ashore more than 1,000 years ago—the first Europeans to step foot in North America. Two Viking attractions make the drive worthwhile, but there's also a fine restaurant and lots of wild and rugged scenery.

L'Anse aux Meadows National Historic Site

Long before archaeologists arrived,

Newfoundlanders were aware of the odd-shaped sod-covered ridges across the coastal plain at L'Anse aux Meadows. George Decker, a local fisherman, led Norwegian scholar-explorer Helge Ingstad and his wife, archaeologist Anne Stine Ingstad, to the area in the 1960s. The subsequent digs uncovered eight complexes of rudimentary houses, workshops with fireplaces, and a trove of artifacts, which verified the Norse presence. National recognition and site protection followed, leading to the creation of the **L'Anse aux Meadows National Historic Site** in 1977 and to UNESCO designating it a World Heritage Site the following year.

A **Visitor Reception Centre** (Rte. 436, 709/623-2608, June and Sept.-early Oct. daily 9am-5pm, July-Aug. daily 9am-6pm, adult $12, senior $10, child $6) has been developed above the site. Here you can admire excavated artifacts, view site models, and take in an audiovisual presentation. A gravel path and boardwalk lead across the grassy plain to the site of the settlement, where panels describe the original uses of buildings now marked by depressions in the grass-covered field. Just beyond is a settlement of re-created buildings overlooking Epaves Bay. Costumed interpreters reenact the roles and work of the Norse captain, his wife, and four crew members.

Norstead

Just beyond the turnoff to L'Anse aux Meadows National Historic Site is **Norstead** (Rte. 436, 709/623-2828, early June-mid-Sept. daily 9:30am-5:30pm, adult $10, senior $8, child $6.50), the re-creation of a Viking port of trade. Aside from the Viking theme, it has little resemblance to how the Vikings of L'Anse aux Meadows lived, but it is still well worth visiting. Right on the water, you can see a full-size replica of a Viking ship, listen to stories in the dimly lit Chieftains Hall, watch a blacksmith at work, and sample bread as it comes from the oven in the dining hall. The costumed interpreters bring this place to life, and you can easily spend an hour or more listening and watching them at work and play.

Food

Amazingly, at the end of the road is one of the finest dining rooms in all of Newfoundland, the ★ **Norseman Restaurant** (709/754-3105, late May-late Sept. daily noon-9pm, $19-36). Admittedly, the ocean views add to the

L'Anse aux Meadows National Historic Site

appeal, but the food is fresh and creative, the service professional, and the setting casual yet refined. Starters include a smooth shellfish-less seafood chowder, smoked char, and lots of salads. Ordering lobster takes a little more effort than usual—you'll be invited to wander across the road with your waitress to pick one from an ocean pound. Other entrées include cod baked in a mustard and garlic crust and grilled Labrador caribou brushed with a red-wine glaze. Still hungry? It's hard to go past a slice of freshly baked pie filled with local berries.

The ★ **Dark Tickle Company** (75 Main St., Griquet, 709/623-2354, June-Sept. daily 9am-6pm, Oct.-May Mon.-Fri. 9am-5pm) uses locally harvested berries to create a delicious array of jams, preserves, sauces, and even chocolates and wines. You can watch the various processes in creating the finished product, but you'll also want to sample and purchase them from the attached store.

Accommodations and Camping

The village of L'Anse aux Meadows comprises just a smattering of homes on the headland. For overnight accommodations, there are a few choices back toward St. Anthony, all more enjoyable than staying in one of St. Anthony's nondescript motels.

The closest accommodations are in Hay Cove, a cluster of houses 2 kilometers (1.2 miles) before the end of the road. Stay in one of four comfortable guest rooms at **Jenny's Runestone House** (709/623-2811 or 877/865-3958, www.jennysrunestonehouse. ca, Apr.-Oct., $100-150 s or d) and enjoy ocean views and a hot breakfast each morning. Also in Hay Cove, **Viking Village Bed and Breakfast** (709/623-2238 or 877/858-2238, www.vikingvillage.ca, $85 s, $110 d) has five en suite guest rooms, ocean views, a TV room, and laundry facilities.

The units at **Southwest Pond Cabins** (Rte. 436, Griquet, 709/623-2140 or 800/515-2261, www.southwestpondcabins.ca, May-Oct., $119 s or d), overlooking a small lake

9 kilometers (5.6 miles) from L'Anse aux Meadows, are an excellent value. Each of 10 spacious wooden cabins has a kitchen, separate bedrooms, satellite TV, and a bathroom. Other amenities include a playground, barbecues, and a grocery store.

At the top of the list for originality is ★ **Quirpon Lighthouse Inn** (Quirpon Island, 709/634-2285 or 877/254-6586, www. linkumtours.com, May-Oct., $425-450 s or d), a converted light-keeper's residence and modern addition that house a total of 11 guest rooms, each with an en suite bath. Rates include all meals and boat transfers (45 minutes) from Quirpon. To get to Quirpon, turn off Route 436, 6 kilometers (3.7 miles) beyond Griquet. Watch icebergs float by and whales frolic in the surrounding waters, or join a Zodiac tour searching out whales and icebergs ($50 extra pp).

One of the few commercial campgrounds this far north is **Viking RV Park** (Rte. 436, Quirpon, 709/623-2425, June-Sept.), where tent campers pay $18 and RVs wanting hookups are charged $28 per night.

Getting There

It's 40 kilometers (25 miles) north from St. Anthony to L'Anse aux Meadows, a 40-minute drive via Route 430 and Route 436. From the ferry terminal in Port-aux-Basques, it's 700 kilometers (435 miles) north to L'Anse aux Meadows, 10 hours via Routes 1, 430, and 436.

RALEIGH

Between St. Anthony and L'Anse aux Meadows, Route 437 branches off Route 436 to the delightfully named Ha Ha Bay and the small town of Raleigh.

★ Burnt Cape Ecological Reserve

Encompassing a barren landscape of limestone, the **Burnt Cape Ecological Reserve** is an unheralded highlight of the Northern Peninsula. The plant life is especially notable, as many species would normally only be found in Arctic regions, while others, such as

Long's Braya and Burnt Cape cinquefoil, are found nowhere else in the world. A geological oddity are polygons, circular patterns of small stones formed by heavy frosts. On the western edge of the cape are sea caves, some big enough to hold pools of water when the tide recedes. Looking straight ahead from the parking lot, you'll see aquamarine pools of water at the base of the cliffs, known locally as the Cannon Holes. The sun reflecting on the limestone bedrock warms the trapped seawater, and you'll often see locals taking a dip on hot days.

To get there, turn left in downtown Raleigh, round the head of Ha Ha Bay, and follow the rough unpaved road up and through the barrens. The end of the road is a semi-official parking lot high above the ocean, 4 kilometers (2.5 miles) from the interpretive board at the entrance to the reserve. As there are no marked trails and many of the highlights are hidden from view, stop by the office at **Pisolet Bay Provincial Park** (just before Raleigh, 709/454-7570) for directions and up-to-date information on access.

Accommodations and Camping

The only accommodation in town is a good one—**Burnt Cape Cabins** (709/452-3521, www.burntcape.com, $129-149 s or d), which is beside a **café** (daily 8am-9pm) serving inexpensive seafood and lobster dinners for $26. Each of the seven modern cabins has a TV, Internet access, and comfortable beds, or choose to rent the affiliated three-bedroom home ($189).

Just before Route 437 descends to Raleigh, it passes **Pisolet Bay Provincial Park** (709/454-7570, June-mid-Sept., $18), which offers 30 sites, a kitchen shelter, washrooms with showers, and a lake with a beach and swimming for the brave.

Getting There

To get to Raleigh from St. Anthony, it's 30 kilometers (19 miles) north, a 25-minute drive via Route 430 and Route 437. From the ferry terminal in Port-aux-Basques, it's 690 kilometers (430 miles) north to Raleigh, 10 hours via Routes 1, 430, and 437.

Labrador

Spanning 294,330 square kilometers (113,640 square miles), two and a half times the size of Newfoundland island and three times the size of the three Maritime provinces, Labrador dominates the geography of Atlantic Canada.

This, the mainland portion of Newfoundland and Labrador, resembles an irregular wedge pointing toward the North Pole, bordered on the east by 8,000 kilometers (4,970 miles) of coastline on the Labrador Sea, and on the west and south by the remote outskirts of Québec. Thorfinn Karlsefni, one of several Norse explorers who sailed the coastline around AD 1000, is said to have dubbed the region "Helluland" for the large flat rocks, and "Markland" for the woodlands. Jacques Cartier

Highlights

Look for ★ to find recommended sights, activities, dining, and lodging.

★ **L'Anse Amour:** North America's oldest known burial site and an imposing stone lighthouse combine to make the short detour to the "cove of love" a highlight (page 425).

★ **Red Bay National Historic Site:** Four Spanish galleons lie in Red Bay; onshore displays tell their story and that of what was at one time the world's largest whaling port (page 426).

★ **Battle Harbour:** Known locally as "outports," dozens of remote communities throughout Newfoundland and Labrador have been abandoned over the last few decades. Battle Harbour is one of the few that encourages tourism (page 427).

★ **North West River:** A short drive from Happy Valley-Goose Bay, this small community is home to the Labrador Interpretation Centre, while down along the river you can watch local Innu hauling in the day's catch (page 430).

★ **Torngat Mountains National Park:** This remote park can only be reached by charter flight, but once there, adventurous visitors can explore the mountains on foot and the coastline by kayak (page 436).

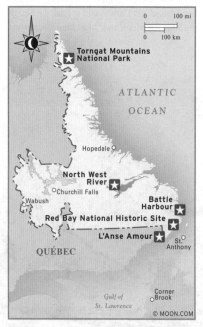

Labrador

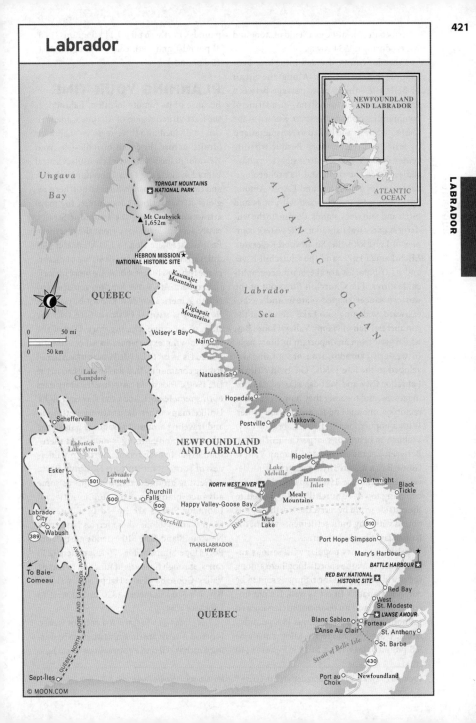

© MOON.COM

described the coastline as a "land of stone and rocks" during a 1534 voyage.

Labrador can be divided into three geographical destinations. Along the Strait of Belle Isle—the narrow passage between Labrador and Newfoundland—is a string of communities fronting the strait. Known as the Labrador Straits and linked to Newfoundland by ferry, this region was a Basque whaling center in the 1500s. Modern sightseers have rediscovered the strait and its archaeological treasures at Red Bay and L'Anse Amour. Spruce forests, interspersed with bogs and birch and tamarack stands, dominate the wilderness of central Labrador. The watery complex of Lobstick Lake, Smallwood Reservoir, Michikamau Lake, and the Churchill River and its tributaries are the main geographical features. The Churchill flows out of the western saucer-shaped plateau and rushes eastward, widening into Lake Melville at the commercial hub of Happy Valley-Goose Bay, which grew from an important military base. In western Labrador, iron-ore mining developed in the late 1950s. The twin cities of Labrador City and Wabush started as mining towns, and together they now serve as the region's economic and transportation center. With a population of 11,300, Labrador City/Wabush is Labrador's largest municipality. Between Labrador City and Happy Valley-Goose Bay, a massive hydroelectric plant, developed in the late 1960s, spawned another company town—Churchill Falls. Linked to the outside world by ferry, the North Coast is dotted with tiny Inuit settlements within the Nunatsiavut land-claim area.

Labrador is very popular with serious anglers, who rank the sportfishing here among the world's best. And the fishing is said to be Atlantic Canada's finest as well: It's not uncommon to land an *ouananiche* (landlocked salmon) weighing 4 kilograms (8.8 pounds). Brook trout here range 3-4 kilograms (6.6-8.8 pounds), lake trout to 18 kilograms (40 pounds), northern pike 9-14 kilograms (19.8-31 pounds), and arctic char 5-7 kilograms (11-15.4 pounds).

PLANNING YOUR TIME

Because of its remote location, Labrador is the least-visited region of Atlantic Canada. It can be divided into three regions—Labrador Straits, across the Strait of Belle Isle from Newfoundland's Northern Peninsula; Central Labrador, along the TransLabrador Highway; and the North Coast. While the northern regions attract serious adventurers, the main attractions lie along the Labrador Straits, easily accessible by ferry from the Northern Peninsula, where along a 120-kilometer (74-mile) stretch of highway is a string of picturesque fishing villages. Some are more historic than others. At **L'Anse Amour,** you can view North America's oldest known burial site; **Red Bay National Historic Site** tells the story of a Basque whaling port. One of the most moving experiences in all of Atlantic Canada is a visit to **Battle Harbour,** an island fishing community that was abandoned in the late 1960s. Today you can relive the glory days of this remote port, and even stay overnight. Unlike many other destinations, getting to and traveling around Labrador is part of the adventure, and nothing is more "out there" than exploring the remote northern wilderness of **Torngat Mountains National Park.**

Getting around Labrador requires some advance planning. The communities of Labrador Straits are linked by Route 510 from Blanc Sablon, where ferries land from Newfoundland. The 510 extends north from Port Hope Simpson for 370 kilometers (230 miles) through Cartwright Junction to Happy Valley-Goose Bay. From Happy Valley-Goose Bay, it's 520 kilometers (320 miles) west to Labrador City.

Deciding *when* to travel to Labrador is easy. July and August are the only two months during which you'll find all attractions open. June

---

Previous: kayaking along Labrador's North Coast; Battle Harbour; Pinware River.

hiking in Torngat Mountains National Park

and September are shoulder months, when the weather is cooler and attractions begin opening and closing. Also be aware that transportation is conducted on a weather-permitting basis. Early-season ice packs and late-season storms can delay the ferries. The region's smaller aircraft need daylight and good visibility. An absence of both may ground flights for days.

Labrador Straits

The communities of Labrador Straits lie across the Strait of Belle Isle from Newfoundland. They are linked by a 160-kilometer (99-mile) stretch of paved road that extends between Blanc Sablon (Québec) and Mary's Harbour. From Mary's Harbour, an unpaved road loops inland and continues north to Goose Bay.

Getting There by Ferry

The ferry **MV Apollo** (866/535-2567, www.labradormarine.com, one-way vehicle and driver $36, extra adult $12, senior and child $10) links the Labrador Straits to Newfoundland. Ferries depart St. Barbe, 300 kilometers (185 miles) north of Deer Lake, once or twice daily early May-early January. The crossing takes around two hours. The arrival point is Blanc Sablon, located in Québec but just a five-minute drive from L'Anse-au-Clair, within Labrador. If the weather is pleasant, find a spot outside and keep an eye out for whales. Inside the ferry are a café and gift shop. Reservations are not required but are definitely recommended for travel in July and August. Even with a reservation, upon arrival at St. Barbe you should check in at the ferry office. It is within the Dockside Motel (on the right before the terminal) and opens two hours before scheduled departures. At Blanc Sablon, the ferry office is at the terminal, along with a craft shop, food concession, and information booth.

L'ANSE-AU-CLAIR

Founded in the early 18th century by French sealers, L'Anse-au-Clair is the closest strait community to the Québec border. Fishing is still the livelihood for the population of

The Grenfell Legend

Labrador's harsh living conditions and lack of medical care attracted Dr. Wilfred Grenfell, the British physician-missionary. Dr. Grenfell worked with the Royal National Mission to Deep Sea Fishermen on the North Sea. A visit in 1892 convinced him that serving the people of remote Labrador and northern Newfoundland was his calling. He established Labrador's first coastal hospital at Battle Harbour the next year, followed by a large mission at St. Anthony. From the mission, he sailed along the coast in boats, treating 15,000 patients in 1900 alone. By 1907 he had opened treatment centers at Indian Harbour, Forteau, North West River, and seven other remote settlements. For his efforts, he was knighted.

Dr. Grenfell initiated a policy of free medical treatment, clothing, or food in exchange for labor or goods. Funded by private contributions and the Newfoundland government, he opened cooperative stores, nursing homes, orphanages, mobile libraries, and lumber mills. He also initiated the Grenfell Handicrafts programs and home gardening projects. In 1912, he formed the International Grenfell Association to consolidate the English, Canadian, and American branches that funded his work. The physician was subsequently knighted a second time, in 1927, and also awarded recognition by the Royal Scottish Geographical Society and other notable organizations.

about 300, although crafts also contribute to the economy. For these, head to **Moore's Handicrafts** (8 Country Rd., 709/931-2086, June-Sept. daily 8:30am-9pm), signposted across from the information center. Pieces to look for include hand-knit woolens, winter coats, cassocks, and moccasins.

Sights and Recreation

The **Gateway to Labrador Visitor Centre** (38 Main Hwy., 709/931-2013, www.labradorcoastaldrive.com, late June-mid-Sept. daily 9am-6pm), the region's interpretive center, seen as you enter town from Québec, is in a handsomely restored, early 20th-century Anglican church. Inside, exhibits, photographs, fossils, and artifacts represent the area's fishing heritage.

The information center staff can also point out two interesting walks. The shorter of the two is to the **"Jersey Rooms,"** site of an early-1700s sealing station operated by men from Jersey. Only stone foundations and a stone walkway remain, but the 2-kilometer (1.2 mile) trail also offers sweeping ocean views. The trailhead is signposted beyond the wharf. At the far end of the beach, a trail leads across the barrens to **Square Cove,** where the boilers are all that remain of a 1954 shipwreck.

In August, wild strawberries are a bonus along this 3-kilometer (1.9-mile) each way walk.

Food and Accommodations

The largest accommodation along the Labrador Straits is the **Northern Light Inn** (58 Main St., 709/931-2332 or 800/563-3188, www.northernlightinn.com, $129-179 s or d), which has 70 comfortable rooms and a few RV sites ($30). The inn's **restaurant** (daily 7am-10pm, $16-35) is well priced throughout the day, with dinner mains topping out at $35 for steamed crab legs with mashed potato and vegetables. Other dinner offerings are as simple as spaghetti and meatballs and as fishy as pan-fried cod.

FORTEAU

Established as a cod-fishing settlement by islanders from Jersey and Guernsey in the late 1700s, Forteau remains a fishing community, not only in the cod industry but also as a base for anglers fishing the salmon- and trout-filled Forteau and Pinware Rivers.

The **Bakeapple Folk Festival,** held over three days in mid-August, is always popular. The gathering includes traditional music, dance, storytelling, crafts, and Labrador foods.

Food and Accommodations

Forteau's accommodations include the **Grenfell Louie A Hall Bed and Breakfast** (3 Willow Ave., 709/931-2916, www.grenfellbandb.ca, May-Sept., $110 s, $120-125 d, including a light breakfast, cottage $165 s or d), in a nursing station built by the International Grenfell Association. The five guest rooms are comfortable but share bathrooms, or choose the adjacent two-bedroom cottage with full kitchen. Other amenities include an antiques-filled dining room and a lounge where you can watch films on the Grenfell legacy or read up on local history.

Along the highway in the center of town, **Seaview Cottages & Restaurant** (33 Main St., 709/931-2840 or 800/931-2840, www.labradorseaview.ca, $100-110 s or d) has motel rooms, not cabins, but they are comfortable, and each has one or two bedrooms, a kitchen, and wireless Internet. The **restaurant** (daily 11am-9pm, $12-24) has simple preparations of locally caught cod, char, and salmon.

Getting There

Forteau is 10 kilometers (6.2 miles) east of L'Anse au Clair via Route 510.

★ L'ANSE AMOUR

Just off Route 510, this tiny community comprises just four houses, all owned by members of the Davis family, residents since the 1850s. The bay was originally named Anse aux Morts ("Cove of the Dead") for the many shipwrecks that occurred in the treacherous waters offshore. A mistranslation by later English settlers resulted quite charmingly in the name **L'Anse Amour** ("Cove of Love").

Maritime Archaic Burial Mound National Historic Site

Turn off Route 510 to L'Anse Amour and watch for a small interpretive board on the right, which marks the **Maritime Archaic Burial Mound National Historic Site.** Here, in 1973, archaeologists uncovered a Maritime Archaic burial site of a 12-year-old boy dated to 6900 BC, which makes it North America's oldest known funeral monument. The dead boy was wrapped in skins and birch bark and placed face-down in a pit. Items such as a walrus tusk were excavated from the pit, and other evidence points to a ceremonial feast. The artifacts found here are on display at The Rooms in St. John's.

Point Amour Lighthouse

Point Amour Lighthouse

At the end of the road is **Point Amour Lighthouse** (709/927-5825, late May-early Oct. daily 9:30am-5pm, adult $6, senior $4, child $3). The strait's rich sea has attracted intrepid fishing fleets through the centuries: The early Basques sailed galleons into Red Bay, followed by English and French fleets, and eventually Newfoundlanders arrived in schooners to these shores. By 1857, shipwrecks littered the treacherous shoals, and the colonial government erected this 33-meter-high (108-foot-high) beacon, Atlantic Canada's tallest. Now restored, the stone lighthouse and light-keeper's residence (now the interpretive center) feature displays and exhibits on the history of those who have plied the strait's waters. The 122-step climb to the top (the final section is a ladder) affords excellent views of the strait and the surrounding land.

Accommodations

One of the village's four homes operates as ★ **Lighthouse Cove B&B** (709/927-5690, $50 s, $60 d), with three rooms open year-round for travelers. The hosts, the Davis family, are very hospitable, spending the evening with guests relating stories of the area and their 150-year history living in the cove. When you make a reservation, be sure to reserve a spot at the dinner table (extra) for a full meal of traditional Labrador cooking, using game such as moose and caribou. Breakfast, included in the rate, comes with homemade preserves.

Getting There

L'Anse Amour is 12 kilometers (7.5 miles) east of Forteau on Route 510.

RED BAY

Little evidence is left today, but 400 years ago, Red Bay was the world's largest whaling port. Not discovered until the 1970s, four Spanish galleons at the bottom of the bay have taught archaeologists many secrets about the whaling industry and early boat construction; an excellent national historic site here brings the port to life. The village itself, 40 kilometers (25 miles) north of L'Anse Amour, has limited services.

It is estimated that between 1540 and 1610, around 2,500 Basque men (from an area of Spain near the French border) made the crossing from Europe each year, traveling in up to 30 galleons that returned to Europe filled with whale oil. The Basques came to harvest right whales, which migrated through the Strait of Belle Isle. Most of the men lived aboard the galleons, but evidence shows that some built simple shelters on the mainland and Saddle Island, where red roof tiles still litter the beaches.

★ Red Bay National Historic Site

Four Spanish galleons lie in Red Bay, including the well-preserved *San Juan*. Archaeologists have done extensive research on all four, and they now lie in the cold shallow water covered with tarpaulins. While you can't view the actual boats, two excellent facilities combine to make up **Red Bay National Historic Site** (709/920-2051, June-late Sept. daily 9am-5pm, adult $8, senior $6.50, child $4). Coming off the highway, the first of the two site buildings is a modern structure centering on a *chalupa*, another wooden whaling boat recovered from the bottom of Red Bay. You can watch a documentary on the galleon *San Juan* and have staff point out where each of the galleons is located. Keep your receipt and head toward the waterfront, where the main collection of artifacts is held. Displays describe how the four galleons, each from a different era, have helped archaeologists track ship design through the 16th and 17th centuries. Highlights include a scale model of the *San Juan*, pottery, and remains of a compass and sandglass.

Food and Accommodations

Down by the harbor but without water views, **Whaler's Station Restaurant** (72 W. Harbour Dr., 709/920-2156, daily 8am-9pm, $12-21) is one of the region's better dining rooms. The seafood chowder is good, as is the beef soup. For a main, the fish-and-chips is as good as it gets in Labrador, while the pork chop dinner is simple and hearty. The same family that operates the restaurant also rents out three **guest rooms** in a historic waterfront building (72 W. Harbour Dr., 709/920-2156, www.redbaywhalers.ca, June-Sept. $95-130 s or d). The best of these is the top-floor Loft room, with sweeping harbor views and a king bed.

The other lodging choice at Red Bay is **Basinview B&B** (Rte. 510, 709/920-2002, $70-100 s or d, including a light breakfast), a modern home overlooking the bay from a rocky shoreline just before reaching the town itself. The three downstairs rooms share a single bathroom. The upstairs guest room has a private bathroom but less privacy, as it is on the main level of the house.

Getting There

Red Bay is 60 kilometers (37 miles) north of L'Anse Amour, a one-hour drive via Route 510.

MARY'S HARBOUR

Beyond Red Bay, Route 510 is unpaved for 80 kilometers (50 miles) to Mary's Harbour. This small fishing village, where the local economy revolves around a crab-processing plant, was isolated until 2000, when the road was completed.

The main reason to travel this far north is to visit Battle Harbour, and since the ferry leaves from Mary's Harbour, the local **Riverlodge Hotel** (709/921-6948, www. riverlodgehotel.ca, $120-135 s or d) makes a sensible overnight stop. The 15 rooms are simple but comfortable (rates include wireless Internet), and the in-house restaurant has pleasant views across the St. Mary's River.

Getting There

Mary's Harbour is about 90 kilometers (56 miles) north of Red Bay, a one-hour drive via Route 510.

★ BATTLE HARBOUR

On a small island an hour's boat ride from Mary's Harbour lies **Battle Harbour,** a remote yet intriguing outport village that is well worth the effort to reach.

Established as a fishing village in 1759, it was one of the earliest European settlements on the Labrador coast. By 1775, Battle Harbour's cod-fishing industry had made the settlement the economic center of the region, a status that faded and then rebounded a century later with the arrival of seasonal fishers from Newfoundland. By 1848 Battle Harbour was the capital of Labrador, an important trade and supply center where up to 100 vessels would be tied up in port at any one time. Thanks to the work of missionary Wilfred Grenfell, the residents had year-round medical services and, by 1904, state-of-the-art communications thanks to the Marconi Wireless Telegraph Company, which erected a station here in 1904.

In the late 1960s, with the inshore fishery in decline, Battle Harbour residents were resettled on the mainland at Mary's Harbour, leaving the community an abandoned outport. A few local families continued to spend summers on the island, but it wasn't until 1990 that the Battle Harbour Historic Trust took over the site and began an ambitious restoration program that continues to this day. Now protected as a national historic site, Battle Harbour allows a glimpse into the past. About 20 structures have been restored, including an Anglican church, the original mercantile salt fish premises, the loft from which Robert Peary told the world of his successful expedition to reach the North Pole, a general store, and a massive fish "flake" (drying platform). A boardwalk links many of the restored buildings, tapering off near the back of the village, where a dozen or so homes stand in varying states of disrepair and a trail leads through a rock cleft to a cemetery.

Visiting Battle Harbour

In addition to restoring many of the most important buildings, the **Battle Harbour Historic Trust** (709/921-6325, www. battleharbour.com) does a wonderful job of providing visitor services, including

accommodations, meals, and transportation. Packages to Battle Harbour comprise two elements: meals/transportation and accommodations. The cost of on-island dining and round-trip ferry fare from Mary's Harbour is set at $175 per person ($80 children ages 6-12, under 6 free) for the first night, with subsequent nights costing $100 ($45 children). Accommodation costs start at $50 per person per night for a bunk bed in the charmingly restored Cookhouse. On a rise overlooking the town and Great Caribou Island, the Battle River Inn is a beautifully restored merchant's home where each of the five guest rooms has double beds or two twins ($195-225 s or d). Cottages cost between $300 and $800 per night and sleep between four and eight guests. They include the Grenfell Doctor's Cottage, which has harbor views; the Constable Forward Cottage; the three-bedroom Isaac Smith Cottage, which is lighted by oil lamps and heated by wood fire; and the very private two-bedroom Spearing Cottage. Meals are provided in a dining room above the general store. All are hearty, with plenty of cross-table conversation between diners. At the general store itself, you can buy snacks and basic provisions.

Getting There and Around

The trip between Mary's Harbour and Battle Harbour takes around one hour aboard a small enclosed ferry (inn guests only). The ferry departs Mary's Harbour in the summer daily at 11am, and the return trip departs Battle Harbour at 9am. The ferry transfer is included in all overnight packages. Once on the island, all lodging is within easy walking distance of the ferry dock.

CARTWRIGHT

Most travelers incorporate Cartwright into their itineraries as part of a loop that includes driving the TransLabrador Highway through to Happy Valley-Goose Bay.

1: Battle Harbour, an abandoned fishing village turned into a tourist destination; **2:** welcome sign at Battle Harbour

From Mary's Harbour, it is 167 kilometers (104 miles) to Cartwright Junction (no services), from where the TransLabrador Highway continues around the Mealy Mountains to Happy Valley-Goose Bay; Cartwright is 87 kilometers (54 miles) north along Route 516.

Sights

The town was named for 18th-century merchant adventurer and coastal resident Captain George Cartwright; **Flagstaff Hill Monument,** overlooking the town and Sandwich Bay, still has the cannons Cartwright installed to guard the harbor 200 years ago.

Gannet Islands Ecological Reserve, off the coast, is a breeding colony for common murres, puffins, black-legged kittiwakes, and the province's largest razorbill population. North of Cartwright lies the spot where Norse sailors first laid eyes on the coast: **Wunderstrands,** a magnificent 56-kilometer (35-mile) stretch of sandy golden beach across Sandwich Bay that is only accessible by boat. The local tour operator, **Experience Labrador** (709/653-2244 or 877/938-7444, www.experiencelabrador.com), offers sea kayaking day trips, but you're missing the local highlight if you simply paddle around local waterways and don't take a day trip to the Wunderstrand. Now protected as part of Mealy Mountains National Park, the beach was named by infamous Viking Erik the Red and to this day receives few visitors. The cost is $500 s or d for the five-hour adventure, booked through Experience Labrador.

Food and Accommodations

The centrally located **Northside Motel** (8 Low Rd., 709/938-7577, $95 s, $105 d) is a simple six-room affair, with a friendly little pub attached to the back.

Getting There

Cartwright is about 250 kilometers (155 miles) north of Mary's Harbour, a 3.5-hour drive via Route 530 and Route 516.

Central Labrador

HAPPY VALLEY-GOOSE BAY

Happy Valley-Goose Bay (pop. 8,000) spreads across a sandy peninsula bordered by the Churchill River, Goose Bay, and Terrington Basin at the head of Lake Melville. Although remote, it is linked to the outside world by the TransLabrador Highway (Churchill Falls is 288 km/180 mi to the west, and Blanc Sablon is 620 km/385 mi southeast) and scheduled air services.

During World War II, Canadian forces selected the Goose Bay site and, with assistance from the British Air Ministry and the U.S. Air Force, built a massive airbase and two airstrips there. Before the war ended, 24,000 aircraft set down for refueling during the transatlantic crossing. Currently operated by the Canadian Armed Forces, 5 Wing Goose Bay Airport serves as a training center for Canadian, British, Dutch, Italian, and German air forces, since the latter four countries have no airspace of their own suitable for low-level flight training. Goose Bay is also an important refueling stop for transatlantic flights, with a runway long enough to accommodate space shuttle landings in an emergency. The town last hit the headlines on September 11, 2001, when the airport filled with commercial flights that were diverted from their intended destinations.

Happy Valley-Goose Bay originally evolved as two distinct areas: Goose Bay, rimming an important air base, and adjacent Happy Valley, which became the base's residential and commercial sector. In 1961 the two areas joined as Happy Valley-Goose Bay and elected the first town council, which was Labrador's first municipal government. The distinction between the two areas remains firm, so be prepared to consult a map as you wander around. Goose Bay connects to Happy Valley by the L-shaped Hamilton River Road, the main drag.

Town Sights

At the **Labrador Institute** (219 Hamilton River Rd., 709/896-6210, call for hours), an arm of Memorial University of Newfoundland, there are often Labrador-oriented artifacts on display, as well as an archive of historical maps and photographs open to the public.

★ North West River

This community of 500, 38 kilometers (24 miles) northeast of Goose Bay on Route 520, was the center of the area until the 1940s. The settlement began as a French trading post in 1743, and the inhabitants are descendants of French, English, and Scottish settlers.

Within town are two worthwhile sights. The **Labrador Interpretation Centre** (2 Portage Rd., 709/497-8566, early May-Sept. Mon.-Sat. 9am-4:30pm, Sun. noon-4:30pm, free) is filled with interesting exhibits that catalog the natural and human history of "the Big Land." Beyond the center, Portage Road leads to piers and pleasant views. If you'd like to meet some of the locals, arrive in late afternoon, when the Innu fishers collect the day's catch from nets strung across the waterway. Within an original Hudson's Bay Company building, the **Labrador Heritage Museum** (Portage Rd., 709/497-8858, July-Aug. daily 8:30am-4:30pm, adult $2, child $1) provides an insight into Labrador's early years with photographs, manuscripts, books, artifacts, furs, native minerals, and other displays.

Food

Fast-food places line Hamilton River Road, including the ubiquitous and ever-popular **Tim Hortons** (220 Hamilton River Rd., 709/896-5666, open 24 hours), a coffee-and-donut chain beloved by Canadians.

The casual **Jungle Jim's** (Hotel North Two, 382 Hamilton River Rd., 709/896-3398,

Happy Valley-Goose Bay

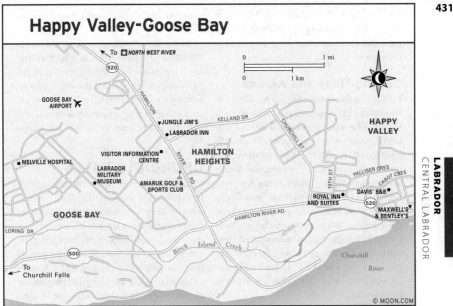

daily 11am-2am, $14-27) features a menu of typical Canadian dishes. Next door in the Labrador Inn, **Larry's Pizza and Waffle House** (380 Hamilton River Rd., 709/896-3351, daily 7am-2pm and 5pm-10pm, $16-29) offers an extensive menu of standard pub fare at prices that are probably a bit higher than you want to pay.

The closest thing to a splurge in all of Labrador would be dinner at **Maxwell's and Bentley's** (97 Hamilton River Rd., 709/896-3565, Mon.-Sat. 11am-9:30pm, $12-27), which combines a restaurant (Bentley's) with a nightclub (Maxwell's). The restaurant section is a semi-stylish, air-conditioned room overlooking the Churchill River. The food is fairly predictable, with the usual array of steak, chicken, pork, and seafood dishes.

Accommodations

B&Bs offer the least-expensive lodgings. **Davis' Bed and Breakfast** (14 Cabot Cres., Happy Valley, 709/896-5077, $70-90 s, $90-110 d) has four guest rooms with private baths and wireless Internet. Rates include a continental breakfast (a full breakfast costs extra).

Facilities include a dining room, laundry, and an outside patio.

Happy Valley-Goose Bay has several motels catering mostly to business travelers. In general, rooms are of an acceptable standard and expensive, but not outrageously so. The **Royal Inn and Suites** (3 Royal Ave., Goose Bay, 709/896-2456 or 888/440-2456, www.royalinnandsuites.ca, $140-260 s or d) is my pick of the bunch. It has 35 smartly decorated guest rooms, including a few with separate bedrooms and kitchens.

Rooms at the **Labrador Inn** (380 Hamilton River Rd., 709/896-3351 or 800/563-2763, www.thelabradorinn.com, $140-180) are of a similar standard. Facilities here include a restaurant, a lounge, and airport shuttles.

Information and Services

Destination Labrador (709/896-6502, www.destinationlabrador.com) operates a helpful information center along the main drag (365 Hamilton River Rd., June-Sept. Mon.-Fri. 8am-8pm, Sat.-Sun. 8am-5pm).

Melville Hospital (also called Grenfell Hospital) is at Building 550, G Street (near

5th Ave.). For the **RCMP** (149 Hamilton River Rd.), call 709/896-3383. **Post offices** are located on Hamilton River Road and at the airport.

Getting There and Around

In 2010, the final link in the **TransLabrador Highway** was completed, and Goose Bay was linked to the rest of the province by road. The highway leading west to Churchill Falls (288 km/180 mi) was already in place, but the section leading south to the Labrador Straits was a much bigger undertaking for engineers (620 km/385 mi to Blanc Sablon). To this day, much of the road is still unpaved and the going can be extremely slow, especially in spring before graders have completed their work. But if you're up for an adventure, the journey along one of North America's newest and most remote highways is well worth considering.

Air Canada (888/247-2262, www. aircanada.com) flies into **Goose Bay Airport** (YYR, www.goosebayairport.com) from Halifax and Toronto. **PAL Airlines** (709/576-3943 or 800/563-2800, www.palairlines.ca) has flights to Goose Bay from throughout the province. **Air Borealis** (709/566-1666 or 800/563-2800, www.airborealis.ca) interlines with PAL and has its own flights as far north as Nain.

Budget (709/896-2976) and **National** (709/896-5575) have rental cars in town and out at the airport, but neither company allows its vehicles on the TransLabrador Highway. **Cooney's Taxi** (709/896-3311) charges around $10 per trip anywhere within Goose Bay, and $20 between the airport and Happy Valley.

CHURCHILL FALLS

Churchill Falls (population 650), 288 kilometers (180 miles) west of Goose Bay, is a relatively modern town constructed to serve the needs of workers at the world's second-largest underground hydroelectric power station. The waters of the Churchill River drop more than 300 meters (984 feet) over a 32-kilometer (20-mile) section—ideal for generating hydroelectric power. In an incredible feat of engineering, the water is diverted underground to the massive generators, which produce 5,220 megawatts of electricity.

The 21-room **Height of Land Hotel** (1 Town Centre, 709/925-3211, www. heightoflandhotel.com, $149 s or d) is a relatively good value for its remote location. Rooms are basic but comfortable, and rates

Labrador Heritage Museum

Laying Claim to Labrador

For centuries the French Canadians have asserted, "Labrador is part of Québec." And the British and the Newfoundlanders have traditionally countered, "Never!"

Labrador is a choice piece of property, and Québec has been a longtime avid suitor of North America's northeastern edge. Québec's interest in Labrador dates to 1744, when the French cut a deal with the British: Québec got jurisdiction over Labrador, but the island of Newfoundland got fishing rights in Labrador's coastal waters. The Treaty of Paris of 1763 went one step further, however, and awarded all of Labrador (not defined by a precise border) to Newfoundland. Newfoundland's claim gained more substance in 1825, when the British North America Act set Labrador's southern border with Québec at the 52nd parallel.

In the 1860s, when the Dominion of Canada was formed, the dispute over Labrador, formerly between France and England, now involved the new Confederation of Canada. Québec never disputed England's sovereignty over Labrador, but instead continued to question the location of the border. In 1898 the Québec border was unofficially as far east as what is now the town of Happy Valley-Goose Bay.

FOR SALE: LABRADOR

Newfoundland put Labrador up for sale in 1909 for $9 million, but there were no takers. In the ensuing years, Labrador's precise border became a tedious issue for England, and so in 1927 a judicial committee in London set Labrador's border at the "height of the land," the watershed line separating the Atlantic Ocean from Ungava Bay, the current provincial border of today. In the decision, Labrador acquired the wedge-shaped "Labrador Trough," a delta area rich in iron ore deposits and rivers perfect for harnessing hydroelectric power.

QUÉBEC'S CLOUT EMERGES

The only road access to Labrador is through Québec, so it is no surprise that the province became a major player in Labrador's economy. Québec bought into Labrador's hydroelectric fortune in the early 1970s. Québec's provincial Hydro-Québec now earns $200 million annually from within Labrador, while Newfoundland, another company shareholder, earns $12 million. Ironically, Newfoundland and Labrador receive none of the energy.

To this day, the province's western border remains to be fully surveyed, and Québec does not consider the issue settled. A fragile status quo exists between the two provinces, but the renaming of Newfoundland to Newfoundland and Labrador in 2001 brought official recognition to Labrador as part of Newfoundland.

NUNATSIAVUT

In 2004, Labrador's Inuit people were successful in a land-claim process that took 30 years to come to fruition. Led by the Labrador Inuit Association (709/922-2942, www.nunatsiavut.com), the indigenous people now have special rights to 142,000 square kilometers (54,825 square miles) of land that extend north from Lake Melville to Torngat Mountains National Park. The latter was established as part of the claim.

---

include wireless Internet and use of an adjacent indoor pool. The attached Height of Land Restaurant (same contact information, Mon.-Sat. 7am-9pm, Sun. 7am-8pm, $11-29) has a wide-ranging menu that is not as expensive as you may imagine—everything from spaghetti and meatballs to baked salmon. If you're in the area to fish, this is the place to stay, as the owner takes guests on guided trips.

Getting There

To drive to Churchill Falls from Goose Bay, it's 288 kilometers (180 miles) west, four hours via Route 500.

LABRADOR CITY AND WABUSH

Continuing west from Churchill Falls, the twin towns of Labrador City and Wabush, 5 kilometers (3.1 miles) apart, lie about 530 kilometers (330 miles) from Goose Bay and just 23 kilometers (14.3 miles) from the Québec-Labrador border. Labradorians knew of the area's iron-ore potential by the late 1800s, and massive ore deposits were discovered in 1958. The Iron Ore Company of Canada and Wabush Mines, served by the two towns, together rank as the Canadian steel industry's largest supplier. The two extract 20 million metric tons of iron ore a year.

Lodging in the two towns is limited to just over 100 rooms in a couple of motels. **Two Seasons Inn** (96 Avalon Dr., Labrador City, 709/944-2661 or 800/670-7667, www.twoseasonsinn.ca, $150 s or d) has the best 54 guest rooms in Labrador, airport shuttle service, a **restaurant** (6:30am-10pm daily), and a small fitness room. The **Wabush Hotel** (9 Grenfell Dr., Wabush, 709/282-3221, www.wabushhotel.com, $165-175 s or d) is an imposing property dating to the 1960s. The 68 rooms have been revamped a few times since, and services include two restaurants, including one serving a Chinese/Canadian buffet dinner.

At **Duley Lake Family Park** (10 km/6.2 mi west of Labrador City, 709/282-3660, late May-Sept., $24), choose between campsites on either the lake or river. The campground has a sandy beach, boating, fishing, and picnicking. **Grande Hermine Park** (45 km/28 mi east of Labrador City, 709/282-5369, June-Aug., $20) offers 45 powered sites and 30 unserviced sites. Facilities include a boat launch, a convenience store, and pedal boat rentals.

Getting There

From Churchill Falls to Labrador City and Wabush, it's a 240-kilometer (149-mile), 3.5-hour drive west on Route 500.

North Coast

Labrador's northern coast evokes images of another world. It's the Labrador you might imagine: raw and majestic, with the craggy mountain ranges of Torngat, Kaumajet, and Kiglapait rising to the north.

The 1763 Treaty of Paris ceded the Labrador coastline to Britain's Newfoundland colony, but the imprint of European architecture only reached the northern seacoast when the Moravians, an evangelical Protestant sect from Bohemia, established mission stations with prefabricated wooden buildings in the early 19th century. It is in these remote North Coast villages—Rigolet, Postville, Makkovik, and Nain—that the original inhabitants, the Inuit, have settled. Few aspects of these towns have changed over the last century, and the lifestyle of northern peoples here remains traditional.

GETTING THERE

Access to Labrador's North Coast is by air or sea. The communities are linked to the outside world by **Air Borealis** (709/566-1666 or 800/563-2800, www.airborealis.ca) from Goose Bay, or by a cargo and passenger ferry that takes two days to reach its northern turnaround point, Nain. Riding the ferry, the **MV Northern Ranger** (709/896-2262 or 855/896-2262, www.labradorferry.ca) is a real adventure. The one-way fare for an adult between Goose Bay and Nain is $220. A single berth in a shared cabin costs $90, while a private cabin costs $290-630 s or d.

MAKKOVIK

After stopping at Rigolet, the MV *Northern Ranger* starts its long haul through open ocean, reaching Makkovik (pop. 400) 18 hours after leaving Goose Bay. The ferry makes a 90-minute stop on the way north and a three-hour stop on the return journey. Makkovik was first settled in the early 1800s by a Norwegian fur trader; the Moravians constructed a mission here in 1896. Today this two-story building holds the **White Elephant Museum** (709/923-2425, July-Aug. daily 1pm-5pm, or by appointment). Local shops such as the **Makkovik Craft Centre** (709/923-2221, call for hours) sell Inuit crafts, including fur caps, boots and mittens, parkas, moose-hide moccasins, and bone and antler jewelry.

Right on the water, the **Adlavik Inn** (7 Willow Creek Ln., 709/923-2389, www. labradorabletours.com, $120 s, $150 d) has the only five guest rooms in town, so call ahead if your itinerary includes an overnight stay in Makkovik. Rooms have TVs and phones, and meals are served in an adjacent dining room.

HOPEDALE

About 110 nautical miles north of Makkovik and 122 miles short of Nain, the MV *Northern Ranger* makes a two-hour stop at Hopedale, just enough time to go ashore and visit the 1782 **Hopedale Mission National Historic Site** (709/933-3864, free), containing the oldest wooden frame building east of Québec.

Here, a restored Hudson's Bay Company storeroom has been converted into a museum; other site highlights include huts, a residence, and a graveyard. It generally opens whenever the ferry is in town.

Accommodations are provided at **Amaguk Inn** (3 Harbour Dr., 709/933-3750, amagukinn@gmail.com), which charges $159-209 s or d for its 18 rooms. Meals are available at the inn for both guests and nonguests.

NAIN AND THE FAR NORTH

With stunning coastal scenery, stops at remote villages, and the chance to see whales and icebergs, the long trip north aboard the MV *Northern Ranger* ferry is a real adventure, but after two days on board, the captain's announcement of imminent arrival in Nain, administrative capital of Nunatsiavut, is welcome. In the early 1900s, an epidemic of Spanish flu—introduced from a supply ship—destroyed a third of the indigenous population on the northern coast. The Inuit who survived resettled at Nain, which now has a population of just over 1,000 and is the northernmost municipality on the Labrador coast. Life is rugged this far north—electricity is provided by diesel generator; fuel and wood are used for

The MV *Northern Ranger* serves communities along the North Coast.

domestic heat; local transportation is by boat in the summer and snowmobile in the winter. The only roads are within the town itself.

Food and Accommodations

For an overnight stay, there's just one option, the **Atsanik Lodge** (Sand Banks Rd., 709/922-2910, $155 s, $165 d). Each of the 25 rooms has cable TV, a phone, and a private bathroom. The lodge also has a lounge, restaurant, and laundry. Other town services include a couple of grocery stores, a post office, and a takeout food joint.

Getting There

If you've arrived on the ferry, you'll have just three hours ashore to explore the town before the return journey. The alternative is to take the ferry one way and an **Air Borealis** (709/566-1666 or 800/563-2800, www.airborealis.ca) flight the other. The one-way fare to Goose Bay is around $520.

Voisey's Bay

Prior to the cod-fishing moratorium, the fishing industry dominated Labrador's Far North Coast, but now mining at Voisey's Bay, 35 kilometers (22 miles) south, appears to be the economic engine of the future. It is home to the world's largest known deposit of nickel and copper. The main processing facility was completed in early 2006, and now around 6,000 tons of nickel and copper concentrate are mined daily by over 400 workers, who live in temporary accommodations on-site.

Hebron Mission National Historic Site

Labrador's northernmost remaining Moravian mission is protected at **Hebron Mission National Historic Site,** on the shores of remote Kangershutsoak Bay, 140 nautical miles north of Nain. Building began on the mission complex, including a church, residence, and store, in 1829. The mission remained in operation until 1959. **Adventure Canada** (905/271-4000, www.adventurecanada.com) can make a stop here on their guided tours along the northern Labrador coastline.

★ Torngat Mountains National Park

Established in 2006 as part of the Nunatsiavut land claim, the remote wilderness of **Torngat Mountains National Park** protects 9,700 square kilometers (3,745 square miles) of the remote coastline and rugged Torngat

Torngat Mountains National Park

Mountains at the northern tip of Labrador. Glaciation dominates the park's geology; its mountains are separated by deep fjords and lakes that have been carved by retreating glaciers, many of which are still present in pockets scattered through the park. The entire park is above the tree line, so instead of trees, its valleys are carpeted in a variety of tundra vegetation, including wildflowers, which carpet large expanses during the very short summer season. Huge herds of caribou migrate across the park's interior, while polar bears are common along the coast.

Unless you are a long-distance kayaker, the only way to reach the park is by charter flight from Goose Bay to Saglek and then a boat transfer into the park. Flights and all ground services are arranged by **The Torngats** (855/867-6428, www.thetorngats.com). Owned by a branch of the Nunatsiavut government, and with a season extending mid-July-early September, this company's on-site camp is at the south end of the park. Although used mostly by park staff and researchers, the facility also offers a variety of services for park visitors. Expect to pay around $5,600 for flights from Happy Valley-Goose Bay, the boat transfer, tent accommodations for three nights, meals, and limited guiding.

The main **park office** (709/922-1290, Mon.-Fri. 9am-4:30pm) is in Nain, although the best source of information for planning your trip is www.pc.gc.ca/torngat, where you can download a visitors' guide and hiking maps.

Background and Essentials

Background

The Landscape

Atlantic Canada forms one-twentieth of the country's total area. The provinces, and the distances separating them, are far larger than they may seem at first glance, compared against the vastness of the whole of Canada. Nova Scotia, for example, is the country's second-smallest province, yet it will take you a long day to drive from Yarmouth, at the southern tip, to Cape Breton Highlands National Park, at the other end of the province. And from Cape Breton, it's a six-hour ferry ride to the next landfall—the island of Newfoundland—which itself lies nearer to Liverpool, England, than to Toronto.

IN THE BEGINNING

Six hundred million years ago, the collision of the North American and European continental plates pushed up the Appalachian Mountains. The range's ribs, starting far to the south in Alabama, extend through New England and the Maritime provinces to the Gaspé Peninsula, whose highlands spread across Cape Breton and as far as Newfoundland. Geologists believe that the range was originally taller and more rugged than the modern Rockies. Glaciation and eons of erosion, however, have ground down the once-mammoth summits such that the rather modest 820-meter (2,690-foot) Mount Carleton, in New Brunswick, is today the Maritimes' highest point. The highest peak in the Atlantic provinces, northern Labrador's desolate Mount Caubvick, rises 1,729 meters (5,673 feet) above the Labrador Sea. Otherwise, great swaths of the region's terrain are mostly low and undulating, dipping and swelling in innumerable variations.

One of the reasons for this is glacial ice, uncountable trillions of tons of it, which formed over the last four ice ages. Glaciers up to an estimated 3 kilometers (1.9 miles) thick weighed down on the elastic bedrock as recently as 14,000 years ago, submerging the coasts and counteracting the inexorable thrust of tectonic uplift.

Some 350 million years ago, as the tectonic plates shifted, a great slab of the Earth's crust slumped, forming the valley that would be flooded by a rising sea to form the Bay of Fundy only 6,000 years ago.

A WATERY WONDERLAND

More than any other region of Canada, the Atlantic provinces are defined by water, which divides as well as unifies them. The planet's mightiest tides surge through the Bay of Fundy between New Brunswick and Nova Scotia. The Cabot Strait separates Nova Scotia's Cape Breton and the island of Newfoundland's southern coastline. The unexpectedly warm Northumberland Strait, heated by the Gulf Stream, is a broad blue parenthesis dividing Prince Edward Island from Nova Scotia and New Brunswick. On the island's north side spreads the Gulf of St. Lawrence. The Baie des Chaleurs, its warmth owing to its shallow depth, lies between northeastern New Brunswick and Québec's Gaspé Peninsula.

Along Labrador's coast, currents from the chilly Labrador Sea move southward and fork into a channel known as the Strait of Belle Isle, which separates the island of Newfoundland from the mainland, while the rest of the current washes along Newfoundland's eastern coast.

If it were possible to walk the profoundly reticulated coastlines of the four provinces, following every cove, bay, point, and peninsula, the footsore traveler would log some 40,000 kilometers (24,855 miles) before eventually returning to the starting point.

The sea's pervasive presence is felt throughout the region, but the ties to the ocean are perhaps strongest in Nova Scotia and Newfoundland, whose outer coasts confront the open Atlantic. The waters off Newfoundland in particular—the Gulf of St. Lawrence and the Grand Banks along the continental shelf—are among the most productive fisheries in the world, for five centuries an unbelievably rich resource for tuna, mackerel, herring, lobster, and cod.

On Prince Edward Island, surrounded by water, fishing is a major industry. But agriculture is an equally important component of the economy, the benevolent result of the last ice age, which blessed the land with a deep fertile loam. New Brunswick faces the sea on two sides and joins the mainland with a massive sweep of land rich in forests and ores, and hence has an economy composed of fishing, forestry, and mining.

Previous: a church in Trinity, Newfoundland; puffins at Witless Bay, Newfoundland.

CLIMATE

Maritime weather varies from province to province, and from region to region within the provinces. As a rule, though, extremes are moderated by proximity to the sea. The months from June through September are generally the most pleasant and popular for visiting. The regions' landscapes and sea-scapes are recast by the changing seasons. In springtime, occasional banks of thick fog blanket the coast from Yarmouth to St. John's. In summer, a pervasive balminess ripens the blueberry fields from Cumberland County in Nova Scotia to Newfoundland's Codroy Valley. Autumn brings the last burst of Indian summer, coloring the forests until winter's sea winds swirl in and send the leaves tumbling away to finish another year.

Nova Scotia

The province has a pleasant, modified continental climate, moderated by air and water currents from the Gulf Stream and the Arctic. Summers are warm and winters are mild. Cape Breton is subject to more extreme weather than the mainland. Precipitation province-wide averages 130 centimeters (51 inches) annually, falling mainly as rain during autumn and as snow in winter.

Spring high temperatures range -2.5-9°C (28-48°F), though the days begin to warm up toward the end of March. Summer weather has a reputation for changing from day to day; daytime highs range up to 30°C (86°F), while nights are cool, averaging 12°C (54°F). Inland areas are generally 5°C (9°F) warmer during the day. The coasts often bask in morning fog. Caribbean hurricanes, having spent their force farther south, limp through the region, bringing to the northwestern Atlantic short spells of rain and wind.

In autumn, the evenings start to cool, but pleasant days continue through September at up to 18°C (64°F). The days are cool and frosty October-mid-November. Winter lasts late November-early March, with temperatures averaging -10-4°C (14-39°F).

New Brunswick

New Brunswick's continental climate contrasts hot summers with cold winters. Extremes are moderated by the surrounding seas, more so near the coast than in the interior. Summer means warm days and cool nights, with an average daytime high temperature of 23°C (73°F) in June, 26°C (79°F) in July, and 25°C (77°F) in August. July is the sunniest month. September and October are

Some of the world's oldest rock is in Labrador.

pleasantly warm, with increasingly cool days toward November. Winter is cold.

Precipitation throughout the province averages 115 centimeters (45 inches) annually. The Bay of Fundy coast is steeped in dense fog about 70 days a year.

Prince Edward Island

The island basks in a typical maritime climate, with one major exception: Its growing season of 110-160 days is Atlantic Canada's longest. The island also gets more than its share of year-round breezes, pleasant and warm in summer but fiercer come fall. Spring is short, lasting early-mid-May until mid-June. Summer temperatures peak in July and August, when temperatures range 18-23°C (64-73°F); an unusually warm day can reach 35°C (95°F), while the other extreme can be quite cool at just 5°C (41°F). Autumn brings with it Atlantic Canada's brightest and most dramatic fall foliage. Winter temperatures can dip below 0°C (32°F) in December and January.

Annual precipitation amounts to 106 centimeters (42 inches), with approximately half of that falling May-October.

Newfoundland and Labrador

The climate is harsher and more extreme here than in the Maritimes. A sultry summer day can be interspersed with chilly breezes, brilliant sun, dark clouds, and showers from light to drenching. The island's eastern and southern seacoasts are often foggy because of the offshore melding of the warm Gulf Stream and the cold Labrador current.

Overall, the island has cool, moist weather. Summer days average 16-21°C (60-70°F), dropping to 9-12°C (48-54°F) at night, but hot spells are common, and the swimming season starts by late June. The island's low-lying interior and coastal areas are warmest and sunniest. Annual rainfall averages 105 centimeters (41 inches). Frost begins by early October on the southern coast, and earlier farther north. Snowfall averages 300 centimeters (118 inches) a year.

Winter high temperatures average -4-0°C (25-32°F), warm enough to turn snow to rain, while nighttime lows can tumble to -15°C (5°F). Expect year-round blustery winds along the Marine Drive and nearby Cape Spear.

Labrador's climate is continental and subject to great extremes. Summers are short, cool to sometimes hot, and brilliantly sunny with periodic showers. A July day averages 21°C (70°F), but temperatures have been known to rise to 38°C (100°F) at Happy Valley-Goose Bay. Temperatures drop rapidly after mid-August. By November, daytime highs at Happy Valley-Goose Bay fall to 0°C (32°F). Winter is very cold and dry. Daytime high temperatures average -20°C (-4°F) in the subarctic, -18°C (0°F) to -21°C (-6°F) in the interior, and -51°C (-60°F) in the western area.

ENVIRONMENTAL ISSUES

The northeastern Atlantic fisheries have been the economic engine driving exploration and development of these coasts for centuries. In days past, codfish were said to carpet the sea floor of the shallow Grand Banks, and those who caught them—first with lines from small dories, then with nets, and finally from great trawlers that scour the sea—have hauled in untold millions of tons of not only cod but also flounder, salmon, pollack, haddock, anchovies, and dozens of other species. Today the fish are in serious trouble and so too, inexorably, are the people and communities whose lives have revolved around them.

Today, the state of local fisheries—most notably the collapse of cod stocks—is the most important environmental issue facing the region. The beginning of the end was the arrival of "factory ships" in the 1960s, which could harvest up to 200 tons of cod per hour. By the late 1980s, the cod stock had been mostly obliterated, and by the early 1990s, a moratorium was put in place until the fisheries had recovered. Unfortunately, what was not fully understood at that time was that overfishing was only part of the problem. Cod are a groundfish, and the factory ships had been

Colossal Fundy Tides

The world's highest tides rise in the upper Bay of Fundy, with up to a 17-meter (56-foot) vertical gain at the head of the bay. The tides work on roughly a six-hour cycle, and each peak or low arrives 50 minutes later each day. Twice daily, six hours after high tide, the bay is empty, but then the Fundy surges onward and water funnels into the bay and up numerous rivers. The upper Fundy is split into two arms by Cape Chignecto, the wedge-shaped point that angles into the bay. On its west side, Chignecto Bay with its raw lonesome coastline penetrates inland and finishes at Cumberland Basin near Amherst. On the cape's other side, the bay compresses itself first into the Minas Channel. It is here in the upper reaches of the bay that the tides are highest. By the time rising water funnels into the head of the bay, it is in the form of a **tidal bore** (lead wave) that rides inland up the area's rivers. The arriving wave can be a dainty, ankle-high ripple or an upright wall of knee-high water, depending on the tide.

Due to the convoluted coastline, viewing the phenomena is possible at dozens of points around the Bay of Fundy, including Truro (Nova Scotia) and Moncton (New Brunswick), where riverside parks have been set aside for watching the bore. At Hopewell Rocks (New Brunswick), you can "walk on the ocean floor" at low tide. If you're feeling more adventurous, you can even take a rafting trip down the Shubenacadie River (Nova Scotia) as the bore moves upstream. Tide tables are posted in shops and storefronts throughout the region. Tides are highest around the full or new moon.

Warning: The Bay of Fundy at low tide can be perilously alluring, when the coastal sea floor looks tranquilly bare and mudflats glisten like glass. High tide's arrival is subtle and hardly noticeable. The distant tidal stirrings alert sea birds, and they cry out and wheel and turn across the sky. But then the sea moves in relentlessly, swelling and pushing forward into the bay at 6 knots per

bottom trawling—scooping up the cod in nets with an opening up to 1 kilometer (0.6 mile) wide that dragged along the sea floor and decimated the very ecosystem that was a breeding ground for the fish. It is widely thought that the cod stock will never fully recover, especially in the waters around the island of Newfoundland.

Plants and Animals

To a great extent, it was the land's natural resources—and the potential riches they represented—that attracted Europeans to Canada over the centuries. Since time immemorial, mammals, fish, and varied plant species had, of course, fed and clothed the indigenous peoples, who harvested only enough to sustain themselves. But the very abundance of the wildlife seemed to fuel the rapacity of the newcomers, driving them to a sort of madness of consumption—and hastening the exploration and settlement of the newfound continent.

Cod, flounder, mackerel, herring, and scores of other fish species in unbelievable numbers first lured brave seafarers across the Atlantic as early as the 15th century. The great whales, too, fell victim to widespread slaughter. Later, the fur-bearing mammals—mink, otters, ermines, beavers, and seals—became a currency of trade and the sine qua non of fashionable attire. Birds, too, by the millions in hundreds of species, represented money on the wing to the newcomers. Some, like the flightless great auk of the northeastern coast, were hunted to extinction.

But much remains, in sometimes astonishing abundance and variety, thanks to each

When the tide goes out, boats are left high and dry on the ocean floor.

hour—and up to 13 knots in tidal rips. The incoming sea can wash across the empty bay faster than a person can swiftly walk. Only a foolhardy sightseer walks the mudflats; the high tide stops for nothing.

species' own unique genius for survival, blind luck, the shifting vagaries of public tastes, and even the occasional glimmer of human enlightenment.

PLANTS

The receding glaciers of the last ice age scoured the land and left lifeless mud and rubble in their wake. Overall, the climate then was considerably cooler than it is today, and the first life forms to recolonize in the shadow of the glaciers were hardy mosses, lichens, and other cold-tolerant plants. Junipers and other shrubs later took root, and afterward came coniferous trees—hardy, fast-growing spruce and fir—that could thrive here despite the harsh climate and relatively brief growing season. In the boggy interiors sprouted moisture-loving willows and tamaracks. As the climate warmed and the soil grew richer, broadleaf deciduous trees arrived, filling in the outlines of the forests still seen and enjoyed today.

Forests

Maritime Canada's forests abound with ash, balsam fir, birch, beech, cedar, hemlock, maple, oak, pine, and spruce. Thick woodlands now blanket over 81 percent of Nova Scotia and 93 percent of New Brunswick, whose interior conifer forests in places resemble vast impenetrable fields of dark green wheat. Prince Edward Island, by contrast, is the country's least-forested province, with its land area about equally divided between farmlands and woodlands.

Newfoundland's forests are dominated by black spruce and balsam fir, with occasional stands of larch, pin cherry, pine, paper and white birch, aspen, red and mountain maple, and alder. In Newfoundland's alpine and coastal areas, you may encounter the formidable "tuckamore," a thicket composed of stunted, hopelessly entangled fir and spruce. Labrador's southern forests are cloaked with spruce, tamarack, juniper, and birch. White spruce 30 meters tall dominate the central area, while stunted black spruce, a mere meter tall, form a stubble along the timberline area. Farther north on the arctic tundra, dwarf birch and willow are common.

With so many provincial tree varieties, visitors may easily become confused. For a helpful general introduction, visit Odell Park Arboretum in Fredericton, New Brunswick, where a 2.8-kilometer (1.7-mile) trail winds through woods made up of every tree native to the area.

Wildflowers and Other Plants

Trees, of course, are only part of the picture. Along the forest margins, raspberry and blackberry thickets proliferate, providing, among other benefits, welcome snacks for summertime hikers. Throughout the spring and summer months, the Maritimes host magnificent wildflower shows that change subtly week by week. Common wildflowers throughout New Brunswick and Nova Scotia—seen especially along roadsides in summertime—include lupine, Queen Anne's lace, yarrow, pearly everlasting, and daisies. The showy spikes of purple loosestrife, a pretty but aggressive and unwelcome pest, can be seen everywhere.

Bayberries and wild rose bloom on the Chignecto Isthmus during June. The bayberry bush grows clusters of dimpled fruits close along woody stems and releases a pleasant spicy aroma, popular in potpourri and Christmas candles. The yellow beach heather colors the Northumberland Strait dunes and sandy plains, and the rhodora (miniature rhododendron) brightens coastal marshes. Another dune resident, the beach plum, grows snowy white to pinkish flowers in June, which produce fruit welcomed by birds, beasts, and man in late summer and early fall. Nutrient-rich bogs in northeastern New Brunswick nurture plant exotics, especially at Lamèque and Miscou Islands, where wild cranberry and sundew grow among peat moss beds. Prince Edward Island is like one large garden when late spring and summer's warm temperatures urge columbines, bachelor's buttons, pansies, lilacs, wild roses, pink clover, and the delicate lady's slipper (the provincial flower) into blossom.

Across Newfoundland's marshes and bogs, you'll see white and yellow water lilies, rare orchid species, purple iris and goodwithy, and insectivorous plants (such as the pitcher plant, the provincial flower). Daisies, blue harebells, yellow goldenrod, pink wild roses, and deep pink fireweed thrive in the woodlands. Marsh marigolds, as bright yellow as daffodils, are native to the western coast's Port au Port Peninsula. Low, dense mats of crowberry are common throughout Newfoundland and Labrador. The late-autumn crop of blue-black fruits is a favorite food of curlews, plovers, and other migrants preparing for their long flights to the Caribbean and South America. Yellow poppies, heather buttercups, miniature purple rhododendrons, violets, and deep blue gentian, mixed among the white cotton grass, brighten Labrador's arctic tundra; farther south, the daisy-like arnica and purple saxifrage grow in plateau-rock niches.

You may encounter poison ivy. Mushrooms are everywhere; be absolutely certain you know the species before sampling—the chanterelles are culinary prizes, but the amanitas deadly poison.

Along the Shore

Near the coasts, familiar plants—spruces, hardy cinnamon ferns, northern juniper—take on a stunted, gnarled look from contending with the unmitigated elements. It can take endurance and adaptation to survive here amid often harsh conditions. Trees and bushes lie cropped close to the ground or lean permanently swept back by the wind as if with a giant hairbrush.

Plants on or near the beach require specialization, too. Marram grass, also called American beach grass, is abundant all along the Atlantic coast. Its extensive root systems stabilize the sand dunes on which it grows. Another important dune plant, the beach heather, grows in low mats that trap sand and help keep the dunes in place. Small, abundant yellow flowers color large patches May-July. Beach pea, seaside goldenrod, dusty miller, and sea rocket are a few of the other plants that can manage on the less-than-fertile soils just above the high-tide line. Lower down grow cord grass and glasswort, whose systems can tolerate regular soakings of saltwater.

Within the intertidal zone, there's a different world altogether amid the surging seawater and tide pools. The great disparities between high and low tides help to make the rocky coasts of the Maritimes among the richest and most varied in the world. Low tide exposes thick mats of tough, rubbery rockweed, or sea wrack, for a few hours each day. Farther out (or deeper down) is the lower intertidal zone of coral-pink to reddish-brown Irish moss and brilliant green sea lettuce, which carpet the rocks and harbor populations of starfish, crabs, and sea urchins.

The deepest stratum of plant life is what marine biologists call the laminarian zone, typified by giant brown kelps, such as the common horsetail kelp. These algae attach to rocks at depths up to 40 meters (131 feet) and grow rapidly toward the surface, their broad leathery fans and air bladders lilting with the rise and fall of the swells. Storms can prune the upper extremities or tear entire plants from their moorings to wash ashore along with the populations of tiny mollusks, crustaceans, and other creatures that made their homes among the fronds.

LAND MAMMALS

About 70 different land mammals call Atlantic Canada home. The ones you're most likely to come across are moose, deer, black bears, and beavers, which are widespread in all provinces except Prince Edward Island (where raccoons, coyotes, and foxes are the largest species present).

Moose

The giant of the deer family is the moose, an awkward-looking mammal that appears to have been designed by a cartoonist. It has the largest antlers of any animal in the world, stands up to 1.8 meters (5.9 feet) tall at the shoulder, and weighs up to 500 kilograms (1,102 pounds). Its body is dark brown, and it has a prominent nose, long spindly legs, small eyes, big ears, and an odd flap of skin called a bell dangling beneath its chin. Each spring the bull begins to grow palm-shaped antlers that by August will be fully grown. Moose are solitary animals that prefer marshy areas and weedy lakes, but they are known to wander to higher elevations searching out open spaces in summer. They forage in and around ponds on willows, aspen, birch, grasses, and all aquatic vegetation. Although they may appear docile, moose will attack humans if they feel threatened.

Moose are present in Nova Scotia and New Brunswick but are most common in Newfoundland, where they are naturally suited to the terrain. Ironically, they are not native to the island. The estimated 150,000 or so that thrive in the province today are descended from a handful of individuals introduced in 1878 and 1904 as a source of meat. On the mainland, they are most common in Cape Breton Highlands National Park (Nova Scotia).

White-Tailed Deer

Populations of deer are not particularly large in Nova Scotia or New Brunswick and were practically nonexistent by the late 1800s, but rose again in the ensuing years. The color of the white-tailed deer varies with the season but is generally light brown in summer, turning dirty gray in winter. The white-tailed deer's tail is dark on top, but when the animal runs, it holds its tail erect, revealing an all-white underside. Whitetails frequent thickets along the rivers and lakes of interior forests.

Black Bears

Black bears number around 8,000 in Nova Scotia, 15,000 in New Brunswick, and 8,000-10,000 in Newfoundland and Labrador (there are no bears on Prince Edward Island). Black bears are not always black in color (they can be brown), causing them to be called brown bears

Caution: Moose on the Loose

Some locals won't drive on rural roads between dusk and dawn. The reason? Moose on the loose.

About 400 moose-and-car collisions occur annually in Newfoundland alone, where the moose population is 150,000 and growing. Rural New Brunswick and Cape Breton Island are other trouble spots. A moose collision is no mere fender-bender. These animals are big and heavy, and hitting one at speed will make a real mess of your car (it doesn't do the unfortunate moose much good either). Consequences can be fatal to both parties.

Seventy percent of collisions occur between May and October. Accidents occur mainly 11pm-4am (but that's no guarantee collisions won't happen at any hour). If you must drive after dark in areas frequented by moose, use the high beams, scan the sides of the road, and proceed with caution.

Provincial governments post signs marked with the figure of a moose along the most dangerous stretches of highway.

when in fact they are not. Their weight varies considerably; males average 150 kilograms (331 pounds) and females 100 kilograms (220 pounds). Their diet is omnivorous, consisting primarily of grasses and berries and supplemented by small mammals. They are not true hibernators, but in winter they can sleep for up to a month at a time before changing position. During this time, their heartbeat drops to 10 beats per minute, body temperature drops, and they lose up to 30 percent of their body weight. Females reach reproductive maturity after five years; cubs, usually two, are born in late winter, while the mother is still asleep.

Polar Bears

Polar bears are often sighted along the Labrador coast during the spring breakup of pack ice, but their range is out of reach to most travelers. The one destination renowned for polar bear sightings are the Torngat Mountains in northern Labrador. These largest members of the bear family weigh up to 600 kilograms (1,323 pounds) and measure over 3 meters (9.8 feet) from head to toe.

Caribou

Standing 1.5 meters (4.9 feet) at the shoulder, caribou have adapted perfectly to the harsh

---

1: white-tailed deer; 2: black bear

arctic climate. They weigh up to 150 kilograms (331 pounds) and are the only member of the deer family in which both sexes grow antlers. The only region of Atlantic Canada where caribou are present is Newfoundland and Labrador; 12 herds roam the island and are most plentiful in the Avalon Wilderness Reserve and across the Northern Peninsula. Four caribou herds inhabit Labrador, the most famous of which is the George River herd. Its 75,000 caribou migrate eastward from Québec in late spring to calve in Torngat Mountains National Park.

Lynx

The elusive lynx is an endangered species across Atlantic Canada. It is present in low numbers in all provinces except Prince Edward Island. Easily identifiable by its pointy black ear tufts and an oversized tabby cat appearance, the animal has broad, padded paws that distribute its weight, allowing it to float on the surface of snow. It weighs up to 10 kilograms (22 pounds) but appears much larger because of its coat of long, thick fur. The lynx is a solitary creature that prefers the cover of forest, feeding mostly at night on small mammals.

Beavers

One of the animal kingdom's most industrious mammals is the beaver. Growing to a

450

BACKGROUND
PLANTS AND ANIMALS

length of 50 centimeters (20 inches) and tipping the scales at around 20 kilograms (44 pounds), it has a flat, rudder-like tail and webbed back feet that enable it to swim at speeds of up to 10 kilometers (6.2 miles) per hour. Once hunted for their fur, beavers can be found in flat, forested areas throughout Atlantic Canada. They build their dam walls and lodges of twigs, branches, sticks of felled trees, and mud. They eat the bark and smaller twigs of deciduous plants and store branches underwater, near the lodge, as a winter food supply.

SEA LIFE

The ocean water that surrounds the four provinces nurtures an astonishing abundance and variety of sea creatures, from tiny, uncounted single-celled organisms up through the convoluted links of the food chain to the Earth's largest beings—whales.

Tidal Zones

Along the shores, the same conditions that provide for rich and diverse plants—rocky indented coasts, dramatic tidal variations—also create ideal habitats for varied animal communities in the tidal zone. Between the highest and lowest tides, the Maritime shore is divided into six zones, each determined by the amount of time it is exposed to air. The black zone, just above the highest high-water mark, gets its name from the dark band of primitive blue-green algae that grows there. The next zone is called the periwinkle zone, for the small marine snails that proliferate within it. Able to survive prolonged exposure to air, periwinkles can leave the water to graze on the algae. The barnacle zone, encrusted with the tenacious crustaceans, while also exposed several hours daily during low tides, receives the brutal pounding of breaking waves. Next is the rockweed zone—home to mussels, limpets, and hermit crabs (which commandeer the shells of dead periwinkles)—and the comparatively placid Irish moss zone, which shelters and feeds sea urchins, starfish, sea anemones, crabs, and myriad other

animals familiar to anyone who has peered into the miniature world of a tide pool. Last is the laminarian zone, where lobsters, sponges, and fishes thrive in the forests of kelp growing in the deep churning water.

Fish

Beyond the tidal zones lie the waters of the continental shelf and then the open sea. Flowing south from the Arctic, cold oxygen-laden currents also carry loads of silica, ground out of the continental granite by the glaciers and poured into the sea by coastal rivers. Oxygen and silica together create an ideal environment for the growth of diatoms, the microscopic one-celled plants that form the bedrock of the ocean's food chain. In the sunlight of long summer days in these northern latitudes, the numbers of diatoms increase exponentially. They are the food source for shrimp and herring, which in turn support larger fish, such as mackerel, Atlantic salmon, and tuna.

Whales

Not all the creatures that swim in the Atlantic Ocean are cold-blooded. About 20 whale species cruise offshore. The so-called baleen or toothless whales—minke, humpback, beluga, and right whales—are lured by the massive food stocks of plankton and tiny shrimp called krill, which the whales strain from the water through their sieve-like curtains of baleen. The toothed whales—a family that includes dolphins, orcas (killer whales), and fin and pilot whales—feed on the vast schools of smelt-like capelin, herring, and squid. In the last three decades, whaling has been halted by Canadian law and international moratoriums, and populations of these beleaguered mammals are undergoing very encouraging comebacks.

Today's lucrative whaling industry is based not on butchering but on simply bringing curious onlookers to observe the wonderful animals up close. Prime whale-watching areas are the Bay of Fundy—especially around Grand Manan Island and Brier Island—and off the shores of Cape Breton. Minke, pilot, finback, orca, and humpback whales are the most populous species. The whales that frequent local waters arrive from the Caribbean between June and mid-July and remain through October; the season peaks during August and September. On Newfoundland's western coast, fin, minke, humpback, and pilot whales are sighted on the shores of Gros Morne National Park.

Seals

Gray and harbor seals inhabit Nova Scotian and Prince Edward Island waters at various times of the year. Whale-watching tours often include a stop at an offshore seal colony, although you may also spot one unexpectedly, such as while dining at a waterfront restaurant in Halifax. One spot you'll be guaranteed sightings is on a seal-watching trip from Eastern Kings County (Prince Edward Island), where the waters are calm and the seals abundant.

Harp seals, after fattening themselves on fish off the Labrador and Greenland coasts, migrate to northern Newfoundland and the Gulf of St. Lawrence in January and February. The females arrive first, living on the ice and continuing to feed in the gulf before giving birth to their pups. These snowy white, doe-eyed pups became the poster children of the conservation movement in the 1970s. The slaughter of the young pups—carried out by sealers who bashed in their heads with clubs—galvanized protests and finally embarrassed the Canadian government into restricting the killing in the mid-1980s. Even with the Canadian government quietly allowing hunting to resume in 1996, seal numbers have rebounded dramatically in the last two decades, and the current population stands at around five million.

BIRDS

If you're an avid birder, Atlantic Canada's birdlife may leave you breathless. In addition to hundreds of year-round resident species, the Atlantic migratory route stretches across part of the region, bringing in millions of seasonal visitors for spectacular and sometimes raucous displays.

Among the richest areas is the Bay of Fundy. In July, waterfowl, such as the American black duck and green-winged teal, and shorebirds, including the greater yellowlegs, descend on the Mary's Point mudflats at Shepody National Wildlife Area. Across Shepody Bay, 100,000 sandpipers stop at the Dorchester Peninsula

Whales are common throughout Atlantic Canada.

to grow fat on their favorite food—tiny mud shrimp—before continuing on to South America. With over 300 species, Grand Manan Island is a prime bird-watching site. The show is thickest during September, when migrants arrive in force. Ornithologist and artist John James Audubon visited the island in 1833 and painted the arctic tern, gannet, black guillemot, and razorbill—annual visitors that can still be seen here.

Even greater numbers of seabirds, the region's densest concentrations, gather on the coastlines of Newfoundland's Avalon Peninsula, most notably at Cape St. Mary Sea Bird Sanctuary. Species found there include common and arctic terns, kittiwakes, great and double-crested cormorants, Leach's storm-petrels, razorbills, guillemots, murres, gannets, and 95 percent of North America's breeding Atlantic puffins.

Each species has found its niche, and each is remarkable in its own way. The black-and-white murre, for example, is an expert diver that uses its wings as flippers to swim through the water chasing fish. This behavior can sometimes get the birds caught up with the fish in nets. The murre's cousin, the comical-looking Atlantic puffin, borrows the penguin's tuxedo markings but is nicknamed the "sea parrot" for its distinctive triangular red-and-yellow bill. Puffins make Swiss cheese of the land, as they nest in burrows they've either dug out themselves or inherited from

predecessors. In Labrador, ruffled and spruce grouse, woodpeckers, ravens, jays, chickadees, nuthatches, and ptarmigans are a few of the inland birds you may spot.

In New Brunswick's interior, crossbills, varied woodpecker species, boreal chickadees, and gray jays nest in the spruce and fir forests. Ibises, herons, and snowy egrets wade among lagoons and marshes. Among Nova Scotia's 300 or so bird species, the best known is the bald eagle. About 250 pairs nest in the province, concentrated on Cape Breton—the second-largest population on North America's east coast after Florida. The season for eagle watching is July and August. Other birds of prey include red-tailed, broad-winged, and other hawks; owls; and the gyrfalcon in Newfoundland and Labrador. Peregrine falcons were reintroduced to Fundy National Park in 1982. They nest in seaside cliffs and attack their prey in "stoops," kamikaze dives in which the falcon can reach speeds of over 300 kilometers (185 miles) per hour.

The noisy blue jay, Prince Edward Island's official provincial bird, is at home throughout the province, but the island's showiest species is the enormous, stately great blue heron, which summers there May-early August. The rare piping plover may be seen (but not disturbed) on the island's national park beaches, and arctic terns nest along the coast near Murray Harbour.

History

THE EARLIEST INHABITANTS

Atlantic Canada's earliest inhabitants arrived in Labrador about 9,000 years ago, camping near the large rivers and hunting seals and walrus during the summer. Archaeological research documents that these Maritime Archaic people hunted seals and whales along the Strait of Belle Isle and hunted caribou inland around 7500 BC.

They eventually crossed the strait to the island of Newfoundland's northern portion and established encampments such as that at Port au Choix, where their burial grounds and artifacts date to 2300 BC. Around 1000 BC, these people died out. A thousand years later, the Dorset people, ancestors of today's Inuit, arrived from the north. They survived until about AD 600. The Beothuk, called Red Indians for their use of ocher in burial rituals, came to Newfoundland around 2,000 years ago.

Mi'kmaq

Culturally and linguistically related to the Algonquian people, the largest language group in Canada, the Mi'kmaq made a home throughout present-day Nova Scotia, New Brunswick, and as far west as Québec. They were coastal dwellers who fished with spears and hook and line while also collecting shellfish from the shoreline. Hunting was of lesser importance for food but earned a great degree of status among other members of the group. Canoes with sails were built for summer travel, while in winter toboggans (a word that originates from the Mi'kmaq word *topaghan*) and snowshoes were essential.

Like aboriginal peoples across North America, the Mi'kmaq practiced a kind of spiritual animism, deeply tied to the land. The trees, animals, and landforms were respected and blessed. Before food could be consumed or a tree felled, for example, it was appreciated for its life-sustaining sacrifice. Mythology also played an important part in spiritual life, along with rituals, shamanism, and potlatch ceremonies.

THE FIRST EUROPEANS

Brendan the Navigator, a fifth-century Irish monk, may have been the first European to explore the area; he sought Hy-Brazil, the "wonderful island of the saints," and later accounts of his voyage, recorded in the medieval bestseller *Navigatio Sancti Brendani*, describe a land with coastal topography similar to Newfoundland's.

Atlantic Canada's link to the Vikings is more certain. Driven out of Scandinavia, it's believed by overpopulation, Norse seafarers settled in Iceland and began to establish settlements in Greenland. Around AD 1000 they sailed in long stout ships, called *knorrs*, southwest from Greenland and down the Labrador coastline, establishing a temporary settlement at L'Anse aux Meadows on Newfoundland's Northern Peninsula. There they built at least eight houses and two boatsheds of cut turf and lived off the land. It is not known how long they lived there, but they stayed long enough to construct a forge for crafting implements from iron ore they dug and smelted. It may have been hostilities with the native people that drove them out. The remnants of their settlement would remain unrecognized until the 1960s.

"Newfoundland" as a place-name originated with the Italian explorer Giovanni Caboto—better known today as John Cabot. Sailing westward from Bristol with a sanction to claim all lands hitherto "unknown to Christians," he sighted the "New Founde Lande" in 1497 and claimed it in the name of his employer, King Henry VII of England. His first landfall probably lay in the northern part of the island. He and his men explored the coast and also sighted Prince Edward Island and Nova Scotia before returning to England. In the summer of 1997, celebrations in St. John's and across Newfoundland commemorated the 500-year anniversary of the event.

The Fabulous Fisheries

So abundant were the cod fisheries of the Grand Banks, the shallow undersea plateaus south and east of Newfoundland, that John Cabot claimed a man had only to lower a basket into the sea to haul it up full. His report exaggerated the truth only slightly. Although the specifics have not been documented, European fishermen are believed to have preceded Cabot by decades. Legends in Newfoundland describe the Basques as whale hunters in the Strait of Belle Isle as early as the 1470s. France's fishing exploits are better known. In the early 1500s, French fleets roamed the seas from the Grand Banks—where they caught cod and dried them on Newfoundland's beaches—to inland rivers such as the salmon-rich Miramichi in what is now New Brunswick. England's fishing fleets were equally active, leading one diplomat to describe Newfoundland as "a great ship moored near the Grand Banks for the convenience of English fishermen."

England also dabbled in other commercial interests in Newfoundland. A group of merchants from England's West Country settled Trinity in the mid-1500s. Cupids, England's first chartered colony on the island, began in 1610. In contrast, St. John's evolved independently and belonged to no nation; the port served as a haven and trading center for all of Europe's fishing fleets, and Signal Hill, the lofty promontory beside the harbor, dates as a lookout and signal peak from the early 1500s.

French Interests

Ultimately, France was more interested in trading posts and settlements than in fishing. The French Crown granted Sieur de Monts a monopoly to develop the fur trade, and in 1604 the nobleman-merchant, with explorer Samuel de Champlain, led an exploratory party to the mouth of the Bay of Fundy. The expedition established a camp on an island in the St. Croix River (the river that now separates New Brunswick from Maine). The group barely survived the bitter first winter and relocated across the Bay of Fundy, establishing Port-Royal as a fur-trading post in the Annapolis basin the following spring.

The grant was canceled, and while most of the expedition returned to France in 1607, a group of French settlers took their place at Port-Royal in 1610. The French dubbed the area Acadia, or "Peaceful Land."

The French settlement and others like it ignited the fuse between England and France. John Cabot had claimed the region for England, but explorer Jacques Cartier also claimed many of the same coastlines for France several decades later. For France, the region was choice property, a potential New France in the New World. On the other hand, England's colonial aspirations centered farther south, where colonization had begun at Virginia and Massachusetts. England didn't *need* what is now Atlantic Canada, though the region offered much with its rich fisheries, but it was a place to confront the expansion of the French, England's most contentious enemy in Europe.

In terms of military strength, the British had the upper hand. An ocean separated France from its dream of settlement, while England's military forces and volunteer militias were located along the eastern seaboard. In 1613, a militia from Virginia plundered and burned the buildings at Port-Royal. The French relocated to a more protected site farther up the Annapolis River, built another fort named Port-Royal, and designated it Acadia's colonial capital in 1635.

Port-Royal

France's Sphere Develops

The French Acadian settlements quickly spread beyond the Port-Royal area to the Fundy and Minas Basin coastlines. The merchant Nicholas Denys, whose name is entwined with France's early exploration, established fortified settlements on Cape Breton at St. Peters and at Guysborough in 1653. So many Acadians settled at Grand-Pré that it became the largest settlement and the hub of villages in the area. Other settlements were established across Acadia on Cape Breton, the Cobequid Bay and Cape Chignecto coastlines, and from the Restigouche Uplands to the Baie des Chaleurs, in what is now northern New Brunswick.

France needed a military center, and created it in the mid-1600s at Plaisance, one of the earliest and most important fishing ports on the Avalon Peninsula in Newfoundland. Here, they erected another tribute to the French Crown and named the new fortification Fort Royal.

British reprisals against the French increased. The British hammered Port-Royal again and again, and in 1654, a militia from New England destroyed some of the Acadian settlements. In Newfoundland, France's presence at Plaisance prompted the British to counter by building forts around St. John's in 1675.

The Treaty of Utrecht

Hostilities between England and France in the New World mirrored political events in Europe. Fighting ebbed and flowed across Atlantic Canada as the powers jockeyed for control on the European continent. Queen Anne's War (1701-1713), the War of Austrian Succession (1745-1748), and the Seven Years' War (1756-1763) were all fought in Europe, but corresponding battles between the English and French took place in North America as well (where they were known collectively as the French and Indian Wars).

The Treaty of Utrecht in 1713 settled Queen Anne's War in Europe. Under the terms of the treaty, England fell heir to all of French Acadia (though the borders were vague). In Newfoundland, Plaisance came into British hands and was renamed Castle Hill. The treaty awarded France the token settlements of the offshore Île Saint-Jean (Prince Edward Island) and Île Royale (Cape Breton). Acadia became an English colony. Nova Scotia (New Scotland) rose on the ashes of New France and the fallen Port-Royal; the British took the fort in 1710, renamed it Fort Anne, and renamed the settlement Annapolis Royal. The town was designated the colony's first capital until Halifax was established and became the capital in 1749.

The French military regrouped. It fled from the peninsula and began to build (but never finished) the Fortress of Louisbourg on Île Royale's Atlantic seacoast in 1719. Once again, the French envisioned the fortification as a new Paris and France's major naval base, port city, and trading center in North America. Simultaneously, they sent 300 fishermen and farmers across the Northumberland Strait to create a new settlement at Port-la-Joye; the enclave, at what is now Charlottetown's southwestern outer edge, was intended to serve as the breadbasket for the Fortress of Louisbourg.

The British quickly responded. A fort at Grassy Island on Chedabucto Bay was their first effort, a site close enough to the Fortress of Louisbourg to watch the arrivals and departures of the French fleets. By 1745, Louisbourg represented a formidable threat to England, so the Brits seized the fortress and deported the inhabitants. But no sooner had they changed the flag than the French were moving back in again. The War of Austrian Succession in Europe ended with the Treaty of Aix-la-Chapelle in 1748, which, among other things, returned Louisbourg to France.

Full-Fledged War

Peace was short-lived. Eight years later, in 1756, the Seven Years' War broke out in Europe, and once more both powers geared up for confrontation in Atlantic Canada. Britain's Grassy Island fort was strategically located, but too small a military base. In 1749 a British convoy sailed into capacious Halifax Harbour, established England's military hub in the North Atlantic there, and named Halifax the capital of Nova Scotia. Fort Edward near the Fundy seacoast went up in the midst of an Acadian area and guarded the overland route from Halifax, while Fort Lawrence on the Chignecto Isthmus, between Nova Scotia and New Brunswick, was built to defend the route to the mainland. The fort defiantly faced two of France's most formidable forts: Fort Beauséjour and Fort Gaspéreau.

The stage was set for war, and the region's civilian inhabitants, the Acadian farmers, were trapped in the middle. Decades before, England had demanded but not enforced an oath of allegiance from the Acadians who lived under their jurisdiction. By the 1750s, however, the British decided to demand loyalty, readying a plan to evict the Acadians from their land and replace noncompliant French inhabitants with Anglo settlers. In 1755, the British swept through the region and enforced the oath. In a show of force, more than 2,000 troops from Boston captured Fort Beauséjour and renamed it Fort Cumberland.

The Acadian Deportation

England's actions unleashed chaos. Those who refused to sign the oath of allegiance were rounded up and deported, and their villages and farmlands were burned. By October, 1,100 Acadians had been deported, while others fought the British in guerrilla warfare or fled to the hinterlands of Cape Breton, New Brunswick, and Québec.

The Acadians being deported were herded onto ships bound for the English colonies on the eastern seaboard, or anyplace that would accept them. Some ships docked in England, others in France, and others in France's colonies in the Caribbean. As the ports wearied of the human cargo, many of them refused the vessels entry, and the ships returned to the high seas to search for other ports willing to accept the Acadians. In one of the period's few favorable moments, the Spanish government offered the refugees free land in Louisiana, and many settled there in 1784, where they became known as Cajuns.

Refugee camps, rife with disease and malnutrition, sprang up across the Maritimes. Beaubears Island, on New Brunswick's Miramichi River, began as a refugee center. About 3,500 Acadians fled from Nova Scotia to Île Saint-Jean (Prince Edward Island); 700 lost their lives on two boats that sank on the journey. Many Acadians returned only to be deported again, some as many as seven or eight times.

Exact deportation numbers are unknown. Historians speculate that 10,000 French inhabitants lived in Acadia in 1755; by the time the deportation had run its course in 1816, only 25 percent of them remained. The poet Henry Wadsworth Longfellow distilled the tragedy in *Evangeline*, a fictional story of two lovers divided by the events.

England's Final Blow

In 1758, the British moved in for the kill. They seized the Fortress of Louisbourg and toppled Port-la-Joye, renaming it Fort Amherst. The French stronghold at Québec fell the next year. In the ultimate act of revenge, the British troops returned to Louisbourg in 1760 and demolished the fortress stone by stone so it would never rise again against England. New France was almost finished; bereft of a foothold in Atlantic Canada, the French launched a convoy from France and captured St. John's in 1762. The British quickly swooped in and regained the port at the Battle of Signal Hill, the final land battle of the Seven Years' War. Finally, the bitter French and Indian Wars were extinguished.

Postwar Developments

Atlantic Canada, as you see it now, then began to take shape. After the British had swept the Acadians from their land, prosperous "planters," gentleman-farmers from New England, were lured to the lush Annapolis Valley with free land grants. Merchants settled Yarmouth in the 1760s, and other Anglo settlers went to Prince Edward Island. The island, formerly part of Nova Scotia, became an English colony in 1769.

Some of the Acadians had evaded capture, and settlements such as the Pubnico communities south of Yarmouth date to the pre-deportation period. But most of the region's surviving Acadian areas began after the refugees returned and settled marginal lands no one else wanted, such as the rocky seacoast of La Côte Acadienne (the Acadian Coast) in western Nova Scotia.

In Canada, England lucked out. Even its inglorious defeat in the American Revolution benefited the British. Loyalists (Americans loyal to England) by the thousands poured into Nova Scotia and New Brunswick. The influx was so great in Saint John and Fredericton that New Brunswick, originally part of Nova Scotia, became an English colony, and Saint John became the first incorporated city in Canada.

An Uneasy Peace

Even as peace settled across Atlantic Canada, the specter of war loomed again in Europe. Ever wary of their contentious enemy, the British feared a French invasion by Napoleon's navies in Atlantic Canada. In Halifax, the British built up the harbor's defenses at the Halifax Citadel and other sites. At St. John's, the British fortified Signal Hill with the Queen's Battery.

As if Britain didn't have enough problems with the Napoleonic Wars, the War of 1812 was sparked at the same time, as England and the United States wrangled over shipping rights on the high seas. More British fortifications went up, this time across the Bay of Fundy in New Brunswick, with harbor defenses such as the Carleton Martello Tower at Saint John, the blockhouse at St. Andrews, and other strongholds at more than a dozen strategic places.

TOWARD CONFEDERATION

The Napoleonic Wars ended in June 1815 with Napoleon's defeat at Waterloo. Atlantic Canada emerged unscathed. The war years had fostered shipping, and Halifax earned a questionable reputation as the home port of privateers who raided ships on the high seas and returned to port to auction the booty at the harbor. In Newfoundland, many ships had been lost on the treacherous shoals outside St. John's Harbour, prompting the British to build the lofty Cape Spear Lighthouse in 1836.

In 1864 a landmark event in Canada's history took place. The "Fathers of the Confederation"—from New Brunswick, Nova Scotia, Prince Edward Island, Ontario, and Québec—met at Province House in Charlottetown. The small city owes its fame as the birthplace of Canada to the discussions of a joint dominion that followed there. In 1867, England gave the union its blessing and signed the British North America Act (now known as the Constitution Act); the Dominion of Canada was born on July 1 as a confederation of Québec, Ontario, New Brunswick, and Nova Scotia united under a parliamentary government.

Under the leadership of its first prime minister, Sir John A. MacDonald, Canada expanded rapidly. The acquisition of Ruperts Land from the Hudson's Bay Company in 1869 increased its total land area sixfold. Manitoba and British Columbia joined the Confederation in 1870 and 1871, respectively. Prince Edward Island, having initially declined to become a Confederation member, joined the dominion in 1873. Alberta and Saskatchewan followed in 1905, and nearly a half century later, in 1949, Newfoundland became Canada's 10th province.

As a condition of participation in the Confederation, British Columbia and New Brunswick insisted that the government build a railroad across Canada to facilitate trade, transport, and communication. Work on the daunting project began in 1881, and in 1885, just four years later, the last spike was driven

Where Canada Began

In the fall of 1864, the colonial capital of Prince Edward Island hosted the Charlottetown Conference, which led to the establishment of the Dominion of Canada. The delegates who became Canada's founding Fathers of Confederation agreed that the city was the ideal neutral site for the conference. Islanders were neither for nor against the idea of a dominion. But just in case the fledgling idea of forming a union did come to something, the islanders appointed several delegates to represent them.

The other delegates arrived by sea in groups from New Brunswick, Nova Scotia, and Upper and Lower Canada, now Ontario and Québec. Their respective ships docked at the harbor, and one by one the delegates walked the short blocks up Great George Street to the Colonial Building, as Province House was then known. The meeting led to the signing of the British North America Act in London in 1867 and the beginnings of modern Canada on July 1 of that year. The initial four provinces were Nova Scotia, New Brunswick, Québec, and Ontario. Prince Edward Island originally passed on membership and didn't join the Confederation until 1873. Other latecomers included Manitoba (1870), British Columbia (1871), Alberta (1905), Saskatchewan (1905), and Newfoundland and Labrador (1949).

Province House

in the Canadian Pacific Railway. Linking Vancouver with Montréal, which in turn connected with regional lines in New Brunswick, Nova Scotia, and Prince Edward Island, the railroad united the country in a way no act of confederation could.

World Wars and the Depression

Atlantic Canada became a hotbed of controversy during World War I, when the sensitive issue of Francophone rights was raised. The federal government had decided to initiate a military conscription, and French Canadians were afraid the draft would decrease their already minority population. The measure was a failure, as both French- and English-speaking men of conscription age avoided the draft. By war's end, however, 63,000 Canadians had died in battle, and another 175,000 were wounded. During the war, the nation had supplied Britain with much of its food and also produced large quantities of munitions,

ships, and planes—an experience that helped move Canada from a primarily agricultural economy to an industrial one. Afterward, Canada emerged stronger, more independent, and with a greater sense of self-confidence. The Atlantic provinces enjoyed a brief brush with prosperity as mining and manufacturing expanded.

But the Maritimes were not immune to the Great Depression of the 1930s, which hit Canada even harder than the United States. Many businesses collapsed under the financial crisis. When World War II erupted, Canada followed Britain's lead in joining the war against Hitler. Nearly one-tenth of the population of about 11.5 million served in the war effort. Atlantic Canada again took part in shipping many of the munitions and food supplies for the Allies, and the regional and national economies were again revived.

In 1959 the completion of the St. Lawrence Seaway, a project jointly undertaken by the United States and Canada, opened a new sea lane between the Great Lakes and the Atlantic. Three years later, the new TransCanada Highway spanned the country from sea to sea. Linking Vancouver Island with St. John's, Newfoundland, the highway joined all 10 provinces along a single route and made the country just a little smaller.

A Constitution and Autonomy

Starting in 1867, the British North America Act required the British parliament's approval for any Canadian constitutional change. On November 5, 1981, Canada's federal government and the premiers of every province except Québec agreed on a Canadian Constitution and Charter of Rights and Freedoms. The Canada Act formally went into effect on April 17, 1982, removing the last vestiges of the British parliament's control. Canada remains, however, a member of the Commonwealth.

Old Divisions in Modern Times

The formation of the Parti Québécois in 1968 signaled a popular new militancy among French-speaking separatists in Québec, who desired a political and cultural divorce from the rest of Canada. The Official Languages Act recognized French as the country's second official language after English, but this act only bandaged over deep wounds. Referenda on the question of Québec secession in the 1980s and 1990s have failed to resolve the issue; a provincial vote on the question in 1995 saw the drive for separation defeated by a margin of barely 1 percent. It's difficult to predict which way the pendulum will swing, should there be another vote, but the national government, in any case, has indicated that it will honor the will of the Québécois. In Atlantic Canada, attitudes toward separation are mixed; the general consensus, even in officially bilingual New Brunswick, seems to run in favor of continued Canadian unity, but that consensus is undermined by a growing impatience with Québec's demands for what many Canadians see as preferential treatment from the federal government.

Government and Economy

GOVERNMENT

Canada is a constitutional monarchy. The federation of 10 provinces and three territories operates under a parliamentary democracy in which power is shared between the federal government, based in Ottawa, and the provincial governments. Canada's three nonprovincial territories (Nunavut, Yukon, and the Northwest Territories) exercise delegated—rather than constitutionally guaranteed—authority. The power to make, enforce, and interpret laws rests in the legislative, executive, and judicial branches of government, respectively.

Federal Government

Under Canada's constitutional monarchy, the formal head of state is the queen of England, who appoints a governor general to represent her for a five-year term. The governor general stays out of party politics and performs largely ceremonial duties, such as opening and closing parliamentary sessions, signing and approving state documents on the queen's behalf, and appointing a temporary replacement if the prime ministry is vacated without warning. The head of government is the prime minister, who is the leader of the majority party or party coalition in the House of Commons.

The country's legislative branch, the Parliament, is composed of two houses. The House of Commons, with 295 members, is apportioned by provincial population and elected by plurality from the country's districts. The Senate comprises 104 members appointed by the governor general (formerly for a life term, though retirement is now mandatory at age 75) on the advice of the prime minister. Legislation must be passed by both houses and signed by the governor general to become law.

National elections are held whenever the majority party is voted down in the House of Commons or every five years, whichever comes first. Historically, it has been unusual for a government to last its full term.

Provincial and Local Governments

Whereas the federal government has authority over defense, criminal law, trade, banking, and other affairs of national interest, Canada's 10 provincial governments bear responsibility for civil services, health, education, natural resources, and local government. Each of the nation's provincial Legislative Assemblies (in Newfoundland and Labrador, the body is called the House of Assembly) consists of a one-house legislative body with members elected every four years. The nominal head of the provincial government is the lieutenant governor, appointed by the governor general of Canada. Executive power, however, rests with the Cabinet, headed by a premier, the leader of the majority party.

ECONOMY

Traditionally, the economy of Atlantic Canada revolved around resource-based industries such as fishing, forestry, and mining. Although communities established around fishing and farming areas continue to thrive, the economy today is a lot more diverse. In addition to the stalwarts discussed below, other growing sectors include information technology, the medical field, and the film industry.

Fishing

Canada was once the world's largest fish-exporting country, but poor resource management and overfishing have destroyed its once-bounteous supplies. Even so, fisheries and fish processing still remain the third-biggest contributor to Nova Scotia's gross domestic product (GDP), and cod, haddock, herring, and lobster are caught inshore and off the Atlantic's Scotian Shelf. The province is Canada's largest lobster exporter.

New Brunswick's fisheries produce groundfish, lobster, crab, scallops, and herring. The newest aquaculture developments are Atlantic salmon farms and blue mussel beds. Blacks Harbour-area canneries on the Bay of Fundy rank first in Canadian sardine production.

Newfoundland and Labrador's fisheries, a chronic boom-or-bust industry, contribute some $300 million yearly to the economy, with catches of mackerel, flounder, capelin, herring, squid, eel, fish roe, sole, salmon, perch, turbot, halibut, lobster, and farmed mussels and rainbow trout. Labrador also produces half of Canada's commercial char. Since the 1990s, when the cod industry came to a standstill, Newfoundland fisheries have diversified. Now scallops and shrimp make up a good percentage of the catch.

Prince Edward Island also has an important fishing industry, especially in lobster and shellfish such as farmed mussels.

Natural Resources

Atlantic Canada's fisheries have declined as a consequence of modern fishing methods as well as foreign competition. As a result, the area has turned to its other resources: timber, coal, and other minerals. New Brunswick harbors Canada's largest silver, lead, and zinc reserves, and also mines potash, coal, and oil shale. Peat moss is collected in northeastern New Brunswick, especially from Lamèque and Miscou Islands—enough to make the province the world's second-largest exporter of this fuel.

Mining contributes $1 billion to New Brunswick's economy and is the second-largest segment of Nova Scotia's. More than 30 mines and quarries in Nova Scotia are worked for their coal, limestone, and tin.

Nova Scotia's extensive forests supply a

1: a commercial fishing boat; 2: potato fields on Prince Edward Island

substantial lumber and paper industry; among the largest operators are Bowater (half owned by the *Washington Post*) on the South Shore and the Irving Forest Products pulp mills at Abercrombie Point, Point Tupper, Brooklyn, Hantsport, and East River.

Western Labrador's mines contribute about 80 percent of Canada's share of iron ore. Other Newfoundland metals and minerals include copper, lead, zinc, gold, silver, chromium, limestone, gypsum, aluminum silicate, and asbestos. Newfoundland's Avalon Peninsula holds Canada's sole commercial deposit of pyrophyllite, used in the production of ceramics. Newfoundland is economically on the bottom rung of Canada's per-capita income, yet the province is sitting on a gold mine when it comes to natural resources. Offshore oil fields started producing in 2001, and the extraction rate is currently 85 million barrels annually, most of which comes from three offshore fields (Hibernia, Terra Nova, and White Rose).

Agriculture

Agriculture contributes $240 million to New Brunswick's GDP; Victoria and Carleton Counties' seed potatoes make up 18 percent of Canada's total potato crop and are exported to Mexico, Portugal, and the United States. The benevolent spring floods wash the Saint John River valley with rich silt, helping to sustain a healthy mixed farming economy. The farms at Maugerville yield two crops each season. Other agricultural products include livestock (exported to France, Britain, Denmark, and the United States), dairy products, and berries.

Although just 8 percent of Nova Scotia's land is arable, agriculture contributes heavily to the economy. The province produces fruit (including Annapolis Valley apples), dairy products, poultry, hogs, and Canada's largest share of blueberries.

Diminutive Prince Edward Island ranks first in Canada's potato production. Half of the crop is grown in Prince County, and the remainder is produced by farms scattered across the province. The province harvests 12 million oysters annually, and most are exported. The island's beauty may be attributed to its investment in agriculture, which contributes about 9.5 percent to the gross domestic product. The sector yields $120 million a year and employs 4,000 islanders on 2,200 farms, each of which averages 140 hectares (346 acres). Grains, fruit, beef, pigs, sheep, and dairy products are other components of mixed farming production.

Power

Water is ubiquitous in the Atlantic provinces (one-third of all the world's freshwater is found in Canada), and hydroelectricity is a cheap, clean export. Québec Hydro alone sells over $1 billion worth of electricity a year to New England. The Mactaquac Generating Station, on the Saint John River near Fredericton, New Brunswick, is the Maritimes' largest hydroelectric station.

Tourism

Tourism ranks as the fastest-growing sector of the economy across Atlantic Canada. Tourism contributes over $2 billion to Nova Scotia's annual economy alone. Most visitors enter the region by road through New Brunswick, Atlantic Canada's land gateway, and arrive by car, RV, or tour bus. Only 25 percent fly in; air arrivals are increasing, however, as air links into the region improve. Most visitors (40 percent) are from the neighboring provinces, while central and western Canada contribute 25 percent, and the United States adds almost 25 percent. Together, these tourists support 95,000 jobs.

People and Culture

While the topography of this region—the dense forests, mountains, and rugged coastline—has tended to separate people and isolate them in scattered settlements, centuries of sometimes turbulent history have bound the Atlantic Canadians together: the mutual grief of the early wars, the Acadian deportation, immigration upheavals, and the abiding hardships common to resource-based economies. In the same sense, these and other factors have given each population an indisputable identity that makes it difficult to generalize about the diverse peoples of this part of Canada. Senator Eugene Forsey's observations on the country as a whole are equally applicable to Atlantic Canada: "I think our identity will have to be something which is partly British, partly French, partly American, partly derived from a variety of other influences which are too numerous even to catalogue."

In spite of diversity, the region still shares a common identity as a place apart from the rest of Canada. A foreign nation borders it to the southwest, and Atlantic Canada is separated from the body of its nation by the insular bastion of Québec. Although the country began in the east and was nourished by its resources for centuries, Canada's general prosperity has not been fully shared here. Atlantic Canada experiences higher unemployment, higher underemployment, and lower income than any of the other provinces. Unlike the rest of the country, the provinces of Atlantic Canada share economies that rise and fall largely on the vicissitudes of the fisheries and other natural resources.

DEMOGRAPHY

A few statistics say much about the region. The entire population of the country numbers some 36.3 million—smaller than California's population. Atlantic Canada's four provinces make up 15.3 percent of Canada's total population, with a combined total of 2,371,000 people.

Nova Scotia

Nova Scotia's population is 943,000. It is the seventh most populous province and is home to 2.3 percent of Canada's total population. Distribution is closely divided between urban and rural, with a full third of Nova Scotians concentrated in and around Halifax.

Almost four of five Nova Scotians trace their lineage to the British Isles. Some 49 original Scottish families, from Archibald to Yuill, are still on the rolls of the Federation of Scottish Clans in Nova Scotia (www.scotsns.ca), which does genealogical surveys.

After the American Revolution, 25,000 United Empire Loyalists poured into Nova Scotia. Several thousand African Americans arrived during the War of 1812, followed by Irish immigrants from 1815 to 1850. Recent worldwide immigration has added more than 50 other ethnic groups (including Poles, Ukrainians, Germans, Swiss, Africans, and Lebanese) to the province's cultural milieu, making it the most cosmopolitan in the region. About 8,000 Black people live in Nova Scotia today, many of them descendants of immigrants from the colonial United States.

New Brunswick

The province, with a population of 754,000, is in a sense a miniature Canada, a provincial composite of Anglophones and Acadian Francophones who harmoniously coexist—the exception rather than the rule in a nation whose two dominant cultures are so often at odds. One suspects the harsh history that divided New Brunswick at its inception has run its course and mellowed. As Canada's only officially bilingual province, it steps to an agreeable duple beat.

The duality repeats itself in numerous ways. New Brunswick has an Anglophone

Magical Music

The thousands of Gaelic speakers who migrated to the New World during the 1700s and 1800s brought many traditions with them, none more distinctive than their **Celtic music.** Many cherished songs describing life on the land have been passed down through the generations, while new, lively tunes create a spirited mix of music heard throughout the region and beyond.

The lively fiddle performances of Cape Breton-born **Natalie MacMaster** bring crowds the world over to their feet. Also from Cape Breton Island are **The Rankins,** who infuse a variety of styles into their music, and grunge-fiddler **Ashley MacIsaac,** whose sound crosses from Celtic to garage rock and heavy metal. Across on "The Rock," **Great Big Sea** is renowned for its energetic rock-meets-Celtic live performances. In addition to the big names, bands like **Beolach** and the **Irish Descendants** are worth watching for, while bands churning out lively foot-stomping, beer-drinking tunes can be heard in pubs throughout Atlantic Canada.

In rural areas of Cape Breton Island, **ceilidhs** (gatherings with Celtic music and dancing) remain an important part of the social scene.

region and another equally distinctive Acadian Francophone counterpart. The distinctions were set in stone centuries ago when the British evicted the Acadians from their original settlements and resettled the Loyalists. The Anglophone cities, towns, and settlements lie along the Fundy seacoast and throughout most of the Saint John River valley. The French-speaking Acadian region lies beyond, on the province's outer rim in the northwestern woodlands along the Saint John River and on the coastlines of the Baie des Chaleurs, the open gulf, and the sheltered strait. Today, English is the first language of about 65 percent of New Brunswickers, while French is the mother tongue for about 33 percent.

Prince Edward Island

Although it's anything but crowded, Prince Edward Island (PEI, population 146,000) is Canada's most densely populated, with around 24 people per square kilometer (60 people per square mile). At the same time, Prince Edward Island is the most rural province, with fewer than two in five residents living in urban areas. PEI's people are also said to be Canada's most homogeneous. The province's ancestry is 80 percent Anglo—a third Irish and the remainder Scottish. Acadians represent 17 percent of the population (5 percent of them speak French). Southeast Asians,

Germans, and a thriving population of about 500 Mi'kmaq (most living on Lennox Island on the north shore and at Scotchfort) together constitute about 2 percent of the population. PEI still lures immigrants, mainly from other Atlantic Canada provinces and Ontario.

Newfoundland and Labrador

In contrast to relatively crowded Prince Edward Island, this province, with a population of 528,000, has fewer than 1.5 people per square kilometer (3.75 people per square mile). Ninety-five percent of the population is concentrated on the island of Newfoundland (known as "The Rock").

In Labrador, Inuit, Innu, and Anglo Labradorians inhabit the sparsely settled eastern coastline and remote central interior. The people of the island of Newfoundland are an overwhelmingly Anglo and Celtic cultural mix (96 percent), whose psyche is linked to the sea and the Grand Banks fisheries. A small number of Mi'kmaq also live on the island.

An insular mentality still informs the provincial character, and nearly 70 years after joining the Confederation, residents of The Rock may still refer to their countrymen as "Canadians"—outsiders from another nation. They even inhabit their own time zone, Newfoundland time, a quirky half hour ahead of Atlantic time.

Though a full-fledged province since 1949,

Newfoundland was a colony of England's for centuries. This is why you'll still hear a clipped King's English accent in St. John's, a West Country dialect in some of the small remote fishing villages (called outports), and a softly brushed Irish brogue on the Avalon Peninsula. Some 60 dialects and subdialects have been documented throughout the province, many of them incorporating colorful expressions and vocabulary that are unique to Newfoundland. In addition, the map of the province is decorated with one-of-a-kind place-names: Blow Me Down, Joe Batt's Arm, Happy Adventure, Jerry's Nose, and dozens of other toponymic oddities.

NATIVE PEOPLES AND MÉTIS

The first European explorers to reach North America found a land that was anything but uninhabited. Tribes or nations of aboriginals had been here for millennia, from coast to coast and up into the continent's subarctic and Arctic regions.

Various names are used to describe aboriginal Canadians, and all can be correct in context. The government still uses the term *Indian*, despite its links to Christopher Columbus and the misconception that he had landed in India. *Native* is generally considered acceptable only when used in conjunction with *people*, *communities*, or *leaders*. *Indigenous* and *aboriginal* can have insulting connotations when used in certain contexts.

Mi'kmaq

When Europeans first arrived, perhaps 20,000 Mi'kmaq lived in the coastal areas of the Gaspé Peninsula and the Maritimes east of the Saint John River. The name Mi'kmaq (also Micmac) is thought to have derived from the word *nikmaq*, meaning "my kin-friends," which early French settlers used as a greeting for the tribe. Mi'kmaq historically referred to themselves as Lnu (meaning "human being" or "the people"). The aboriginal Mi'kmaq fished and hunted, and became involved with the fur trade in the 18th century.

The Mi'kmaq historically had practiced little or no agriculture, and attempts by the British to convert them into farmers fared poorly. Later, they found employment building railways and roads and in lumbering and fisheries. Today the Mi'kmaq number an estimated 15,000 in the Maritime provinces, Newfoundland, and parts of New England.

Maliseet

Culturally and linguistically related to the Mi'kmaq (both are members of the widespread Algonquian language group), the Maliseet (or Malicite) inhabited the Saint John River valley in New Brunswick and lands west to the St. Lawrence and what is now Maine. For the first century after contact, the Maliseet got on well with European fishers and traders, although Old World diseases greatly reduced their numbers.

As the fur trade dwindled, Maliseet women adopted agriculture, while the men continued to hunt and fish. Increasing white settlement along the Saint John, however, displaced the Maliseet from their traditional lands, eventually leaving them destitute. In the 19th century, the first Indian reserves were created for the Maliseet at Fredericton, Oromocto, Kingsclear, and other New Brunswick locations.

Inuit

The Inuit (formerly known as Eskimos—a name many consider pejorative) inhabit the northern regions of Canada, as well as Alaska and Greenland. Their ancestors arrived in the Arctic in the 11th century. Today they number roughly 25,000 in eight main tribal groups and share a common language—Inuktitut—with six dialects. Until the late 1930s, when a court ruled that their welfare was the responsibility of the federal government, the Inuit were largely ignored by Canada, principally because they occupied inhospitable lands in the far north.

In the late 18th century, Moravian missionaries in Labrador established the first lasting contact with the Inuit, followed by commercial whalers and explorers. The Europeans initiated cultural and technological changes in the traditional societies (including almost universal conversion to Christianity) that continue to this day. Although the Inuit of northern Labrador gained self-governing status with the creation of Nunatsiavut in 2005, they continue to live in small, remote settlements while maintaining traditional practices: hunting seals, caribou, and whales and continuing other aspects of Inuit culture.

Métis

The progeny of native people and Caucasians, the Métis (named for an old French word meaning "mixed") form a diverse and complex group throughout Canada. They date from the time of earliest European contact: in Atlantic Canada, unions between European fishermen and native women—sometimes casual, sometimes formal—produced Métis offspring by the early 1600s.

In the 17th century, the French government encouraged this mixing, seeing it as conducive to converting the native people to Christianity and more speedily increasing the population of New France. Samuel de Champlain said, "Our young men will marry your daughters, and we shall be one people." That policy had changed by the 1700s, however, and France then *discouraged* mixed unions, in part because of the increased presence of European women in North America. This policy led to the development of distinct Métis settlements, mainly around the Great Lakes (these settlements would later grow into cities such as Chicago, Milwaukee, Sault Ste. Marie, and Detroit).

Recent census figures estimate Métis numbers at about 60,000. Some identify themselves with the aboriginals, some with Whites, while others consider themselves members of a society and culture distinct from both.

LANGUAGE

Although Canada is constitutionally bilingual, English is the language of choice for most of the country and for the majority of Atlantic Canadians. (In 2016, French was the mother tongue of about 22 percent of Canadians, while the figure in Québec was 88 percent.) The Official Languages Acts of 1969 and 1988 established French and English as equal official languages and designated rights for minority language speakers throughout the country.

In Atlantic Canada, English is the first language for the majority. But in officially bilingual New Brunswick, French is the home tongue for a substantial portion of the population—about 28 percent—and the province's two languages and cultures have managed to coexist in reasonable harmony. Francophones are smaller minorities in Prince Edward Island (about 5 percent), Nova Scotia (4 percent), and Newfoundland (less than 1 percent).

The French spoken here is not a patois; it's closely tied to the language that was brought to the continent by the original settlers from France. Visitors who have studied standard Parisian French may have a little trouble with the accent, syntax, and vocabulary (the differences are not unlike those between American and British English). Still, travelers who make an effort at speaking French will find Francophones patient and appreciative.

Some Dutch is spoken on Prince Edward Island, and with the arrival of Asian immigrants starting around the 1960s, Chinese, Vietnamese, Punjabi, Hindi, Urdu, and other tongues can be overheard in urban areas. The Inuit of Labrador continue to speak Inuktitut, and the Mi'kmaq of the other provinces maintain their native language with varying degrees of success.

Canada, Eh!

Canadian English is subtly different from American English, not only in pronunciation but also in lexicon. For instance, Canadians may say "serviette," "depot," and "chesterfield" where Americans would say "napkin," "station," and "couch." Spelling is a bit skewed as well, as Canadians have kept many British spellings—colour, kilometre, centre, and cheque, for example. "Eh?" is a common lilt derived from British and Gaelic in which each sentence ends on a high note, as though a question had been asked. At the same time, Canadian English has been profoundly influenced by its neighbor to the south. Nevertheless, language variations pose no serious threat to communication.

RELIGION

Atlantic Canada's cultural diversity is also reflected in religion. Though Christian faiths have predominated since the first Europeans settled here, and despite Canada's less-than-sterling history of religious tolerance, the Maritime territories have offered sects and a variety of denominations—including oppressed minority groups such as Mennonites, Doukhobors, Eastern European and Russian Jews, and others—an opportunity to start anew. The domination of organized religions (primarily the Roman Catholic Church and various Protestant churches) over the lives of Canadians has waned substantially since the 1960s. Partly this is due to the overall national drop in church membership over the past several decades, but it could also be an effect of Canada's increasingly multicultural population. In the Atlantic provinces, church affiliation is still high, and the Catholic and Protestant churches, in particular, still play substantial roles in the lives and communities of people throughout the region.

Essentials

Transportation

GETTING THERE

Visitors to Atlantic Canada have the option of arriving by road, rail, ferry, or air. The main gateway city for flights from North America and Europe is Halifax (Nova Scotia), from where flights leave for other provincial capitals. Ferries land at Yarmouth (Nova Scotia) from Maine, while the main rail line enters the region in New Brunswick and terminates at Halifax.

Unless otherwise noted, telephone numbers given in this section are the local (North American) contacts.

Air

Most long-haul international and domestic flights into eastern Canada set down at Toronto, Ottawa, or Montréal, with connecting or ongoing flights to Atlantic Canada.

AIR CANADA

Air Canada (888/247-2262, www.aircanada.com) is one of the world's largest airlines, serving five continents. The company has one of the world's easiest-to-understand fare systems, with five fare levels and multiple ways of searching for online flights and fares. It offers direct flights to Halifax from Fredericton, Saint John, Moncton, St. John's, Montréal, Ottawa, Toronto, Calgary, and Boston. All other flights from North America are routed through Toronto, Ottawa, or Montréal, where connections can be made to Halifax. From Europe, Air Canada flies from London to Halifax. From the South Pacific, Air Canada operates flights from Sydney to Vancouver for onward connections to Halifax. Asian cities served by direct Air Canada flights include Beijing, Hong Kong, Nagoya, Osaka, Seoul, Shanghai, Taipei, and Tokyo. All terminate in Vancouver. Air Canada's flights originating in South America are all routed through Toronto.

WESTJET

Canada's second-largest airline, **WestJet** (403/250-5839 or 888/937-8538, www.westjet.com), is the main competition to Air Canada. Based in Calgary, its flights extend as far east as St. John's, with flights routed through Toronto to Halifax, Fredericton, Moncton, Charlottetown, Deer Lake, and St. John's.

U.S. AIRLINES

Air Canada offers direct daily flights from Boston to Halifax, but the city is also served by **Delta** (800/221-1212, www.delta.com) from New York (LGA), **American** (800/433-7300, www.aa.com) from Philadelphia, and **United** (800/538-2929, www.united.com) from Chicago and Newark. Delta also flies between New York and Charlottetown, and United between New York and St. John's.

Rail

Amtrak (800/872-8725, www.amtrak.com) has service from New York City to Toronto (via Buffalo), and from New York City to Montréal.

VIA RAIL

Once you're in Canada, rail travel is handled by **VIA Rail** (416/366-8411 or 888/842-7245, www.viarail.ca). Best known for the transcontinental rail route, the spectacular journey from Vancouver to Toronto through the Canadian Rockies, VIA Rail has replicated that route's deluxe trappings and service with its Sleeper Plus class aboard the *Ocean.* The *Ocean* departs Montréal, follows the St. Lawrence River's southern shore to northern New Brunswick, cuts across the province to Moncton, speeds into Nova Scotia via Amherst and Truro, and finishes at Halifax. The trip takes 21 hours. The train has a variety of classes, but it is the Sleeper Plus class that gets all the attention. These luxuriously appointed carriages include a domed car with three small salons (one of which is a replica of the transcontinental's mural lounge), a dining car with art deco trappings, and a more informal car designed for lighter dining. Fares from Montreal to Halifax range from $205 each way in Economy class to $675 in Sleeper Plus class, the latter including sleeping-car accommodations and all meals.

Bus

North America's main bus line, **Greyhound** (800/231-2222, www.greyhound.ca or www.greyhound.com), doesn't provide service to Atlantic Canada. Instead, you will need to catch a Greyhound bus to Riviere-du-Loup on the Québec/New Brunswick border and connect with **Maritime Bus** (902/429-2029

Air Taxes

The Canadian government collects a variety of "departure taxes" on all flights originating from Canada. These taxes are generally not in the advertised fare, but they will all be included in the ticket purchase price. First up is the **Air Travellers Security Charge,** $7-14 each way for flights within North America and $25 round-trip for international flights. At the time of writing, both major Canadian airlines were adding $25-100 per domestic sector for a fuel surcharge and $3 for an insurance surcharge. Although fees were reduced in 2016, **NAV Canada** still dips its hand in your pocket, collecting $9-20 per flight to maintain the country's navigational systems. Additionally, passengers departing Halifax International Airport must pay an **Airport Improvement Fee** of $28, while those departing Bathurst (New Brunswick) pay $40, the highest such fee in Canada. Additionally, if your flight transits through Toronto, you pay a $4 improvement fee for that airport.

or 800/575-1807, www.maritimebus.com), which provides service from Riviere-du-Loup to locations throughout New Brunswick and Nova Scotia.

Car

The majority of visitors drive to Atlantic Canada. From the United States, Highway 9 heads east from Bangor, Maine, and enters New Brunswick—Atlantic Canada's principal land gateway—at St. Stephen, near the Fundy Coast. The Trans-Canada Highway from central Canada (another main entry route) is more roundabout, following the St. Lawrence River through Québec to enter northwestern New Brunswick at Saint-Jacques near Edmundston. Once in New Brunswick, you can take the Confederation Bridge to Prince Edward Island or continue driving east into Nova Scotia.

Labrador can be reached from Québec on Highway 389, from Baie-Comeau, on the St. Lawrence River's northern bank. The 581-kilometer (360-mile) drive takes nine hours; the two-lane road wends through Québec's northern wilderness to enter western Labrador at Labrador City.

GETTING AROUND

Driving, whether with your own vehicle or a rental car, is by far the best way to get around Atlantic Canada. This section talks about driving in Canada, as well as public transportation options.

Air

Halifax International Airport (YHZ, www. flyhalifax.com), 35 kilometers (22 miles) from Halifax, serves as Atlantic Canada's principal regional air hub. Other airports are located at Saint John, Moncton, Bathurst, Yarmouth, Sydney, Charlottetown, and St. John's. **Air Canada** (888/247-2262, www.aircanada.ca) and its subsidiary, Rouge, saturate the region with frequent flights. **WestJet** (403/250-5839 or 888/937-8538, www.westjet.com) also flies between all major Atlantic Canada cities.

PAL Airlines (709/576-1666 or 800/563-2800, www.palairlines.ca) serves all of Newfoundland and Labrador with direct flights into the province from Halifax and Montreal. Based in Happy Valley-Goose Bay, **Air Borealis** (709/566-1666 or 800/563-2800, www.airborealis.ca) links the remote towns of Labrador's North Coast to the outside world.

Air travel is the public transportation mode of choice throughout the provinces. While the airlines haven't put bus or ferry travel (or trains, yet) out of business, the airports are usually crowded and regional flights are often filled.

Bus

Getting around Nova Scotia and New Brunswick by bus is made possible by **Maritime Bus** (902/429-2029 or 800/575-1807, www.maritimebus.com), which links all major cities and towns as well as many minor ones (although there is no service along Nova Scotia's South Shore or Fundy Coast). It operates seven days a week year-round. No passes are offered, but fares are reasonable.

All major cities have public transportation systems that revolve around scheduled bus service. If you have a day on your hands and no other plans, consider an early morning bus to an unexplored area and a late afternoon or early evening return to the city. Few outsiders do it, but mixing among the locals on a bus circuit is a terrific way to explore a city.

Ferry
FROM MAINE
Between mid-June and October, **CAT** (877/762-7245, www.ferries.ca, adult $107, senior $102, child $65, vehicle under 6.6 feet $199) departs Portland, Maine, daily, for Yarmouth, Nova Scotia, a 5.5-hour crossing.

ACROSS THE BAY OF FUNDY
Bay Ferries (902/245-2116 or 888/249-7245, www.ferries.ca) handles the busy Bay of Fundy crossing between Saint John (New Brunswick) and Digby (Nova Scotia), a shortcut that saves drivers a few hours' driving time. Operating once or twice daily year-round, one-way high-season fares are adult $46, senior and youth $36, child under five free, vehicle $92 plus a $20 fuel surcharge. Reservations are essential through summer.

TO PRINCE EDWARD ISLAND
Northumberland Ferries (902/566-3838 or 877/762-7245, www.ferries.ca) operates 5-9 sailings daily between Caribou (Nova Scotia) and Wood Islands in eastern Prince Edward Island. The crossing takes just over one hour. The fare is $78 per vehicle, regardless of the number of passengers. You pay when leaving the island, so take the ferry to PEI and return on the Confederation Bridge to save a few bucks.

TO AND AROUND NEWFOUNDLAND AND LABRADOR
Marine Atlantic (902/794-5254 or 800/341-7981, www.marineatlantic.ca) operates two routes between North Sydney (Nova Scotia) and Newfoundland. The shorter passage, to Port-aux-Basques, takes 5-6 hours (adult $44, senior $40, child $20, vehicle under 20 feet $115). Summer-only sailings between North Sydney and Argentia take around 14 hours (adult $125, senior $115, child $62, from $253 for vehicles).

The **Department of Transportation and Works** (www.tw.gov.nl.ca) operates ferries on 16 routes within Newfoundland to Labrador. The region's most adventurous ferry trip is the 4.5-day round-trip to remote Nain operated by **Nunatsiavut Marine** (709/896-2262 or 855/896-2262, www.labradorferry.ca).

Driving in Canada
U.S. and international driver's licenses are valid in Canada. All highway signs give distances in kilometers and speeds in kilometers per hour (km/h). Unless otherwise posted, the maximum speed limit on the highways is 100 kilometers per hour (62 miles per hour).

Infants weighing up to nine kilograms must be strapped into a "bucket"-style car seat. Use of a child car seat for larger children weighing 9-18 kilograms is also required. Before venturing north of the 49th parallel, U.S. residents should ask their vehicle insurance company for a Canadian Non-resident Inter-provincial Motor Vehicle Liability Insurance Card. You may also be asked to prove vehicle ownership, so be sure you have your vehicle registration form.

If you're a member in good standing of an automobile association, take your membership card—the Canadian AA provides members of related associations full services, including free maps, itineraries, excellent tour books, road- and weather-condition information, accommodations reservations, travel agency services, and emergency road services. For more information, contact the **Canadian**

Confederation Bridge

Confederation Bridge

The 13-kilometer-wide (8.1-mile-wide) strait between New Brunswick's Cape Jourimain and Prince Edward Island is spanned by the Confederation Bridge, Canada's longest bridge (and the world's longest continuous multispan bridge). Replacing a busy ferry route that had been in operation since 1832, the bridge was completed after four years of construction and at a cost of $1 billion. Building a road link to the rest of Canada was a subject of debate for decades, with passionate opinions running on both sides of the issue. Open now since 1997, there's little question that the link has increased traffic to the island. Whether the growing volume of visitors will dramatically alter the island's way of life, as opponents warned, remains to be seen.

The bridge toll is $47 per vehicle, including passengers. The fee is collected upon leaving the island—in effect, the amount is for the round-trip. Payment can be made in cash or by debit or credit card. Check out the bridge at www.confederationbridge.com.

Automobile Association (613/247-0117, www.caa.ca).

Note: Drinking and driving (with a blood-alcohol level of 0.08 percent or higher) in Atlantic Canada can get you imprisoned for up to five years on a first offense and will cost you your license for at least 12 months. Those caught driving with a blood alcohol level between 0.05 and 0.08 percent automatically lose their license for seven days.

CAR RENTAL

All major car rental companies have outlets at Halifax International Airport, in downtown Halifax, and at airports and cities across Atlantic Canada. Try to book in advance, especially in summer. Expect to pay from $50 a day and $250 a week for a small economy car with unlimited kilometers.

Major rental companies with outlets in Halifax include the following: **Avis** (800/331-1212, www.avis.ca), **Budget** (800/268-8900, www.budget.ca), **Discount** (800/263-2355, www.discountcar.com), **Enterprise** (800/261-7331, www.enterprise.ca), **Hertz** (800/654-3131, www.hertz.ca), **National** (877/222-9058, www.nationalcar.com), and **Thrifty** (800/847-4389, www.thriftycanada.ca).

RV AND CAMPER RENTAL

You might want to consider renting a camper-van or other recreational vehicle for your trip.

With one of these apartments-on-wheels, you won't need to worry about finding accommodations each night. Even the smallest units aren't cheap, but they can be a good deal for longer-term travel or for families or two couples traveling together. The smallest vans, capable of sleeping two people, start at $185 per day with 100 free kilometers (62 miles) per day. Standard extra charges include insurance, a preparation fee (usually around $60-80 per rental), a linen/cutlery charge (around $60 pp

per trip), and taxes. Major agencies with rental outlets in Halifax include Cruise Canada (800/671-8042, www.cruisecanada.com) and Canadream (888/480-9726, www.canadream. com). Both of these companies also have rental outlets across the country.While you can take these vehicles across to Newfoundland on the ferry, you can also rent from St. John's-based Islander RV (709/738-7368 or 888/848-2267, www.islanderrv.com, May-Oct.), which charges from $250 per day for campers and RVs.

Recreation

In Atlantic Canada's great outdoors, just about every form of recreation is feasible and first-rate: bicycling and hiking, mountaineering, scuba diving, houseboating, river rafting and canoeing, ocean and river kayaking, sailing, windsurfing, rockhounding, bird-watching, fishing, hockey, tennis, golf—you name it. No matter what the temperature—35°C (95°F) in summer or -15°C (5°F) in winter—people can be found enjoying some form of recreation throughout the year.

Spectator sports popular in the Atlantic provinces include minor-league professional ice hockey, harness racing, and rugby.

PARKS

The region's national and provincial parks come in a wide range of personalities and offer an equally eclectic array of activities and facilities, from wilderness backpacking at New Brunswick's Mount Carleton Provincial Park to lounging in luxury at Cape Breton Highlands' Keltic Lodge resort.

National Parks

Atlantic Canada has 9 of Canada's 45 national parks. Cape Breton Highlands National Park, in Nova Scotia, is one of the most spectacular, but it is also very accessible: ocean panoramas, abundant wildlife, and an extensive network of hiking trails are the highlights. Best known for its wild horses, Sable

Island National Park, off the Nova Scotia coast, is much more remote and requires an air charter to access. In the same province, Kejimkujik National Park is the only one not on the ocean, which means visitors trade kayaks for canoes to explore the extensive system of freshwater lakes. In New Brunswick, Fundy National Park is renowned for the world's highest tides, while Kouchibouguac National Park fronts the calm waters of Northumberland Strait. The beaches of Prince Edward Island National Park are a popular destination for vacationing families. Newfoundland and Labrador has three parks—Terra Nova, renowned among kayakers; Gros Morne, where spectacular cliffs rise above inland "ponds"; and Torngat Mountains, protecting the remote northern tip of Labrador.

For information on these parks, including detailed trip planners, visit the Parks Canada website (www.pc.gc.ca).

Provincial Parks

Protecting areas of natural, historical, and cultural importance, Atlantic Canada's many hundreds of provincial parks also provide a wide variety of recreational opportunities. All provide day-use facilities such as picnic areas and washrooms, while many also have playgrounds, canoe rentals, and concessions. A good number also have campgrounds and summer interpretive programs.

You'll find lots of information about provincial parks at local information centers and in general tourism literature. You can also contact the following:

- **Nova Scotia:** 902/662-3030, http://parks. novascotia.ca

- **New Brunswick:** 506/462-5924, www. tourismnewbrunswick.ca

- **Prince Edward Island:** 902/368-4444, www.tourismpei.com

- **Newfoundland and Labrador:** 709/729-2664, www.tcii.gov.nl.ca/parks

HIKING

Hiking is one of the most popular activities in Atlantic Canada. Not only are there hundreds of trails to explore, but it's free and anyone can do it. The hiking season in the Maritime provinces spans spring-fall; hiking in Newfoundland and Labrador is relegated, for the most part, to the height of summer, except for the hardiest adventurers. Coastal areas throughout Atlantic Canada are generally free of pesky insects, but insect repellent is wise inland May-September. As national and provincial parks protect the most spectacular scenery, it'll be no surprise that this is where you find the best hiking. One standout is **Cape Breton Highlands National Park,** on Nova Scotia's Cape Breton Island. Here you can find anything from short interpretive trails along raised boardwalks to strenuous slogs that end at high ocean lookouts.

FISHING

Sportfishing in Atlantic Canada is legendary, especially for Atlantic salmon in Newfoundland and Labrador, New Brunswick, and Cape Breton Island. Fishing guides, tours, lodges (from rustic to luxurious), and packages are available throughout these regions. Expect to pay $250-500 a day for a guide. An all-inclusive week's package has the highest price and usually includes license fees, lodging, meals, a guide, and, for remote locations, fly-in transportation. Typical is Labrador's **Rifflin' Hitch Lodge** (www. rifflinhitchlodge.com), a 50-minute flight southeast from Goose Bay. Located on the Eagle River, one of the richest Atlantic salmon rivers in North America, the lodge supplies anglers with some of the world's best fishing and all the comforts of home. Guests enjoy luxuries such as gourmet meals and a hot tub, comfortable private rooms, and fishing from

Prince Edward Island National Park

National Park Passes

Permits are required for entry into all Canadian national parks. These are sold at park gates, at all park information centers, and at campground fee stations.

Day passes (less than $10 per person) are the best deal for short visits, but if you're planning to visit a number of parks throughout Atlantic Canada, consider an annual **Parks Canada Discovery Pass,** good for entry into all of Canada's national parks and national historic sites for one year from the date of purchase. The cost is adult $67.70, senior $57.90, child $33.30, up to a maximum of $136.40 per vehicle. For more information on park passes, check the Parks Canada website (www.pc.gc.ca).

the shore or boats at a ratio of one guide to every two guests.

Salmon

Just one species of salmon is native to the tidal waters of Atlantic Canada—the Atlantic salmon. It is anadromous, spending its time in both freshwater and saltwater. The salmon spend up to three years in local rivers before undergoing massive internal changes that allow them to survive in saltwater. They then spend 2-3 years in the open water, traveling as far as Greenland. After reaching maturity, they begin the epic journey back to their birthplace, to the exact patch of gravel on the same river from where they emerged. It is the returning salmon that are most sought after by anglers, with New Brunswick's **Miramichi** watershed the most famed of all river systems. Atlantic salmon grow to 36 kilograms (79 pounds), although their landlocked relatives rarely exceed 10 kilograms (22 pounds).

Other Saltwater Species

Flounder are caught in shallow waters, where they bury themselves in the sand. Growing to 40 centimeters (16 inches) long, these groundfish are easily caught, and just as easy to lose. Clams and worms are favored baits. **Mackerel,** living in shallow waters throughout summer, are easy to catch using spinning rods. Mackerel charters departing from North Rustico Harbour (Prince Edward Island) are extremely inexpensive.

Freshwater Fish

Speckled trout (also known as brook trout) are widespread throughout the region, and are fun to catch and tasty to eat. They tend to gravitate to cooler water, such as springfed streams, and can be caught on spinners or flies. A 3.4-kilogram (7.5-pound) specimen, one of the largest ever caught, is on display in Halifax's Museum of Natural History. Introduced in the late 1800s, **rainbow trout** are in lakes and rivers across Atlantic Canada. Many easily accessible lakes across Atlantic Canada are stocked with trout each spring. Most are rainbows because they are easy to raise and adapt to varying conditions. You can catch them on artificial flies, small spinners, or spoons. Sherbrooke Lake and Dollar Lake, both near Halifax, have healthy populations of **lake trout,** but the biggest of the species are in Newfoundland and Labrador. Introduced from Europe, **brown trout** are found in some streams and larger lakes, with the regional record a 13-kilogram (28.7-pound) fish caught in Newfoundland.

Long and lean, **striped bass** inhabit rivers and estuaries throughout the region. There is a definite art to catching the species—it is estimated it takes an average of 40-50 hours of fishing to catch one. The regional record is a 28.6-kilogram (63-pound) monster pulled from the lower reaches of the Saint John River (New Brunswick). **Smallmouth bass** are a popular sport fish introduced to the waterways of New Brunswick and southwestern Nova Scotia from farther west. They live in clear, calm water that usually has a gravelly bottom. Common throughout North America, **whitefish** are easily caught in most rivers and lakes, although they rarely exceed 15 centimeters (6 inches) in length. **Atlantic** whitefish (also called Acadian whitefish) are endemic to southwestern Nova Scotia. The fish is a protected species, so angling for them is prohibited; carry an identification chart if fishing these waters. Yellow perch (also known as lake perch) are identified by wide vertical stripes. Most often caught in shallow rivers and lakes in Nova Scotia and New Brunswick, they are fun to catch and tasty.

Fishing Licenses and Regulations

Each province has its own licensing system and regulations with which you should familiarize yourself before casting a line.

Nova Scotia: The recreational fishery is managed by the Department of Fisheries and Aquaculture (www.novascotia.ca/snsmr/paal/ndxfish.asp). A freshwater license for nonresidents costs $13 for one day, $34 for seven days, or $64 per year. Residents pay $28 for an annual license.

New Brunswick: A three-day nonresident license to fish for salmon is $38; to fish all other species for three days is $20. A seven-day license is $75 and $26, respectively, and an annual license is $138 and $38. It is illegal for nonresidents to fish for salmon in New Brunswick rivers without a guide, while other waters are set aside as "Crown Reserve"—for the fishing pleasure of residents only. For information, check the government website, www.gnb.ca.

Prince Edward Island: The Department of Communities, Land, and Environment (www.princeedwardisland.ca) charges $10 per annum plus a $20 Wildlife Conservation Fund fee ($13 for seniors) for a trout fishing season that runs mid-April-mid-September.

Newfoundland and Labrador: Contact the Department of Environment and Conservation (www.flr.gov.nl.ca) for information on fishing in both fresh and tidal waters. A license for trout angling is $12 per year, while a nonresident salmon license costs $80. An important point to note is that nonresidents are prohibited from fishing farther than 800 meters from a provincial highway without a guide or direct relative resident.

Fishing in national parks requires a separate license, which is available from park offices and some sports shops near major parks ($9.80 for a seven-day license, $34.30 for an annual license).

CYCLING AND MOUNTAIN BIKING

Reasonably good roads and gorgeous scenery make Atlantic Canada excellent road biking territory, while mountain biking has caught on among the adventurous as a way to explore more remote areas of the region. Except on main arteries, particularly the Trans-Canada Highway, car traffic is generally light. Cyclists, nonetheless, should remain vigilant: Narrow lanes and shoulders are common, and in some areas, drivers may be unaccustomed to sharing the road with bicycles.

Touring opportunities through a variety of terrain are numerous in Nova Scotia; probably the ultimate trip is the 5-6-day trek around Cape Breton Island's Cabot Trail. In New Brunswick, following the Saint John River valley and the complex of lakes north of Saint John makes for pleasant touring. The narrow roads that slice through Prince Edward Island's gentle countryside are sublime avenues for biking, while the Confederation Trail, extending from one end of the island to the other, is specifically designed for biking; Outer Limits Sports (330 University Ave., Charlottetown, 902/569-5690, www.ols.ca) is a good source of trail information. The shop also rents bikes decked out with panniers and provides drop-offs to points along the trail.

Many shops rent decent- to good-quality road and mountain bikes, but if you plan to do some serious riding, you'll probably want to bring your own. An outstanding information resource is Atlantic Canada Cycling (902/423-2453, www.atlanticcanadacycling.com). The organization publishes extensive information on cycling routes (including descriptions and ratings of highways and byways throughout Atlantic Canada), tours, races, clubs, and equipment, while its website has links to local operators and a message board.

A Photographer's Dream

Atlantic Canada has incredible light for photography. The sky turns from a Wedgwood color to sapphire blue—a beautiful background for seacoast photographs. Rise at dawn to take advantage of the first rays of sunlight hitting picturesque villages such as popular **Peggy's Cove,** near Halifax, and **St. Andrews,** in New Brunswick, as well as remote gems such as **Battle Harbour** in Labrador. Nature photographers will revel in the fall colors of **Cape Breton Highlands National Park,** the red-sand beaches of **Prince Edward Island National Park,** and Newfoundland's rugged **Gros Morne National Park.**

While photography is simplest when the weather is favorable—and that's more often than not—don't pass up a morning basking in thick mist, as bright sun illuminates the sky behind the thick clouds. The fog breaks apart gradually, and when it does, the sun radiates like a spotlight, illuminating the sparkling dampness that briefly clings to the landscape.

Guided Tours

Nova Scotia-based **Freewheeling Adventures** (902/857-3600 or 800/672-0775, www.freewheeling.ca) leads guided trips in small groups, each accompanied by a support van to carry the luggage and, if necessary, the weary biker. Owners Cathy and Philip Guest plan everything—snacks, picnics, and meals at restaurants en route, as well as overnights at country inns. Expect to pay around $300-400 per person per day for the all-inclusive tour. The trips pass through some of Atlantic Canada's prettiest countryside, including the Cabot Trail and South Shore, Prince Edward Island, and Newfoundland's Northern Peninsula.

WATER SPORTS

This ocean-bound region has no shortage of beaches, and most waterside provincial parks have a supervised **swimming** area. The warmest beaches are found along the Baie des Chaleurs ("Bay of Warmth") and the Northumberland Strait. The Bay of Fundy and Atlantic shores tend to be much cooler, although conditions vary considerably throughout the region.

With so much water surrounding and flowing through the provinces, **boating** opportunities are nearly infinite. Sailing is popular in the Bay of Fundy, around Passamaquoddy Bay, and in the spacious Halifax and Sydney harbors, as well as in protected inland areas such as Bras d'Or Lake and the extensive inland waterways of New Brunswick's Saint John River and Mactaquac Lake.

Canoeing and Kayaking

Canoeing is a traditional form of transportation that remains extremely popular throughout Atlantic Canada. You can rent canoes at many of the more popular lakes, including those protected by Kejimkujik National Park. If you bring your own, you can slip into any body of water whenever you please, taking in the scenery and viewing wildlife from water level. Coastal kayaking is another adventure, especially among the rock towers at Hopewell Rocks and along Cape Breton Island's turbulent Atlantic coast.

Tidal Bore Rafting

Instead of white-water rafting, Atlantic Canada is known for wild and woolly trips on the tidal bore created by the world's highest tides in the Bay of Fundy. **Tidal Bore Rafting Resort** (Hwy. 215, Urbania, 902/758-4032 or 800/565-7238, www.raftingcanada.ca) offers trips for varying levels of adrenaline rush in motorized Zodiacs, riding the bore as it rushes upriver before blasting back across its face.

Surfing

Nova Scotia is home to a small but dedicated population of surfers who hit the waves of the province's east coast year-round. **Lawrencetown Beach** (known as "L-town" to the locals), less than an hour's drive north of Halifax, is the best-known spot, with beach breaks along the long stretch of sand and a right-hander breaking off the rocky point. Other surf spots are scattered along the province's east coast. Water temperatures rarely rise above 16°C (61°F), meaning a 4/3-millimeter or 3/2-millimeter wetsuit is necessary, even in midsummer. Boards and wetsuits can be rented from **Kannon Beach Surf Shop** (4144 Lawrencetown Rd., 902/434-3040, https://kannonbeach.com), ideally located within walking distance of Lawrencetown

Beach; and from **Rossignol Surf Shop** (White Point Beach Resort, 902/354-7100, www.rossignolsurfshop.com) on Nova Scotia's South Shore. Lessons can also be arranged through both these outlets or the **East Coast Surf School** (902/434-3040, www.ecsurfschool.com) at Lawrencetown Beach.

WINTERTIME SPORTS

Winter is definitely low season for tourism in Atlantic Canada. Outdoor recreation is severely limited by the weather, although snow-related sports are popular with the locals. In addition to downhill skiing and boarding, skating on frozen ponds is popular, while locals cheer for minor-league ice hockey teams scattered throughout the region.

Skiing and Snowboarding

The alpine resorts of Atlantic Canada may lack the vertical rise of their western counterparts, but snowfall is high and outsiders will be greeted with open arms wherever they choose to ski. Day passes top out at $40, and each resort has day lodge facilities and rentals. Vertical rises range 180-300 meters (590-985 feet), and the season generally runs Christmas-late March.

Nova Scotia has three downhill resorts. Closest to Halifax is **Ski Martock,** south of the Annapolis Valley; **Wentworth** is near the New Brunswick border; and **Cape Smokey** has spectacular ocean views from its Cape Breton Island location.

In New Brunswick, **Crabbe Mountain,** west of Fredericton, and **Ski Mont-Farlagne,** near Edmundston, have loyal followings.

Atlantic Canada's biggest and best-known resort is **Marble Mountain,** in western Newfoundland (709/637-7601, www.skimarble.com), which has impressive enough mountain statistics to attract skiers and boarders from throughout eastern and central Canada. The resort receives up to 5 meters (16 feet) of snow each season. Four lifts (including the region's only high-speed quad) offer a vertical rise of 520 meters (1,706 feet), with the longest run being over 4 kilometers (2.5

miles). Amenities include a massive day lodge, on-hill accommodations, a terrain park, and a respected ski school. On the mainland, just outside Labrador City, **Smokey Mountain** is a small hill developed in the 1960s by the local mining company.

Cross-Country Skiing

The region's national parks and many of the provincial parks stay open year-round. In winter, hiking routes are transformed by snow into excellent cross-country ski trails, many of which are groomed by local ski clubs that charge a nominal fee for their use. **Ski Tuonela** (902/929-2144, www.skituonela. com), on Nova Scotia's Cape Breton Island, is one of North America's only lift-served telemark hills. In addition to a rope tow, the resort has 20 kilometers (12.4 miles) of groomed trails, a day lodge, and overnight accommodations. Organizations with handy websites loaded with information and links to ski clubs are **Canada Trails** (www.canadatrails.ca) and **Cross Country Canada** (www.cccski.com).

SPECTATOR SPORTS

Windsor, Nova Scotia, claims its place in history as the birthplace of ice hockey (known simply as "hockey" in Canada). Although the region is home to no National Hockey League (NHL) teams, the exploits of the Toronto Maple Leafs, Montréal Canadiens, and other NHL franchises are passionately followed here. In the Atlantic provinces you can also see lively play from NHL-affiliate team the St. John's IceCaps. Québec Major Junior Hockey League teams based in Atlantic Canada include the Halifax Mooseheads and Moncton Wildcats. The season runs October-March; check with local tourist information offices for game schedules and ticket information.

SHOPPING
Arts and Crafts

Quilts, sweaters, hooked rugs, porcelains, and wooden carvings are deftly mixed among the watercolors, oils, and sculptures in many arts and crafts venues. The hand-woven tartans of Loomcrofters (the weavers who designed the New Brunswick provincial and Royal Canadian Air Force tartans) at Gagetown, New Brunswick, and the work of the Madawaska Weavers, in New Brunswick's Acadian northwest, are well known on the provincial fashion scene.

New Brunswick's craftspeople specialize in yarn portraits, glass-blowing, pottery, wood sculptures, and pewter goods. The tourism department publishes the *Crafts Directory*, available at any tourism office. Antiques buyers should head to Nova Scotia, where many historic sites and homes have been converted into antiques shops. The Nova Scotia tourism department produces a buyer's guide, available at tourism offices. Newfoundland is known for a wide selection of labradorite jewelry as well as down jackets. The basketry work of the Mi'kmaq of Lennox Island (Prince Edward Island) has received much attention. PEI shops also carry beadwork, leather goods, silver jewelry, pottery, handcrafted furniture, and woodcarvings.

On Prince Edward Island, *Anne of Green Gables* is a common theme, but there is also a wide range of more traditional crafts. The best of these are knitted sweaters created by **Northern Watters Knitwear** (150 Richmond St., Charlottetown, 902/566-5850). The **PEI Crafts Council** website (www. peicraftscouncil.com) has an online address book of island craftspeople.

Business Hours

Shopping hours are generally Monday-Saturday 9am-6pm, with city malls open on Sundays also. Late shopping in most tourist areas is available until 9pm on Thursday and Friday, and supermarkets open 24 hours are found in the larger cities. Generally, banks are open Monday-Wednesday 10am-4pm and Thursday-Friday 10am-5pm. A few banks may open on Saturday, but all are closed on Sunday.

Accommodations

Atlantic Canada has all the chain hotels you know, as well as a range of accommodations that showcase the region—historic bed-and-breakfasts, grand resorts, riverside cottages, and luxurious fishing lodges. This section will give you a taste of the choices and some hints on reserving a room. Throughout the travel chapters of this book, I detail my favorites in all price ranges.

Many large local, national, and international hotel, resort, and motel groups have properties in Atlantic Canada; if you want to make advance reservations at any of their lodgings, simply phone the toll-free reservation center or book online using their websites.

Rates quoted through this guidebook are for a standard double room in the high season (usually July and August, but sometimes as early as June and as late as September). Almost all accommodations are less expensive outside of these busy months, with some discounting their rates by up to 50 percent. You'll enjoy the biggest seasonal discounts at properties that rely on summer tourists, such as those along the Northumberland Strait or in Cavendish. The same applies in Halifax on weekends—many of the big downtown hotels rely on business and convention travelers to fill the bulk of their rooms; when the end of the week rolls around, the hotels are left with rooms to fill at discounted rates Friday, Saturday, and Sunday nights.

While you have no influence on the seasonal and weekday/weekend pricing differences detailed above, *how* you reserve a room *can* make a difference in how much you pay. First and foremost, when it comes to searching out actual rates, the Internet is an invaluable tool. All hotel websites listed in this book show rates, and many have online reservation forms. Use these websites to search out specials, many of which are available only on the Internet. Don't be afraid to negotiate during slower times. Even if the desk clerk has no control over rates, there's no harm in asking for a bigger room or one with a better view. Just look for a vacancy sign hanging out front.

Most hotels offer auto association members an automatic 10 percent discount, and whereas senior discounts apply only to those older than 60 or even 65 on public transportation and at attractions, most hotels offer discounts to those ages 50 and older, with chains such as Best Western also allowing senior travelers a late checkout. "Corporate Rates" are a lot more flexible than in years past; some hotels require nothing more than the flash of a business card for a 10-20 percent discount.

When it comes to frequent-flyer programs, you really do need to be a frequent flyer to achieve free flights, but the various loyalty programs offered by hotels often provide benefits simply for signing up.

HOTELS, MOTELS, AND RESORTS

International, Canadian, and regional lodging chains are represented in Atlantic Canada. At the more expensive properties, expect all the requisite amenities and services—swimming pools, air-conditioning, in-room Internet access, room service, complimentary toiletries, restaurants, and bars. This type of accommodation can be found in central locations in all cities and major tourist areas. Rates at four- or five-star hotels start at $180 s or d in high season. Prices for a basic motel room in a small town start at $65 s or d, rising to $140 for a room in a chain hotel within walking distance of a major city's downtown core.

The big chains are represented in Atlantic Canada, as well as the following, some of which you may not be familiar with.

Best Western

Presumably you've heard of the world's largest motel chain, but the website www. bestwesternatlantic.com provides direct links to 15 local properties.

Choice Hotels Canada

Over 300 properties across Canada are marketed under the Choice Hotels (800/424-6423, www.choicehotels.ca) banner. It operates 10 brands, including Sleep, with smallish but clean, comfortable, and inexpensive rooms; Comfort, where guests enjoy a light breakfast and newspaper with a no-frills room; Quality, a notch up in quality with a restaurant and lounge; and Econo Lodge, older properties that have been renovated to Choice's standard and often have a pool and restaurant.

Delta Hotels

Owned by the Marriott company but still branded by their Canadian name, at Delta Hotels you can expect fine hotels with splendid facilities in notable downtown settings. Locations include Saint John, Fredericton, and Moncton, New Brunswick; Halifax, Nova Scotia; and St. John's, Newfoundland. Reservations can be made by calling 888/236-2427 or online at http://deltahotels.marriott. com. Check the Marriott website for package deals offered year-round.

Maritime Inns and Resorts

With package deals and locations in Antigonish, Port Hawkesbury, and the Cape Breton resort town of Baddeck, these properties (902/863-4001 or 888/662-7484, www. maritimeinns.com) are popular with holidaying Maritimers. Generally, packages include meals and activities such as golfing for around $150 per person per day.

Rodd Hotels and Resorts

This locally owned hotel company (902/892-7448 or 800/565-7633, www.roddvacations. com) is Prince Edward Island's lodgings standard bearer. The handsome Rodd Charlottetown in the capital is the oldest.

Two full-facility resorts are situated on the island: Crowbush Cove in the northeast and Brudenell River in the east. Other Rodd locations include another property in Charlottetown, two in New Brunswick, and one in Yarmouth, Nova Scotia.

Signature Resorts

Nova Scotia's provincial government owns two stunning resorts. They appeal to the carriage trade—travelers who like the understated ambience of a resort lodge with a tony rustic setting and furnishings, gourmet dining, a remote location with manicured grounds, and the genteel sports of golf or fly-fishing. Provincial resorts in Nova Scotia are the Pines Resort at Digby and Liscombe Lodge at Liscomb Mills. The website www. signatureresorts.com has links to both.

BED-AND-BREAKFASTS

Atlantic Canada is blessed with hundreds of B&Bs. Concentrations are located across Prince Edward Island and in historic towns such as Annapolis Royal (Nova Scotia) and St. John's (Newfoundland and Labrador). Styles run the gamut from historic mansions to rustic farmhouses, and as a result, amenities can also vary greatly. Regardless, guests can expect hearty home cooking, a peaceful atmosphere, personal service, knowledgeable hosts, and conversation with like-minded travelers. B&Bs are usually private residences, with hosts that live on-site and up to eight guest rooms. As the name suggests, breakfast is included in quoted rates; ask before booking whether it is a cooked or continental breakfast. Rates fluctuate enormously—from $55 s, $65 d for a spare room in an otherwise regular family home to over $200 in a historic mansion.

Finding and Reserving a Room

My favorite B&Bs are recommended within the travel chapters of this book. You can also use provincial accommodations guides and local information centers to find out about individual properties. **Select Atlantic Inns** (www.selectinns.ca) is an organization of mid- to top-end B&Bs, with online reservations and lots of information on specific properties. **Bed and Breakfast Online** (www.bbcanada.com) doesn't take bookings, but links are provided, and an internal search engine helps you find the accommodation that best fits your needs.

Before reserving a room, it is important to ask a number of questions of your hosts. The two obvious ones are whether or not you'll have your own bathroom and how payment can be made (many establishments don't accept debit cards or all credit cards).

BACKPACKER ACCOMMODATIONS

As accommodation prices are reasonable throughout Atlantic Canada, there is less of a need to find a dorm bed than in other parts of North America. While privately operated backpacker lodges come and go with predictable regularity, Hostelling International operates twelve hostels in the region.

Hostelling International

The curfews and chores are long gone in this worldwide nonprofit organization of 4,200 hostels in 60 countries. Hostelling International Canada has hostels in Nova Scotia at Halifax, Wentworth, and two on Cape Breton Island; in Charlottetown on Prince Edward Island; and in Newfoundland and Labrador at St. John's, Trinity, and Bonavista.

For a dorm bed, members of Hostelling International pay $22-30 per night; nonmembers pay $26-34. Generally, you need to provide your own sleeping bag or linens, but most hostels supply extra bedding (if needed) at no charge. Accommodations are in dormitories (2-10 beds), although single and double rooms are often available for an additional charge. Each hostel also offers a communal kitchen, a lounge area, and laundry facilities, while some have wireless Internet access, bike rentals, and organized tours.

You don't *have* to be a member to stay in an affiliated hostel of Hostelling International, but membership pays for itself after only a few nights of discounted lodging. Aside from discounted rates, benefits of membership vary from country to country but often include discounted air, rail, and bus travel; discounts on car rental; and discounts on some attractions and commercial activities. For Canadians, the membership charge is $35 annually, or $175 for a Friend Membership (lifetime). For more information, contact **HI-Canada** (604/684-7111, www.hihostels.ca).

Joining the Hostelling International affiliate of your home country entitles you to reciprocal rights in Canada, as well as around the world; click through the links at www.hihostels.com to your country of choice.

CAMPING

Camping out is a popular summer activity across Atlantic Canada, and you'll find campgrounds in all national parks, many provincial parks, on the outskirts of cities and towns, and in most resort areas. Facilities at park campgrounds vary considerably, but most commercial operations have showers and water, electricity, and sewer hookups.

National parks provide some of the nicest surroundings for camping. All sites have picnic tables, fire grates, toilets, and fresh drinking water, although only some provide showers. Prices range $18-38, depending on facilities and services. A percentage of sites can be reserved through the **Parks Canada Campground Reservation Service** (877/737-3783, www.pccamping.ca). Backcountry camping in a national park costs $8 per person per night.

Private campgrounds are generally located in popular tourist areas and open between May and October. Prices range dramatically, with tent sites from $20, but expect to pay up to $60 for an oceanfront site with all services.

Whenever possible, reservations for campsites—especially at the national parks and most popular provincial parks—should be made at least six weeks in advance. Most provincial parks, however, do not accept reservations, but instead assign sites on a first-come, first-served basis. At those parks, it's best to arrive before noon to ensure yourself a spot. Most provincial parks are open mid-May–mid-October. Most privately owned campsites accept reservations, which are more likely to be held if you send a small deposit.

Travel Tips

WHAT TO PACK

You'll find little use for a suit and tie in Atlantic Canada. Instead, pack for the outdoors. At the top of your must-bring list should be **hiking boots.** Even in summer, you should be geared up for a variety of weather conditions, especially at the change of seasons or if you'll be spending time along the coast. Do this by preparing to **dress in layers,** including at least one pair of fleece pants and a heavy long-sleeved top. For breezy coastal sightseeing, a sweater or windbreaker, hat, sunscreen, and comfortable shoes with rubber soles will come in handy. For dining out, **casual dress** is accepted at all but the most upscale restaurants.

Electrical appliances from the United States work in Canada, but those from other parts of the world will require a **current converter** (transformer) to bring the voltage down. Many travel-size shavers, hair dryers, and irons have built-in converters.

EMPLOYMENT AND STUDY

International visitors wishing to work or study in Canada must obtain authorization *before* entering the country. Authorization to work will only be granted if no qualified Canadians are available for the work in question. Applications for work and study are available from all Canadian embassies and must be submitted with a nonrefundable processing fee. The Canadian government has a reciprocal agreement with Australia for a limited number of **holiday work visas** to be issued each year. Australian citizens ages 30 and younger are eligible; contact your nearest Canadian embassy or consulate. For general information on immigrating to Canada, check the **Citizenship and Immigration Canada** website (www.cic.gc.ca).

VISITORS WITH DISABILITIES

A lack of mobility should not deter you from traveling to Atlantic Canada, but you should definitely do some research before leaving home.

Access to Travel (www.accesstotravel. gc.ca) is an initiative of the Canadian government that includes information on travel within and between Canadian cities. If you haven't traveled extensively, another good Internet source is www.wheelchairtraveling. com, where you will find a wide range of tips on accessible travel, as well as firsthand stories of Canadian travel. The **Society for Accessible Travel and Hospitality** (212/447-7284, www.sath.org) supplies information on tour operators, vehicle rentals, specific destinations, and companion services. For frequent travelers, the membership fee (US$49 per year) is well worth it. *Emerging Horizons* (www.emerginghorizons.com) is a U.S. quarterly online magazine dedicated to travelers with special needs.

For vision-impaired visitors, **CNIB** (www. cnib.ca) offers a wide range of services from its Halifax office (902/453-1480 or 800/563-2642). Finally, **Spinal Cord Injury Canada** (www.sci-can.ca) is another good source of information; provincial head offices include Halifax (www.thespine.ca), Moncton (www. abilitynb.ca), Charlottetown (www.sci-pei.ca), and St. John's (www.sci-nl.ca).

TRAVELING WITH CHILDREN

Regardless of whether you're traveling with toddlers or teens, you will face decisions affecting everything from where you stay to your choice of activities. Luckily for you, Atlantic Canada is very family-friendly, with indoor and outdoor attractions aimed specifically at the younger generation, such as Magnetic Hill just outside Moncton. Children familiar with *Anne of Green Gables* will love Cavendish, Prince Edward Island, the setting of the tale and now a major tourist destination packed with places highlighted in the book and also many commercial attractions.

Admission prices for children are included throughout the travel chapters of this book. As a general rule, reduced prices are for those ages 6-16. For two adults and two-plus children, always ask about family tickets. Children under 6 nearly always get in free. Most hotels and motels will happily accommodate children, but always try to reserve your room in advance and let the reservations desk know the ages of your brood. Often, children stay free in major hotels, and in the case of some major chains—such as Holiday Inn—eat free also. Generally, B&Bs aren't suitable for children, and in some cases they don't accept kids at all. Ask ahead.

Let the children help you plan your trip; look at websites and read up on Atlantic Canada together. To make your vacation more enjoyable if you'll be spending a lot of time on the road, rent a minivan (all major rental agencies have a supply). Don't forget to bring along favorite toys and games from home—whatever you think will keep your kids entertained when the joys of sightseeing wear off.

The various provincial tourism websites have sections devoted to children's activities within each province. Another handy source of online information is **Traveling Internationally with Your Kids** (www.travelwithyourkids.com).

Health and Safety

Atlantic Canada is a healthy place. To visit, you don't need to get any vaccinations or booster shots. And when you arrive, you can drink the water from the faucet and eat the food without worry.

If you need an ambulance, call 911 or the number listed on the inside front cover of local telephone directories. All cities and most larger towns have hospitals—look in each travel chapter of this book for locations and telephone numbers.

INSURANCE AND PRESCRIPTIONS

Intraprovincial agreements cover the medical costs of Canadians traveling across the nation. As a rule, the usual health insurance plans from other countries do not include medical care costs incurred while traveling; ask your insurance company or agent if supplemental health coverage is available, and if it is not, arrange for coverage with an independent carrier before departure. Hospital charges vary from place to place but can be as much as $3,000 a day, and some facilities impose a surcharge for nonresidents. Some Canadian companies offer coverage specifically aimed at visitors.

If you're on medication, take adequate supplies with you, and get a prescription from your doctor to cover the time you will be away. You may not be able to get a prescription filled at Canadian pharmacies without visiting a Canadian doctor, so don't wait till you've almost run out. If you wear glasses or contact lenses, ask your optometrist for a spare prescription in case you break or lose your lenses, and stock up on your usual cleaning supplies.

GIARDIA

Giardiasis, also known as "beaver fever," is a real concern for those who drink water from backcountry water sources. It's caused by an intestinal parasite, *Giardia lamblia*, that lives in lakes, rivers, and streams. Once ingested, its effects, although not instantaneous, can be dramatic: Severe diarrhea, cramps, and nausea are the most common. Preventive measures should always be taken and include boiling all water for at least 10 minutes, treating all water with iodine, or filtering all water using a filter with a small enough pore size to block the *Giardia* cysts.

WINTER TRAVEL

Travel through Atlantic Canada during winter months should not be undertaken lightly. Before setting out in a vehicle, check antifreeze levels, and always carry a spare tire and blankets or sleeping bags.

Frostbite can occur in a matter of seconds if the temperature falls below freezing and if the wind is blowing. Layer your clothing for the best insulation against the cold, and don't forget gloves and, most important, a warm hat, which can offer the best protection against heat loss. Frostbite occurs in varying degrees. Most often it leaves a numbing, bruised sensation, and the skin turns white. Exposed areas of skin, such as the nose and ears, are most susceptible, particularly when cold temperatures are accompanied by high winds.

Hypothermia occurs when the body fails to produce heat as fast as it loses it. Cold weather combined with hunger, fatigue, and dampness create a recipe for disaster. Symptoms are not always apparent to the victim. The early signs are numbness, shivering, slurring of words, and dizzy spells; in extreme cases, these can progress to violent behavior, unconsciousness, and even death. The best treatment is to get the patient out of the cold, replace wet clothing with dry, slowly give hot liquids and sugary foods, and place the victim in a sleeping bag. Prevention is a better strategy; dress for cold in layers, including a waterproof outer layer, and wear a warm wool cap or other headgear.

CRIME

The provinces of Atlantic Canada enjoy one of the country's lowest crime rates. Violent crimes are infrequent; the most common crime is petty theft. If you must leave valuable items in your car unattended, keep them out of sight, preferably locked in the vehicle's trunk. Women have few difficulties traveling alone throughout the region.

Remember that cities such as Halifax, Saint John, and St. John's are international ports with seamy (albeit interesting) bars and taverns at or near the working area of the waterfront; keep your wits about you, especially late at night. Better yet, leave these night scenes to the sailors and others who frequent the areas.

Both possession and sale of illicit drugs are considered serious crimes and are punishable with jail time, severe fines, or both. Furthermore, Canadians consider drinking while driving equally serious; the penalty on the first conviction is jail, a heavy fine, or both. A conviction here or in your home country can be grounds for exclusion from Canada.

Royal Canadian Mounted Police (RCMP)

Despite the romantic image of the staid redjacketed officer on horseback, Mounties (as they are most often called) nowadays favor the squad car as their mount of choice and wear a less colorful uniform. They are as ubiquitous a symbol of the country as the maple leaf, and they are similar to the highway patrol or state police in the United States. They operate throughout all the country's provinces and territories (except Ontario and Québec), complementing the work of local police.

Information and Services

MONEY

Unless noted otherwise, **prices quoted in this book are in Canadian currency.** Canadian currency is based on dollars and cents, with 100 cents equal to one dollar. Canada's money is issued in notes ($5, $10, and $20 are the most common) and coins (1, 5, 10, and 25 cents, and $1 and $2). The 11-sided, gold-colored $1 coin is known as a "loonie" for the bird featured on it. The unique $2 coin ("toonie," for "two loonies") is silver with a gold-colored insert.

Credit and debit cards are readily accepted throughout Atlantic Canada. By using these cards, you eliminate the necessity of thinking about the exchange rate—the transaction and rate of exchange on the day of the transaction will automatically be reflected in the bill from your bank or credit-card company. On the downside, you'll always get a better exchange rate when dealing directly with a bank. You should always carry some cash, as places like farmers markets and some bed and breakfasts do not accept debit or credit cards.

Costs

The cost of living in Atlantic Canada is lower than elsewhere in the country. For you, the visitor, this will be most apparent when paying for accommodations and meals. By planning ahead, having a tent, or traveling in the shoulder seasons, it is possible to get by on around $120 per person per day or less. Gasoline is sold in liters (3.78 liters equals 1 U.S. gallon) and is generally $1.20-1.50 per liter for regular unleaded.

Tipping charges are not usually added to your bill. You are expected to add a tip of 15 percent to the total amount for waiters and waitresses, barbers and hairdressers, taxi drivers, and other such service providers. Bellhops, doormen, and porters generally receive $1 per item of baggage.

Harmonized Sales Tax (HST)

A 13 percent Harmonized Sales Tax is levied on most goods and services purchased within Nova Scotia, New Brunswick, and Newfoundland and Labrador. The HST includes the 5 percent goods and services tax (GST) applied across Canada. At 9 percent, the provincial sales tax on Prince Edward Island is 1 percent higher than the other three provinces, for a combined total of 14 percent HST.

COMMUNICATIONS AND MEDIA

Postal Services

Canada Post (www.canadapost.ca) issues postage stamps that must be used on all mail posted in Canada. Letters and postcards sent within Canada are $1, to the United States $1.20, and to other foreign destinations $2.50. Prices increase with the weight of the mailing. You can buy stamps at post offices (closed weekends), some hotel lobbies, airports, many retail outlets, and some newsstands.

Telephone Services

The country code for Canada is 1, the same as the United States. Provincial area codes are: Nova Scotia, 902; New Brunswick, 506; Prince Edward Island, 902; Newfoundland and Labrador, 709. These prefixes must be dialed for all long-distance calls, even in-province calls. Toll-free numbers have the 800, 888, 877, or 866 prefix and may be good for the province, Atlantic Canada, Canada, North America, or, in the case of major hotel chains and car rental companies, worldwide.

To make an international call from Canada, dial the prefix 011 before the country code or dial 0 for operator assistance.

Public phones accept 5-, 10-, and 25-cent coins; local calls are $0.35-0.50, and most long-distance calls cost at least $2.50 for the first minute. The least expensive way to make long-distance calls from a public phone is with

Tourism Offices

The website of the **Canadian Tourism Commission** (www.canada.travel) is loaded with general information and provides travel information for individual provinces. The following provincial government offices provide more detailed information and will send out free information packages and maps:

- **Tourism Nova Scotia** (902/425-5781 or 800/565-0000, www.novascotia.com)
- **Tourism New Brunswick** (800/561-0123, www.tourismnewbrunswick.ca)
- **Tourism Prince Edward Island** (902/368-4444 or 800/463-4734, www.tourismpei.com)
- **Newfoundland and Labrador Tourism** (709/729-2830 or 800/563-6353, www. newfoundlandlabrador.com)

a **phone card.** These are available from convenience stores, newsstands, and gas stations.

Internet Access

All major hotels and most B&Bs have wireless Internet access. You'll also find free wireless Internet along the Halifax harbor front and in most airports and cafés.

Newspapers and Magazines

Atlantic Canada is too expansive and diverse to be well covered by one newspaper, but plenty of regional and big-city papers are available. The *Globe and Mail* and *National Post* are distributed throughout the Atlantic provinces, and Halifax's *Chronicle Herald* is found throughout Nova Scotia. Publications for the other provinces are listed under each specific province.

Canada's best-selling and most respected newsmagazine is *Maclean's*. *L'Actualité* is the French counterpart. *Newsweek*, *Time*, and other big American publications are available at drugstores, bookstores, and corner groceries.

WEIGHTS AND MEASURES

Canada uses the metric system, with temperature measured in degrees Celsius; liquid measurements in liters; solid weights in kilograms and metric tons; land areas in hectares; and distances in kilometers, meters, and centimeters. This newfangled system hasn't completely taken hold everywhere, and many locals still think in terms of the imperial system; expect to hear a lobster described in pounds, local distances given in miles, and the temperature expressed in Fahrenheit degrees.

The electrical voltage is 120 volts. The standard electrical plug configuration is the same as that used in the United States: two flat blades, often with a round third pin for grounding.

Time Zones

Even though Nova Scotia was home to Sir Sandford Fleming, the man who devised time zones, the province didn't receive any special favors. It is on **Atlantic Standard Time (AST),** the same as New Brunswick and Prince Edward Island. Officially, all of Newfoundland and Labrador is on **Newfoundland Standard Time (NST),** 30 minutes ahead of Atlantic Standard Time, although in reality only the island of Newfoundland and the southeastern Labrador communities on the Strait of Belle Isle adhere to NST.

Atlantic Standard Time is one hour ahead of Eastern Standard Time and four hours ahead of Pacific Standard Time.

Resources

Suggested Reading

NATURAL HISTORY

Fitzhugh, William W., and Wilfred E. Richard. *Maine to Greenland: Exploring the Maritime Far Northeast*. Washington DC: Smithsonian Institution Scholarly Press, 2014. A big, beautiful, hardcover book filled with essays that delve into the natural and human history of the region's coastline.

Grescoe, Taras. *Bottomfeeder*. Toronto: HarperCollins, 2008. An insight into the fisheries industry made more readable by the author's firsthand accounts of visits to the world's most important fisheries, including Nova Scotia.

MacAskill, Wallace R. *MacAskill Seascapes and Sailing Ships*. Halifax: Nimbus Publishing, 1987. Cape Breton's famed photographer captures the misty moods of fishermen, schooners, seaports, and seacoasts.

Primrose, Mary, and Marian Munro. *Wildflowers of Nova Scotia, New Brunswick & Prince Edward Island*. Halifax: Formac Publishing, 2006. A glorious combination of text by Munro and stunning color photography by Primrose—a must for every naturalist who revels in wildflowers.

Scott, Peter J. *Edible Plants of Atlantic Canada*. Portugal Cove, Newfoundland: Boulder Publications, 2014. A detailed field guide to around 60 edible plants and berries present in the region. Includes details on finding each one as well as recipes.

Thurston, Harry. *Tidal Life: A Natural History of the Bay of Fundy*. Halifax: Nimbus Publishing, 1998. The lavishly illustrated contents describe natural habitats formed by the Fundy.

HUMAN HISTORY

Andrieux, J. P. *St. Pierre and Miquelon: A Fragment of France in North America*. Ottawa: O.T.C. Press, 1986. One of the most thorough books about France's overseas province, the small volume details sightseeing within a historical context and is illustrated with historical photographs.

Brasseaux, Carl A. *The Founding of New Acadia*. New Orleans: Louisiana State University Press, 1997. A little academic, but this book will make interesting reading for anyone from the South who wants to learn about the links between Cajuns and the Acadians of Nova Scotia.

Campbell, Gary. *The Road to Canada*. Fredericton, New Brunswick: Goose Lane Editions, 2005. Tells the story of how river transportation—specifically on the Saint John and St. Lawrence Rivers—opened up central Canada for settlement.

Campey, Lucille H. *After the Hector: The Scottish Pioneers of Nova Scotia and Cape Breton*

1733–1852. Edinburgh: Birlinn Publishing, 2005. An account of those who arrived in Pictou aboard the *Hector* and how their Scottish Highlands heritage helped them adapt and thrive in the New World.

Collie, Michael. *New Brunswick.* Toronto: Macmillan, 1974. Much has changed in the 40-plus years since this book was written, but much still rings true. Collie provides a poetic, highly personal, and often moving overview of the province, its history, and the psyche of its people.

Crooker, William. *Oak Island Gold.* Halifax: Nimbus Publishing, 2011. One of many books devoted to the world's longest treasure hunt, this one does a noble job of unraveling the story—and even suggests an explanation to the secrets of the island.

Daigle, Jean, ed. *Acadians of the Maritimes.* Moncton, New Brunswick: Chaire d'Études Acadiennes, Université de Moncton, 1995. The history of the Acadians in Atlantic Canada is a tangled tale of upheaval and survival, cultural clashes and passions. Daigle's collection of Acadian literature is among the best on the bookshelves.

De Mont, John. *Citizens Irving: K. C. Irving and His Legacy, The Story of Canada's Wealthiest Family.* Toronto: Doubleday Canada, 1991. The Irving family is very private, and this unofficial biography is stuffed with well-documented unfavorable and favorable facts, legends, and speculation.

Duivenvoorden Mitic, Trudy. *Pier 21: Gateway that Changed Canada.* Halifax: Nimbus Publishing, 2011. As a child of parents who emigrated through Pier 21 and who was employed as a director with Employment and Immigration Canada, Duivenvoorden Mitic is well qualified to author a book on this important Halifax site.

Faragher, John Mack. *A Great and Noble Scheme: The Tragic Story of the Expulsion of the French Acadians from Their American Homeland.* New York: W. W. Norton, 2005. In this hefty 560-page book, Faragher describes the evolution of Acadia, the horrors of the deportation, and the resulting pockets of Acadian culture that thrive to this day.

Hamilton, William B. *Place Names of Atlantic Canada.* Toronto: University of Toronto, 1996. Includes definitions for thousands of place-names throughout the region. Divided by province and then sorted alphabetically.

Hicks, Brian. *Ghost Ship: The Mysterious True Story of the Mary Celeste and Her Missing Crew.* New York: Random House, 2005. Just one of dozens of books devoted to unraveling the story of the world's most famous mystery ship, including its early history and launch from Nova Scotia.

Irwin, Rip. *Lighthouses and Lights of Nova Scotia.* Halifax: Nimbus Publishing, 2011. Nova Scotia is renowned for its photogenic lighthouses—and this new edition details all 164, complete with historical facts.

Kert, Faye. *Trimming Yankee Sails.* Fredericton, New Brunswick: Goose Lane Editions, 2005. Stories of privateers from Saint John, including the 1863 capture of the passenger liner SS *Chesapeake*.

Ledger, Don. *Swissair Down.* Halifax: Nimbus Publishing, 2000. The story of the September 1998 crash of a Swissair jetliner off the village of Peggy's Cove from a pilot's point of view.

Major, Kevin. *As Near to Heaven by Sea: A History of Newfoundland and Labrador.* Toronto: Penguin, 2002. Lively yet full of detail, this is an excellent introduction to Newfoundland and Labrador's long and colorful history.

Nunn, Bruce. *History with a Twist*. Halifax: Nimbus Publishing, 2002. Light yet interesting reading that covers a few dozen tales from Nova Scotia's past. And if you're looking for more, there's *More History with a Twist* by the same author, as well as a third volume released in 2008.

Poliandri, Simone. *First Nations, Identity, and Reserve Life: The Mi'kmaq of Nova Scotia*. Lincoln: University of Nebraska Press, 2011. A big, beautiful book that tells the story of the Mi'kmaq from their arrival in the province.

Rompkey, Ronald. *Grenfell of Labrador: A Biography*. Toronto: University of Toronto Press, 1991. Sir Wilfred Grenfell, the physician-missionary whose work left an indelible imprint on the province's remote areas, has had several biographers, but none as meticulous and incisive as Rompkey.

Slumkoski, Corey. *Inventing Atlantic Canada: Regionalism and the Maritime Reaction to Newfoundland's Entry into Canadian Confederation*. Toronto: University of Toronto Press, 2011. This hefty hardcover book tells the story of Newfoundland's 1949 entry into the Canadian confederation and its effect on the three Maritime provinces.

Tuck, James A., and Robert Grenier. *Red Bay, Labrador: World Whaling Capital, A.D. 1550–1660*. St. John's, Newfoundland: Atlantic Archaeology, 1989. Archaeological discoveries provide the grist for relating the early Basque whaling industry. Splendid color photography and black-and-white graphics.

SPORTS, CULTURE, AND CRAFTS

Buist, Ron. *Tales from Under the Rim: The Making of Tim Hortons*. Fredericton, New Brunswick: Goose Lane Editions, 2011. Although non-Canadians may not be familiar with the Tim Hortons chain of fast-food restaurants, you'll see them everywhere on your Nova Scotia travels, which makes this book an interesting read for those interested in a marketing success story.

Coldrick, Helen. *New Brunswick's Covered Bridges*. Saint John: Neptune Publishing, 2013. This fact-filled guide highlights nearly all the province's covered bridges, complete with construction details and their history.

Elliot, Elaine. *The Chowder Trail Cookbook*. Halifax: Formac Publishing, 2014. One of the best-loved meals in Atlantic Canada is seafood chowder. This hardcover book takes readers on a journey through Nova Scotia, searching out the best ingredients and recipes.

Harper, Marjory. *Myth, Migration and the Making of Memory: Scotia and Nova Scotia*. Halifax: John Donald Publishers, 2000. Explores Nova Scotia's Scottish heritage and the importance of the province's links to Scotland through the years.

Heibron, Alexandra, ed. *Lucy Maud Montgomery Album*. Markham, Ontario: Fitzhenry and Whiteside, 1999. Thoroughly researched, this huge compilation includes everything there is to know about Montgomery, her writing, and her home province. It was released in 1999 to commemorate the 125th anniversary of her birth.

Hollingsworth, Paul. *Sidney Crosby: The Story of a Champion*. Halifax: Nimbus Publishing, 2011. Hockey's current superstar has already been the subject of many books, but this one, published by a local company, includes much detail of growing up in Nova Scotia's Cole Harbour.

Lief, Charles. *Taste of Nova Scotia Cookbook*. Halifax: Nimbus Publishing, 2011. An in-depth look at local cuisine, including many traditional dishes, with recipes supplied by local restaurants, inns, and bed and breakfasts.

Lucas, Paul. *Prince Edward Island Seafood: Local Fare, Global Flavours.* Charlottetown, Prince Edward Island: Acorn Press, 2011. Lucas, head chef at Charlottetown's Lobster on the Wharf Restaurant, dishes on his favorite recipes, many influenced by the tastes of Asia and Central America.

MacDonald, Edward. *If You're Stronghearted: PEI in the Twentieth Century.* Charlottetown, Prince Edward Island: PEI Museum Heritage Foundation, 2000. This hardcover book tells the story of the people of Prince Edward Island, their culture, and a changing economy through a turbulent 100 years that ended with the construction of a bridge to the outside world.

Montgomery, Lucy Maud. *Anne of Green Gables Library.* New York: Aladdin, 2014. A beautifully presented box set of the four books that sparked Montgomery's popularity as an author, and are as interesting today as when they were written.

Montgomery, Lucy Maud. *The Alpine Path.* Halifax: Nimbus Publishing, 2005. Some of Montgomery's most vivid descriptions of the island are found in this recounting of the author's life.

Mowat, Claire. *The Outport People.* Toronto: Key Porter Books, 2005. The wife of famed Canadian writer Farley Mowat describes the couple's time living in a remote Newfoundland village in the form of a fictional memoir.

Nightingale, Marie. *Out of Old Nova Scotia Kitchens.* Halifax: Nimbus Publishing, 2011. Beloved by Nova Scotians for decades, this is a reprint of a classic known for its simple approach to preparing comfort food with locally available ingredients.

Perlman, Ken. *The Fiddle Music of Prince Edward Island.* Pacific, Missouri: Mel Bay Productions, 1996. More than 400 traditional Celtic and Acadian tunes.

Proulx, E. Annie. *The Shipping News.* New York: Touchstone, 1994. Pulitzer Prize-winning story of a widowed journalist rebuilding his life on the Newfoundland coast.

Rootland, Nancy. *Anne's World, Maud's World: The Sacred Sites of L. M. Montgomery.* Halifax: Nimbus Publishing, 1998. This thought-provoking book reflects on how Montgomery's island home was reflected in her writing, with references to many sites that remain today.

Story, G. M., W. J. Kirwin, and J. D. A. Widdowson, eds. *Dictionary of Newfoundland English.* Toronto: University of Toronto Press, 1990. The Newfoundlanders use their own version of the King's English—from "Aaron's rod," a roseroot's local name, to "zosweet," a Beothuk word for the ptarmigan. This remarkably researched compilation translates words and adds historical, geographical, and cultural insights.

Sylvester, John. *Prince Edward Island: Landscape and Light.* Charlottetown, Prince Edward Island: Acorn Press, 2014. Among the best of the photography books depicting Canada's island province.

RECREATION GUIDES AND GUIDEBOOKS

Broadhurst, Katie, and Alexandra Fortin. *Hikes of Western Newfoundland.* Portugal Cove, Newfoundland: Boulder Publications, 2014. Details 60 hiking trails from Port-aux-Basque in the south to the tip of the Northern Peninsula and as far east as Twillingate. A large section of the book is devoted to Gros Morne National Park.

Eiselt, Marianne, and H. A. Eiselt. *A Hiking Guide to New Brunswick.* Fredericton, New

Brunswick: Goose Lane Editions, 1999. Extensively detailed with abundant maps, the guide describes 90 hikes throughout the province.

Gadd, Ben. *The Canadian Hiker's and Backpacker's Handbook*. Vancouver: Whitecap Books, 2008. Authored by a renowned expert, this is the best book for reading up on your backcountry and hiking skills.

Gillis, Rannis, and Ken Aiken. *Motorcycle Journeys Through Atlantic Canada*. Conway Center, New Hampshire: Whitehorse Press, 2011. A travel guidebook for motorcycle enthusiasts, the book covers routes through all four provinces, including the Cabot Trail.

Haynes, Michael. *Hiking Trails of Mainland Nova Scotia*. Fredericton, New Brunswick: Goose Lane Editions, 2012. The ninth edition of this comprehensive yet compact guide details about 50 trails throughout the province. Each description, up to five pages long, is accompanied by a map.

Haynes, Michael. *Trails of Halifax Regional Municipality*. Fredericton, New Brunswick: Goose Lane Editions, 2010. This comprehensive guide to hiking trails in and around Halifax includes maps, photos, GPS coordinates, and useful offerings such as cellphone coverage for each trail.

Lawley, David. *A Nature and Hiking Guide to Cape Breton's Cabot Trail*. Halifax: Nimbus Publishing, 1994. The first half of this 200-page book covers all major trails along the Cabot Trail. The second half delves into the region's natural history, complete with descriptions of all flora and fauna.

Lebrecht, Sue. *Trans Canada Trail Guide to Prince Edward Island*. Ottawa: Canadian Geographic, 2004. On the island, the Trans Canada Trail follows an abandoned rail bed and is known as the Confederation Trail. This book details everything you'll need to know for a walking or biking trip along its length.

Maybank, Blake. *Birding Sites of Nova Scotia*. Halifax: Nimbus Publishing, 2005. This thorough field guide makes the province's birdlife easy to identify through detailed descriptions and habitat maps.

National Geographic. *Guide to the National Parks of Canada*. Washington DC: National Geographic Society, 2011. This full-color guide was published to celebrate the centenary of the Canadian national park system.

O'Flaherty, Patrick. *Come Near at Your Peril: A Visitor's Guide to the Island of Newfoundland*. St. John's, Newfoundland: Breakwater Books, 1994. Often hilarious and always insightful, the author meanders across the island, explains the sights as no one but a Newfoundlander sees them, and reveals travel's potential tangles and torments.

Tracy, Nicholas. *Cruising Guide to the Bay of Fundy and the Saint John River*. Toronto: Stoddart Publishing, 1999. A useful guide to Fundy and Saint John sailing.

MAGAZINES, MAPS, AND ATLASES

Canadian Geographic. Ottawa: Royal Canadian Geographical Society (www.canadiangeographic.ca). Bimonthly publication pertaining to Canada's natural and human histories and resources.

Cummins' Atlas of Prince Edward Island, 1928. Charlottetown, Prince Edward Island: P.E.I. Historical Foundation, 1990. All the details are here, from maps and lists to history.

Downhome. St. John's, Newfoundland. Monthly magazine of everything Newfoundland and Labrador, from family stores to hints on growing gardens in northern climes (www.downhomelife.com).

Explore. Toronto. Bimonthly publication of adventure travel throughout Canada (www. explore-mag.com).

MapArt. Driving maps for all of Canada, street atlases for major cities, and folded maps of Atlantic Canada (www.mapart. com).

Nature Canada. Ottawa. Seasonal e-newsletter of Nature Canada (www.naturecanada.ca).

Nova Scotia Atlas. Halifax: Formac Publishing, 2006. This comprehensive atlas breaks the province down into 90 topographical-style maps, including geographical features and all public roads. The back matter includes an index of 14,500 place-names and a short description of all provincial and national parks.

Rand McNally. Products include the *Atlantic Canada Road Atlas* and *Halifax* and *Nova Scotia Communities StreetFinder*, as well as folded maps of various Atlantic Canada regions (www.randmcnally.com).

Saltscapes. Bedford, Nova Scotia. Classy lifestyle magazine for Canada's east coast. Seven issues annually (www.saltscapes. com).

Internet Resources

TRAVEL PLANNING
Canadian Tourism Commission
www.canada.travel
Official tourism website for all of Canada.

Newfoundland and Labrador Tourism
www.newfoundlandlabrador.com
The first place to go when planning your trip to the region's largest province. This site includes a distance calculator, order forms for brochures, and detailed events calendars.

Nova Scotia Tourism Agency
www.novascotia.com
Everything you need to begin planning your trip to Nova Scotia.

Prince Edward Island Tourism
www.tourismpei.com
Visitor guides are available online, along with information especially for children, online reservations, and package deals.

Tourism New Brunswick
www.tourismnewbrunswick.ca
A searchable database of accommodations, information on provincial parks, and event listings make this a worthwhile site for planning your trip.

PARKS
Department of Natural Resources
www.novascotiaparks.ca
This department manages Nova Scotia's provincial park system. The website details seasons and fees, and has a handy search tool to make finding parks easy.

Department of Tourism, Culture, Industry, and Innovation
www.tcii.gov.nl.ca/parks
Newfoundland and Labrador is dotted with provincial parks and wilderness preserves, and this website details them all.

Parks Canada
www.pc.gc.ca
Official website of the agency that manages Canada's national parks and national historic sites. Information includes general information, operating hours, and fees.

Parks Canada Campground Reservation Service
www.pccamping.ca
Use this website to make reservations for campsites in national parks.

GOVERNMENT
Atlantic Canada Online
www.acol.ca
An alliance of the four provincial governments created to disseminate databases of information to the public.

Citizenship and Immigration Canada
www.cic.gc.ca
Check this government website for anything related to entry to Canada.

Environment Canada
www.weather.gc.ca
Seven-day forecasts from across Canada, including more than 200 locations across Atlantic Canada. Includes weather archives such as seasonal trends, hurricane history, and sea ice movement.

Government of Canada
www.gc.ca
The official website of the Canadian government.

ACCOMMODATIONS
Bed and Breakfast Online
www.bbcanada.com
Easy-to-use tools for finding and reserving B&Bs that suit your budget and interests.

Hostelling International–Canada
www.hihostels.ca
Canadian arm of the worldwide organization.

TRANSPORTATION
Air Canada
www.aircanada.ca
Canada's national airline.

Halifax International Airport
www.hiaa.ca
The official airport website, which includes images of departure and arrival boards, tools to help reach Halifax using the most direct flights, and virtual flight maps that show the location of all incoming and outgoing flights.

Marine Atlantic
www.marineatlantic.ca
Use this website to make advance reservations for ferry travel between Nova Scotia and Newfoundland.

Maritime Bus
www.maritimebus.com
Where Greyhound buses terminate, Acadian takes over, with inexpensive service through Nova Scotia, New Brunswick, and Prince Edward Island.

Northumberland Ferries
www.ferries.ca
Use this website to find out schedules and make reservations on routes between New Brunswick and Nova Scotia, and across to Prince Edward Island.

VIA Rail
www.viarail.ca
Passenger rail service across Canada, including from Montréal through New Brunswick to Halifax.

WestJet
www.westjet.com
Before booking with Air Canada, check out this airline for flights into Atlantic Canada from points west.

CONSERVATION
Atlantic Canada Conservation Data Centre
www.accdc.com
Some good information on what species you're likely to see and where, but mostly composed of charts and databases.

Canadian Parks and Wilderness Society
www.cpaws.org
A national nonprofit organization that is instrumental in highlighting conservation issues throughout Canada.

Ducks Unlimited Canada
www.ducks.ca
Respected wetlands protection organization represented by chapters in each of the four Atlantic Canada provinces.

Sierra Club Atlantic
www.sierraclub.ca/en/atlantic
Dedicated to preserving wilderness throughout the region. Currently active in fighting oil and gas development in the Gulf of St. Lawrence.

Starving Ocean
www.fisherycrisis.com
Filled with Canadian content, this private website contains articles related to seals, humpback whales, and the decline in cod stocks.

PUBLISHERS

Acorn Press
https://acornpresscanada.com
The most prolific publisher of Prince Edward Island–related books, including both fiction and nonfiction.

Breakwater Books
www.breakwaterbooks.com
A Newfoundland Labrador publishing house that specializes in producing works by local authors.

Creative Book Publishing
www.creativebookpublishing.ca
This St. John's book publisher has expanded from its stable of local titles to include a catalog of over 200 books, many related to life in Newfoundland and Labrador.

Goose Lane Editions
www.gooselane.com
While all the best books on Atlantic Canada are detailed under *Suggested Reading*, check the website of this prolific Fredericton-based publisher for contemporary titles about the region.

Nimbus Publishing
www.nimbus.ca
Respected publisher of numerous Nova Scotia books, including lots of natural and human history titles.

OTHER INTERNET RESOURCES

Acadian Genealogy Homepage
www.acadian.org
One of the best websites for everything Acadian. Includes detailed census reports dating to 1671 and links to books about this unique culture.

Lucy Maud Montgomery Institute
www.lmmontgomery.ca
This institute promotes everything Anne (as in *Anne of Green Gables*). The webpage www.tourismpei.com/lucy-maud-montgomery is a source of tourist-oriented information about the famous author.

Titanic in Nova Scotia
www.novascotia.ca/titanic
Maintained by the government of Nova Scotia, this website includes everything from full passenger lists to local links as obscure as a plaque in the Halifax YMCA that commemorates the sinking with the wrong date.

Index

List of Maps

Photo Credits

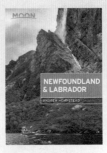

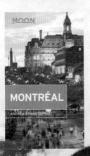

MAP SYMBOLS

═══	Expressway	○	City/Town	✈	Airport	♫	Golf Course
───	Primary Road	◉	State Capital	✗	Airfield	P	Parking Area
───	Secondary Road	✹	National Capital	▲	Mountain	⬥	Archaeological Site
─ ─ ─	Unpaved Road	★	Point of Interest	✦	Unique Natural Feature	⬦	Church
───	Feature Trail	•	Accommodation				Gas Station
- - - -	Other Trail	▼	Restaurant/Bar	⬧	Waterfall		Glacier
··········	Ferry	■	Other Location	♣	Park		Mangrove
═══	Pedestrian Walkway			⬛	Trailhead		Reef
▭▭▭	Stairs	ʌ	Campground	⬲	Skiing Area		Swamp

CONVERSION TABLES

°C = (°F – 32) / 1.8
°F = (°C x 1.8) + 32
1 inch = 2.54 centimeters (cm)
1 foot = 0.304 meters (m)
1 yard = 0.914 meters
1 mile = 1.6093 kilometers (km)
1 km = 0.6214 miles
1 fathom = 1.8288 m
1 chain = 20.1168 m
1 furlong = 201.168 m
1 acre = 0.4047 hectares
1 sq km = 100 hectares
1 sq mile = 2.59 square km
1 ounce = 28.35 grams
1 pound = 0.4536 kilograms
1 short ton = 0.90718 metric ton
1 short ton = 2,000 pounds
1 long ton = 1.016 metric tons
1 long ton = 2,240 pounds
1 metric ton = 1,000 kilograms
1 quart = 0.94635 liters
1 US gallon = 3.7854 liters
1 Imperial gallon = 4.5459 liters
1 nautical mile = 1.852 km

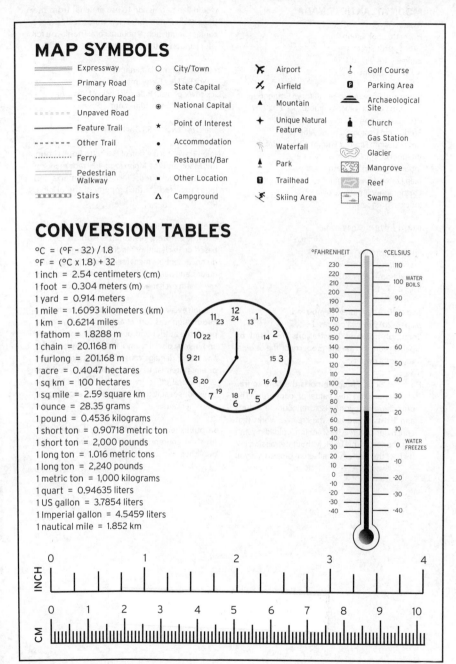

MOON ATLANTIC CANADA
Avalon Travel
Hachette Book Group
1700 Fourth Street
Berkeley, CA 94710, USA
www.moon.com

Editor and Series Manager: Kathryn Ettinger
Acquiring Editor: Grace Fujimoto
Copy Editor: Ann Seifert
Production Design: Suzanne Albertson
Cover Design: Faceout Studios, Charles Brock
Interior Design: Domini Dragoone
Moon Logo: Tim McGrath
Map Editor: Albert Angulo
Cartographer: Andrew Dolan
Indexer: Greg Jewett

ISBN-13: 978-1-64049-024-6

Printing History
1st Edition — 1995
9th Edition — May 2019
5 4 3 2 1

Front cover photo: Lunenburg Harbour
© Rick Hicker / Getty Images
Back cover photo: Hopewell Rocks at low tide
© Rndmst / Dreamstime.com

Printed in China by RR Donnelley

All recommendations, including those for sights, activities, hotels, restaurants, and shops, are based on each author's individual judgment. We do not accept payment for inclusion in our travel guides, and our authors don't accept free goods or services in exchange for positive coverage.